CONFLICT AMONG NATIONS

CONFLICT AMONG NATIONS

BARGAINING, DECISION MAKING,
AND SYSTEM STRUCTURE IN
INTERNATIONAL CRISES

Glenn H. Snyder and Paul Diesing

PRINCETON UNIVERSITY PRESS

PRINCETON, NEW JERSEY

Library of Congress Cataloging in Publication Data will be
found on the last printed page of this book

This book has been composed in Linotype Times Roman

Printed in the United States of America by
Princeton University Press, Princeton, New Jersey

CONTENTS

List of Figures

List of Tables

PREFACE

This is the first book-length study to emerge from the Center for International Conflict Studies, SUNY–Buffalo, founded in 1967 and directed by Glenn H. Snyder. The Center's research activity from the beginning has centered on the theme of negotiation and bargaining, especially the empirical testing of bargaining theory in various types of conflict situations. This choice of theme reflected a common interest of the four senior faculty members who were "present at the creation": Glenn Snyder, Department of Political Science; Paul Diesing, Department of Philosophy, later Political Science; Paul Guinn, Department of History; and Dean Pruitt, Department of Psychology. Guinn and Pruitt have separate projects underway; they also participated in the research for the present volume.[1]

This book presents a theory of international crisis behavior, conceived chiefly as bargaining behavior, but including also the effects of international system structures and the decision-making activities of the actors on the bargaining process. We developed our theory by testing and linking a number of primarily deductive theories and models via sixteen case studies of international crises that occurred from the late nineteenth century to the present. This is not the first book to analyze crises from the bargaining perspective,[2] but we believe our effort is unique in the scope, formality, and variety of the theories applied, in its systematic attempt to test existing theory (and some that we invented ourselves) against the record of history, and in the span of history covered.

It was an enormous task, and would indeed have been impossible for the two co-authors alone. We were assisted, however, by nine other

---

[1] Except for the completion of work begun earlier, the Center is presently inactive due to the termination of University support.

[2] That distinction belongs to Oran Young, with his *The Politics of Force: Bargaining during International Crises* (Princeton, N.J.: Princeton University Press, 1968). Other persons to whom we owe a special intellectual debt include Thomas Schelling, whose theories of strategic bargaining inspired the senior author to undertake this project; Anatol Rapoport and Daniel Ellsberg, for their work with game theory; Alan Coddington, whose bargaining model is the starting point for our Chapter IV on information processing; Herbert Simon, James March, and Richard Cyert, for decision theory; Graham Allison and Morton Halperin, for their innovative work on bureaucratic politics; Robert Jervis, for his studies of international perception and communication; Kenneth Waltz, for his theoretical essays on international system structure; and Alexander George and his collaborators, whose empirical studies of coercive diplomacy and deterrence have, like Young's book, broken new ground in the use of historical cases for theory development.

persons—three faculty members, one research associate, and five gradu-
ate student research assistants. Each member of the team wrote one,
and some two, case studies of crises that form the empirical base of
the book. Since most of these studies were themselves book-length,
it was impossible to include them in this volume. We have, however,
included as Appendix A highly condensed summaries of 12 of the cases.
The reader who is not familiar with some or all of the cases we have
used should read this appendix first, in order to comprehend better our
references to case materials in the book. The case studies and their
authors are as follows:

The Fashoda Crisis of 1898—Kenneth Fuchs
The Morocco Crisis of 1905–1906—Glenn Snyder
The Morocco Crisis of 1911—Charles Lockhart
The 1914 Crisis—Dennis Yena
The Ruhr Crisis of 1923—Paul Guinn
The Munich Crisis of 1938—James Smith
The Iran Crisis of 1946—Charles Planck
The Berlin Blockade of 1948—Clark Murdock
The Suez Crisis of 1956—Kenneth Fuchs
The Berlin Crisis of 1958–1961—Paul Diesing
The Quemoy Crisis of 1958—Jane Holland
The Lebanon Crisis of 1958—William Stover
The Cuba Crisis of 1962—Charles Lockhart

Glenn Snyder and Paul Diesing also researched, but did not write up,
three others cases: Bosnia, 1908; United States–Japan, 1940–1941; and
the Yom Kippur "alert crisis" of 1973. They studied less intensively
the Balkans crises of 1912–1913, and the Syria–Jordan crisis of 1970.

Because we were chiefly interested in studying bargaining, the principal criterion for selection of cases was that they have a considerable
degree of bargaining content. Also, since we wanted to study the effects
of different system structures on bargaining behavior, we spread our
selection over a considerable span of history beginning in 1898. This
means, of course, that many of our findings do not apply to crises not
characterized by bargaining. And the findings may not be valid for
crises earlier in the nineteenth century, although a cursory examination of a few earlier crises showed that they probably would hold rather
well for crises after 1870.

The case research was guided by a set of questions and hypotheses,
and a checklist of theory-relevant themes developed by the co-authors.[3]

[3] To save space, these guidelines for the case research were not included in the
book. Interested readers may obtain them from the Department of Political
Science, SUNY-Buffalo, Buffalo, N.Y. 14261.

The research team met frequently in seminar during the early years of the project, roughly 1969 to 1972. In the initial phase, the co-authors presented their theoretical ideas and received useful criticism. Later, the case researchers presented their findings to the group. These sessions were invaluable in revealing cross-case similarities and differences and generating new theoretical insights. Professor Pruitt participated in some of these seminars and contributed psychological perspective. Professor Guinn kept us down to earth when bursts of theoretical exuberance threatened to lead us too far from the historical facts. Professors Murdock, Planck, and Diesing, moderately sympathetic with revisionist history of the Cold War, provided a useful counterpoise to the more traditional views of Snyder and Guinn; our discussions of certain controversial points helped to produce a balance interpretation of the post-World War II cases.

Glenn Snyder conceived, designed, and directed the study, considerably assisted in the design and direction by his co-author, Paul Diesing. In writing up the final results, the co-authors divided the labor according to their particular skills—Diesing on formal models, Snyder on less formal theories. Snyder wrote the first drafts of Chapters I, III, VI, VII, and part of II; Diesing, Chapters IV, V, and most of II. In the revision process, however, each made contributions to the other's drafts, so the book is truly a joint product, though some chapters are more joint than others. The collaborative revision process was sometimes difficult, owing primarily to the differing intellectual backgrounds and outlooks of the co-authors. Snyder's field is international relations; Diesing's, the philosophy of social science and political theory. These different perspectives were on the one hand beneficial, in that we each learned much from the other. On the other hand, we sometimes found ourselves at odds on either theoretical preferences or interpretation of the empirical data. Working in a spirit of mutual respect, we managed to reach common ground on most of our differences. When disagreements could not be resolved, it was decided that the author of the first draft of a chapter would have the last word. The other party would write a dissent if he felt it necessary for integrity's sake. There are not many such dissents, and they are on major theoretical points where the reader may well benefit from the juxtaposition of two contrasting viewpoints. With the exception of points where dissents are raised, and the separately authored case summaries in Appendix A, we both assume full and sole responsibility for the contents of this book.

We wish to express our thanks to several scholars who read and commented helpfully on earlier drafts of the book or parts of it: Lowell Dittmer, Lawrence Finkelstein, William T. R. Fox, William Gamson,

Robert Jervis, James King, Peter Kodžić, Charles Lockhart, Clark
Murdock, George Quester, Dean Pruitt, and Kenneth Waltz.

For efficient secretarial assistance, we are indebted to Chris Black,
Cindy Breeden, Roslyn Capisco, and Diane Biggins, all secretaries in
the Department of Political Science, and to Donna Iverson, Carol
Breitenbach, and Judith Wagner in the Philosophy Department.

The National Science Foundation supported this project over a
five-year span with a grant to Glenn Snyder that also provided support
to Paul Diesing and our research assistants. When the NSF grant ex-
pired, the Advanced Research Program of the Naval War College gen-
erously provided full support to Glenn Snyder during the fall of 1974
to permit completion of the book. We also thank the Free Press for
permission to use revised portions of Snyder's chapter on "Crisis Bargaining" in Charles F. Hermann, ed., *International Crises: Insights from
Behavioral Research,* 1972, and a large part of his essay on "Crises and
International Systems" in James Rosenau, Kenneth Thompson, and
Gavin Boyd, eds., *World Politics,* 1976.

A note on sources and footnotes: we have not cited sources for our
historical references in the main body of the book, except for certain
specific points revealed by recent research that may not yet be generally
known. A selected list of sources consulted for the case studies is
given in Appendix A, following the summary of each case. The sources
are mostly secondary, although some primary sources, chiefly memoirs,
were used for the post-World War II cases.

GLENN H. SNYDER
PAUL DIESING

GLOSSARY

GAME MODEL SYMBOLS

A First player

B Second player

C A strategy of accepting the other player's demands in whole or in part; making concessions, either all at once or gradually

CC The outcome when both players each accept the other's demands in part; a compromise outcome

CD The outcome when A accepts B's demands completely or almost completely

CD A mixed strategy of making certain limited or conditional concessions, coupled with firmness on essentials

D A strategy of refusing to compromise; standing firm on one's initial demands, except for minor adjustments

DC The outcome when B accepts A's demands completely or almost completely

DD Deadlock; the outcome when both sides refuse to reduce their initial demands, and negotiations break down

DE A mixed strategy of standing firm on initial demands and preparing to attack if the other player does not accept those demands within a specified time

E Military attack

P The payoff to either A or B of a breakdown of negotiations (DD)

R The payoff to either A or B of a compromise outcome (CC)

S The payoff for accepting the opponent's demands completely

T The payoff for getting one's initial demand accepted by the other player; payoff for winning

TYPES OF DECISION-MAKING STRUCTURES

Type 1.   Decision made by one or two persons pretty much according to their own judgment

Type 2.   Decision made by one person within limits set by his colleagues, who may also get involved

Type 3.   Decision made by one person after getting advice from several quite influential advisors

Type 4.   Decision made by 3 or more persons: a committee or Cabinet or Presidium

Type 5.   Decision made by a committee that is sharply and continuously divided, cannot agree on anything

CONFLICT AMONG NATIONS

CHAPTER I

INTERNATIONAL CRISES AND INTERNATIONAL THEORY

This book may be viewed from two different perspectives. On the one hand, it is a study of how states and statesmen behave in international crises, and it uses several kinds of theory to describe and explain that behavior. From this perspective, the purpose of the analysis is to increase our understanding of crises, and the theories are used as analytical tools. From another point of view, the purpose is to improve and integrate the theories—chiefly systems, bargaining, and decision-making theories—using crises as an empirical source for the testing, revision, augmentation, and synthesis of theory. Here the empirical phenomenon —crisis—functions more as a means than an end of analysis.

We did not feel a need to choose between these two perspectives, since they are not opposed but complementary. When one theorizes about any empirical phenomenon, the theory will have broader prima facie applicability to the extent the phenomenon has some elements in common with other phenomena in its general empirical field. And when one tries to improve general theory in the field by focusing on a particular aspect of the field, one is bound to learn a good deal about that aspect. Thus we conceive of our work *both* as a theory of crisis behavior and as a contribution to the theory of international conflict or international politics generally. Our conscious attempt to integrate several types of theory in an empirical context strengthens, we hope, the latter contribution.

Progress toward a general theory of international politics will proceed fastest, one supposes, by focusing empirical research initially on phenomena that lie at the center of the field. Theory thus developed can then be extended outward, with appropriate qualifications, to the more peripheral aspects. Crises admirably meet this criterion of centrality. Conflict is central to all politics, especially international politics, and crises are conflict episodes *par excellence*. Lying as they do at the nexus between peace and war, crises reveal most clearly and intensely the distinguishing characteristic of international politics and the logical starting point for theorizing about it: the pervasive expectation of potential war,[1] which follows from the "anarchic" structure of

---

[1] We prefer this phrase to Stanley Hoffmann's (and Thomas Hobbes's) "state of war," which is a bit too hyperbolic, although it nicely dramatizes the essential consequences of structural anarchy. Stanley Hoffmann, *The State of War: Essays in the Theory and Practice of International Politics* (New York: Praeger, 1965).

the system. Since war is always possible, the implicit or explicit threat of war is the ultimate form of political pressure and the ultimate means to security and other values. What most urgently needs theoretical description and explanation is how the perpetual shadow of war affects the behavior of states, and how they manipulate that shadow to advance and protect their interests. In placid peacetime this expectation of potential war remains in the background of the statesman's consciousness and its effects are muted, diffuse, and not easily observable. In a crisis, the expectation is dramatically elevated and its behavioral effects stand starkly revealed. Related core elements, such as power configurations, interests, images, and alignments tend to be more sharply clarified, to be activated and focused on a single well-defined issue. The policy choice between coercing or conciliating adversaries, which is a perennial and central dilemma in diplomacy even in ordinary times, comes to a head in a crisis and urgently demands resolution. Thus a crisis distills many of the elements that make up the essence of politics in the international system. It is a "moment of truth" when the latent product of all these central elements becomes manifest in decision and action.

The case for using crises as a data source for the empirical development of general theory rests also on the generality of the primary form of interaction between states in a crisis—that of *bargaining*, broadly defined to include coercion and deterrence as well as mutual accommodation. Bargaining is pervasive in political life, and especially so in international politics, where centralized authority is absent. The external and internal parameters of crisis bargaining, namely the power structure of the international system and the domestic politics and decision-making processes of the actors, are also parameters of non-crisis bargaining. Thus, whatever theory we can develop about crisis bargaining, as bounded and influenced by these parameters, should have some validity, with appropriate modification, for diplomatic bargaining in other contexts.

Of course, we cannot claim to be presenting here a "general theory" of international politics. Theories about international systems, bargaining, and decision making are not the only theories that would have to be linked on the road to that (possibly illusory) goal, though we contend that they must be central to any general theory. And despite what we have just said about the generalizability of theory developed from the study of crises, such wider relevance pertains mostly to the "strategic" dimension of international politics—i.e., the search for security and promotion of other interests by sovereign states via the accumulation, use, or threatened use of military force. The theory is less relevant, for example, to such things as the politics of international economics, revolution, "transnational" relations, international organizations, and other elements of international community. And of course crises have certain special characteristics—notably a high degree of conflict, the perception of a dangerous probability of war, and a high emotional content—which limit the general relevance of theory based on them. We would argue, nevertheless, that it is possible to "factor out" empirical features peculiar to strategic crises and hence to increase the general applicability of the present theory. Some of the non-strategic aspects mentioned above do often appear tangentially in our crisis cases—e.g., revolutionary disturbance of some kind occurs in almost all cases, international organizations occasionally get involved, and community restraints such as international law often moderate the coercive behavior of the parties. While this does not mean that a theory centered on crises contributes much to a *general* theoretical understanding of such matters, it does help to show their relationship to the strategic dimension. And it further supports the point made above that a strategic crisis tends to galvanize, clarify, and concentrate many important elements in international politics, and to reveal the interaction between them more explicitly than in other empirical contexts.

Our methodology was quite straightforward. We took certain abstract, deductive theories and models about bargaining, decision making, and international systems and tested their empirical validity, or at least their plausibility, against 16 case studies of crises, ranging from Fashoda, 1898, to the Yom Kippur "alert crisis" of 1973. Much of the theory was available in the existing literature; some of it we invented. We also developed a list of specific hypotheses—some of them deduced from the general theories, some abstracted from "conventional wisdom," others merely hunches—and also a checklist of theory-relevant items for our researchers to look for in the cases. We sought to maximize comparability of the cases by defining the concept "crisis" as precisely as possible and by choosing cases that essentially matched the definition. The range of cases spans two different international systems—the multipolar, non-nuclear system that preceded World War I and continued during the interwar years, and the bipolar, nuclear system that followed World War II. Thus we were able to observe the effects of international systemic variables on bargaining and decision making, and to determine what aspects of such behavior seemed to be similar across both systems.[2]

The results of this confrontation of theory and history amount to a set of judgments about the empirical validity and usefulness of the various theories, and explicit or implicit suggestions for their revision,

---

[2] Appendix A gives short summaries of 12 of the cases studied.

augmentation, and combination, at least for the study of crises and potentially for the study of international politics in general.

THE ANATOMY OF INTERNATIONAL CRISES

The term *crisis* has been used in so many different ways, in personal and domestic social contexts as well as in international affairs, that it has no generally accepted meaning. Consequently, we must stipulate a definition that suits our research purposes.

An international crisis is a sequence of interactions between the governments of two or more sovereign states in severe conflict, short of actual war, but involving the perception of a dangerously high probability of war.

We use the term *sequence of interactions* rather than *situation* because of the ambiguity and emptiness of the latter term. *Sequence of interactions* is more meaningful, first, because it is the kind of interaction going on between the states that gives their relations the character of "crisis" and because the term *interaction* ties in nicely with our dominant theoretical theme of bargaining. Second, the word *sequence* clearly denotes a span of time and also a certain relatedness between the specific instances of interaction—each instance is affected by the instances just past and by the contemplation of possible following instances.

Note that our definition says nothing about the amount of time covered by a crisis. Most previous analysts have emphasized shortness of decision time as one of the defining conditions of crisis, along with a related sense of urgency. While the notion of urgency is supportable in terms of a sense of danger and risk that the parties feel must be alleviated as soon as possible, short decision time is not a necessary characteristic of crisis. Many historical crises lasted for months, even a year or longer—e.g., the Morocco crisis of 1905–1906 or the Berlin crisis of 1958–1960.

The term *governments of sovereign states* needs no elaboration except to note what it excludes. Principally, it excludes revolutions and internal war except when intervention by outside governments leads to a danger of war between the intervenors or between one intervenor and the incumbent government. Thus the Dominican "crisis" of 1965 was not a crisis by our criteria because it was a revolutionary situation in which only one outside power intervened and essentially on the side of the incumbent government. However, a crisis under our definition— one between sovereign governments—may involve some revolutionary elements or even be precipitated by them, as the 1914 crisis was precipitated by Austria's fear of revolution fomented by Serbian intrigues.

Quite obviously, a crisis always involves "severe conflict." There is, first, a deep *conflict of interest* between the parties. However, conflict of interest in itself is not sufficient to bring about a crisis. One of the parties must initiate some form of *conflict behavior* in an attempt to resolve the underlying conflict of interest in its favor. Usually, a crisis erupts when one party attempts to coerce the other with threats of violence and the other party resists.

The centerpiece of our definition is "the perception of a dangerously high probability of war" by the governments involved. Just how high the perceived probability must be to qualify as a crisis is impossible to specify. But ordinary usage of the term *crisis* implies that whatever is occurring might result in the outbreak of war. The perceived probability must at least be high enough to evoke feelings of fear and tension to an uncomfortable degree.

Several corollaries are implied here. First there are various forms of disputation (conflict behavior) between great powers that cannot be called crises because, if there is any chance of war at all, it is below the "crisis threshold." Such low-intensity forms of conflict behavior may be referred to as "disputes," "disagreements," "press wars," or simply "bad relations."

Second, the probability-of-war element excludes so-called "crises" between allies, such as the Skybolt affair of 1962. Our crises are between governments who identify each other as enemies or at least potential enemies, and the kinds of political processes we shall be analyzing are primarily adversary processes. However, the adversaries usually have allies, so we include some analysis of alliance relations.

Third, the term *probability of war* excludes war itself from the concept "crisis," although minor forms of violence "short of war" are included as potential instruments of coercive bargaining. In the modern age, when the line between peace and war has become increasingly blurred, it may in some empirical cases be difficult to determine precisely when "crisis violence" becomes transformed into "war." And, as Thomas Schelling has emphasized, war itself, especially limited war, has become increasingly an affair of bargaining, similar in many respects to crisis bargaining.[3] Despite such occasional ambiguity, we simply stipulate that cases of large-scale violence (war) lie outside the class of events we call "crises," although war may be a consequence of crises. The distinction corresponds closely enough to ordinary language usage and to empirical reality.

The exclusion of war, per se, from the concept, does not exclude crises that accompany or arise out of war between states that are aligned or

[3] Thomas C. Schelling, *The Strategy of Conflict* (Cambridge, Mass.: Harvard University Press, 1960), pp. 53–81.

allied with the warring protagonists, or between one of the states at war and a third state. For example, the 1973 Yom Kippur war in the Middle East triggered a brief crisis between the United States and the Soviet Union. Similarly, almost a hundred years earlier, the Russo-Turkish war of 1877–1878 set off a crisis between England and Russia. The Korean war stimulated a crisis between the United States and China that eventually led to China's entry into the war.

Finally, the term *probability*, in the loose, subjective sense in which we use it here, suggests the element of *uncertainty,* an element stressed by Thomas Schelling: "The essence of the crisis is its unpredictability." [4] One kind of unpredictability is that arising from the participant's lack of full control over events, the possibility of "things getting out of hand." But even if the parties do have firm control (over their own behavior at least), uncertainty also arises from their very imperfect information about the other party's values and intentions. To a considerable extent it is this element of uncertainty, in both the forms mentioned, that lends to an event its "crisis atmosphere," i.e., to feelings of fear, tension and urgency. If each party *knew* what the other intended to do—in simple terms: yield, stand firm, or fight—and also knew its own intentions in the light of that knowledge, there could be no crisis. Either no coercive challenge would be issued, or, if issued, it would be followed inexorably either by the opponent's capitulation or by war. Even if some length of time occurred between challenge and outcome, it would be characterized not by feelings of "crisis" but by the parties' preparation to do what their values and certain knowledge dictated. Thus, it is largely because of the lack of complete information that crises occur at all. A corollary is that if one of the parties thinks it *does* have accurate information about the other's intentions, the situation does not *become* a crisis for that party until it realizes it has misestimated those intentions or loses confidence in its initial estimate. For example, the Cuban crisis of 1962 did not become a crisis for the Soviet Union until President Kennedy issued the U.S. challenge in a television speech and confounded Soviet expectations. It had already been a crisis for the U.S. government for a week while secret decisions were being made.

Our definition is quite different from those typically employed by students of the effects of crisis on decision-making behavior. A definition of this latter type is the one advanced by Charles F. Hermann: "a crisis is a situation that (1) threatens high-priority goals of the decision-making unit, (2) restricts the amount of time available for response before the decision is transformed, and (3) surprises the

---

[4] Schelling, *Arms and Influence* (New Haven, Conn.: Yale University Press, 1966), p. 97.

members of the decision-making unit by its occurrence." [5] While this definition usefully points to certain characteristics of crisis that presumably affect decision making, it obscures the state-to-state interaction aspect of crises, which we regard as fundamental. Only when this aspect is central to the definition do all the dimensions of crisis as an international political phenomenon come into view.[6]

Of course, we do not assert that crises have no effects on the context of internal decision making, or that these effects are not important. For example the feeling of tension that always accompanies a crisis is subjectively felt within states, although it is a consequence of the objective tension between the interests of the states involved. Thus, Edward L. Morse includes in his definition of crisis the notion of "a situation requiring a choice between mutually incompatible but highly valued objectives." [7] That is, a crisis not only is a severe conflict of interests between states but also sets up a sharp conflict of values within the states. Each party faces the uncomfortable choice between preserving its politico-strategic *interests* by standing firm at the risk of war, or ensuring *peace* by sacrificing important interests. It is probably the difficulty and distastefulness of this choice, combined with the quality of uncertainty mentioned above (notably uncertainty about how the other party will choose), and the perception of the possible imminence of war, that produces the general sense of crisis. Moreover the internal value conflict may give rise to an internal struggle between individuals, factions and agencies, each favoring different ways of resolving the conflict along a "hard-soft" continuum. Thus the Morse component is a useful supplement to our own definition because it points to internal effects in a way that links them to the central interaction process between the state adversaries.

So much for the definition of crisis. We turn now to a discussion of how crises fit into the wider pattern of diplomatic-strategic events and to some further characteristics of their "anatomy."

[5] Hermann, ed., *International Crises: Insights from Behavioral Research* (New York: The Free Press, 1972), p. 13.

[6] James L. Richardson has made a similar point in "The Definition of Crisis: A Working Paper" (mimeographed) 1973, p. 9.

[7] Morse's complete definition is "the sudden emergence (whether or not anticipated) of a situation requiring a policy choice by one or more states within a relatively short period of time, a situation requiring a choice beween mutually incompatible but highly valued objectives." We exclude the notions of suddenness and short time for decision from our own definition because they are not logically necessary and some empirical crises do not have these qualities. See Morse, "Crisis Diplomacy, Interdependence, and the Politics of International Economic Relations," in Raymond Tanter and Richard H. Ullman, eds., *Theory and Policy in International Relations* (Princeton, N.J.: Princeton University Press, 1973), p. 127.

It is useful to conceive of a crisis as an intermediate zone between peace and war. Almost all wars are preceded by a crisis of some sort, although of course not all crises eventuate in war. A crisis is a sort of hybrid condition, neither peace nor war, but containing elements of both and comprising the potential for transformation from peace to war. Thus a study of crisis behavior should cast some light on the age-old problem of the causes of war, especially if we consciously ask ourselves: under what conditions are crises resolved peacefully and what conditions tend to make them escalate to war? Beyond this, the "intermediate zone" conception highlights an interesting characteristic of crisis behavior: it tends to be a mixture of behavioral elements typical of war and other elements typical of peacetime diplomacy. War in its extreme form is the ultimate form of coercion—the raw, physical clash of armed forces—in a context where the pursuit of objectives in conflict greatly predominates over the pursuit of common interest. Accommodation occurs only in the terminal phase in negotiating the terms of surrender, although in limited war, the parties also tacitly agree during the war about the nature of the limits. Non-crisis peacetime diplomacy, even between adversaries, is generally accommodative; attempts to realize common interests predominate over the use of coercion to win conflicts. Relations between adversaries are colored by some sort of conflict of interest, but conflict behavior takes relatively mild or passive forms: mutual deterrent postures, minor disputes, and so on.

In a crisis, these contrasting types of behavior tend to converge, merging in a complex blend of coercion and accommodation. Diplomacy becomes more actively coercive, and the emotional climate shifts toward greater hostility and fear. Aims center on winning the conflict rather than realizing common interests. When accommodation occurs, it is not "amicable settlement" but "backing down" or "painful compromise," forced by the risk of war. Pressure is exercised not by brute force, as in warfare, but by manipulating the risk of war and the fear of escalation. The risk of violence if one stands his ground is analogous, in function, to the actual violence suffered as one tries to take or hold ground in war. Backdown or facedown are the analogues to defeat or victory. The outcome is determined not by relative physical strength, but by psychological strength—the relative ability of the parties to stand risk. The well-known terms *coercive diplomacy* and *force short of war,* each from a different perspective, express the notion of a blend of peace-like and war-like behavior. The central problem of crisis statesmanship is how to achieve an optimum blend of coercion and accommodation in one's strategy, a blend that will both avoid war and maximize one's gains or minimize one's losses.

How and why do crises occur? What is it that causes conflicts of interests and mild conflict behavior to escalate to the point where war seems possible and a crisis exists? How does one identify the beginning and end of a crisis? Are there more or less regular phases within a crisis, as well as immediate pre-crisis and post-crisis phases, each with its own typical characteristics? Questions such as these seem to call for a phase model of crisis interaction over time, which can be compared with the course of events in actual cases.

Typically, the immediate cause of a crisis is an attempt by one state to coerce another by an explicit or implicit threat of force. The first act of severe coercion may be called the *challenge;* technically it starts the crisis by posing a distinct possibility of war. A challenge is stimulated or motivated by a *precipitant,* of which there are two broad types, external and internal. In the external type, a state perceives an intolerable situation developing in its environment as a result of action by another state or states. It may be intolerable for a variety of reasons: it is threatening to the state's external or internal security, it threatens the state's economic viability or affronts its national dignity and prestige. We may call this the *general* precipitant, which provokes the challenge. There is usually also a *specific* precipitant, a particular and especially provocative act by the opponent that is seen as the "last straw," or perhaps as the pretext for the challenge.

Thus, to illustrate, the general precipitant of the 1914 crisis was the intriguing of Serbian-based revolutionaries within the Austro–Hungarian empire; the specific precipitant was the assassination at Sarajevo; and the challenge was the Austrian ultimatum to Serbia. The two Morocco crises of 1905 and 1911 were precipitated generally by increasing French penetration and control, specifically in each case by the sending of missions to the capital to make demands on the Sultan and "restore order." The German challenge that started the first crisis was a visit by the Kaiser to Tangier during which he expressed support for the Sultan against the French; in the 1911 case the challenge was the anchoring of a German gunboat in the harbor of Agadir. As the latter examples indicate, the act of challenge may not explicitly state the demand and threat; these may be left for later elaboration. In a more recent case, the Cuban missile crisis of October 1962, the general precipitant was the flow of Russian armaments into Cuba during the summer and early fall, the specific precipitant was the Soviet attempt to deploy long-range missiles, and the challenge was a televised speech by President Kennedy demanding that the missiles be withdrawn.

The identification of specific precipitants is useful in developing a pattern of crisis events, but in most cases little causality should be imputed to them. They function more as convenient occasions for, or as legitimizers of, the challenge than as causes of it. When McGeorge Bundy was asked about the importance of the Communist raid on the

Pleiku base in triggering the start of U.S. bombing of North Vietnam, he replied "Pleikus are like streetcars"—one will come along eventually if you wait long enough. The real causes of a crisis challenge are more likely to be found in the general precipitant—the larger and longer-term developments in the challenger's environment that create an intolerable conflict of interest between the challenger and some other states(s).[8] But a full statement of the "causes" of any particular crisis would have to go beyond even the general precipitant, to whatever it was that caused the "intolerable situation" to develop, and this would lead into a host of factors in the general historical background. In short, our "precipitant" does not mean "cause" in any complete sense, but only in a partial proximate sense: those developments that finally caused a developing conflict to boil over into crisis.[9]

We have so far discussed only precipitants external to the challenger; the challenger's interests and values do not necessarily change; they are threatened or violated by the actions of other states or some other outside forces. Another type involves changes internal to the challenger— e.g., changes in the values and perceptions of leaders, or of the balance of power between factions within the regime, or a change of the regime itself. In these cases, the state's leaders come to perceive opportunities for change by coercion and place a high value on such change. The purpose of the challenge that starts the crisis is to revise the status quo to the state's advantage, not to preserve it against the efforts of others to change it, as in the first type.

Examples of such an internal precipitant may be seen in the crises of the 1930s in Europe. Although many Germans no doubt were dissatisfied with the boundaries of Germany as drawn by the Versailles treaty, it was only after Hitler came to power, with his special values and perception of the external environment, that a series of crises occurred. The external environment was not changing to Germany's disadvantage; it became "intolerable" and was challenged because of changes within Germany that produced an expansionist foreign policy.

An internal precipitant will also have both general and specific aspects. In the Munich case, for example, the general precipitant was Hitler's desire to "smash Czechoslovakia," or even more generally his

---

[8] The Cuban missile crisis is a notable exception to this statement. There was more real causality in the specific precipitant—the introduction of Soviet missiles into Cuba—than in the general precipitant, defined as Soviet military aid to Cuba in general.

[9] We are indebted to Robert Jervis and Lawrence Finkelstein for the point made in this paragraph, and to Jervis for the Bundy comment. The latter is quoted in Townsend Hoopes, *The Limits of Intervention* (New York: David McKay, 1969), p. 30.

desire to expand the boundaries of the Reich. The specific precipitant, which, it seems, brought on his actual decision to attack Czechoslovakia by a certain date, was the "May crisis" when the Czechs infuriated Hitler by mobilizing and causing the French and British to issue stiff warnings to Germany.

In some cases the crisis arises out of a combination of external and internal precipitants. An example would be the Berlin crisis of 1958. To a considerable degree, Khrushchev's challenge was motivated by factors internal to the Communist bloc: the weakness of the East German government and the perception by the Soviet leadership that getting the Western powers out of West Berlin and/or gaining the formal recognition of the German Democratic Republic would both strengthen East Germany and give the Soviet Union a great diplomatic triumph. However, there was also a degree of external precipitation in the anti-Communist propaganda, espionage, and subversive activity that the Soviets perceived to be emanating from West Berlin, and perhaps also in the rearmament of West Germany and the U.S. deployment of tactical nuclear weapons on West German territory.

In a broad sense, almost every crisis would have a mixed precipitant, since with the external stimulus, it is certain of the challenger's values and perceptions that impel him to react. With the internal stimulus, the shift in the internal perspectives of the challenger tends to focus his attention on some aspect of the external environment that presents an opportunity for gain. Thus, the external–internal distinction refers in most cases to a preponderance of motivation one way or the other.

Once a challenge is given, it must be *resisted* by the challenged party in order for a crisis to occur. If the victim were to cave in immediately, there would be no crisis. Sometimes resistance is immediate, overt, and clear: a vigorous "no" is issued to the challenger's demand. Sometimes it is more diffuse, consisting of an absence of official response to the challenge, a defiant outcry in the press and public opinion, simple continuance of an activity that the challenger has demanded be stopped, or perhaps a quiet increase in military readiness. Even in the barely conceivable case of neither clear nor diffuse signals of resistance, a crisis will generally be perceived to exist as a consequence of the challenge alone, since it will be clear both to the immediate parties and to outside observers that important interests of the victim have been threatened, and that he therefore can be *expected* to resist, at least initially.

The resister is not only resisting but also deterring. That is, besides saying "no" to the challenger's demands, he is also explicitly or implicitly threatening to fight if the challenger carries out his threat. It may also be said that the issuance of the challenge constitutes a kind of failure of deterrence for the resister—a failure to deter coercive action against itself.[10]

The collision of challenge and resistance produces a *confrontation,* which is the core of the crisis. The confrontation may continue for a short or fairly long time (from days to months) and is characterized by high or rising tension and predominantly coercive tactics on both sides, each standing firm on its initial position and issuing threats, warnings, military deployments, and other signals to indicate firmness, to undermine the other's firmness, and generally to persuade the other that he must be the one to back down if war is to be avoided.

There may be several peaks of tension of varying intensity during the confrontation phase, each centering perhaps on a particular issue, or perhaps following an especially severe and provocative coercive act. At these peaks, the likelihood of war appears to rise, and the feelings of anxiety associated with tension become more intense.

In general, there are three possible outcomes of the confrontation phase: war, capitulation by one side, or negotiated or tacit compromise. If it is war, the crisis is over, as we define it, and the parties move into a different type of interaction. If it is capitulation or compromise, the confrontation is followed by a *resolution* phase during which the details of settlement are arranged, and accommodative tactics—bids, concessions, settlement proposals—become preponderant over coercive behavior, although the latter may not entirely disappear. This phase will involve capitulation by one party if the other has clearly established its dominance of resolve during the confrontation phase; it will involve compromise if neither has established such dominance and both mutually decide to retreat from the brink to avoid disaster. In the former case, "accommodation" often includes some sort of minor facesaving concessions by the victor to allow the loser to rationalize his yielding; in the latter case, accommodation will require some hard bargaining, with one or both sides making displays of determination and mild coercive moves somewhere along the road toward settlement. Accommodation may settle both the crisis and the underlying conflict of interest; or it may only settle the crisis, leaving the conflict of interest unresolved or only partially resolved. There usually is a fairly clear breakpoint between the two phases of confrontation and resolution, resulting from the recogni-

---

[10] Alexander George and Richard Smoke have clearly explained and demonstrated that deterrence is a complex, multilevel phenomenon. The theory of deterrence began at the level of deterring strategic nuclear attack, then was extended downward to the deterrence of limited war. George and Smoke, in *Deterrence in American Foreign Policy: Theory and Practice* (New York: Columbia University Press, 1974) have developed a valuable theory of how deterrence operates at "lower" levels of conflicts—i.e., in crisis-prevention and crisis resolution.

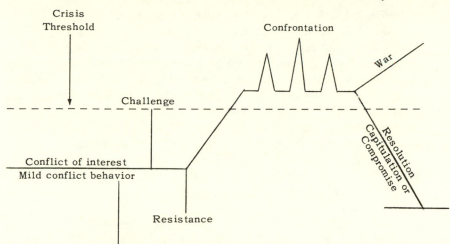

Figure 1-1. Crisis Phases

tion by one or both sides that further coercive and countercoercive tactics based on the initial challenge–resistance positions will either be unsuccessful or too dangerous, or both.

Figure 1–1 summarizes our model of crisis phases. The solid horizontal lines represent the degree of "tension" or intensity of conflict behavior. It is low or mild up to the challenge–resistance point, when it rises above the "crisis threshold" (long dotted line). It varies in intensity during the confrontation phase, then either sharply increases with the transition to war, or falls back to something approximating the pre-crisis level during or following the resolution phase.

The pattern we have just sketched probably fits a majority of crises, but there are also many variations, and some totally different types. Alexander George has emphasized that crises are heavily context-dependent [11] and their political contexts may differ greatly. First, to examine the way a crisis begins, our phase model has an aura of deliberateness about it; the challenger who starts the crisis does so deliberately in an attempt to coerce another party. But are there also *accidental* crises, the parties "stumbling into" a confrontation through a series of actions that neither expected to reach crisis proportions? We find no examples in our sample where the challenge move is accidental, and by

[11] Alexander F. George, David K. Hall and William R. Simons, *The Limits of Coercive Diplomacy* (Boston: Little-Brown, 1971), p. 217. Our phase model is adapted from a similar one by Charles Lockhart in his "A Bargaining Conceptualization of International Crises," Center for International Conflict Studies, State University of New York at Buffalo (mimeographed), April 1970.

definition it hardly could be. However, the prior precipitant sometimes is, either because it is an unauthorized act or because, though itself intended, it is not expected to be challenged severely enough to produce a crisis. Marchand's expedition to Fashoda in 1898 was unintended by the French government as a unit, though it was intended by a part of that government, the Ministry of Colonies. The French government did intend to begin taking over Morocco in 1905, but although it expected protests from Germany, it did not expect a crisis. However, the idea of an accidental crisis seems to connote something more than surprise at being challenged; it implies that both protagonists get drawn into a confrontation by contextual factors beyond the control of either. This would seem to be best exemplified by two major powers being dragged into a crisis by the actions of their clients or allies. For example, the Soviet–U.S. "alert crisis" in the fall of 1973 was precipitated by actions of the Arabs and Israelis. There are elements of accident surrounding the beginning of other crises: e.g., the assassination at Sarajevo was "accidental" from the point of view of the highest officials, at least, of the Serbian government. But the *general* precipitant—the Serbian agitation within Austria–Hungary—was hardly accidental, nor was the Austrian response. In general, while elements of accident, surprise, chance, and imperfect control are often present in our cases, we find no clear example of a crisis beginning entirely by accident, and, in all cases, elements of deliberateness predominate over elements of inadvertence, even though the deliberateness may be premised in very inaccurate perceptions of the situation.

A different type of crisis from the coercive bargaining type portrayed in our model is what might be called the "war scare" or "security dilemma" crisis. Here, tension arises not because one party makes a coercive demand upon another but because one or both parties begin to fear that the other is about to attack. Typically, the parties are already in a fairly high state of hostility and tension. Then one side takes some action that looks like preparation to attack, the other side reacts with partial mobilization, the first side responds with further measures, which confirm the second side's fears and cause it to mobilize further, etc. The preparedness measures are undertaken not to bring coercive pressure upon the opponent but simply to be ready to defend against a possible attack. But the defensive measures on both sides self-confirm each side's fears that the other is preparing an attack, in the familiar dynamics of the security dilemma. Examples of this type of crisis are the war scare of 1875, the "May crisis" that preceded the Munich crisis in 1938, and the Syria–Turkey war scare in 1957. (Such war scares have been frequent in the perennial Israeli–Arab conflict.) Since typically in these cases neither side intends to attack or coerce the other, they are, in a sense, "illusory" crises; yet they are still crises by our definition. Bargaining activity may occur once they get started, as, for example, a firm show of resistance by the "defenders" in the 1875 and 1938 cases forced the presumed "aggressor" to stop his threatening activity. Or a security dilemma subcrisis may emerge out of a crisis that begins with a coercive challenge—for example, the Anglo–German naval war scare that occurred during the Franco–German crisis over Morocco in 1905.

Another non-bargaining variant is the crisis that begins as a prelude or pretext to an intended attack. Hitler's creation of a crisis over Czechoslovakia in 1938 is an example. The reverse twist is illustrated by Bismarck's editing of the Ems telegram in 1870, designed to *provoke* the French into starting a crisis and a war that Bismarck wanted.

There is also considerable variation in the onset of crises that generally fit our coercive bargaining model. First, the parties may not begin to feel a sense of crisis at the same time. When the precipitant is external to the challenger—i.e., when it is some action by the challenger's opponent—the challenger may feel he is in a crisis when he first becomes sensitive to the precipitating actions and before he issues the challenge, while the precipitating actor remains unaware that a crisis is looming. This was the pattern in the Cuban missile crisis, for example. Second, not all crises erupt as suddenly as our diagram might suggest. Sometimes tension rises gradually through a series of actions and reactions, and it is difficult to identify a specific precipitant or a single clear challenge. For instance the U.S. "challenge" to Japan in 1940–1941 was really a series of increasingly severe restrictions on exports of strategic fuel and materials; the increasing application of actual harm that at some point generated a crisis and finally drove Japan to war. Which specific measure should be labeled the "challenge" is hard to say. Usually, however, the challenging act is clearly identifiable, both to the participants at the time and to researchers in retrospect. Even so, it may be preceded by a build-up phase of gradually rising tension. During this phase there may be protests, recriminations, warnings, and even mild acts of coercion by the incipient challenger, and expressions of mild defiance or reassurance by the precipitating actor. Our diagram would be somewhat more realistic, therefore, if the conflict behavior line sloped upward gradually to the challenge point, then sharply upward. As a final qualification, the sense of "crisis" may be felt in different degrees by each party during the crisis. One side may be surer of its superior coercive power and thus confident of prevailing. Hitler in 1938, for example, felt much less of the sense of fear and tension associated with crisis than did Chamberlain, Daladier, or Beneš. Or one side may place a higher value on the things at stake and thus face a much more difficult choice between firmness and yielding, especially if its military power is questionable. It is clear, for example, that the Japanese government agonized more over its decisions in 1941 than did the U.S. government.

Note, incidentally, that our terms *precipitant, challenge,* and *resistance* are strictly technical and skirt the subjective and emotion-laden issue of who is the "aggressor" or who is "to blame" for starting a crisis. They simply denote the sequence of acts that create the actors' perception that the likelihood of war has risen dangerously high. The challenge is the crucial act that starts the crisis, but we do not intend the implication that the challenger is an "aggressor." Either the challenger or the precipitator may be seeking to change the status quo, and both may perceive the other as the "aggressor," but this is irrelevant to our purpose. Further, in postulating that the crisis starts with the clash of specific challenge and resistance moves that push tension over the "crisis threshold," we avoid the elusive and fruitless issue of "who started" a possibly long action-reaction sequence leading up to the crisis.

There are many variations in the way a crisis may be terminated peacefully, e.g., by a simple act of yielding by the loser, by explicit negotiation of varying duration, by tacit bargaining, or by just "fading away." Broadly, there are two alternative conditions for crisis termination: (1) the weaker party realizes its weakness, or (2) neither party is obviously overpowered, but both recognize that continued confrontation is too dangerous. In the first case, if the weaker party is the challenger, he may prefer to let the matter drop rather than negotiate a settlement that is sure to be unfavorable. (Example: China in the Quemoy crisis of 1958.) If the target of a challenge turns out to be the weaker, he must of course perform some act of yielding, which may or may not be done in the context of negotiation. If there is hope of salvaging something, as for the Soviets in the Cuba, 1962, case, there will be some sort of negotiation. Explicit detailed negotiation is most likely when the parties are roughly equal in bargaining power [12] and there must be some give and take in fashioning a settlement. Tacit bargaining may occur when the parties wish to end the crisis but are as yet unwilling to formalize a settlement of the underlying issue in conflict. Here the closest example is the tacit settlement of the Berlin crisis of 1961 by Western acceptance of the Wall and Khrushchev's dropping his deadline for settling the West Berlin issue. Explicit negotiation should not be identified exclusively with the resolution phase: negotiations may occur just before or just after the onset of the crisis, or during the heat of the confrontation, though they are generally unproductive

---

[12] Henceforth, whenever we use the term *power* in the book we mean bargaining power or political power, not military power, for which we will use the terms "military capability" or "military strength."

until the confrontation reveals the true balance of bargaining power. We define the resolution phase as beginning when this revelation takes place; then the denouement may be long or short, depending on the context. It was very short in the Cuban missile crisis, for example, because of the urgency of reaching a settlement before the missiles became operational.

We should not forget that crises are sometimes "resolved" by war. From our two cases of this type—1914 and United States–Japan, 1941 —we can see two general reasons why a war may erupt from a crisis: (1) recognition of power realities comes too late to abort the preemptive logic of military mobilization already begun (1914), and (2) interests are so deeply incompatible that no peaceful settlement is possible (1941). Of course there are other reasons for the outbreak of war, whether or not preceded by a crisis, that our cases do not reveal.

There is also much variation in the aftermath of crises that are resolved peacefully—in their effects on the subsequent relations between the protagonists and third parties and on the general state of the international system. Some crises embitter and worsen subsequent relations, others improve them. An important variable here is whether the crisis resolution also resolves the underlying conflict of interest; another is whether the loser is "driven to the wall" and humiliated or given some face-saving concession that can be presented as a "compromise." Still others are the effects of the crisis on the alignments and on the "images" the parties develop of each other. The Bosnia crisis of 1908–1909 illustrates several of these variables. It did not settle the issue between Russia and Austria in the Balkans. It was a humiliating defeat for Russia at the hands of Germany, unleavened by any "consolation prize." Russia felt it necessary to ease the pain of defeat for her client, Serbia, by promising support in a future crisis, and Germany, likewise, gave a virtual blank check to Austria. Germany developed an image of Russia as a bluffer who could be faced down. Aehrenthal, the Austrian foreign minister, instructed his ministers to spare Russia's feelings and told the press not to describe the outcome as a German–Austrian victory. (Kennedy's instructions to his subordinates not to "gloat" over the U.S. victory in the Cuban missile crisis comes to mind as a parallel.) Nevertheless the crisis left Russia embittered, determined never again to back down to German and Austrian threats, and more closely committed to a client who was a thorn in Austria's side. These factors, combined with almost the mirror image on the German–Austrian side—an impression of Russian weakness of will, and closer ties between these two countries —contributed much to the outbreak of World War I.

The opposite result, an improvement of relations, is illustrated by Fashoda, 1898, and Cuba, 1962. The Fashoda defeat made clear to the French that they had to choose between their conflicting policies of deterring Germany on the continent and competing with England in the colonial arena. Perceiving that the latter was probably a losing enterprise, they decided to mend their fences with England. Although it took a few years for anti-British public opinion to grow used to the idea, the new relationship was consummated in the Entente Cordiale of 1904. Somewhat similarly after 1962, the Soviet Union perceived some contradiction between crisis competition with the United States, where she was not having much success, and a new threat, China. The result was movement toward détente with the United States, which reached its fullest development in the Nixon-Brezhnev agreements of 1972. Of course, there are several differences between these examples, notably that the Cuban crisis occurred in a bipolar context. Since China was not a serious enough threat to require alliance or informal entente with the United States, the reorientation of Soviet policy was limited to the mixed and somewhat fragile relationship of détente. The détente in turn caused further deterioration in Sino-Russian relations and a certain uneasiness among the NATO allies about U.S. reliability. In both China and Western Europe the spectre of collusion loomed between the two duopolists to the detriment of the allies' interests; the lesser allies then began to mend *their* fences with both the behemoth and his clients on the opposite side. As Stanley Hoffmann has remarked, crises "are like rocks thrown into a pond: the stones disappear, but the reverberations ruffle the waters all around." [13]

Aftermath effects could be classified in four categories: effects on relative power between the main protagonists, effects in reducing or increasing conflict of interest, effects on alignments, and emotional effects. Effects on power relations include what material power resources are lost or gained as a consequence of the outcome, effects on images of the other's general resolve, and effects on internal preparedness. As noted above, reduction of the basic conflict of interest may or may not occur. Even when a crisis settlement also settles the interest conflict that underlay it, this may not be sufficient to eliminate or even reduce enmity and hostility if the enmity is a consequence of larger factors such as system structure or alignments in the system. Thus the Agadir crisis of 1911 did settle the Morocco issue between Germany and France, but it did not end, in fact it increased, their enmity because that was more a function of alignments and the perception of the other as a generalized threat than of particular conflicts of interest. Domestic factors, also, may be important determinants of aftermath effects. Again, in the Agadir case, although Germany had more reason

[13] Hoffmann, *Gulliver's Troubles* (New York: McGraw-Hill, 1968), p. 62.

to be dissatisfied with the compromise settlement than did France, the settlement created a popular uproar in France that overthrew a moderate government and installed a hard-line one resolved never again to compromise with Germany. The result was increasing tension and stepped-up arms competition.

Some of the alignment effects have been mentioned. Aside from new alignment or realignment, a crisis may either loosen or solidify existing alliances. The Berlin blockade crisis hastened the consummation of NATO. The 1905 Morocco crisis transformed the Anglo-French entente from a rather vague pledge of friendly cooperation and colonial collusion to a quasi-alliance. Conversely, the Bosnia crisis caused disenchantment with the French connection in Russia because of France's lack of support, which Russia reciprocated in the Agadir affair. But then France, partly because of this sign of Russia's questionable reliability and partly because of the change of regime just mentioned, vowed unconditional fealty to Russia to hold Russia in line—another important input to the tragedy of 1914.

Emotional aftermath effects seem to vary according to the tactics used by the winning side. If the winner employs unnecessarily severe or humiliating threats, or if the loser is not allowed some loophole or face-saving device that permits him to retreat with some semblance of dignity, future relations will be embittered. The unnecessary and excessively brusque German ultimatum to Russia in the Bosnia crisis is a case in point. If the more powerful party does not flaunt his power but uses it in a spirit of quiet firmness without hostility, does not try to glorify his victory publicly, and follows it up with conciliatory moves—as exemplified by Salisbury in 1898 and Kennedy in 1962—the emotional aftermath will be much more benign.

Much more could be said about aftermath effects—Hoffmann's "ruffles in the pond." However, since this is a book primarily about behavior *during* crisis, we rest content with the above observations.

SYSTEMS, BARGAINING, DECISION MAKING: A THEORETICAL SYNOPSIS

It has been frequently noted that international relations theory suffers from an excess of fragmentation. Some theories are advanced to account for some sorts of phenomena, others for other kinds. Some theories are said to be useful at one "level of analysis," others at some other level. In our teaching and research, we are like travelers in a houseboat, shuttling back and forth between separate "islands" of theory, whose relatedness consists only in their being commonly situated somewhere in the great "ocean" of "international behavior." Some theorists take up permanent habitation on one island or other, others continue to shuttle, but few attempt to build bridges, perhaps because the islands seem too far apart.

We are attempting in this book to build bridges between three of these islands: systems theory, bargaining theory, and decision-making theory. We choose these three because between them, underdeveloped as they may be, they seem to encompass the central (most significant) aspects of international behavior. If we can achieve some degree of synthesis between these three bodies of theory, we will have fashioned a core, to which, we hope, other kinds of theory might be linked.[14]

BARGAINING

The central element of the core, as we see it, is bargaining theory. Bargaining theory is central because its constitutent elements correspond to what are widely regarded as the most important elements in international behavior—e.g., power, interests, conflict, and cooperation —and because, being a theory about the interaction of entities in a condition of interdependence, it is directly relevant to what we are presumably most interested in theorizing about, the interactions between sovereign states. The content of these interactions consists largely of the interplay of influence in the prosecution and resolution of conflicts (violently or otherwise) and the establishment of mutually beneficial collaborative arrangements, and that is also what bargaining theory is all about. In this book, we apply bargaining theory chiefly to adversary interaction in situations with a high conflict content—crises—but bargaining theory is just as relevant to other contexts, some of which, such as relations between allies, will appear around the periphery of our analyis.

We construe bargaining theory in a somewhat larger sense than the term "bargaining" normally implies. In everyday language (and in some bargaining theories) bargaining usually refers to a process of give-and-take between parties who both would benefit from some agreement but who would suffer no harm or cost if no agreement is reached. This is an important kind of bargaining—we call it the accommodative aspect—

[14] We remind the reader, however, that our synthesis is empirically focused on the politico-strategic dimension of international politics, with states as the acting units. A good deal of contemporary theory lies outside this focus. In particular, theories of transnationalism, stimulated by the rise of economic interdependence and the increasing importance of private actors, represent a new paradigm that may not be readily assimilable to the one we are developing here. Alternatively, one can argue that the state will remain the dominant actor in an international system that now has two subsystems of roughly equal importance—the politico-military and the politico-economic. We shall be satisfied if we contribute something to theory about the first, but it is not inconceivable that some of our analysis and synthesis could be applied to the different subject matter of the second.

but there is also the *coercive* aspect, which in ordinary discourse is usually considered something else—intimidation, blackmail, the use of power of some kind to force (persuade, influence) another party to do something that he ordinarily would not wish to do. He is persuaded to do so essentially by a threat of harm whose effects he considers worse than the sacrifice or behavior change that is being demanded of him. What coercion and accommodation have in common is that, in both contexts, one party is presented with a choice between accepting the other party's proposal (offer, demand) or rejecting it and holding out in the hope of getting something better at the risk of getting something worse. In accommodative bargaining the "something better" is a better offer from the other bargainer; in coercive bargaining it is a withdrawal of the threat or reduction of the demand. The "something worse" in accommodative bargaining is "no deal"; in coercive bargaining it is the harm suffered if the threat is carried out. In many bargaining situations there are elements of both accommodation and coercion; in crisis bargaining the coercive element tends to be dominant, and may be exercised by the defensive as well as the offensive side.

One would expect crisis bargaining to exhibit certain features that distinguish it from, say, bargaining over the purchase of a house or bargaining between factions in a legislature or in an election campaign, or international bargaining in non-crisis situations. First, crisis bargaining is typically "redistributive" or "distributive" bargaining—to borrow terms coined by Iklé, and Walton and McKersie, respectively.[15] Distributive bargaining, the more general term, refers to bargaining over the division of a good that is mutually desired. Redistributive bargaining is a subclass: the object(s) at issue are already possessed or in the process of being acquired by one of the parties; the other party tries to force the possessor to give up all or part of it, or to stop acquiring it. International crises are almost always cases of redistributive bargaining; the "challenge" that triggers the crisis is a demand that a government give up to the challenger something that it already has or controls or that it stop an ongoing process of acquiring possession or control. A few crises, however, may involve simply distribution, not *re*distribution, when the object at stake is controlled by neither of the protagonists before the crisis. The crisis erupts when they collide in their simultaneous attempts to gain control. One would expect to find such a crisis historically in colonial competition, and in fact the only one of our cases that approach the distributive rather than the redistributive type—the Fashoda crisis of 1898—was essentially a colonial dispute.

[15] Fred C. Iklé, *How Nations Negotiate* (New York: Harper & Row, 1964); Richard F. Walton and Robert B. McKersie, *A Behavioral Theory of Labor Negotiations* (New York: McGraw-Hill, 1965).

As the terms *distributive* and *redistributive* imply, in crises the parties' attention tends to center more on their conflicting interests—on making gains and avoiding losses—than on their common interests, although their minimum common interest in avoiding war acts as an important constraint on their conflict behavior. This is to be contrasted with Walton and McKersie's "integrative bargaining" and Iklé's "innovative bargaining," virtually equivalent classes in which the parties strive to reach some new arrangement that is mutually beneficial. Here, the common interests are at the forefront, although there are elements of conflict in the fact that alternative forms of the new arrangement may benefit one party more than the other. Some typical examples of integrative or innovative bargaining are arms control negotiations and negotiation of trade treaties and customs unions. While crisis bargaining, almost by definition, is never integrative-innovative in its essential nature, there may be integrative phases in the bargaining process or integrative elements in the outcome. For example, an outcome might be termed integrative or at least mixed integrative-distributive (again borrowing from Walton and McKersie) if it definitively settled a serious source of friction between the parties, and the shared gains from this considerably exceeded the losses suffered by the "losing" party in the conflict dimension. Or a crisis might begin as a redistributive affair and become transformed into integrative bargaining if during its course one or both parties came to recognize the other's claims as "legitimate" or devalued its own goals to a degree that the costs of compromise appeared minor compared to the mutual gains to be had from a long-range improvement of relations. Finally, one of the parties might sincerely perceive its proposals as integrative in nature even though they are perceived by the other as an attempt at redistribution. For example, the Soviet Union may have really believed that its "free city" proposal for West Berlin in 1958 would produce mutual benefits in stabilizing the situation in Central Europe, far outweighing the Western sacrifice. The West, of course, saw the proposal as redistributive: hence the outbreak of a crisis. A less sympathetic interpretation of Soviet perceptions and motives would be that they pretended to be proposing integrative bargaining (get rid of the "abnormal" status of West Berlin as a tag-end of World War II that was a continual source of friction) in order to obscure their essentially redistributive aims.

The conception of crisis bargaining as essentially or usually redistributive implies certain asymmetries between the parties that are not present in most other bargaining contexts. The initial bid of the "challenger" is a demand for change in the status quo, or for a stop to his adversary's attempts to change the status quo unilaterally.[16] In the first case, the

---

[16] Parties may sometimes disagree about what the status quo is, who is trying to change it, and who is defending it.

"resister" or "defender" would appear to be at a bargaining disadvantage since logically he can make no counterdemand other than to stand firm on the status quo itself. In other words, he lacks flexibility. If he wants to appear firm, yet "reasonable," he has little scope for demonstrating "reasonableness" and runs the risk of appearing excessively intransigent to third parties and world opinion; whereas the challenger can moderate his demands and, by appealing to the convention that "concessions should be reciprocated," bring pressure on the resister of a kind that is not available to the latter. This asymmetry may, however, be more than counterbalanced by others. First, the status quo has a certain aura of legitimacy, whereas an attempt to change the status quo by threat of force is generally considered illegitimate in international tradition. Second, usually the party who already possesses something will value it higher than another who covets it. The possessor's valuation may even increase by his knowledge that it is coveted or by an attempt to extort it from him. Third, the defender cannot make concessions without sacrificing something of substance, while the revisionist party's concessions are merely reductions in the amount of change demanded. Fourth, if the defender yields the object in dispute, he is likely to consider it lost permanently, while a revisionist challenger can more easily yield, expecting to get another chance later.[17] All four of these latter asymmetries increase the resister's motivation to stand firm and hence increase his bargaining power.

However, when the challenge is to some ongoing activity that is changing the existing state of affairs (by far the more frequent situation in our cases—12 of 16), the shoe tends to be on the other foot. The challenger can then cite the sanctity of the long-term status quo as justification for his challenge (as Kennedy did in 1962), and the other side may be hard put to find some equally potent source of legitimacy for change. When the status quo is only recently established or in the process of being changed, the challenger may be more powerfully motivated to force a return to the long-run state of affairs than the resister is motivated to hold on to his recently acquired gain. However, in this class of cases, the asymmetry is not so regular or clear-cut. Legitimacy may be attributed to some sort of ongoing change in the status quo. France, for example, in 1905 and certainly by 1911, could count on general diplomatic and public acceptance of the idea that she was destined to control Morocco, and this enhanced her bargaining power against the German challenge. And, as the Germans calculated in 1914

[17] We are indebted to Lawrence Finkelstein for this fourth point. Bernard Brodie makes the first point, concerning legitimacy, adding that the sanctity of the territorial status quo has increased in the nuclear age, in Europe at least, because the responsibility for disturbing the peace is much heavier when it involves some risk of catastrophe. B. Brodie, *Escalation and the Nuclear Option* (Princeton: Princeton University Press, 1966), pp. 77, 81.

when they urged Austria to attack Serbia quickly, even a short-term change established by fait accompli may be difficult to reverse; the fait accompli shifts the burden of the initiative for coercion or violence to those who would reverse it, and this, as Schelling has pointed out, is a source of bargaining weakness.[18]

A distinctive feature of crisis bargaining is the prominence of coercion. A crisis normally begins with an attempt to coerce, and much of the bargaining activity in a crisis is the coercive variety, including, as coercion, the negative form of resisting and deterring offensive challenges. In most other bargaining contexts, the coercive aspect is only latent or implied; the explicit bargaining activity takes the form chiefly of bids, concessions, proposals for settlement. In a labor-management contract negotiation, for example, everyone knows that a strike will be the result of failure to reach agreement; the union need not explicitly or repeatedly threaten to strike. In other contexts, e.g., bargaining about the price of a used car, varying degrees of firmness may be expressed in holding out for a certain price, but still there is only one basic coercive threat— to refuse the other's bid and walk away—and it is only latent in the situation, not part of the bargaining activity. The coercive aspect in crises is manifest, prominent, and highly variable and, most important, involves explicit or implicit threats of physical violence, not just threats of "no agreement." This is not to say that the non-coercive aspect of bargaining—mutual accommodation converging toward a settlement— is not present in crisis bargaining; it is, but it is commingled with coercive activity in a unique manner.

The fact that crises have a high degree of emotional content introduces further distinctive features. The two principal emotions involved are anger (hostility) and fear. Anger generated by the opponent's coercive activities may lead to a semi-autonomous hostility spiral—i.e., a non-calculated action-reaction escalation process more or less independent of the calculated process of bargaining. More likely, it may distort the bargaining process itself, cause it to deviate from rationality in various ways, as the protagonists "get their backs up," overreact to threats perceived as "provocative," determine to stand firm "whatever the cost," etc. The emotion of fear may also distort calculating processes and perceptions, leading perhaps to overreaction in military moves and preparedness, which then generates exaggerated fear in the opponent and similar countermoves, resulting in an illusory "fear spiral."

An important special element in some crises is shortness of *time* for decision. While we reject the view that scarcity of time is a defining characteristic of crises, it is true that a feeling of urgency is a prominent

[18] Schelling, *The Strategy of Conflict,* Ch. 2.

aspect of most crises. This feeling may stem from a deadline in the opponent's demand, from some more impersonal feature of the crisis context (e.g., the imminence of the Russian missiles in Cuba becoming operational), or from a diffuse fear that the longer tension is allowed to continue or increase, the more likely that the governments will lose control of events. In addition, the prominent "compellent" element in most crises inherently carries with it a certain time urgency, since logically any threat intended to force an adversary to do something (as opposed to "deterrent" threats to dissuade him from some action) must bear some sort of time limit, however vague and implicit.[19] If this were not so—if the victim knew that he had unlimited time within which to comply—he would have no incentive to comply, and the threat would be worthless.

Crisis bargaining is unique in the size of the stakes involved. The objects being bargained over, the interests in conflict, are valued very highly, so highly that it is plausible that a war might be fought to gain them or hold them. In some cases the interests at stake are so "vital" that the parties (or one of them) refuse to bargain about them at all in the ordinary sense; preserving the interest is seen as an absolute imperative. Indeed as suggested earlier it is largely the extreme tension between these interests at stake and the possibly calamitous consequences of "no deal" that gives to the situation its character of "crisis."

Finally, crisis bargaining differs from most other bargaining contexts in that the actors feel they have only limited control over the course of events. Like inexperienced canoers shooting the rapids, they feel caught in a rush of events that has a dynamic and momentum of its own only marginally subject to control; a false move could lead to disaster. This is related to the emotional element mentioned above—part of the out-of-control fear is that passions of public and leaders will become so aroused that rational controlled interaction is overwhelmed. But fundamentally the feeling stems from the knowledge that war is near, and from decision makers' imperfect grasp of the processes that lead to war.

DECISION MAKING

Decision-making theory is closely related to bargaining theory, since obviously the interactions between states are consequences of decisions made by the governments of states. Specifically, bargaining "moves" are the outcomes of choices from a set of alternatives, and each move in turn becomes an input to the opponent's decision-making apparatus leading to a choice and a move by him. Moreover, each choice may include a process of bargaining between individuals and groups within

[19] Schelling, *Arms and Influence,* pp. 69–72.

the government, each of whom may favor a different alternative. Thus bargaining appears as an important component of intragovernmental decision making as well as of intergovernmental relations, and we shall have a good deal to say later about the interaction between bargaining processes at these two levels. The most salient link between intergovernmental bargaining and internal bargaining is the flow of information. A large part of bargaining between governments consists of the emission of "signals" of various kinds, verbal or otherwise, designed to influence the other party's perceptions and expectations. The interpretation or perception of such signals and other information is in turn a crucial part of the decision-making process within the governments. We shall devote a later chapter to information processing, with particular emphasis on the important phenomenon of misperception. In reality, intergovernmental bargaining and intragovernmental decision making form virtually a unitary process; it is only the theories about them that heretofore have been artificially separated. One of our aims in this book will be to integrate them.

We shall test against our crisis data three theories of decision making: utility maximization, bounded rationality, and bureaucratic politics. The first two are theories of the "intellectual" component in decision making —i.e., the mental processes that individuals employ in making choices, abstracting from their interaction with other individuals in the decision-making unit. The third, bureaucratic politics, is a theory of the "political" aspect of decision making, sometimes referred to as the "policy formulation" process. This is a theory of how decisions are made by groups, composed of individuals with different governmental roles, values, perceptions and degrees of influence.

Intergovernmental bargaining and intragovernmental decision making together constitute the basic dynamic *processes* in the theoretical synthesis we are attempting to develop. These processes do not operate in a vacuum. They are constrained and conditioned by two sets of relatively static factors (static in the short run at least), the structure of the international system and the structure and general political make-up of the domestic systems involved. These may be considered the external and internal parameters, respectively, of the bargaining and decision-making processes.

THE EXTERNAL PARAMETER: INTERNATIONAL SYSTEM STRUCTURE

By "structure of the international system" we mean essentially the *number* of major actors in the system and the *distribution of power* between them. In a "multipolar" system there are three or more "great powers" whose potential military strength is roughly equal, plus a number of weaker states whose systemic role is usually that of objects of competition among the great states, although other roles (e.g., neutrality) are also possible. In a "bipolar" system, there are two "superpowers" whose military strength dwarfs that of all others, the latter clustering as client-allies in "blocs" around the superpowers or at least being the implicit beneficiaries of security guarantees by one or the other superpower.

International structure affects the bargaining and decision-making processes in many ways, a few of which will be broadly stated here by way of introduction. First, a multipolar system provides a range of *alignment options* for each actor. The number of options, logically, is a function of the number of actors, but this maximum logical range is narrowed by tangible *interest conflicts* that either foreclose or make unlikely certain alignments. Alignments are characterized by various possible degrees of firmness, from "good relations" to "alliance." The less firm, i.e., the more tentative, the alignments in the system, the wider the range of operational options. But even when alignments are apparently firm, there is always the possibility of realignment.

When a conflict of interest develops into a crisis, the behavior of the immediate adversaries will be strongly influenced by the degree of support expected from allies, both one's own and the opponent's. A considerable part of the bargaining activity will be directed toward gaining a firmer commitment from one's own allies and weakening the commitment of the opponent's allies, and manipulating the opponent's perception of such commitments on both sides. The relative bargaining strength of the parties, and the crisis outcome, will depend considerably on these commitments and the perception of them. The bargaining strategies and tactics of the direct adversaries will be constrained by their perceptions of the interests of their allies in the immediate issue of the crisis and in the preservation of the alliance or alignment. They will be subject to influence, typically restraint, from their allies to the degree that the latters' commitment or interest is uncertain, and to the degree that their support is needed or valued.

The ally will typically be willing to make greater concessions than his directly involved partner because he will have less interest in the immediate stakes of the conflict. The partner can therefore expect pressures from his ally to moderate his demands and to make greater concessions in the interest of settlement. However, the ally may be inhibited from exerting such pressure by his more general interests—i.e., his interests in preserving the alliance. Too much pressure for concessions may alienate the partner, reduce the apparent value of the alliance for him, and perhaps lead to his realignment later. The degree of this risk, and the consequent inhibition of pressure will depend largely on the alliance alternatives open to the partner. Often, in the interest of preserving the alliance, the ally will be willing to extend firm support for a somewhat tougher bargaining position than he would wish his partner to assume. And, of course, if the partner realizes this, he will be able to resist pressures for concession.

Consider now the bipolar structure. The most obvious differences from multipolarity are the much lower prominence of realignment potential and alliance-preserving considerations in crisis bargaining. A crisis confrontation between the superpowers themselves tends to be largely a bilateral affair because the behemoths depend so little on the military support of their small allies. Alliances in bipolarity are really unilateral guarantees by the superpowers to their clients: guarantees given usually because the territories of the small allies are seen as power and security assets in the balance of power between the giants, not because of any expectation of reciprocal support from the smaller allies in case a superpower itself is under attack or threat of attack. Realignment is only a remote possibility, since alignments are virtually ordained by geography and the power structure of the system, if not by ideological considerations; and even should a small ally desire or succeed in realignment, this would have little effect on the fundamental balance of power. For all these reasons, the superpowers need not feel much constrained by the interests of their allies (on power considerations at least) and can brush aside as either incredible or inconsequential the latters' possible threats of withdrawal of support or realignment. However, some deference may be given to allies' interests on normative or conventional grounds, or to avoid dissension in the alliance, or because allies' approval is useful for mobilizing domestic support.

When the crisis is between clients on opposite sides, not directly between the superpowers, the situation takes on more of the characteristics of multipolarity. The small protagonists *do* have to be concerned about support from their protectors, especially if the other superpower enters or may enter the fray. This support is obviously even more important to them in this case than it is among allies in multipolarity. Therefore, in bargaining with their immediate opponent, they are highly constrained by the attitude of their protector; the corollary is that the superpower protector has a high capacity for restraint of the client. Restraint may in fact shade into virtually absolute control if both superpowers become heavily engaged. The crisis is then transformed into a superpower crisis and the clients are transformed from principals to objects. The client may retain some freedom of action, however, to the degree that he believes the superpower's support will be automatically available in any case. Such a belief would be plausible given the superpower's basic interest in protecting its own bloc members. Thus the superpower's capacity for restraining the client may be somewhat ambiguous: the low credibility of the superpower's threat to withdraw support may undermine the restraining effect of the essentiality of that support.

THE INTERNAL PARAMETER: DOMESTIC SYSTEMS AND POLITICS

We conceive of both the international system and domestic systems as embracing different sets of relatively static factors that constrain and shape the dynamic processes of interstate bargaining and internal decision making. The domestic factors we have chiefly in mind are such things as national style in foreign policy, governmental structures, political party philosophies, bureaucratic roles, the personalities of decision makers (particularly as they generate preferences for "hard" and "soft" bargaining strategies), and public opinion. These factors obviously affect decisions, but they are not, strictly speaking, part of the *process* of decision making. They constitute the context within which the process occurs, or they generate substantive variation in perception, values, and influence that individuals and groups bring to the process. As factors that affect the outcome of the decision-making process, they are roughly analogous internally to the external factors in the structure and nature of the international system that affect the bargaining process between states. Of course, the external systemic variables affect the bargaining process *through* their effects on the minds of decision makers. They stand in relation to the internal variables as sources of general compulsions and constraints that establish the range of choice within which the internal forces peculiar to each state combine to produce decisions.

The reason we distinguish between the decision-making process per se and the substantive variables that shape or enter into the process is that the theories about decision making that we wished to examine implicitly claim to be relevant to any domestic political context. In order to find and describe regularities in process across a number of cases, it is necessary to ignore for analytical purposes the substantive variables peculiar to each state-actor. Otherwise, each decision appears unique, explainable only in terms of the particular "political forces" that produced it. Some of these variables, however, e.g., bureaucratic roles, images, and strategic preferences of individuals, and the number of participants and distribution of power within the decision-making unit, are hard to separate from process. We shall therefore take special account of those structural and substantive factors that cast light on the validity of theories about process or suggest limitations and revisions; otherwise we use such factors only to illustrate the workings of a theory. We shall also have something to say about how some of the substantive elements enter directly and fairly regularly into the interstate bargaining process—as when, for example, one government's perception of domestic political conditions in another state affects its choice of bargaining moves. Beyond this, any further independent analysis of matters such as political party differences, public opinion, or national styles would take us too far afield.

We turn in the following chapter to an application of certain formal models of bargaining and strategic interaction—utility models and game models. This is appropriate since bargaining is our central theoretical concern, and since, in developing a theory, it seems logical to start with the most rigorous and abstract formulations that capture the essential structure of the phenomena being analyzed. One can then move to less formal variants and extensions that encompass more details of the bargaining process; this we do in Chapter III. Information processing, the subject of Chapter IV, is the principal link between state-to-state bargaining and internal decision making. In Chapter V, the three decision-making theories—utility maximization, bounded rationality, and bureaucratic politics—are compared, applied, and somewhat integrated. Chapter VI deals with the effects of different international system structures and military technologies on crisis bargaining. The final chapter attempts to develop further links between interstate bargaining, system structure, and internal decision making, and to summarize the results of our theory-testing in earlier chapters.

CHAPTER II

FORMAL MODELS OF BARGAINING

In this chapter we summarize, test, and revise the various formal conceptions of bargaining appearing in the literature. A formal conception is one that can be expressed as a mathematical or computer model, that is, as a highly abstract logical construct, composed of postulates, definitions, and logical deductions.

The various formal conceptions of bargaining in the literature all describe pretty much the same kind of process, but they emphasize different aspects of the process. For instance, no theorist denies that bargaining takes place over time, but time is entirely absent from some models, is present incidentally in computer models, and is the fundamental variable in one model.[1] Consequently these models do not disagree with one another over what bargaining is in general, but rather over what factor or factors are essential to understanding or explaining actual bargaining.

We intend to determine the strengths and weaknesses of each model for understanding crisis bargaining. We will ask, for each model, are the factors it focuses on fundamental and persistent ones, or are they superficial and trivial? If they are fundamental, are they described properly or are revisions of the model necessary? For instance, we will ask, Is time pressure important in crisis bargaining? If so, is it one or more of the three kinds of pressure John Cross lists in his model? In any case, does it operate in the fashion specified by Cross's model, or in some other fashion?

From a survey of the strengths we should be able to locate the two or three best models, the ones that in combination best describe and explain the whole process of crisis bargaining and its outcome. From a survey of the weaknesses and especially the weaknesses of the best models we should locate the revisions that need to be made in these models to improve their descriptive and explanatory power. This will enable us to construct improved or supplementary models in Chapters IV and V.

UTILITY MODELS

These models focus on the utilities or goods that are allocated during bargaining. They treat bargaining as a process of deciding on a distribution of utilities between two parties, and the bargain or outcome as an

---

[1] John G. Cross, *The Economics of Bargaining* (New York: Basic Books, 1969).

allocation of utilities. Other aspects of bargaining are either described by reference to the utilities involved or are ignored.

Specifically, the bargaining problem—the situation that induces bargaining—consists of conflicting wants or demands. Two parties both want the same good or set of goods, and they cannot both have the whole set. Consequently the more that one has, the less is left for the other. The bargaining process consists of a series of bids, each proposing a certain distribution of the disputed goods; and it ends when a bid is accepted.

Conflict or struggle is thus an essential component of bargaining. There would be nothing to bargain about if two parties did not desire the same thing. However, conflicting interests always occur in a setting of common interests. The minimum common interest is the interest in reaching agreement, or rather an agreement in which both parties get something rather than nothing. In crisis bargaining there is an even stronger common interest in avoiding war and various other disastrous consequences. Further, some agreements may be better for both parties than others, so they have a common interest in reaching the better rather than the worse agreements.

Common interests are not only the setting for conflict, they also provide the instruments used in the conflict. Each party uses the threat of destroying some common interest to achieve a private gain, and one can also use the promise of achieving some common good to win in the conflict. If the only common interest is to reach agreement, each party can threaten no agreement or can promise agreement to achieve a private gain. If there are disasters, such as war, that both parties wish to avoid, one can warn or threaten war or risk of war, etc., to win the struggle, and similarly one can promise other mutual benefits such as entente or détente to win the struggle. The converse process is also possible: the occurrence of conflict can draw attention to threatened common interests, help to define them, and thus produce a basis of shared experience for achieving them.

In short, bargaining always occurs in a setting of interdependent common and conflicting interests, with the conflict providing the immediate occasion and focus and the community providing the ground or setting.

Formally this means that bargaining takes place in a two-dimensional utility space (see Fig. 2–1). Each point in this space represents one possible bid. The coordinates of the point measure its utility to the two bargainers; the A dimension measures its utility to A and the B dimension measures its utility to B. The zero point, where the two lines intersect, we define arbitrarily as the no agreement point; that is, we define no agreement, continuation of the status quo, as having zero

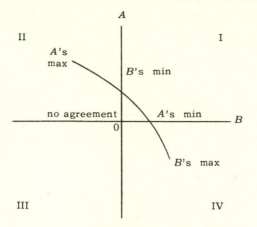

Figure 2-1. The Bargaining Space

utility for both. All points in the third quadrant have negative utility for both, while points in the first quadrant have positive utility in comparison with no agreement. Wars and other disasters are located in the third quadrant and possible agreements in the first. (Later we will come to cases in which wars, etc., are located in II or IV.)

All eastward movement in this space represents an increase of utility for B, and northward movement represents an increase of utility for A. This means that a move straight east increases B's utility without changing A's, and conversely a northward movement is good for A but neutral for B. All northeast moves increase the utility of both parties, and SW movements leave both worse off. That is, the NE–SW axis is the axis of common interests and the NW–SE axis is the conflict axis. There is a common interest in achieving agreements in the first quadrant, as far up as possible, and in avoiding outcomes in the third quadrant. Any movement diagonally toward the second quadrant benefits A at B's expense and vice versa for movement toward the fourth quadrant.

The curved diagonal is the conflict line, running mainly parallel to the conflict axis. We define this as the empirically possible limit of NE movement. When the bargainers reach this line in the bidding process, the available common interest has all been achieved and only conflict remains. In principle one could extend this line through all four quadrants to form the empirically possible bidding space, as Kent does.[2] This extension says that there is also some empirical limit to the damage the bargainers can do to each other. The limit of mutual damage is represented by the segment in the third quadrant, and the limit of uni-

[2] George Kent, *The Effects of Threats,* Mershon Center Pamphlet Series (Columbus: Ohio State University Press, 1967).

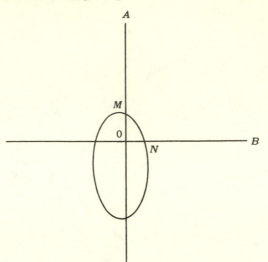

Figure 2-2. The Bargaining Space, after Kent

lateral damage is represented by the II and IV quadrant segments. In Figure 2–2, *B* can do much more damage to *A* than *A* can do to *B*, which presumably gives *B* a bargaining advantage.

One can abstract out the conflict line (I quadrant) to study only the conflict aspects of bargaining, though this can produce misleading results if one forgets the common-interest background from which the line was abstracted.

As Figure 2–3 shows, the conflict line is subdivided into several segments: *A*'s estimated bargaining range, *B*'s estimated range, and the actual range. *A*'s estimated bargaining range stretches between his minimum disposition, namely the settlement that he regards as no better than no agreement, and his maximum hope of what *B* might concede— i.e., his estimate of *B*'s minimum disposition. The actual bargaining range stretches from *A*'s minimum to *B*'s minimum. If an actual range

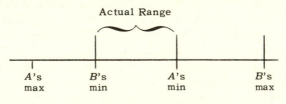

Figure 2-3. The Conflict Line

exists, the final bargain must lie within it, since at all points outside it either *A* or *B* prefer no agreement to agreement. If no actual range exists, agreement is impossible.

The bargaining process consists of a series of bids—i.e., settlement proposals—plus perhaps threats or other conditional statements. (If you do *A*, I will. . . .) Each bid, threat, or other conditional statement is represented as a point, whose location represents the estimated utility of the bid, etc., for both bargainers. By definition all bids must be located within the empirically possible bidding space. If one is using only a conflict line, all bids must somehow be located on the line. Presumably the initial bids of both parties are far apart, and they may even be located beyond the two minima, in the II and IV quadrants. Later bids presumably move into the bargaining range and converge to agreement.

A three-dimensional model adds time as a third dimension to the two utility dimensions. That is, it is assumed that the utilities of possible bargains decrease over time. The decrease may be uniform for both *A* and *B*, or asymmetrical, and the rate of decrease may also vary. There may also be situations in which utilities may increase for one bargainer and decrease for the other.

The decrease of utility over time provides an incentive to reach agreement rapidly; or conversely, an increase over time provides an incentive to stall. The pressure to reach agreement rapidly may induce *A* to make concessions to *B* at an increasing rate, in hopes of inducing rapid acceptance, or it may induce *A* to risk a costly threat for the same purpose. Conversely, increasing utility over time enables *A* to wait *B* out and forces *B* to redouble his efforts for rapid agreement. The three-dimensional model says that time pressures and the tactics resulting from them are important characteristics of a bargaining process, in the sense that they are the primary determinants of the outcome along with the initial utility distribution.

MODELS OF STRATEGIC INTERACTION

These are "game" models that focus, not on bidding sequences converging toward settlement, as utility models do, but on strategies available to the players, each of whom is trying to maximize his own gain (or minimize his loss) in the knowledge that the other is trying to do the same. The parties are interdependent in the sense that the outcome depends on the opponent's choice of strategy as well as on one's own. The outcome is simply the intersection of the two strategy choices. An outcome favorable to one party need not be entirely at the expense of the other; it can involve mutual advantage (though perhaps in different degree), or it may be disadvantageous to both.[3]

Bargaining, in this context, consists of two kinds of activity—*information search* and *influence*—both of which closely commingle in practice. Each party, recognizing that the outcome will depend on the other's choices as much as his own, will want to understand as accurately as possible the factors and circumstances affecting the other's choices—his preferences, his resources, his estimates and expectations, his perceived strategy alternatives, etc.—and will try to gather information about those factors and circumstances. At the same time, each will be using this knowledge to influence the other's choices in a direction favorable to himself. The commingling of the two activities consists in the fact that what is "influence" from one party's point of view is "information reception" for the other. In other words, influence tactics are largely attempts to convey information to the other about one's own probable strategy choice, or about the nature and value of possible outcomes, so they appear to the other as information. Conversely, the response of the other to these influence tactics is a source of information for oneself.

Influence tactics may include factual statements about one's own position, resources, intentions; predictions about the consequences of one's own or the opponent's tactics; statements about the probable outcomes and their value to self and opponent, and comments about the opponent's persuasive statements; strictly coercive threats or ultimata; troop movements, recall of ambassadors, and other symbolic acts; and violence.

All communications may be deceptive as well as truthful, and may or may not be believed by the other party, or correctly perceived or misperceived as to what the communicator intended to convey and what his underlying motive was.

A strategy is a set of tactics. Strategies may be ranged roughly along an accommodative-coercive dimension. An extreme accommodative strategy would consist of making a series of concessions until the opponent finally accepts; tactics might include a search for those concessions most valuable to the opponent and most likely to produce rapid agreement. A more moderate or mixed strategy would consist of concessions on details or acceptance of minor demands but refusal to concede on essentials. A firm strategy would be to make no concessions; an escalating strategy would be to make no concessions and to move

---

[3] We are speaking of course of the "non-zero-sum game"; the zero-sum game, in which the gain of one party is exactly equal to the loss of the other, is not to be found empirically in international politics. A non-zero-sum game is "mixed motive" in that the parties have common as well as conflicting interests.

steadily toward war until the opponent either yields or fights; and an attack strategy would be to pretend negotiations until one is ready to attack, then attacking.

Bargaining strategies also vary along a completeness-incompleteness dimension. At the one extreme, a strategy may be worked out in considerable tactical detail in advance, for example Germany in 1914; or the general principles may be fixed but the tactical details left to be improvised, for example Britain in 1938; or the strategy may be worked out only a few moves ahead and revised as more information comes in; or, at the other extreme, a player may be unable to agree on a strategy, for example Germany in 1905 and the United States in 1940–1941, and will respond to each move as it occurs. Bargaining, then, is the playing out of two or more interacting strategies.

In applying strategic interaction models to bargaining in crises, we erase the distinction between "preplay communication" and "play of the game," which some game theorists insist upon. The "game" for us is bargaining in crises, and such bargaining is largely communication. Some purists might argue that the game starts only when one party decides to initiate some action strategy, such as "attack," and that what comes before is preplay communication and by implication thus relatively inconsequential. Not only does this conception not fit our focus of interest but it also misportrays reality.

Verbal bargaining and action are interspersed during a crisis, so one does not stop when the other starts. Actions such as building the Berlin Wall or convoying supplies to Quemoy are preceded and followed by verbal communications, and are indeed themselves also communications. Even war does not put an end to verbal communication but merely changes the balance of talk and action. For some purposes, however, a distinction between the "bargaining game" and the "action game" is useful—we will show this formally later on. In most of what follows, we are concerned only with the "bargaining game," which ends with one of three outcomes: (1) capitulation by one party, (2) compromise, or (3) no agreement (cf. Fig. 2–4). The latter outcome subsumes the *possibility* of an action game (violence), which may or may not follow.

We now survey the various types of strategic models that we have attempted to apply to crises, some of which proved more useful than others. Some of them, such as Prisoner's Dilemma or Chicken, were available and quite thoroughly analyzed in the existing literature before we did the case studies; others we invented to fit situations that emerged from our empirical research.

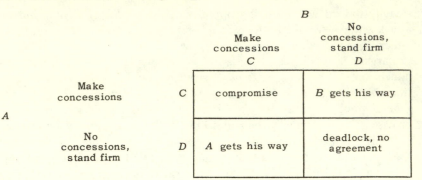

Figure 2-4. A Generalized Bargaining Game

Normal Form, 2×2.

In this type of model one focuses on the basic strategic situation and leaves out all details. The whole temporal development of a crisis is ignored and with it all particular tactics, communications, and changes of tactics. The obvious disadvantage is that the model leaves out the whole of the bargaining process, and all strategies that may be available to the players except the very simplest ones—"make concessions" or "stand firm." Moreover, these two labels are so simple that they obscure the variety of actual behavior that might be employed in following them.

The advantage of this drastic simplification is that it brings out the basic structure of crises. Also on the positive side, these models may be used, as we shall see later, as frameworks to classify tactics, and they allow us to describe a greater variety of bargaining situations than do the utility models. We can also make use of the conclusions reached in experimental gaming, most of which uses 2×2 models.

The basic structure of a generalized crisis is given in Figure 2–4. The two essential strategic possibilities are to hold pretty much to one's original demands, D, and to make some concessions or accommodations to the opponent's demands, C. Holding to one's original demands usually requires the use of various coercive tactics to induce the opponent to accommodate. We shall therefore refer to C as the accommodative strategy and to D as the coercive or stand-firm strategy.

Since there are four possible outcomes, each player has four possible payoffs, one for each outcome. We use the standard labels originated by Rapoport for these payoffs. The payoff for deadlock, DD, we label P; the payoff for compromise, CC, we label R; the payoff for making unilateral concessions, yielding, we label S; and the payoff for getting one's way is T. The four payoffs are always arranged as given in

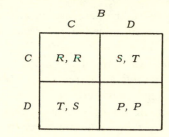

Figure 2-5. Payoffs from a Generalized Game

Figure 2–5, with the first letter of a pair representing *A's* payoff and the second representing *B's* payoff.

These letters all originally had a heuristic meaning in the Prisoner's Dilemma game, but since the meanings are more or less misleading when applied to other games, we omit them.

Note that a matrix formalization of bargaining distinguishes four kinds of outcomes, while a utility space formalization presents a continuity of possible outcomes. The matrix formalization is a simplification, perhaps a distortion, that creates difficulties of empirical interpretation at the *CD* boundary. A crisis may end with *A* essentially getting his way but with *B* receiving a few face-saving concessions after *B* has capitulated. Is this *CC* or *DC*? Technically it is *CC*, since both have made concessions; but also *A* has gotten what he wanted by redefining "what he wanted" to allow a slightly better *S* payoff to *B*. This suggests that there is really a hidden continuum from *DC* through *CC* to *CD*, which is made explicit in utility space models.

Utility models in fact tend to call attention to the *CC* cell, which in a matrix formalization is only one of four possible outcomes. Accounts of bargaining based on utility models tend to focus on the process of making concessions and on the convergence toward agreement in *CC*, while game models suggest that the basic issue is the continuing choice between *C* and *D* strategies, and by implication the choice of influence tactics designed to affect the opponent's choice of *C* or *D*. Which of these two emphases, on the continuum of possible concessions or on the *C–D* choice, is more illuminating depends of course on the empirical situation.

Symmetric Games: The Four Mixed Motive Games.

Anatol Rapoport and Melvin Guyer have shown that if the numbers in a 2 × 2 game matrix are considered to represent the ordinal preference rankings of the players over the four possible outcomes, rather than cardinal utilities, then there are exactly 78 2×2 games.[4] Out of these, 12 are *symmetric* games in the sense that the ordinal rankings are the same for each player. All the rest are *asymmetric*—the preference orderings are different. Of the 12 symmetric games, eight are of little or no theoretical interest, either because there is no conflict (both players give highest preference to the same outcome) or because the outcome is completely determined. The remaining four are "interesting"; Rapoport calls them the "archetypes" of the 2×2 game.[5] We chose to start with these four in attempting to apply game models to crises; they are shown in Figure 2–6. A few of the other games, both symmetric and asymmetric, turned out to be useful when we explored the empirical cases; they will be shown subsequently. Since the payoffs represent ordinal rankings rather than cardinal magnitudes, we show them by the positive numbers 1 through 4, i.e., from "least preferred" to "most preferred," even though in real play some of the outcomes may be losses and thus have negative utility. Each game is strictly defined by the ordinal ranking of the four payoffs, and the four games together represent all possible rankings of mixed-motive games. T is always the most preferred payoff, $T = 4^{\text{th}}$, since we defined T as "win" or "get one's way." This requires a rearrangement of Hero, which at one time was defined as $S > T > R > P$.[6]

In all four games the 1st payoff is more or less disastrous; 2^{d} is the minimax payoff, the minimum a player can insure for himself no matter what the other does; 3^{d} is the best accommodative payoff; and $T = 4^{\text{th}}$ is the best coercive payoff. The games are mixed motive not just in the sense that both common and conflicting interests are present; this is true of all bargaining. Rather, the common and conflicting interests are so intermingled that neither kind of interest can be pursued without inducing a reversal of attention to the other. In other words, the players are caught between opposite inducements and must vacillate between them. $T = 4^{\text{th}}$ induces them to play against each other, to struggle and coerce, since T can be achieved only at the cost of a lesser payoff to the other. However, the payoff for both yielding to this inducement is $P = 1^{\text{st}}$ or 2^{d}, and both could do better than 2^{d} by coordinating their strategies. In other words, a strategy of struggle induces a reversal of strategy to accommodation. But the attempt to

[4] Rapoport and Guyer, "A Taxonomy of 2 × 2 Games," *General Systems* (1966), pp. 203–214.

[5] Anatol Rapoport, "Exploiter, Leader, Hero, Martyr: the Four Archetypes of the 2×2 Game," *Behavioral Science,* 12 (1967), pp. 81–84.

[6] Our definition, $T > S > P > R$ is mathematically identical with the earlier definition, since by the rules of matrix algebra the mathematical structure remains the same when rows and columns are transposed. In our definition the difference between Hero and Leader is located entirely in the P, R ranking, a point that did not come out clearly in earlier treatments of Hero and Leader.

HERO
$T>S>P>R$

	C	D
C	1, 1	3, 4
D	4, 3	2, 2

LEADER
$T>S>R>P$

	C	D
C	2, 2	3, 4
D	4, 3	1, 1

Player *B*

	C	D
C	R, R	S, T
D	T, S	P, P

Player *A*

PRISONER'S DILEMMA
$T>R>P>S$

	C	D
C	3, 3	1, 4
D	4, 1	2, 2

CHICKEN
$T>R>S>P$

	C	D
C	3, 3	2, 4
D	4, 2	1, 1

Figure 2-6. The Four Symmetric Mixed-motive Games

coordinate strategies inevitably leads back to conflict. In Prisoner's Dilemma and Chicken there is the danger of a double cross, a switch to *D,* which induces suspicion and a temptation to preempt *D;* in Hero and Leader there are two opposed ways to coordinate, and the players must struggle over the question of how to coordinate. But if both struggle, they are back at *DD;* there is no guaranteed way out.

Prisoner's Dilemma and Chicken are adversary games in that the interest of the parties are more completely opposed than in the other two. If one player plays D or commits himself to it, the other can do no better than minimax, which usually in actual cases has negative utility. In Prisoner's Dilemma, he gets this by playing D to avoid the disastrous 1 payoff. In Chicken, he gets it by accommodating to the other's coercive pressure. The chief difference between the two games is that in Chicken the worst outcome is mutual coercion, and yielding to the other's coercive pressure is only the second worst, whereas in Prisoner's Dilemma the reverse is true. In both of these adversary games compromise is quite possible, in Prisoner's Dilemma because of the knowledge or fear that a D strategy will be reciprocated, and in Chicken because of the inability of the parties to commit themselves credibly.

We should mention at this point that we are *not* assuming simultaneous play, which takes us another step away from game theory orthodoxy and toward real world conditions. Our players move in sequence; thus the second player's choice is taken in full knowledge of what the first has already chosen. The difference is particularly important with respect to the way we shall be using the Prisoner's Dilemma model. Most discussions of the Prisoner's Dilemma assume simultaneous play. With this assumption, either or both players are either tempted to play D to exploit an opponent who is expected to cooperate or they are driven to play D in fear that the other will succumb to such temptation. From either or both of these motivations both players must logically choose D strategies, and the outcome is mutual "punishment" —worse than what they might have achieved had each cooperated. However, in a sequential-move game, the "dilemma" in the Prisoner's Dilemma disappears. That is, there is no problem about guessing whether or not the opponent is trustworthy and whether to double-cross him if he is or to preempt if he isn't. This is because even if the opponent proves to be non-cooperative—plays his D strategy— there is time to counter with one's own D strategy, thus avoiding the disastrous CD or DC outcomes. Since both parties know that such countering is inevitable, neither has any incentive to play D and the logical outcome of the Prisoner's Dilemma with sequential moves is CC, mutual cooperation. One would expect, therefore, that there would be no crises with a Prisoner's Dilemma structure. As we shall see, however, this is not the case, since one or both parties may initially misperceive the other's preference ordering, believing he is playing a Chicken game, for example. Moreover, there are Prisoner's Dilemma situations in some crises where the simultaneous move version of the game is approached in the sense that, although it is possible to counter the opponent's D strategy in time to avoid the *worst* outcome, it is still

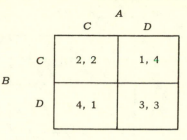

Figure 2-7. Deadlock

costly to let him play it first and thus there is some incentive to preempt.[7]

Hero and Leader would appear to be alliance games since even though one party plays coercively, the other can still achieve the fairly high payoff of 3 by accommodating. In contrast to the two adversary games, both 3 and 4 payoffs for both parties lie in NE or SW cells. Accommodating the other in his attempt to gain his best payoff is better than resisting it by attempting to get one's own best payoff. As a working hypothesis, it seemed to us that this was roughly analogous to the position of allies during a crisis, wherein the partners might each favor different strategies for dealing with the opponent, but value the preservation of the alliance over the adoption of their preferred strategy vis à vis the opponent. Hence they might argue or bargain about the optimum crisis strategy to adopt, but each would, in the end, prefer to go along with the other's preference rather than disrupt the alliance. Compromise (*CC*) is not a logical outcome in Hero and Leader because its payoff is less than going along with the partner's preferred strategy.

There may also be alliance games that take a Prisoner's Dilemma or Chicken form, that is, games in which compromise is possible.

A fifth symmetric game that showed up in our cases is Deadlock (Fig. 2–7). This is not a mixed-motive game, since both players prefer firmness (*D*) to either appeasing the opponent or compromising with him. Mathematically the outcome of Deadlock is *DD*, since *D* dominates *C* for both players, and empirically the outcome is war. However, there can be complications in actual play that do not appear in the mathematics

---

[7] We shall continue to use the traditional name "Prisoner's Dilemma" for the sequential-play $T > R > P > S$ game, despite the fact that the dilemma disappears when one substitutes sequential play for simultaneous play. Mathematically the game remains the same despite the auxiliary rule change. If one were to change names every time an auxiliary rule was changed, there would be a proliferation of games whose mathematical similarity was obscured. We shall occasionally use the simultaneous-play *PD*, but shall in that case identify it as a simultaneous-play game.

B

	C	D
C	3, 3	1, 4
D	4, 2	2, 1

A (label at left for rows)

Figure 2-8. Called Bluff

of the game. The essential difference between Deadlock and Prisoner's Dilemma is that in the latter there is some compromise (R, R) available, which both parties would prefer to no agreement (P, P).

Asymmetric Games [8]

Called Bluff (Fig. 2–8) is Prisoner's Dilemma for player A and Chicken for player B. Player A can play a D strategy confidently, knowing that player B, who is playing Chicken, must ultimately play C. Although this game seems to combine Chicken and Prisoner's Dilemma, its dynamics are different from either of them and therefore it deserves its own heuristic name. We name it "Called Bluff," because from A's standpoint, if B threatens to play D he is a bluffer whom A can and must call, although A must do it carefully to avoid an accidental DD outcome. In our cases, this game also appears frequently as a misperception game; that is, the "caller" thinks the game is Called Bluff when actually it is Prisoner's Dilemma or Deadlock.

In the game shown in Figure 2–9, A's preference ordering is the same as in Deadlock; he prefers no agreement (possibly war) to any conceivable compromise, though his highest preference is T (4), resulting from B playing C to his D. However, the game itself is not Deadlock, since B is in Chicken and prefers compromise or even capitulation to no agreement. We call this game "Bully" because A, who is assured of a 3 payoff regardless of B's strategy, can bully and threaten B with impunity. He can in fact force B to yield, play C to his D threats, and thus obtain his maximum payoff of 4.

In Big Bully (Fig. 2–10), B is again in Chicken, but A prefers no

---

[8] By "asymmetric" games we mean games that have a different ordinal structure for each player. This should be distinguished from the asymmetry in cardinal values that may exist in games which are ordinally symmetrical. For example, both players may be in Chicken (and the game is Chicken) but P might be much lower, and/or S much higher, for one than the other, so that the first player is at a serious bargaining disadvantage when the asymmetry becomes known to his opponent.

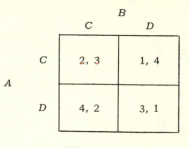

Figure 2-9. Bully

agreement and probably war not only over any conceivable compromise but also over *B*'s total capitulation. This distinguishes the game from Bully, where *A,* though unwilling to compromise, would accept *B*'s yielding to his (*A*'s) demands rather than no agreement or war. *A* is a "big bully" because his demands on *B* are intended only as a pretext for the use of force. Big Bully is exemplified by Austria vs. Serbia, 1914, and Germany vs. Czechoslovakia, 1938, abstracting out the complicating alliance relationships in both cases. *B*'s game may become transformed into Prisoner's Dilemma as a consequence of *A*'s humiliating threats and insults, which prompt him to prefer fighting a losing war, thereby salvaging some dignity, to knuckling under to *A*'s demands.

Protector (Fig. 2–11) is an alliance game between two unequal partners. *A,* the great power "protector" has preferences ordered as in Bully, while *B*'s (the client's) are ranked as in Leader. Assume that *B* is in conflict with some other state; *A* plays the role of supporter (in varying possible degrees). *B*'s *D* strategy is to stand firm against the other state's demands and make demands himself; his *C* strategy is to make concessions desired by *A*. *A*'s *C* strategy is to support *B*'s position fully; his *D* strategy is to provide limited defensive support. *A* can enforce concessions by threatening to withhold support because

		B	
		C	*D*
A	*C*	2, 3	1, 4
	D	3, 2	4, 1

Figure 2-10. Big Bully

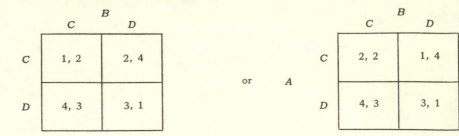

Figure 2-11. Protector

B's alternative of standing firm alone against the opponent is disastrous. In short, since *A*'s *D* strategy is dominating, *B* must follow his "protector" and make the concessions demanded by *A* as the condition for the latter's support.

The Critical Risk Model

Of considerable interest is the "critical risk" model developed by Daniel Ellsberg to show the dynamics of coercion and persuasion.[9] The model requires the use of cardinal utility numbers and precise probability figures to show its workings. Of course, this is "unrealistic," but the usefulness of the model does not depend on being able to find statesmen actually making such precise calculations. The purpose of the numbers is to make the model run so we can analyze its logic. The logic thus revealed and highlighted is, plausibly, the same logic a rational bargainer would have in mind in cruder form.

Structurally, the model is Chicken or Leader—each party prefers to accept the other's terms, or some compromise, to suffering the consequences of no agreement. It can also be adapted to the other models presented in this chapter. What it adds to the basic Chicken model is that the parties make probability estimates, not either-or estimates, of the other's strategy choices in choosing their own strategies.

Figure 2–12 portrays a rather simple crisis precipitated by a challenger's demand that a defender yield something worth 10 "utiles" to

[9] "The Theory and Practice of Blackmail," unpublished lecture delivered at Lowell Institute, Boston, March 1959, in a series entitled "The Art of Coercion: A Study of Threats in Economic Conflict and War." Similar models that emphasize the accommodative process are presented by Frederick Zeuthen, in *Problems of Monopoly and Economic Warfare* (London: George Routledge and Sons, 1930), Ch. 4; and by Walton and McKersie, *A Behavioral Theory of Labor Negotiations,* Ch. 3. See also Glenn H. Snyder, "Crisis Bargaining," in Charles F. Hermann, ed., *International Crises: Insights from Behavioral Research* (New York: The Free Press, 1972), Ch. 10; and Douglas Hunter, "The Decision-Making Model in Nuclear Deterrence Theory," *Journal of Peace Research* (1972), pp. 209–222.

B (defender)

	Yield or make a concession	Stand firm	
Yield, or make a concession	−1, 1	−5, 5	A's critical risk = .50
Stand firm	10, −10	−20, −20	B's critical risk = .60

A (challenger)

Figure 2-12. Critical Risk

each player, under threat of war. If state *A,* the challenger, stands firm and *B,* the resister, yields, the payoffs are 10 and −10, respectively. If the resister is firm and the challenger yields (fails to carry out his threat and lets the matter drop), the challenger loses and the defender gains bargaining reputation, prestige, loyalty of allies, domestic support, etc., worth five to each. The consequence of both standing firm is war at a mutual cost of 20. The outcome comply-comply (*CC*) is a compromise settlement, which yields a small net loss for *A* and a small gain for *B*. (Say, the challenger gets a small bit of territory, but its value is less than the intangible values lost in backing down from his original demand; the defender suffers a small tangible loss, more than offset by intangible gains from having successfully resisted the challenger's main demands.)

A central assumption of the model is that, although each party knows its own payoffs, it does not know the opponent's. However, each can make rough, uncertain estimates of the other's payoffs, which enter into estimates of the probability whether the other will stand firm or yield. A further assumption is that the parties' payoffs and estimates of the other's payoffs are subject to change and can be manipulated by bargaining tactics.[10]

[10] Thus the model drops certain standard game theory assumptions: that the preference schedules of the parties remain fixed during bargaining and that each party knows or can find out the preference schedule of the other. Thus it takes small steps toward "real life," in which values do change during interaction and there is always uncertainty about the other bargainer's values. The model is still "unrealistic" in its use of cardinal utilities and precise probability estimates. But this is of no consequence, since the purpose of using the model is not detailed empirical application but simply to show some of the logical dynamics of crisis bargaining and to classify tactics.

The concept of "critical risk" as developed by Ellsberg expresses the notion that there is some threshold of risk that is the maximum risk a party can stand without capitulating or conceding. If the credibility (probability) of the adversary's being committed to stand firm is perceived as higher than this threshold, the party must give in; if it is lower, the party will continue to stand firm. In other words, the party estimates whether the likelihood of the adversary's being really committed to firmness is too high to take a chance or low enough to be worth risking.

Formally, the critical risk for either side is derived from its *own* payoffs—specifically from a comparison of its payoff for yielding with its payoff for standing firm. In our example, B loses 10 by yielding. If he stands firm, he either gains 5 or loses 20 depending on A's choice. If he estimates a .40 chance that A will yield and a .60 chance that A will be firm, B's expected value for standing firm is −10, just equal to the cost of compliance. In other words, when B estimates the credibility of A's threat at .60, B is indifferent between yielding or standing firm. This is B's critical risk—the credibility of A's threat must be higher than this to force B to back down. A similar calculation will show that A's critical risk is .50. If A estimates the probability of B's firmness at higher than this, A must retreat.

The formula for critical risk is $\frac{T-S}{T-P}$, where $S < 0$, $P < 0$. For B the calculation is

$$\frac{5-(-10)}{5-(-20)} = \frac{15}{25} = .60.$$

Having calculated his critical risk level, B must next estimate the credibility of A's threat to stand firm and compare it with his critical risk. He asks himself, "Is A's credibility as high as .60?" In part he answers this from what he can guess about A's payoffs, which are also the determinants of A's critical risk. There is some relationship therefore between a party's critical risk and the opponent's estimate of his degree of resolve to stand firm.[11] However, even in the model, credibility cannot be calculated precisely like critical risk because each party has only a vague impression of the other's payoffs. Supplementing these impressions, the bargainers may base credibility estimates on

[11] It is worth noting that "resolve" and "credibility" are close to being opposite sides of the same coin. Resolve is a party's own degree of determination to carry out a threat; credibility is the opponent's perception of that determination. Theoretically, resolve is likely to be more absolute (less probabilistic) than credibility because, presumably, a party knows more about his own incentive structure than his opponent does. On this point, see Kent, *The Effects of Threats,* pp. 84–86.

TABLE 2–1

AN ACCOMMODATIVE BIDDING SEQUENCE

Bids		Critical Risk	
A	B	A	B
10	5	.50	.60
7	5	.44	.48
3	5	.39	.32
3	1	.17	.19
−1	1	0	0

empirical evidence they possess about the opponent's positions—e.g., civilian morale, the economy, military preparedness, the popularity of the government, intercepted communications. Third, credibility estimates may be based partly on each party's judgments as to how credible he has made his own position, since the more credible his position is, the more likely the opponent will decide he must yield.[12]

The critical risk model can also be used to represent the accommodative process—concessions converging toward settlement. Returning to Figure 2–12, suppose that A finds B's arguments fairly persuasive and realizes that B is rather unimpressed with A's arguments—then it appears that the credibility of B's threat of firmness is higher than A's critical risk, and for B, the credibility of A's threat is lower than B's critical risk. Then A must yield. Suppose A reduces his claim to 7, what then happens to the critical risk levels? From Table 2–1 we see that both critical risks go down, but B's more than A's. However, A's critical risk is still lower than B's. Logically, after each concession, the party with the lower critical risk must make the next concession, since it is less able to stand the risk of holding firm. Hence, A concedes again, to 3, but after this concession, B's critical risk is lower, so it is his turn to concede. He reduces his claim to 1, which makes A's critical risk lower. A then makes a concession to minus 1, which lowers both critical risks to approximately zero (neither party has any further incentive to stand firm) and a settlement is reached at −1,1.

Note that this accommodative version of the model is less determinate than it appears because it leaves out credibility estimates. A party makes a decision to concede only by comparing critical risks.

[12] We enter here the familiar thicket of "infinite regress of expectations." B's resolve to stand firm depends on how resolved he thinks A is, but this depends in part on how resolved A thinks B is, and this depends on how resolved A thinks B thinks A is, and so on. Empirically, the bargainers probably cut the regress short after two or at most three steps. Robert Jervis has discussed this regressive phenomenon in "Bargaining and Bargaining Tactics," in J. Roland Pennock and John W. Chapman, eds., *Coercion*, Nomos XIV, (Chicago, New York: Aldine, Atherton, 1972), Ch. 14.

But since the adversary's critical risk cannot be known, the perception of his degree of firmness, and his perception of one's own—and hence whose "turn" it is logically to concede—depends on credibility estimates that are derived from factors in addition to estimates of each other's actual payoffs and critical risks. Yet the table does show an important element in the accommodative process; *if* a party believes it is less able at any point to stand the risk of breakdown than the opponent, and thinks the opponent believes likewise, the party must concede. It is also quite plausible psychologically that after one party makes a concession, the other will feel obliged to make the next one, not just because of some convention that "concessions should be reciprocated" but because the expected value of standing pat now looks comparatively worse than before, since the adversary is now offering something better as an alternative.

Linkage of Game Models to Utility Models

Only four of these nine or ten games—Chicken, Prisoner's Dilemma, Called Bluff, and Bully—can be translated in any direct way into the "bargaining range" of utility models. A bargaining range requires that there be a possibility of negotiated compromise that both parties would prefer to no agreement at all. This rules out Deadlock, Leader, and Hero, where no compromise is possible, and also the asymmetrical games except Called Bluff. The translation of Chicken into a one-dimensional utility diagram is shown in Figure 2–13. The limits of the bargaining range, i.e., the possible settlements at which each party is indifferent between agreement and no agreement, are established by the value of *P* (*DD* outcome) for each party. Both prefer accepting the other's "win" (*CD* or *DC;* alternatively, *S*) to no agreement or risk of war, and of course a compromise (*CC*) somewhere between the two "win" points is also possible.

Each point on the line represents a possible bid, i.e., a possible distribution of the disputed goods. The right end of the line is the lowest utility for *A,* and the left end is *B*'s lowest utility. *A*'s initial bid by definition is *DC* and *B*'s initial bid is *CD*. As bidding continues, *A* and *B* may remain at their initial bids or may make concessions

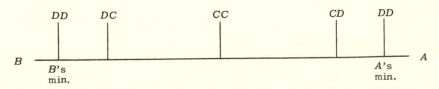

Figure 2-13. One-dimensional Chicken

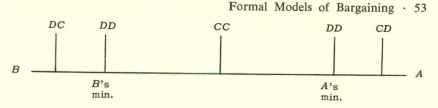

Figure 2-14. One-dimensional Prisoner's Dilemma

(move toward *CC*). Agreement occurs when the bids of both parties coincide. Breakdown, no agreement, occurs at the two *DD* points. The two *DD* points are differentiated by who precipitates the "no agreement" outcome. As one moves right along the line, *A* shifts from *D* to *C*—he reduces his initial demand—and continues to reduce it until he reaches the limit of his available concessions. At this point he breaks off negotiations, stops offering concessions (*DD*). Conversely, at the left-hand *DD* point *B* breaks off negotiations. In Chicken, of course, agreement can be reached at either *CD* (*A* accepts *B*'s initial demand) or *DC*, and there is no reason to reach either *DD* point.

In the Prisoner's Dilemma translation, the limits of the bargaining range are still set by the values for the *DD* outcome, but the "win-lose" outcomes in the strategic model (*CD* and *DC*) are outside the range (Figure 2–14). It is easy to see that no settlement is possible here as long as at least one of the parties stands firm on his initial *T* claim; the other prefers no agreement to acceptance of this claim (*CD* or *DC*). Therefore, a prerequisite to reaching a settlement is that both parties reduce their *T* claims past the "Chicken-*PD* boundary"—i.e., past the point where acceptance of the claim by the opponent (his *S*) is higher than (or less costly than) his utility for *P*—no agreement. Then, in effect, the strategic game is transformed into Chicken, and the conflicting claims are within the bargaining range. We shall have more to say about the nature of this process when we discuss our actual Prisoner's Dilemma cases.

In a Called Bluff game only one of the outcomes is outside the bargaining range, in Figure 2–15, the *CD* outcome.

In Bully most of the *CC* segment is also outside the bargaining range because the minimum of *A*, the "Bully," is so close to his initial

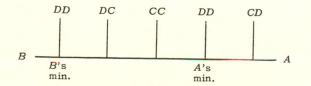

Figure 2-15. One-dimensional Called Bluff

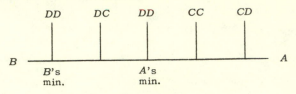

Figure 2-16. One-dimensional Bully

bid (Figure 2–16). The bargaining range, practically speaking, is from *DD* (*A*'s minimum) to *DC*. That is, *B* can either accept *A*'s initial bid (*DC*) or he can try to improve it a little bit, until he reaches *A*'s minimum.

The process of reaching agreement in the critical risk model could also in principle be plotted on a one-dimensional utility space. Each successive concession would be shown at a point within the bargaining range, accompanied by the changed critical risks of the parties as a consequence of the concession, converging to zero critical risks at the agreement point. This could be superimposed on either of the cruder Chicken and *PD* adaptations shown above.

If one uses a two-dimensional utility space, more games can be translated into utility language (see Figure 2–17). Each game becomes a certain kind of bidding space whose shape is determined by the preference ordering of the game. The two minima of the conflict line (Figure 2–13) become the horizontal and vertical axes of the two-dimensional space. We assume here that the two initial bids, *DC* and *CD*, represent the maximum possible utility for *A* and *B,* respectively, so they are located at the farthest north and east points of the bidding space. *DD* in our cases is worse than the status quo so we locate it in Quadrant

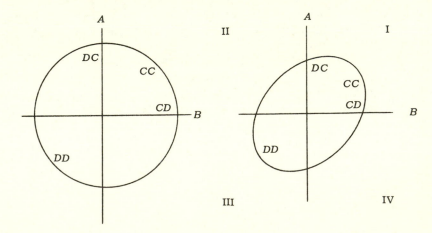

Figure 2-17. Two-dimensional Chicken

III. Since in Chicken, *DD* is the worst outcome for both parties, it must be left of *DC* and below *CD*. The bargaining space must therefore be circular or oval and have a general NE–SW orientation.

The *DD* area of Quadrant III is the area of threatened or actual coercive measures, which are worse than the status quo. Thus the two-dimensional representation of Chicken enlarges the meaning of a *D* strategy. *D* includes not merely a firm stand on one's initial bid but also threatened or actual coercive tactics. This shift of meaning also enlarges the bargaining range. The bargaining range still runs between the two *DD* payoffs, but this now includes the whole bargaining space, not just the first quadrant.

The Prisoner's Dilemma space (Figure 2–18) has a predominant II–IV orientation. Since both *DC* and *CD* are outside the "bargaining range" of the conflict line, they must be located in Quadrants II and IV. Moreover, their utility to the loser is lower than *DD,* so the bargaining space must be stretched out along a NW–SE axis. In general *DD* is worse than the status quo, since it includes the possibility of war or other unpleasantness, as in Chicken, so it is in Quadrant III.

The II–IV orientation of the bargaining space shows graphically the ineffectiveness of threats, as long as the bidding is in the *DC* and *CD* areas. That is, as long as a bargainer follows a *D* strategy and holds to his initial demand, any threats by the opponent about the consequences of no agreement (*DD*) are useless and worse than useless. Since *DD* is preferred to the acceptance of the opponent's initial demand, any message that suggests the opponent is committed to his initial demand can only hasten the breakdown of negotiations. Threats become effective only after the bidding has moved beyond the two dotted lines toward the I Quadrant and the game has been transformed into Chicken.

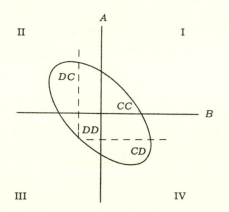

Figure 2-18. Two-dimensional Prisoner's Dilemma

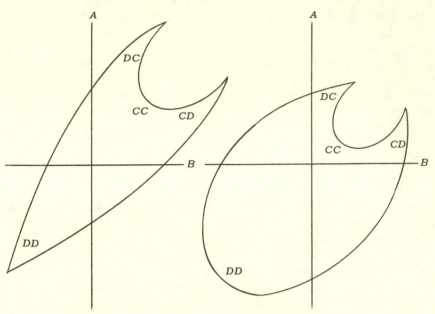

Figure 2-19. Two-dimensional Leader

In Leader (Figure 2–19) the *DC* and *CD* outcomes are preferred to *CC* by both parties, while *DD* is the least preferred outcome for both. Therefore *DC* and *CD* must curve around and beyond *CC* in the I Quadrant, while *DD* remains in III. The resulting NE–SW orientation brings out the similarity between Leader and Chicken. Leader in fact is Chicken without the possibility of reaching a compromise from the *DC-CD* positions. Compromise can be reached from *DD,* but remains unstable because both parties prefer to move toward *CD* or *DC.*

Hero cannot be diagrammed in a two-dimensional space because the *CC* boundary must dip below *DD,* thus turning the Leader space inside out. Similarly, Deadlock would be an inside-out *PD* space, with the *CC* boundary crossing the *DD* boundary. Finally, Protector is just barely reducible to two dimensions.

Chicken is the most natural and obvious of the various bidding spaces. If one wishes to draw a plain, simple bidding space one would tend to draw a circle or an oval, and that would immediately be Chicken. For example, Kent proposes to use a two-dimensional utility model to study the effects of threats on bargaining. He begins by drawing the two utility axes and then superimposes an oval bidding

[13] Cf. R. Duncan Luce and Howard Raiffa, *Games and Decisions* (New York: Wiley, 1957), p. 116.

space on them.[14] This immediately makes Chicken the setting of his whole argument and means that all his conclusions apply only to Chicken games and perhaps, with modification, to Leader games. Whether any of them apply also to other games must be investigated step by step using the appropriate bidding spaces. This brings out a serious defect of utility models, for they induce the modeler to think in terms of Chicken and to overlook several other possible—and actual —kinds of strategic situations in crisis bargaining. The result can be seriously and dangerously misleading conclusions, such as Kent's tacit implication that his argument applies to bargaining in general, and therefore to Prisoner's Dilemma and Deadlock as well as to Chicken.

EXTENSIVE FORM.

This is a detailed model in which specific tactical moves are laid out in time sequence. *A* chooses one of several tactical alternatives; for instance, he chooses either to stay put or to make a concession. This choice leaves *B* with two or more alternatives, from which he chooses one. Then *A* chooses again, and so on. Each choice can be called a move, a move being anything that changes the real alternatives open to the other player. If one diagrams the whole set of alternatives over several moves, the result is a game tree or graph, as shown in Figure 2–20. This model could be used to describe the sequence of choices and

[14] Kent, *The Effects of Threats,* p. 18.

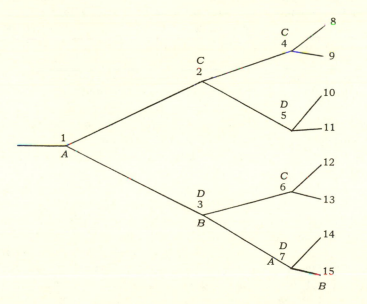

etc.

Figure 2-20. An Extensive Form Game

their consequences during the crisis, and also to estimate the expected value of a tactic by summing its consequences a short way into the future. It is good for detailed description of some restricted segment of a crisis, enabling one to sort out the strategic complexities. However, it could be extended to a whole crisis only by leaving out many details, and even then the larger picture would not come out clearly from all those branches and numbers. Another difficulty is that one must always decide, more or less arbitrarily, which empirical events are to count as a discrete move or, in other words, what is to count as a change of situation for the other party. One must distinguish actions that change the set of available alternatives from actions or communications that merely change the nature of existing alternatives, but this distinction is one of degree. We did not find this model to be useful.

EXPANDED NORMAL FORM, M × N.

If there is a limited set of m options available during a crisis, one might build one's description around this set. The intersection of the m options open to A with the n options open to B constitutes an $m \times n$ matrix of possible outcomes. Because of its size, such a matrix becomes too complex to work with when more than two players are included. The options are arranged in order of decreasing utility to the opponent. For example, in the Cuban crisis, the U.S. option set included: do nothing, demand removal of the missile bases, blockade to stop increase of missiles, bomb missile sites, limited ground raid, full invasion and occupation, etc. The Soviet Union had a different set of options. Some outcome cells make no empirical sense and can be blocked out. A strategy, actual or contingent, consists of a series of moves up and down the option set, and a complete game is the interaction of two strategies. The game continues until agreement is reached or time runs out, or play may peter out without any explicit agreement.

The rows and columns of an $m \times n$ matrix can be derived mathematically by expanding a 2×2 matrix. One can either put the four cells in the NW corner of the $m \times n$ matrix and extrapolate or put them in the four corners of the $m \times n$ matrix and interpolate. This is a simple process if one is using cardinal numbers, but if one is using ordinal numbers, the rankings get indeterminate. However, if one is constructing a matrix empirically, the outcomes and their preference ranking can be estimated directly. This will undoubtedly produce a somewhat irregular matrix, but (1) if it closely resembles some regular expanded matrix the irregularities can be ignored or treated ad hoc, and (2) if it is completely irregular, at least each 2×2 submatrix is a regular game whose dynamic properties are known. One can then use the mathematical dynamics of either the whole matrix or of the sub-matrices to explain the actual sequence of bargaining moves through the matrix.

Empirically the option set, the rows and columns of an expanded matrix, probably consists of varying levels of coercion. Thus U.S. options in the Cuba, 1962, case range from the noncoercive "do nothing" to the highly coercive invasion of Cuba and bombing of the missile sites and, hypothetically, after escalation, to the extremely coercive bombing of Soviet bases. There is a close similarity to Kahn's escalation ladder,[15] each row or column representing one rung on the ladder. This means that the expanded matrix is an escalation matrix, and treats bargaining as an interaction of two escalation-deescalation processes. If we wish to translate this conception into utility terms we must refer to a two-dimensional bargaining space, in which escalation would consist of SW movement into and in quadrant III.

This type of model has the advantage of summarizing the whole situation without losing too many details. It also enables one to bring in time and communication indirectly. Communication moves can be described as conditional undertakings to choose or persist in a certain option, and basic moves can be described as revocable choices of an option. Each basic move then represents either an escalation or a de-escalation. In this way one can reconstruct something of the bargaining sequence that is laid out in extended-form models. However, none of the sequence actually appears in the expanded matrix, though it is described by reference to the matrix. The advantage of this way of describing the bargaining sequence is that it distinguishes (as extended-form models do not) escalatory moves, de-escalatory moves, and continuation of an option, and thus puts more order into the otherwise interminable sequence of moves. Also it relates each move to the total picture, thereby clarifying both the detail and the total picture.

One particular expanded model should be of special interest. That is expanded Chicken, which has a very interesting mathematical property—its upper left hand corner is Prisoner's Dilemma.[16] As one moves down the main diagonal the submatrices rapidly shift to Chicken, thus providing a continuum between the two types of game. For example, in Figure 2–21 the I, II submatrix is *PD,* and from III on the dynamics are Chicken. A plausible interpretation of what such a game might look like empirically would be as follows: the players begin with their maximum initial demands (II, II), allowing some room for compromise and each expecting the other to reduce his demand (I, I). But at II,

---

[15] Herman Kahn, *On Escalation* (New York: Praeger, 1965).
[16] Henry Hamburger, "Separable Games," *Behavioral Science,* 14 (1969), pp. 121–132.

B

	I	II	III	IV	V	VI
I	2 2	−1 3	−4 4	−7 5	−10 6	−13 7
II	3 −1	−½ −½	−4 0	−7½ ½	−11 1	−14½ 1½
III	4 −4	0 −4	−4 −4	−8 −4	−12 −4	−16 −4
IV	5 −7	½ −7½	−4 −8	−8½ −8½	−13 −9	−17½ −9½
V	6 −10	1 −11	−4 −12	−9 −13	−14 −14	−19 −15
VI	7 −13	1½ −14½	−4 −16	−9½ −17½	−15 −19	−20½ −20½

A (row label at left)

Figure 2-21. Expanded Chicken

II, analogous to *DD* in Prisoner's Dilemma, they are immediately in trouble. Threats to break off negotiations at II, II are useless to induce the opponent to shift to I, and the alternative of a shift to I oneself is unattractive. However, the model offers a way out of the "*DD* trap" that looks more immediately rewarding than the "martyr route" of playing I. Either player can escalate or threaten to escalate to III or IV. This looks rewarding because there is not only an immediate small gain from escalation (from $-\frac{1}{2}$ to 0 or $\frac{1}{2}$), but also the prospect of additional large gains as the other player cuts his losses by moving to I. The immediate gain from escalation might consist empirically of an improvement in one's resolve image or increasing domestic support from hard-line groups. The prospect of other gains arises from the opponent's possible preference for yielding rather than to accept the escalated costs or risk further escalation. This model thus implicitly moves from the non-violent bargaining of "crisis" to the violent bargaining of "war." However, instead of submitting, the threatened player can counterescalate at a slight additional penalty to himself and can impose great damage on his opponent; and so on down to VI, VI and disaster. From IV, IV on, the motive for escalation is no longer to achieve an immediate gain, since further escalation is self-punishing; the motive is rather the prospect of forcing the other to submit and thereby retrieving a large win out of the crisis. However, the opponent always has the option of upping the stakes at slight additional cost to himself and great additional cost to the other. Near VI, VI or in general near m, n the motivation probably shifts to that of pulling the opponent down to mutual disaster: "We may be destroyed, but England shall at least lose India," the German Kaiser raged as the 1914 crisis went over the brink.

The numbers in the matrix are significant only in sequence, not individually; they express rates of increase of cost or benefit, not absolute quantities. All the sequences together represent the dynamics of the model; the straight lines are the dynamics of unilateral escalation-deescalation, and the main diagonal is the dynamics of mutual escalation, the "slippery slope to destruction."

The slippery slope is always a curve with $d<0, d^2>0, d^3=0$.

The dynamics of the model depend on three parameters: (1) rate of increase of escalation benefits (T), the sequence from I, I to m, I; (2) the rate of increase of submission cost (S), the sequence from I, I to I, n; (3) rate of increase of escalation cost (P), the sequence from I, I to m, n. Parameter no. 3 is the crucial d^2 of the slippery slope. Note that these three parameters are the same that determine critical risk in the critical risk model. Expanded Chicken is an expansion of the critical risk model.

An empirical instance of expanded Chicken cannot be expected to be mathematically regular; the slippery slope has bumps and plateaus in it. In other words, the option set or "rungs on the escalation ladder" will be irregularly spaced and will contain salient thresholds. One would expect that these irregularities in the three parameter sets would determine the detailed bargaining dynamics.

SUPERGAME MODELS.[17]

These consist of a set of 2×2 matrices arranged in a larger matrix or vector. Each matrix has different payoff properties, and the changes of payoff properties form regular sequences in the supermatrix. Each payoff has two parts, an immediate payoff and a statement directing the players to the next game. The statement might direct the players to play the same game again or it might direct them to a different game in the supergame. Play of a supergame consists of a series of plays of component subgames, the exact sequence depending on the instructions

[17] Amnon Rapoport, "Optimum Policies for the Prisoner's Dilemma," *Psychological Review*, 74 (1967); "Effects of Payoff Information in Multi-stage Mixed Motive Games," *Behavioral Science*, 14 (1969).

	C	D	C	D	C	D	C	D
C	4, 4 Stay	−10, 5 Stay	3, 3 to I, 25%	−9, 6 Stay	2, 2 to II, 25%	−9, 8 Stay	1, 1 to III, 25%	−10, 10 Stay
D	5, −10 Stay	−9, −9 to II, 25%	6, −9 Stay	−7, −7 to III, 25%	8, −9 Stay	−5, −5 to IV, 25%	10, −10 Stay	−3, −3 Stay
	I		II		III		IV	

Figure 2-22. A Hypothetical Supergame

in the outcome cells. For example, a supergame might look like Figure 2–22. This supergame consists of four subgames. Note the double payoff in each cell. The numbers on top are immediate payoffs, and the words below are instructions on which game to play next. "Stay" means play the same game again; the "25%" instructions are to flip a coin or some other probability device and move to some other game with 25% probability and stay put with 75% probability.

If we look only at the numerical payoffs, each subgame is Prisoner's Dilemma. However, I is a fairly cooperative version in which CC should be easy to achieve because of the weak temptation and strong punishment for playing D. Cooperation is more difficult to achieve in each successive subgame until in IV it is very difficult. If we look at the total payoffs the nature of the subgames depends on the number of subgames to be played and on the probabilities.

Play might begin in either II or III and move in either direction or stay in the same game, according to the outcome and probabilities associated with it. Suppose it began in II and the outcome of the first three plays was DD; then by the fourth play the players would probably (58%) have shifted to III. A series of CC outcomes would shift them back to II again, from which they could shift either to I or III. The consequence of a series of CC outcomes is to move the players toward game I, that is toward games in which CC is progressively easier to achieve. Conversely a series of DD outcomes moves the players eventually to game IV in which DD is almost impossible to avoid. One would expect players to end the supergame in either I at CC or IV at DD.

Plainly the supergame is useful for modeling long-run changes of relationship between two parties. Each subgame could represent one crisis with its immediate outcome, and the shift to a different subgame would represent a change in the relationship as an indirect result of how the crisis was handled and resolved. The supergame of Figure 2–22 would represent a series of changes in the level of conflict between two countries. Game I represents a relatively cooperative relationship, say entente, in which common interests are strong and occasions for conflict unimportant; game IV represents an intense conflict of interests in which bargaining is all but useless. If additional games were added to both ends, the supergame would move out of Prisoner's Dilemma to Chicken in one direction and to Deadlock in the other direction. The supergame could also be used to model changes of relative bargaining power by showing how the winner of one game increases his relative power and thereby is more favorably placed to win the next game. The component subgames would move from Chicken to Called Bluff to Bully to Big Bully.[18]

THE METAGAME.[19]

This type of bargaining theory takes complete bargaining strategies as its unit, rather than bids, moves, or options. A metagame takes the form of a matrix in which each row and column is a complete strategy. The set of rows and columns represents "all possible" strategies for both players.

A metagame is derived from a simple, normal-form game by assuming sequential rather than simultaneous play. This has the effect that the later player has more strategies available than an earlier player. If A plays first, he has two strategies to choose from, while B has four. A's alternatives are simple: C or D. B's alternatives are conditional on A's and constitute metastrategies: if C then C, if D then C; if C then C, if D then D; if C then D, if D then C; if C then D, if D then D. These may be more generally described as (1) play C whatever A does; (2) play the same strategy that A chooses (tit-for-tat); (3) play the opposite of what A chooses, and (4) play D whatever A does. Similarly, A has sixteen metastrategies conditional on B's four. If we convert this to normal form, for a 2×2 simple game, the first metagame is 2×4 and the second metagame 16×4, and so on to infinity.

To see how a metastrategy or conditional strategy might work, consider experimental gaming conditions. If the game is Prisoner's Dilemma and preplay communications are allowed, it is possible for the players to construct conditional strategies and communicate them before play. B can say, "If you play C I'll play C, but if you play D I'll play D." If

[18] For example, see Glenn H. Snyder, "Prisoner's Dilemma and Chicken Models in International Politics," *International Studies Quarterly,* Vol. 15, No. 1 (1971), p. 97.

[19] Nigel Howard, "The Theory of Metagames," *General Systems* (1966), pp. 167–186; *Paradoxes of Rationality: Theory of Metagames and Political Behavior* (Cambridge, Mass.: MIT Press, 1971); Thomas Saaty, *Mathematical Models of Arms Control and Disarmament* (New York: Wiley, 1968); Henry Bain, N. Howard, and T. Saaty, "Using the Analysis of Options Technique to Analyze a Community Conflict," *Journal of Conflict Resolution,* 15 (1971), pp. 133–144.

A believes this, it is to his advantage to choose C; B then chooses C, and both benefit. The point of communicating the metastrategy is to induce the opponent to choose a mutually favorable alternative. On the other hand B can still double-cross A with D. This possibility is prevented by A's metastrategy, which might run, "If I play C and you reciprocate, as you say, then I shall continue to play C; but if I play C and you double-cross I'll shift to D." That is, A's metametastrategy can induce a favorable metastrategy choice by B, just as B's can induce a favorable strategy choice by A.

We see from this gaming example that there are two components to a successful conditional strategy. One is the positive inducement, the carrot, namely a promise to reciprocate a favorable action of some sort. The other is the sanction, the stick, namely a threat to punish an unfavorable action. Such a concept is familiar in bargaining, and all the metagame does is to focus our attention on it and provide a mathematical formalization of it.

In crisis bargaining we drop some artificial rules that are useful only for gaming experiments. We drop the distinction between preplay communication and actual play and the rule commanding sequential choice of complete metastrategies. What is useful, however, in metagame theory is the idea of a stable settlement. Metagame theory tells us that bargaining is a process of searching for or constructing a settlement that is stabilized, guaranteed, by conditional strategies of each player. Each player must be able to say, "If you continue to play C (respect the settlement) I will too, but if you double-cross then I'll play D in turn." It may be that a settlement is constructed piece by piece during bargaining, or possibly the settlement is constructed as a whole package somehow. Note that this conception is entirely different from the one underlying utility models, where bargaining appears as a process of creeping up on some midpoint from two opposite sides. The utility models focus on the sequence of bids and attempt to provide a formal explanation of the specific sequence, while the metagame focuses on the underlying carrot-and-stick tool that each bargainer uses to defend the settlement.

The one application of metagame theory developed so far is the "analysis of options," which conforms generally to the above account. It drops the mathematical complexity of the infinite metagame (2×4, 16×4, 16×64, . . .) and works instead with the familiar $m \times n$ expanded game. The unit of analysis is not metastrategies at all, but rather options, and the analysis is a technique for locating stable, defensible settlements in the expanded matrix. The principle that emerges from the published analyses is that a settlement is stable if each player has available a sanction, a stick, that can prevent the other players from shifting to a different outcome more advantageous to themselves. This is by no means a new idea, but the analysis of options provides a formal way of working with it. It provides an algorithm for searching through N-person $m \times n \times o$ . . . matrices, matrices so complex that they cannot be written down. This technique enables us to work with a four- or five-country bargaining process in which each country has half a dozen or so options, which is indeed a technical advance.

THE N-PERSON GAME.[20]

N-person theory deals with situations involving three or more bargainers. The bargaining problem here is one of forming coalitions and agreeing on the payoff to each coalition member. Presumably two or more bargainers attempt concurrently to form coalitions by making offers to prospective members, and the recipient of an offer must decide whether to accept, ask for a better payoff, or wait for a better offer from another coalition. Bargaining does not end when a coalition is formed; coalition members can try to renegotiate the coalition agreement in their own favor, and outsiders can try to lure away a member. One important empirical discovery in coalition experiments is that coalition members are most reluctant to accept an outside offer and to desert their coalition, because they realize that their resulting reputation for fickleness will be hard to live down.

To discuss coalition bargaining we need a number of concepts from N-person theory. First, there must be a *leader* who attempts to form a coalition. His objective is a *winning coalition,* one strong enough to have its way against any or all of the other players. There must be some rule which specifies how strong a coalition must be to win. For instance in voting situations the rule might be that 50% plus one vote wins; this would be a *majority coalition.* The strength of a coalition consists of the combined strengths of its members; each member has a *weight,* which is the amount of strength or power he adds to the coalition. In voting situations each member's weight consists of his vote, and all weights are equal. Normally, however, in non-voting situations weights are unequal. A coalition not yet strong enough to win is a *protocoalition;* although not strong enough to win, it may be strong enough to prevent any other protocoalition from winning, in which case it is a *blocking coalition.* A player's weight for blocking may be different from his weight for winning, for instance if he has veto power (1-person blocking coalition) but does not otherwise vote. In this case a leader need only to induce him to abstain rather than join a coalition. Finally, if all players unite they form a *grand coalition.*

We also need some concept of a *decision point*—a point in time when

[20] Anatol Rapoport, *N-Person Game Theory* (Ann Arbor: University of Michigan Press, 1970).

the winning coalition is determined and payoffs are awarded to it and divided among its members. *N*-person theory is vague about the location of this point, but we need it for empirical application. For international alliance bargaining, it is sufficient for our present purpose to locate it at the terminal point of a crisis, whether that is the resolution of the crisis peacefully or its eruption into war. For coalition bargaining within governments—i.e., in internal decision making—the decision point occurs when an external bargaining strategy is adopted or significantly revised.

In summary, the models considered in this chapter differ more in their focus of attention than in their assumptions about what bargaining is. They all assume that bargaining is an interaction between two or more rational actors with unitary preference functions and adequate information; that bargaining is precipitated by a conflict of interest that occurs in a setting of common interests; and that it ends in an agreement over how to distribute the disputed goods, or in disagreement. The utility models focus on the actual bargaining, the sequence of bids, and attempt to provide a formal explanation of the sequence and perhaps a prediction of the outcome. The game models focus on the strategies that produce a bidding sequence and on the strategic and tactical choices that must be made before and during bidding. The expanded game focuses on one specific tactical choice, that of escalation and de-escalation. The metagame in its current application focuses on the settlement, i.e., on the characteristics a settlement must have if it is actually to resolve the dispute and keep it resolved. The supergame focuses on the effect an outcome of one game has on the characteristics of the next game.

EMPIRICAL INTERPRETATION AND EVALUATION OF UTILITY MODELS

So far we have described the various formal models of bargaining available in the literature and indicated briefly how each might be applied to crisis bargaining. In the remainder of the chapter we attempt to test each model against the empirical evidence.

The testing of a mathematical model is a quite different process from the testing an empirical hypothesis. A mathematical model is an arbitrary construction that of itself says nothing about the empirical world and thus makes no truth claim that can be tested. To test a model, it is first necessary to give its various terms an empirical interpretation; and for all but the most complex models, several alternative interpretations are possible. Also most models, including game models, have several variants—alternative rules for games, alternative definitions and postulates—and one of these must be selected or constructed. This preliminary process of interpretation and selection, which we have already begun in preceding sections, serves to make a model relevant to some empirical situation. If one cannot devise an interpretation and a variant that makes a model relevant, the model must be discarded—not as false but as inapplicable in this empirical area.

But even an interpreted model cannot be directly falsified. The derivations of the model follow logically from the postulates, so if the "predictions" of the model do not hold good empirically, this merely shows that the postulates were not all empirically exemplified. For example, a 2×2 Prisoner's Dilemma game necessarily ends in *DD*. When we find instances of *PD* crises that end in *CC* this does not falsify Prisoner's Dilemma; it shows that one or more of its postulates—simultaneous play, a certain kind of rationality in the players, a certain level of information—was not exemplified in the crisis.

What we look for is not correct predictions but rather fruitfulness and relevance. Each of our models calls attention to certain factors, implicitly says that these are the important ones, and ties them together into a neat mathematical package. If we find (with the help of other models) that important factors have been omitted by some model and that when these are included the resulting package looks quite different, we are justified in saying that the model is superficial, incomplete, misleading, beside the point, but not false. The same model that is misleading for crisis bargaining may be quite useful in other situations.

The result of testing should be the selection of one or two models as most relevant and fruitful for understanding crisis bargaining and the rejection of others as less relevant or beside the point. The relevant models may also be extended and adapted by changing their postulates to improve their fit with the data. Finally, testing and adaptation should be followed by the construction of an improved model or models that capture more of the actual dynamics in the cases.

We begin our interpretation with the simplest utility model, the one-dimensional conflict line.

One advantage of utility models in comparison with game models is that their empirical interpretation is easy. One simply estimates the relative utility of some bid and plots it in the utility space. This makes utility models especially useful for describing a bidding sequence and a settlement. For example, Figure 2–23 uses the conflict line to describe the bids in the Fashoda crisis of 1898. The bids are shown in the figure with "E" representing England and "F" representing France.

Several points of clarification are necessary. First, the bargaining space can be treated as one-dimensional because the issue was geographical, the location of the boundary between French and British

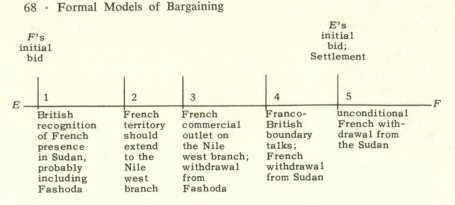

Figure 2-23. The Bidding Sequence, Fashoda, 1898

possessions. Second, the space was not continuous but consisted of four salient points at which the boundary could plausibly be drawn. On the other hand, it would be possible to locate additional points between any pair of points on the line if necessary. Third, the two initial bids were not geographically specific, and thus the two points adjacent to the initial bids were partly clarification and partly concession. Fourth, the minima of both sides are unknown to us and to the bargainers as well.

The bargaining process began with ambiguous initial bids by both sides (points 1, 5), and continued with a series of clarifications or concessions by the French (points 2, 3, 4). The British eventually accepted the French proposal for boundary talks (point 4), but only after the French had unconditionally withdrawn their force from Fashoda (point 5). The French hoped for some small British concessions during the talks but got none. The final settlement, therefore, was geographically identical to the initial British demand (point 5) or rather constituted a clarification of that demand that specified the exact line of French withdrawal.

The conflict line can only rarely be used to describe a bidding sequence accurately because it abstracts from common interests. That is, it assumes that all bids are on an essentially straight conflict line, and this is almost always false. Of our cases, only Fashoda plus portions of a few other cases can be so described. And we shall argue later that even in these few cases, and especially for Fashoda, the conflict-line formalization is misleading and superficial. The reason is that power relationships cannot be included in the conflict line, and without these a mere portrayal of the bidding space remains superficial.

The two-dimensional model, to which we turn next, can be used to portray relative power, though not as effectively as certain game models. However, a two-dimensional model is good for describing the combina-

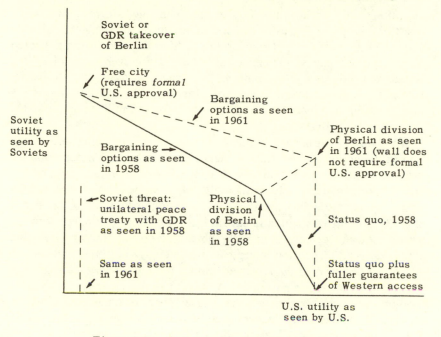

Figure 2-24. Options with Respect to Berlin

tion of common and conflicting interests. For example, Figure 2–24 is Pruitt and Holland's description of the Berlin situation in 1958 and 1961.[21]

If one treats the status quo, 1958, point as the zero point, all the bidding except the Berlin Wall bid is located in the II and IV quadrants, which makes the game *PD*. Note that the conflict line has empirical kinks in it that are important for describing the bargaining process. Note also that one can describe changes of utility estimates over time.

This example also illustrates the use of a utility model to explain bids and responses to bids. It says that both sides accepted the wall (which Ulbricht had already considered in 1958) because it was the only option preferred to no agreement by both sides. It also says that the United States rejected Khrushchev's 1958 threat (unilateral peace treaty) because it could not distinguish his three options (GDR takeover, free city, and peace treaty) as to their utility, and therefore rejected all three equally. Khrushchev's reluctance to carry out the threat is explained as due to its considerably lower utility for him as compared with the free

[21] Dean G. Pruitt and Jane Holland, "Settlement in the Berlin Crisis, 1958–1962" (mimeographed), Center for International Conflict Studies, SUNY–Buffalo, June 22, 1971.

city alternative, as he himself asserted. The diagram also suggests a question: why did Khrushchev choose to make an ineffective threat? Probably his estimates of United States utilities differed from the United States' own estimates. Or conceivably he did not even think of it as a threat, but only as another option. This suggests that it would be desirable to construct two diagrams, one for the utilities of both parties as estimated by the Soviet Union and another for the utilities as estimated by the United States.

If we take Khrushchev's public and diplomatic statements seriously— and in the absence of contrary evidence, that is the best we can do—he estimated that the threat point was a bit NE of the status quo, and the free city bid considerably farther NE. He supposed that the United States would settle for something in the neighborhood of the free city point because it was mutually advantageous, both as compared with the status quo and as compared with the threat point. He supposed that both sides had a common interest in a free city-type settlement, though of course he reserved the larger advantage for the Soviet Union and assigned a much smaller advantage to the United States, only the elimination of an anomalous situation that was a source of undesirable friction. A separate peace treaty, he supposed, was less desirable for both sides; its sole advantage was that the Soviet Union could carry it out unilaterally. Khrushchev was officially saying, in effect, "If you do not wish to share with us the advantages of a Berlin settlement we shall have to do the best we can by ourselves."

Khrushchev's move miscarried because his estimate of United States utilities was vastly different from Dulles's estimate. Khrushchev's estimate was based on his distinction between "realists" and "madmen" in international politics. The madmen, including some United States military leaders, some West German leaders such as Franz Josef Strauss, and the Chinese, were trying to work up a U.S.S.R.–U.S. war over Germany. They were stirring people up with inflammatory speeches and writings and movies, sending agitators and saboteurs into East Germany, and urging military moves on their respective governments. The realists, including especially Eisenhower, realized that nuclear war was unthinkable and that U.S.–U.S.S.R. differences had to be settled peacefully by compromise. To Khrushchev's way of thinking, Soviet and the United States realists had a common interest in restraining the madmen on both sides, and the best way to do this was to reach a definitive settlement of the Berlin issue based on mutual recognition of the 1958 status quo of two Germanies. This would leave the madmen with no disputed areas in which to stir up trouble. In Khrushchev's view, his 1958 free city proposal was essentially a way of removing a source of conflict, and therefore was of advantage to both sides (though mainly to the Soviet

Union). It was perhaps also a way of persuasively reminding the U.S. "realists" of the 1958 realities, in case they were still dreaming of past hopes. The unilateral peace treaty would define boundaries, but would be a less effective restraint on the U.S. "madmen" because the United States would not be officially bound by it. For Dulles and Adenauer, in contrast, the free city proposal, whether unilateral or not, was a brazen Soviet grab for territory that legitimately belonged to the West, not a mutually advantageous normalization of an abnormal situation.

EVALUATION OF THE TWO-DIMENSIONAL UTILITY MODEL

The interplay of common and conflicting interests on which this model focuses is indeed present in all our cases. In this respect the utility model is very useful. In nearly all cases there is a negative common interest in avoiding war. Positive shared interests and the opportunity for joint benefits other than avoiding war were present in 1905–1906, 1908, 1911, the 1913 Balkan conferences, the 1922–1923 Ruhr crisis, 1947 Iran, and 1958–1962 Berlin. They were less important in 1898, 1914, and Berlin 1948, and remained in the background in 1941, Quemoy, Lebanon, and Cuba. It would be incorrect to assert that crisis bargaining is concerned essentially with achieving shared interests; but the interplay between conflicting and common interests is a pervasive and central feature of our cases.

Specifically, in the Fashoda case there was some mutual fear or at least reluctance to engage in warfare. This reluctance provided time for negotiations to run their course because each side knew that the other side would not begin hostilities unless negotiations failed. Conversely, the possibility of war provided an impetus to keep the negotiations moving, and this was the chief basis for the successive French concessions. There was also a weak joint interest in the possibility of future cooperation, an interest that came to fruition in the 1904 entente, and the French used this interest in their bargaining tactics.

The primary deficiency of the utility model is its neglect of cognitive factors. Of course the model does not pretend to deal with cognitive factors; it is not that kind of model. However, theorists who use this model are implicitly saying that cognitive factors are a separate issue, probably a secondary one, and perhaps one that can be handled ad hoc. We find, on the contrary, that cognitive factors are an essential and inseparable part of crisis bargaining. One set of cognitive processes that always occur are those devoted to understanding the opponent: interpreting his various communications and actions, estimating his intentions, estimating his preference function. In addition one must predict his interpretation of one's own messages, estimate his image of one's own intentions and preferences, and predict his probable response to one's actions.

These processes could be ignored if they usually produced a correct result, but the opposite is the case. Our bargainers consistently misinterpret each other's communications, intentions, preferences, and images of each other, so much so that misinterpretation must be treated as a normal part of the bargaining process. There are a few exceptions (such as British Foreign Secretary Grey in 1905–1906 and 1911 and Iranian Premier Qavam in 1946, who were remarkably correct in their interpretations and estimates), and there are variations in the rate and extent of error, but error is the norm. Nor are cognitive errors confined to the Cold War period; they are just as prominent in the earlier cases. Cognitive errors were of minor importance only in 1898 Fashoda, 1922–1923 Ruhr, and 1948 Berlin.

A second kind of cognitive process neglected by the utility models is the search process—i.e., the active search for information about the interests of and tactical options available to each party. These factors, assumed to be given in utility models, are not in most cases given at the start of bargaining; they must be discovered or in some cases constructed. Interests are not usually arranged in a preference order, but must be searched out, evaluated, and ordered. The bargaining range is of course not known in advance, but in some cases it does not even exist in any obvious way and must be created by deciding on minima or by changing minima. Nor do interests remain fixed once they have been ordered; they change in a variety of ways, mostly involuntary. A bargaining range that existed initially may disappear through such changes before agreement can be reached. Finally, in at least two cases, Lebanon 1958 and Berlin 1961–1962, the parties did not even know that a settlement had occurred, and had to discover this fact.

The neglect of cognitive factors by utility theorists betrays them into some discussions that are misguided and even meaningless. Their formal assumptions suggest problems that are mathematically interesting but turn out to be empirically meaningless, while screening out some empirically important problems. One example is the discussion by Kenneth Boulding and others [22] of the expected sequence of bargaining tactics. In a two-dimensional utility model, two different kinds of movement are possible, movement toward the conflict line and movement along the conflict line. The former kind benefits both parties in varying degree while the latter benefits one at the expense of the other. Here is a clear distinction that suggests an interesting puzzle: which kind of movement will come first in a rational bargaining process? Both Boulding and Walton and McKersie argue that the former kind of movement should come first. This may make sense in labor-management or busi-

[22] Kenneth Boulding, *Conflict and Defense* (New York: Harper, 1962), pp. 16–17.

ness bargaining, but in political crises the distinction and therefore the discussion is meaningless. The conflict line does not exist (or is not known) prior to bidding but is constructed (or discovered) during bidding as the bargainers clarify for themselves the issues in dispute and their importance. The two initial bids establish the two limits of the conflict line and later tactics explore portions of the intervening space. A creative compromise bid (which Walton and McKersie would call "integrative bargaining") can be described indifferently as a shift of the conflict line, or the discovery of an unsuspected kink in and therefore a movement *along* a kinky conflict line, or as movement from a false to a real conflict line. And since the bargainers can never know when they are on the real or ultimate conflict line, they cannot know which sort of bargaining is going on at any time. Another example is Nash's (and Harsanyi's) involved discussion of how to predict the exact point on the conflict line at which agreement will occur. Since the conflict line does not exist (is not known) prior to bidding, and since the parties cannot know whether they are on it, the computations he requires cannot be performed for our cases.[23]

Another factor neglected by utility models is the interplay between adversary and alliance bargaining. We all know that adversaries often have allies or try to get allies, and we know that alliance considerations often play some sort of role in moves against adversaries, but this knowledge is not normally incorporated in our formal bargaining models. But if we focus on the alliance-adversary interplay we come to see in case after case that adversary bargaining interacts closely with alliance bargaining and that both kinds of consideration enter into each move. A move may be officially directed at an adversary but actually intended primarily to affect one's allies; for example Adenauer's anti-Soviet moves in 1958–1961 were probably intended primarily as NATO alliance-strengthening moves. Adenauer's concern was to integrate Germany firmly within NATO and demonstrate Germany's trustworthiness to NATO allies. Conversely, moves officially directed at allies usually take their main meaning from an adversary context; for example the French-British sparring in 1904–1914 always had reference to Germany, and often to Russia as well. Khrushchev's travels in France and England in 1959–1960 were probably a move (weaken opponent's alliance) in his adversary confrontation with the United States, which in turn was mainly intended to strengthen an ally (East Germany) and an alliance (Warsaw Pact and perhaps also Soviet Union–China).

[23] John C. Harsanyi, "Approaches to the Bargaining Problem Before and After the Theory of Games: A Critical Discussion of Zeuthen's, Hicks' and Nash's Theories," *Econometrica*, 24 (1956), pp. 144–157; Kent, *The Effects of Threats*, pp. 24–25.

In addition to the endlessly ramified interplay between adversary and alliance considerations, we note also the continual presence of opposed interests between allies and common interests between adversaries, so that allies are to some extent adversaries and vice versa. This is a more generalized version of the interplay between common and opposed interests mentioned earlier. At the extreme, opposed and common interests are so nearly balanced in a specific situation that one can see the parties both as allies and adversaries; they are antagonistic partners or allied adversaries. Three examples are Austria–Russia 1897–1908, Bulgaria–Serbia 1912–1913, and United States–Soviet Union 1942–1945. Then there are cases in which alliance considerations slightly predominate such as Austria–Italy 1908–1914, and cases in which adversary conditions are becoming dominant such as United States–Soviet Union in Iran 1946; and so on through varied mixes to the extreme cases of nearly pure allied or adversary relations. To omit the alliance element in bargaining, as utility models do, may be justified as a single step in a larger theory of bargaining, but in the absence of such a larger theory, the result is inevitably some degree of distortion. The alliance element expands the number of bargainers to more than two; hence an adequate treatment of it formally requires an adaptation of N-person game theory, which we shall attempt in a later chapter.

Specifically, Bulgaria and Serbia, in 1912, had a common interest in taking territory from Turkey and an opposed interest in the allocation of the occupied territory. They also had a common interest in avoiding Austrian domination and an opposed interest in gaining Austrian support or neutrality. Austria and Italy, 1908–1914, had a common interest in taking territory from Turkey, a common interest in preventing a Serbian military port on the Adriatic, and therefore a common interest in an independent Albania. Italy had an interest in maintaining its relative power position in the Adriatic and was therefore opposed to unilateral increase of Austrian influence. Italy had a grievance over the Italian population in Austrian South Tyrol and in Trieste. Austria had an interest in maintaining the alliance with Germany and was therefore a potential opponent of France, but Italy had a secret non-aggression treaty with France.

Another limitation of utility models is that they assume a unitary bargainer with known and moderately stable preference functions. Our crisis bargainers however are committees or hierarchies, or even competing groups within a government. The preference functions of these groups, bureaus, or committee members differ greatly and are sometimes direct opposites. Some may have preferences that are closer to members of the opposing side than to some of their own colleagues. Consequently, the preferences of the whole bargainer vary according to the shifting power distribution of his component parts and may in fact shift suddenly as a former minority coalition becomes predominant. An example is the shift of French policy 1922–1924 as Briand was replaced by Poincaré, who in turn was replaced by a Left coalition. Sometimes the components of a bargainer are also internally divided, for example Japanese navy leaders in 1941 and the West German foreign office in 1961.

Consequently the crisis bargaining process is as much a struggle within governments as between them. The preferences, specific objectives, maxima and minima, images of the opponent, and strategies are not given at the start of bargaining but are determined and changed during it. The moves of a dominant group within a government may be directed as much to maintaining or improving their internal position as to winning against the opponent or ally. To illustrate from the Fashoda case: British and French interests did indeed conflict in the Sudan once the French soldiers were there; but how did this conflict come about? We find that the French expedition was a project pushed by the French Colonial Office and disapproved by the Foreign Office. The project and its vague objective was redefined in an attempt to get Foreign Office approval; finally in 1895 a new foreign minister knowing little about the project approved it. His instructions limiting the scope of the expedition were reversed in practice by Colonial Office subordinates, and the French and British governments found themselves, to their surprise and dismay, in a confrontation. The French expedition shows resemblances to the U.S.-sponsored invasion of Cuba in 1961.

A further implication of these internal factors is that the basic postulate of utility models, the postulate of rationality, fails in most cases. Governments do not usually choose between alternative tactics in such a way as to maximize expected returns as these might be estimated by a single decision maker. Tactical and strategic decisions are rather the result of internal coalition bargaining reflecting, at most, the rationality of N-person game theory rather than that of utility theory. A bargainer's "strategy" is usually a shifting or internally inconsistent compromise among the majority coalition members, and includes side payments, ambiguities representing postponed disagreements (such as the 1905 German demand for a conference), and symbolic gestures. Change of strategy is a result of internal pulling and hauling, as the members try to improve strategy according to their varied specifications. Much of this change occurs in the carrying out of a chosen strategy, so that a bargainer's actual behavior may be quite different from what he "decided" to do. A well-known example is the U.S. blockade line in 1962, which Kennedy decided to move closer to Cuba but which in practice stayed where it was. Then there were the Turkish missiles, which

Kennedy had ordered removed but which the State Department decided should stay there because of Turkish objections. Other examples are the Russian commandant's sabotage of a vague currency agreement Stalin had just made for Berlin 1948, and in 1945 General Clay's revision of agreements Truman had made at Potsdam.

Another difficulty with utility models is that in practice the object at stake is often not divisible, or is divisible only into a few discrete parts. This means that the "utilities" that are being bargained over do not lie on a smooth continuum so that trade-offs (e.g. between risk and concession) can be considered in small marginal amounts. They must be considered in large chunks. In the extreme cases of complete indivisibility—as in Cuba, 1962, when the Russians either had to take all their missiles out or none—the idea of a compromise is difficult to formulate practically. Theoretically, compromises in such cases might be fashioned out of tie-ins with other issues, or side-payments (as occurred in the Cuban case), but we did not find this happening very often, and when it does occur it is not easily represented in a two-dimensional utility model.

A virtue of utility models is that they allow more possible outcomes to be shown graphically than do game models.

In summary, the two-dimensional model is useful for studying the interrelations of common and conflicting interests. It is useful for describing a sequence of bids and in some cases in explaining the response to a bid. It permits the display of all plausible outcomes. Its deficiencies are: (1) it neglects cognitive factors, including information processing, making estimates about the opponent, and searching for one's interests and for tactics and strategies; (2) it assumes pure adversary bargaining and thus neglects the interplay between adversary and alliance bargaining; (3) it assumes an integrated bargainer and thus neglects internal politics; (4) it assumes that bargainers try to maximize expected utility, whereas actually bargaining decisions are often made by coalition tactics and other more haphazard procedures; and (5) it obscures the imperfect divisibility and compromisability of the issues in dispute. These deficiencies lead one to suppose that the utility model must either be (1) rejected for crisis bargaining, or (2) radically restructured, and/or (3) supplemented by models dealing with the neglected aspects of crisis bargaining. We choose the first option.

EVALUATION OF THE THREE-DIMENSIONAL UTILITY MODEL.

Some economists have argued that time is an essential third dimension of any bargaining process since utilities continually change over time. In particular, Cross states, "The most important characterization which we, in this study, will apply to the bargaining process is that it is fundamentally time dependent." [24] Cross distinguishes three effects of time on utility: (1) the utility of a future agreement may be discounted to the present on the assumption that the bargainer would rather enjoy the benefits of an agreement now than to postpone enjoyment, so that a postponed enjoyment is worth less than a present one; (2) the utility of the issues in dispute may decrease over time—the cake gets moldy while we bargain over how to cut it, the value of the blocked Suez Canal decreases as alternative oil transport techniques are developed; (3) the total cost of bargaining increases over time.[25] All three of these effects have the consequence that the more distant the agreement is estimated to be, the lower is its expected utility. They therefore provide the incentive for the bargainers to speed up the bargaining, to make concessions faster, so they can reach agreement before the benefits dissolve.

Although we did not have such a model in mind initially, the case studies provided several examples of time-dependent effects. The time-dependent effects are nearly all instances in which the utility of no agreement for one bargainer is declining rapidly. That is, the status quo is rapidly deteriorating. The danger here is that the other bargainer, B, can use the threat of no agreement to get a better and better outcome for himself. In order to avoid this, A must press for rapid agreement either by making concessions, or by coercive tactics, or by some preemptive combination of the two. Note that this is a different sort of utility change from the three listed by Cross; Cross thinks of the deterioration over time of the future goods to be secured by agreement, whereas our bargainers are impelled to act by rapidly approaching disaster.

In Cuba, 1962, the U.S. position was rapidly deteriorating. The Soviet missiles would be operational in a matter of days, at which point "no agreement" could mean millions of American deaths in Kennedy's estimation. Consequently, the United States had to press for rapid agreement, and chose the coercion-escalation-ultimatum route. In 1961 the GDR position was deteriorating daily due to refugee movements, and it was up to Ulbricht to speed the bargaining process. In this case he chose a preemptive combination of concession and fait accompli that proved successful. The U.S. freezing of Japanese assets July 26, 1941, plus coordinated Dutch moves, effectively stopped Japanese imports of a series of vital raw materials. The military estimated that they had an eighteen-month supply of oil, two years at most, and were similarly short on other materials, so that each month's delay made military and economic collapse more likely. Consequently, they pressed ever more urgently for a rapid end to negotiations one way or the other,

[24] Cross, *The Economics of Bargaining,* p. 12.
[25] Ibid., pp. 13, 45.

and when agreement could not be reached they pressed for a desperate gamble on war. On November 5, 1937, Hitler estimated that the German military position would begin deteriorating rapidly by 1943 at the latest, so that he had to speed up the solution of the German living-space problem, with special reference to Austria, Czechoslovakia, and Poland. In July 1914 the Austrian mobilization and declaration of war caused the Russian military situation in the Balkans to deteriorate daily, and this pressured them into their own disastrous mobilization decision. In 1905 and 1911 the French preemptive moves aimed at taking control of Morocco forced the Germans to take decisive actions to forestall total German loss in Morocco. In 1913 the Austrian military position in the Balkans was deteriorating due to the imminent Montenegran capture of the town of Scutari. The Austrians made several border concessions at the Balkan Conference in a vain attempt to achieve agreement before the fall of Scutari. These hasty concessions proved to be unnecessary, because the surrender of Scutari during the negotiations had no effect on the demands of the other bargainers. In August 1922 the British demand for debt repayment from France, plus the German request for a moratorium on reparations payments, put France into a financial squeeze that called for quick action. In this case France decided on coercion, and in December–January began the disastrous occupation of the Ruhr. In addition, there are several examples, especially before 1914, of military figures arguing that the opponent's military posture is improving rapidly so if a war has to come, it should come quickly.

If a deteriorating status quo produces an effort to speed up bargaining, does an improving status quo produce a stall? A stall is not identical with refusal to negotiate, since such refusal may be accompanied by vigorous coercive action. It consists rather of slowing down whatever moves are under way, whether they are talks, signals, internal consultations, or military moves. The most likely places to find stalls would be the examples listed above, since a deteriorating situation for one bargainer is presumably an improving situation for his opponent. However, there were stalls in only two of the above examples—United States, 1941, and Germany, 1914—and the latter stall was decided in advance as part of the German fait accompli strategy. We have one other example of a stall due to an estimated improving situation—the Soviet Union in Berlin, 1948. In this case Stalin's estimate that time was on his side was disastrously wrong: when he discovered his error, he began to press for rapid agreement, but now the United States was in no hurry, and even withdrew its previous concessions.

The other examples of stalling in our cases do not fit into Cross's scheme at all. They are cases in which the status quo is neither deteriorating nor improving; it is hopeless. Faced with a hopeless and dangerous situation, a utility-model bargainer withdraws to cut his losses, but our bargainers do not withdraw; they stall. Examples are France in September 1923 at the moment of victory, faced with an impossible German situation and suddenly isolated from its allies; Japanese peace advocates in 1941, faced with a choice between economic collapse and a war Japan was sure to lose; the United States in Berlin in 1948, faced with a blockade that was impossible to break or circumvent short of war. Note that the United States was rewarded for its "irrational" behavior with an unexpected victory. These examples, plus other hopeless situations that suddenly become visible once one sees what is going on (France, 1898) point away from utility models in a different direction. They show that some of our bargainers at least are not operating according to a utility model but on some quite different basis.

In summary, we find one regular time-related process, the speeding up of bargaining by a bargainer faced with rapidly approaching disaster. However, the correlative opposite process, a stall by a bargainer faced with rapidly approaching bliss, is rare, and stalling is as often associated with a hopeless situation as with bliss. This shows that Cross is correct in asserting that time is an important variable in bargaining. But it also shows that his particular bargaining model does not apply to crisis bargaining, for two reasons: (1) Our cases have a different kind of time pressure from the cases Cross has in mind. Cross's model deals with bargaining whose point is to allocate some good that will benefit both parties. Our cases involve an intricate combination of expected goods and feared disasters, and the time pressures come more from the disasters than from the goods. A crisis may begin with the hope of positive gain on one or both (or three, etc.) sides, but as it develops its own momentum the danger of disaster provides the time pressure that produces a settlement. (2) Bargaining behavior in hopeless situations, where time pressure is presumably the strongest, is the opposite of that prescribed by Cross's model—stall rather than speedup. This behavior makes no sense in utility terms and again suggests that utility models are missing much of what goes on in crisis bargaining.

EMPIRICAL INTERPRETATION AND EVALUATION OF GAME MODELS: 2×2 GAMES

Game models and utility models both give the same basic picture of bargaining, but with reversed emphases. Utility models focus on the payoff space, that is on the issues in dispute, while game models focus on alternative bargaining strategies, that is the ways of dealing with the issues. Utility models focus on the bargaining situation while game models focus on strategy and tactics, or so it seems. Each kind of model can be used to describe the whole bargaining situation and process by reference to its own focal point. With a utility model one can describe a strategy indirectly, as a series of points plotted on the utility space, as for instance Kent does with threat strategies.[26] The actual bargaining process again can be described as a series of bids or threats plus shifts in the conflict line and the minimum lines. Conversely with a game model one can describe the issues in dispute indirectly as the payoff matrix, that is the set of all possible outcomes of alternative bargaining strategies. The actual bargaining process can be described as a sequential selection and carrying out of strategies, or as attempts to change, or actual changes in, payoff values.

The payoff space of utility models is continuous while the payoff set of game models is a set of discrete points, but this is a trivial difference since a continuous space can always be treated as a set of points, and a set can be treated as a sample from a continuous space. Our examples of utility models in the previous section treated the utility space as a set of points.

The reversal of emphasis means that aspects of bargaining that are central in one kind of model are peripheral in the other. For utility models the conflict line and the minima are salient features, while for the mixed-motive game models the interplay between common and conflicting interests and between accommodative and coercive strategies are salient, as we shall argue shortly. From this standpoint the game models are of superior usefulness in understanding crisis bargaining, because conflict lines and minima are either non-existent or hard to find in our cases while the accommodative-coercive alternation is continually and obviously present and is of central importance (see Ch. III). Another advantage of game models is that they present a much greater variety of possible strategic situations, distributions of power and interests, than utility models, which, as we have indicated, tend to focus attention on chicken-like situations.

Despite their difference of emphasis, both kinds of models give us the same basic picture of bargaining: they treat it as an interaction between two rational maximizers. As we saw with utility models, the assumption of minimax rationality, as defined in pure game theory, is unrealistic. As usually postulated, the players each have a known, clearly defined, and limited set of alternatives available at the outset; they have perfect information, or can acquire it, about the consequences of their choice (given the other player's choice); they can attach precise value payoffs to each set of consequences; and they also know the payoffs of their rational opponent over all the possible outcomes. Such qualities are superhuman, so far from the way real human beings calculate and

---

[26] Kent, *The Effects of Threats.*

behave that a model that assumes them cannot be used even as an ideal-type "benchmark" from which to measure behavioral "deviations."

However, it is possible to define "rationality" in a less rigorous way, closer to the ordinary meaning of the term, and yet preserve a modest role for game models. One may define it, for example, as the choice of means (strategies) so as to maximize expected value across a given set of consistently ordered objectives, given the information actually available to the actor or which he could reasonably acquire in the time available for decision. This definition loosens information requirements, leaves room for the discovery or "creation" of new alternatives during the course of decision making, and drops the requirement for precise (i.e., cardinal) payoff estimates. Our use of game models, as will be seen presently, is consistent with this more modest definition.

It should be noted that the assumption of pure minimax rationality is much more severe for a one-play 2×2 game than it is for other models of rational behavior. Models of economic competition need not assume that any particular person is rational at any particular time, or even that anybody is ever rational; they work if there is a selective process in the economy that rewards and preserves those who act as if they are rational and that eliminates the others.[27] Voting models work if a few marginal voters are rational.[28] Experimental gaming with iterated play does not deal with minimax rationality at all, but with learning and teaching; the players use their repeated experience to learn the structure of the game situation, to work out an effective strategy, and in some cases to teach the opponent an effective joint strategy.[29] Only at asymptote, when the learning and teaching are complete, can one expect rationality of the players. In contrast, a one-play 2×2 game assumes that both players, that is *all* players, are rational right from the start.

The cases show that players usually misperceive their opponent's intentions, misinterpret his messages, miscalculate the effects of their actions on the opponent, misestimate or neglect to estimate their own utilities, fail to examine some alternatives, ignore or miscalculate long-term consequences, fail to compare alternatives impartially, and sometimes fail to carry out chosen strategies. In most cases the players are not even unitary actors, but are committees or hierarchies, or sets of competing organizations. A player's "strategy" is often a shifting or

[27] A. A. Alchian, "Uncertainty, Evolution and Economic Theory," *Journal of Political Economy,* 58 (1950), pp. 211–221; Gary Becker, "Irrational Behavior and Economic Theory," *Journal of Political Economy,* 70 (1962); Paul Diesing, *Patterns of Discovery in the Social Sciences* (Chicago: Aldine, 1971), pp. 58–62.

[28] William Riker, *The Theory of Political Coalitions* (New Haven, Conn.: Yale University Press, 1972), pp. 20–21.

[29] Anatol Rapoport and A. Chammah, *Prisoner's Dilemma* (Ann Arbor: University of Michigan Press, 1965).

internally inconsistent compromise among the player's component members, reflecting more the internal politics of the player than the external realities of the bargaining situation. To treat all these characteristics of crisis bargaining merely as deviations from an ideal of perfect rationality would mean that the norm itself would be lost from sight under the great mass of "deviations," and thus be useless.

In other respects, however, crisis bargainers are more rational than the postulated players of game theory. Game-theoretic players are passive in the face of given alternatives and given utilities; they accept the game that is given them and try only to make the best of it. Actual crisis bargainers do not passively accept a given situation; they search for or construct new alternatives, sometimes abandon strategies that are not working, and frequently try to change their own or their opponent's utilities.

2×2 models have the additional disadvantage of pretending that each player has neither more nor less than two strategies available at all times. But how then do we deal with the Cuban crisis, where the U.S. group considered at least five clear alternatives? Or what do we do with cases such as the United States in 1948 and Germany in 1905, where the bargainers had no strategy but tried to "play it by ear"?

Finally the traditional conception of game play as consisting of one move made simultaneously by both players is an obvious simplification. Such a conception distinguishes much too sharply between maneuvering and rigidity, change and fixity; it locates all the probing, maneuvering, threatening, bidding, and demonstrating in the preplay communication and locates all the irrevocability in the one basic move that constitutes the game. This is obviously a fiction, not intended to describe empirical game play. Experimental gaming treats game play in an entirely different fashion, reducing a total complex strategy to a single simultaneous choice, but such a redefinition is not suitable to a one-play diplomatic game. One can reduce some crises to two or three basic moves plus much interspersed communication and maneuvering, but the basic moves are never simultaneous, even if they are treated as secret decisions on an irrevocable strategy.

If the 2×2 game is to be used at all in describing or explaining crises, it must be considerably reinterpreted. It cannot be treated as an account of an actual playing process between two actual players, nor can the two alternatives be treated as actual alternatives. Nor can the payoffs be treated as fixed or even as ordinal numbers that are known to both parties. What remains? The proper interpretation of the 2×2 game is similar to the proper interpretation of other models of rational behavior. Models of economic competition, properly interpreted, do not describe the actual decision processes of actual businessmen; they describe the dynamics of social institutions, which select and reward some people, punish others, and gradually redistribute resources in a certain pattern. Gaming models do not describe the actual play of experimental subjects; they set up a pattern of constraints on the players' choices, and these constraints reward and punish the players in certain ways and induce them to behave in certain ways as they learn to master its dynamics. Similarly, a 2×2 model can be used to describe the *basic structure of the crisis situation,* that is, the *game.* The game is simply the preference orderings of the two players over the four possible outcomes. Each preference ordering in turn is based on the estimated relative military capabilities of the parties, plus the interests they believe are at stake, plus their valuation of these interests. The structure of the situation is not fully known to the players or understood by them, but it constrains their behavior in characteristic ways and determines the sometimes unexpected outcomes of their decisions. The structure of the situation may change during a crisis, again perhaps unknown to the participants; for instance in a Chicken game it is possible to reduce the opponent's S payoff so much, through diplomatic bungling, that the ordinal values of S and P are reversed and the game changes to Prisoner's Dilemma. Conversely the structure of the situation can stay the same while the players' understanding of it changes, a common occurrence.

The 2×2 alternatives are not specific strategies but general directions that specific strategies may take. They represent the two basic modalities of accommodation and coercion that run through all crisis bargaining. Each specific mixed-motive game represents a different mix of these two modalities, while all four games together with their asymmetric variants bring out the rich dialectical interplay of accommodation and coercion in its varied aspects. In Chicken the two alternative directions can be conceived heuristically as "stand firm" and "yield," or escalate and compromise; in Leader they are "lead" and "follow"; in Hero they are "take on burdens" and "receive benefits"; in Prisoner's Dilemma they are "trustfully cooperate" and "unilaterally defect." Any number of specific strategies can be classified in these two dimensions and described in a 2×2 matrix. Thus in the Cuban crisis, which we estimate was Called Bluff, the diplomatic moves considered by the United States, including the offer to trade missile removals, were all some degree of compromise (C), and the other moves including ultimatum, blockade, air strike, and invasion, were steps in the defensive-firm-escalate direction (D). In the 1905 crisis, which moved between Called Bluff and Chicken, the German lack of strategy consisted of vacillation between firm and compromise, with the compromise moves being carried out coercively and the firm moves consisting of bluffs.

The ordinal numbers in the four cells represent the estimated value to the two players of the estimated outcomes of intersecting strategy choices.[30] Thus in Chicken if both players stand firm (D) the empirical outcome is deadlock followed perhaps by war or some sort of military move, and the numbers in the DD cell represent the estimated value of a deadlock with its probable consequences, to both players. In Leader if both players insist on leading (D), the empirical outcome is failure of coordination, and the numbers in the DD cell represent the estimated value of independent action to the two players.

Ideally we would have liked to construct an objective matrix and two or more subjective matrices for each crisis, the objective matrix representing the real or objective structure of the situation and each subjective matrix representing one player's estimate of the situation. The objective structure of the situation consists of the ways in which the military, diplomatic, and economic acts of each player actually affect the other, and these ways are determined by the actual resources of the players, the manner in which the resources are deployed, and the resources and probable actions of other participants. In short, the objective situation is what will happen or what will probably happen in various strategic circumstances given the actual resources of the various participants. For example in the Fashoda crisis the number and composition of both British and French fleets is known; their deployment in 1898, the location of naval bases, and the available supplies are also known. We also know the approximate political strength of imperialist pro-war forces in Britain 1898, also the strength of the Russian navy and its lack of interest in a confrontation with Britain. On the basis of this information, we can state that the outcome of a DD deadlock would have been a Mediterranean naval war, which Britain would have won and which would have included the isolation of French colonies.

One difficulty in constructing an objective matrix is that we cannot usually say with confidence what would have happened had the players chosen differently than they did, although we can of course see the consequences of their actual choices. In addition it is not clear whose valuations we should put on these hypothetical and actual outcomes—ours, the Emperor's, his chancellor's, the chief of staff's, the successor government's, or the judicious historian's. In short, the objective situation in its totality is not fully known to us, even with the benefit of hindsight. Another more crucial difficulty is that even if we could

---

[30] The kinds of values that enter into these outcomes will be discussed more fully in Ch. III.

reconstruct with confidence the "might-have-beens" from the possible but unchosen strategies, combining these with the actual consequences of actual choices in an "objective" matrix, such a reconstruction might be so far from the awareness or possible awareness of the participants as to have no bearing on their behavior during the crisis. None of the 1914 participants had the remotest idea of how bad the war was going to be for them, nor did Hitler in 1938 have the remotest idea of the price Germany would pay for his Czech strategy, so these objective facts contribute nothing to understanding what the participants actually thought and did. The subjective estimates and valuations of the participants are all we need to explain actual behavior.

Consequently, we abandoned the idea of trying to construct an "objective" matrix for each crisis, and we constructed "subjective" matrices instead. A complete portrait of a crisis would have to show a subjective matrix for each player, consisting of his own valuations of possible outcomes and his estimate of the valuations of the other player. Each player's matrix describes his estimate of the situation and to a certain extent explains his behavior, though the estimate may change during the crisis as he acquires new information. Of course, the subjective matrices will be different if one or both players misestimate the other's payoff rankings. Rather than deal with two or more subjective matrices, we found it more convenient to construct a single *composite* subjective matrix for each crisis, consisting of each player's estimates and valuations of *his own* outcomes. It is this composite matrix that describes the basic *structure* of a crisis. Each player's estimates of *other* players' predictions and valuations of outcomes are then dealt with verbally in terms of their correspondence or lack of correspondence to the actual (subjective) structure. This means, of course, that when a player misestimates another's payoff ordering, a common occurrence, he thinks he is playing a different game than he actually is. As we shall see, a good part of crisis behavior can be explained in terms of the correction or non-correction of such misestimates.

We do not completely abandon the idea that there is an objective situation "lying behind" the subjective structure that often constrains the behavior of the players via feedback information about the effects of chosen tactics and strategies; when this occurs, however, we describe it in terms of a change in the player's subjective matrix. The subjective-objective distinction we make here is similar to Harold and Margaret Sprout's distinction between the "psychological environment" and the "operational environment" of nation-states: the psychological environment—i.e., the statesman's subjective picture of the world—affects *decisions;* the operational environment—the actual world—affects the *outcomes* of decisions and through a learning process may eventually change the psychological environment.[31]

In summary, we interpret the 2×2 matrix as describing the basic structure of the crisis situation. By "structure" we mean the two preference orderings over the four possible intersections of accommodative and coercive strategies for each side. Each game matrix represents a particular pattern of preferences that poses a unique bargaining problem. The matrix describes a *bargaining problem,* in other words; it does not describe any particular solution or indeed any specific strategy. We abandon the idea of a single complete strategy chosen irrevocably from exactly two alternatives, the idea of simultaneous play, the separation of play and communication, and the idea that the objective structure is fully known to the players. Consequently we also abandon the idea that one can read off or predict game play directly from the matrix. Nor can we compute the "value" of a game.

Actual play has several components. (1) We conceive the players to be building up a subjective matrix in the early stages of a crisis as they try to estimate the specific intentions and long-range objectives of the opponent and/or the ally, collect information about the military situation, and estimate their own governmental and non-governmental political situation. Some subjective estimates are extremely mistaken, others moderately mistaken, and a few are essentially correct as far as we can tell. (2) The players try to work out a satisfactory strategy on the basis of their initial estimate of the situation. Some players work out a basic strategy in advance and change only details as a crisis develops (Germany, 1914); others work out or improvise a strategy step by step, or even act without knowing exactly what they are doing (Germany, 1905). If the player's subjective picture of the crisis is relatively correct, his strategy is likely to be as successful as conditions permit since he is able to take account of the objective constraints of the situation; if his picture is incorrect, his strategy may or may not be successful, and in fact he may not be able to judge correctly whether it was successful. For example, in 1911 extremists on both sides estimated that their side had "lost," based on exaggerated estimates of their own military power and exaggerated valuations of the national honor and Congo swampland at issue. On September 30, 1938, Chamberlain was convinced that he had won; he had gotten everything he wanted—peace and a friendship agreement with Hitler—at negligible cost, self-determination for the Sudetenland. Only six months later did Britain begin to correct its mistaken valuations. (3) The primary pur-

---

[31] Harold and Margaret Sprout, "Environmental Factors in the Study of International Relations," in J. Rosenau, ed., *International Politics and Foreign Policy* (New York: The Free Press, 1969).

pose of all strategies is to influence the other players to change their subjective estimates (or to preserve them against changes by third parties). This is done partly by communication (direct talks, notes, public speeches, messages by third parties, conversations meant to be overheard), partly by tacit communication (visible troop movements, budget allocations, recall of emissaries), and partly by acts to change the objective situation publicly. Thus there is an essential influence and communication aspect to all crisis action, and every strategic move is in part a communication. This puts communication in the very center of game play and reverses the standard separation of communication and game play. In any case, experimental gaming has shown that this distinction is empirically inapplicable, since all experimental subjects communicate anyway. A secondary aim of some strategies is to prepare for war in case bargaining fails; but all such preparations have a communicative aspect too. (4) As a strategy is being carried out, information feedback enables a player either to revise his estimates of payoffs or to preserve them against others' efforts at revision. Some players in our cases carry out several corrections of previous estimates during a crisis, and other players are so confident of their first estimate that they ignore or reinterpret disconfirming information. Most corrections of estimates bring a subjective picture closer to the actual situation, but some leave it about as inaccurate as before. (5) Some revised estimates lead in turn to strategy revision. (6) The members of a player pull and haul at a strategy while it is being carried out, trying to improve it according to their own varied specifications; it may emerge quite different in practice from what it was on paper, without the player knowing it.

None of these components is possible in a game played by perfectly rational players with perfect information, fixed preferences, and given alternatives; and in this sense the assumption of rationality obscures *all* the important characteristics of actual crisis bargaining. We are speaking here of the technical and severe definition of "rationality" associated with game theory. Of course, one can think of looser definitions of rationality that would allow one to say that most people (including most statesmen) are rational most of the time. The purpose of our revised interpretation of game matrices has been mainly to increase their operational usefulness in the limited role we assign to them—depicting the structure of a crisis. In addition, they begin to correct some of the deficiencies we noted earlier for both utility models and game models, namely the neglect of information processing, search, and feedback. Cognitive processes will become the center of attention in later models (Chs. IV, V), but it is useful to include them as far as possible even in game models so that the relation of game models to other aspects of crisis bargaining is brought out.

PRISONER'S DILEMMA

In the original formulation of this game the C, D alternatives have the heuristic meaning of cooperate and defect. The payoffs have also been given heuristic names: R is the reward for cooperation, T is the temptation to try for a win, P is the punishment for double defensiveness or double yielding to temptation, and S is the sucker's payoff for trying to cooperate unilaterally. One can also think of S as surrender. But the names should not be taken seriously (Fig. 2–25).

The cooperative aspects of this game are concentrated in the CC cell, while the competitive aspects are on the secondary diagonal (NE–SW). There is one common good, approaching CC, and two private goods, approaching T and avoiding S, both on the secondary diagonal. The standard version of this game is based on assumptions that C and D are specific strategies, that all payoffs are known to both players, and most notably that the players make one and only one simultaneous choice. With these assumptions, as explained earlier, there is no possibility of a cooperative (CC) outcome. Both parties play D, either to gain T or avoid S, and the outcome is DD, a P payoff for both, which is less than they could have had from cooperating. There are some specific situations in international politics where this tragic dynamic tends to operate because these assumptions, particularly that of simultaneous play, are approached. For example, disarmament agreements are not made, and even modest "arms control" arrangements are difficult, because of suspicions of secret defection by the opponent, which cannot be countered in time. Preemptive war resulting from the "reciprocal fear of surprise attack" [32] is also possible. The mobilization race that was the immediate cause of World War I could also be modeled by this version of the game.

B

	C	D				
C	3, 3	1, 4			R, R	S, T
D	4, 1	2, 2	$T > R > P > S$		T, S	P, P

A

Figure 2-25. Prisoner's Dilemma

[32] Thomas Schelling's term; see *The Strategy of Conflict*, Ch. 9.

However, the above assumptions do not fit most crises; consequently we have modified them. In place of perfect information, we assume considerable ignorance and misinformation. In place of one instantaneous play, we assume a time period in which a number of moves can be made by both players. In place of two specific strategies, we assume two general strategies—"make concessions" or "stand firm"—out of which an indefinite number of variants can be constructed. Of these revised assumptions, the second one, enough time, proves to be crucial in determining bargaining tactics for Prisoner's Dilemma crises. Insofar as the players have enough time, say several months, they can devise a solution to the game; insofar as playing time is reduced to days or hours, that is insofar as it approaches the limit of simultaneous play, there is an increasing tendency to a defensive play of D and the DD outcome. Generally, in PD crises, the parties have enough time to counter a coercive D strategy with a resistant D strategy, or to counter an attack with defense, so that the "dilemma" and compulsion to preempt with D disappear. What remains are simply two preference structures in which war or risk of war is preferred to accepting the opponent's initial demand.

If we interpret Prisoner's Dilemma as a general description of a certain type of conflict situation, the specific characteristics of this situation are as follows:

1. There is a bargaining dimension, that is, there is some incrementally divisible good such that the more A has of it, the less B has of it. However, the parties may not realize at first that this good is divisible; all they perceive at first is that either A or B must give way.

2. The two initial bids of the parties (T) are outside of the bargaining range or contract zone. That is, each party prefers no agreement (DD) to its payoff (S) from the opponent's initial bid. Nor do the parties know at first whether there is a bargaining range between these initial bids. There may not be any; the game may be Deadlock.

3. It is possible for both parties to reduce their initial bids (reduce T or, if persisted in as a deliberate strategy, shift to C). However, if one party so reduces his bid, this does not necessarily lead to agreement. The opponent may wait on D, repeating his initial bid, in hopes of further concessions, and the first party may find it easier to try another tentative concession, and another one, than to hold firm at some arbitrary intermediate bid. After all, each new bid (R) is still preferable to no agreement (P), and the opponent may finally reciprocate.

4. This suggests a D strategy of pretended concessions designed to induce the opponent to reciprocate with a genuine concession. The concession may consist of hints or promises that may later be reneged upon,

conditional concessions such that the conditions later nullify the concession, reductions of an artificial initial bid, or concessions on some trivial side issue. The corollary of this strategy is that one must be on guard against the opponent's trying it; that is, one must be suspicious of the opponent's apparent concessions and wait for a genuine concession before one reciprocates.

Points 3 and 4 reinforce each other and combine to make it advantageous to wait on D and induce the opponent to concede first.

Of the crises we studied, the following are estimated to be Prisoner's Dilemma:

> 1911, Morocco: France–Germany
> 1958–1962, Berlin: Soviet Union–United States

The following is estimated to be Bully-Prisoner's Dilemma, a variant:

> 1914, Germany–Austria–Russia–France

These estimates are reached by combining the considered judgments of the leading decision makers on each side.

The composite matrix for the 1911 crisis is estimated to be as given in Figure 2–26. In this matrix, the terms "self-assertion," "defiance,"

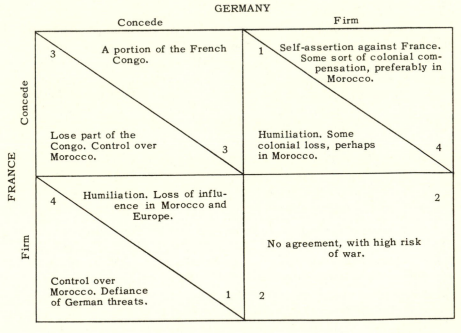

Figure 2-26. Morocco, 1911

and "humiliation" are to be taken politically as well as psychologically. They refer to effects on the country's reputation for resolve, that is, its international reputation as a power whose interests must be taken into account by other countries. If France could "humiliate" Germany by ignoring it (DC), this would suggest that other countries could also ignore Germany in making their colonial policies. Conversely, if Germany could demonstrate "self-assertion" against France by forcing concessions from it (CD), this would suggest that other countries had better be careful not to antagonize Germany or they might find themselves forced to yield concessions as well. If France could successfully defy German threats (DC), this would suggest that it could successfully resist threats by other countries, who had therefore better keep out of France's way. Conversely, a French humiliation by Germany (CD) would suggest that other countries could safely ignore French interests and protests.

The issue of the crisis for Germany was France's failure to consult Germany before taking a decisive step to control Morocco. Britain, Spain, and Italy had been consulted years earlier, and each had received compensation for approval of French actions, but Germany had been left out. When Germany had protested, the result was the 1906 Algeciras conference, in which France had gotten everything it wanted in Morocco except formal control, while Germany had received nothing. Now the French were moving to take over formal control, again without offering Germany compensation. Plainly one French objective was to humiliate Germany once again.

The initial French bid, T, took the form of French military action near the Moroccan capital, in which the French suppressed a revolt against the Sultan of Morocco. This was a tacit claim to establish a protectorate over Morocco and the immediate precipitant of the crisis. The German payoff from this bid, humiliation and complete loss of influence in Morocco, was estimated by Germany to be intolerable, worse than a military confrontation of some sort ($S < P$). The German counterbid, T, the "challenge," was expressed by the anchoring of the German gunboat *Panther* in Agadir harbor. To the French this meant that Germany was demanding compensation, probably southern Morocco, where Agadir was located. But the French estimated that the humiliation of giving up part of Morocco just as they were taking it over, to a country that had no rights in Morocco anyway, and under military pressure at that, was intolerable and worse than war ($S < P$). Thus the issue of the crisis for France was the German attempt to humiliate France by forcibly taking away something that "belonged" to France.

In addition, both sides recognized the possibility of some other form of French compensation to Germany, either economic advantages, financial compensation, or some other French colonial territory (*CC*). This possibility had arisen in preliminary French diplomatic feelers in which the French ambassador had suggested the possibility of some sort of French compensation, and the German foreign minister had expressed interest without committing himself.

The matrix is Prisoner's Dilemma because for each side *T*, a win, > *R*, compromise, > *P*, high risk of war, > *S*, loss of resolve reputation and loss of colonial territory. One may disagree with some of these valuations, but they are the valuations of the participants and therefore the ones that determined their behavior.

The "precipitant" of the 1958 Berlin crisis was a combination of factors internal and external to the challenger, the Soviet Union (see Fig. 2–27). The internal factor was simply a desire to clear up the anomalous status of West Berlin as an island of capitalist democracy within the Socialist camp, thus to stabilize the Ulbricht regime in East Germany

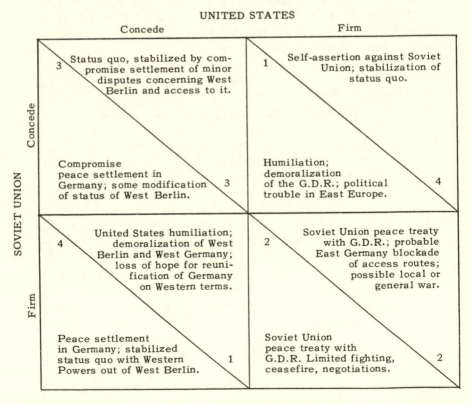

Figure 2-27. West Berlin, 1958

and to gain recognition of that government by the West. There is no reason to doubt Khrushchev's sincerity when he pictured this situation as "abnormal," an artificial tag-end of World War II, and an autonomous source of instability and conflict that the Western Powers as well as the Soviet Union ought to have an interest in terminating. For Khrushchev, the external precipitants were the use of West Berlin by West German "revenge-seekers" to stir up trouble in the Socialist camp and to agitate for military preparations and eventual war in the Western camp, the build-up of a West German army, and possibly recent NATO decisions to place atomic weapons in West Germany.

Khrushchev's "challenge" in November 1958 was a proposal and a threat. He proposed a general peace settlement with each of the two Germanies separately, which would include removal of Western troops from Western Berlin and making the latter a free city. If the Western Powers refused to negotiate a peace treaty, the Soviet Union would make a unilateral peace treaty with East Germany, thus legally turning over control of the access routes to West Berlin from the Soviets to the East German government. In game terms, this was an initial bid of T, demanding a Western response of C (DC). However, Khrushchev also stated explicitly that he was willing and eager to negotiate a compromise settlement acceptable to both sides (CC). He estimated that if it came to a deadlock (DD), there would be some brief but intense tank and air battles, a cease-fire, and then negotiations on the CC pattern. The worst outcome, CD, would be a continuation of Western aggressive agitation leading to a gradual weakening of the Socialist camp and perhaps a collapse of the Ulbricht regime. This was a Prisoner's Dilemma structure, with T, a settlement on Soviet terms, $> R$, a compromise settlement, $> P$, some fighting and a compromise settlement, $> S$, demoralization and retreat.

From the U.S. standpoint, the picture looked entirely different. Khrushchev's initial bid was a coercive grab for Western territory (West Berlin), an "ultimatum" only thinly disguised by the talk about "negotiations" and the free city fig leaf. It was an attempt to humiliate the West, which, if allowed to succeed, would destroy its reputation for resolve to defend its vital interests and perhaps lead to the eventual collapse of NATO. The U.S. payoff, S, would be intolerable and worse than the risk of war that might arise from East German harassment or blockage of the access routes: $S < P$. A highly preferable outcome would be R, a compromise settlement that would satisfy legitimate Soviet grievances and fears and thus stabilize the status quo; and best of all would be a firm rebuff to the "aggressor" with no concessions. In short $S < P < R < T$.

The 1914 crisis is difficult to portray in 2×2 form because there were five or six Great Power actors. However, we get a rough approximation if we consider Russia–France as one actor and Germany–Austria the other, with England and Italy as uncertainly aligned countries "outside" the matrix, estimates of whose intentions nevertheless affected the payoff structures of the main protagonists (see Fig. 2–28). (The high degree of solidarity between France and Russia and Germany and Austria makes it plausible to consider the pairs as unitary actors.)

The immediate crisis precipitant was the assassination of the Austrian Archduke Ferdinand. This was merely the most dramatic episode in the long-run or general precipitant, the continual Serb agitation in Bosnia, which, in the opinion of Austrian and German decision makers, threatened to escalate to general Slav revolution throughout the empire and cause its likely dissolution. The Austrian challenge followed: an ultimatum to Serbia that, if accepted, would have turned Serbia into an Austrian protectorate; if not accepted, would serve as a pretext to destroy Serbia by force.

At this stage, the crisis structure was either Bully or Big Bully for Austria–Germany—that is, there was vacillation and difference of

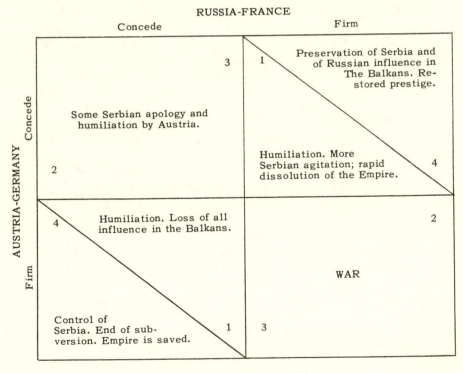

Figure 2-28. Europe, 1914

opinion internally in both countries as to whether the preferable outcome was war (Big Bully) or Serbian acceptance of the entire ultimatum (Bully). However, since the Serbs did not accept unconditionally, it is sufficient to call it Bully: T, control of Serbia, $> P$, a brief victorious war against Russia–France, with Britain undoubtedly remaining neutral and Serbia destroyed and partitioned. R would consist of a compromise in which Serbia accepted some amount of humiliation and punishment and promised to stop bothering Austria. This sort of solution had been established in 1909 and continued since then. However, the 1909 compromise had failed to end Serb subversion: Serbia had promised to be good but the subversion had continued and even intensified. Consequently compromise with Serbia was no longer acceptable; $P > R$. The worst outcome would be S, passive Austrian acceptance of continued Serb agitation leading to the rapid dissolution of the Austrian empire. Initially, Austria–Germany believed Russia–France would not fight—that their preference ordering was Chicken—which made the Austro–German P quite high. But even later, when they corrected this misestimate, they remained in Bully, preferring war to compromise.

From the Russian standpoint the story was altogether different, beginning with the Russian S. Russian reputation for resolve was very low. Russia had been brazenly double-crossed by Austria in 1908; had been forced to back down, humiliated, by Germany in 1909; had been pretty much ignored in the 1912–1913 Balkan wars and conferences; had been unable to protect her client, Bulgaria, in 1913, and had lost the Bulgarian clientship to Austria. If Russia now acquiesced in the destruction of her last client, Serbia, she would have no more influence in the Balkans, the balance of power would turn dangerously against her, and her resolve reputation and general influence in world politics would be demolished. Russia felt she had to fight to prevent the loss of Serbia; however, she was willing to make some concessions on the ultimatum to preserve peace, so long as Serbian sovereignty remained intact. Thus Russia was in Prisoner's Dilemma: T, coercing Austria to leave Serbia alone, $> R$, compromise, $> P$, war with uncertain outcome, since British participation was uncertain, $> S$, humiliation and loss of relative power. France shared these preferences (as she quickly made known to Russia) with a somewhat different S-cost: failure to support Russia would mean the defeat and loss of a badly needed ally.

PD STRATEGY AND TACTICS

It is important to note that a PD crisis is always characterized by an initial misperception, by the challenger at least, that the opponent is in

Chicken, that he would rather accept one's demands than push the dispute to the point of war. In other words, in the subjective matrices of one and possibly both sides, the game appears to be Called-Bluff: the opponent is a bluffer who can be faced down. This is logically necessary in the mathematics of the *PD* game: if both sides had correct knowledge of the other's payoff structure, a crisis would not occur (except in the special case of the "inadvertent" or accidental crisis), since a potential challenger would know that the other party would resist even at the cost of war, and war is worse than the status quo. This is also an important distinction between Prisoner's Dilemma and Chicken crises. The latter could occur even if the actors have full knowledge of each other's payoff structures; one party could rationally challenge in the knowledge that the other's $S > P$, even though his own payoffs have the same ordering, plausibly hoping to best the other in a contest of "nerve."

In Morocco, 1911, the French miscalculated that the Germans would accept French control of all Morocco with only token compensation rather than risk war. The Germans failed to perceive that the *"Panther's spring"* would be taken by the French, not as "insurance" for moderate compensation outside Morocco as it was primarily intended (although some German factions *did* want a piece of Morocco) but as a tacit demand for part of Morocco itself, which was unacceptable to France. Both sides perceived the other to be playing Chicken, when in fact each saw the other's claim as intolerable and worth risking war to frustrate— i.e., each was in *PD*. Similarly, in Berlin, 1958, Khrushchev mistakenly believed that the West would concede most of his demands rather than risk the fulfillment of his unilateral peace treaty threat since West Berlin was not worth a war to them; while there was disagreement among the Western powers about the credibility of that threat, in general they underestimated the costs to the Soviets and East Germans of continuation of the status quo in Berlin, and they failed to realize that their defensive military build-up could be perceived as threatening by the Soviet Union. In 1914, the misperception was more one-sided: the Central Powers were quite confident, at the outset, that Russia would not fight for Serbia even with French support, and after this misestimate was corrected, they continued to believe until the eleventh hour that England was "chicken." The Russians more accurately estimated the Austro–German preference structure; yet the partial mobilization move indicates some hope, at least, that Austria might be faced down by threats.

The effect of this initial misperception is to move the game directly into deadlock. The challenger, perceiving the game as Called Bluff, initiates a *D* strategy in the expectation of an eventual *C* response by the opponent. The opponent, perceiving this as a bluff, responds with *D* and there is a deadlock. Or if he realizes that the challenger is serious, as in 1914 Russia realized that Germany–Austria was serious, his own preference structure requires a D response accompanied by much frantic signaling about the imminent danger of war. These signals, in turn, are likely to confirm the challenger's estimate that the signaler is chicken.

Resolution of this deadlock without war requires the correction of the misperception that produced it. Once the correction occurs, the second requisite is a reduction of initial demands (T) to the point where the opponent's $S > P$. The actual game is then transformed into Chicken—or, to put it differently, the claims are moved into the bargaining range and a compromise settlement becomes possible.

To understand the resolution process that occurred in the two PD crises that *were* resolved peacefully, we need some new concepts.

Earlier in this chapter we stated that, from the perspective of strategic interaction, bargaining is primarily a process of persuasive communication. Communications may be verbal and explicit, or they may consist of actions—troop movements or budget decisions—whose meaning is fairly clear, or they may be the tacit byproduct of seemingly trivial actions such as omitting reference to something in a speech or press release. The usual purpose of communication is to *influence* the opponent to move toward a desirable bargaining outcome. One does this by communicating information about one's demands, about one's power and readiness to act if the demands are not met, about the favorable consequences to the opponent if he makes certain moves, about the impossibility of his achieving certain of his apparent goals, about the availability of other desirable outcomes he may have overlooked, and so on. These communications are intended to revise the opponent's estimates of the bargaining situation in such a way that the outcome one desires seems desirable or at least unavoidable to him as well. The opponent's response provides feedback about how effective the influence attempt was, which can be used to make future influence attempts more effective.

However, there are times when the usual emphasis is reversed. The usual emphasis is on influencing the opponent, and information feedback is a secondary consequence. But when a bargainer realizes he does not know what is going on and needs to find out what the opponent is up to or what his real interests are, the primary emphasis is on getting information. Messages are then sent for the sake of feedback, and the influence on the opponent is a secondary result. We call the attempt to get specific information, *search*.

We now divide the general bargaining process, that is, the influence/search process, into four subprocesses according to the four cells of the 2×2 matrix. We label the four subprocesses P-, R-, S-, and T-bargaining, respectively. If we wish to emphasize either the influence or the search aspect, we can refer to P-influence and P-search and so on.

Resolution of a *PD* deadlock, as we see it in the two *PD* crises that *were* resolved peacefully, consists of three of these subprocesses, namely *P*-, *T*-, and *R*-bargaining. It is important that the subprocesses occur in the right order—*P-T-R*—and that the parties follow them roughly symmetrically. Each subprocess clarifies or changes its corresponding cell of the payoff matrix, thereby correcting initial misperceptions step by step. In general, *P*- and *T*-bargaining clarify the coercive aspects and *R*-bargaining clarifies the accommodative aspect of the bargaining situation.

P-influence comes first. It involves continuing the initial *D* strategy through various coercive and firmness-indicating moves. These tactics are tested sequentially on the opponent, using the feedback to correct one's estimates about how determined the adversary is, and devising improved coercive tactics on the basis of the initially more successful ones.

When the initial play of *D* strategies leads to deadlock, the first reaction on both sides is likely to be "That bluffer still does not realize how resolved I am to stand firm. I have to make myself understood better." Threats and other communications then become more strident and explicit, armaments may be increased, troops deployed, statements of support secured from allies, etc. The effect of this stepped-up coercion is to increase tension and mutual hostility, but more importantly, to make both sides begin to realize, as the brink of war comes into view, that the opponent may *not* be bluffing. Coercive tactics then tend to shift to probes (*P*-search), limited moves against specific targets that are withdrawn if they meet serious resistance. Probes are carefully focused and controlled coercive tactics whose purpose is to test and clarify the opponent's interest and degree of resolve associated with specific interests, rather than to bowl him over by generalized displays of one's own resolve.

The effect of each specific *P*-tactic is coercive for the opponent and, by feedback, informational for the self. When both sides use these tactics, the effect is to clarify the *P*-situation—not just the probable outcome of escalation or war in general but also the likely consequences of specific coercive moves by each side.

P-bargaining leads of itself directly into the next phase, *T*-search. *T*-search is primarily a clarification of one's own goals, both maximum and minimum, and subsequently a communication and clarification of one's goals to the opponent. It begins at the point where the *P*-situation is sufficiently clarified so that the decision maker realizes there is a considerable danger of war and he had better be careful with his coercive moves and responses. He needs, not undifferentiated coercion, but carefully focused specific coercion. Thus, coercive bargaining continues, but the bargainer's attention turns also to examination of his own goals from two perspectives: (1) what points will the opponent believe I will stand firm upon? (clarified minimum), and (2) what can I afford to sacrifice, if necessary to avoid war? (reduced maximum). The frustrated coercer begins to realize that instead of a generalized firm stand he must find a specific minimum point at which he could credibly commit himself to war, a point so clearly important to him that the opponent cannot help but see he is committed to it. At the same time, he is deciding for himself exactly what additional items in his goal set are really worth risking war over. In the continuing coercive bargaining, the target of a coercive act is also forced to reevaluate his goals. Ideally, he should repulse all probes and tests of resolve, but with imminent danger of war he must decide in each case whether this specific point is worth a war. In addition, if the deadlock is going to be protracted, it is more efficient to save one's "coercive capital"—military forces, the most severe threats, and riskiest moves—for the important issues and areas, the places that one is really resolved to defend.

The outcome of T-search is a clarification of one's own goals, a differentiation between those that are essential even at the risk of war and those that are important but not essential. Whereas at the time of one's initial bid, one may have had visions of victories, consolidation or expansion of one's position, and a decisive put-down of the opponent, these grander goals give way to the sober decision that certain issues are worth war and others are not. The results of this clarification are communicated to the opponent by one's actions, by one's responses to probes, and by one's specific coercive acts and statements. The opponent discovers that one is not determined to conquer the world after all, at least not this year (reduced maximum), and could in fact be persuaded if worst came to worst to settle for rather limited results (clarified minimum). The cost of yielding, S, is thus not complete disaster but a rather specific moderate loss. When both players make this discovery, the crisis is under control; it has shifted from Prisoner's Dilemma to Chicken.

This argument for the importance of T-search agrees with the conclusion of George, Hall, and Simons in their study of coercive diplomacy.[33]

The reduction and clarification of T and consequent moderation of opponent's S is the decisive turning point in a Prisoner's Dilemma crisis. It consists of the realization by both sides that: (1) the opponent is not aggressively bent on conquest and humiliation at this specific time, so he

[33] George, Hall, and Simons, *The Limits of Coercive Diplomacy*.

would in principle be willing to compromise. (2) There are, however, specific issues on which he is probably willing to fight a war. These issues are "off limits," and one may as well give them up. On the other hand, if both parties discover they are willing to fight rather than yield on the same specific issue and if there is no way of compromising the issue, the game is Deadlock, and both sides reluctantly go to war. (3) In between these specific off-limit issues, there is a bargaining range or set of issues that is not worth a war to either side and on which compromise is therefore possible.

This turning point is accompanied by changes in the bargaining "atmosphere" and the parties' images of each other. The image of the opponent shifts from "aggressor" or "unreasonable enemy" to "reasonable partner in seeking a settlement." The atmosphere shifts from mutual coercion to mutual accommodation. Each sees the other as only protecting its legitimate interests that are not incompatible with one's own interests. Affective attitudes change from hostility to some degree of mutual empathy or even sympathy.

R-bargaining is the cooperative investigation of the intermediate area or set of issues. Its purpose is to work out an optimum allocation of the disputed issues, in which each side wins the items most important to it but an overall balance between the two sides is maintained. One R-tactic is to insist on getting a certain item; the other side must then concede that item, with the clear understanding that a return concession elsewhere is now due. If both sides insist on a certain item, another tactic is to decompose the item to find parts of special value to each side. If there is a deadlock, the bargaining process moves back to the stage of T-search, in which each side is forced to ask itself, "Is this specific item really worth a war to me?" There may even be a return to P-influence, renewal of threats, affirmations of firmness, and the like, intended to force the opponent to reassess (R-search) his current objectives. R-bargaining is most appropriately carried on by soft-line elements on each side because the hard-line preference for coercive tactics tends to disrupt it and return it to P-bargaining. Thus the ideal Prisoner's Dilemma crisis is one that is started by flexible hard-line or middle-line actors on each side and ended by soft-line or middle-line actors.

The evidence from our cases shows that one cannot begin the solution to a PD crisis with R-bargaining, as a soft-line actor might wish, but must precede R by T and P-bargaining. There were early attempts at negotiation in each of our three cases, the 1911 Cambon–Kiderlen talks, the 1959 Geneva negotiations, and Grey's proposals in 1914. The first two exhibited the reluctance of both sides to make the first genuine concessions that we would expect from the mathematics of the game (points 3 and 4, p. 89). The danger of being the first to make a real concession is that it may confirm the opponent in his possible belief that one is weak and can be forced to yield; if he does have aggressive intentions, any sign of weakness will only encourage his aggressiveness. Our 1911 and 1959 negotiators were not prepared to do this; they hinted and listened, waited, and avoided committing themselves. Grey's unilateral search for a possible compromise in 1914 had precisely this effect of confirming the opponent's misperception. His attempt to compromise reinforced the German belief that Britain would not fight and that they could safely continue their *D* strategy. Consequently they did not need to compromise and could in fact afford to double-cross Britain.

The essential prerequisite to cooperative negotiations in these cases was reduction of *T* and clarification of one's minimum essential goals, and communication of both to the opponent. This removes the opponent's danger of being double-crossed if he risks accommodative tactics, since one has given up one's desire for a big win. Consequently both sides, having faced the danger of war together, can now cooperate in *R*-bargaining. *T*-search in turn can only be induced by the real danger of war that is revealed in the clarified *P*-situation.

Incidentally, *P*-bargaining may also reveal that the game is Chicken or a variant of Chicken right from the start, and this is an entirely different kind of bargaining situation, which will be discussed in the next section.

We turn now to strategy and tactics in the three cases by way of illustrating the general *P-T-R* scheme. The 1911 crisis began with both sides choosing a coercive strategy, which after some inconclusive attempts at negotiation led directly to deadlock. Deadlock occurred when the French troops in the vicinity of Fez, the capital, had shown that they were the real power in the country and when the German warship *Panther* was in Agadir harbor. It was clear that the French troops could not really leave Morocco and did not intend to; that they could not control Morocco so long as the *Panther* was at Agadir; and that the *Panther* could not be forced out without war. At this point *P*-bargaining began on both sides. The first step was to check alliance support (*P*-search). Here the French got the usual ambiguous reply from Britain and a negative reply from Russia, while Germany got a negative reply from both Austria and Italy. The next step was coercive moves (*P*-influence) to convince the opponent that he had better back down. These included mobilization of French public opinion for war, and threats by both sides. The coercive moves had the opposite effect from that intended: instead of forcing the opponent to back down, they produced a hostility spiral including war panic in England. The hostility spiral plus the allies' replies provided feedback that clarified the *P*-situation for the Germans. Kiderlen, the German leader, realized that if war came the British would fight on the French side and Germany would be without support, and that war would come if Germany insisted on compensation in Morocco. The French also discovered that Germany would probably fight if it did not get substantial compensation, and that British support in such a case was doubtful. Both sides therefore realized that things were serious and that any further coercive moves would have to be very carefully selected. This realization set off a process of *T*-search on both sides. Both Caillaux and Kiderlen intended to continue to stand firm, but they now had to be clear exactly what they were willing to risk a war over. On the French side, there had always been vague intentions to compensate Germany in some way, but it was now quite clear that substantial compensation was unavoidable since the compensation issue was not worth a war. On the other hand it was clear that the compensation could not come from Moroccan territory; the humiliation to the French would be too great, given all the German insults that France had already endured. On the German side, there had always been an interest in having a piece of Morocco, but given the *P*-fact that insistence on Moroccan territory would lead to war, it became clear that a piece of the Congo would be sufficient to preserve German honor and reputation for resolve. Other, grander goals—a place in the sun as a Colonial Power, humiliation of France, destruction of the Anglo–French entente—would have to wait.

The clarified goals of each side were communicated during the July–August negotiations. The first German demand for all of the French Congo was probably a sham bid, and when the French reacted strenuously against it, Kiderlen dropped it. Caillaux then became convinced that Kiderlen really would settle for part of the Congo and had given up interest in Morocco, and Kiderlen saw that Caillaux was serious about substantial compensation. This was the crucial turning point, in which each side realized that the other was not aggressively determined to get a humiliating victory but would be willing to compromise. At this point *R*-bargaining set in; the two *D*-strategies were abandoned, and both sides concentrated on *C*. Although there were one or two flare-ups of threats and displays of firmness (*P*-influence) along the way to settlement, these were largely an expression of Kiderlen's hard-line bargaining style. Kiderlen insisted on two items, access to the Congo River and part of the Atlantic coast. However in so doing he automatically implied that other issues, such as amount of territory, were less important to him. So he got 100 meters of Congo access and a few kilometers of coastline, plus substantial hinterland. A settlement had been achieved, though at great cost in hostility and disappointment on each side. Consequently it was also necessary for the principal negotiators to cooperate in selling the settlement to their disappointed supporters.

In the 1958–1962 Berlin crisis, the years 1958–1960 saw no progress toward a settlement. Both sides were attempting to work out a compromise settlement through negotiations, that is, each side gave out hints of possible concessions and waited for a genuine concession from the other. Both sides were disappointed at the failure of the opponent to negotiate seriously, which led to suspicion of his aims and hardening of positions. There was no clarification of aims and no correction of initial misperceptions.

Progress toward a settlement began with the 1960 probes—P-search—initiated by Ulbricht, which showed that U.S. firmness was not entirely undifferentiated. The United States still insisted on air access to Berlin and on no diplomatic recognition, but was not as interested in canal taxes and other details of commercial traffic, nor even in temporary civilian travel restrictions. This clarified the U.S. P-situation for the Soviet Union. Even if a player is determined to be absolutely firm on every issue, he cannot avoid giving away his preference schedule to the probing opponent. There are some probes that he does not resist because he cannot see them as probes, tests of his resolve, because the issues are not important to him. The United States was on the lookout for the slightest interference with military traffic and air access and the slightest hint of tacit recognition, but did not feel that changes in canal tax schedules or inspection of commercial shipments constituted a threat to its position. Consequently Ulbricht learned what specifically the United States was willing to fight over.

Further progress was made in 1961, when Kennedy, disturbed by the high level of Soviet coerciveness, realized that the United States had to increase the credibility of its stand in order to convince Khrushchev to back down. This required not merely additional coercive moves (P-influence), of which there had been plenty on both sides, but rather the development of a specific position that even Khrushchev could see was vital to the United States. Further, it had to be a position on which the United States would be willing to risk war if Khrushchev refused to back down. This meant that the position had to represent the irreducible minimum U.S. position in Berlin. The search for such a position produced the "three essentials": this was a T-search. It turned out that the essential U.S. interests all lay in West Berlin—self-determination and economic viability for the West Berliners; continued presence of Western troops; and freedom of access. Other interests in four-power control, liberation, free elections, lost territories, etc., were important but not worth risking a war. The rest of the Kennedy strategy, involving military measures and firm talk, was the coercive punch that emphasized U.S. determination to fight if the three essentials were attacked.

A reevaluation of goals was simultaneously occurring in East Berlin under the pressure of the economic situation. It became clear to

Ulbricht that although diplomatic recognition would provide the basic guarantee against West German attack, and although West Berlin was a desirable piece of property, there was a more immediate problem of protecting his economy against the subversive influences located in West Berlin. That is, Ulbricht's minimum goal was in East Berlin. His information about what the United States would fight for and what it might settle for, derived from previous probes and from Kennedy's July 25th speech (which spelled out the "three essentials"), enabled him to work out a solution. It was clear that the United States did not intend to destroy the German Democratic Republic and then the whole Socialist camp, at least not this year, and that it would in fact be willing to settle for the three essentials if worst came to worst. These were compatible with the security of East Germany, Ulbricht's immediate problem; compromise was possible. Ulbricht's perception that the minimum goals of the two sides were compatible enabled him to devise a bid, the Wall, that ultimately provided a settlement and saved the peace.

Khrushchev was drawn into the process of goal reevaluation in early August. According to our evidence [34] he came to realize during the August 3–5 meetings or shortly before that the free city goal was less important than protection of the German Democratic Republic because it was intended after all as a GDR security measure, and he agreed on August 4 to give it up if necessary to secure U.S. acceptance of the Wall. Information about the reevaluated goals was exchanged by Kennedy and Khrushchev in late September and early October. Kennedy sent a message through President Kekkonen of Finland stating that he was not interested in unifying Germany, and therefore by implication not interested in subverting the German Democratic Republic; Khrushchev wrote that he could get along without a formal free city arrangement, and therefore by implication that he could accept U.S. troops in West Berlin. This mutual clarification of goals stabilized Ulbricht's settlement. The decisive turning point of the crisis thus occurred toward the end of September, when the leaders of each side received information about the clarified goals of the other, the consequence of the T-search both sides had undertaken. Each leader found that, as Ulbricht had earlier perceived, the other was not out for victory and humiliation but would settle for moderate defensive goals if worst came to worst. Consequently it was now possible to risk a cooperative attempt to achieve some less than essential goals for each side.

R-search began with the exploratory Rusk-Gromyko talks of late

---

[34] Herman Zolling and Uwe Bahnsen, *Kalter Winter in August* (Oldenburg, Germany: Stalling, 1967), pp. 111–115; Stefan Dörnberg, *Kurze Geschichte der DDR* (Berlin: Dietz, 1968), p. 448; Hans Kroll, *Lebenserinnerungen eines Botschafters* (Cologne: Kiepenheuer und Witsch, 1967), pp. 511–512.

September 1961 and continued, unsuccessfully, for another ten months or so. The United States tried to get some sort of access guarantees, and Khrushchev tried to get some sort of indirect recognition of the German Democratic Republic. Successful R-bargaining did not occur till ten years later, in 1971. As a result of this bargaining, the German Democratic Republic received recognition of the essential political independence of West Berlin and some recognition of its own existence, the Soviet Union got recognition of the postwar borders, the West got its access guarantees, and Bonn got the right to handle West Berlin's foreign affairs. The free city package was opened up, and each side got the elements that were most important to it. This was perhaps the sort of negotiations that Khrushchev had in mind in 1958, though he would undoubtedly have found the eventual Soviet Union concessions unacceptable in 1958.

Why could Khrushchev's program not be carried out in 1958–1959, when he intended, or in 1961–1962, when our ideal scheme called for it? The answer illustrates the importance of P and T-bargaining. R-bargaining was impossible in 1958–1959 because of the objective conflict of interest, which Khrushchev underestimated. This conflict, a T-conflict, could not be resolved by R-search, but required a lowering of T payoffs first. T-clarification in turn could be induced only by P-bargaining, coercion and probes. The two sides had to be forced to lower their own aspirations (T) by jointly facing the P-situation in detail. In other words, Ulbricht's "hard" strategy culminating in the Wall had to precede Khrushchev's "soft" strategy of negotiations. The United States and West Germany had to give up their aim of a unified capitalist Germany with recovery of lost territories before they could negotiate details about Berlin that weakened its value as a symbol for eventual reunification and a forward base for intelligence and propaganda activities. Kennedy gave this aim up in 1961, making the interim settlement possible, but the German Christian Democratic strategists did not. Consequently R-bargaining was not yet possible in 1962; Adenauer would not permit it. A Social Democratic election victory was a necessary prerequisite to R-bargaining. And on the Soviet side it was necessary to see the Western powers' presence in West Berlin as defensive and therefore harmless (rather than as part of a plan to destroy the German Democratic Republic).

In 1914, the P-T-R processes as described above, which might well have resolved the crisis peacefully if more time had been available, were cut off by two factors: the German fait accompli strategy and the virulent simultaneous-move Prisoner's Dilemma that was inherent in military plans and technology. German pressure on Austria to attack Serbia quickly and present the European powers with a fait accompli produced the Austrian declaration of war on July 25; this declaration turned the attention of governmental leaders in all parties toward preparation for war and away from bargaining strategies that might, in time, have corrected misperceptions and led to a peaceful resolution. The fait accompli strategy itself was a function of the German misperception that the game was Chicken for the entente powers; the Austrian halfway response, though short of what the Germans wanted, was nevertheless an extreme committal move that pretty effectively preempted the kind of probing and feedback that would have been necessary to correct the misperception in time.

Still, some P-bargaining did take place, correcting the German misperception before the outbreak of war but too late to stop it. Sazonov, the Russian foreign minister, urged England almost daily to give a firm commitment to Russia, which he thought would put Germany in a Chicken game and convince German leaders that the entente powers were not playing Chicken. However, Grey, the British foreign minister, held back because of division in his cabinet and because he mistakenly believed that there was plenty of time, due to his ignorance of the preemption logic in continental military and mobilization plans. Finally, on July 29, Grey did come through with such a commitment and communicated it to Germany. This clarification of the P-situation immediately changed the German game to Prisoner's Dilemma or perhaps Chicken, and the German chancellor frantically tried to persuade Austria to halt mobilization and accept a compromise. But it was too late; the mobilization Prisoner's Dilemma had taken over. According to military thinking, the side that mobilized first, even by one day in the case of Germany and France, would have a decisive advantage in war, so neither side could afford to let the other mobilize first. Consequently the slower Austrian mobilization was followed by Russian mobilization, then immediately by German and French mobilization.

So far we have not taken up S-bargaining because it did not contribute to the solution of our Prisoner's Dilemma crises. However, it does occur. S-search is a search for cheap ways to increase the opponent's S payoff so it will be easier for him to back down—i.e., the search for "face-savers." Both sides at the 1959 Geneva negotiations engaged in S-search; the Soviet Union searched for painless Western troop withdrawal procedures from West Berlin after establishment of the Free City, and the United States offered an anesthetic to ease the Soviet troop withdrawal from the Soviet-occupied zone after reunification and free elections. S-bargaining is unsuccessful and irrelevant in Prisoner's Dilemma crises for several reasons, but principally because the bargainers prefer no agreement and possibly war to surrender $(P > S)$ and are therefore not interested in inducements to surrender.

CHICKEN AND CALLED BLUFF

As in Prisoner's Dilemma, the cooperative aspects of Chicken are distributed along the main (NW–SE) diagonal, while the competitive aspects are on the secondary diagonal. There are two common goods, avoiding *DD* and approaching *CC,* and there is a private good in achieving *T* at the expense of the opponent. This distribution of common and private goods suggests a coercive strategy of exploiting a common good to achieve a private good, hence the alternate title "exploiter." That is, by playing *D* one threatens to destroy the common good of avoiding *DD,* and the opponent must then play *C,* preserving the common good and yielding one a private good as well. However, if both players exploit the common good in this way, it is destroyed. There is also a conflicting accommodative strategy of giving up private goods to achieve the compromise common good, *CC.*

In crisis bargaining situations, these characteristics produce the following bargaining characteristics:

1. There is a bargaining dimension; that is, there is some incrementally divisible good such that the more *A* has of it, the less *B* has of it.

2. There is a bargaining range or contract zone that includes both initial bids plus the space between them; all points in this range are preferable to no agreement for both parties. *DD,* no agreement, sets the outer limits of the bargaining range; it is also the worst outcome for both parties. This contrasts Chicken with Prisoner's Dilemma, in which the worst outcomes are *DC* and *CD*–surrendering to the opponent's demands.

3. It is possible for both parties to reduce their initial bids (*C*). One way to reach agreement is for one party to reduce his claim until it matches the initial bid of the other party (*CD* or *DC*), that is, to back down entirely.

4. Another way to reach agreement is for both parties to reduce their bids until they match (*CC*). This is compromise, the *R* payoff, which

		B					
	C	D		C	D		
C	3, 3	2, 4	C	R, R	S, T		
D	4, 2	1, 1	D	T, S	P, P	$T>R>S>P$	

A (row label at left)

Figure 2-29. Chicken

is better for both sides than *S* or *P*. That is, it is possible to untie the package of disputed items and award some to each party, and it is more profitable to get some items (*R*) than to get none (*S*). This distinguishes Chicken from Leader.

5. It is possible to offer the opponent positive inducements (heuristically, the carrot) to yield. Such an inducement consists in increasing the opponent's *S* payoff.

6. It is also possible to increase the cost of no agreement, that is, to threaten increased harm (heuristically, the stick). However, the stick hurts both parties.

In summary, the worst possible outcome in this game is no agreement. Agreement can be reached by some combination of tactics 3, 4, 5, and 6. However, the exact point of agreement cannot be specified on the basis of the above characteristics.

Experimental work with Chicken [35] offers some heuristic suggestions about how Chicken is played, but because of the difference between a one-play diplomatic game and an iterated experimental game, these suggestions have little force. Rapoport and Chammah's article, as we interpret it, offers the following suggestion: The tendency to stand firm (*D*), which if unchecked leads to *DD*, no agreement, war, is not checked by appeasement (unilateral *C*). It is checked by a fear of future retaliation (*DD*), which is greater as the cost of *DD* increases. That is, a large subjective risk of war induces caution and a tendency to compromise, but appeasement by itself does not.

Of the crises we studied, the following are estimated to be Chicken:

Munich, 1938	Britain/France–Germany
Berlin, 1948	Soviet Union–United States
Lebanon, 1958	United States–Soviet Union

We add one shorter Chicken episode to this list, the East German–West German trade negotiations of Fall 1960.

The following are estimated to be Called Bluff:

Morocco, 1905–1906	France–Germany. Germany in Chicken; France in *PD*
Quemoy, 1958	United States in *PD*; China in Chicken
Cuba, 1962	United States–Soviet Union. Soviet Union in Chicken; United States in *PD*

In the top three of these crises a perceived conflict of interest occurred which could be compromised, in which failure to reach agreement could

[35] Anatol Rapoport and A. Chammah, "The Game of Chicken" in I. Buchler and H. Nutini, eds., *Game Theory and the Behavioral Sciences* (Pittsburgh: University of Pittsburgh, 1969).

lead to war, and in which capitulation was preferable to war and compromise preferable to capitulation. This estimate is reached by combining the final, considered judgments of the leading decision makers of each side. However, some of these judgments were hypothetical, and Quemoy and Lebanon are especially ambiguous.

For the next three crises we accept the judgment of the leading decision maker on one side that war or high risk of war was preferable to capitulation.

The estimated payoffs of the 1905 Morocco crisis are delineated in Figure 2–30. The general precipitant of the crisis was France's failure to consult Germany before taking steps to control Morocco. Britain, Spain, and Italy had been consulted and had each received compensation for approval of French actions, but Germany had been left out.

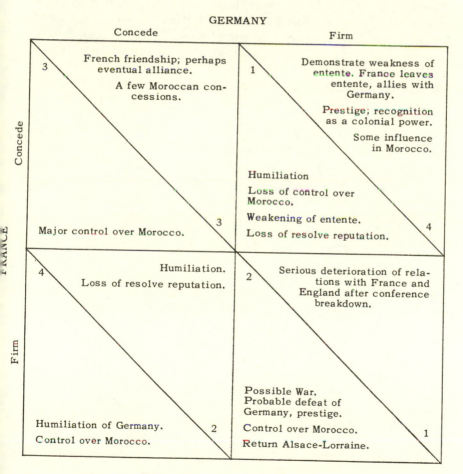

Figure 2-30. Morocco, 1905-1906

Germany sought to rectify this by declaring support for Moroccan independence (the "challenge") and later demanding a share in the control of Morocco. Part of the "win" payoff to France (T) would have been a certain amount of prestige and self-esteem for standing up to Germany. The value of this self-esteem was relatively small at the beginning of the crisis, except for Germanophobe groups, because apparently most of the population felt friendly toward Germany and had little interest in humiliating her. But German bullying and threatening during the crisis aroused a hostile, defensive reaction that increased the value of standing up to the enemy greatly (increase French T, decrease S). Control over Morocco, the other T component, had some economic value and some prestige value. For Germany the main prospective T payoff was the breaking of the entente by demonstrating that Britain would not support France in a showdown. However, this German goal proved to be illusory—Britain *did* support France, and the entente was strengthened instead of weakened. The other German T payoff was its recognition as a colonial power, a member in good standing of the European Great Power club with the right to be consulted about changes in the status quo outside Europe.[36] The main German R payoff, French friendship, was as illusory as breaking the entente, but it also was subjectively important in determining German tactics. There was internal disagreement on R; the emperor placed high value on French gratitude at German generosity and urged concessions (C), while Holstein did not expect any French gratitude and urged firmness (D). The conflict between these two R estimates was one cause of German vacillation during the crisis. The other R payoff, minor influence in Morocco, was of negligible importance.

DD, no agreement, had quite different meanings for Germany and France. France expected that if the conference broke up in disagreement Germany might declare war; but given assurances of British support, France expected a decisive victory. Germany however had no intention of starting an unpopular and costly war over Morocco. The German P-cost was: (1) worsened relations with France and an end to the possibility of a Continental Alliance against Britain (another German illusion); (2) the general diplomatic disgrace of breaking up a conference Germany herself had demanded.

The matrix is Chicken for Germany, since T, breakup of the entente, $> R$, some French goodwill, $> S$, humiliation, $> P$, ruptured relations with France and diplomatic disgrace. The matrix is Prisoner's Dilemma for France; $T > R$, partial control over Morocco, $> P$, victory in war with British support, $> S$, humiliation, loss of Morocco, weakening of the entente and possible dependence on Germany.

[36] This sentence can also read ". . . a member in good standing of the European gang of thieves then engaged in looting Africa."

The German strategy was based on their misestimate that Britain would not support France, that France could not risk war against Germany, and that the game overall was therefore Chicken. They estimated their own critical risk as higher than the French; that is, they estimated that the French would have to back down first in a showdown, and this misestimate was one reason for their adoption of a D strategy. Another reason was their misjudgment of the effects of their threats and displays of firmness, particularly their tone and manner, which was blatantly coercive and peremptory. The Germans judged, on the basis of misinterpreted evidence, that threats would make the French concede more and more, whereas actually they increased the French T payoff and lowered their S payoff, thus increasing the French resolve to stand firm. German strategy was not only ineffective, it was self-defeating. The Germans however did not know this; they misread the feedback from the objective situation and thought they were winning.

The objective situation, which had been misestimated by both sides all along, finally constrained the outcome during the Algeciras Conference. Germany found herself isolated and deserted except for her ally Austria, and the French found themselves continuously supported by the British. The actual game was Called Bluff. When this finally became clear to the Germans, they saw that they had to yield; and yield they did, step by step.

The 1938 crisis involved five players, but we can simplify this to two. Hitler was attempting to make the two players himself and Czechoslovakia, a Big Bully relationship in which German demands would be used simply as a pretext for attack. However, he was in a latent Chicken relationship with Britain–France. He tried to hold off Britain and France through fake negotiations and real military preparations. However, at the end of September he was forced into real negotiations with Britain–France, and at this point the Chicken structure became dominant in the crisis. Britain–France can be treated as a single player in the late September negotiations, with Russia a potentially available ally and Czechoslovakia a client state in a Protector game. The British–French alliance bargaining took place prior to the late September joint negotiation with Germany. Thus at the very end of the crisis, two dominant players had emerged, Britain–France and Germany, in a Chicken relationship. The subjectively estimated payoffs in this relationship are given in Figure 2–31.

What makes this crisis so difficult to interpret is the great divergence between the subjective estimates of the players and the quasi-objective estimates we can make with hindsight. Britain and France overestimated Hitler's military power and therefore made only defensive plans. Hitler half-expected a French attack, but underestimated the Czech defenses and thought he could move his troops west in time to stop the French.

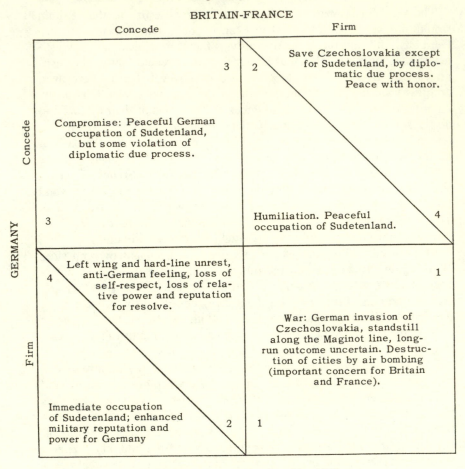

Figure 2-31. Czechoslovakia, 1938

Hitler knew that there was opposition to him in the army, but it is doubtful that he knew of the plan to arrest him in the event of war, and in any case we do not know whether the plan would have succeeded. Subjectively, thus, the two sides agreed that Germany had a military advantage; but the hindsight estimates reverse this. As for valuations, Chamberlain and his group could not appreciate Hitler's mad desire to destroy the hated Czechs and his fear of encirclement by inferior races; they saw him as a conservative nationalist, a moderate who was restraining the radical Nazis and who needed support in this task. Nor can we appreciate Chamberlain's valuations of Czechoslovakia as a nullity, of Hitler as a rather respectable but very touchy fellow Conservative, and that the main dangers were the Labour–Socialist–Communist menace and the rising anti-German war sentiment in Britain. When we read our values into the 1938 situation, the bargaining behavior of both sides becomes unintelligible. The value rankings for Chamberlain's group and Bonnet's group were P, war, $< S$, domestic turmoil and loss of national honor, $< R$, peaceful solution of the Czech question with some compromises in diplomatic due process, $< T$, German take-over of the Sudetenland by means of fully legitimate diplomatic procedures. The value rankings for Hitler's group were P, general war, $< S$, limited and gradual occupation, $< R$, immediate occupation of territory that included Czech defense lines, $< T$, victory. Not much attention was given to S and R until late in the crisis, and in any case there was strong disagreement within the German group, so these valuations are not definite.

The West Berlin blockade crisis of 1948 was Chicken, with Stalin apparently guaranteeing himself a win by credible physical commitment to D on his challenge move. It was Chicken because both sides would probably have preferred giving up their goals to a serious outbreak of violence, risking a major war. The blockade passed the initiative for taking such risk to the West and thus gave Stalin a powerful initial advantage. (See Figure 2–32.)

The Soviets had both a maximum and a minimum goal. Their maximum objective was to force the West to give up its project for a separate West German state (which the Soviets denounced as a violation of the Potsdam agreements), to return to four-power control of all Germany, and to resume reparations payments to the Soviet Union—and perhaps beyond this, to frustrate Western plans for the economic and military strengthening of Western Europe. The minimum objective was to force the Western powers out of West Berlin and incorporate it into the Soviet zone. Apparently Stalin believed at first that this minimum objective was assured; he might then be able to trade it for his maximum, but if such negotiations failed he in any case had West Berlin.

Just as for Stalin the issue of West Berlin was settled, so for the United States the issue of a separate West German state was settled. The United States had no intention of giving that up; for it the issue was finding some way of staying in West Berlin. Its preferred maximum (T) was preservation of its rights in West Berlin but it was prepared to give up something on currency reform to preserve access and the right of occupation (R).

As a result of the differences of bargaining agenda there was no real negotiation during the crisis. The bargaining process consisted essentially of coercion and resistance; from each side's separate perspective both parties stood firmly on D until Stalin yielded. Stalin thought he was negotiating about Potsdam and Yalta, but the United States had no

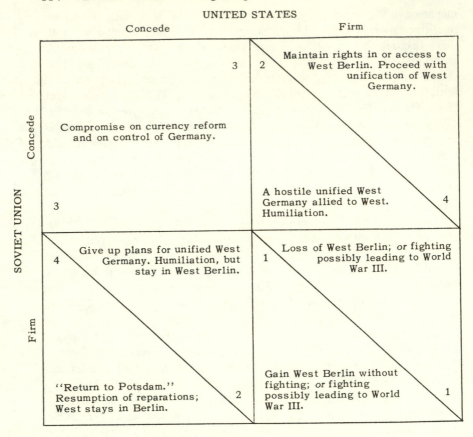

Figure 2-32. Berlin Blockade, 1948-1949

interest in that topic and would not agree to put it actively on the agenda. The United States thought it was negotiating a Berlin settlement through currency concessions, but Stalin had no interest in these; he was waiting for his blockade to work so that he could trade West Berlin for a "return to Potsdam." Finally the surprising success of the airlift swept all these misperceptions away and imposed its own solution by eliminating Stalin's blockade leverage. The airlift passed the initiative for risking war to Stalin, and he chose to yield instead.

The Cuban crisis of 1962 is still too recent to permit a reliable reconstruction. In particular, information about the Soviet estimates of the situation, objectives, preference structure, and decision-making process is weak. On balance, we are inclined to interpret it as Called Bluff, with the Soviet Union the bluffer, though *PD* is a possibility on the assumption that the Soviet Union perceived the United States as intending to take over Cuba. In this case the Soviet *S,* loss of Cuba, would be worse than some limited fighting (*P*).

The precipitant of the Cuban missile crisis was the secret emplacement of long-range, ground-to-ground missiles in a country that was already a thorn in the U.S. side. (See Fig. 2–33.) These missiles were judged to be an intolerable threat to the United States, both directly, in shifting the balance of nuclear power to the U.S. disadvantage, and indirectly for what they symbolized—Russian contempt for U.S. resolve. If Khrushchev could place missiles this close to the United States and get away with it, the United States would look like a paper tiger. It would lose heavily in the "balance of resolve," that intangible equation of comparative "nerve" and determination in which the United States had

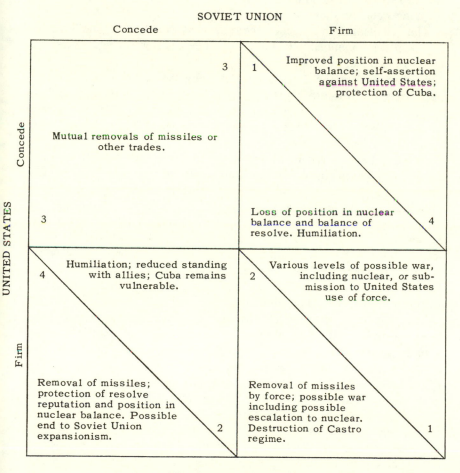

Figure 2-33. Cuba, 1962

already lost some ground via the Bay of Pigs and Berlin Wall incidents. For both of these reasons the U.S. S (allowing the missiles to stay) was very low, lower than P, the risk of nuclear war if they had to be removed by force. The U.S. T-goal was simply to get the missiles out. Although a few advisers also had visions of toppling the Castro regime and therefore favored military action at the outset rather than bargaining, this additional goal did not enter into the bargaining game except as a plus factor in P. The value of R, some sort of compromise or exchange, is uncertain, chiefly because the evidence does not show conclusively whether the United States would have (or did) accept a private trade of Turkish missiles for Cuban missiles rather than undertake direct military action. We assume that $R > P$ by a small margin: thus the United States was in Prisoner's Dilemma: $T > R > P > S$, though there is room for the interpretation that she was in Bully: $T > P > R > S$.

The "challenge" that opened the crisis was President Kennedy's television speech announcing the naval blockade and demanding removal of the missiles under threat of "further action."

For the Soviets, the T-goals were the obverse of the U.S. S-components, namely to improve their position in the nuclear balance and to demonstrate superior resolve, plus the additional item, which was underestimated by the United States, of deterrence of U.S. attack on Cuba. S was the humiliation, loss of resolve reputation, and increased vulnerability of Cuba involved in having to remove the missiles. R was the Turkey-Cuba exchange or the no-invasion pledge in exchange for missile removal, and P was either some sort of warfare in the Caribbean, perhaps escalating to nuclear war, or meekly submitting to U.S. destruction of the missile sites and possible removal of Castro. We estimate the Soviets were in Chicken: $T > R > S > P$, although admittedly this judgment is based rather unscientifically on the outcome itself—the fact that the Soviets did remove the missiles—in the absence of data on Soviet decision calculations prior to the outcome. The composite game was therefore the hybrid Called Bluff.

The Lebanon crisis was a crisis only in a subjective sense because there was only one Don Quixote out on the playing field, namely Dulles–Eisenhower assisted by Malik–Chamoun. The opponent was that hydra-headed devil, the "International Communist Conspiracy" as Dulles and Eisenhower saw it. New heads had recently sprouted in Egypt, Syria, and Iraq and were about to gobble up Lebanon by fomenting and aiding a revolution, with the main head, the Soviet Union, in ultimate control. Objectively, a crisis occurs when two powers make incompatible demands on each other and when the cost of no agreement is some risk of war. There were two Great Powers involved in the Lebanon crisis, but their demands were not incompatible. The Soviet Union demanded that the United States leave Syria alone, and the United States demanded that the Soviet Union leave Turkey and Lebanon alone, enforcing its demand with troops. These demands were not incompatible. The objective situation constrained the "crisis" process and outcome; after the U.S. troops had landed, there was nothing for them to do, and they presently went home again. Admittedly, however, we cannot say for certain that the landing did not discourage revolutionary activity. Subjectively, as an imaginary construct of U.S. misperceptions, the crisis was Called Bluff. The Communist Conspiracy's aim was to take over the whole Middle East and eventually the world, and U.S. passive acceptance of this program (S) was worse than war (P). R would be a division of influence in the Middle East, with the United States protecting some countries including Lebanon and the Soviet Union getting the rest; $T > R > P > S$. Or if we just consider the United States and the Soviet Union as the protagonists we can call the crisis Chicken because Lebanon by itself was not worth a risk of war to either side.

The 1958 Quemoy crisis is difficult to put in matrix form because the Chinese made no explicit demands, and it is still uncertain what their objective was in shelling Quemoy island. Perhaps their aim was to apply enough pressure to force Chiang to evacuate the island—an illusory goal since Chiang's troops had enough supplies to last for many months. In this case the game would be Chicken, analogous to the Berlin blockade; the United States not willing to bomb the shore batteries if the blockade worked, and China not willing to attack Quemoy or the U.S. escort vessels if the blockade did not work. Or the Chinese aim may simply have been to keep Chiang's troops pinned down in their underground bunkers, thereby demonstrating that mainland invasion from Quemoy was impracticable. In this case the game was Called Bluff, China defending the mainland in PD and Taiwan being the bluffer with its announced intention to invade the mainland from Quemoy. Their aim could also have been to test U.S. resolve to defend the island; if the United States failed the test, an invasion might have followed at some future date though there were no invasion preparations in 1958. The latter interpretation was the one adopted by the U.S. government, which passed the test convincingly by dramatically convoying supply ships to the island and by other military maneuvers and declaratory statements. In this interpretation the game was Called Bluff, China being the bluffer with its announcement that Quemoy would shortly be invaded, while the United States was committed to defend the island.

A fourth possibility is that this crisis was primarily alliance bargaining between the United States and Taiwan—a Protector game—with the United States attempting both to reassure Chiang of U.S. support and to restrain him from attacking the mainland. This interpretation is suggested by the puzzling fact that U.S. officials were pretty sure by the end of August that no invasion even of Quemoy was intended, let alone Formosa, but they continued to proclaim defiance of China and resolve to defend Formosa against expected Chinese attack.[37] Perhaps the speeches were mainly for Chiang's benefit.

The Lebanon and Quemoy cases bring out a difficulty in the subjective interpretation of game models. Interpreting game payoffs objectively leads to peculiar results, we have found; but if we interpret them subjectively we seem to be forced to accept even the most fantastic delusions as a real expected payoff. And worse, even pretenses made to enable a bargainer to reassure an ally or to demonstrate resolve or express a commitment cannot easily be distinguished from real expectations.

CHICKEN AND CALLED BLUFF TACTICS

The early stages of a Chicken or Called Bluff crisis proceed exactly like those of a Prisoner's Dilemma crisis. In our cases, since the parties are operating mainly on initial misperceptions, their initial strategies are based on these misperceptions rather than on the actual payoff structures. A Chicken crisis therefore proceeds through initial D strategies to confrontation and P-bargaining. This is the first point at which the actual crisis structure can break through by feedback, and it is therefore at this point that the distinctive characteristics of a Chicken crisis begin to appear.

If P-bargaining discloses to both parties that the opponent is serious and powerful and really resolved to fight in certain circumstances, the outlines of a Prisoner's Dilemma crisis begin to appear and the parties are forced to move on to T-search. On the other hand, P-bargaining might disclose that one party is dangerously overpowered and cannot afford to risk war (or ruptured diplomatic relations), and this reveals that the crisis is Chicken or Called Bluff. The weaker party then yields, shifts to C. There is consequently no need for the stronger party to reexamine his goals; nor is there the shared experience of facing the danger of war together that would induce a shift to an accommodative orientation and R-bargaining. All that is left is S-search. After one party has yielded, the victor may look for inexpensive ways of increasing the loser's S payoff (face-saving) in order to stabilize the situation and prevent the loser from thinking of revenge; this is S-search. In short, the formula for Chicken tactics is first the coercive P, then perhaps the accommodative S.

[37] Johnathan T. Howe, *Multicrises: Sea Power and Global Politics in the Missile Age* (Cambridge, Mass.: The MIT Press, 1971), pp. 198, 211, 212, 223, 351, 360, 361.

The other possible outcome in Chicken games is for both players to face the possibility of war, recoil from it simultaneously, and shift directly to *CC*. We have one apparent example of such an outcome—Munich, 1938.

The shortened search process allows for less correction of misperceptions than the longer Prisoner's Dilemma process. The loser has his mistaken estimates of the power situation corrected; but neither side is forced to examine its objectives and rerank them. Consequently, neither party learns the minimally essential goals of either itself or the other that might provide a basis for compromise. As a result the winner continues to think that he has put down a bluffer by his firmness, and the loser is faced with the necessity of increasing his power so he can do better on the next round. If there is no opponent, as in the Lebanon case, there is no correction of misperceptions at all. Our Don Quixote enters the field with banners of resolve flying and, when nothing happens, concludes that he has successfully deterred his opponent. There is of course nothing wrong with deterrence as a policy goal, but real deterrence is that undertaken against an actual threat.

We next illustrate the *P-S* scheme from the cases. The 1905–1906 crisis was characterized by a series of deadlocks interspersed with partial concessions by both sides. The German coercive strategy, consisting of threats and refusals to make concessions, was based in its detailed workings more on bureaucratic traditions and on the value-perception set of one man in the foreign office, Holstein, than on conscious decision at the top. The continuous feedback that his strategy was having the opposite effect from that intended was ignored or misinterpreted, until finally the conference votes in which Germany was in a minority of two (with Austria) provided unambiguous feedback. When the Germans finally were forced to perceive the *P*-situation correctly, namely that they would have to take the blame for breaking up the conference, they yielded and the crisis was over. There was no *S*-search by France to moderate the sting of defeat. At the end France rejected the almost pitiable German pleas for some face-saving cosmetic; and Germany returned to the attack a few years later when its military forces were stronger.

On the French side, *P*-bargaining consisted mainly of trying to get an explicit commitment of support from England and communicating it to Germany. When Rouvier was finally satisfied that he would get British support, he saw that the *P*-situation was in his favor and so refused to make any further concessions.

The Munich crisis was unusual in that *both* parties, faced with the prospect of war, backed down at the last moment. The outcome can be called a compromise of sorts, though Britain-France did nearly all the compromising. The dominant Chamberlain group, supported by Bonnet in France, chose a *C* strategy from the start: they offered a series of concessions, first mediation, then Sudeten autonomy, then limited annexation. Hitler's *D* strategy was to pretend to negotiate "for the record" by making impossible negotiating demands until he was ready to invade Czechoslovakia. At the September 22 Bad Godesberg meeting Chamberlain unwittingly upset this strategy by accepting Hitler's terms, forcing Hitler lamely to increase his demands.

Hitler's refusal to reciprocate British concessions angered even Chamberlain momentarily and increased hard-line influence in both the British and French cabinets. Both cabinets shifted momentarily to *D*: France and Czechoslovakia mobilized; France rejected the increased demands; Halifax inquired about Soviet military support, with the usual positive response; Britain sent several war warnings to Hitler; and the British fleet was mobilized.

Thus both sides faced the prospect of war on September 26–27, and both sides drew back. Hitler's first response on September 26 was a bellicose speech, but then after a very agitated morning he sent a polite letter to Chamberlain thanking him for his efforts and suggesting that they might possibly be continued. Meanwhile the British waverers were disturbed both by their own boldness and by Hitler's apparent failure on September 26 to back down, and they once more allowed Chamberlain to make a new concession. The French also shifted back to *C* on September 28, offering Hitler almost all he had demanded. Meanwhile Hitler was under internal pressure to back down too, and, faced with the French offer, he agreed on September 28 to call off the invasion and give up his dream of a triumphal entry into Prague. The September 29 Munich meeting itself was a formality that spelled out and ratified the tacit agreement of September 28.

There was little real bargaining between Hitler and the West until the final phase of the crisis. Chamberlain thought he was engaged in mutual *R*-search with Hitler, but since Hitler was not interested in bargaining, only in setting up a pretext for attack, these efforts were fruitless. Brief *P*-influence occurred with the British–French coercive moves of September 25–27, which were intended to force Hitler to back down. However, the timid coercers gave Hitler no time to back down, but backed down themselves at the first bit of negative feedback— Hitler's bellicose speech of September 26. Hitler's more leisurely (two days) back-down was prompted as much by an additional French concession as by fear of war.

The 1948 Berlin case was essentially a contest of physical commitments, the second (airlift) circumventing the first (blockade) and producing a win for the West. Beyond this, there was little bargaining.

There was talk, but no real negotiation. The Soviet strategy was to maintain the Berlin blockade until the Western powers surrendered, at which time Stalin would demand as his price a halt in the movement toward a West German state. If the price was not met, he would at least have West Berlin. The U.S. strategy was to circumvent the blockade, postponing the choice between surrender and attack as long as possible in hopes that something would turn up. The success of the airlift clarified the P-situation: Stalin saw that he had to choose between yielding and risking war, and he yielded, the West providing a small S-crumb in a promise to hold a future conference.

The 1960 Berlin trade dispute began with Bonn's September 30 cancellation of the East–West trade pact effective January 1. This was a response to the German Democratic Republic's September 8 temporary travel restrictions, one of Ulbricht's probes to which the United States responded with an airlift. Bonn's aim was to demonstrate power and resolve as a deterrent to future travel restrictions. East Berlin's reply on November 7 was the inspection of commercial shipments to West Berlin (escalation). The two powers were now in DD, and both engaged in P-search, beginning with checks on alliance support. Bonn found no active alliance support, and East Berlin received Soviet support in the form of an underwriting of trade losses. Having found itself short of power, Bonn on December 1 proposed "compromise": renew trade agreement and end travel restrictions and inspections; this would achieve Bonn's original aim minus the demonstration of power and resolve. East Berlin's reply on December 18 was a threat to block access totally, a bluff. However, Bonn was in no position to call this bluff and yielded before the December 31 deadline, agreeing to renew the trade pact unconditionally. East Berlin then increased Bonn's payoff to stabilize the situation; they reduced the classes of shipments to be inspected and made the inspections unobtrusive. They had preserved (or established) their right to control trade and traffic to West Berlin, but quietly and without continually rubbing in the humiliation for Bonn.

Aside from the partial example of the Berlin, 1960, trade dispute, we found no clear-cut case among those we studied in depth of a Chicken crisis won by successful bluffing, an outcome which one would expect, from the logic of the game, to be natural, even the norm. The closest to it was the Munich crisis. Quite probably Hitler was bluffing when he indicated indifference whether or not Britain and France fought for Czechoslovakia, and a firm stand by these two powers early in the crisis would have saved the Sudetenland. What makes this an ambiguous example is that the Western powers did not yield to Hitler's demands *primarily* out of fear of war and the belief that Hitler's threats of war were credible, although they did indeed hold such fear and belief. The

British, at least, "yielded" to (more accurately, collaborated with) Hitler, chiefly because they thought his demands were legitimate. Granting them was therefore not only costless but positively valuable in re-arranging the map of Central Europe according to the moral norm of "national self-determination." British–German relations in this crisis thus do not fit the notion of "successful bluffing," which implies that the victim of the bluff gives up something he values highly out of a (mistaken) belief that the opponent will inflict worse consequences if he does not. And the British did, in a sense, *call* Hitler's demand to take the Sudetenland by force of arms.

Very probably, history contains crises that were resolved by successful bluff. One example, which we did not investigate thoroughly, was the Rhineland crisis of 1936. Hitler was bluffing: he gave instructions to his military commanders to retreat if the French showed signs of resisting. The French, grossly exaggerating German military strength, believed Hitler was serious and, inhibited by a defensive military doctrine, failed to call. But this example, like Munich, is also somewhat "impure" because of the widespread belief in the West, especially in England, that the demilitarization of the Rhineland was abnormal and that Hitler had a right to occupy it.

Another logically possible outcome of a Chicken crisis is that both parties establish the credibility of their threats (bluff successfully) and mutually withdraw to an evenly balanced compromise in the *CC* cell, in a process similar to the one we found in the Prisoner's Dilemma cases. We find no good examples of this either. If we separate the conclusion of the Munich crisis from the larger picture, we get an imperfect example, imperfect because the compromise was hardly "evenly balanced".

From this meagre set of cases we conclude tentatively that the typical dynamics of a Chicken crisis and its Called Bluff variant are, first, a confrontation with mutual coercive tactics (*P*-bargaining), which leads to the realization by one party that the opponent's power and resolve are greater than its own; then the weaker party gives way entirely, with the stronger party perhaps providing some minor or apparent concession (*S*-bargaining), which the loser can use and magnify afterward to obscure the extent of his defeat.

BULLY

Bully games (Fig. 2–34) are characterized by very unequal power between the two players, so unequal that the stronger player could easily win a war or other confrontation. He prefers to gain his objectives without war, but if the opponent refuses to surrender peacefully he can easily gain his objectives by force. Consequently he has no motive to

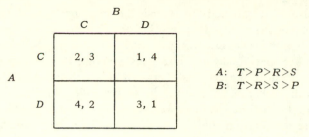

Figure 2-34. Bully

compromise and can afford to bully his opponent rather than to bluff or conciliate him.

Because of the inequality of power; there are no important co-operative aspects of this game and therefore no mixed motives. The game is purely competitive, with the competitive goods distributed on the secondary diagonal (NE-SW). Player A, the bully, has available a dominating coercive strategy whose force lies in the threat of disaster (DD) to player B. Player B has no effective counterstrategy and must yield (C) to avoid disaster. This game represents Chicken dynamics in their extreme form.

These dynamics produce the following bargaining characteristics:

1. As in Chicken and *PD,* there is a bargaining dimension.

2. Technically, the bargaining range is the range between the *DD* pay-offs for both sides, as in other games. However, since A's *DD* payoff (P) is so high, the range is small and in practice is limited to the difference between his third and his fourth payoff. That is, he may be willing to reduce his initial demand a little to avoid the bother of war. As Bully intensifies toward Big Bully ($P > T$) this range shrinks toward a point, and disappears in Big Bully.

3. Because of 2, the only way to reach agreement is for B to accept A's bid with at most minor modifications. The only available solution is *DC*.

The Fashoda crisis is our example of Bully. The balance of forces in the Nile area and in naval forces was such that the British could easily win any fight that might start. The eight French and 120 Senegalese soldiers isolated in the vast Nilotic swamps were no match for the 20,000-man British army that had just reconquered the Sudan, though they had enough champagne on hand for a lengthy stay. The French fleet was no match for the British navy in the Mediterranean or else-where. Both sides knew this; there was no misperception to complicate game play. Play consisted of the French incrementally reducing their initial bid until it matched the British bid, thus ending the crisis. The British then contributed several face-saving gestures such as announcing the French withdrawal casually as though it were a trifle, which raised the French S payoff slightly and thus stabilized the situation. It is interesting to note the contrast between this account of the Fashoda crisis and the utility model account in the preceding section. This model focuses on the distribution of power and on the resulting strategic situation, while the utility model stays on the surface, the specific steps by which the French moved toward the British opening bid. The game model says that the specific steps the French used to climb down were unimportant; what was important was the strategic situation which awarded France a loss and Britain the opportunity to stabilize their win.

DEADLOCK

In Bully one player is the Bully and the other is Chicken. What happens when both players are Bully? We have one such case, United States–Japan, 1941. This is a symmetric but not a mixed-motive game, which we call Deadlock (see Fig. 2–35). This game is mathematically uninteresting, since there are no mixed motives. There is nothing to bargain about; the necessary outcome is *DD,* and no maneuvers can make any difference. Empirically, however, the story is not that simple. The outcome may indeed be inevitable, but many interesting and frustrating things can happen on the reluctant journey to the inevitable outcome.

If we define this crisis in terms of each party's perceptions of the other, it was a clash between two capitalist empires, the U.S.–British–Dutch empire established by force in the nineteenth century and the new Japanese empire being established by force since 1910. In both cases, industry was concentrated in the metropolitan area that controlled the empire, and raw materials were to be supplied by the outlying areas, the Indies and Indo-China plus China. The economic conflict therefore was over which countries would control the raw material areas. The power-strategic corollary was, who was to be dominant in the East Asian balance of power. (See Fig. 2–36.)

$$B$$

		C	D
A	C	2, 2	1, 4
	D	4, 1	3, 3

$T > P > R > S$

Figure 2-35. Deadlock

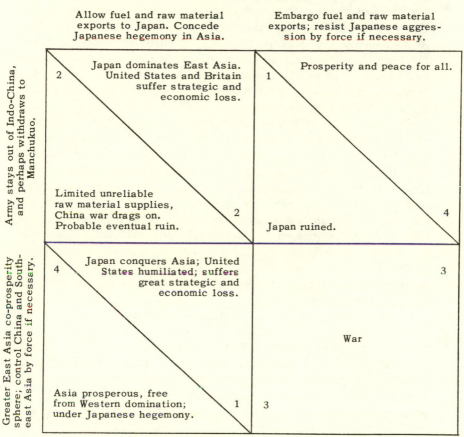

Figure 2-36. United States-Japan, 1940

Neither side, however, saw itself as imperialist; it was the other side that was imperialist. The U.S. leaders and especially Hull believed in free trade (except for unfair Japanese low-wage competition) and favored freeing the British and Dutch colonies. They believed that if the ex-colonies were to offer their materials to the highest bidder, everyone would profit and nobody would dominate anybody. U.S. interests in Asia were primarily moral and strategic; they were there to protect innocent countries against Japanese aggression and to protect the raw materials our allies needed for the European war. Economically, the United States was interested only in preventing Japanese domination, not in securing domination for itself.

For Japan the issue was Western domination of East Asia, which had reduced Asiatics to an inferior status, robbed them of their raw materials and their indigenous culture, and assigned them the low-paying jobs and low standard of living. So far only Japan had avoided this wretched fate. The West controlled more than enough raw materials in America and Africa and could in fact export surplus raw materials from America to Japan profitably, so their selfish control of East Asia raw materials was nothing more than racist domination. The purpose of the Co-prosperity Sphere was to throw off Western domination and produce a prosperous, cooperative Asiatic free trade area.

Each side could see through the hypocrisies of the other but sincerely believed in the justice of its own cause. The Japanese could see that "free trade" was a fraud: Japanese products were systematically excluded from Western markets by a variety of devices, Japanese surplus populations were excluded by immigration laws, and the raw materials were owned by Western corporations interlocking with Western industrial corporations. There was no free trade. The United States could see that, if Japan established military domination over East Asia, they would take whatever they wanted and their subject populations would get the leavings. "Co-prosperity" was a fraud. The Japanese military and the Zaibatsu industrialists would get the "prosperity" and everyone else would get the "co."

For the Japanese leaders the strategic alternatives were self-assertion as an independent Great Power (D) or acceptance of domination by the United States, Britain, and France (C). Japan could be an independent great power only if it had an army and navy strong enough to repel Western (including Soviet) military attack, an industrial base strong enough to support the military forces, and raw materials sufficient to support the industrial base. Hence the co-prosperity sphere. If a self-sufficient independence could not be established, the army would have to retreat to Manchukuo or even the home islands, industry would stagnate and decline for lack of materials and markets, the population would starve, and eventually the Western imperialists would divide Japan as they had divided China and the rest of Asia. Domination (CD) was thus unthinkable. The only real issue was whether the United States and its allies would accept Japan's need for raw materials (DC) or whether they would block Japan's access (DD). Japanese bargaining strategy aimed at the preferred DC outcome: they made requests of French Indo-China, Dutch Indies, and the United States, for guaranteed raw material deliveries, to be paid for by Japanese industrial exports. With guaranteed deliveries the army would complete the pacification of China and then withdraw to its permanent bases. If raw materials were refused Japan must fight for its existence (DD); and even if defeat by the United States were almost certain, as some Japanese navy leaders estimated, an honorable death was preferable to surrender and national ruin (CD). In short, $T > P > S$.

From the perspective of the U.S. leaders, the strategic alternatives were to support Britain and China against Japan (*D*) or to continue appeasing Japanese aggression (*C*). *C* consisted of supplying Japan the war materials it demanded, materials that consequently would not be available for Britain and China. As a result China would soon be defeated, as Chiang's desperate calls for help made clear; Japan would go on to take the British supply area in the Indies; Britain would eventually be defeated; and the United States would be isolated and weak in a hostile world. The only real bargaining issue therefore was whether Japan could be persuaded to halt its program of conquest (*CD*) or whether it would continue its aggressive advances until war became inevitable (*DD*). U.S. leaders had some hope for *CD*, since they were informed by Ambassador Grew that an antimilitarist faction in the government, including the prime minister, was desperately trying to overcome the military faction and reverse Japanese policy. In short, U.S. preference ordering was $T > P > S$.

What is missing from both preference orderings is a concept of compromise, *CC*. But without information on *CC* we cannot complete our account of the game structure. If there is a potential area of compromise that is preferable to war, then $R > P$, and the game is Prisoner's Dilemma. In this case we would have to inquire why bargaining took such a sharply different form from our other Prisoner's Dilemma cases. But if no such possibility of compromise exists, then $P > R$, and the game is Deadlock. From hindsight we can see an obvious compromise, the one adopted after the war; the United States took in Japan as junior partner in its sphere of economic influence. (Today, of course, the "junior partner" has become transformed into a "senior competitor.") But as we work our way into the world-views of the decision makers on both sides we realize that none of them could have conceived of such an arrangement in 1941, except Grew. The United States could not take a junior partner into its empire because it had no empire; if the Japanese were not getting enough raw materials, that was how the free market worked. And the Japanese military leaders could not conceive of a national independence not based on military power. Speaking subjectively, therefore, compromise was not actually available.

DEADLOCK TACTICS

We cannot generalize from one case, so the following is pure description. We begin with misperceptions, which were essential determinants of both bargaining strategies. The previous section shows that, as usual, each side thoroughly misperceived the subjective concerns and alternatives of the other. But there is also a new wrinkle. The Japanese leaders could hardly be said to have any clear perception of the United States as a bargaining partner at all. Theirs was not a bargaining or strategic outlook, in which one estimates what the other person is trying to do and then calculates how best to deflect or block or induce him. It was more of a duty or absolute constraint outlook, in which there were things that had to be done no matter what the cost or consequences. The task of the negotiators was not to explore possible compromises or to seek out the opponent's weak spots, but to explain Japan's sincerity and earnestness to the United States. The U.S. bargainers, of course, with their bargaining outlook, misperceived the Japanese bargaining style, finding deception rather than sincerity in almost every utterance. The task of the military in Japan was not to estimate the relative costs of war for both sides and advise an appropriate coercive strategy; it was to prepare for war regardless of consequence, even if the likely consequence was suicide (though they hoped for a negotiated peace after initial Japanese victories).

Two other misperceptions were crucial. The United States, based on Grew's "soft" advice, thought that the Japanese soft-line faction wished to play C with CD outcome, and would do so as soon as it overcame the Japanese military-hard-line faction. Consequently, the U.S. strategy was to wait for a soft-line victory in Japan and meanwhile to S-search for ways to encourage the soft group. This was a typical instance of soft-line underestimation of the amount of conflict of interests. The Japanese soft faction had a similar underestimation, expecting the United States to play C as soon as it understood Japan's true position. The members of this faction were encouraged in this belief by a U.S. bargaining proposal of April 1941. They did not know that this proposal had originally been written by a Japanese diplomat as a hypothetical basis for discussion and in no way represented the U.S. position. Consequently they were disappointed when the United States backed away from its formerly reasonable position but remained hopeful that the United States would reconsider. The U.S. hard-line faction, finally, thought the crisis was Called Bluff with Japan the bluffer.

Given the misperceptions on both sides, play is easily summarized. Soft-liners on both sides dominated negotiations, with hard-liners ready to veto any substantial concessions. Each side remained on D but hoped and expected the other to play C. Consequently each side engaged in S-search to find inducements that would facilitate the shift to C. When no shift occurred, disappointment gradually grew, accompanied by more frantic S-search. The soft groups saw this as exploring all possibilities for peace, however slight. Time pressure was operating on the Japanese side to make the hard-liners more restless, and reverse time pressure on the U.S. side induced a stall. As Japanese softs got more discouraged and hards more frantic, a shift of power occurred in which the hards took over and moved into the action game (war). The inevitable occurred, but only after a tremendous amount of frantic, confused negotiation.

ALLIANCE GAMES

The distinguishing characteristic of alliance games in a crisis is that they are played by reference to a third party, the opponent. In adversary games the bargaining problem is to distribute some disputed good between the parties; in alliance games the problem is to coordinate strategy against or toward a third party. The external, third-party reference introduces an objective constraint, a reality principle, that is not present in adversary bargaining. When the problem is to distribute some divisible good, the criterion for a satisfactory settlement is the desire of the two parties. A settlement is good for A to the extent that he gets what he wants of the disputed good, and similarly for B. But when the problem is to coordinate strategy, the criterion for a satisfactory settlement is the effectiveness of the strategy against the opponent. A settlement is good for A and B to the extent that the adopted strategy is effective in dealing with the opponent.

This contrast appears in the two-dimensional utility model as a contrast in the slope of the conflict line. The conflict line runs from A's optimum settlement to B's optimum settlement. In adversary bargaining, if we begin at A's optimum and move toward B's optimum, each successive point represents a possible settlement that is a little worse for A and a little better for B. This means that the conflict line slopes from NW to SE in the utility space. In addition, the successive settlements usually have diminishing marginal utility for either A or B. That is, some components of the disputed good are of greater value for A and others are of lesser value, and so also for B. Since the interests of the two parties are opposed, the components of greatest value to A, whose loss would be a great loss, are usually of least value to B, and their possession would be only a small gain, and vice versa. This means that the conflict line is usually convex (see Fig. 2–37).

In alliance bargaining, the slope of the conflict line depends on the relative effectiveness of alternative strategies against an opponent. "Relative effectiveness" refers to the expected net benefits to the alliance, regardless of how these benefits are divided among alliance members. If one strategy is estimated to be the most effective one, with effectiveness decreasing with distance from the best strategy, the conflict line will peak at the best strategy and the conflict line will be convex as in adversary bargaining (Fig. 2–38, left). The alliance bargaining games would then be Chicken, Prisoner's Dilemma, or Called Bluff.

The British–French bargaining games in the 1905 and 1911 Morocco

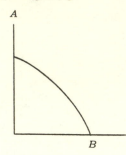

Figure 2.37. Adversary Bargaining

crises probably illustrate this situation. The issue was how to deal with the German demands on France, demands backed by threats of war. The optimum strategy was probably some combination of moderate French concessions plus firm joint resistance to further demands. The cost of the concessions would go to France, while the cost of firmness, namely the risk of war, would fall most heavily on Britain, which would otherwise have no quarrel with Germany. A reduction in the concessions offered would increase war risk or, even if Germany backed down as in 1906, increase the danger of future war because of German frustration and anger. An increase in the concessions offered would reduce immediate war risk but would increase the cost to French interests and the cost to both alliance partners in resolve reputation and alliance solidarity. In both these cases the alliance game was probably Chicken: for both parties, acceptance of the ally's preferred strategy or some compromise was better than risking the collapse of the entente.

The optimum strategy in other cases might be joint uncompromising firmness against an opponent who is believed to be systematically expansionist. In still other cases the optimum might be full accommodation to the opponent's demands, if they are seen as limited and legitimate, and if settlement of the dispute would remove a serious source of future conflict. In these variants, the peak of convexity would lie near one end or the other of the conflict line, rather than near the center as in the example given.

Allies are likely to disagree about what the optimum strategy is for at least two possible reasons: (1) they disagree about the nature of the opponent and his ultimate aims, and (2) each strategy carries a different allocation of costs, risks, and benefits, and each partner is likely to be more concerned about his individual benefits than joint ones. Thus, we distinguish between the joint optimum strategy, that which maximizes total net benefits to the alliance, and individual optima that maximize net benefits to one party. The strategy chosen will reflect the

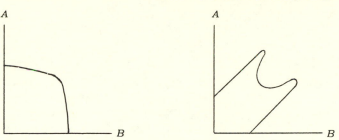

Figure 2-38. Alliance Bargaining

relative bargaining power of the allies—a function primarily of their relative dependence on the alliance. France achieved *its* optimum in 1905–1906 because England needed or thought it needed the entente more than France, and the French knew this. The joint optimum was more nearly approached in 1911, partly because the French premier at that time was more skeptical of British loyalty. Degrees of mutual dependence (interdependence) also determine which game the allies are playing. When both are highly and about equally dependent on the alliance, the game is Chicken; when interdependence is less, the game may be Prisoner's Dilemma (each would risk an alliance break-up rather than accept the other's preferred strategy); and when the interdependence is asymmetrical, the game is Called Bluff.

When there are two opposite ways to deal with the opponent effectively, and intermediate strategies are less effective, the conflict line will be concave between two peaks. The bargaining game then will be Leader, Hero, or Protector. In these games the issue usually is not what combination of firmness and conciliation to adopt toward the opponent, as in the type just discussed, but a choice between two discrete strategies that cannot be effectively combined. Thus we distinguish between two general classes of alliance bargaining games (Fig. 2–38). Since we have already analyzed the first class in the adversary context, we turn now to the second class.

LEADER

Leader is identical to Chicken except that the relative value of the two C payoffs is reversed for each player. In Chicken $R > S$; in Leader $S > R$. This also means that the heuristic names associated with $T, S, R, C,$ and D in Chicken and Prisoner's Dilemma are misleading and should be ignored. P, however, still means "punishment" heuristically. S can be thought of heuristically as "support," D is "lead," and C is "follow."

The reversal of R and S changes the distribution of cooperative and

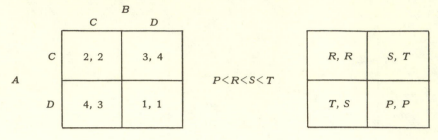

Figure 2-39. Leader

competitive elements. In Chicken there is a common good in avoiding *DD* and approaching *CC*, while competition is distributed along the secondary diagonal (*DC–CD*). This implies a coercive strategy of manipulating the common good of avoiding *DD* in order to achieve a win on the secondary diagonal, and an opposing accommodative strategy of giving up private goods to compromise on *CC*. In Leader there is a common good in avoiding *both DD* and *CC,* with competition again located on the secondary diagonal. This implies a coercive strategy of manipulating *both* common goods to achieve a competitive win, with no opposing accommodative strategy. However, a competitive win is simultaneously cooperative, since it achieves both common goods. The competitive and cooperative elements are more completely fused than in Chicken or Prisoner's Dilemma.

Translated into bargaining terms, the structure of forces is as follows:

1. Unlike Chicken, there is no single bargaining dimension. In Chicken, the player uses force or threat of force to push the opponent back along the bargaining dimension to gain advantage for himself (*CD, DC*) *or* both players compromise on some midpoint (*CC*). In Leader, there are two discrete solution spaces (*CD, DC*) with no intervening bargaining space and no means of compromising (*CC*); the players must coordinate their strategies to move to one of the two solution spaces. However, a small amount of accommodation is possible within each space (*S*-bargaining).

2. Like Chicken, failure to agree (*DD*) is the worst outcome.

3. Therefore like Chicken, escalation or threat of escalation (decreasing partner's *P*) is possible to force a win.

4. Like Chicken, positive inducements (increasing *S*) can also be used to stabilize a win.

5. In contrast with Chicken, inducements are more readily available than threats and are the primary ingredient of a successful strategy.

In short, Leader is Chicken without the possibility of compromise.

This means that the conflict is an almost zero-sum affair—either *CD* or *DC*—except that the whole struggle rests on a cooperative 3d payoff base. This in turn means that the positive inducement of a high *S* is more available than in Chicken.

Guyer and Rapoport reported in 1969 on experiments with iterated Leader and provide information on typical strategies used by experimental subjects. The strategies conform to the mathematical structure of the game. There is a tendency to preempt or lead, that is, play *D* unilaterally, and to persist in playing *D* as long as the follower reciprocates with *C*. Reversal of roles, from *DC* to *CD,* occurs when the follower shifts to *D* and persists in it; the former leader then shifts to *C*. In other words, reversal moves through *DD.* These results suggest that in one-play games, the kind we observe in our crisis cases, when both players are relatively equal they will both try to lead, with a *DD* outcome, but when the two players are clearly unequal, the stronger will lead and the weaker follow.

We found five examples of Leader, all five of them occurring in alliance or détente bargaining. From this uniformity we induced the hypothesis that Leader ordinarily occurs in alliance or détente bargaining. The five examples are: Germany–Austria, 1914; Austria–Russia, 1908; England–Russia, 1908; Soviet Union–United States, 1945–1947 Iran (a questionable example); and France–England 1922–1924.

The bargaining for Germany–Austria, 1914, dealt with the distribution of military forces in the impending showdown with Russia (Fig. 2–40). Germany is player *A,* Austria is player *B.* The *CD* alternative is Germany concentrating or threatening to concentrate its army on the Russian border to deter Russia, while the Austrian army invades Serbia. The *DC* alternative is Austria concentrating most of its army on the Russian border while the German army invades France. *CD* mainly benefits Austria and *DC* mainly benefits Germany. The *CC* alternative, both armies deterring Russia, costs little but gains nothing, and *DD* is the disastrous alliance break-up with each army operating independently and being defeated. The cost of *P,* independent operation, is much greater for Austria than for Germany, and this difference is an important determinant of game outcome.

Here as elsewhere *C* stands not for a specific strategy but for a range of possible strategies involving some degree of acceptance of the ally's position. The extreme would be complete acceptance of his position, as in Figure 2–40. Short of the extreme, *CC* could represent a compromise in which each partner gives in partly to the wishes of the other. Austria would send part of the army to the Eastern front and attack Serbia with the rest, and Germany would send part to the Eastern front and attack France with the rest. This again would be no gain. The weakened

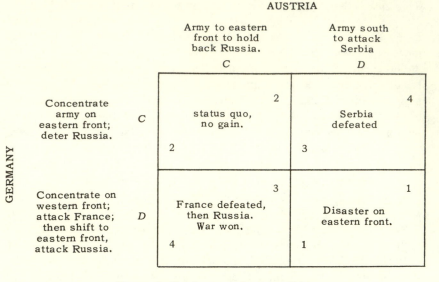

Figure 2-40. Germany-Austria, 1914

Austrian attack would be insufficient to conquer Serbia, and the weakened German attack would similarly fail in France. It is characteristic of Leader that compromise is fruitless; the two partners can achieve a win only by coordinating their forces in one of two opposed directions. Austria would get a quick victory in Serbia only by sending most of its army south, and Germany would have to use nearly all of its army to defeat France.

The bargaining for Austria and Russia in the 1908 Bosnia crisis concerned the manner of implementing the Aehrenthal–Izvolsky agreement whereby Austria would support Russia on the Turkish Straits question and Russia would support Austria on the Bosnian annexation (see Fig. 2–41). The Russian preference, *CD,* was for both supports to occur in the diplomatic bargaining at a European conference. The Austrian preference, *DC,* was for each country to devise its own strategy and confidently call on the other's help when needed. *CC* is pointless, and *DD* is each party pursuing its own aim with no help from the other.

The bargaining issue for the United States and the Soviet Union in 1945 over Iran was a manifestation of the more general issue of how the two powers would run the world for their mutual benefit. The wartime alliance was ended, but both parties hoped to cooperate in the postwar period of reconstruction, and Iran was one of the test cases. The Soviet Union plan (*CD*) was for the powers to agree on spheres of influence, with disputes to be settled at regular Big Three conferences as

RUSSIA

	Recognition of Bosnia annexation	Mutual diplomatic support at a conference
Mutual diplomatic support at a conference	2 no compromise possible; no gain. 2	4 Straits opened; Bosnia annexed at cost of Austrian concessions. 3
Immediate annexation of Bosnia; Russia takes up Straits later	3 Annexation successful; conference becomes unnecessary. Serbian hostility toward Russia. Straits opened eventually. 4	1 Annexation difficult, dangerous. Conference dropped. Straits remain closed. Russian-Austrian-British-German enmity; general war more likely. 1

(left margin label: AUSTRIA)

Figure 2-41. Austria-Russia, 1908

during the war. The United States plan (*DC*) was for independence and neutrality of small powers (except Latin America), fair economic competition for the world's resources, and disputes to be settled by the United Nations, where the United States had a comfortable majority.

It is difficult to compromise these two sets of principles: the Soviet Union either has a sphere of influence in northern Iran, excluding U.S. oil companies, or it does not. Similarly, disputes are either settled privately or they are brought into the open at the United Nations; one cannot half-bring them into the open. One could imagine some sort of *global* compromise in this case—spheres of influence in some areas, competition in others. *DD* is the break-up of postwar cooperation, with the Soviet Union securing a sphere of influence where it can, and the United States using economic penetration and United Nations diplomacy. Since effective compromise is at least imaginable in this case, it could also be interpreted as Chicken.

The bargaining issue for France–England in 1923 was how the two powers could maintain security against a revival of German power. The British plan was for financial control of German industry, achieved by a large German loan at 10 percent interest from British–American bankers, and a British financial adviser in Berlin to guarantee the loan repayment. This plan would produce a prosperous Germany that could trade with the West, pay heavy and continuing reparations to France and Britain, and eventually repay its loan with interest. The French plan was for military control, namely a puppet Rhenish state militarily and economically integrated with France. This plan would ruin the truncated German state and make reparations payments impossible, but on the other hand would provide France with control over the coal and iron of the Ruhr, and insure French security against German attack.

There was no effective way to compromise these two plans. In order to be able to pay continuing reparations and to participate in international trade, Germany had to be relatively prosperous, and this required a fully functioning Ruhr industry. Conversely, a viable Rhenish state tied to France could not be constructed out of superfluous scraps of the Germany economy, but must be a functioning unit, the whole Rhine valley. A compromise would produce a weakened, struggling German state unable to trade or pay reparations plus uneconomic pockets of Rhenish territory that would be a burden to France. A U.S. observer summarized the impossibility of compromise: "It is not practicable to obtain steak and milk from the same cow."

DD again is the breakdown of collaboration, with the French occupying the Rhineland and the British supporting Germany financially against France.

BARGAINING TACTICS

There are three possible outcomes to a Leader game. (1) One player can lead and the other follow. (2) Both players can insist on leading, with *DD* the outcome. (3) The initial follower can turn the tables and become leader. All three outcomes are exemplified in our five cases: (1) in Germany–Austria, 1914, and England–Russia, 1908; (2) in Austria–Russia, 1908, and Soviet Union–United States, 1945, Iran; (3) in France–England, 1923. The outcome is determined partly by the particular distribution of payoffs and partly by the particular pattern of misperception. We consider misperception first.

An identical pattern of misperception appears in the first four cases. In each case both parties perceived that an agreement had been made that they intended to keep. However, each party to the agreement interpreted the agreement in a way favorable to itself; and no party (with the possible exception of Stalin in 1945) recognized the possibility of an alternative interpretation. In game-theoretic terms, no party perceived the situation as a Leader game: each perceived it as Prisoner's Dilemma or Chicken, with both players committed to play *C*. As play proceeded, each party perceived its partner reneging, playing *D,* but perceived itself as playing *C.* Each reacted with disappointment and sorrow at one extreme to bitter anger at the other.

In Germany–Austria, 1914, misperception was minimal but was certainly present. Austria had been assured of complete German support in whatever action it chose to take against Serbia. Austria interpreted this to mean that Germany would deter Russia, with an army if necessary, so Austria could concentrate on Serbia (*CD*). Germany intended to give Austria complete diplomatic support; but if it came to troop movements and war (which Germany did not expect), there was only one plan for that, the Schlieffen plan. This plan depended on Austrian troops holding their Russian frontier until after Germany defeated France (*DC*). When, on July 30, Moltke notified the Austrian government of the German mobilization and specified the expected Austrian contribution, the Austrians changed their plans, canceled the Serbian invasion and took a defensive stand against Russia. The German misperception consisted of the fact that the German diplomats did not know the exact German military plans and therefore were not clear on what the German blank check to Austria meant in military terms.

Misperception also occurred in the Aehrenthal–Izvolsky bargain of 1908. Aehrenthal wrote down his understanding of the agreement immediately thereafter: Austria would immediately annex Bosnia with Russian diplomatic support; when Russia chose to move on the Straits question, Austrian diplomatic support was available. He had however not told Izvolsky that the annexation was imminent, as the timing was solely Austria's business. Nor did he apparently realize that the annexation would make Izvolsky's strategy ineffective, as it did by causing a furore in Russia and making England unwilling to raise the Straits issue with Turkey so soon after the loss of Bosnia. Izvolsky's actions reveal his understanding of the agreement: he arranged a tour of European capitals to prepare for a conference that would deal with both Bosnia and the Straits. In his various discussions he was trying to line up votes for a proposal to open the Straits; presumably Aehrenthal would also have to line up votes on Bosnia and could count on Russia's vote. The surprise Austrian annexation announcement appeared to Izvolsky as a renege, a unilateral move, while the Russian refusal to recognize the annexation appeared to Aehrenthal as a renege, a stab in the back that greatly complicated his problems. Both men were bitterly angry at being double-crossed, and each tried to get revenge on the other. Outcome: *DD,* no joint action, followed by a "Called-Bluff" adversary crisis, with Germany and Austria successfully calling the Russian bluff.

A subsidiary Leader game also was played between Britain and Russia in the Bosnia crisis. Britain and Russia had reached an agreement in

1907 in which Russia made concessions in Central Asia and Britain, in return, agreed to assist Russia on the Straits question at some future time. The success of Izvolsky's strategy in the game with Austria depended on his being able to cash this check. Izvolsky's idea was to have a European conference at which the Straits would be opened to Black Sea countries. The British role would be to enforce this agreement if Turkey objected. But when Izvolsky requested England's support at a conference to open the Straits (*CD*), Grey demurred, saying this was not the same proposal he had agreed to a year earlier. Grey did not wish to exert pressure at this time on the new liberal Turkish regime, for which there was much sympathy in England. He proposed instead an indefinite delay and then opening the Straits to all countries, not just to those bordering the Black Sea (*DC*), and doing it by friendly negotiations involving Russian concessions to Turkey, not by coercion. This was not what Izvolsky had in mind, but he had to follow Grey's lead because Russia could not open the Straits unilaterally. Russia received a follower's payoff (*S*) in the form of British diplomatic support in the subsequent crisis with Austria. Actually, this British–Russian game approached Protector in structure because of Russian dependence on England on the Straits issue.

The Iranian case is more complex, and also rather difficult to reconstruct with confidence, but components of the same type of misperception are present. The United States perceived itself as carrying out a Big Three agreement to cooperate in peacetime (*CC* in Prisoner's Dilemma). The agreement as interpreted by the United States was for the Great Powers to respect the independence and neutrality of small powers, and in fact to provide them economic assistance, financial and military advice, and trade. The United States was living up to this agreement in Iran: it provided a number of advisory missions in Tehran, which supervised the Iranian economy, army, police, and social services. Also U.S. oil men were trying to negotiate concessions to explore for oil in northern Iran, a form of economic assistance to Iran. The Soviet Union had formally accepted the wording of the various postwar cooperation agreements, but always with explicit reservations for the lands bordering the Soviet Union. Stalin's preferred interpretation of the agreements to cooperate was that the Big Three would each mark out spheres of influence for themselves, would respect each others' spheres of influence, and would resolve other differences privately at foreign ministers' meetings. He had several times between 1941–1944 explained his position; later he pointed out at Potsdam that he was not interfering in Belgium and Greece, and his allies should not interfere in Poland. At the Teheran conference, Stalin and Molotov had attempted to map out the various spheres of influence in more detail, again claiming the lands bordering the Soviet Union as the Soviet sphere. However, the West misunderstood the Soviet explanations, because the Soviets employed the euphemism "friendly states" knowing that the idea or term "spheres of influence" was anathema to the United States.

It is not clear whether Stalin was under the illusion that the United States had accepted or would tacitly accept his sphere of influence idea. Certainly he had plausible grounds for thinking that the British had accepted it, since they were moving to reestablish their prewar spheres of influence, and Churchill had worked out with Stalin in 1944 an explicit definition of Russian and British spheres in the Balkans. Also the United States and Britain had excluded the Soviet Union from discussions about the provisional Italian government, thereby treating Italy as a U.S.–British sphere. Also from Stalin's standpoint the United States was in fact trying to set up a sphere of influence in Iran (including Stalin's north Iran) with its military and police advisers, trade agreements, and oil concessions. The United States perceived these actions as respecting the independence and neutrality of Iran; but from a Soviet standpoint they were in fact setting up a sphere of influence. But whatever Stalin's perceptions were, his military moves in Iran were one more attempt to get his spheres of influence interpretation accepted in practice by the United States. He was playing D in Leader, hoping that the United States would follow his lead.

The United States, however, did not perceive the game as Leader because it did not recognize the existence of two alternative ways to cooperate. There was only one way to cooperate, the U.S. way. The United States was cooperating (C), but the Soviet Union was not; its military moves in Iran constituted a renege (D) in a Prisoner's Dilemma.

The Soviet Union play of D was perceived by the United States as reneging on the agreement to cooperate. Instead of respecting the independence and neutrality of Iran, the Soviet Union was taking control of its zone militarily and politically. Consequently the United States had to defend itself against possible future U.S.S.R. encroachments. After some warnings, the United States supported Iran in the United Nations against the Soviet Union. This action was in accordance with the U.S. conception of Big Three peace keeping, though in this case the action had to be taken unilaterally (D) because the Soviet Union had defected (D). To the Soviet leaders it was a U.S. double-cross; its ally was publicly supporting an opponent instead of discussing differences privately at a Big Three meeting. As in the Aehrenthal–Izvolsky agreement, the Soviet leaders reacted to this double cross with bitter complaints at the next foreign ministers' conference. U.S. leaders were apparently also angry and disappointed at Soviet duplicity. The outcome was unilateral actions by both players and recriminations that contributed to the end of postwar cooperation (*DD* in the Leader game). Cooperation would have ended anyway because of ideological differences and strategic circumstances, but the Leader game in the Iran crisis describes the type of episode, of which there were several, which led up to the final breakdown.

The occurrence of the same pattern of misperception in four of the five Leader examples suggests that this type of misperception is associated with Leader. A comparison of these four examples with the fifth example (1923), where there was no misperception, suggests that the effect of the standard misperception is to rigidify the struggle for dominance characteristic of Leader. The leader does not realize he is playing *D*; he thinks he is carrying out an agreement in good faith. The follower's choices are then limited to following (*C*) or to insisting on his version of the agreement (*D*). Bitter anger at having been betrayed by an ally makes it easier to insist on *D,* and the leader's subsequent anger at what *he* sees as betrayal makes it easier for him to stand firm on his interpretation (*D*). In addition, if the two powers are relatively equal, the double-crossing ally may come to be perceived as a threat, a new opponent, against whom one must go on the defensive. So there is an end to cooperation.

The follower's choice between *C* and *D* is affected by the relative payoffs as well as by his anger at being betrayed. In Germany–Austria, 1914, and Britain–Russia, 1908, the follower's choice of *C* is influenced by the relatively high advantage of continuing the alliance (*S* payoff). He cannot afford to act independently and so must accept the leader's interpretation. This situation illustrates the close fusion of competition and cooperation characteristic of Leader. The leader chooses the major advantage for himself; but he also is cooperatively providing a positive payoff for the ally by activating the alliance agreement and contributing to it his superior resources. Germany committed great resources to support Austria, and England had a considerable fund of goodwill in Turkey, which it was willing to commit to the Russian cause.

In the other two cases, Austria–Russia, 1908, and United States–Soviet Union, 1945, the follower's choice of *D* is presumably related to the comparatively lower value of the détente or alliance to a follower (*S* only slightly larger than *P*). Austrian support for Russia on the Straits question was valuable; but the value was diminished by the British reinterpretation and canceled (for the Russian government if not Izvolsky himself) by the cost of submitting to Austrian domination of the Balkans. Moreover, there were no other advantages to increase the *S* payoff. Similarly, the Soviet Union's place in a world dominated by the United States through the United Nations was distinctly a minor one and perhaps a diminishing one. In the 1908 case, the anger at (misperceived) betrayal presumably diminished the perceived value of S farther, until the situation was perceived as Prisoner's Dilemma by the follower ($S < P$). Conversely, the leader's anger at misperceived betrayal, combined with low alliance value, perhaps made $S < P$ in appearance, so that both players perceived themselves in Prisoner's Dilemma. Here again the Iranian case is difficult to interpret clearly. The Soviet withdrawal from Iran may represent a shift to C induced by positive valuation of Big Three cooperation; the outcome would then parallel that of Germany–Austria, 1914, and England–Russia, 1908. Alternatively it may have been forced by fear of U.S. reprisal, in which case cooperation was already dead and the Soviet withdrawal may be interpreted as yielding in a game of Chicken or Called Bluff. A third interpretation is that the Soviet Union's minimal objective in Iran was an oil concession, which it achieved by using troop withdrawal as a bargaining concession (see Ch. V). In this case the U.S. stand merely weakened the Soviet bargaining position, forcing concessions Stalin would otherwise not have had to make, or make as rapidly as he actually did.

The fifth example, France–Britain 1922–1924, illustrates some of the complexity possible in a one-play Leader game when the situation is not simplified by misperception. The outcome depended on a combination of bargaining strategies, shifting resources, domestic politics, and shifts of payoff values, and could hardly have been predicted.

The divergent policy proposals of France and Britain were well known to each other. In 1919 France proposed a separate Rhenish state, which Britain and the United States rejected. In December 1921 Britain supported German desires for a reparations moratorium, and proposed financial support for German economic recovery, which France rejected January 1922. In addition French and British arguments in various meetings made clear the details of their respective preferences and the likely consequences of each. By mid-1922 the picture was as follows:

British proposal (CD): economic recovery for Europe, based on U.S.–British loans. British financial advisers in Berlin would supervise German economic planning. Payoffs would be:

(1) To the alliance, a cooperative payoff. Security against German rearmament and military production. Reparations payments to France and Britain.

(2) To Britain, a leader's payoff. Security for previous British loans to Germany. 10 percent interest on economic recovery loans. Expanded world trade, which was more important to Britain than to France.

French proposal (*DC*): A separate Rhenish state economically and militarily integrated with France. Payoffs would be:

(1) To the alliance, security against Germany, but no reparations.

(2) To France, a leader's payoff. Franco-Rhenish predominance in coal and steel and in military power.

(3) To Britain, a follower's payoff. French military protection and assistance to Britain.

At this point, August 1922, the British asked for French repayment of wartime debts. This represents a shortening of bargaining time, a demand to begin collecting payoffs, and was designed to induce France to follow British policy, to get the reparations payoffs. In September British troubles in Turkey increased the value of the follower's payoff—Britain needed French military support, which France refused (threaten *D*). On August 22 France had also threatened *D*, stating that, if Britain still refused to cooperate in occupying the Ruhr, France would occupy unilaterally. When Britain failed to reply, the French felt obliged to carry out their threat, and in December they announced military occupation of the Ruhr and rejected a British proposal for economic assistance to Germany. Britain then played *C*; it accepted the French occupation. The reason for acceptance was twofold. First, Britain needed the alliance ($S > P$); it needed French military assistance and support against Germany and Turkey. Second, Britain realized that France thought it did not need the alliance ($S \approx P$) and would play *D* regardless of what Britain did. Its critical risk level was higher than Britain's. The British hope was that some experience with military occupation and Rhenish separatism would show the French that they had overestimated their *D* payoffs and would make them realize they still needed the alliance.

Payoff values changed significantly in September–November 1923. For Britain the solution of the Turkish dispute reduced Britain's immediate need for French military support, and the German economic collapse reduced Britain's follower's payoff by stopping German loan repayments. For France, achievement of the Rhenish state goal revealed that its value would be less than anticipated. The state had little popular support and was economically in bad shape, and the lack of reparations payments hurt France financially. France in fact needed British financial support. Interacting with the decline in perceived payoff value was a decline in domestic support for French policy. At that point Britain shifted to *D*. It reactivated its plan for financial control, secured alliance support, and threatened to break the alliance with France (*DD*) unless France complied. The combination of reduced *D* payoff, declining domestic support, and the British threat induced France to comply, shifting from *D* to *C*. The outcome was *CD*, with Britain taking over leadership and France following.

To sum up, we find the Leader game being played in essentially two sorts of situations: "solid alliance" and "fragile alliance" or "détente." In the solid alliance, exemplified by the 1914 Austro–German case, the follower follows because the value of preserving the alliance is seen as better than the cost of competitive defection (DD).

The more general Leader situation is the fragile alliance or détente. This situation may occur near the close or immediately after the close of a war, when the victorious allies still perceive themselves as allies, or at least as collaborators in dealing with the defeated enemy and arranging the postwar world. However, the value of the alliance itself is sharply lowered by the impending or actual defeat of the opponent. The allies make agreements, or think they have agreed, about how to deal collaboratively with the various postwar problems, but inevitably the allies have different interests and consequently interpret the agreements differently. A sequence of Leader games follows. At first, one party preempts with its own interpretation, and the other follows reluctantly, still believing in the possibility of general collaboration. But with each successive episode, the partners become more disillusioned with the value of collaboration—S declines below R. At some point in the sequence, the value of S may even drop below $P;$ after this, the parties conceive themselves as opponents rather than as allies, and their disputes take on the character of Prisoner's Dilemmas: no agreement and further deterioration of relations is seen as better than the much devalued fruits of following the other's lead. Subsequent disputes are more likely to be seen as power struggles involving some prospect of violence of war, i.e., adversary games such as Chicken or high-stakes Prisoner's Dilemma, in which yielding is perceived as worse than risking war. In short, in this interpretation, the Leader game is typically a transitional game that punctuates the normal deterioration of relations between allies once the main raison d'être for the alliance—a powerful common enemy—has been eliminated.

This pattern can be illustrated by some of the events surrounding the close of World War II and the emergence of the Cold War. As we mentioned in discussing the Iran case, the basic Leader relationship and its associated misperception were established by the existence of two opposed plans for postwar cooperation. These plans were embodied in the ambiguous Yalta–Potsdam agreement, which each side interpreted as embodying its own plan for cooperation. Each side then proceeded to take the lead in carrying out the agreement as opportunity permitted. The handling of the Italian surrender and setting up the Allied High Command in Italy was a Leader game in which the Western powers led and the Soviets—excluded from real participation—reluctantly followed. The analog occurred in Rumania, this time the Russians excluding the Western powers, who followed under protest. In Poland the Russians led with their interpretation of what a democratic government meant; the West followed because it had no other choice, but protested sharply. Throughout this period each partner was disappointed again and again by the other's failure to live up to the Tehran–Yalta–Potsdam agreements, not realizing that those agreements were open to selective emphasis and dual interpretation, but each partner continued to hope that the other would finally repent and return to cooperation. The Iran case is the period of transition in which the hope for renewed cooperation died. The parties moved into a Chicken relationship, as in Berlin 1948, and thence gradually into Prisoner's Dilemma.

Leader as a détente game is also illustrated by the Bosnia case of 1908. Though they were formally opponents in the alliance lineup, Russia and Austria had fashioned a détente some years earlier, the leading principle of which was consultation over any change in the Balkan status quo. The 1908 agreement concerning reciprocal support for each country's acquiring a piece of Turkish territory (Bosnia and the Straits) was an attempt to implement the détente, but by this time mutual trust had deteriorated. When Austria led, Russia chose not to follow, and this left the parties in a state of deep antagonism, culminating in World War I. This example indicates that Leader games may occur in a détente relationship other than the type that normally occurs as a transition state before a wartime alliance breaks up. They could also occur in a transition the other way, i.e., when adversaries negotiate a détente on the road to alliance. Our closest example of this is the 1908 negotiations about the Straits between England and Russia. The incident weakened the détente that had been negotiated the previous year, but it was saved by power-strategic necessities and subsequently developed into quasi-alliance.

HERO

The Hero game (Fig. 2–42) is identical with Leader except that R and P are reversed. This reversal, however, makes little difference in either the structure of forces or the distribution of cooperative and competitive elements. Like Leader, there is a common good in avoiding both CC and $DD,$ and competition is located on the secondary diagonal. This means that Hero, like Leader, is empirically a game of coordination against a third player. There are two opposed ways to deal effectively with the third player, and combinations or compromises between the two (CC) reduce their effectiveness.

The structure of forces is almost the same as Leader:

(1) Like Leader, there is no bargaining dimension, no possibility of effective compromise beyond minor modifications of the two effective strategies.

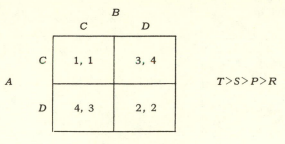

Figure 2-42. Hero

(2) Unlike Leader, independent action (DD) is more effective than compromise (CC).

(3) Therefore lowering P or the threat of doing so is not as effective as in Leader. This tactic simply transforms the game to Leader, where the same problems of coordination remain.

(4) Like Leader, positive inducements (increasing S) are important in producing or stabilizing a win.

The difference between Hero and Leader turns on the relative valuations of R and P, and since estimation of R is always difficult in our alliance cases, we did not succeed in finding any unambiguous examples of Hero.[38] Since in both Hero and Leader, compromise (R) is either impossible or less effective than coordinating on the preferred strategy of one player, and such coordination is better than independent action (P), the two games are virtually identical formally. They are both Chicken with the possibility of compromise eliminated. The original heuristic illustrations associated with both games [39] are also identical upon close inspection. In Leader, one player "takes the lead" by playing D and the other must follow (play C) to avoid the undesirable DD. In Hero, one party waits on D until the other "plays the hero" by choosing C, which yields the joint payoff with the hero getting the smaller share. There is no difference. We conclude therefore that for empirical application there is little to choose between the two games, although Leader fits our cases somewhat better.

PROTECTOR

Protector (Fig. 2–43) is the alliance version of Bully, representing an alliance between two partners of very unequal power. In contrast with Bully, S>R for both players or at least for B, the weaker; the alliance payoff of S is the best accommodative payoff. In Bully the best accom-

---

[38] Britain-Zambia, 1965, coordinating against Rhodesia, provides an interesting apparent example of Alliance Deadlock T>P>S>R, a variant of Hero, but was not included in our case studies.

[39] Rapoport, "Exploiter, Leader, Hero, Martyr," pp. 81–84.

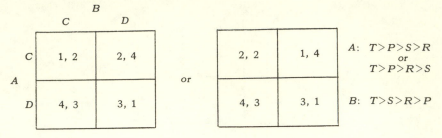

Figure 2-43. Protector

modative payoff is *R* for both parties; this indicates that cooperation consists of compromising an issue in dispute between two players. In Leader and Protector, cooperation consists of coordinating activities against an opponent. There are two different ways to cooperate against the opponent, each favored by one of the partners. In either case both partners get the cooperative *S* payoff, the alliance payoff, but the leading partner gets in addition the leader's payoff.

In ordinary Leader the partners cooperate competitively; there is a struggle for dominance, since each partner wishes to get the leader's payoff. If the two partners are relatively equal in power (United States–Soviet Union, 1945, and Britain–France, 1922), each will insist on being leader, threatening alliance breakup if necessary to get its way, and the alliance may break up. If there are inequalities of power or other salient differences, for instance Britain–Russia, 1908, on the Straits issue, the struggle for dominance is muted and the weaker partner soon accepts the follower's role. In Protector the inequality of power is extreme and no struggle for dominance is possible. The dominant player, the protector (A in Fig. 2–43), automatically becomes leader and the other player, the client, follows of necessity. There is only one bargaining solution, *DC*.

Since *DC* is the only solution, the protector's preference over *R, S* is irrelevant to the dynamics of the game and may not even be clearly formulated by the protector. Consequently there are two possible versions of Protector (Fig. 2–43), both with the same dynamics.

As in Bully, the stronger player automatically gets his way, but the reasons differ in the two versions. In Bully he wins because of his threat potential; the weaker party must concede to avoid disaster, the *P* payoff. In Protector he wins because of his alliance potential; the weaker party cooperates voluntarily to get the alliance *S* payoff. However, if the weaker party shows reluctance to cooperate, threat potential is also available. There is a double motive to cooperate.

Stated more formally, Protector has the following bargaining characteristics:

(1) As in Leader, there is no bargaining dimension but only two discrete solution spaces (*CD, DC*). The two partners cooperate competitively to move to one of the solution spaces.

(2) As in Bully, *DD* or alliance breakup is the worst outcome for player *B* only. Player *A* does not need the alliance to survive, but player *B* does.

(3) Therefore player *A* can safely play *D* and player *B* has no defense. He must accept the follower's role and the alliance payoff of *S*.

(4) In addition, the large *S* payoff gives *B* a strong positive inducement to accommodate *A*'s demands. Since *B* has no way to achieve *T*, *S* is the largest payoff he can hope for, and the *DC* solution is extremely stable.

The following alliances are estimated to be Protector: Russia–Serbia, 1908, 1914; France–Czechoslovakia, 1938; United States–Taiwan, 1958; United States–England and France, 1956; United States–West Germany, 1961; Soviet Union–East Germany, 1961; Soviet Union–Cuba, 1962. Each is an alliance between a strong protector and a weak client state. Insofar as we have evidence on these cases, they all seem to follow a similar pattern, with some variation. The pattern brings out characteristics of the game that are indeed present in the mathematical structure but could not easily have been deduced from it a priori. United States–Taiwan is typical and has the matrix displayed in Figure 2-44.

The favored Taiwan strategy, *CD,* was for an aggressive campaign to reconquer the mainland with U.S. support, with hopes that the population would welcome their liberators and the Soviet Union would stand aside. The United States had no interest in getting entangled in an endless war on the Chinese mainland, to say nothing of risking a nuclear encounter with the Soviet Union. It preferred the defensive strategy of conciliating China by negotiated partial withdrawal from the offshore islands but of defending its ally against any direct Chinese attack. This strategy would preserve the status quo at the cost of Chiang giving up publicly his hopes of mainland conquest. If Chiang insisted on an aggressive attack anyway (*DD*), the United States could publicly stand aside while the attack failed, then step in to protect Taiwan from retaliation. This is apparently what happened in the case of Soviet Union–Syria and Egypt, 1967; the Soviet Union stood aside until its clients were losing badly, then stepped in to protect them. The *CC* compromise might be Chiang attacking the mainland a little bit with a limited U.S. military support. This sort of strategy would neither be coercive enough to get Chiang back on the mainland nor accommodative enough to

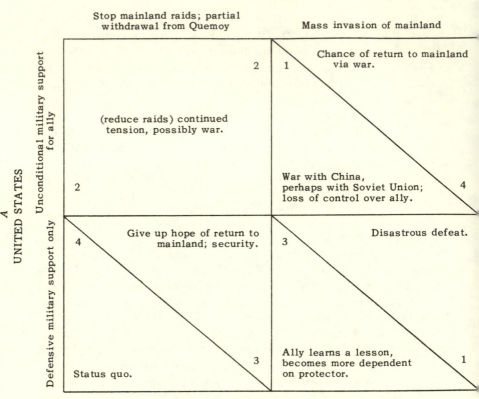

Figure 2-44. United States-Taiwan, 1958

reduce tension and preserve the status quo. At best it might provoke a dangerously tense situation as in 1958, and at worst it might set off a war under worse military conditions than the deliberately planned *CD* war.

The Suez, 1956, case is interesting because the British and French initially misperceived the game as Leader (see Fig. 2-45). They believed that once they had committed themselves to a military solution the United States would follow, at least by tolerating such action, rather than incur damage to the NATO alliance by opposing it. After all, the United States ought to have an interest in deposing Nasser too, now that he had become a Communist dupe, and ought to appreciate her allies' assuming the onus of doing the job. Retaking the Suez Canal would also set a good precedent for the Panama Canal. In short, they overestimated the U.S. payoff for alliance collaboration (*S*), and underestimated the U.S. payoff for independent action (*P*). Dulles's ambiguous diplomacy,

BRITAIN-FRANCE

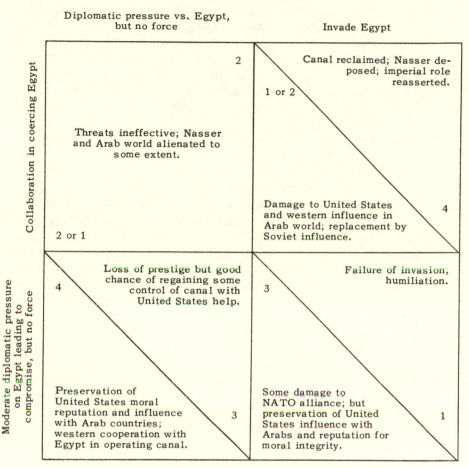

Figure 2-45. United States-Britain and France, 1956

interacting with Eden's and Mollet's wishful thinking, produced this misperception. When Britain–France–Israel initiated their *D* strategy, they were surprised to find the United States not only refusing to follow but actively opposing them with diplomatic and economic pressure. The game was Protector, and the denouement followed the logic of that game. The United States preferred to get its way by coercing its allies, even at the cost of straining alliance bonds, and the U.S. coercive power was too strong for the allies to resist. From this crisis dates the full realization by Britain and France that their time of imperial glory was over and that they could no longer play an independent role on the world stage, at least not without U.S. sufferance. (In this short sketch, we omit some other things that contributed to the British–French backdown, such as U.N. opposition, internal disunity in Britain, and the ineptitude of the military operation.)

To generalize, the disputed issue in all of these protector–client alliances is the client's interest in either expansion or security against a powerful and threatening neighbor, with the protector paying most of the cost. Achievement of the client's interest would also make it more independent of its protector. Taiwan wanted to return victoriously to the mainland in a war fought mainly by the United States; England and France wanted to reassert their imperial influence in the Middle East and beyond, with the United States restraining the Soviet Union; Western Germany wanted to recover its Eastern territories with U.S. support; East Germany wanted international recognition as an independent state; Serbia wanted to develop a Greater Serbia at Austria's expense with Russian backing; Czechoslovakia wanted Britain and France to fight a war for its independence; and Cuba wanted U.S.S.R. protection against U.S. economic and military pressures. These goals were all more or less unattainable short of a major war fought by the protector, the likeliest exceptions being G.D.R. recognition and Cuban and Czech independence.

The protector is always ambivalent about the client's goal. He supports it publicly, in part to retain the client's loyalty and in part out of genuine sympathy with the client's aims. But he is reluctant actually to commit resources to the goal, mainly because he does not want to get involved in a war and partly because a strong, independent ally could no longer be controlled and might cause problems. For instance, Kennedy argued in October 1961 that an independent West Germany might turn nationalist and then stir up trouble in Europe, and Dulles and Eisenhower in 1956 were more than a little suspicious that Britain still had imperialist ambitions in the Middle East, which would impel the Arabs to seek Soviet support. The protector's favored strategy, therefore, is to maintain the dependence of the client by a limited defensive support involving concessions by the client, while publicly supporting the client's aims in the abstract. This status quo strategy yields as T payoff a dependent and dependable ally at little cost, and as S payoff to the client, security.

Specifically, Russia was ready to advise Serbian concessions to Austria in 1908 and 1914, while consistently warning Austria that Serbian sovereignty itself was not negotiable. The United States was willing to sacrifice some of the Chinese offshore islands in the 1950s and to reduce Quemoy to an outpost status if China would agree to leave Taiwan itself alone. In 1961 the United States was willing to give up its interests in

East Berlin and indeed East Germany and with them the West German reunification goal, if the Soviet Union would leave West Germany and West Berlin alone; and the Soviet Union found it could get along without formal recognition of the German Democratic Republic if the West would halt its subversive penetration of that state. In 1962 the Soviet Union was willing to tolerate continuing economic blockade and the U.N. inspectors poking around in Cuba (something it would never tolerate on its own soil) as long as the United States promised not to invade Cuba. In 1938 England and France were willing to cede German areas of Czechoslovakia to Germany, following the principle of national self-determination, on condition that Germany would promise to leave the rest of Czechoslovakia alone. In 1956 the United States was willing to sacrifice its clients' control over their vital oil supplies and supply line in order to preserve U.S. influence in the Middle East.

The play of these games is more complex than one might expect. Mathematically the client's position is hopeless, and he must follow the protector's advice to make concessions. Empirically, our clients have refused to give up hope and have tried a variety of D strategies in the attempt to get their protector to follow with C. These strategies all failed. Taiwan tried massing its army on Quemoy and making invasion-of-mainland pronouncements, hoping to somehow get a war started. England and France tried a fait accompli at Suez, and were undone by the difficulty of coordinating their complex scheme and by U.S. and U.N. pressures. East Germany tried "diplomatic recognition" probes, only to find its protector urging caution so as not to spoil the negotiating atmosphere. Serbia tried defiance of Austria in 1908, and found it would get Russian–British support only after it had yielded to Austria. West Germany tried a trade boycott of East Germany in 1960, found itself without U.S. or allied support, and had to back down in direct negotiations with a government it did not recognize.

Indeed, in some cases the client's D strategy resulted in the mathematically unbelievable DD outcome with the client giving himself a 1 payoff. The cases are Suez, 1956, and the West German trade boycott of 1960, plus perhaps Soviet Union-Egypt and Syria, 1967.

However, these strategies become intelligible if we remember that our games are played, not by omniscient players, but by ordinary statesmen with imperfect information and misinformation. The mathematical matrix represents the composite structure of the crisis situation, the objective pattern of constraints, but this structure is not fully known to the players at the start of a crisis. Consequently any successful strategy will have to include information-gathering components of various sorts. It happens that in Protector (as in Bully) there is no way out for the weaker party, but he does not know this in advance, and may not know definitely that the game is Protector. He may think it is Leader, as Eden did in 1956. Consequently it is reasonable to explore the matrix to locate possible effective tactics. There is no point in beginning with *P*-search, as in Chicken, *PD,* and sometimes Leader, because the client knows that *P,* independent action, is unsatisfactory for him. Consequently he begins with *S*-search, studying the protector's payoff for supporting him and trying to increase that payoff. He may also try *S*-influence, persuasive messages that emphasize the protector's reward for supporting the client (for example Ulbricht's July-August, 1961, messages that if East Germany lost any more manpower it would no longer be able to guarantee its industrial deliveries to Poland and the Soviet Union). If *S*-bargaining is carried out cautiously and incrementally (like Ulbricht and unlike Eden in 1956, who limited himself to wishful thinking about the size of the United States' *S*) nothing need be lost by it. And, after all, there may be a way out.

EMPIRICAL INTERPRETATION AND EVALUATION OF GAME MODELS: EXPANDED GAME AND METAGAME MODELS

The advantage we expected from expanded models was their combination of realism and mathematical tractability. Obviously there are always more than two alternatives open to a participant in a crisis, and it seemed arbitrary and unrealistic to insist on always reducing alternatives to two. With an expanded matrix we could list the actual alternatives considered by each side, arranged in order of increasing coerciveness. Then we could estimate the outcome in each cell and rank them in order of preference for each side. The resulting payoff matrix would be somewhat irregular, but each 2×2 segment would be a simple game with known dynamics, so we could plot the dynamics of the whole crisis situation. It might even be possible to impose a regular expanded matrix on the empirical alternatives by simplifying a bit here and there, so that the mathematics of the 2×2 game and the experimental results with expanded games could be brought directly to bear.

We tried fitting the expanded model to several of our crises with mixed results.

Our experimentation did lead us to recognize an ambiguity or complexity in the *DD* cell of a 2×2 game when applied to a crisis situation. We had supposed at first that this cell simply meant "war" or violence of some kind. However, if the 2×2 game is used to represent bargaining in advance of violence with the *C* and *D* alternatives "make concessions" and "hold firm," respectively, then logically the *DD* cell represents simply "no agreement" with some degree of likelihood that war

might follow. For example the bargaining at the 1906 Algeciras conference could easily have ended in no agreement if both France and Germany had continued to stand firm. What then? Presumably the French
would have continued with the program of "reforms" that Germany had
halted by its challenge to France. Germany then would have had the
option either of tacitly accepting the French protectorate over Morocco
or of sending an ultimatum and attacking if the French refused to leave
Morocco alone. The British and French were fully aware of both possibilities. British delegates urged the French to make some concessions
to get agreement, arguing that if there were no agreement Germany
might start a war. The French rejected the advice, contending that
Germany would not dare to attack both Britain and France. The disagreement was over the probability of German attack if the conference
ended in *DD,* no agreement. This probability was therefore located in
the *DD* cell. In other words, the *P* values in the *DD* cell subsume the
"expected costs" of war in the strict logical sense; anticipated absolute
costs discounted by the probability that war will occur as the consequence of both parties' "standing firm." Or to put it still another way,
strictly speaking even the simplest crisis logically involves two games in
the parties' calculations and perhaps also in actuality, a bargaining game
and an "action game." The action game is the game that follows "no
agreement" in the bargaining game. When there is no agreement, the
challenger must decide whether or not to "attack" in fulfillment of his
threat, and the resister must decide whether to "defend." ("Attack"
and "defend" may of course take the form of minor violence, escalating
verbal or tacit threats into the zone of violence.) This is not just a
formal distinction, made only for logical completeness. The size of the
stakes—the actual content and valuation of *T, S, R* and *P*—usually
change radically once the parties move from "peaceful" coercive bargaining to war. For example, in the Munich crisis, *S* for the Western
powers (give Hitler all he wanted) was a satisfactory payoff, better than
P, no agreement. But if Hitler had attacked Czechoslovakia as he actually intended up until the eleventh hour, the British and French *S* in the
action game—complying in his total conquest of Czechoslovakia—
would have dropped well below *P*—the cost of war—and they would
have defended the country they had previously been collaborating in
partitioning. For them, the bargaining game was Chicken but the action
game was Prisoner's Dilemma.

Clearly this is a distinction of quite general validity. If states *A* and
B are in conflict over some object, such as a small state "pawn" *C* lying
between them, and if *A* attacks the pawn, *B* may be in Prisoner's Dilemma in the "action game": *B* may very well defend, preferring war to
A swallowing *C.* But if *A* merely makes some limited demand on *C,*

threatening to attack if C does not comply, B may be in Chicken—i.e., he may prefer that the demand be granted rather than accept the *risk* of war involved in resisting it or encouraging C to resist it. In the bargaining game, for the resister, S is defined by the adversary's claim and P is the anticipated absolute cost of war discounted by its probability. In the action game, S is the loss from not opposing attack—probably the complete conquest of C by A—and P is the full anticipated cost of war. For the challenging party, $A,$ in the bargaining game, S is the loss from non-compliance with his demand, and P is the estimated cost of war discounted by the subjective probability that B will defend. In presenting our abstract models and empirical examples thus far, we have shown only the bargaining game, with the action game subsumed within the DD cell "no agreement," i.e., the parties' P estimates logically include some probabilistic calculation of the play and outcome of the action game that may or may not follow. But this somewhat obscures the fact that the parties have a new decision to make—to fight or not—if the bargaining game ends up in no agreement. The full situation is shown more clearly by the 3×3 matrix of Figure 2–46.

To illustrate how the matrix works, we put in ordinal numbers in a preference ranking that makes the bargaining game Chicken and the action game Prisoner's Dilemma.

In this matrix, the bargaining and action games intersect in the DD cell, which is an unstable outcome. Logically the parties must move out of this cell; one cannot "stand firm" forever. The challenger A must eventually "put up or shut up." If he "puts up," he attacks (E). The resister, $B,$ then must decide whether to defend (E). If he does, the

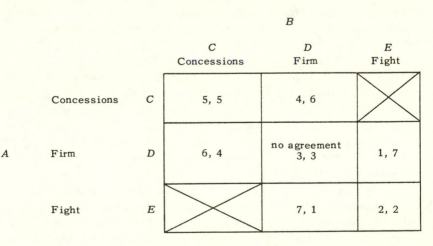

Figure 2-46. The 3×3 Matrix

outcome is *EE,* if not, it is *ED.* According to the numbers in Figure 2–46, he does fight; he is playing Prisoner's Dilemma in the action game, though he is Chicken in the bargaining game. If the challenger "shuts up," he in effect yields in the bargaining game, and the outcome is *CD;* conceivably he may propose a compromise, which if accepted produces a *CC* outcome. The *DE* outcome is shown for logical completeness, to cover the case where either party may attack. The *EC* and *CE* outcomes are crossed out because they are logically impossible in this situation where the bargaining game is Chicken. If it were Big Bully, *EC* at least might have some content (the challenger attacks even after his victim yields).

The 3×3 matrix introduces another logical possibility into a bargaining game, namely an initial *E* strategy. With a 2×2 matrix the players are limited to *D,* standing firm on initial demands; *C,* making concessions; and a mixture of the two. An *E* strategy might consist of making sham negotiating demands until one is ready to attack, then attacking. Hitler's initial strategy in 1938 was *E,* and in 1914 some German and Austrian leaders proposed immediate attack on Serbia. The actual Austrian strategy was *E* with a *D* component (*DE*): Austria sent an ultimatum (*D*) that was mainly a pretext for attack (*E*) but that Serbia could in principle have accepted (*C*) and thus avoided war.

With this modest expansion of the matrix that seems necessary to fully represent *any* crisis, the logical next step seemed to be to subdivide further the "fight" strategy (*E*) into various levels or intensities of violence. This would show the escalation from minor forms of violence used strictly for coercive bargaining purposes (probes, token blockades, force demonstrations) to limited warfare in various degrees, on up to nuclear war. This would conform to the familiar theory that nuclear weapons and the fear of nuclear war have caused the introduction of various forms of "force short of war" in between mere threats of force and actual full-scale war. While the 3×3 matrix is a fairly accurate portrayal of choices in a prenuclear crisis, a further expansion seemed necessary to show the increased number of violent and quasi-violent bargaining strategies that the parties have available or actually use in nuclear age crises. Or such would be implied at least by the theory and its corollary that the line between peace and war, or between "crisis bargaining" and "warfare," has been blurred in the nuclear age, with warfare itself, especially limited war, taking on more the character of forcible bargaining than a physical contest. To what extent this supposed multiplication of forcible strategies has actually occurred in the calculations and behavior of crisis actors since 1945 was one of the matters we sought to investigate in our empirical research. As part of this effort, we tried out a larger expanded matrix on some of the nuclear age crises, notably Berlin, 1958–1962 and the Cuban crisis of 1962 (Fig. 2–47). Here is one example of the Berlin crisis as it might have appeared to the Soviet Union and the United States decision makers soon after Khrushchev's "ultimatum" of November 1958.

In Figure 2–47 the numbers are ordinal, with 12th the most preferred payoff. However, the spaces between numbers increase rapidly below 6 or 7. The cost of payoffs from III, III on down derive partly

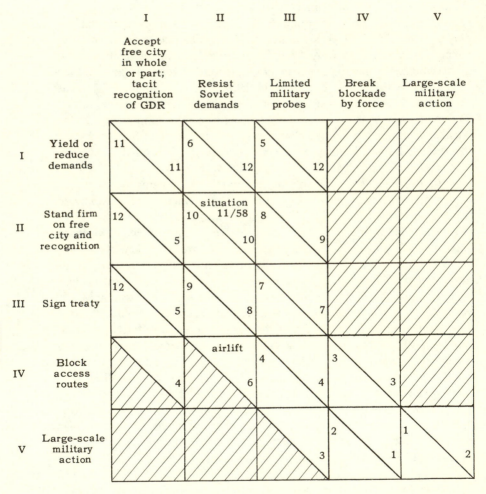

Figure 2-47. Berlin, 1958

from the possibility of accidental war. The matrix is expanded Chicken, with additional possible rows and columns beyond V up to nuclear war. The upper left submatrix is Prisoner's Dilemma. Play begins November 1958 at II, II. Some cells are foreseen as empirical possibilities by only one player; IV–II, blockade with airlift, figured prominently in U.S. contingency planning but was not seen as a possibility by Khrushchev. As with our 2×2 matrices, Option I means either compromise (I, I) or yield (I, II or II, I).

The corresponding subjective matrices are given in Figures 2–48 and 2–49. The subjective matrices of Clay, Acheson, Kozlov, etc., were different again.

Khrushchev's strategy was to stand on II, threatening a move to III. His hope was that the U.S. realists would then move to I, whereupon he in turn would move to I. The risk in strategy III was that the United States would move to III (ignore the treaty) and impose an unacceptable payoff of 7 in the hope of forcing the Soviet Union to back down to I—e.g., guarantee continued Western presence in Berlin. Because of this risk, Khrushchev was most reluctant actually to play III and was willing to move directly from II, II to I, I via negotiations. At I, I the United States has no incentive to escalate because 11 is a

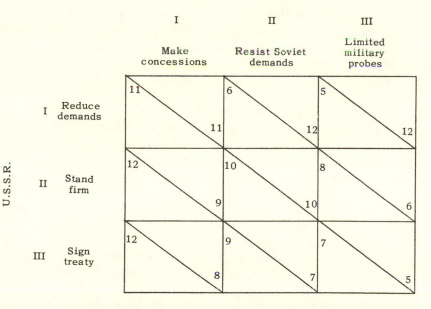

Figure 2-48. Khrushchev's Subjective Matrix

UNITED STATES

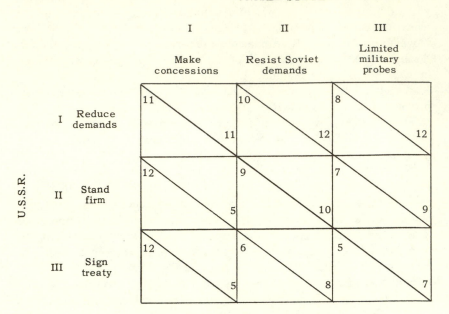

Figure 2-49. Dulles's Subjective Matrix

very good payoff; at III, II the United States might escalate because of the poor payoff. Khrushchev postponed his announced move as long as possible, waiting for a U.S. commitment to play I. The matrix does not apply after March 1961 or so.

The crisis did not go according to Khrushchev's plan because the U.S. estimates of its payoffs and of the strategic alternatives were different from Khrushchev's estimates.

This example brings out several characteristics of empirically derived expanded models. First, the expansion beyond III, III is principally or entirely along the main diagonal; the secondary corner areas are not empirically relevant except possibly as routes of retreat. Second, the reason is that expansion consists empirically of escalation. The possibility of escalation is always implicitly present in a crisis. Bargainers are aware of the possibility as a vague risk, but they do not construct a complete escalation ladder in their strategic thinking, planning only a step or two ahead. Third, some expanded models will consist of Prisoner's Dilemma expanded into Chicken by escalation, as in the above example; others consist of Chicken expanded into *PD*. Fourth, the typical escalation ladder after 1945 has about four areas: negotiations, or accommodative bargaining (*CC*); coercive bargaining

(*DD*) including non-violent probes, threats, marshaling of alliance support, troop movements, small faits accompli, etc.; limited violence over a short time period (*EE*); full war. *EE* may have several steps. Before 1945 the ladder had only three stages, omitting the limited violence stage. The first two stages are the normal bargaining area with which we are concerned, and the third and fourth stages are the action game. Escalation to the third stage and beyond becomes a possibility only if bargaining breaks down in *DD* or time runs out in some way. Even then escalation into violence, into the action game, is not automatic but requires a separate, painful decision.

Because expanded models focus entirely on escalation, their usefulness would seem to depend on the relative importance of escalation in crisis bargaining. We find that the possibility of escalation is always present in adversary crises; it enters into calculations and provides an essential basis for coercive tactics, including warnings, threats, guarantees, alliance support, and military buildups. However, all our statesmen except Hitler are extremely reluctant to move into the action game, even when they have promised or threatened or committed themselves to do so. The escalation ladder beyond *DD* thus serves as a forbidden danger area, by reference to which the bargainers make threats and clarify their own risks, as in the Khrushchev example, but not as an area into which they enter freely and in which they maneuver confidently. But this means that in our cases coercive tactics that threaten or allude to the danger of escalation are of enormously greater importance than actual escalation tactics. Recent escalation theory, therefore, provides little or no clarification of crisis bargaining as it has actually been practiced in the twentieth century.

Another difficulty with the expanded matrix is the empirical status of the options listed in it. This question arises immediately when one is constructing an expanded matrix for a specific crisis. Does one list all the potentialities for escalation that were inherent in the situation, as seen by 20–20 hindsight? Or does one list only the alternatives that were actually perceived and considered by decision makers as they formulated their strategies?

The first approach has some value for locating "blind spots" in decision makers' calculations, for specifying alternatives that might plausibly have been considered but were not, hence stimulating research on the question, why not? Such a usage would highlight one party's failure to conceive of certain options being available to the opponent and thus unprepared with a response when such an option is chosen. A good example would be the U.S. failure to conceive of the Wall as a Soviet-East German option in 1961. More ambitiously, one might try to list options and possibilities that were not perceived by either side:

the consequent "why not" question might throw light on actual perceptions and decisions. The fact that an option is not perceived could help to explain why another one was perceived and chosen.

While the first approach would thus have value for some purposes, the second seems to have the most utility for empirical research, since it attempts to portray the situation as the actors see it. What *they* see, what they introduce into their own calculations has the most direct bearing on their own behavior. But if we adopt this approach, we find that the alternatives are not perceived as spread out before the decision maker at the start of a crisis, waiting for a decision. They are usually devised one or two at a time, to deal with the situation as perceived at that time; but the situation changes, and as it does, new alternatives pop up and others drop out of consideration. Thus if the expanded matrix is taken to mean that the decision makers have all those alternatives and potential outcomes in mind at the start of the crisis, and do all their calculating, at the beginning and subsequently, with this complete picture in their hands, the model is misleading. One might correct this by specifying that the model shows all the options and consequences that were considered at some time during the crisis, further specifying the point at which each was first perceived or overtaken by events. Then one would have a crude picture of what was actually in the minds of the actors at any stage in the development of the crisis. But for a clear picture, a matrix of this sort probably would have to be broken up into matrices for each time segment, which might grow rather unwieldy.

A more serious difficulty is the problem of ignorance and misperception. Neither we, the historians, nor the participants could reconstruct accurately the lists of alternatives on both sides, assuming such lists existed. The lack of data for us, the researchers, was particularly acute for just those crises to which the expanded model would hypothetically be most appropriate, those since 1945. The paucity of information about Soviet and Chinese internal decision making needs no comment, but in most cases, even U.S. internal data—e.g., on the Berlin contingency plans—are not fully available. As for the participants, not only did they not know the opponent's options, they did not even perceive him as choosing among three or four alternatives; they perceived him as having already decided on a detailed course of action, but as subject to deflection or frustration by a well-chosen move.

Among our cases, only in the Cuban missile crisis, and in that case for one side only, can we say with some confidence that all the major options were out on the table at or near the beginning of the crisis. The U.S. decision makers rather thoroughly canvassed five or six options more or less simultaneously and came up with the blockade. They weighed the costs, advantages, and risks of other options, carrying their calculations out sometimes two or three moves and countermoves ahead. (If we bomb the missile sites, the Russians will hit the Turkish sites or take Berlin, this would require U.S. retaliation against missile sites or airbases in Russia in the first case, a general European war in the second. After this nuclear war would be very likely.) But even in this crisis, the actual course chosen, the blockade, did not emerge in the calculations until the other options had been pretty thoroughly explored and found wanting. And one reason why we see the options rather clearly from the start on the U.S. side is that the U.S. leaders managed to "stop the clock," so to speak—i.e., keep their deliberations secret from the opponent so that they were not really interacting with him while they were deliberating. Had it been otherwise, their array of options, and their calculations, would have been much less complete at the start and would have emerged out of evolving events. Of course, even in this crisis the "clock did not stop" for the Soviet Union, so its list of alternatives undoubtedly had to be devised in sequence in a much more haphazard way: furthermore in studying the Soviets we run into the second difficulty mentioned—simple lack of information about their decision-making process.

Despite the modest fit in the Cuban case, we conclude that the expanded matrix has less descriptive utility than the simpler 2×2 or 3×3 matrices. It does not describe either the objective or the subjective situation realistically. It pretends to list actual or nearly actual alternatives, but these usually do not exist as an array of comparable alternatives either at the start of the crisis or at any point during its progress. It pictures the players as maneuvering against each other by successive choices in a matrix of possibilities, but they neither act this way nor perceive the opponent as acting this way. It portrays crises as escalation–de-escalation contests, and thus tends to exaggerate the importance of escalation in crisis bargaining.

What we need is not a static chess board that shows the complete set of options and considerations upon which the parties base their calculations from the start, but a model that takes account of the continual *transformation of the situation*. The 2×2 matrix, or at most 3×3 (explicitly showing the action game), allows for this. It points to the clarification of the situation resulting from P and T-search as well as S and R-search and says that that is what a crisis is about. The smaller matrix makes more modest claims and thus is less misleading. It cannot pretend to describe actual strategies, but provides only an abstract structure, which is filled in by actual strategies. The numbers then represent the actual strategic situation at the time without pretending to list an imaginary complete set of "alternatives." The 2×2

or 3×3 matrix still has several serious deficiencies, but for all its simplicity it proves to be more realistic and flexible than the unwieldy static expanded matrix. On the other hand, the expanded game model has a definite use, to clarify the escalation process and possibilities in some cases, for which it should be retained.

THE METAGAME

Despite the claims made by some that the metagame is *the* key to conflict analysis, our attempts to apply metagame concepts to crisis data were unsatisfactory. First, the "analysis of options" technique meets the same difficulty as the expanded matrix, only more so. An analysis of options for A consists roughly of taking one of A's options and running through the list of B's possible replies, A's possible replies to these, etc. The strength of the technique is that it enables one to accomplish this seemingly endless task quite rapidly. But if the options are not all spread out before A, if A misestimates B's options and preference ordering, and if A or B or both, being committees, do not make decisions in this fashion, then the analysis is pretty hypothetical. If an analysis of options is applied to decision makers *during* a crisis, it can have the effect of inducing them to search for neglected options and perhaps even to make a decision in the manner required by metagame theory, but this is a normative rather than an empirical use of the analysis.

Metagame theory seems most useful in illuminating the notion of a "stable settlement." A settlement is stable if it dominates all other options for all bargainers, that is if no side has any option available that would improve its own position. In practice this means that a settlement is stable if each side has a sanction available that can punish any attempt by another bargainer to improve his position unilaterally. This proposition seems intuitively plausible and even important at first. Bargaining is not simply a matter of reaching agreement; it is a matter of finding an agreement that cannot be unilaterally broken, an agreement that each bargainer can defend. For example, Chamberlain and Hitler easily reached agreement September 30, 1938, to settle their future differences by negotiation; but Britain had no sanction available in case Hitler chose to ignore the agreement, so it did not settle anything. In contrast, the Munich agreement of the previous day had implicit sanctions attached: if Hitler chose to attack Czechoslovakia on October 1 as scheduled, he knew he would be at war with France and Britain, in domestic turmoil or revolt, and without alliance support—and all to no purpose, since he was getting Sudetenland free of charge anyway.

Despite this initial plausibility, the concept of a settlement that is stable because it dominates all other options is inadequate and misleading. It fails because of the assumption that the option set is given at any one time. An agreement may dominate all known options but be dominated by some option not yet devised; in this case the agreement will last only until the new option is devised.

A settlement is stable, then, not because it dominates all known options, but because it both dominates them *and* ends the search for better options. But the search for better options ends when an agreement is satisfactory to all sides, that is, when it meets the minimum aspiration level of each bargainer. An unsatisfactory agreement may dominate all *existing* alternative options; that is, the defeated party may be unable to better his position by breaking the agreement *at that time,* but he will continue searching for five, ten, twenty years until he finds a way to improve his unsatisfactory position.

We have several examples of agreements that dominated known options but were unsatisfactory and did not last. The 1906 Algeciras agreement was the best option for Germany at the time, since the choice was between a humiliating defeat, diplomatic outlaw status, and a war against France and Britain. But since a humiliating defeat was unsatisfactory, the lesson Germany learned was to increase its military strength and strengthen its alliance bonds so it could avoid further colonial humiliation by France. The result was the second Morocco crisis. Other examples: the 1909 Bosnian agreement was unsatisfactory to both Serbia and Russia, hence the Russian rearmament program; the 1912 Balkan agreement was unsatisfactory to all four belligerents, hence the 1913 war; Munich 1938, did not satiate Hitler's ambitions, and the 1949 Berlin agreement did not solve the Soviet problem with West Berlin. Other well-known unsatisfactory agreements were Versailles, 1919, the Saar agreement of 1945, the various Palestine agreements, and the 1973 pseudo-agreement in Vietnam.

In general, a compromise settlement is likely to be more stable then a unilateral backdown outcome because the compromise involves a resolution of the underlying conflict of interest. That is, when a settlement is arrived at by a process of give-and-take, it carries a tacit legitimacy, and both parties achieve their minimum level of aspiration. In contrast a settlement by back-down leaves the loser frustrated; he bides his time pending accumulation of power sufficient to raise the issue again.

The implication is that one should understand settlements not by analyzing known options but by investigating levels of aspiration and their determinants. We contribute to such an investigation in Chapter V.

THE INTERNATIONAL SUPERGAME

The supergame model presented earlier (p. 61) turned out to be useful but it was not "super" enough for our purposes. We wanted a more comprehensive model that would subsume all the 2×2 games previously discussed, show how they relate to each other logically, and locate them in the context of more general, long-term relations between states. In short, we wanted no less than a model of the strategic dynamics of the international system as a whole that would show how the play of crisis games fits into these larger dynamics. Since such a model does not exist in the literature, we had to invent one. We then found, in pleased surprise, that the typical supergame model in the game theory literature fitted naturally into our own creation as one of its dimensions. What we are about to present can thus be considered an enlargement of existing supergame theory applied to international relations.

We started with the familiar assumption that nation-states exist in a condition of "anarchy"; there is no super-ordinate authority that can enforce order and provide security. This condition places them in a "security dilemma": for security against attack by others, each state must look to its own power and diplomacy; but unilateral security measures are at least partly self-defeating because power accumulation by one or some states will appear threatening to others, causing them to feel more insecure and to accumulate power themselves, which in turn increases the insecurity of those who initiated the competition, and so on in a vicious circle. This tragic outcome is similar to the logic of the Prisoner's Dilemma: all-around cooperation is the best collective solution, but this outcome is not possible since each party fears that its own attempt to cooperate will be exploited by others. Thus each is driven to "defect" from cooperation (i.e., to accumulate power) in order to be secure against the potential defection of others. The result, of course, is that all defect, and the outcome is all-around competition, which is a worse condition for all than general cooperation, but not as bad as being double-crossed while attempting to cooperate.[40] It appeared, therefore, that the Prisoner's Dilemma was the appropriate model for our grand supergame. We assumed, however, consistent with both laboratory experimentation and diplomatic history, that some states, some of the time, can escape the logically dominant "DD trap" and cooperate profitably at CC. Security, in other words, may be obtained cooperatively as well as competitively, e.g., by adversaries agreeing to settle disputes or to moderate their power competition.

Strategic [41] activity in the supergame has three dimensions: armament,

[40] The Prisoner's Dilemma we are discussing here is the familiar type in which there is some advantage in defecting first if one fears defection by others. Its dynamics are therefore different from those of the Prisoner's Dilemma bargaining games discussed earlier, in which there is no such preemptive incentive to defect and therefore no "dilemma." The latter games appear, however, as episodic encounters within the supergame, as will be shown presently.

[41] The word *strategic* denotes that we are focusing here on behavior designed

alliance formation, and "adversary action." Competitive activity in the first two is obvious enough: armament is an internal means of accumulating power vs. opponents; alliance formation is an external means—the pooling of power with others. Adversary action refers essentially to the acquisition of additional power resources through expansion, carried out by the use or threat of military force, or conversely, to the resistance to others' expansion by similar means. If we look at each dimension from the cooperative point of view, security may be obtained in the armaments dimension by agreed upon measures of arms control and limitation, in the adversary action dimension by détente or rapprochement with an opponent, and in the alliance dimension, theoretically, by a collective security arrangement that obviates the need for competitive coalition building. Although, for simplicity, we say that the basic value of security is the only value involved in the three dimensions, states do of course pursue other values, either competitively or cooperatively.

We considered the alternative of the N-person game as the appropriate model for our supergame. Crises, wars, and settlements might then be viewed as "decision points" at which payoffs are awarded to winning coalitions and distributed among their members, and losses (negative payoffs) are similarly suffered and apportioned by losing coalitions. However, we rejected this approach because it would have meant postulating the alliance dimension as the dominant dimension of the supergame. Clearly the action game is dominant; alliances as well as armament are only means for accumulating power for potential action against an opponent. However, we do consider the N-person game the appropriate model for the coalition dimension of the supergame, and we will employ some "N-person logic" in Chapter VI to explain alliance elements in our crises, and also in Chapter V to analyze bureaucratic bargaining.

We conceive the overall supergame as a network of interdependent two-person supergames between each pair of major actors in the system. Each of these two-person games tends to be a Prisoner's Dilemma. This is most clearly seen if we imagine, first, a system containing only one pair. Each member of the pair fears attack by the other. Out of such fear, each member seeks security by accumulating power, either by armament or by expansion at the other's expense—i.e., each plays D, and they wind up in the DD cell in their supergame, which is the normal outcome of a Prisoner's Dilemma. In such a system, the extreme form of bipolarity, relations would normally take the form of con-

---

to increase or preserve security or power position as the central activity in international relations; economic competition and other non-strategic aspects of international relations are excluded.

tinuing rivalry and competitive struggle for power in the preparedness and action dimensions. If we imagine now a system of several actors with equal power potential (ideal-type multipolarity) each actor sees all others as potential enemies, but also as potential allies. Coalition-formation is introduced as a means of accumulating power. Each state is in a two-person supergame with each other state, but it is now likely that some pairs will move into a *CC* relationship via alliance to increase their power and security in their *DD* relationships with common opponents. Realignment with a former opponent, against a former ally, shifts the relationship to *CC* with the former and to *DD* with the latter. In other words, when two states form an alliance, they simultaneously "play *C*" in their supergame with each other and play *D* against the target of the alliance. Thus, some of the dyadic supergames are linked via tacit or formal alliances, and the typical dynamics of the *N*-person game—coalition formation and dissolution—are transmuted into shifts between *CC* and *DD* in the two-party supergames.

The alliance dimension of the supergame also is essentially a Prisoner's Dilemma. Alliances are burdensome, and all actors would prefer the freedom and independence of "isolation." But when others may ally against oneself (play *D*), to abstain from alliance may be to invite disaster. Hence states are driven to seek allies out of the familiar Prisoner's Dilemma incentive "If I don't, he might, therefore I must." The result is a generalized competition for allies (the *DD* outcome), which is worse for all than *CC*, general abstention from the competition, but better for each than abstaining when others do not.

The Prisoner's Dilemma character of the adversary action dimension is seen most simply in the necessity to resist the adversary's attempt to expand lest he become powerful enough to attack one's own state successfully. His use of force or threat of force against others is a play of *D*, which there is a considerable incentive to counter. The aphorisms "the cause of war is war itself" [42] and "better to fight them now than later" both express the general Prisoner's Dilemma compulsion to take the second worst in order to avoid the worst. Crises short of war may or may not be Prisoner's Dilemmas in themselves, depending on the values involved, but the resistance that makes them crises reflects the defensive Prisoner's Dilemma incentives in the supergame. The offensive incentive shows up in the temptation to increase power when easy opportunities present themselves. Power "vacuums" tend to be filled competitively, if only to preempt the rival from filling them unilaterally. Thus the Soviet Union asserted control over the Eastern

[43] R. G. Hawtrey, *Economic Aspects of Sovereignty* (London: Longmans, Green and Co., 1930), p. 105. Hawtrey's meaning is that most wars are fought chiefly to preserve or increase one's capacity to fight future wars.

European countries after World War II largely to preempt their moving into the orbit of the United States or a possibly resurgent Germany; the United States responded with an alliance with inevitable hegemonial overtones. Germany itself became divided because arrangements for four-power control (CC) could not withstand the compulsion on the controllers to "defect" by asserting unilateral control over their own zones. In an earlier period, collaborative attempts to keep the "sick man of Europe"—the Ottoman Empire—alive as long as possible finally broke down beginning in 1911 as one rival after another sought to grab its share of the carcass before someone else did. Generally rivals' competition for power and security places them in the DD area of the supergame, and they find it difficult to move into, or stay in, the CC area because of mutual mistrust. They may succeed in settling some of their disputes, moving to the relationship of détente. But détentes are fragile as long as the basic relationship is one of rivalry, and the pair are subject to a persistent pull back deeper into the DD area by the conflicts which still divide them.

Figures 2–50 and 2–51 show two versions of the supergame model. Figure 2–50 is an impressionistic version that displays verbally various kinds of relations that may exist between the players and the types of crisis or alliance bargaining episodes (subgames) that are likely to be played in each type of relation. This is not technically a "game" since no payoffs are shown. Figure 2–51 is a true game, an expanded Prisoner's Dilemma, which specifies payoffs for any point, i.e., any particular relationship that the parties are in, in any of the four quadrants of Figure 2–50. It does not, however, show payoffs for the episodic subgames within parentheses in Figure 2–50. Figure 2–51 may be superimposed over Figure 2–50, or vice-versa. Since the two matrices represent substantially the same things empirically, the term *supergame* in the following discussion refers to either one, unless otherwise specified.

The supergame, in our empirical interpretation, has two variables; degree of conflict of interest and relative power. The conflict variable appears on the NW-SE diagonal. Movement SE to NW represents decreasing conflict between the parties. The relative power variable lies on the NE-SW diagonal. Power is equal at the midpoint of the matrix, highly unequal favoring A at the extreme SW corner, unequal favoring B at the NE corner, with gradations of inequality in between. Power is defined as "political power" consisting of asymmetries of dependence between allies and inequalities of military capability and resolve between adversaries.

Thus any point at which the parties find themselves within the matrix represents the confluence of the two variables: the degree of conflict (or

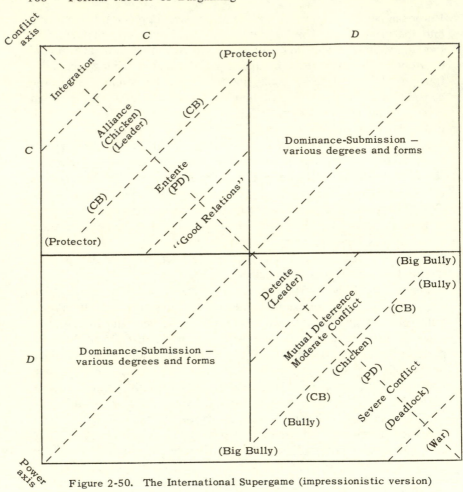

Figure 2-50. The International Supergame (impressionistic version)

harmony) between them, and their relative power positions. As we move down the NW-SE diagonal, the parties' relations change through increasing degrees of conflict, but they remain roughly equal in power. Similarly as we move from SW to NE, power relations change but the degree of conflict does not.

In Figure 2–50, the labels in the quadrants that are not in parentheses represent different types of general relations on the conflict-harmony dimension, the NW-SE diagonal. *CC* is the cooperative quadrant, in which conflict is generally low and common interests are predominant. In the lower right-hand corner, the parties are experiencing "good rela-

Conflict axis

	C				D			
C	6, 6	4, 7	2, 8	0, 9	−2, 10	−4, 11	−6, 12	−8, 13
	7, 4	5, 5	3, 6	1, 7	−1, 8	−3, 9	−5, 10	−7, 11
	8, 2	6, 3	4, 4	2, 5	0, 6	−2, 7	−4, 8	−6, 9
	9, 0	7, 1	5, 2	3, 3	1, 4	−1, 5	−3, 6	−5, 7
D	10, −2	8, −1	6, 0	4, 1	2, 2	0, 3	−2, 4	−4, 5
	11, −4	9, −3	7, −2	5, −1	3, 0	1, 1	−1, 2	−3, 3
	12, −6	10, −5	8, −4	6, −3	4, −2	2, −1	0, 0	−2, 1
	13, −8	11, −7	9, −6	7, −5	5, −4	3, −3	1, −2	−1, −1

Power axis

Figure 2-51. The International Supergame (technical version)

tions." Their conflicts are minor; they are generally behaving cooperatively; but they have no strategic common interest in defense against a
third-party threat, hence they do not perceive themselves as allies or
even incipient allies. The entente relationship is that of incipient or
tentative alliance. The parties have resolved all significant conflicts of
interest; they do feel a common interest in opposing the ambitions of
some opponent; but they have not formalized this common interest.
In the category "alliance," the common interest has been formalized
in a contract that specifies the conditions and contingencies of common
action. The "integration" category is mentioned mainly for completeness. The parties have so many interests in common, beyond common
defense vis-à-vis an opponent, that they believe the partial or full

integration of their economies and policies will most fully realize these values. There is no necessary link between "alliance" and "integration" since integration may develop out of a sense of community or values other than security. However, security alliances, and integration centered on other values, may be mutually supporting, as between the United States and Britain or among the West European countries.

Pairs whose relations are in the *DD* quadrant clearly identify each other as adversaries, but they experience this relationship with varying degrees of intensity. In the upper left corner, détente is a relation in which the parties see themselves basically as rivals, but they have settled some of their particular conflicts and have agreed generally to dampen their competition so as to realize and maximize common interests. That is, they have managed to overcome to a considerable extent the inherent compulsion of rivals to play *D* strategies and have moved close to the *CC* quadrant. Moving SE, "mutual deterrence" reflects greater conflict, little collaborative behavior but also little conflict behavior of the "action" type. The parties have feelings of mutual hostility, engage in competitive armament and alliance building and have disputes that, however, seldom reach crisis proportions. The next relational category, severe conflict, is the one where most crises occur. Finally, conflict is most extreme, of course, in war.

Movement on the NW-SE diagonal could also be described in terms of increasing or decreasing *interdependence,* a general concept that correlates with both conflict of interest and political power, and thus provides a link between the two supergame variables. Interdependence means that the parties are dependent on each other for the preservation or realization of important values. In the *CC* quadrant, interdependence is low with merely "good relations" since the parties perceive no third-party threat that makes them need military aid from the other. In entente, such a threat is perceived, though perhaps uncertainly, and the parties are interdependent to a higher degree. Interdependence is greater in an alliance, since then the outside threat is clearly perceived and the parties have reduced the availability of alternatives to their present alignment by formalizing the relationship.

The interdependence between allies is also a function of the unresolved conflicts among them; each is dependent on the other's goodwill in settling them, though there is a tendency for their interdependence in opposition to a common opponent to dampen these intramural conflicts. Interdependence is very high in an integrated relationship, though perhaps in terms of values other than, or in addition to, security.

Directly on the NW-SE diagonal, the interdependence is symmetrical, whether high or low—the parties need each other equally much. Away from this diagonal, it is asymmetrical: one party needs the alliance or entente more than the other. Asymmetrical dependence is equivalent to asymmetrical political power; hence changing asymmetry of dependence is equivalent to movement parallel to the NE-SW axis of the supergame.

Adversaries located in the *DD* quadrant are also interdependent, but in a different way. They are interdependent, first, in the amount of harm and loss each could inflict on the other in war—i.e., the continued enjoyment of certain values currently held depends on the other's refraining from destroying them or taking them. Opponents are interdependent also via their conflict of interest; realization of one's interests is dependent on the acquiescence of the other. In the *DD* quadrant, interdependence increases symmetrically with SE movement for either or both of the above reasons—conflict of interest increases and perhaps mutual capacity to harm as well. Indeed, the normal tendency is for mutual increases in military power to exacerbate conflict, in contrast to the alliance relation, where increasing interdependence tends to moderate conflict between the allies. The capacity to harm physically or to threaten harm, in the adversary relationship, and the capacity to withhold support or to threaten non-support, in an alliance relation, are analogous sources of political power. In the adversary quadrant, too, dependence becomes asymmetrical (power becomes unequal) at locations away from the NW-SE diagonal, i.e., with movement parallel to the opposite diagonal.

The various power-dependence relations that are possible in the alliance or adversary relations are not shown in Figure 2–50. They do appear in Figure 2–51, however, in the increasing gap between the payoffs for each party, as they move away from the NW-SE diagonal in either direction.

Extremes of dependence are shown in the *CD* and *DC* quadrants of Figure 2–50 as the domination of one party by another in a hegemonial or imperialist relationship. Figure 2–51 makes clear the degrees of domination that may be involved, and also shows that they lie on a continuum with the lesser power inequalities in the *CC* or *DD* quadrants.

We may locate various contemporary relations at appropriate points in the matrix. The United States' relationship with each of the West European countries is about in the center of the *CC* quadrant on the conflict axis and a bit to the right of center on the power axis (some degree of U.S. dominance). With the Latin-American countries the relationship is further NE (greater dominance) on the power axis. The United States–Canada and Soviet–Finland positions are near the boundary of the *CC* and *CD* quadrants (cooperation with strong elements of dominance). The relations between the Soviet Union and the Eastern European Communist countries (except Yugoslavia) might be located just over the boundary into the dominance (*CD*) quadrant. Yugoslavia is in an ambiguous relationship, somewhere between détente and "good relations" with both the Soviet Union and the United States. The United States and Soviet Union are in a détente position at the present time, and the United States and China are in the "good relations" area, but the emergence of each pair from its previous *DD* competitive stance is still tentative and unstable. Typically a détente *is* unstable, tending to move either upward toward entente or alliance or downward into *DD* competition. Conceivably, if the present international system is evolving toward multipolarity, the relations between any power in this triangle could move further "upward" toward entente or implicit alliance, but this is unlikely to happen for some time.

The play of the supergame is best described by reference to Figure 2–51, which brings out clearly its prisoner's dilemma dynamics. The parties do not move in huge leaps from *C* to *D* or vice versa (as might be implied by Figure 2–50), but gradually step-by-step. For example, state *A* buys an increment of armament to which state *B* responds in kind, then *A* builds another increment, and so on. Or *A* makes a move toward alignment with third party *X,* which *B* may counter, leading to a tightening of the *A-X* connection, etc. These are moves away from *C* toward *D,* or from a moderate *D* posture to a more extreme one. Movement may take place in the opposite direction as well, when a party seeks to reduce conflict. In any case, adversaries normally are located in one of the cells in the *DD* quadrant, while allies or tentative allies will be somewhere in the *CC* quadrant. The numbers in the cells represent the values and costs the parties derive from the particular relation they are in at any given time, e.g., security or insecurity, alliance risks, preparedness costs. These are not payoffs from any particular interaction episode, such as a crisis, but payoffs from a *relationship,* enjoyed or suffered in a continuing stream through time, until the relationship changes, at which time the payoffs also change.

There are two dynamics in the game, corresponding to two possible directions of movement: either up the NW-SE diagonal, or away from this diagonal parallel to the NE-SW axis. Starting from any cell, upward NW movement reduces conflict or increases realization of common interests, as shown by the increasing payoffs for both parties. Movement away from this diagonal in either direction—i.e., up or down along the NE-SW diagonal—increases power inequality, as shown by the widening gap between the parties' payoffs with such movement. But each type of movement tends to be frustrated by a countertendency. A unilateral attempt to increase power (perhaps in fear of unilateral increase by the other) prompts the opponent to counter, and the result is no change in relative power. A unilateral attempt to reduce conflict is frustrated by an opponent who exploits the attempt in order to improve his relative power position.

To illustrate: if *B,* starting from the upper left cell of the *DD* quadrant (with payoffs of 2, 2) attempts to increase his relative power by moving right, *A* is likely to respond by moving down and the result is increased conflict (SE movement to 1, 1) with no change in relative power. This dynamic was predominant during the Cold War period and between the Triple Alliance and Triple Entente in the decade before 1914. Or, if *A,* starting from the 1, 1 cell representing moderate conflict, attempts to move upward to détente at 2, 2, the attempt will be frustrated unless *B* reciprocates by moving left. Since *B* gets a better payoff (3) by standing pat, he is likely not to move, leaving *A* not only frustrated but in a poorer relative power position. *A* then logically corrects his misplaced optimism by moving back down to 1, 1. This was the predominant dynamic in the relations between Chamberlain's England and Hitler's Germany during the 1930s.

Thus the logical tendency, for adversaries, is to move SE in the *DD* quadrant, or at least not to move NW. These are the normal dynamics of the Prisoner's Dilemma. However, the parties may be able to move from 1, 1 to 2, 2 and stay there, frustrating the countertendency, if they sufficiently fear the consequences of further power competition. This seems to have been the case with the current United States–Soviet détente, although the SE pull is obvious. In a multipolar system, if *A* and *B* are at 1, 1 and both perceive a threat from *X,* then NW movement is not frustrated since a payoff higher than standing pat is visible at the 4, 4 or 5, 5 cells in the *CC* quadrant—the increased security payoff to be had from alliance. However, the countertendency appears as SE movement in the supergames that *A* and *B* are playing with *X* and *X*'s allies. And if the perceived threat from *X* declines, say by the settlement of disputes with him constituting NW movement in the game with *X,* then the payoff from the *AB* alliance will decline, the conflicts between *A* and *B* will become more salient, and they will be pulled back SE-ward into the *DD* quadrant of their own supergame. Thus we see how the dyadic supergames are dynamically linked: reduced conflict in one or some is accompanied by increased conflict in others. The linkage appears in a bipolar system as well as in a multipolar one: we note how the U.S.–Soviet détente has increased the level of conflict within the alliance systems of both superpowers, although a complete change of role from ally to adversary does not occur.

The crisis and alliance games described earlier in this chapter appear within this framework as episodic subgames in the *CC* and *DD* quadrants of the supergame, each associated with a particular kind of general relationship. Their outcomes yield payoffs of two kinds: intrinsic gains or losses not closely associated with the long-term strategic relationship of the parties, and other values which *are,* and which therefore enlarge or reduce the continuous stream of values deriving from the relationship, or change the nature of the relation. Between adversaries, among the "supergame values" are military power resources on territory gained or lost and "reputation for resolve," both of which affect the likelihood and likely outcome of future crises. Other supergame values are associated with settlements that reduce the general level of conflict, and with failures to settle a disputed issue. Between allies, prominent supergame values are "reputation for loyalty" and reduction in alliance dependence. Of course there are other kinds of subgames besides crises; e.g., non-crisis disputes or wars in the *DD* quadrant, and bargaining episodes over the scope of commitment or sharing of defense contributions between allies in the *CC* area. Before a crisis or other type of encounter, the parties are located at a certain cell in either the *DD* or *CC* quadrants of the supergame, defined roughly as their relative power or dependence and the degree of conflict between them; the encounter reflects these prior relations, and its outcome may change the relations— i.e., move the parties to a different cell. Crises and their outcomes may be considered a primary source (though not the only source) of movement in the "adversary action" dimension of the supergame.

The 2 × 2 subgames appear in parentheses in Figure 2–50, in the general area of conflict-power relations where each is likely to occur. The adversary crisis games are shown in the *DD* quadrant in the area of "severe conflict" relations. Moving NW-SE, we move from Chicken through Prisoner's Dilemma to Deadlock. The movement reflects increasing conflict of interest while power relations remain roughly in balance. In the Chicken game, the degree of conflict is relatively low since both parties would rather accede to the other's demands than fight or risk a war. Logically, a settlement is fairly easy to achieve. In Prisoner's Dilemma the degree of conflict is greater. Both sides prefer war or risk of war to giving in to the other's demands. Compromise is possible, however, and both prefer compromise to war. But a settlement is harder to reach than in Chicken because of the greater conflict of interest. In Deadlock, the conflict of interest is so deep that no settlement is possible; any conceivable settlement would be unacceptable to at least one of the parties, i.e., it is considered worse than war, so war is the inevitable outcome.

The asymmetric 2 × 2 games are located to the left and right of the NW-SE diagonal because they reflect substantial asymmetry in bargaining power; i.e., they reflect a power advantage for one player or the other along the NE-SW "power axis." In Called Bluff, where the asymmetry is moderate, the party with a *PD* preference structure is enough stronger in military resources and/or has enough greater interest in the disputed object to be willing to stand firm at the risk of war, whereas his opponent is not. But there is still some possibility of compromise, with the chicken party getting the worst of it. Moving further NE (or SW), we come to Bully, where the bully is so far superior in power that he would rather fight than concede anything substantial, while the chicken party is so weak that he would rather concede everything than fight. Moving still further up or down the power diagonal, we reach Big Bully, where the stronger party prefers war to achieving even his maximum bargaining demands. We place Big Bully athwart the boundary between the *DD* and *CD* (*DC*) quadrants of the supergame because the bully's apparent "bargaining" is designed only to establish a pretext for the use of force to dominate the victim completely.

The alliance subgames are shown in parentheses in the *CC* quadrant. They may occur as non-crisis disputes between allies, as well as during crises with adversaries. Those centered on the NW-SE diagonal are games in which bargaining power is relatively equal. That is, each ally is equally dependent on the other though the degree of interdependence varies. For example, in an alliance Chicken game, interdependence is high; neither party can afford to risk alliance break-up or non-support from the other, so disputes between them are likely to be settled by one party's giving in or by compromise—logically by compromise, since bargaining power is equal. In alliance PD there is less interdependence; alliance break-up is not as disastrous as in Chicken because each of the parties has greater independent power vis-à-vis the adversary. In a dispute, each party prefers alliance dissolution to accepting the other's terms in full. Still, both prefer continued collaboration to dissolution, so the dispute is likely to be compromised. *PD* subgames are placed in the area of the entente relationship in the diagram because, presumably, informal or quasi-allies are less dependent on each other than formal ones. This may not always be the case, however; before 1914, Britain was more interdependent with France and Russia than Italy was with her formal allies, Austria and Germany.

Asymmetric alliance subgames are those in which one ally is significantly more dependent on the alliance than is the other. Hence they are located NE and SW of the center on the power axis. In Called Bluff, alliance version, the asymmetry is moderate: one party needs the alliance less than its partner and consequently has preponderant bargaining power but not so much that it is able to dominate the partner or call the tune completely in alliance conflicts. But in Protector, the alliance analog to Bully, the asymmetry is extreme: the protecting party has virtually complete control over the client's foreign policy and thus over the policy of the alliance. Protector is therefore placed near the boundary between the *CD* and *DC* quadrants. Protector relationships, as between the United States and Taiwan, or the Soviet Union and the

Eastern European countries, may be equivalent to, or may evolve into, an imperial relationship. That is, the parties may move into the *CD* or *DC* quadrants.

Leader is a special subgame that typically is played high on the NW-SE diagonal—i.e., when alliance interdependence is high. Its structure is similar to Chicken, the principal difference being that there is no empirical possibility of compromising the issue in dispute. One party grabs the lead, and the other must follow, since not following and acting independently yields a worse outcome than following. As discussed in an earlier section, Leader games may also occur in détente, when the rival-partners prefer different strategies for realizing collaborative projects but will still accept the other's strategy rather than sacrifice the détente itself.

The formal supergame model discussed in the early part of this chapter (p. 62) can be adapted to represent movement on either the power or conflict axes of the more comprehensive supergame we have constructed here. That model, it will be recalled, was a sequence of subgames, with the *CC* and *DD* outcomes in each subgame carrying, besides their immediate payoff, a certain probability that the parties would move to a different subgame on the next play. Movement consisted of moving toward other games where cooperation was either easier or harder to achieve. Repeated successes in cooperation in one game produced an increasing likelihood of moving to another game where the rewards for cooperation were greater and the rewards for non-cooperation were lower, so that the incentives for cooperation were strengthened cumulatively. Conversely, non-cooperative (*DD*) outcomes increased the chances of moving to future games in which payoffs for cooperation were lower.

This game is a mathematical model of adversary action behavior on the NW-SE axis of our supergame. That is, the consequence of repeated crises might be that the parties, by successive compromise settlements, gradually reduce the amount of conflict of interest between them. When their interests are highly incompatible, crises between them may be Deadlock; if the incompatibility can be reduced to a moderate level, they are more likely to be Prisoner's Dilemma; if reduced further, crises will tend to be Chicken. Such NW movement need not occur only via crisis settlements but also from negotiated settlement of differences in a non-crisis context.

Movement can also go the other way, the degree of conflict increasing and the chance of peaceful settlement decreasing with each successive encounter. Something like this seems to have occurred in the sequence of crises between 1905 and 1914. Conflict between France and England, on the one hand, and Germany on the other, was increased by the 1905–1906 crisis, still further by the 1911 replay, and both contributed much to transforming the Entente Cordiale into a practical alliance directed at Germany. (Germany vis-à-vis the other two moved NW-SE on the conflict axis, while France vis-à-vis England moved SE-NW.) At the other end of the continent, the 1908 and 1912–1913 crises heightened conflict between Russia and Austria–Germany, failed to resolve the Austro–Serbian tension, and brought Russia more firmly into the entente. Again, the movement was heightened conflict and greater alliance solidarity. War developed out of this situation when a spark ignited a conflict that was becoming intolerable, and allies had become so interdependent that they could not restrain each other.

The model can also be adapted as a "power supergame," to represent adversary action movement along the opposite NE-SW axis of the grand supergame. In this version, the model would show cumulative changes in the power relations between the parties rather than changes in the amount of interest conflict and incentives to cooperate. This adaptation requires placing the "go to the next game" probabilities in the CD and DC cells rather than in CC and DD. In ordinary language, when a state loses a crisis, yields to the opponent's pressure, it loses not only the intrinsic values at stake, but also some of its power, whether in the form of material resources or reputation for resolve. If the adversary is expansionist-minded, this increases the probability that he will challenge again on some other issue; if the victim backs down again, he loses more power, and the chances of facing another challenge increase; and so on through the sequence until finally the challenger is in a position to impose his will easily and completely. In Figure 2–50 this corresponds to movement from crisis subgames of Chicken or PD to Called Bluff to Bully to Big Bully as power relations become more and more asymmetrical. The end-game in the sequence results in absolute domination by the stronger party—CD or DC in the comprehensive supergame. Of course, the weakening side may decide to call a halt to this process before the end-game is reached, at which point either the expansionist power is deterred or war results.

This version fits well the sequence of European crises in the 1930s. Hitler's material power, resolve, and contempt for the resolve of his adversaries progressively increased with several episodes of appeasement. His game in the Rhineland crisis was Chicken, but he believed it possible that France was in Prisoner's Dilemma or Bully; hence he instructed his generals to retreat if France intervened. He could have been stopped also in the 1938 crisis, when he was again playing Chicken. But by 1939 the "balance of resolve" had shifted so far in his favor that he saw himself as Bully or Big Bully and his opponents as Chicken. Then the British decided to call a halt, but Hitler's image of them as "worms" was now so firmly set that he could not be stopped. Unlike the pre-1914 series, the 1930s sequence ended in war because of a failure of deterrence, too little (defensive) coercion employed against a state whose expansionist aims went too long unrecognized.

The reader may have noticed on the power axis of the supergame a certain similarity with the familiar "domino theory." True, the model does reflect what is valid in the crude domino theory (which, incidentally, is a very old theory in international relations, though not as well articulated as its antithesis, the "balance of power"). What is valid about it is that successive victories for one side in crises and wars may indeed result in a cumulative shift in material power and resolve in favor of the victor. The supergame model improves upon it, makes it more precise, by specifying in the *CD* and *DC* cells the *probability* that the next domino will be pushed, and by reference to the structure of the next subgame in the sequence, the likelihood that it will fall. Thus, it is possible to construct a power supergame that represents a more moderate and sophisticated domino theory by showing various possibilities short of the inexorable collapse of the whole domino stack. For example, if the "go to the next game" probability assigned to yielding in the present encounter is placed (correctly) at zero or near zero, the next domino very probably does not fall. The model thus leaves room for the possibility (i.e., subjective expectation) that the adversary's aims are limited, that he will be satisfied with gaining his objectives in the present game, and push no further. Of course, the estimated probabilities may be quite wrong, as Chamberlain was wrong in putting the "go to next game" probability close to zero at Munich, and as Eisenhower was probably wrong in putting it close to 1.00 in Southeast Asia, 1954. Empirically, we find that decision makers either do not estimate such probabilities at all, or place them at near-zero or near-1.00.

A micro-version of the balance of power can also be linked to the power supergame. The idea of "balancing" here means stopping the opponent's accumulation of power and resolve before it goes too far. At any subgame in the sequence, the defender may foresee that another backdown will shift the power balance decisively against him, and that the adversary will take advantage of the shift. The "go to next game" probability then is high, and combined with the disastrous consequences that the defender sees in future games if he yields now, produces a very low payoff for yielding. His subgame structure, which might have been Chicken on the immediate stakes alone, becomes Prisoner's Dilemma. Then, of course, he stands firm, with the result that either the revisionist adversary retreats or he miscalculates and war results. A far-sighted defender who perceived the adversary as systematically expansionist would stand firm in the first game of the sequence, anticipating that firmness would be less credible and more dangerous the next time. This defender would be a Churchill rather than a Chamberlain type—which suggests the obvious point that the probabilities and payoffs in each subgame are subjective, depending heavily on a decision maker's image of the long-term intentions of the adversary.

In our crisis cases, the power supergame does not show up empirically as clear scenarios of sequences of future subgames, with precise estimates of payoffs and go-to-next game probabilities in each one. Rather it manifests itself much more crudely and qualitatively in the players' concern about the effects of the crisis outcome on their future power positions. That is, the players' knowledge that they are playing an infinite sequence of games introduces power values into their payoffs for the immediate game and thus affects the structure of that game. Such power values (to be distinguished from the intrinsic, non-instrumental values involved) include tangible power resources inherent in territory that may be given up or gained, the general image of resolve and willingness to take risks that is projected, and the loyalty of allies and the allies' beliefs about one's loyalty to them.

There are certain complexities involving interactions between the two subordinate supergames. It may not be at all clear to both participants which one they are playing, or one party may be playing one while the adversary is playing the other. Thus in the 1930s, Hitler was playing the power supergame while Chamberlain was playing the conflict-cooperation version. Chamberlain was working for a "general settlement" with Germany, based largely on the principle of national self-determination, and he believed the Munich settlement was a step toward that goal. His error, of course, was in thinking that Hitler was playing the same game; Hitler's error was in believing Chamberlain was playing *his* (Hitler's) game—hence his misinterpretation of Chamberlain's behavior at Munich as mere weakness in a power struggle. The prerequisite for stability in the power supergame and success (conflict reduction) in the conflict-cooperation game is that both parties correctly perceive what game the other is playing and both play the same game. A state that attempts conflict reduction vis-à-vis a power-hungry adversary is liable to be double-crossed; a state that misperceives the game as a power struggle against an opponent who really wishes to build cooperative relations may create a real enemy out of an imaginary one.

The two subsidiary supergames are intermingled in practice. The power game presumes the existence of conflict between the rivals. When the interests in conflict are asymmetrically valued, and the asymmetry is mutually perceived, the party with the greater values at stake gains some advantage in bargaining power.[43] The conflict-cooperation game presumes that the players have power; their conflict is usually over something with power-content, or it may arise simply from fears of the other's power. The players' objectives in reducing conflict and increasing cooperation are either to reduce the chances that their power will be used against each other, or to pool their power against a common third-party threat. Any major state is likely to be playing both games at the same time.

If we analytically separate the two games, we can say that playing the power game all-out calls for maximizing power gains (or minimizing power losses) in every encounter at the cost of continuing hostility and conflict. Unadulterated play of the conflict-reduction game calls for the accommodation of conflicts and conciliatory behavior at the risk of losing position in the balance of power. At bottom the *prescriptive* issue between hawks and doves, hard-liners and soft-liners, is which game one's own state ought to be playing against the presumptive adversary. The factual or *descriptive* issue is what kind of adversary he is. If he is a relatively permanent opponent with unlimited expansionist aims, obviously the power game is the one to play, since the conflict is irreconcilable. If he is possibly a temporary opponent with limited grievances or objectives, the conflict-reduction game may be more appropriate: the gains from reducing possible causes of war, and other cooperative benefits, are greater than the risks to one's power position. For most major states, most of the time, the appropriate game is a mixture: play the power game at least hard enough to preserve ultimate security in the inherent condition that the adversary's larger aims can never be known with certainty, but play the conflict-reduction game to the degree that gains from reducing the chances of war and the costs of power accumulation offset the risks of losing ground in the balance of power and resolve. This is a macro-statement of the main theme we shall take up in the next chapter in micro-terms: the problem of finding the proper combination of coercive and accommodative strategies in crisis bargaining.

SUMMARY

The bargaining models examined in this chapter vary greatly in usefulness for understanding crisis bargaining. First, the utility models proved to be of very limited usefulness. They are useful for describing a sequence of bids and threats in a few cases; but bidding sequences

---

[43] Robert E. Osgood has invented the useful term "balance of interests" to cover the power significance of such asymmetries. Robert E. Osgood and Robert W. Tucker, *Force, Order and Justice* (Baltimore, Md.: The Johns Hopkins Press, 1967), p. 148.

are on the surface, and one must look elsewhere for explanations of both bidding and outcome. Moreover, the conflict line and the two minima, which figure so prominently in the literature, are either non-existent for the bargainers or unknown to us in most cases. The three-dimensional model is correct in calling attention to time but does not accurately describe how time pressure operates in a crisis. All utility models are misleading in their neglect of various cognitive factors including information search and processing, which are an integral part of crisis bargaining. They also assume a unitary rational calculator and thus neglect political processes internal to the bargainers.

The expanded game models are a little more useful. In particular, the 3×3 model is a handy expansion of the 2×2 models, bringing in the action game and E strategies. But the larger $m \times n$ models, which focus on escalation-deescalation, are misleading descriptively and not as realistic as they at first seem to be. Escalation beyond DD, but short of war, occurs only rarely, and the possibility or danger of escalation is vastly more important than the actuality. Most important, the escalation ladder as a series of preexisting escalation options usually does not exist for the bargainers and is not used in crisis decision making. However, contingency planning in the nuclear age does involve consideration of escalation options that can be modeled by the expanded game.

The metagame proved to be entirely useless. The options on which it focuses are almost never known at the start of bargaining, and crisis decisions are not made by choosing from an array of options (detailed data will be presented in Chapter V). The concept of a stable settlement is also misleading. A settlement is stable, not when it dominates all other options as in metagame theory, but when the aspiration levels of all bargainers have been met. This point will be developed in Chapter V.

The most useful model examined in this chapter was one of the simplest, the 2×2 game. It goes directly to the heart of the crisis bargaining problem, the choice between accommodation and coercion. This choice is so central that Chapter III will be devoted to it; in addition much of the internal bargaining discussed in Chapter V turns on the disagreement between those decision makers who prefer accommodation and those who prefer coercion (soft-liners and hard-liners). The hard-line/soft-line disagreement also proves to be central in information processing (Chapter IV).

Because its focus is exactly correct, we adopt the 2×2 model (and its 3×3 extension) as the basic model of the bargaining situation. Its flexibility enabled us to distinguish and analyze nine different kinds of bargaining situations, each one a unique combination of power and interest relations between the bargainers, each therefore having its own dynamics and problems, each one requiring a different combination of accommodation and coercion for its solution.

In order to adapt the 2 × 2 game to model the bargaining situation, it was necesary to make several changes in the standard interpretations. We drop the postulate that the players are calculators of expected utilities, and leave the whole decision making and bargaining process for later study. We drop the rule of simultaneous play, the limiting of play to a single move, and the distinction between play and preplay communication. We also drop the assumption that payoffs and even the game are fixed, as these do change during bargaining. We drop the assumption that the payoff matrix is known to the players. This means that the cells of the matrix must be searched during bargaining, in a certain sequence demanded by the game itself. The bargaining process then includes the subroutine of building up a subjective estimate of the matrix, testing it, and correcting it. The estimate deals with the empirical content of the various possible outcomes and of the opponent's preference ordering over them.

The other useful model we found was the supergame. This can be used to model the effects of individual crisis outcomes on long-term relations between the parties. The supergame has two dimensions—relative power and degree of conflict of interest—and a crisis outcome may change relations in either or both dimensions. Conversely, the supergame also shows what type of crisis or other bargaining encounter will occur in each type of relation. We found that supergame considerations were prominent and persistent in the calculations of crisis bargainers. However, equally persistent was the inability of crisis bargainers to estimate correctly the effects of their bargaining tactics and strategy on long-term relations. We found instead a persistent preference in many, though not all, bargainers for either the power dimension or the conflict dimension of the supergame, reflecting personal preferences for hard or soft strategies. This bias persisted almost independently of changes in the objective situation.

The shortcomings of the models considered in this chapter point to the need for a different kind of model to deal with the bargaining and decision-making process. This model must incorporate various cognitive processes—search, information processing, building up and revising subjective estimates of the bargaining situation, constructing and revising strategies. We shall describe, test, and revise such a model in Chapters IV and V. In addition, our revisions of the 2 × 2 game have already incorporated some of the cognitive categories, so that the game structure model and the cognitive process model can each connect to the other.

CHAPTER III

CRISIS BARGAINING: STRATEGIES AND TACTICS[1]

In this chapter we chiefly take up the bargaining process in crises, employing a less formal mode of analysis than in the preceding chapter. Since bargaining is largely a process of manipulating values and perceptions of them, we begin with a statement of the value structures involved in crises, which also links the discussion here to the formal game structures presented in Chapter II. We then attempt to define the notion of "bargaining power." Then we move to an analysis of specific strategies and tactics in the bargaining process, grouped into the categories of persuasion, accommodation, and coercion. The last two correspond to the C and D strategies in the game models of Chapter II.

VALUE STRUCTURES

What crisis bargaining has in common with all bargaining is that it takes place within a context of values, interests, and power relations that are inherent in the situation but that are not fully known to the parties at the outset. The values and interests[2] of the parties have a triple function in bargaining. First, they provide the content of the conflict the bargaining attempts to resolve as well as of the common interests that motivate the bargaining. Second, they are the essential ingredients in the relative bargaining power that largely determines the outcome (a point we will elaborate in the next section). Third, it is these values and interests already inherent in the situation, and the parties' perceptions of them, that bargaining strategies and tactics attempt to manipulate during the bargaining process.

It is convenient to speak of these inherent values and interests as the parties' "value structures"—defined as the net value each party places on each possible outcome, including war. The value structure subsumes both the "interests" of the parties and their military power relations. Interests at stake in a crisis may be conveniently divided into three categories: *strategic* interests, which are interests derived from the material power content of the object in dispute; *reputational* interests, which are also power-related, but have to do with effects of outcomes upon others' images of one's resolve, flexibility, trustworthiness, alliance reliability, predictability, etc.; and *intrinsic* interests, which,

---

[1] Portions of this chapter draw upon Snyder's "Crisis Bargaining," in Charles F. Hermann, ed., *International Crises: Insights from Behavioral Research*, Ch. 10.

[2] The terms *value* and *interest* are closely related but not quite the same. *Interest* refers to the tangible or intangible things that are at stake for the parties; *value* connotes the kind and amount of utility that are attached to those things. The stakes in a crisis really consist therefore of a set of "valued interests."

unlike the other two, are not instrumental to one's future power and bargaining capability but are valued for their own sake: self-respect, prestige, economic values, etc.

Military power relations may be translated into values as the parties' utility for war. This is compounded of two elements: (1) a party's expectation whether it would win or lose and the value of whatever would be won or lost, and (2) its estimate of war damage, human and material, and the disutility attached to it. (For example, in the 1930s France and England had a much greater disutility for war damage than did Germany, quite apart from the possible war outcome.)

Another component is the value the parties place upon settlement of the dispute per se—i.e., upon eliminating the source of conflict and thus improving their future relations—independently of the terms of settlement.

Admittedly, these values are not entirely independent. A state that believes it has a high interest in the disputed stake may be inclined to discount the cost or risk of war incurred in standing firm. Conversely, the state that is highly fearful of war may rationalize a low interest in the object at stake and place a high value on settlement, per se, in order to eliminate the seeds of future conflict and war risk. A powerful state may inflate its perceptions of its interests to make them commensurate with its power, or a state that has recently suffered a chastening revelation of the limits of its power may reduce its perceived interests, e.g., the United States after the Vietnam war. Yet, even though they are not entirely separable, or may not be entirely distinct in the minds of decision makers, and may change during the course of interaction with the adversary, these values are fundamental determinants of a state's crisis bargaining behavior.

A special aspect of value structures is the legitimacy the parties ascribe to each other's claims. By *legitimacy* we mean not only legality but the broader and more subjective beliefs about the justice of one's own and the opponent's cause. Generally, of course, states believe their own aims are legitimate and the opponent's illegitimate, but there are sometimes asymmetries. One source of asymmetry is the status quo— the state that defends a clear and long-established status quo will generally have an edge in the perceived "balance of legitimacy." There are other sources of legitimacy beliefs, e.g., principles, conventional rules of behavior, tradition. The Munich crisis of 1938 vividly illustrates how a principle—that of national self-determination—can strengthen one state's bargaining position and weaken another's. The weight of tradition in the Monroe Doctrine strengthened U.S. determination in the Cuban missile crisis. For simplicity, we will consider legitimacy beliefs as part of the "intrinsic interests" of an actor, the moral aspect that determines his sense of the relative rightness and wrongness of his own and his opponent's aims and actions.

REPUTATION FOR RESOLVE

The strategic interest in preserving a future reputation for resolve deserves special attention since it appears frequently in our cases and it is not at all obvious how it stands in relation to other more immediate interests. It would appear that *if* states were quite clear about the magnitude of each other's interests (other than resolve reputation) in any crisis, there would be no need for concern about preserving a reputation for firmness. One would be expected to be as firm in any crisis as "justified" by one's known interests and capabilities—more precisely, by the relative "balance" of interests and forces between the parties. If one had backed down in a previous crisis, the reason would clearly be seen as an asymmetry of interests and/or forces favoring the opponent, not in a general want of courage, and no inferences could logically be drawn about one's likely behavior in the present or future crises when the configuration of interests and forces were different. However, a closer look shows that even in this fantasy world it would be possible to acquire a general reputation for firmness or weakness independently of the other interests at stake. In any bargaining situation, even when the values of each party are known to the other (and known to be known) the outcome cannot simply be "read off" from these values but is indeterminate within a certain range. Within this range, in any single episode, a party may be able to convince his opponent that he is dominant in "pure resolve," more daring, more willing than the opponent to risk a breakdown, and thus force an outcome better for himself than a 50–50 split of the indeterminate range. If this is accomplished once, presumably it affects the adversary's expectations concerning future encounters. Thus, generating an "image of resolve" to be drawn upon in future conflicts becomes one of the party's interests in the current conflict—its general value depending, one supposes, on whether future confrontations are expected. Of course, if building such an image is an important interest of both parties, the range of indeterminacy narrows and may disappear entirely, and the determinate outcome is breakdown—in a crisis, war.

If we drop the assumption of perfect knowledge of other states' interests and adopt its opposite of complete uncertainty, either of two logical conclusions may be drawn—that a reputation for resolve is completely unimportant or all-important. Given such uncertainty, statesmen may feel that it is too risky to draw any confident inferences about another state's firmness in a crisis from its behavior in a previous one. On the other hand, it may be precisely when states are most uncertain about each other's degree of interests in particular cases that they are most likely to draw inferences about each other's resolve from their *behavior* in previous encounters. The human mind abhors a "belief vacuum" (it could be argued), and when another state's interests in a present crisis cannot be estimated directly, its resolve will be inferred from the only hard evidence available—its behavior in past crises.

The real world is obviously closer to the pole of uncertainty than that of certainty. Yet statesmen do have *some* basis for estimating the magnitude of others' (non-reputational) interests in particular conflicts. They are probably able at least to rank them in some sort of hierarchy— some vital, some moderately important, some peripheral, and so on. A state that yielded on one issue would then be expected to yield again when confronted with a similar level of risk on issues at the same level or lower in its interest hierarchy. But no reliable inferences could be drawn about its probable resolve on higher valued interests. Conversely, a firm stand on a particular issue would imply firmness on other interests at the same level or higher in the hierarchy, but not necessarily for lesser interests. This reasoning implies that a state may be especially motivated to demonstrate resolve in a crisis over some object the adversary believes is low in its interest hierarchy, since firmness there would leave no doubt about its determination on higher valued issues; in short, resistance on small issues yields the highest resolve image payoff; on important issues, the least.

There is a flaw in this reasoning, however. The ability to rank an adversary's interests is of dubious predictive value for the following reason. When a state yields on any issue, it is more likely to be because it believes its adversary's interest to be stronger than its own (and/or because it is weaker in military strength) than because its independent valuation of the stake is low. That is, a state's resolve in a particular case is a function of how it perceives the *comparative* interests of itself and its opponent. The opponent's estimate of the state's hierarchy of interests across issues will be of little help in predicting this perception. Thus, when a state yields in a conflict where its own values at stake are of intermediate importance, it may also yield on issues of greater importance if it thinks the adversary's stake is greater still; and conversely, it may be firm on lesser issues when it thinks the balance of interests favors itself. Inferences can therefore not be drawn from another state's behavior in previous encounters because behavior in each case depends on the balance of interests perceived by the state in *that case.*

There are other reasons for doubting the actual importance of a "reputation for resolve." With the passage of time and shifts in the climate of public opinion, a nation's behavior in a past crisis becomes an increasingly unreliable indicator of future behavior. Regimes change, and it is at least problematical whether one government's reputation for resolve carries over to its successor. Common sense seems to argue that a government's degree of resolve will be influenced considerably by the peculiar circumstances and context of each crisis. Since crises tend to be diverse in structure, background, emotional content, and so on, predictions of a state's behavior from one case to another would seem unreliable. Perhaps the most reasonable hypothesis is that a state's resolve reputation is most likely to be undermined for future crises in the same geographical area or the same type of issue on which it has backed down before, and least likely for those in other areas over distinctly different issues. Thus the U.S. refusal to play the "end-game" in South Vietnam probably damaged its resolve image in Southeast Asia, but not with respect to crises in the Middle East.

Robert Jervis has pointed out that it is possible for a state to "decouple" its resolve reputation from its actions in a particular case.[3] The state may argue, after a crisis, that its apparent backdown was really a compromise, as Khrushchev did after Cuba, 1962. (Conceivably, for him it did appear as something of a compromise.) Or a state may be able to convince others that it really did not think the issue very important, or that it yielded because it believed the other's claim was legitimate.

We have been speculating, however. What do our cases tell us about the actual importance of resolve reputation, or the related idea of the "interdependence of commitments," in the thinking and behavior of statesmen? Not a great deal, but something. What stands out is the discrepancy between the little evidence that statesmen *do* infer an opponent's resolve from his behavior in previous cases and the massive evidence that decision makers *think* such inferences are made. We found only one recorded statement of an actual inference: Hitler's remark just before he invaded Poland, "Our enemies are little worms. I saw them at Munich."[4] Of course there may be other instances that do not appear on the record. For instance, the German leaders' easy confidence that Russia was bluffing in 1914 probably stemmed in part from the fact that Russia had backed down in several earlier crises, beginning with Bosnia, 1909. The enormity of the Russian misestimate in 1962 may be explainable in part by a Soviet perception of general U.S. weakness from the Bay of Pigs fiasco and the feeble U.S. response to the erection of the Berlin Wall. The absence of any serious direct

[3] Robert Jervis, *The Logic of Images in International Relations* (Princeton, N.J.: Princeton University Press, 1970), pp. 190–191.

[4] Quoted by Iklé, *How Nations Negotiate*, p. 82; and by Chester Wilmot, *The Struggle for Europe* (London: Collins, 1952), p. 21.

Soviet challenge since Cuba, 1962, including the easing of pressure on West Berlin, probably can be attributed at least partly to the U.S. firmness demonstrated on that occasion. But this is circumstantial evidence at best.

On the other hand, in almost all of our crises, some participant warns that giving in or making a concession will be taken as evidence of general weakness and will encourage further challenges. On the evidence available, statesmen are apparently overly concerned about resolve reputation. This is explainable partly in terms of personal bias, partly in terms of the nature of the international system. The concern is always voiced by "hard-liners." The hard-liner tends to focus on the power consequences of the outcome of the current dispute; the opponent's expectations about one's future firmness is an element of power. Furthermore, his image of the opponent is that he is a relatively permanent and aggressive opponent who is constantly probing for indications of weakness, and with whom one is engaged in a long-term power struggle that dwarfs in importance the "merits" of the immediate issue. The soft-liner is less concerned with the power considerations and more with the merits; the opponent is not necessarily a persistent aggressor, but a party with legitimate grievances whose satisfaction can turn him into a friend.

Aside from personal bias, the systemic factor that produces a concern for resolve reputation is ultimately the anarchic nature of the international system. This induces a constant concern for security and power and a conservative tendency to think of the future in "worst possible" or "worst plausible case" terms. The opponent *may* think we will be weak in the future if we give in now; to be safe we must *assume* he will. For the more extreme hard-liner, the assumption easily becomes a *belief*—i.e., an assumption that logically must be made for insurance against uncertainty becomes a resolution of the uncertainty itself. The tendency to resolve uncertainty conservatively also relates to what we said earlier about statesmen having at least *some* capacity to estimate the intensity of others' interests. *Some* capacity is not enough; what looms more prominently is the uncertain capacity of others to estimate one's interests. That is, one assumes that the opponent is above all uncertain about one's own interests; that he will therefore not try to estimate them at all in predicting one's future firmness, but will rely instead on the only real evidence he has—one's firmness or weakness as demonstrated by *behavior* in past encounters. Of course there is a certain asymmetry here in that the actor deals with his own uncertainty conservatively by assuming that the opponent does not think conservatively in dealing with his. Conservative thinking for the opponent, cast in the role of potential aggressor, would be not to dare to challenge at all if he is not sure of the interests of his prospective victim.

Another general finding that emerges from our data is what might be called the "never again" phenomenon. A state that has backed down on several occasions finally comes to think that, if it yields once more, its future threats of firmness toward an opponent or pledges to allies will be worth nothing; therefore it *must* stand firm now, whatever the risk, to avoid political disaster. The Russian leaders were clearly in this mood in 1914 as they looked back on their previous capitulations and weak behavior vis-à-vis Germany and Austria in the Balkans during the previous five or six years. When such a state becomes engaged with an opponent who expects the state to back down again, obviously the stage is set for disaster through miscalculation. It is quite clear that Kennedy's determination to stand firm in Cuba, 1962 was influenced by his apprehension that Khrushchev had judged him weak by the Bay of Pigs fiasco, his failure to react firmly to the erection of the Berlin Wall, or his failure to respond in kind to Khrushchev's verbal bellicosity at the Vienna summit of 1961. It was imperative that Kennedy stand firm *this* time. An alliance example is provided by Germany, 1914, whose leaders reasoned that they could not again restrain Austria as they had during the Balkan Wars lest they lose their only reliable ally.

BARGAINING POWER

Since we shall be using the term *bargaining power* throughout this chapter and the rest of the book, it is important to define it. A simple definition would say that bargaining power is political power held and exercised bilaterally. The typical definition of political power says that A has power over B to the extent A can persuade B to behave as B would not otherwise wish to do, by the threat of harm or the promise of reward. This conception is "unilateral" in that it does not take into account B's counterpower over A, for instance, B's possible capacity to threaten harm to A if A carries out his threat. This fits some real-life situations, but not bargaining situations. In bargaining, each state's power is limited by the power of the other; the relative bargaining power that determines the outcome is a resultant of the opposed power of the two sides.

However, we must probe a little deeper and ask what the sources of bargaining power are—for present purposes, in an international crisis. Bargaining power, like political power generally, refers to a capacity to achieve results—i.e., to gain or avoid losing some portion of the object in conflict—a capacity that becomes manifest in the outcome. The source of this capacity, in the main, is the value structures of the parties, described in the preceding section, as these structures are mutually perceived. Leaving perception aside for the moment, the elements in those structures may be collapsed into two broad categories: the parties' relative military strengths and their "interests" engaged in the conflict.

These two general factors determine the "resolve" of each party, its degree of motivation to stand firm. As a first analytical step we may speak of the "inherent resolve" of each party, independent of its estimate of the other's resolve. Inherent resolve is a function of a party's expected cost (or value) of war (which in turn is a function of military strength ratios), compared with the value of what it would lose if it yields and the value of what it would gain if the other party yields. Such a calculation, carried out by an omniscient observer for both parties, would yield an estimate of comparative inherent resolve.

Obviously, the protagonists may compare asymmetrically on the two gross dimensions of strength and interests. If one party is superior in military strength and also clearly has more at stake in the conflict, it will be the more resolved. But the military inferiority of one party may be compensated by its greater interests engaged, thus making the parties equally resolved. A militarily stronger party may be less "resolved" in the crisis than its opponent if it does not value its interests as highly as the opponent values his.

The notion of "resolve," it seems clear, is conceptually different from "bargaining power" since it is an attribute of the bargainer—his degree of determination to stand firm on a position—which says nothing about the degree of influence he has over his opponent or what he can achieve in exercising such influence. However, bargaining power is a close function of resolve and comparative resolve. To make the connection clear, we may usefully distinguish between *inherent* bargaining power, *actual* bargaining power, and bargaining *skill*. Inherent bargaining power is how much influence each party would have given its inherent resolve as just defined, i.e., independent of each party's perceptions of the other's resolve, and independent of manipulative tactics intended to change it. This concept is useful as a kind of benchmark that expresses what the relative bargaining power would be if the parties had perfect information about each others' values and strengths and consequently each other's "resolve." Also, it sets a certain limit on what the parties can achieve by manipulative tactics during the bargaining process. It represents what the parties "have to work with" in bargaining, the base from which they start in employing these tactics, a base that may be raised or lowered by the interplay of moves during the bargaining process, but only up to a point.

But the actual relative bargaining power, the parties' real capacities to influence each other, is a function of *perceived* comparative resolve, not "inherent" resolve as it might be calculated separately by each party. Put simply, each party knows with some confidence how resolved it is itself, but it cannot have the same assurance about the other party's resolve, since it does not know the other party's values. In practice, the parties will estimate each other's resolve from whatever indicators are available—past and present behavior, military strengths, verbal statements, etc. Each will then compare these estimates with its own resolve. The result will be separate perceptions of what the relative bargaining power is—that one or the other is superior and approximately to what degree. It is these perceptions (which may change, of course, during the bargaining process) that determine the actual outcome. The outcome may well deviate from what it would have been under conditions of perfect information—i.e., if the "inherent" power relations had been known. In an extreme case, one side might yield when it could have forced the other to yield, if it had estimated inherent power correctly. However, as we will show in the following chapter, there is a tendency for misestimates to be corrected during the bargaining process, so that, near the end of bargaining, perceived power approximates inherent power.

A precise definition of both inherent and actual (perceived) bargaining power may be derived from Ellsberg's critical risk formula, presented in the previous chapter. We show in Figure 3–1 a version of that model with the *CC* compromise cell blocked out for simplicity.

A party's "inherent resolve" is its critical risk: the maximum risk of bargaining breakdown (in a crisis, risk of war) that the party is willing to accept in standing firm. It is a function of three values: the loss in conceding to the opponent's demands, the possible gain from standing firm, and the possible loss from standing firm. The first two are a party's interests at stake; the third is its estimated net cost of war, derived from comparative military capabilities. In Figure 3–1 party *A*, a crisis challenger, would lose 5 by giving in (resolve reputation, prestige), would gain 10 if he stands firm and the defender yields, and would lose 20 if the defender does not yield and violence results. *A*'s critical risk is .50; he will stand firm at this probability of war or less, but will yield

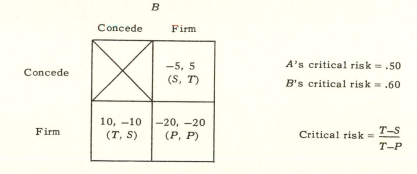

Figure 3-1. Critical Risk

if the probability is higher. This follows from a simple expected value calculation: when the probability of war is .50, A's expected value of standing firm is -5 (.50 $\times$ -20 plus .50 $\times$ 10), which is exactly equal to his payoff for yielding. B's critical risk is calculated similarly. B loses 10 by yielding, and he may get either the status quo plus prestige and reputational values worth 5, or war with a loss of 20 if he stands firm, depending on what A does. B's critical risk, or resolve, is .60— he will stand firm so long as his estimate of A's probability of standing firm is less than this. Each party's critical risk is the base for its "inherent" bargaining power, since it is a function entirely of its own values, involving no comparison with the opponent's values. The *relative* inherent bargaining power is shown by comparing the two critical risks: B is more powerful by .10, that is, he can "stand" that much more risk than A.

Actual bargaining power derives implicitly in the critical risk model from each party's *perception* of the credibility of the other's threat to stand firm, compared to its own critical risk.[5] If this credibility seems higher than the party's own critical risk, the party concedes—the other side is superior in bargaining power. If the credibility estimates are reasonably accurate, i.e., close to the other party's real degree of resolve, the actual bargaining power manifested in the outcome will more or less coincide with inherent bargaining power, but if the estimates are mistaken, the "actual" will deviate from the "inherent" in either direction and by varying amounts.[6]

It is worth noting also that the perception of comparative resolve and its derivative, relative bargaining power, is not simply a matter of each party's determining its own resolve by its own values, then estimating the opponent's resolve and comparing these estimates. We have been speaking of resolve as if it were an independent attribute of each side— independent of the perceived resolve of the opponent—more or less as the military forces of two opposing armies can be independently and objectively estimated and compared. In the case of resolve, however,

[5] Estimating "credibility" is logically equivalent to estimating the other's critical risk, but since the mental operations involved in estimating attributes of the opponent may be quite different than those used in estimating one's own values, the different term is employed. On the difference between "resolve" and "credibility" see Kent, *The Effects of Threats,* pp. 84–86.

[6] Three types of ordinal deviation are possible. Suppose A's resolve is "inherently" superior to B's. (1) If A estimates this correctly but B does not, B is firmer than he "should" be and either he gets more out of the bargain than he "deserves" or there is inadvertent war. (2) If A is incorrect while B is correct, B also gets more than the inherent power relations justify, but the situation is much less dangerous. (3) If both parties estimate incorrectly, B gets an actual superiority in bargaining power and a much greater share in the outcome than "justified."

the act of comparison changes it. If a party sees itself as less resolved than the opponent it is likely to *become* even less resolved and vice versa. (The military analogy might be that unequal forces become even more unequal by attrition during the battle.) A still further complexity is that a party's own resolve may be somewhat affected by the party's estimate of how resolved the opponent thinks he is. Bargainer A may see himself as "inherently" more resolved than B, but because he thinks B is underestimating his (A's) resolve, perceiving himself (B) as the more resolved, A becomes less resolved out of fear of the war that B's miscalculation might precipitate. Here we enter the thicket of "infinite regression," but since we find no good evidence of the phenomenon in our cases we need not pursue the trail further.[7]

Logically, when the inherent bargaining power heavily favors one side, and the asymmetry is correctly perceived by both sides, a conflict of interest does not erupt into crisis. Either the favored side deters the other from attempting change, or it can force change to its own advantage without the other carrying its resistance to the level of crisis, defined in terms of a high probability of war. A crisis occurs only when the net balance of interests and material power is even enough that both sides can plausibly see some chance of winning, or at least, for the challenger, some chance of improving his position, or for the resister, some chance of salvaging something better from resisting than he would lose by immediate capitulation. Alternatively, the balance may be quite asymmetrical, but one side misperceives this, miscalculating that there are gains to be made either by challenging or resisting. In either case, the crisis outcome ordinarily will register the relative bargaining power that both parties perceive after a period of interaction, during which initial misperceptions are adjusted.

An analysis of crisis bargaining power must not overlook the contextual advantages that may be possessed by one side or the other. Every crisis has its unique contextual features that may permit one side or the other to carry out faits accompli, deploy forces more easily, retract initiatives with less loss of face, shift the onus of initiating violence to the opponent, etc. These features are generally of some geographical or locational character. For example, the easy ability of the United States to deploy forces in the vicinity of Cuba in 1962, compared to the Soviets' difficulty of doing so, undoubtedly contributed to the U.S. bargaining power in that crisis. In each of the Berlin crises, the location of West Berlin deep inside East Germany gave the Communist side special coercive options not available to the West.

Finally, for crises between nuclear powers, comparative military

---

[7] Robert Jervis has discussed the infinite regress phenomenon in "Bargaining and Bargaining Tactics," Pennock and Chapman, eds., *Coercion*, pp. 285–287.

strength has become a less reliable indicator of crisis bargaining power in modern times. For prenuclear times, one can say with fair confidence that when each side had about the same interest in the disputed object, the side with the greater overall military capability would have a bargaining edge. But in a crisis between nuclear superpowers, each with a powerful second-strike capability, a comparison of overall *nuclear* forces is of dubious relevance to bargaining power. Although conventional force ratios are still relevant, even their relevance has become ambiguous because of possibly asymmetrical fears of escalation. Thus, for the great nuclear states, estimates of relative bargaining power in a crisis must rest primarily on the subjective factor of interest comparisons, observations of each other's behavior as an indicator of interests, and contextual factors that affect the deployability of conventional forces and the burden for initiating violence. Reputation for resolve has become more important as an element in bargaining power. In Chapter VI we take these matters up again in more detail.

What about "bargaining skill"? Do we include, as an aspect of bargaining power, a party's virtuosity in the bargaining process, its skill in making threats, commitments, or concessions, in deception or clarification, in gaining information about the opponent? Common sense might say "yes," for is not anything that increases a bargainer's capacity to make gains or avoid losses an element in his "bargaining power"? However, we reject this interpretation in favor of the equally reasonable notion that "skill" is not power itself, but efficiency in using and manipulating the power available. Bargaining tactics may be employed either ineptly or with finesse, producing outcomes either better or worse than the inherent power relations would suggest.

Strategies and tactics in the bargaining process mediate between value structures and outcomes. They do so necessarily because the parties are uncertain about each other's values and interests and because they are subject to change. If value structures were fully known and immutable, the relative bargaining power of the parties, and hence the inevitable outcome, could simply be read off from them without going through the process of bargaining, just as there would be no need to fight wars if the outcome could be reliably predicted from a comparison of forces at the outset. Bargaining mediates between value structures and outcomes in at least four different ways. First, because of uncertainty, tactics may be employed to communicate one's own values and consequently one's resolve to the opponent, either truthfully or deceptively—i.e., the adversary's *perception* of one's own value structure may be manipulated. Second, because the kind and amount of values engaged are not given and immutable, bargaining may *change* the values at stake for both sides; for each bargainer the intention normally will be to increase the value of interests engaged for the self and reduce the value of the opponent's interests; conversely for the prospective costs of war. These first two functions are those of coercive and persuasive bargaining. Third, bargaining also *clarifies* values for the self, both one's own values and the opponent's. At the start of bargaining, a party's own interests may be quite ill-defined; they become clarified in the crucible of struggle. Each party is also interested in getting a correct picture of the adversary's interests and resolve. This is accomplished by tactics of information search and by feedback from coercive and persuasive tactics. Finally, after the parties develop fairly clear (though not necessarily correct) images of each other's value structures and resolve, values are sacrificed or exchanged in the process of resolving the conflict. This is the function of accommodative strategies and tactics.

THE BARGAINING PROCESS: COERCION, ACCOMMODATION, PERSUASION.

We think of any bargaining process as having three broad dimensions: accommodative, coercive, and persuasive. The accommodative dimension is the convergence of the "bargaining positions" of the parties toward a settlement, through a sequence of "bids" or proposals for settlement—i.e., demands, offers, concessions. Most theorists of bargaining have concerned themselves primarily with this dimension, either analyzing the *process* of convergence (including the parties' mental processes in deciding whether to concede or to continue holding out for their current demand) or attempting to devise formulas that predict the point within a bargaining range at which a settlement is likely to take place. The process of accommodation toward some agreement is also the dominant image of "bargaining" in ordinary discourse.

Coercive bargaining is the bilateral process of asserting firmness, making threats and warnings, and exerting pressure in various ways to influence the other party to accept one's will or one's latest bid. It includes the threat of harm; in crises, the threat of war. To speak of coercion by threats of harm as a form of bargaining is somewhat alien to ordinary usage, and even to most theoretical analyses, in which coercion generally means the unilateral exercise of power by one party over another.[8] Only one party does the coercing; the other merely responds by yielding or not. Sometimes it is postulated that both parties have power over each other and the outcome is a function of their relative power. However, such analyses hardly ever admit the

---

[8] It may not seem so alien to those who have seen the movie "The Godfather" in which the gangster gives a man "an offer he can't refuse" by holding a gun to the victim's head.

possibility of bargaining in the form of the "victim" resisting the first demand but offering something less, or the coercer reducing his original demand and some sort of dynamic process continuing beyond the initial confrontation.

Apparently the first theorist to include coercion by threat of force explicitly as a kind of bargaining, thus expanding the concept of bargaining beyond the notion of mutual accommodation, was Thomas C. Schelling. In his seminal "An Essay on Bargaining," [9] Schelling dealt with a variety of tactics by which bargainers might commit themselves to a given position, not only in what he called "ordinary bargaining"—i.e., when the parties attempt to reach an agreement that would benefit both, and the consequence of no agreement is simply the failure to realize these benefits—but also in the more purely coercive situations of enforcing one's will upon an adversary by threats of harm. In the latter area, Schelling initially dealt with "deterrence," dissuading the other from doing something (what might be called "negative coercion"); later he invented the term "compellence" for the obverse "positive coercion," persuading another to do something that he would not of his own incentives wish to do.[10] Schelling brought both deterrence and compellence into the bargaining rubric by taking the view that *all* conflict situations that contain an element of common interest between the parties are essentially bargaining situations. The conflict element in both negative and positive coercion is obvious; the common interest is the *mutual* desire to avoid the harm that would befall both parties if the coercive threat is carried out. This formulation made coercive bargaining theoretically equivalent to ordinary bargaining.

However, some acts of coercion logically fall outside the bargaining umbrella. For example, if the carrying out of a certain compellent threat were costless or positively beneficial to the threatening party, but costly to the victim, the parties would have no common interest in avoiding the fulfillment of the threat and thus no *mutual* incentive to reach a bargain. The threatener would have no incentive to withhold the threatened harm even if the victim met his demand in full; in fact he might have a positive incentive to carry it out despite the victim's acquiescence. We might call this situation one of pure conflict; since there is no element of common interest, it is not bargaining. The outer limit of coercive bargaining is the situation in which the threatener is indifferent between carrying out his threat or accepting the victim's compliance. Within this limit, where threat-fulfillment promises a net gain somewhat less than the gain from the victim's compliance, there is some range wherein the victim may make offers short of the threatener's

---

[9] Schelling, *The Strategy of Conflict,* Ch. 2.
[10] Schelling, *Arms and Influence,* pp. 79–80.

demand that may be acceptable to the latter. The limit is roughly equivalent to the boundary between the Bully and Big Bully models presented earlier, Bully lying just inside it and Big Bully outside. A case which was outside the limit was the German–Czech crisis of 1938 until its final stages. Whatever one might call the interaction between Germany and Czechoslovakia, it was not bargaining until certain eleventh-hour developments, including a higher risk of war with England and France, made Hitler perceive that his planned forcible occupation was less desirable than gaining his objective at the conference table.

The outer limit of bargaining on the accommodative side is the "game of pure coordination," which the values and goals of the parties are identical. In this situation there is no conflict, only common interest, and the interaction between the parties is better labeled "problem-solving" than "bargaining." That is, the parties simply collaborate in devising an arrangement that maximizes their fully shared values. Pure empirical examples of this in international relations are difficult to find, but they are most closely approximated in relations between allies. The game of Leader falls just inside the outer limit, since, though the parties share interests and values to a high degree, the sharing is imperfect.

Within these outer limits, a bargaining process is primarily accommodative when the common interest is high relative to the conflicting interests. Since the parties have so much to gain mutually, they are more interested in reaching an agreement that will realize these gains than in getting their way on the issues in conflict. They adopt accommodative strategies, with only occasional displays of firmness to make sure they get their fair share of the benefits. The process is primarily coercive if the conflicting interests are valued highly compared to the common interests and when the coercion is exercised by explicit or implicit threats of harm. The parties are more interested in imposing their will on the adversary than in getting an agreement per se, though there are some agreements they would prefer to no agreement at all. They adopt coercive strategies at the start, with perhaps an occasional accommodative gesture to dampen the provocative effects of their coercion. But real accommodation does not take place until one party makes clear its superior resolve, and the accommodation then adopted by the weaker party is forced, not freely given, and will be mixed with a considerable element of defensive coercion as he seeks to minimize his losses. Or it occurs when the parties find themselves about equally resolved: then both give ground grudgingly until a mutually acceptable settlement is found. Bargaining in an international crisis is, of course, primarily coercive.

Still another broad element in crisis bargaining (or any bargaining) is that of *persuasion*. Persuasion is akin to coercion in that its aim is to influence the adversary to concede, to accept one's own demands. Unlike coercion, however, it does not involve threatening harm to the other party if he does not concede. One form of persuasion is to attempt to change the adversary's estimate of the empirical consequence of possible outcomes, or the value he places on these consequences. For example, the persuader tries to show the other party that backing down would not be as costly as he might think, that a war would have terrible consequences, that his (the persuader's) military capabilities are superior, etc. Persuasion also includes trying to change the adversary's estimates of how oneself predicts the nature of outcomes and values them. In short, persuasion attempts to influence the adversary's value structure and his perception of one's own values—for given outcomes. Both coercive and accommodative moves (threats and concessions) present the adversary with a *choice* between a pair of outcomes, one of which is certain, the other uncertain. That is, a coercive threat gives him a choice between accepting the demand or taking the risk that the threat will be carried out. A concession gives him a choice between accepting the offer or holding out in the hope of getting more. Persuasion helps him make these choices to one's own advantage, by changing his valuation of the outcomes and his estimate of one's own valuations, as well as his prediction of the likelihood of uncertain outcomes.

PERSUASION, COERCION, AND THE CRITICAL RISK MODEL

Bargaining tactics, especially persuasion and coercion, can usefully be related to Ellsberg's critical risk model.[11] Its usefulness derives from its fairly realistic assumption that (1) each party knows its own payoffs for different outcomes but does not know those of the other party, and (2) each party's payoffs are subject to change during the bargaining process. As will be recalled, (see Fig. 3–1), a party's "critical risk" is derived entirely from its own values and expresses the degree of war risk that the party can "stand." Theoretically, the party compares his own critical risk with his perception of the probability (credibility) that the other will stand firm or attack if the party does not concede. The estimate of the opponent's threat credibility is derived in part from estimates of the opponent's payoffs, but since these estimates are uncertain, the opponent's past and present behavior may influence credibility estimates directly. If the credibility of the other's threat is higher than the party's critical risk, the party must yield; if it

[11] Ellsberg, "The Theory and Practice of Blackmail."

is lower, he will stand firm. Thus, both bargainers are interested in reducing the adversary's critical risk and increasing their own threat credibility. Such manipulation may be done by a variety of bargaining tactics, most of which fall into the "persuasive" category. They come in three subclasses: (1) those that attempt to change one's own payoffs or the opponent's estimates of them for possible outcomes, (2) those which tend to increase the credibility of one's firmness but without changing payoffs, and (3) those that attempt to change the opponent's payoffs. The first two types are aimed at increasing one's own credibility of firmness, the third at reducing the adversary's critical risk. (There is some overlap, i.e., some tactics may work both ways.)

The following list shows the tactics that appeared most frequently in our cases. Each is accompanied by a brief statement of the crises where it appeared most prominently. A few are tactics we expected to find when we began our research, but found no instances.[12]

I. *Increase credibility of own firmness by changing one's apparent payoffs*

Here the attempt is to change the adversary's estimate of one's own payoffs—e.g., to minimize the adversary's estimate of one's own net costs of war, to maximize one's apparent valuation of winning, and to maximize one's apparent cost of yielding. Some of these tactics may actually change one's payoffs; others merely change the opponent's perceptions of them. For bargaining effect it is, of course, the adversary's perceptions that count.

  A. *Reduce one's apparent net cost of war*
    1. Increase capabilities (United States and Soviet Union, Berlin, 1961)
    2. Increase readiness of capabilities (U.S., 1962; 1973)
    3. Various verbal statements
      a. "We don't fear war" (Hitler, 1938)
      b. "We will win" (no instances)
      c. "Your ally will not support you" (Germany to France re England, 1914; England to Germany re Italy, 1914)
      d. "Our ally will support us" (Austria to Russia, 1914)
      e. "We believe the war will be limited" (no instance)
  B. *Increase one's apparent valuation of the stakes* (increase costs of backing down, increase the apparent value of winning)
    1. Make threats that engage prestige, honor, and future bargaining reputation (instances in all cases studied)

[12] Many of the tactics in the list are suggested in the writings of Thomas Schelling, esp. *The Strategy of Conflict*. Some others are discussed by Robert Jervis, in *The Logic of Images*. Some simply appeared in our cases, not having been mentioned in the theoretical literature.

2. Couple the present issue with other issues; make it appear as an aspect of a larger confrontation (United States 1958—coupling Quemoy to Formosa)
    a. Cite need to preserve reputation for resolve in general, or reputation for loyalty to allies (United States, Berlin, 1948; United States and Soviet Union, Berlin, 1961; United States, Quemoy, 1958)
3. Cite the legitimacy or fairness of one's position
    a. Inviolability of the status quo (United States, Cuba, 1962)
    b. The right of consultation (Germany, Morocco, 1905)
    c. The right of compensation (Germany, Morocco, 1911)
4. Tie one's position to moral principles (United States, Berlin, 1948, 1958, 1961; Hitler, 1938—persecution of Sudeten Germans, their right of national self-determination)
5. Invoke legal rights (France and England, Fashoda, 1898; United States and Soviet Union, Iran, 1946; United States and Soviet Union, Berlin, 1948, 1958, 1961)
6. Invoke alliance obligations (moral principle as well as political value of alliance preservation and cohesion) (England to Germany, 1905; Germany to Entente powers, and France and England to Central Powers, 1914; Soviet Union and United States, Berlin, 1958–1962)
7. Invoke "national honor" (England, 1911; Germany, 1914; Soviet Union, 1946)
8. Cite danger of internal revolution if oneself capitulates (Austria to Russia, 1914)
9. Invoke historical tradition (United States, Cuba, 1962—Monroe Doctrine)

II. *Increase apparent probability of firmness without changing payoffs.*
Although some of the tactics in this category may carry indirect implications about one's payoffs, their primary intent or effect is to modify the opponent's direct perceptions of the probabilities of one's choice. Most are coercive rather than persuasive.

1. Irrevocable commitment (physically or administratively eliminate the alternative of compliance, or make compliance physically or administratively difficult; "relinquish the initiative") (Berlin blockade, 1948; Berlin Wall, 1961; German Schlieffen Plan, 1914).
2. Claim lack of control over subordinates or inability to resist their pressure (Aehrenthal, 1909; Czar, 1914; Hitler, 1938).
3. Devolve decision-making authority to lower levels in the command hierarchy to persons whose incentive structure is more

favorable to firmness than that of the governmental leadership (or appear to do so) (to General Clay, Marshall Konev, Berlin, 1961; General Kitchener, 1898; U.S. Seventh Fleet Commanders, Quemoy, 1958).

4. Devolve decision-making authority to a proxy state or ally whose incentive structure more obviously favors firmness than one's own (or threaten to do so) (Germany to Austria, 1914; Soviet Union to E. Germany, 1958, 1961).

5. Claim that one's constituency will not allow compliance or compromise (the constituency may be the cabinet, Congress, public opinion, allies, etc.) (England to Germany, 1905, 1914; Germany to France, 1911).

6. Parliamentary votes and resolutions supporting one's position (U.S. Formosa Resolution of 1955).

7. Pretend irrationality (Hitler, 1938).

8. Express confidence in the adversary's rationality and good sense ("since you are reasonable you are surely not going to fight over this minor issue") (Khrushchev, 1958, 1961, 1962).

9. Express disbelief in the opponent's commitment, or skepticism about his resolve ("my resolve is high because I think yours is low") (Soviet Union, Berlin, 1958–1961).

10. Emphasize uncertainties in the situation, or the unpredictability of one's own behavior, e.g., "keep them guessing" (England, 1938; United States, 1941; United States, Quemoy, 1958).

11. Show of force; minor use of force. (England, 1898; Germany, 1911; United States, 1946; United States, 1948; Britain, France, Israel, 1956; United States, Lebanon and Quemoy, 1958; United States and Soviet Union, Berlin, 1961–1962; United States, 1962).

12. Represent oneself as a "force of nature," totally committed and immune to persuasion (Hitler, 1938; Eisenhower, Berlin, 1958; Khrushchev, Berlin, 1961).

III. *Reduce the adversary's critical risk*

The adversary's critical risk is a function of *his* payoffs—his cost of war and his valuation of the stakes. These utilities can be manipulated, although perhaps to a lesser degree than the adversary's perception of one's own utilities.

A. *Increase the adversary's estimate of his net costs of war.*

1. Increase one's own capabilities and readiness (United States and Soviet Union, Berlin, 1961; United States and Soviet Union, Cuba, 1962; Germany, 1938)

2. Verbally exaggerate one's capabilities, claim that the balance

of military power favors oneself (Soviet Union, Berlin, 1958–1962)

3. Emphasize the loyalty of one's own allies and the unreliability of the adversary's allies (Germany and France, 1914—unreliability vs. reliability of England; France to Germany, 1905—English loyalty to France)

4. Stress the danger of escalation (Soviet Union, Lebanon, 1958; Soviet Union, Berlin, 1958–1962)

5. Stress danger of revolution as consequence of war (Germany to Russia, 1914)

6. If we fight, state X will be the beneficiary (England to Germany, 1938—X = Soviet Union)

B. *Devalue the stakes for the adversary* (decrease his cost of compliance, reduce his estimate of the value of winning)

1. Stress limited nature of aim (Hitler, 1938—"this is my last demand"; Austria, 1914—"we will not take any Serbian territory")

2. Provide a loophole or rationale that permits the adversary to back down or de-commit himself with minimum humiliation (United States to Soviet Union, 1946—show of belief that Soviet troops' actions in Iran were not sanctioned by government; Mussolini and Chamberlain to Hitler, 1938—suggestion of conference allowed Hitler to decommit himself from attacking)

3. Invoke community values that adversary would serve by backing down (United States to Soviet Union, 1962—how Khrushchev would contribute to world peace by retreating)

4. Mobilize support of international community institutions for one's own position (United States, 1946; United States, 1962)

5. Undermine the legitimacy of the opponent's position (Soviet Union, 1958—the status of West Berlin is "abnormal"; Hitler, 1938—Sudeten Germans should be in the Reich by right of "national self-determination")

6. Challenge the legality of the opponent's position (United States, Berlin, 1958–1962; England and France, 1898; Russia and England, 1908; Germany, 1905 and 1911; United States, 1946; United States and Soviet Union, 1948; Soviet Union, 1962)

7. Minimize the element of duress or provocation in one's demands and threats (England, 1898; England, 1905, 1914; England and France, 1938; United States, 1946; Soviet Union, 1958, 1961; United States, 1962)

    a. Assert that the crisis has arisen autonomously rather than by deliberate challenge (Soviet Union, 1958–1960, 1961; Hitler, 1938)

    b. Give a non-coercive rationale for coercive moves (Germany, 1911; Soviet Union and United States, 1948; England and France, 1956)

    c. Use non-provocative diplomatic "code language" (almost all parties in all crises)

8. De-couple the present issue from other or future issues ("This issue is special. I will not draw any conclusions about your general resolve if you concede on this issue") (Soviet Union, Berlin Wall, 1961)

9. Help the adversary undo his commitment by arguing that the situation does not meet the conditions specified in his threat or commitment (Soviet Union, Cuba, 1962—"the missiles are not offensive")

10. Stress the common interests in settling the dispute and avoiding war (United States and Soviet Union, Berin, 1958–1962; United States and Soviet Union, Cuba, 1962; England to Germany, 1914; Germany to Russia, 1914—appeal to "monarchical solidarity")

    a. Promise improvement in relations if demands are accepted (Germany to England, 1905, 1914, 1938; England to Germany, 1914; Soviet Union to United States, 1961; France to England, 1898)

11. Suggest plaudits to be gained from third parties or neutrals by giving in (Kennedy to Khrushchev, 1962)

12. Use proxy state to present the challenge (devalues the stakes for the adversary because it is not a test of resolve with his primary opponent) (U.S. use of Israel in Syria–Jordan crisis of 1970)

Persuasive communication attempts to magnify in the adversary's mind one's own interests at stake and minimize one's own costs of war, and to change in the opposite direction the adversary's estimate of his own values and costs. With some of the tactics just listed, there is a problem in how to change one's own apparent valuations without changing the adversary's in the same direction. For example, citing the need to preserve one's reputation for firmness may remind the opponent that he has a resolve reputation to protect, too, or more subtly, the more one emphasizes one's resolve-reputational values, the more the issue itself is transformed into a resolve contest, automatically engaging the adversary's resolve reputation. Either way, the effort is futile, and indeed dangerous, which is perhaps why we find few invocations of need-to-preserve-resolve-image as a bargaining tactic, although it is a value in internal decision making in most crises. Pretty much the same point can be made about invocations of "national honor" or "prestige"; to engage such values for oneself automatically engages them for the opponent as well. Similarly, to suggest how the opponent can serve common interests or general community values by giving in, naturally makes him wonder why *he* is the one who has to make the sacrifice.

Persuasive tactics, therefore, are potentially effective only when they change payoffs or perceptions of them asymmetrically, as Robert Jervis has pointed out.[13] Most of the moves and declarations listed above do have asymmetrical effects. Obviously, increasing the size or readiness of military forces reduces one's potential net war costs and increases the adversary's. Most of the verbal items point to values or empirical elements in the situation that are important only or primarily for one side. For example, to insist on the sanctity of the status quo emphasizes the values of the defending side. To stress the legitimacy of change ("the status of Berlin is abnormal") tends to expand the apparent stake of the challenger. Emphasizing the moral principle and legal rights in one's position tends to enhance one's own stake, but not automatically that of the opponent. In general, the trick in all these tactics is to point to elements that suggest that one's own interests, and hence one's own costs in backing down, are greater than the adversary's.

Similarly, the mobilization of international institutions in support of one's position adds legitimacy to it, and denies legitimacy to the adversary. It tends to increase the cost of intransigence for the opponent, for he is then placed in the position of flaunting the will of a wider community that presumably speaks for objective justice rather than the self-interest of a particular adversary. It also decreases his cost of backing down because conceding to the will of the "community" is less humiliating than conceding to the will of another state. He can present his withdrawal as obedience to an impersonal set of generally valid rules rather than capitulation to the superior power of a peer. For example, the Soviet withdrawal from Iran in 1946 was made easier by the fact that the Western powers exercised their pressure through U.N. procedures more than by direct coercion. U.N. involvement has been significant in several post-World War II crises, notably in our sample (in addition to the Iran case), Suez, 1956; Cuba, 1962; and the Middle East, 1973. The unanimous Organization of American States endorsement of the U.S. position in the Cuba case strengthened the U.S. bargaining power.

---

[13] Jervis, "Bargaining and Bargaining Tactics."

The effectiveness of persuasive tactics varies widely. Generally, the verbal tactics are most likely to be effective when the adversary is already predisposed to believe what the persuader is saying. Thus Hitler was effective when he pointed out to Chamberlain that although his own interest in change in Czechoslovakia was high, he did not believe Britain had any interests there. Conversely, in 1914, officials of the French and German foreign offices failed to change the other's belief that England would or would not fight. But the British argument to Germany that Italy would defect did add something to the trepidation felt among German officials in the last days of the crisis, since they already had their doubts about Italy. If a country already perceives some legitimacy in the adversary's position, the latter's assertions of such legitimacy will have some effect in changing, to its advantage, the first country's perceptions of comparative valuations and comparative firmness. Germany's assertion of its "right" to consultation about Morocco in 1905 and its "right" to compensation in 1911 activated latent French guilt feelings, and Hitler's assertions of the injustices of the Versailles Treaty activated British ones in 1938. Perhaps the major reason why the United States agreed to negotiate about Berlin in 1958 and 1961 was that there was a good deal of suppressed agreement with Khrushchev's claim that the situation *was* abnormal.

Finally, persuasive arguments are more likely to be effective if there are empirical elements in the situation that support their plausibility. Berchtold's statement to the Russian government in 1914 that the Austrian government would be "swept away" if it modified its demands on Serbia probably was effective in convincing the Russians early that negotiations would be futile, given their knowledge of the instability of the Austrian regime. In the Cuban missile crisis of 1962, Khrushchev was fairly easily convinced of the superiority of U.S. values at stake because of certain obvious facts, such as geographical location, a large U.S. base on the island, and the fact that the missiles would have increased Soviet nuclear striking power against the United States by something like 50 percent. By contrast, a claim that a crisis is a special case, that therefore the adversary will not impair his resolve image in future crises by retreating, is likely to be ineffectual because of the difficulty in adducing empirical support for the argument.

Accommodative tactics are not included in the list given above, because the critical risk model, or formula, does not describe very well what actually occurs in a process of accommodation, in crises at least. According to the formula (p. 51), first each bargainer calculates both critical risks, then the party with the lower critical risk reduces its claim. This reduces both critical risks: the conceder's because he is now demanding less than before and logically will risk less to get that than his earlier larger claim; the other party's too, because what he can now get as an alternative to standing firm is greater than it was before. Though both critical risks are reduced by a concession by either party, that of the firm party falls more, so that if the concession is large enough his critical risk drops below the conceder's. Then it is the other party's "turn" to make a concession, which again reduces both critical risks, but the first party's more, which forces him to make another concession, and so on until a settlement is reached at the point where both critical risks have dropped to zero. Although the mathematics are impeccable, this formulation does not fit the actual convergence process in empirical cases. One obvious reason is that the decision to concede in the model rests so heavily on a precise calculation of critical risks, whereas the parties in reality do not have the information about the opponent's payoff values and even their own values that is necessary to calculate critical risks. (This debility does not seriously affect the linkage of persuasive and coercive tactics to the model, since the motivation to use these tactics rests simply on the desire to change the critical risks in a certain direction, not upon a precise calculation of what they are.) Second, either party's motivation to concede or stand firm during the accommodation process depends on psychological factors not included in the values that would go into critical risk calculations. These include high or low risk-taking propensities, a determination not to concede more because of having conceded much already, a perception that the opponent "looks weak" after he makes a concession so that he can be "pushed to the wall," or oppositely, increasing feelings of friendliness toward an accommodating adversary, causing greater reciprocal concessions than warranted by the relative critical risks, etc. In only one of our 16 cases do we find the "turn-and-turn-about" pattern of the critical risk formula. Usually, one party simply concedes everything, although it may receive a "carrot" or "face-saver" along the way. The reason may be that when the value-power relations finally become clear, they are so asymmetrical that the party with the lower critical risk cannot concede anything less than the opponent's full claim to get the latter's critical risk below its own. More likely, the explanation is the "psychological" one given above: once superior resolve is established, it is not affected or is even enhanced by the other parties' concessions; there is no reason for the superior party to stop pushing until it has gotten everything. In the one case— Agadir, 1911—where there was a pattern of alternating concessions, it could be argued that the parties "sensed" shifting critical risks. The record, however, shows a quite different mental process. France: Kiderlen needs to show the Reichstag a concession at this point; Germany: if we don't give France something now, the government will fall and a tougher one come to power; both sides: now that we have decided to settle, it's only fair that both sides concede something.

DIMENSIONS OF CRISIS MANAGEMENT

The term *crisis management* is usually taken to mean the exercise of detailed control by the top leadership of the governments involved so as to minimize the chances that the crisis will burst out of control into war. But statesmen in a crisis are interested in more than just avoiding war. They also want to advance or protect their state's interests, to win or at least to maximize gains or minimize losses, and if possible to settle the issue in conflict so that it does not produce further crises. We therefore adopt a broader conception of the problem of crisis management. The problem is to find the optimum mix or trade-off between coercion and accommodation in the particular crisis context, given the distribution of values and military power among the participants. Coercion and accommodation are viewed as contrasting, though intermingled, dimensions of crisis bargaining, each directed toward a characteristic goal and bounded by a characteristic constraint, the goals and constraints reflecting the conflicting and common interests involved. Persuasive tactics are largely supportive of coercion, so we do not consider them as a separate dimension here.

The goal of both parties in the coercive dimension is to win, either offensively or defensively—to gain or retain for their side the whole, or at least the essence, of whatever is in dispute. The constraint is to do this without war or excessive risk of war. In this dimension the goals of the parties are in conflict and the constraint represents a common interest. In the accommodative dimension, the goal is to reach some settlement that promises to defuse the issue as a potential source of future crises. The constraint is to accomplish this with minimum concessions by one's own side. Here, the goal reflects the common interest and the constraint reflects the conflicting interests. Thus, in theory, the mixed motive character of any bargaining situation—the coexistence of conflict and common interest—appears in a crisis as a complex interaction between these two sets of goals and constraints. Each state wishes to manage the crisis so as to maximize its values in the outcome, which means it wants to coerce prudently or accommodate cheaply, or some combination of both.[14]

---

[14] The term *crisis management* has been used rather vaguely in the literature, with a variety of meanings and emphases. The most precise formulation is in George, Hall and Simons, *The Limits of Coercive Diplomacy*, pp. 8-11. The tension between the requirements of "crisis management" and "coercive diplomacy" is a central theme of this work. The authors use the term *crisis management* in more or less the same sense as our constraint of "war risk avoidance." Although their usage has merit, we prefer to broaden the meaning of "management" to encompass the totality of the crisis decision-maker's problem.

	GOAL	CONSTRAINT
Coercion:	Win (conflicting interests)	Avoid risk of war (common interest)
Accommodation:	Settle (common interest)	Minimize losses (conflicting interests)

Figure 3-2. Goals and Constraints in Crisis Management

Admittedly, there is some overlap between the two dimensions. Winning in the coercive dimension is not qualitatively different from "minimizing sacrifices" in the accommodative dimension: both involve maximizing one's ultimate share of the substantive stakes. Coercive tactics, including simply protestations of firmness, are appropriate for both. Similarly, seeking a settlement in the accommodative dimension is on the same value continuum as avoiding risks in coercive bargaining; obviously, a settlement eliminates the possibility of war. Accommodative moves are appropriate both for achieving the goal of compromise settlement and for meeting the risk-avoidance constraint when a party is trying to "win." In dichotomizing coercive and accommodative dimensions of crisis bargaining, we are really pointing to two types of generalized *strategies* that are open to the parties, differentiated according to the dominant goal of the bargainer. Whichever strategy is adopted, some mixture of coercive and accommodative *tactics* may be involved in its implementation. Thus a party seeking to win, pursuing a primarily coercive strategy, may yet feel it necessary to show some flexibility and willingness to negotiate in order to avoid provoking the adversary into counterthreats and a dangerous spiral of hostility. Similarly, a party bent on accommodation in search of settlement may yet feel compelled to take firm stands and even issue threats at certain points along the accommodative road, in order that the settlement not be too one-sided to its disadvantage. In a primarily coercive strategy, coercive tactics are used to achieve the goals, accommodative ones to meet the constraint. In an accommodative strategy, accommodative tactics serve the goals, while coercive ones play the secondary role of dealing with the constraint.

The overlap is minimized empirically by the fact that most crises pass through two distinct phases: first, a confrontation phase in which both parties are following coercive strategies, attempting to win either offensively or defensively; then a resolution phase in which either one party, clearly overpowered, perforce adopts a clearly accommodative strategy, while the stronger party continues on a clearly coercive track, or both parties, finding themselves roughly equal in bargaining power, converge toward a compromise settlement. The latter cases are less frequent and involve more complex strategy mixtures.

In game-theoretic terms, pure coercive bargaining is characterized by both parties' holding out for the *CD* or *DC* outcome, but constrained in this by the risk of the *DD* outcome. In accommodative bargaining, one or both have dropped hopes of a win (*CD* or *DC*) and aim for some version of *CC,* but each wants the substance of the latter to be as close as possible to a win for itself, and this constrains them from offering too much or appearing too eager in their *CC* proposals.

We turn now to a logical examination of specific tensions or dilemmas between goals and constraints in coercive and accommodative bargaining. This will be accompanied by a statement of empirical findings from the cases about how nations in crises actually resolve these dilemmas.

COERCIVE: WIN VS. RISK-AVOIDANCE

Coercion is obviously conflict-oriented. The common interest is involved chiefly as something to be manipulated, typically via a threat to destroy it (e.g., a threat of war), as a means of exerting influence. Most contemporary theorizing about strategic bargaining tends to emphasize the coercive aim of winning in the conflict dimension, under-emphasizing the common interest as something to be realized or preserved, rather than manipulated.

This perspective overlooks the point that states in a crisis may well be as concerned about their common interest in avoiding war as they are about getting their way. Statesmen are likely to have prominently in mind that they are in a dangerous, unpredictable situation, from which a war could possibly erupt that neither side wants. This awareness introduces a set of considerations that tends to temper their coercive efforts. That is, it creates a number of antinomies between tactics that are useful for winning the conflict, and other behaviors that tend to reduce the risk of war.

Risk-avoidance considerations fall into two broad categories. One set of risks is inherent in the bargaining process itself, conceived as a controlled process based on reasoned calculation. The key risk is that of *miscalculation.* The parties calculate and have their behavior under control, but for a variety of possible reasons, including misperceptions of the adversary's interests and intentions, they calculate badly. They commit themselves to violence if the adversary does not behave as demanded, expecting him to concede in the knowledge of the commitment; however, the adversary either does not get the message or is already committed himself. The parties become locked into a disastrous course that they would have wished to avoid. Given imperfect information, possible misperception and unreliable communication channels, any coercive strategy based on commitment logically involves this risk as a constraint.

The other general type of risk is "autonomous" risk, the danger that the parties will lose control of events. Such risks are analytically external to the bargaining process, if the latter is conceived as a deliberate, controlled affair, although they do impinge on the bargaining in various ways. What, precisely, people have in mind when they refer to the danger of "events getting out of control" is somewhat obscure, but there is no doubt that in many crises it is a prominent consideration in statesmen's minds, usually focused on the possibility of some violent incident that would touch off uncontrollable escalation. One can imagine several possible sources of "uncontrollability." There is, for example, the collective human experience that, once significant violence occurs between states, it develops to its fullest possible extent. Khrushchev had something like this in mind during the Cuban missile crisis when he told Kennedy that "if indeed war should break out, then it would not be in our power to stop it, for such is the logic of war." [15] The implication is that once violence breaks out, a whole new set of forces takes over, with an inner dynamic of its own which develops to its fullest extent, more or less autonomously. The notions of controlled limited wars or violent crises have not sunk very deeply into the consciousness of the race, despite recent experience; but the idea that some spark can ignite an uncontrollable conflagration when tensions are high is deeply ingrained, and could act as a self-fulfilling prophecy.

A more specific source of "events out of control" could be "subordinates out of control," especially military subordinates. When violence begins, there is at least the possibility that military commanders will act and react independently of political control, according to preset plans. However, very few, if any, cases of war in modern history appear to be directly attributable to unauthorized military action. A more plausible possibility is that political leaders retain control technically but cannot resist the imperatives built into military plans for certain contingencies, or the pressures from military commanders to implement them. A good example of this would be the Russian and German mobilization and war plans prior to World War I. Perhaps the most likely cause of loss of control is the effect of violence on popular passions or on the emotions of statesmen themselves. Violence may trigger automatic psychological compulsions to react in kind, feelings of "no choice" based essentially on emotional or irrational factors such as pride, "face," rage or even "duty." [16] The statesman loses control

---

[15] Robert F. Kennedy, *Thirteen Days* (New York: Signet, 1969), p. 87.

[16] In many primitive social systems, with no strong central authority, it is considered a "duty" to exact reprisal in kind for injury done to oneself or one's kinsman. The international system is, of course, a "primitive social system."

here by losing control of himself; he stops calculating rationally, emotions replace reason, he can only be "provoked," not coerced.

Subsumed within the overall tension between coercion-to-win and avoidance-of-war are several subdilemmas of which we shall discuss two. The first, *commit vs preserve options,* relates to the first kind of risk discussed above—the danger of mutual commitment. The other one, *manipulate vs. minimize autonomous risk,* relates to the second kind, the danger of losing control of events. The first, commit vs. preserve options, may be divided into the categories of physical and verbal coercion. As will be seen presently, these dilemmas are not always clearly separable in actual cases, but for purposes of theoretical stage-setting, it is useful to separate them.

Commit vs. Preserve Options: Coercion

This dilemma reflects certain tensions between coercion and war-avoidance in the bargaining process itself, strictly conceived as the interplay of rationally calculated moves, i.e., abstracting from the non-rational and accidental elements. Moves that commit a party to stand firm, or to fight if the opponent does not behave as desired, are powerful coercive tactics. But for a variety of reasons they may jeopardize the common interest in settling a crisis short of war.[17]

First there are many ways a commitment can fail to coerce the adversary as intended. A successful commitment has three elements: (1) the act of committal, (2) communication to the adversary that one is committed, and (3) a decision by the adversary to behave in the way one desires, as a result of the communication. Between each of these steps many things can go awry. The enemy may not perceive that one's alternatives or incentives have been altered so that one is now committed, especially if the committal act is not physical and highly visible (e.g.,

---

[17] The term *commitment* has several meanings in ordinary usage, and even in the theoretical literature its meaning is often ambiguous. Writers tend to shift back and forth between the notion of commitment as something a party "is committed" (would prefer) to do, given its existing preference structure, and commitment as a type of strategic *move* that creates a commitment in the first sense, without distinguishing clearly between the two meanings. We use *commitment* in the first sense only and the terms *committing move* or *committing threat* for the second meaning. All coercive moves, verbal or physical, attempt to communicate that one is committed to a firm stand, but the move as an *act* should be separated analytically from its *effect* in increasing the threatener's cost in backing down. This effect may or may not create a commitment. A move creates a commitment—i. e., is a committing move—when it raises the cost of yielding higher than the potential cost of standing firm, when that was not the case before the move. A state may be committed to stand firm in a crisis without making any "moves" at all. If so, its coercive moves are intended only to communicate the commitment; they are themselves neither commitments nor committing moves. When we pose the dilemma of "commit vs. preserve options" we refer to the choice between making a newly *committing move* or refraining from doing so to preserve flexibility.

like the troops in Berlin). Efforts to communicate the commitment to him have to be processed by his preexisting image, expectations, and emotional state. Even if the commitment is successfully communicated, there is still no guarantee that he will behave in the manner one expects or demands of him. One may have misestimated his incentives, and his decision-making system may be subject to vagaries or rigidities of various kinds. Thus a commitment is inherently risky. It fully determines *one's own* subsequent behavior but by no means determines his. If the commitment fails to "work," the outcome could be disastrous or at least more costly than if freedom of action had been preserved.

Second, a committing move, especially a provocative one, may trigger a countercommitment by the opponent, who either feels he must respond to preserve his prestige or thinks the only way he can force one to back down on *one's* commitment is to make a commitment even more firm and less revocable. There can be dangerous escalation in the making of threats and commitments just as there can be escalation in violence. This may produce the familiar situation of becoming "locked in," each side hoping and believing that its commitment will effectively intimidate the other and each failing to realize until too late that the other party has become committed, too.

The obvious alternative to a strategy of commitment is to preserve a maximum range of options so that one is free to react flexibly to the opponent's moves at minimum cost and risk. But option preservation may detract from coercive potency: the adversary can be fairly confident that if he misbehaves or fails to concede to our desires, we will choose the option which costs us least, which will probably also be the one that damages him the least. Moreover, we may be vulnerable to the opponent's coercion; *he* may be able to commit himself to precipitating mutual disaster unless we yield to him, safe in the knowledge that our flexibility gives us the option of yielding. In short, the dilemma is this: commitment maximizes the chances of winning but flirts with disaster; option preservation maximizes the chances of avoiding war or extreme levels of destruction but risks being bested in the crisis contest of wills.[18] A large part of the crisis management problem is to resolve this dilemma optimally. In verbal coercion, the dilemma appears mainly as the choice between clarity and ambiguity. In the domain of physical moves, it appears as the choice whether to begin high or low on the escalation ladder.

[18] This dilemma is roughly analogous to the choice in preparedness policy between "deterrence by nuclear threat" and "defense by flexible response," an issue that was thoroughly debated in the late fifties and early sixties. Cf. Glenn H. Snyder, *Deterrence and Defense* (Princeton, N.J.: Princeton University Press, 1961). The dilemma in its bargaining form is implicit in much of Thomas Schelling's writing; see especially *Arms and Influence*, Ch. 2.

Commit vs. Preserve Options: Verbal. The difference in function or effect between verbal and physical coercive acts is not entirely clear. It is generally believed that "actions speak louder than words," and some argue that words alone are ineffective, but our cases do not bear this out. A show of force may be quite weak, and some threats and other verbal statements may be strongly committing. What is important is the amount of value apparently engaged by the act, whether verbal or non-verbal—i.e., the cost of non-fulfillment. Often the most potent moves or strategies combine verbal and non-verbal acts—the words explicate the contingency that will activate the threat and describe the specific nature of the sanction; the physical moves provide credibility by giving the impression of "seriousness," and perhaps by taking steps toward actual fulfillment of the threat. However, for convenience, we shall take up the verbal and physical techniques separately.

The most obvious verbal coercive move is the *threat.* In form a threat states a demand on another party, plus a sanction that will be inflicted if the demand is not met. The purpose may be either compellent ("do that or else") or deterrent ("don't do that or else"). Either the demand or the sanction may be quite vague, and one or the other may even be left unstated for inference. In terms of the threatener's real intention (i.e., his "commitment"), three kinds of threats may be specified logically. First, there is the "committing threat," the threat that creates a commitment for the threatener that he did not have before, via the engagement of additional values (honor, resolve reputation, etc.) that would be lost if the threat were not fulfilled. Second, there is the "warning threat," which merely states, and perhaps strengthens, a commitment that already existed before the threat was made.[19] The third type is the "bluff," the threat that neither states nor creates a commitment. Bluffs may be divided into "pure" and "problematic" varieties. The pure bluff is a threat the threatener knows he will not carry out. The problematic bluff covers cases where the threatener does not know at the time of making the threat whether he would fulfill it or not, should the occasion for fulfillment arise.

[19] We use the term *warning threat* rather than simply *warning* as Schelling labels this category, because we wish to give the term "warning" a somewhat different meaning later. In actual diplomatic parlance the distinction between *threat* and *warning* rests more on the form and tone of the utterance than on whether or not the threatener is already committed to do what he is threatening. Implicitly, we are distinguishing here between the *communicative* quality of a threat and its *committal* quality. The communicative quality refers to the informational structure of the threat—size and nature of the demand, severity of the sanction, time limit for compliance, degree of explicitness, etc. Its committing quality refers to its *effect* on the preference structure of the threatener and perhaps also the threatenee. These effects may or may not commit the threatener; via the "backlash effect" (to be discussed below) new values may also be engaged for the threatenee that may or may not commit him to resist.

We found no *clear* instances of the committing threat in our cases. The distinctive quality of such a threat is that, if the occasion for fulfillment arrives (i.e., the threatenee fails to comply with the demand), the threatener may wish he had not made the threat but is forced to fulfill it nonetheless by the fact that the issuance of the threat has made non-fulfillment more costly than fulfillment. There are one or two instances which come close to this quality, or which leave the researcher uncertain as to whether a commitment was actually created. One is the British and French threats to Germany during the "May crisis" over Czechoslovakia in 1938. These threats may well have committed the two countries to defend Czechoslovakia had Germany attacked. But this is not certain; the utterances could have been "warning threats" or "problematic bluffs."

The reason that committing threats are so rare [20] is not so much that threats do not or cannot engage sufficient values to commit, but rather that statesmen prefer not to commit themselves as a purely "strategic move." That is, they prefer not to commit themselves to a course of action that, prior to the threat, they would rather not take, hoping that the threat-commitment will persuade the adversary to behave so that the threatened action need not be carried out. They want to have it both ways—to influence the adversary but to avoid committing themselves.

It follows that virtually all the threats in our crisis cases are of the second and third types—those that declare an already existing commitment and those that are either pure or problematic bluffs. The severest, most explicit threats usually fall into the first category; the milder and more ambiguous ones in the second.

---

[20] The reason, other than logical completeness, why we included this type of threat in our typology is that it is quite prominent in the existing theoretical literature; therefore we expected to find quite a number in our cases. For instance, Thomas Schelling at one point seems to define threats in general as necessarily *creating* a commitment: "Like the ordinary commitment, *the threat is a surrender of choice, a renunciation of alternatives* that makes one worse off than he need be in the event the tactic fails" (italics ours). Schelling, *The Strategy of Conflict,* p. 123. However, Schelling in other passages clearly implies that threats may be bluffs. Fred Iklé employs a definition of threats similar to Schelling's; *How Nations Negotiate,* p. 63.

Incidentally, while we shall note later that there are not many empirical instances of the more dramatic tactical options discussed by Schelling—irrevocable commitment, manipulation of shared risk, pretending irrationality, etc.—we do not intend this as a criticism of Schelling's work. Schelling did not pretend to describe what states actually do (nor to prescribe what they should do); his intent was to lay bare the inherent logic of coercive bargaining, including a list of pure types of tactics that this logic suggested. No one should expect the real world to conform closely to deductive logic, but a deductive theory like Schelling's provides an excellent benchmark for exploring and describing how real actors *do* behave. Without Schelling's prior theoretical work this book could never have been written, and it was his work which largely inspired our project. We have tried to discover how far the tactics of real actors deviate from Schelling's ideal types, and to explain why.

For example, the severest possible threat is the ultimatum, which demands the unconditional acceptance of certain terms within a short time, with war the consequence of non-compliance. There were six ultimata in our 16 cases, all issued by a fully committed state: Germany to Russia, 1909 (demanding Russian recognition of the Austrian annexation of Bosnia); Austria to Serbia, 1914; Germany to Russia, 1914; Germany to France, 1914; Germany to Czechoslovakia, 1938; and United States to the Soviet Union, 1962. The three 1914 ultimata were simply preludes to a war that had already been decided upon. They were so severe that compliance was not expected; they were intended simply to satisfy the convention of the time that the party to be attacked have a final opportunity to come to terms. Hitler's ultimatum to Czechoslovakia of September 26, 1938, also had this conventional quality; on this date Hitler was still determined to attack although two days later the British, the French, and Mussolini were able to undo his commitment. The other two, the Bosnia and Cuba, 1962, ones, were not pro forma preludes to war, but genuine coercive bargaining moves. In the first case, Germany was fully committed to fight if necessary, but knew it would not be necessary since Russia, not being ready for war, would have to comply. In the Cuban case, the United States was committed to an air strike on the Cuban missile sites should the Soviets not comply, but was not absolutely certain of Soviet compliance.

Other variants of the warning threat, less severe than ultimata, were quite common in our cases. In some of these instances, the threat was almost immediately successful in communicating the underlying commitment, in others not; in some it required a sequence of threats sometimes accompanied by physical moves to instill belief in the adversary. For example, in the Fashoda case, the French did not fully believe Salisbury was serious until the British began mobilizing their fleet, and it took a while for the Germans to believe the British threats in 1905.

While we can be sure the total of committing threats is zero, it proved impossible to make a precise count of warning threats, problematic bluffs and pure bluffs for two reasons: (1) no good operational criteria could be found to enable us to distinguish between threats and merely bellicose language, and (2) it was often impossible to distinguish between problematic bluffs and pure bluffs, since our empirical materials did not always disclose whether the state, when it made the threat, was sure it would not carry it out or was merely undecided. However, we can say with confidence that warning threats were more frequent than either problematic or pure bluffs. Examples of problematic bluffs are the rather timid British threats to Germany in 1938 and the vague threats the U.S. government made to Japan in 1941 before the government had decided it would defend Southeast Asia. The clearest example of the pure bluff was the German threat to France in 1905. And Kennedy must have been bluffing in 1962, when he said a missile fired from Cuba to any target in the Western Hemisphere would result in "full retaliation" against the Soviet Union.

EXPLICITNESS VS. AMBIGUITY: The dilemma between commitment and option-preservation appears in the domain of verbal coercion primarily as the choice between explicitness and ambiguity. Maximum explicitness and clarity in threats tends to produce maximum credibility. Values such as national prestige and bargaining reputation are then engaged to the highest degree, and a failure to fulfill the threat would result in maximum losses to these values. Knowing this, the threat recipient will expect the threatener to fulfill the threat to avoid these losses. The threatener is then most likely to be or to seem committed as a result of having made the threat. On the other hand, an ambiguous threat leaves the threatener an out; he can reinterpret the threat, imply that it really didn't mean what it seemed to mean, claim that the contingency or behavior of the other party is not what was intended to activate the threat, or even claim that he never really threatened at all. If, when making the threat, the threatener was not clear about what he would do if his demand were resisted, ambiguity leaves him free to act as he wishes when the respondent's compliance or non-compliance is clear. Thus, ambiguity "preserves options"; the threatener can avoid fulfillment with minimum value loss or can act at a lower lower of mutual cost and risk than he had threatened.

But the threatenee, perceiving that the threatener has left himself an out, may then believe that the threat is not intended to be executed—that it is a bluff. At least, in his eyes, it will have low credibility, and he is less likely to be influenced. He will feel safer in becoming more committed himself. In short, clarity and explicitness maximize coercive power but at the cost of closing off the option of non-fulfillment, or of increasing the cost of that option, if the threat fails to work. Ambiguity minimizes costs and risks if the threat fails in its aim, but at the sacrifice of some coercive potency.

This dilemma is most relevant for crises structured as Chicken. Each party has the option of gambling with a commitment in the hope of a win if the opponent does not become committed or of playing it safe by not committing. It is not so relevant to Prisoner's Dilemma crises because the parties are already committed to fight rather than yield. They lose nothing by making this much clear at the start. However, they are not committed to fight rather than *compromise,* so both sides have an interest in not committing themselves so strongly as to foreclose compromise, and this may in some cases conflict with their interest in communicating their commitment to fight rather than give in entirely.

We have already hinted how states who do face this dilemma tend to resolve it, when we said we found no example in our cases of the "committing threat," the threat that, by its clarity and explicitness commits a party who was not committed before by its interests. The dilemma is always resolved on the side of preserving options by retaining elements of ambiguity in verbal declarations.

However, there is still the choice of how much ambiguity. A state may choose to make its threats moderately explicit in the hope of presenting at least the appearance of commitment. This has its potential costs, of course, in the extra values lost if the threat fails to influence the adversary and is exposed as a bluff. The dilemma here is not the extreme one of "commit vs. preserve options," but rather "maximize coercive power vs. minimize costs of being caught bluffing." Actors who consciously make threats with this trade-off in mind often describe their function as "keeping them guessing." For example, in August 1938, the British cabinet feared that Hitler was about to commit himself to attack Czechoslovakia. They considered issuing a clear explicit threat that might deter the commitment. However, Chamberlain argued that a nation should not commit itself to go to war unless it was actually prepared to do so, as Britain was not. A solution was found in a public statement that if war broke out "it would be quite impossible to say where it would end and what governments would be involved." [21] The idea was that this statement would at least "keep Herr Hitler guessing" about British intentions while keeping British options open. However, the statement had no effect on Hitler's firm belief that Britain and France would not act; he assessed the ambiguous threat as simply a bluff. Given Hitler's firm image of Chamberlain as a soft appeaser, it would have required an explicit threat to create even uncertainty in his mind about British intentions.

The "keep-em-guessing" formula attempts to give some coercive mileage by introducing uncertainty into the opponent's calculations, when the state wishes to keep its options open. As the example shows, whether the gambit works depends on the opponent's image of the threatener. Or, more precisely, the amount of clarity required to induce even uncertainty in the opponent is a function of that image. If the threatener has compiled a record of toughness in the past, or of acting tougher than his previous declarations had indicated (e.g., as when the United States defended South Korea after Acheson's declaration that it was outside the U.S. "defense perimeter"), or of generally acting unpredictably, the state can get maximum coercion out of ambiguous threats. Since Chamberlin had compiled exactly the opposite record,

[21] J. W. Wheeler-Bennett, *Munich: Prologue to Tragedy* (New York: The Viking Press, 1963), p. 85.

he could get none; he had either to commit himself explicitly or not threaten at all; the "keep-em-guessing" straddle was not a viable option.

The dilemma we have just been discussing relates only to the effects of threats on the threatener. There are, however, other aspects of the more general "win vs. avoid risks" tension in coercive bargaining that involve the effects of threats on the opponent. For example, successful coercion while minimizing risks also requires avoiding provocativeness in one's threats and declarations, preserving and maximizing the opponent's options for compliance, and increasing his sense of the risks incurred by his own coercive tactics. The general choice between clarity and ambiguity also bears on some of these aspects.

MINIMIZING PROVOCATION: Between status equals an explicit threat is typically provocative to the recipient. The threatener appears more resolved but this gain is offset by the "stiffening" effect on the adversary —his prestige and resolve image are engaged as well as the threatener's, and the net effect is to make concessions more difficult for both sides. The threatenee may feel it necessary to make a counterthreat to preserve status and equality of resolve, or he may refuse to negotiate at all "under duress." The problem for the threatener, therefore, is to fashion his threat so as to get his message across credibly without provoking the recipient to firmer resistance. Vagueness may help resolve this dilemma by avoiding, for the recipient, the connotation that he is being dictated to by a peer.

There are several instances in our cases of bargainers refraining from making threats, or manipulating the context or timing of the threats, so as to minimize the element of provocation. The best-known instance perhaps is the U.S. government's decision against sending an ultimatum to Khrushchev early in the Cuban missile crisis because "no great power could accept" it.[22] In 1914, Austria delayed presenting her ultimatum to Serbia until after the French president and prime minister had left Russia, partly because it might be regarded as a contemptuous affront if delivered when the top French and Russian leaders were in consultation. After the ultimatum, the Russian foreign minister, Sazonov, avoided brusque language in dealing with Austria for fear of irritating her. He was similarly cautious when he instructed his ambassador in Vienna not to deliver the Russian protest jointly or simultaneously with those delivered by France and England. In diplomatic tradition, a *joint demarche* was more potent but also more challenging than notes delivered separately—thus Sazonov sacrificed coercive power to avoid provocation. Later in the crisis, Lord Grey refused Russia's request for a pledge of support partly from fear that it would provoke Germany.

[22] Theodore Sorenson, *Kennedy* (New York: Bantam, 1966), p. 772.

When he belatedly took a firm stand, he made it in the form of a "private statement" to the German ambassador, fearing that a threat made as an official statement would provoke Germany to war. These last examples illustrate how the mere labeling of declarations can modify their provocative implications.

In 1938 Chamberlain and Halifax used extremely delicate language in most of their infrequent warnings to Hitler, carefully avoiding anything that might "set Hitler off." In other ways, too, they sought to avoid provoking the Fuehrer, e.g., in refusing the French request for staff talks and by "forbidding" the Czechs to mobilize after their mobilization in May had sharply increased tension.

Hitler, too, was sensitive to the "avoid provocation" constraint. When he perceived, at Godesberg, that he had made Chamberlain angry by raising his demands, he extended his time limit for three days, saying that Chamberlain was the only man for whom he had ever done such a thing, and complimenting Chamberlain on his brilliant diplomacy. Chamberlain was then able to persuade himself that Hitler had made a "concession" to balance off his new demands; remarkably, his ire subsided immediately.

A technique for avoiding provocation of the other party is to frame threats in the form of "warnings." The critical distinction between a threat and a warning, as these terms are understood in actual diplomatic practice, is whether the utterance appears to be an act of deliberate coercive pressure when the threatener has the option of not exerting pressure, or is simply a statement of what the communicator would *have* to do in a contingency, having no choice to do otherwise. It is this difference in *perceived intent* between warnings and threats—the one merely conveying information, the other clearly intended to intimidate—that gives rise to the subjective or affective difference between the two, which is more significant empirically than the objective criterion of whether the threatener (warner) was actually committed before making the declaration. The warning generates less hostility than a threat because the warner appears to be merely explaining, in a "friendly spirit," what he would have to do to make sure the recipient, out of ignorance, does not precipitate consequences harmful to both sides. When the message is perceived as a threat, however, the recipient feels anger because the threatener is saying he would deliberately choose to inflict harm and is saying it in order to force the other to bend to his will, which, as an equal, he has no right to do. Thus a threat will often increase the spirit of resistance in the recipient because it implicates status values that can be saved only by resistance. To avoid this, governments often state their actual threats in the form of warnings.

Thus the United States informed the Soviet government during the

Iran crisis of 1946 that it would have "no choice" but to place the issue before the U.N. Security Council unless the Soviets withdrew their troops. Similar statements were made by Germany to Russia in 1914, warning of the inevitable consequences of Russian mobilization. In 1962, when Robert Kennedy demanded of the Soviet ambassador a promise "by tomorrow" that the missiles in Cuba would be removed, otherwise the United States would have to remove them, he said he "was not giving them an ultimatum but a statement of fact." [23]

Obviously, it is the interpretation of a statement by its recipient that is crucial, and curiously, the simple labeling of a statement by the issuer as a "warning, not a threat" is often sufficient. The incantation tends to relieve the recipient of the need to counterthreaten in defense of his prestige. It neutralizes the element of challenge, and if the recipient does not really want to "get his back up" he can refrain, without losing status values; he joins the warner in the mutual pretense that no real coercion has taken place.

Still another variable in the practical distinction between warnings and threats is the degree of bellicosity of the language (apart from the choice-or-no-choice variable). When the German government referred to the strident, chauvinistic Lloyd George speech in the 1911 Morocco crisis as a "warning bordering on a threat" they apparently meant that Lloyd George had used "fighting words," close to the kind of language that could provoke a war.

Threats and warnings are not of course the only kinds of verbal coercive declarations. A state may simply declare its firmness, or re-iterate its demand, or adduce reasons why it cannot concede or reduce its demands, without any mention of sanctions to be inflicted upon the opponent if he does not concede. Indeed, statements of this sort are far more frequent than threats and warnings as forms of verbal pressure, although naturally the possibility of sanctions may be implicit. States-men are generally aware that outright threats are counterproductive except in special circumstances: when the adversary is so obviously weak that he cannot afford to let himself be provoked by the threat.

The wisest bargainers prefer "quiet firmness" over noisy bellicosity when exercising pressure, whether verbally or non-verbally. One reason is to avoid provoking the opponent, but there is another reason, too: quiet firmness is more credible than dramatic threats and declarations. It is more credible because a blatant threat (or an over-flamboyant non-verbal maneuver) implies that one feels a special need to "make an impression." In other words, it implies actual weakness: one is really not resolved but is trying to make menacing language do the job of real intent. The very "bluster" carries a suggestion of bluff. A show of quiet

[23] Kennedy, *Thirteen Days,* p. 108.

firmness is more effective in communicating real determination because it gets across that one contemplates the prospect of fighting with equanimity and feels no special need to overpower the adversary with bellicose language in order that fighting be *avoided*. Henry Kissinger probably had this in mind when he advised President Kennedy not to declare a national emergency during the Berlin crisis of 1961. He argued the Soviets would be more impressed by a gradual sustained build-up of U.S. readiness and apparent resolve than by such a single dramatic gesture, which would appear "unnecessarily bellicose, even hysterical." There was evidence that Khrushchev might so interpret it in the latter's remark after the United States declared a military alert at the time of the 1960 U-2 incident: "We have not declared an alert and will not declare one. Our nerves are strong." Eisenhower writes that he deliberately delayed the U.S. response to Khrushchev's "ultimatum" that opened the Berlin crisis of 1958, because he did not want the American government to appear "edgy." [24] Thus we see that moderation in the tone of coercive statements, or delay, or an appearance of calmness may be useful for defensive or offensive coercion as well as for minimizing provocation of the opponent.

PRESERVING OPPONENT'S OPTIONS: Both the goal of winning the crisis and the risk-avoidance constraint counsel preserving options for the opponent. On the one hand, this may mean avoiding severe threats that engage so much emotion, prestige, and reputational value for the opponent that he cannot concede. On the other hand, it means including in one's coercive communications rather specific "loopholes" through which the adversary can retreat with minimum loss. Examples of the latter include Bulow's statement to the French in 1905 that the German demand for a conference on Morocco was a mere formality; once the conference was convened, the French would get all they desired. Another was the U.S. statement in 1946 that it believed the Russian troops in northern Iran were acting without official authorization in supporting the rebel government and preventing Iranian troops from entering the area. Also in the Iran case, a United States-sponsored resolution in the United Nations, which called upon the Soviet Union and Iran to report *jointly* on the arrangements for the Soviet troop withdrawal, enabled the Soviets to present their compliance as resulting from amicable negotiations with a small power, rather than coercive pressure from

[24] The Kissinger quotation is from Arthur M. Schlesinger, *A Thousand Days: John F. Kennedy in the White House* (Boston: Houghton Mifflin, 1965), p. 363; the Eisenhower quote is from his memoirs, *Waging Peace, 1956–1961* (Garden City, N.J.: Doubleday, 1965), p. 331; and the Khrushchev quote is from Jervis, *The Logic of Images,* p. 175, originally quoted in Hans Speier, *Divided Berlin* (New York: Praeger, 1961), p. 109. Jervis gives the Khrushchev remark a slightly different interpretation.

outside big powers. If an opponent is already committed but would like to get out of the commitment, he may need help in doing so. The whole Munich conference, for example, was an elaborate device for relieving Hitler of his commitment to attack Czechoslovakia.

MANIPULATING ADVERSARY'S RISK CONSTRAINTS: Some coercive leverage may be gained by manipulating the *adversary's* risk-avoidance constraints—i.e., by enlarging his perception of the risk involved in his own coercive attempts, either the risk of inadvertent mutual commitment or the risk that the crisis will get out of control.[25]

Thus the French foreign minister, Delcassé, warned the British ambassador during the Fashoda crisis that, if Britain persisted in her coercive course, France would be boxed in by her "honor," unable to retreat. The tactic did not work in this case because the French were so weak militarily that they could not fight even for honor. Khrushchev may have had more success with his famous "knot of war" analogy during the Cuban missile crisis. "Mr. President, we and you ought not to pull on the ends of the rope in which you have tied the knot of war, because the more the two of us pull, the tighter the knot will be tied. And a moment may come when that knot will be tied so tight that even he who tied it will not have the strength to untie it, and then it will be necessary to cut that knot, and what that would mean is not for me to explain to you." [26] Since both parties know that threats engage values for the threatenee as well as the threatener, to point this out explicitly may inhibit the opponent's coercive strategy.

The tactic of feigning irrationality or high emotionality may be used to play upon the opponent's fears that the crisis will get out of control. Schelling had something different in mind when he discussed this possible tactic: when a party makes a threat that would be irrational to carry out, its credibility is enhanced if the party appears to be irrational.[27] We find, however, that the primary function of apparent irrationality, recklessness, emotional instability, etc., is not to make the irrational threatener's threats more credible, but to deter his opponent from making threats. It activates the adversary's risk-avoidance constraint, inhibiting his capacity to exert coercive pressure. To be sure, the Schelling interpretation is not without substance. Hitler, the prize exhibit, cultivated an image of tenuous control over raging passions for both purposes. However, the primary effect of his emotional dis-

[25] This seems to be partly what Schelling had in mind in his discussion of "the manipulation of risk," although his central meaning there was somewhat different and will be taken up in the next section. Schelling, *Arms and Influence,* Ch. 3.

[26] Kennedy, *Thirteen Days,* pp. 89–90.

[27] Schelling, *Arms and Influence,* pp. 36ff.

plays was to inhibit his adversaries from warning him or taking firm stands for fear of sending him off the deep end. To a lesser degree Khrushchev's natural impetuousness, which he let "hang out" on appropriate occasions—e.g., when he banged his shoe on a desk during a U.N. meeting—chiefly instilled in his adversaries the thought that here was a man who might quite easily be provoked to rash behavior. Hence Kennedy worried during 1961 that the firm, coercive aspects of his Berlin policy might be too strong, might be taken by Khrushchev as insulting, and he carefully hedged his firmness with fervent statements of a desire to negotiate. In the Cuban crisis, as well, Kennedy's fears of a Soviet "spasm response" to any violent U.S. act probably were linked at least as closely to his picture of the highly emotional and provokable Khrushchev, as to a theory of how states generally react to violence in a crisis.

MULTIPLE AUDIENCES: The clarity-vs.-ambiguity choice is relevant not only to bargaining with the adversary but also to dealings with allies and to the preservation or mobilization of domestic support—i.e., to the whole range of goals and constraints a party faces in a crisis. For example, in the Quemoy affair of 1958 the U.S. government felt the need to be explicitly firm to deter the Communist Chinese, ambiguously supportive to restrain Chiang Kai-Shek, and vague to calm the timid British and to avoid congressional criticism. These multiple constraints were met by vaguely linking up Quemoy to the Formosa Resolution of 1955, combined with firmer expressions of determination in newspaper leaks and by subordinate officials, and a military build-up in the local area. The mixture was successful in getting across to the Communists that the United States probably was committed, while the lack of an explicit public declaration of commitment by either Eisenhower or Dulles met the allied and domestic constraints.[28]

Also illustrative of the mixed motives for ambiguity was the British warning to Germany on August 27, 1938, which was mentioned above. Chamberlain and Halifax wanted to issue some kind of warning to Hitler and deter him from an expected commitment to attack Czechoslovakia. However, they knew that a clear statement of British intent to fight would rouse a storm in British public opinion, they feared it would produce intransigence in the Czechs, and they wished to avoid commitment to a war they were not prepared to fight. They were wary also of provoking Hitler with excessively blunt language. Out of these con-

---

[28] Howe, *Multicrises*, pp. 208, 210. Avoidance of an explicit verbal commitment was urged by the Joint Chiefs of Staff because an explicit warning limited to Quemoy and Matsu would only invite the Communists to take smaller islands. Dulles would have preferred a stronger statement. Eisenhower, *Waging Peace*, p. 295.

flicting considerations came the decision to issue the highly ambiguous warning—its impact reduced further by the fact that it was not a new statement but merely a reiteration of something Chamberlain had said earlier.

A firm, explicit threat may not always be in conflict with the constraint of risk-avoidance. When the risk to be avoided is inadvertent mutual commitment, such a threat may be employed to enlighten an apparently miscalculating opponent. This was the essential motive for Lloyd George's speech in the Morocco crisis of 1911. Lord Grey approved the speech because he feared Germany was mistakenly assuming British indifference. Alexander George has pointed out that a highly coercive threat may also be employed to deal with the other component of the risk-avoidance constraint, the risk of accidental war. When a U-2 plane was downed over Cuba in 1962, President Kennedy feared that another such incident might set in motion an uncontrollable train of events leading to war. It was this incident that prompted him to instruct his brother to deliver an ultimatum to the Soviet ambassador demanding a commitment to remove the missiles the following day.[29] A strong coercive action was taken, despite its risks, in the dimension of controlled bargaining, in order to preempt the onset of disaster from uncontrollable elements.

Whether a state chooses to commit itself explicitly depends also on the time-phasing of a crisis. We find in our cases a general tendency for threats and other coercive declarations to be vague during the early part of a crisis, increasing in explicitness as the crisis progresses. When a party is unsure of his opponent's resolve, keeping verbal declarations ambiguous early in the crisis allows for feedback that tells him how explicitly committed he may safely become. Pressure can then be escalated gradually by more explicit statements. At the end of the confrontation stage, if one side had clearly established its superior resolve, it can safely make a firm committing threat to turn the other party toward accommodation. The other, realizing it is overpowered, and perhaps having gotten too uncomfortably committed to an ally, or its domestic public, may even welcome such a threat because it "takes him off the hook." This was the case with the harsh "yes or no" ultimatum that Germany delivered to Russia in 1909; it was not unwelcome because Russia could then say to Serbia she had "no choice" but to withdraw her support.

There is some tendency for statesmen to want to preserve their verbal "big guns" for when they are most necessary—e.g., for when the op-

---

[29] Another motive for the ultimatum was the fact that the missiles were fast approaching operational readiness. George, Hall, and Simons, *The Limits of Coercive Diplomacy*, p. 59.

ponent makes, or seems about to make, some strongly coercive or dangerous move. Thus, in the Berlin crisis of 1961, Kennedy vetoed Acheson's suggestion of a declaration of "national emergency" early in the crisis, because he felt it would appear provocative, over-reactive, and because he wanted to save it for when the Soviets actually signed a peace treaty with the East Germans or made a move to blockade access to West Berlin.[30]

Commit vs. preserve options: physical action. Physical coercive moves in a crisis may be arrayed on an "escalation ladder": [31] from symbolic shows of force, to increases in military capabilities, to alerts and deployments that increase one's readiness to fight, to physical moves that apparently create a commitment to fight if the opponent initiates violence, to the actual use of violence short of war. With physical moves, the choice between commitment and preservation of options involves whether to start low or high on the escalation ladder.

STARTING LOW VS. STARTING HIGH: The logic of starting low is that it keeps open a wide range of options and thus minimizes the risks of mutual commitment and of violence escalating out of control. Action at a low level of risk may be enough to persuade the adversary to comply, and, if he does not, one can always move higher. The more potent but more dangerous moves higher up are reserved for use only if necessary. The adversary's response to the initial moves provides information about his resolve—how he is likely to react to higher-level moves. Starting low also enables a state to communicate its own resolve gradually so that its determination is clearly established if a more drastic action or commitment has to be undertaken later. A commitment taken suddenly, when an image of resolve has not been cultivated previously, may not seem credible. With few exceptions, states in our cases preferred to start low if they manipulated or used physical force.

The Cuban missile crisis provides a good illustration. If we had dealt with the problem summarily by an air strike the consequences could have been disastrous. The Russians would have been maximally provoked and might have felt impelled to take some violent counteraction, perhaps in Berlin or Turkey, or conceivably against the United States itself. Even a threat or warning of an air strike early in the crisis (which was considered and rejected) might have provoked the Soviets to make a strong countercommitment. Even if they had remained calm and calculated rationally, they would have faced a simple one-step calculation: was the United States really willing to take such a high risk of nuclear war? Lacking hard evidence about U.S. resolve (in fact, pos-

[30] Sorenson, *Kennedy,* p. 664.
[31] Kahn, *On Escalation.*

sibly holding a low estimate from U.S. behavior in recent confrontations in Laos, the Bay of Pigs, and Berlin), they might have guessed wrong. And the United States could not have been sure just how they would guess.

The naval blockade initiated the confrontation at a low level of risk by focusing on a subsidiary issue where the United States demand as well as the damage threatened were both limited. Above all, coercion was exercised by the threat of damage rather than by actual damage. And just what the blockade committed the United States to do, in what specific contingencies, was left somewhat ambiguous. The ambiguity preserved for the United States a considerable range of options in its implementation. Kennedy manipulated the blockade so as to keep open as long as possible his own options short of violence and to maximize the time available to his opponent to consider *his* options. But the time made available to Khrushchev had a double-edged significance: if it kept him from making rash moves and gave him time to realize he was overpowered and to get his decision-making apparatus to reverse course, it contributed to "risk-avoidance." On the other hand, as Alexander George has pointed out, Khrushchev might have used the time to get himself committed to leaving the missiles in and he *did* use it to bring the missiles closer to operational readiness. Thus in delaying resort to violence, Kennedy served his risk-avoidance constraint at the price of a potential loss in the balance of coercive power.[32] He won his gamble, and it paid off not only in avoiding violence but also in increasing his bargaining power for the main event—actually forcing the missiles out. The superior U.S. resolve that was demonstrated on the blockade issue "spilled over" into the Soviet assessment of U.S. resolve on higher rungs of the escalation ladder, notably the air strike. When an ultimatum was issued a few days later, demanding removal of the missiles, it carried high credibility because of the previous build-up of the U.S. resolve image. Thus the tension between "winning" and "risk-avoidance" is not unequivocal; preserving options and stretching out the course of events may increase coercive potency as well as minimize risks.

The opposite logic, which favors "starting high," holds that starting low on the escalation ladder may seem timid, indecisive. As it was argued in the debate about Dulles's "massive retaliation" policy, keeping options open might be interpreted as a lack of will to use the most costly or risky ones. Moreover, it prolongs the confrontation, providing time for the opponent to develop countercoercive tactics and to demonstrate his resolve. It may start a process of escalating violence, or of deepening commitment and progressive magnification of the values

[32] George, Hall, and Simon, *The Limits of Coercive Diplomacy,* pp. 233–234.

at stake so that the adversary becomes less coercible and the ultimate disaster becomes more difficult to avoid. As argued by the air strike advocates in the Cuban case, the preferable course may be the fait accompli, which resolves the issue swiftly and summarily and provides no time for the opponent to make counterthreats and commitments. The game is over, he has lost, and he had best accept it. With this logic, the Germans urged the Austrians to march quickly into Serbia in 1914 to preempt the mobilization of counterpressures from the Entente powers. (For technical military reasons, the Austrians were unable to carry out the advice.) An advantage of the fait accompli strategy is that it brings about a switch in roles: the former challenger is now the defender of a new status quo with the bargaining advantage that usually comes with that role; the former defender is now the potential challenger, carrying the burden of having to initiate the risks of a further confrontation. The fait accompli is at the high end of the start low vs. start high continuum. If it does not resolve the crisis it at least sharply increases the bargaining power of the party accomplishing it, but at the risk of war with an opponent who either is already committed or who becomes committed by the provocative effect of the fait accompli.

The choice between starting low or starting high with the fait accompli thus depends heavily on the actor's estimate of the adversary's value structure, specifically whether he is playing Chicken, or some other game that commits him to fight in response to the fait accompli, and the degree of confidence with which this estimate is held. The Germans were (mistakenly) certain the Russians were chicken in the early part of the 1914 crisis; Kennedy was not sure of the Soviets in 1962, in fact he was inclined to believe they would be provoked by the air strike to violent reprisal.

THE "IRREVOCABLE COMMITMENT":   The tactic of the physical irrevocable commitment, suggested by Thomas Schelling, is similar to the fait accompli in that it shifts the burden of initiating violence to the opponent. It differs in that it does not directly resolve the crisis issue by force, but rather positions one's forces in such a way that they cannot retreat; one's own option of yielding is therefore foreclosed, and the opponent knows it is he who must yield if violence is to be avoided.[33]

Our cases supply only four fairly clear examples of this tactic: the Soviet blockade of surface access routes to Berlin in 1948, the U.S. airlift that followed, the deployment of U.S. troops in Lebanon in 1958, and the raising of the Berlin Wall in 1961. Had any of these moves been countered by force, war was distinctly possible if not probable. The 1948 Berlin blockade placed a physical barrier across highways and rail-

[33] Schelling, *The Strategy of Conflict,* Ch. 2.

roads; a U.S. attempt to breach them by force would have dangerously risked bringing Soviet troops into action. The Soviet move was ineffective because it was circumvented by the U.S. airlift, which shifted the initiative for violence to the Soviets. A forcible interference with the airlift would have created a probability of war higher than the Soviets were willing to risk. It is worth noting, however, that the airlift was not *intended* as a coercive commitment by the United States, but only as a stop-gap measure to supply Berlin for a few weeks, until (it was hoped) negotiations would resolve the issue. The United States itself was surprised when the airlift worked—i.e., proved capable of supplying West Berlin's essential needs indefinitely.

The Berlin Wall was certainly "irrevocable" once it was erected, but like the airlift, it does not quite fit Schelling's ideal-type, since it was not really intended to coerce the Western powers but rather to deal directly with the internal East German problem that had triggered the crisis of 1961—the outflow of people to the West. It did not constitute a commitment to the move that the Soviets had been threatening if they did not get their way in *West* Berlin—signing a peace treaty unilaterally with East Germnay. Rather it was a partial *resolution* of the crisis by fait accompli even though its immediate effect was to heighten tension: It was a physical commitment only with respect to a forcible Western attempt to recover their lost rights in East Berlin. It did increase Western apprehension that the Soviets were about to try something tougher with regard to the West Berlin issue, but it did not constitute a commitment to do so.

The Lebanon landing is the purest case. The United States intended it as a commitment to fight in the event of a Lebanese revolution supported by outside forces, hence as a move to deter such revolution or intervention. Whether it worked depends on whether there was any real possibility that the events to be deterred would have happened had the troops not landed; the weight of the evidence indicates otherwise, but this is irrelevant to the fact that the move itself did create a commitment.

There are a few borderline instances: moves that bear some of the markings of the physical commitment, or "passing the initiative," but for one reason or another do not match Schelling's description of such moves.

The Chinese artillery blockade that started the Quemoy crisis was somewhat similar to the Berlin blockade. The Chinese possibly calculated that the blockade would force the United States to choose between bombing the mainland artillery batteries or persuading Chiang to evacuate the island, and that U.S. leaders would opt for the latter rather than enlarge the conflict. However, as in Berlin, the United States successfully passed the initiative back to China by a combination of convoying and sophisticated landing techniques. The Communist Chinese were then faced with the choice of either firing on the U.S. convoy ships (analogously to the airlift in Berlin) or invading the island, neither of which they were prepared to do.[34] Objectively, the example is less "pure" than the Berlin blockade case because Chiang's troops had enough supplies to last for many months (although the Communists probably did not know this), and Chiang probably could have gotten enough supplies ashore on his own to alleviate any shortages. Thus, in the early part of the crisis the United States was not so clearly saddled with the initiative for violence as in the Berlin case. The U.S. convoy operation was less important as an act of "reversing the initiative" than as a political demonstration of support for the Nationalists.[35]

The U.S. naval blockade in the Cuban missile crises of 1962 did commit the United States to use force had the Soviets attempted to run the blockade with missile-carrying ships. But the reason it did so was not that it physically closed off the United States' option to choose otherwise. It was physically possible to let the Soviet ships pass. The U.S. was committed not by a physical inability to avoid forcible action, but by the political costs of inaction. The blockade dramatically and visibly placed U.S. resolve on the line, and it was this fact that produced the commitment. The blockade is thus most accurately described as a threat by show of force that engaged values not previously engaged to a degree that the United States would, in fact, have had no choice.

The German anchoring of the gunboat *Panther* in the Agadir harbor during the Morocco crisis of 1911 is another instance of a show of force that had some of the characteristics of commitment. The high visibility of the move, and the fact that the ship symbolized German prestige, would have made its withdrawal extremely costly for Germany had the French conspicuously failed to meet their demands for compensation. In that case, the Germans would have been forced to occupy the port of Agadir, in which case they *would* have been physically committed. However, Germany left her options open to some extent by not tying the withdrawal of the gunboat to the satisfaction of any particular demand; since the contingency that would lead to the occupation of the town was not specified, the Germans were free to declare themselves satisfied with any number of possible settlements and withdraw the boat.

There are other instances of deployment of forces at a crisis locale that definitely did *not* create a commitment, e.g., the French at Fashoda in 1898, the Soviets in Northern Iran in 1946, and the German occupation of the Rhineland in 1936. In the first two of these, the governments involved were persuaded to withdraw the forces by a combination of verbal bargaining and shows of force. In the Rhineland case, Hitler was prepared to withdraw if the French intervened. However, the Germans *looked* committed, so the French did not intervene. Hitler got the best of both worlds: the appearance of commitment with full preservation of options.

From all these examples three general points emerge. First, the physically committing move is appropriate only for crises structured as Chicken, or as Called Bluff where the adversary is believed to be Chicken.[36] These conditions did not hold for the French at Fashoda, the Russians in Iran, or the Germans at Agadir. Second, Schelling's archetype of "burning one's bridges" so that it is physically *impossible* to retreat, is difficult to arrange in practice—the Western "hostage" troops in Berlin and the mines around Haiphong harbor in the terminal phase of the Vietnam war are the closest approximations one can think of. In nearly all instances it is physically possible to withdraw the supposedly committing forces or to refrain from fighting if a physical barrier is breached. Third, and related to the second point, the committal quality of such moves lies not in the physical foreclosure of the option to retreat but in the engagement of additional values that would be lost in retreating. The substance of the commitment lies in the total political *costs* of not reacting to a physical challenge, costs that are largely a function of the committing party's interests at stake, but which are heightened, of course, by the physically committing maneuver.[37] Thus, such moves are not essentially different from verbal threats that commit by changing the threatener's preference structure, although they are probably more effective committal moves than threats because they engage more values and are so highly visible.

Probably the reason we find so few physically committing moves, even when the game structure and physical context are appropriate, is that statesmen generally prefer to keep their options open. In the miasma of confusion, misperception, and emotionality of crises, there is simply not enough assurance that the commitment, even though highly visible and apparently at least difficult to revoke, will deter the opponent from committing himself or attacking.

When a physical commitment is undertaken, it is established gradually and sometimes with a non-coercive covering rationale that provides the committer an "out." Thus the Soviets closure of the surface access

---

[36] Although the 1961 Berlin crisis was Prisoner's Dilemma overall, in the subcrisis surrounding the erection of the Wall, the United States was Chicken.

[37] This point is made by Daniel Ellsberg in "The Theory and Practice of Blackmail," p. 1–26. Schelling would probably agree with it, although he does not explicitly state it.

routes to Berlin in 1948 was only the last in a series of delaying and harassing measures. These earlier measures provided time for feedback about the probable Western response. Only when the Soviets were confident that the blockade would not be breached by force did they implement and announce a full blockade. And then they announced it as only a technical necessity: the roads and railroads needed repairs. This covering rationale not only left the Soviets a loophole through which they could lift the blockade without severe bargaining losses in case they had guessed wrong about the Western allies' passivity but it also minimized the provocativeness of the move, allowing the West to collaborate with the technical pretense should it wish to minimize the mutual engagement of "face" and resolve. Interestingly, the allies' counterblockade of traffic from West to East Germany was given a similar non-coercive rationale, and when General Clay proposed using force to break through the Soviets' blockade he also proposed announcing beforehand that the forces carried tools for effecting the needed repairs! Of course, no one really believes such covering rationalizations, but that is not the point; the point is that values such as prestige, face, and resolve become engaged only when the adversary believes they are engaged; but he may be glad to have an excuse for pretending not to believe it. Curiously, these intangible status and reputation values can be decoupled from the confrontation, and full commitment thereby avoided, by the flimsiest of pretenses, provided the opponent wishes to collaborate, and often he does. Sometimes, the opponent actually suggests the rationale himself, as when Lord Salisbury in 1898 referred to the French force at Fashoda as "travellers."

In the case of the Berlin wall, again the East Germans set up the commitment in a series of steps. They started with administrative restrictions, then began setting up barbed wire fences. But several gaps were left at first, so that traffic was not entirely cut off. Only after several days of inaction by the West did the Russians become confident that no violent response would be forthcoming and proceed to erect a full concrete barrier.

SHOWS OF FORCE AND PREPAREDNESS MOVES: Symbolic displays of force appear quite frequently in our cases, although they are also sometimes rejected when proposed, for fear of provoking the opponent. Their usefulness lies in the sense of menace they convey, combined with the ambiguity about what is being threatened in what contingency, which preserves flexibility. Some of these moves are designed mainly to show an *intent,* which makes them functionally equivalent to verbal threats of intent. U.S. "flyovers" in the Lebanon crisis and the Cuban crisis, and the dispatch of the battleship *Missouri* to the Eastern Mediterranean in 1946 were threats of this type. (In the last example, a proposal to send the whole Mediterranean fleet was vetoed by the State Department as "too provocative.") The meaning of such intent-demonstrations is less precise than threats, and this sometimes makes them a useful substitute for threats when a party wishes to exert pressure with less provocative effect than might be entailed by an explicit verbal threat. Also, they allow the continuous prolonging of threats; so long as the demonstrating instrument is visible, such as the *Panther* at Agadir, the opponent knows the threat is outstanding, whereas verbal threats may have to be reiterated lest the opponent think the threatener has changed his mind. However, such demonstrations probably have maximum potency when combined with verbal statements. The verbal warning or threat provides some precision about what is being demanded and threatened, and the demonstration reinforces the threat's credibility by actually doing something (at some cost) consistent with fulfillment of the threat.[38]

Other demonstrations chiefly display *capability,* and imply intent only indirectly. They are designed mainly to increase the adversary's perception of the harm that one is physically able to inflict, as with the Soviets' explosion of a 50-megaton bomb during the Berlin crisis of 1961, or the stationing of U.S. B-29s in Britain during the 1948 crisis, or the emplacement of nuclear-capable howitzers on Quemoy in 1958. In none of these cases was the demonstrator actually contemplating the use of the capability displayed, but hoped to derive some coercive value from the display of its availability.

Still another type of display are moves that increase one's readiness to fight, usually in the actual conflict locale, when there is a real intent to use the forces if necessary. Examples are the U.S. conventional military build-up in Florida and the Caribbean during the Cuban missile crisis, the naval build-up around Formosa and Quemoy in 1958, and the concentration of the British fleet in 1914. These are preparedness moves whose coercive bargaining effect is incidental. But precisely because they show that the actor is actually preparing to fight and is not just saber-rattling, they have a greater coercive effect than the merely symbolic kinds of demonstrations.

It has been remarked, by Henry Kissinger among others, that the stationary quality of nuclear missiles and the inherent invisibility (to the opponent) of increasing their state of readiness, makes them poor instruments for force demonstration.[39] (This point is often stressed by

[38] For a fuller discussion of force demonstrations see Snyder, *Deterrence and Defense,* pp. 252–258; also Alfred Vagts, *Defense and Diplomacy* (New York: King's Crown Press, 1956), Ch. 7.

[39] Henry A. Kissinger, "Reflections on Power and Diplomacy," in E. A. Johnson,

the Air Force in requesting funds for bombers.) However, Kissinger's conduct of the "alert crisis" during the Yom Kippur war of 1973 shows that the calling and publicizing of alerts according to certain graduated stages may compensate for the missiles' physical immobility. When missiles and their command and control apparatus are moved up one level of "alertness," the adversary knows that they are that much closer to actual firing, which is likely to have a sobering effect.

Shows of force may be given additional potency by other kinds of symbolism which are attached to the instruments used or the ways of using them. For example, the German gunboat *Panther* had acquired a special reputation, via previous incidents in South America and elsewhere, as *the* ship the Germans used when they wanted to make threats-by-demonstration, a fact which gave a special significance to its appearance in Agadir harbor.[40] President Nixon's visit to the flagship of the Sixth Fleet, when it was concentrated off Syria during the Syria–Jordan crisis of 1970, added pointedness and authority to that maneuver. A similar combination of personal and military symbolism was Vice President Johnson's visit to West Berlin in 1961 at about the same time Kennedy sent a battle group up the *Autobahn* to reinforce the U.S. garrison.

"Risk-avoidance" constrains both symbolic force demonstrations and military readiness measures. Demonstrations are sometimes inhibited by the possibility of emotionally provoking the other party or because they would set up an accident-prone situation. There are several instances in our cases of demonstrations being considered but rejected for these reasons. When actual preparedness measures are undertaken, often they are carried out as unobtrusively as possible, or efforts are made to assure the opponent that the measures are necessary precautions for defense, not intended for coercion or aggressive attack. In 1898, Lord Salisbury directed the British naval mobilization to be carried out quietly to minimize the provocative effect. When France carried out certain preparedness measures during the Munich crisis, the German military attaché was informed "as a friend" that they were done because of "technical necessity."

In the nuclear era, there seems to be less concern about the provocative effects of force displays, maneuvers, and readiness measures. They are not only done more frequently, but are deliberately publicized. The reason, apparently, is that such moves are now considred more

---

ed., *The Dimensions of Diplomacy* (Baltimore: The Johns Hopkins University Press, 1964), p. 24. Robert Jervis has argued, against Kissinger's point, that since dispersal of bombers is only a conventional signal, it can be replaced in principle by any signaling device involving missiles, so long as both sides accept the signal as part of the "code." Jervis, *The Logic of Images,* pp. 228–229.

[40] Vagts, *Defense and Diplomacy,* p. 236.

"legitimate" than in former times, since the nuclear powers, at least, feel the need for a greater ensemble of coercive moves short of war to resolve conflicts, war itself having become excessively risky and costly. More rungs have been put into the lower part of the escalation ladder to increase the chances of resolving crises short of the higher rungs.

The additional rungs may have to be put in during the crisis itself. Thus Kennedy, worried by the lack of U.S. low-level military options during the 1961 Berlin crisis, increased conventional forces both at home and in Germany. This was part of a new general strategy of "flexible response" to substitute for the Eisenhower administration's option-scarce "massive retaliation." It had two important coercive functions as a crisis move, however. First, it gave Kennedy the option of starting low in case the Berlin crisis escalated from verbal to violent bargaining. Second, it demonstrated to Khrushchev that Kennedy *had* this option and consequently was more likely to risk or initiate violence than to back down. He realized, in other words, that it raised Kennedy's "critical risk": Kennedy could now afford to stand firm at a higher risk of violence than before, since the violence would be conventional and could be kept conventional for a longer period before the decision whether to use nuclear weapons had to be faced. Kennedy also reasoned, as he did later in the Cuban crisis, that slowing down the pace of escalation would give his opponent more time to reconsider his behavior. Khrushchev's cancellation of his previously planned reduction in Soviet conventional forces, in response to Kennedy's move, could be interpreted as an attempt either to lower Kennedy's critical risk or raise his own.

Manipulate Risk vs. Minimize Risk

One of the more dramatic coercive tactics suggested by Schelling [41] is to raise the level of shared risk so that the opponent prefers to back down rather than accept continuation of the risk. The risks Schelling had chiefly in mind are what we have called autonomous risks—the risks of inadvertent war through loss of control. Pressure is exerted on the adversary not by threatening deliberate violence but by raising the danger that war will occur through autonomous processes beyond the control of either party. The device can be considered a probabilistic substitute for violence or a commitment to violence.

However, certain logical doubts arise about the effectiveness of such risk manipulation as a coercive tactic. First, the risk created is a *shared* one, and it is not clearly apparent why the other party should be less willing to tolerate the risk than the party initiating it. Perhaps the reasoning is that the act of creating the risk demonstrates the high risk

[41] Schelling, *Arms and Influence,* Ch. 3.

tolerance of the initiating party and his determination to continue it; then, if the adversary feels the risk is intolerable, he also believes that only he can terminate it, by complying with whatever is demanded of him. But if the adversary is being asked to give up something of substance as the price of ending the danger, this may seem more costly to him than stopping the risky behavior will seem to the risk initiator. He may feel compelled to start some risky behavior of his own to maintain his position in the balance of resolve. The coercive value of this tactic would seem to depend on a known asymmetry in the parties' tolerances for risk—that is, the tactic will be used only by the party who is confident that the risk will be more burdensome to the opponent than to himself. This confidence, in turn, would depend on a belief that the object at stake is worth considerably more to him than to the adversary,[42] or that the subjective cost of war looms greater to the adversary, or some combination of these two asymmetries. Thus, the tactic is useful and rational only for the party with the higher threshold of "critical risk," and the degree of risk created must lie somewhere in the gap between the two thresholds.

However, even if escalation of autonomous risk is conceded to have some coercive value, it is obviously inconsistent with the constraint of risk-avoidance. Our cases clearly show that statesmen are usually more concerned with avoiding or minimizing autonomous risks than with deliberately heightening them. They are aware of and fearful of the possibility of losing control, and a good deal of their behavior is aimed at reducing this risk, often at some cost in potential coercive power. The specific risks they chiefly have in mind are (1) popular passions forcing them into undesired commitments, (2) emotionally provoking the opponent's leadership into rash behavior, (3) accidental or unauthorized military incidents that could escalate to war, (4) irresistible pressure for war from military bureaucracies, and (5) being dragged into war by a small ally or "proxy."

In fairness to Schelling, he did not assert that states *often* use the tactic of increasing shared risk—"the threat that leaves something to chance"—but apparently advanced it only as a logical possibility. Also, he emphasized that conflict situations usually carry an *inherent* risk of things getting out of control and that the risk can be exploited for bargaining purposes. We do find considerable support for the latter proposition.

The few positive instances will be mentioned first. We find the tactic first used by Hitler during the Munich crisis, in his manipulation of the

[42] This is argued by Stephen Maxwell in "Rationality in Deterrence," Adelphi Paper No. 50 (London: Institute of Strategic Studies, 1968), p. 15. Robert Jervis also discusses the problem in *The Logic of Images*, pp. 240–242.

Sudeten German party as a proxy actor. The party took orders from Berlin, but Hitler's control was somewhat less than complete. Partly by egging them on, partly by verbally exploiting what they were doing autonomously, Hitler created an apparent risk that their disruptive activity might provoke severe repression by the Czech government, which would "force" him to intervene. The tactic was successful in stimulating a sense of urgency in the French and British governments, inducing them to step up their pressure on the Czechs to concede. Hitler was not unmindful of the "minimize risk" constraint, however. In mid-September, at the peak of the crisis, the Sudetens became difficult to control and committed some acts, such as capturing several small towns, that Hitler feared might trigger war before he was ready. He then sought to bring them under tighter control, with only partial success.

The next example is the Russian harassment of the Western airlift to Berlin in 1948–1949. Fighters buzzed the transport planes, creating some apparent risk of collision, and a few barrage balloons were put up in the air corridors. Whether any appreciable risk of accidental violence was created by these acts is doubtful; they were more in the nature of visible warnings of greater risks that the Soviets might create should they choose to do so. At any rate, they had no discernible effect on either the operation of the airlift or Western diplomatic behavior.

The Soviets also harassed the air corridors in the later Berlin crisis in the winter and spring of 1962. This included reserving air space and filing flight plans for Soviet military aircraft, flying MIGs into the path of allied aircraft, buzzing civilian airliners, dropping metal chaff to interfere with allied radar facilities, and causing sonic booms in the air corridors. The activity was apparently a probe to test the U.S. resolve to defend the access routes to Berlin. The test was passed when allied military and civilian transports continued to fly on schedule in airspace the Soviets had "reserved" for themselves.[43]

There is massive evidence on the other side. Statesmen in most crisis are seriously concerned about events getting out of hand because of some accidental or unauthorized act, and often take measures to minimize this risk.

When the British government sent General Kitchener's force up the Nile to meet the French force at Fashoda in 1898, there was some risk that the two expeditionary bands would inadvertently clash. However, Salisbury's motive was not to create this risk but rather to demonstrate British determination and capability to oust Marchand by force if necessary. The risk of inadvertent violence was seen as an undesirable byproduct, which the British cabinet sought to minimize by instructing Kitchener not to attack the French and to avoid all acts that might lead

[43] Jack Schick, *The Berlin Crisis* (Philadelphia: University of Pennsylvania Press, 1971), p. 190.

to violence. However, Salisbury did not tell the French about this instruction when they expressed worries about a clash; thus he got some "risk manipulation" benefits while actually minimizing risk.

In the first Moroccan crisis, 1905–1906, leaders of Germany, England, and France all exhibited real fears that the crisis might get out of control, and these fears induced considerable restraint. For instance, Bulow, out of fear of provoking an emotional reaction in his opponents or a spiral of military mobilization, notified the German military not to take any special preparedness measures. Similarly, Lord Grey instructed the British navy not to undertake any unusual fleet maneuvers that might be interpreted as a threat of attack; specifically, he canceled a scheduled fleet exercise in the North Sea for fear it might lead to an inadvertent clash with the German fleet. These moves of restraint were taken against the background of a "press war" in the German and British newspapers, and wild rumors in Germany that the British fleet was about to descend on the German coast. Thus statesmen on both sides sought to diminish popular panic, which might at some point have undermined their own control of events.

There was a considerable danger of unauthorized violence breaking out between Austrian and Serbian military forces during the Bosnian crisis of 1908–1909. The Austrian military exerted very strong pressure for war on Serbia. The foreign minister, Aehrenthal, was able to keep the military in check, and at the same time derive considerable bargaining value against Serbia's supporters, England and Russia, by calling attention to the fragility of his control.

At first glance, the 1914 crisis would appear to be the clearest possible case of war breaking out because statesmen lost control of events. It was a "war which nobody wanted"; yet it occurred. However, as analyzed in the previous chapter, the proximate cause of the war's outbreak was not fundamentally a loss of control by statesmen either over their subordinates or their own emotions, but rather that the parties became caught up in an "action" Prisoner's Dilemma,[44] the mobilization

---

[44] The word *action* is used here to differentiate the mobilization race Prisoner's Dilemma from the "bargaining" Prisoner's Dilemmas that we employed in Chapter II to represent some types of overall crisis structures. The dynamics of the action *PD* are those of the familiar *PD* model: there is a compulsion for both parties to "defect" (play *D*) to preempt the opponent's defection, in order to avoid the worst outcome, which occurs if the opponent defects and oneself does not. The compulsion (and the "dilemma") follow from the assumption in the model that moves are simultaneous and the payoffs are "paid" immediately after both parties have moved. This dynamic was approximated in the 1914 mobilization race, in that the party who started mobilizing first immediately gained an advantage in a subsequent war. In the bargaining *PD*, these dynamics are not present (there is no incentive to defect preemptively and therefore no "dilemma") because the payoffs are not paid until the bargaining process comes to a conclusion, and there is some "outcome."

race, which created strong incentives not only to mobilize but also to attack once the opponent started mobilizing. It is true, of course, that at a certain point the military leaders on both sides began to exert strong pressure toward war, but it is less correct to say that the civilians "capitulated" to this pressure and thus lost control, as that they were simply informed by the military of the dilemma in which they were trapped and then proceeded to act, however reluctantly, according to the inexorable logic of that dilemma. Of course, it could be argued that a Prisoner's Dilemma of this kind is itself a situation "out of control" since the parties are unable to avoid a mutually undesired outcome, but for analytical clarity we reserve the term "out of control" for the unilateral loss of control of one's own state machinery or one's own rational calculating faculties.

There were indeed some elements of lack of control in 1914 which helped bring about the catastrophe. An important reason why the statesmen of 1914 let themselves slide into the mobilization PD was that they had not fully informed themselves in advance of the logic of existing military plans. They thought they had control but actually they did not because they lacked this critical information. However, there was no instance during this crisis of a deliberate increase in the out-of-control risk by leading statesmen as a means of coercing their adversaries. The Russian partial mobilization order was not intended to have this effect but rather to demonstrate Russian commitment.

There was some danger that events might have spiraled out of control in the Quemoy crisis of 1958, because this was a crisis in which a good deal of actual violence was employed and because the direct protagonists were client states who had some interests in dragging in their superpower protectors. There was some risk that a stray Chinese Communist artillery shell might have struck one of the U.S. ships that convoyed Chiang's supply transports to Quemoy; this might have triggered a U.S. reprisal and further escalation. The risk was enhanced by the fact that U.S. naval forces in the area were given considerable autonomy of decision and were under the general order: "If shot at, shoot back." Another possible source of inadvertent escalation was the air battles between Communist and Nationalist air forces; the most prominent risk here was that Nationalist pilots might decide on their own to strafe Communist artillery batteries on the mainland.

What is most noteworthy, however, is first, that these out-of-control risks were not deliberately created by the United States for coercive purposes and, second, that both sides made considerable effort to minimize the risk of inadvertent escalation. The purpose of the U.S. convoying was to shore up the morale and capability of the Nationalist forces on Quemoy, to help break the artillery blockade, and to underline the U.S. commitment to defend Quemoy. The risk of an accidental hit on a U.S. ship was simply an undesired by-product. The United States sought to minimize this risk by escorting only up to the three-mile limit of Chinese territorial waters, which happened to be out of range of most of the major artillery batteries on the mainland. U.S. caution was reciprocated by the Chinese Communists, who carefully avoided shelling in the vicinity of U.S. vessels and refrained from using naval and air forces to stop the flow of supplies after the artillery blockade began to fail. The United States kept a close rein on Chiang Kai-shek throughout the crisis by physical (e.g. restricting supplies of jet fuel) and political means.

The potential for loss of control of events played a significant part in both phases of the Berlin crisis of 1958 to 1962, at least in the perceptions and bargaining behavior of the parties, if not in terms of actual danger. It appeared first in the Russian threat that opened the crisis; the threat to sign a separate peace treaty with East Germany which would have turned over to them the control of the access routes to West Berlin. This was in effect a *threat* to "manipulate risk." If the West did not comply with the Soviet demand, they would be placed in the dangerous situation where an unpredictable and possibly irresponsible party, with interests more immediately involved and more prone to risk-taking than the Soviet Union, might harass and restrict traffic so as to create a serious risk of inadvertent war. The West took this threat quite seriously, and it was an important element in their decision to negotiate.

The renewal of the Soviet threat kept the risk alive during the second phase in 1961–1962, but there were several additional elements and occasions for possible loss of control during this phase. First, the instability within the German Democratic Republic and consequent large outflow of refugees via West Berlin in the summer of 1961 seemed to point up the possibility of an East German revolt in which West Germany might become involved, and drag in the military forces of NATO and the Soviet Union. The international crisis stimulated the refugee flow, and the exodus, in turn, increased tensions in the international crisis via the fears of accidental war it generated on both sides. It was largely for this reason that most Western leaders perceived the erection of the Wall at first as a mutually beneficial measure to reduce autonomous risk, offsetting losses of Western rights in Berlin. Later, Western and Soviet forces engaged in shows of force and minor confrontations in Berlin and on the *Autobahns* that carried some risk of inadvertent violence, but again this was an unwanted by-product of the main purpose, which was either to demonstrate resolve or, on the Western side, to claim what vestiges of rights remained to them in East Berlin.

Out-of-control fears were prominent on both sides during the Cuban missile crisis of 1962. Kennedy was fearful of triggering some unconsidered "spasm response" by the Soviets that might send the crisis out of control. The naval blockade was chosen as the initial U.S. move, rather than an air strike on the Russian missiles, largely because of fear that any violence might precipitate uncontrollable escalation. Implementation of the blockade was also heavily influenced by risk-minimization. The first Soviet ship to approach the blockade line, a tanker, was allowed to pass. The first ship actually boarded was carefully selected as a vessel of non-Soviet registry. Kennedy ordered that the blockade line be pulled back 300 miles and that interception of Soviet ships be delayed until the last possible moment. Planning for enforcement of the blockade, should it be necessary, involved minimal violence: first a "shot across the bow," then a disabling of the ship's rudder.

A clear choice between "risk manipulation" and "minimizing risk" was posed by the presence of six Soviet submarines in the blockade area. The President's inclination was toward minimizing risks: "Isn't there some way we can avoid having our first exchange with a Russian submarine?" he asked, "almost anything but that?" Secretary McNamara replied: "No, there's too much danger to our ships. There is no alternative." He said the submarines must be forced to surface, if possible by sonar-signaled demands; if necessary by small depth charges.[45] All six of the Soviet submarines were forced to surface by Navy "harassment"; the public record does not reveal the nature of this harassment, specifically whether depth charges were used. The point to be made here is that even if depth charges were used—with clear risk that a Soviet sub might be hit—it was done not for purposes of "manipulation of risk," i.e., for coercive or bargaining purposes, but simply for the safety of U.S. ships. Nevertheless, it can be argued, as Alexander George does, that the harassment of Soviet submarines, with its attendant though undesired out-of-control risk, was the critical move that convinced Khrushchev of the reality of U.S. resolve.[46] Later in the crisis, when a U-2 plane was shot down over Cuba, Kennedy canceled an earlier decision to retaliate against air defense installations in Cuba out of fear of provoking a violent response by the Soviets. He also canceled planned flare-drop flights over the offensive missile sites for fear the flares might be mistaken for air-to-ground fire and provoke a violent response.

During the Cuban crisis, especially in its final, tensest days, both Kennedy and Khrushchev seemed to think of themselves as partners in disaster-avoidance—both sitting on top of a volcano containing powerful explosive forces that might erupt out of control. Each implored the

[45] Kennedy, *Thirteen Days,* pp. 69–70.
[46] George, Hall, and Simons, *The Limits of Coercive Diplomacy,* p. 113.

other not to do anything that would set loose these forces. The event that would spark the eruption would be some sort of violent clash, but just what sort of dynamics would cause a small bit of violence to blow the top off the volcano did not seem very clear in the mind of either leader. However, the fears were strong, and they effectively restrained both sides.

The same sense of partnership in avoiding inadvertent disaster was found also in the Morocco crisis of 1911 between Lord Grey and Bethmann-Hollweg in an agreement to abstain from mentioning the Lloyd George speech in their public utterances in order to calm down the public uproar that followed that speech in both countries. The British and German foreign offices also agreed to play down the seriousness of the situation in their statements to the press. These efforts were only partly successful because of activities of firebrands in the press and the Reichstag and Parliament.

Although the weight of our evidence shows that decision makers do not deliberately increase autonomous risks for coercive purposes, it also shows that when such risks do become uncomfortably high inadvertently, or as a side effect of other coercive moves, they do exert some influence on the party who is either the most fearful of the risk or the most capable of alleviating it, and sometimes they induce accommodative tendencies in both parties. In the Agadir case the French at one point were motivated to offer a concession out of fear that unless Kiderlen could present some gains to the Reichstag, excited German public opinion might force a decision for war. The Soviet settlement offer during the Cuban crisis, and the United States' quick acceptance of it, no doubt were largely precipitated by the feeling on both sides that the risk of losing control was increasing hour by hour.

As with the fear of military bureaucracies out of control it seems that diplomats are prone to overestimate the risks of war breaking out because tempers get out of control. We found no instances of a crisis erupting into war, or nearly so, for this reason, in the span of history we studied. A possible exception was the Dogger Bank incident of 1904 when the Russian navy, on its way to fight the Japanese, sank some British fishing trawlers in the North Sea by mistake, bringing British blood to a boil. Lamsdorff, the Russian foreign minister, believed that a "single word of menace would have made war inevitable." [47] In fact, Balfour, the British prime minister, was about to utter that word in a speech when a telegram arrived saying the Russians had agreed to arbitrate.

The *fear* that events may get out of hand, however exaggerated, pro-

[47] G. P. Gooch, *Before the War* (London: Longmans, Green, 1938), Vol. I, p. 131.

vides material for coercive warnings that play upon such fears. Such "warnings" are different from those discussed in the preceding section—warnings of "no choice" as a means of minimizing provocativeness. Here the warning is that one may lose the power to choose at all, or to choose rationally, because subordinates or proxies or one's own passions may get out of hand. We do find such warnings quite frequently in our cases, sometimes sincerely meant, sometimes as bargaining ploys. (It is not always easy to distinguish the "sinceres" from the "ploys.") In the spring of 1938, Hitler's adjutant, on instructions, told British leaders that Hitler's "power to restrain himself" would be exhausted in six months. Hitler and other German officials also spoke of the danger of that the suffering Sudeten Germans would take matters in their own hands: Czech repression would then force Germany to act. At Berchtesgaden, Hitler promised Chamberlain he would not set his military machine in motion at least until the two men had a second talk, but added that "incidents" might make it impossible to keep the promise.[48] In 1909, the Austrian chancellor Aehrenthal told Lord Grey that he could not hold his military back from attacking Serbia much longer; soon Grey agreed to support a settlement humiliating to Serbia and Russia. In 1914, the Czar pleaded with the Kaiser to restrain the Austrians, referring to the tremendous pressure being placed upon him by his own military. These last two cases were not contrived, since both Aehrenthal and the Czar *were* under heavy pressure. Khrushchev, during the 1961 Berlin crisis, apprised Kennedy, through an intermediary, of the intense pressure being brought upon him to sign a peace treaty with East Germany, and also warned that the danger of a military incident in Berlin was too great to delay a settlement much longer.[49]

To summarize:

1. In almost all of our 16 cases (13, to be exact) decision makers felt fears of varying intensity that the crisis might go out of control, either because of unauthorized acts by subordinates or client states or because of spiraling anger and hostility, popular or governmental. (The exceptions are the Ruhr, 1923; Iran, 1946; and Suez, 1956.)

2. However, in most cases, these fears were highly exaggerated. The only possible exception, where the fears were lower than the actual loss-of-control possibilities, was the 1914 crisis.

3. In only three cases—Germany, 1938, and Soviet Union, Berlin, 1948 and 1961–1962—were there significant attempts to coerce by deliberately increasing shared autonomous risks.

[48] Keith Middlemas, *The Strategy of Appeasement: The British Government and Germany, 1937–1939* (New York: Quadrangle, 1972), pp. 341–342.
[49] Arthur M. Schlesinger Jr., *A Thousand Days*, p. 454.

4. In almost all cases, decision makers sought to minimize risks of accidental or unauthorized violence; i.e., when facing the choice between coercion by increasing autonomous risks, and avoiding inadvertent war by minimizing such risks, they chose the latter.

5. When autonomous risks did become uncomfortably high in a few instances (again excepting the ambiguous case of 1914) the effect was to speed the peaceful resolution of the crisis, either by motivating statesmen to moderate their coercion and begin accommodating, or by stimulating a strongly coercive move by the dominant power, which forced the weaker side's capitulation.

6. Warnings that events might get out of control were used quite frequently for coercive purposes, sometimes quite effectively (as in the Bosnia case), sometimes not.

ACCOMMODATIVE: SETTLEMENT VS. LOSS-AVOIDANCE

When we shift from the coercive dimension to the accommodative dimension, the roles of the conflicting interests and the common interests are reversed. In coercive bargaining the *purpose* of the parties is to make gains or minimize losses to their self-interests that are in conflict with the self-interests of the opponent; the *constraint* is to do this while still protecting the common interest in avoiding war or excessive risks of war. In accommodative bargaining, the primary aim is to achieve a settlement and terminate the crisis, thus realizing the common interest in peace; the constraint for each party is to arrange this while at the same time avoiding or minimizing unilateral losses to self-interest.

The extreme accommodative move is capitulation. This preserves the common interest but at the high price of sacrificing all of one's substantive interest concerning the issue in conflict. If the self-interests and inherent power of the parties are roughly symmetrical, they will each hope to do better than this. They will hope to get by with a minor or moderate concession—ideally, one which minimizes their losses in self-interest. A concession is a proposal for settlement that the other bargainer may or may not accept; the uncertainty about his willingness to accept is the essence of the conceder's problem, just as uncertainty about the other's response to threats and commitments is the essence of the threatener's problem in coercive bargaining.

As a general rule, the greater the concession offered, the more likely that the adversary will accept it, but this runs counter to the conceder's interest in minimizing his loss. Therefore he offers an "optimum" concession, one that seems to strike the best balance between three factors: the probability of the other's acceptance, unilateral loss if he does accept, and unilateral loss if he doesn't. This third factor includes at least two items: the inability or difficulty for the conceding party to move back to his previous position, and the possibility that the adversary will interpret the concession as a sign of weakness, which will encourage him to stand firm on his own position in the expectation of further concessions.

Two different logics are operating here. According to one, the conceder hopes that, once his concession is made, the adversary will expect him to stand even firmer on the new position, so that he (the adversary) will prefer to accept the concession rather than run the higher risk of war. This hope is based partly on the logic of diminishing marginal utility. Some items around the periphery of the issue are valued lower by the conceding party than are other items closer to the core of the issue. Presumably, the closer to the core a party moves, the firmer he will stand. Also, and supporting this reasoning, the opponent's threshold of critical risk (with respect to continued confrontation) is lowered because the concession grants him a portion of his objective, and he is less willing to risk war in hopes of obtaining the remaining portion. If the effect of these two opposite movements is to raise the conceder's apparent resolve higher than the other's new critical risk, the other party will accept the concession or make a counteroffer rather than continue to stand on his original position. Logically, of course, the conceder wants to limit his offer to just that amount of concession that will bring this about.

The reverse logic is that, when the party offers a concession, the other may interpret it as a sign that the party's resolve is weakening and that more will be forthcoming if he just stands firm and waits. The other may reason that, if the party wants to settle, it will first offer only a small concession, hoping to get by with that, but it will be willing to offer more. If the accommodator has already made several concessions, the other's reasoning is supported by the thought that he will certainly not fight over the small remaining issues that still divide the parties. The accommodator may reason oppositely of course, and ask why it is *he* who must make the final sacrifice over minor issues to bring the parties together, after he has sacrificed so much already. The critical risk model supports this latter reasoning in specifying that the parties make alternate concessions as they approach the settlement point. However, this logic may be overridden by a kind of "psychologic" derived from one party's being in a coercive mood and wanting above all to win, while the other is in an accommodative mood, desiring above all to settle. This was the situation, for example, in the closing stage of the Munich crisis of 1938. After the Western powers had made substantial concessions, Hitler was convinced that he could get everything if he held out; and some of the appeasers argued that once they had given Hitler everything he wanted on the "substance," it would be ridiculous to threaten or fight a war over mere "procedure" (Hitler's demand for immediate occupation of the Sudetenland). However, for the majority in the British cabinet, "procedure" was a major not a minor issue, and the firm stand they put up on the issue helped induce Hitler to accept a conference and a procedural compromise. Thus the qualitative character of the "small remaining issues" may be different than those already conceded, and if this is recognized by the coercer, it may work against the "concession means weakness" logic.

Commit vs. Preserve Options: Accommodation

The choice between commitment and preserving freedom of action appears in the accommodative dimension in the same two forms it takes in coercive bargaining: clarity vs. ambiguity, and starting low vs. starting high.

A clear, explicit concession is more likely to facilitate a settlement than is an ambiguous one. The principal reason is that a clear offer is committing; it cannot be retracted without serious costs to one's future bargaining reputation, especially if the opponent reciprocates. The opponent, realizing this, is likely to believe the offer is seriously meant; therefore he can accept it or make a counteroffer without much risk of being left out on a limb. Moreover, a clear offer is more likely than an ambiguous bid to penetrate the "noise" in the opponent's communication system and to change his perhaps contradictory image of one as intransigent, and it presents a clear option that can readily be analyzed and evaluated by his decision-making system.[50]

On the other hand, a clear, explicit offer risks violating the self-interested constraints of minimizing one's sacrifices. It may result in two kinds of losses, which Dean Pruitt has called "position loss" and "image loss."[51] Position loss is simply the loss incurred in moving from one's original position to something less, when it is possible the original demands might have been achieved by waiting. Image loss is the projection of a general appearance of weakness by having made the concession, which may encourage the opponent to stand firmer or even to increase his demands.

An ambiguous offer, or a mere hint that one is ready to concede, protects against both position loss and image loss because it can easily be disavowed if the opponent does not accept or make a reciprocal concession. The conceder can retreat to his original position with little

---

[50] Roger Fisher, *International Conflict for Beginners* (New York: Harper & Row, 1970) p. 80. Fisher emphasizes the value of presenting clear "yes-able" proposals in the accommodative process.

[51] Dean G. Pruitt, "Indirect Communication and the Search for Agreement in Negotiations," *Journal of Applied Social Psychology*, Vol. 1, No. 3 (1971) p. 207.

or no reputational cost. However, an ambiguous proposal is less likely to elicit a reciprocal concession and move the parties toward settlement because (1) the other thinks the party is not really serious and is trying to trick *him* into making a concession, (2) the signal may not be strong enough to overcome communications "noise" or to alter the other's image of oneself, and (3) the offer does not present a clear-cut option to the other's decision-making system.

In sum, clarity in offers and concessions tends to promote the common aim of reaching a settlement, but works against the constraint of protecting self-interest. There is an obverse parallel to coercive bargaining, where clarity in threats enhances their credibility and prospect of success but runs counter to the constraint of preserving flexibility, in the common interest of avoiding mutual commitment to war.

There is also a parallel with the "start low vs. start high" choice in coercive bargaining. In the latter, a coercing party may wish to begin low on the escalation ladder in the hope that a small amount of pressure, damage, or risk may be enough to induce the opponent to capitulate. Likewise, in accommodation a party may start out with an offer much smaller than he really is willing to concede in the hope of buying a settlement cheaply. If the first offer is not accepted, he can always concede more, step by step, up to the limit to which he is willing to go. There is a further parallel with the notion, in coercive bargaining, that starting at a low level of pressure, then gradually increasing it, pays dividends by demonstrating resolve, which can be "banked" and then drawn upon if and when a high-level threat has to be made. In similar fashion, starting with a high negotiating demand preserves accommodative "capital" that can be drawn upon at the critical point where concessions are absolutely necessary to prevent breakdown.[52] Also, starting high, then making a few concessions, may create the impression that a party has moved closer to his "non-negotiable" core values than he actually has. If the tactic works, he may get a more favorable settlement than if he had begun with a more "reasonable" offer. In sum, the parallel to "starting low" in coercion is "starting high" in accommodative bargaining; it may gain a settlement with minimal real concessions; just as the analogous policy in coercive bargaining may gain a win short of excessive strain on the constraint of war-risk-avoidance.

Conversely, the counterpart to "starting high" in the coercive process —threatening or committing oneself to major violence or carrying out a fait accompli—is "starting low" in the accommodative process, i.e., making one's final offer at the beginning of negotiations and holding firmly to it. In coercive bargaining, the tactic of "starting high" accepts

[52] Ibid., p. 212.

more risk of escalation and war than might have been necessary in the interest of getting a quick and decisive win. In the accommodative process, "starting low" means offering a greater concession than might have been necessary, a concession labeled "final," in the interest of a quick settlement. In labor-management bargaining, this accommodative tactic is known as "Boulewareism" after its originator, Lemuel Bouleware, at one time the management negotiator for the General Electric Company.[53] The tactic requires the previous development of expectations on the other side that one's first offer *is* indeed the final offer, and the building up of such a reputation may incur costs in prior negotiations and in the resentment aroused by its "take-it-or-leave-it" flavor. Analogously, "starting high" in coercive crisis bargaining is risky unless a strong resolve reputation has been previously constructed, especially since it is likely to seem provocative to the opponent.

A good statement of "Boulewareism" in an international crisis was made by Khrushchev in 1959 during the Berlin crisis:

> They [the Western powers] say that negotiations with the Soviet Union should follow the principle of concession for concession. But that is a mercantile approach. When working out our proposals we did not approach the matter as hucksters would, who name the price with a "margin" at thrice the cost, and then, after bargaining, sell their goods at a much cheaper price than the one they named at the beginning. . . . We have no reason to make any concessions, since we have not made our proposals for the purpose of bargaining.[54]

There is also a parallel between bluffing in the coercive mode and bluffing in the accommodative mode. If one makes a threat and fails to carry it out, one loses reputation for "resolve." If a party makes an offer and then retracts it, it loses reputation for "trustworthiness." Future offers are less likely to be interpreted as sincere and more likely to be suspected as tricks to lure the other bargainer into making concessions. Thus they are less likely to be accepted or reciprocated. A threat-bluff is an attempt at cheap coercion, which runs the risk, if called, of rendering future threats less effective, whether they are bluffs or not. An offer-bluff is an attempt to deceive the other party into making most of the sacrifices in a settlement; its cost is that it makes settlements more difficult to achieve in future encounters.

---

[53] Carl M. Stevens, *Strategy and Collective Bargaining Negotiations* (New York: McGraw-Hill, 1963), pp. 34–37.

[54] Speech in Tirana, May 30, 1959. In N. S. Khrushchev, *World Without Arms, World Without Wars,* Book I, p. 374. Quoted by Iklé in *How Nations Negotiate,* p. 208.

Settlement vs. Loss-Avoidance: Empirical Evidence

In 9 or 10 of our 14 crisis cases that did not lead to war, the accommodative process was mostly one-way—i.e., one party did virtually all the accommodating, after realizing it was the weaker in bargaining power. Most settlements, in other words, were a clear win for the stronger party, with sometimes a face-saving concession being awarded the loser to make it possible for him to accept defeat. In only one case—Morocco, 1911—was there a phase of give-and-take negotiation leading to a compromise settlement. In another—Berlin, 1958–1961—there emerged a tacit compromise, although the compromise was a unilateral fait accompli, the raising of the wall, which itself triggered a subcrisis, and the crisis in general did not simmer down until about a year later. Whether this pattern of many more back-downs than compromises is also characteristic of non-crisis bargaining we cannot be sure, but our general impression is that it is not. Therefore the empirical evidence must be considered peculiar to crises pending further research. Apparently the main reasons we find it in crises are, first, that the value of the stakes is so high for both sides that "settlement" per se has little value compared to the value of "winning," and, second, that an imbalance of bargaining power usually emerges. Hence, when the weaker side begins to bend, the other sees it as confirmation of its superior strength and keeps pushing until it achieves its whole objective, whether it be some change in the status quo or its preservation.

The cases show overwhelmingly that the only good way to meet the loss-avoidance constraint on accommodation is *first* to establish a convincing image of firmness. That is, a state that desires to settle with the opponent at minimum cost to itself must first demonstrate that it is resolved to hold firm on issues it considers vital, though it will concede on others. If concessions are offered before this resolve image is established in the opponent's mind, he will not accept them or offer counter-concessions, since he still believes himself the more resolved and therefore capable of winning the whole prize. The concessions will be considered signs of general weakness, to be exploited.

A good example of a premature accommodative attempt was France's behavior in the early part of the 1905 Morocco crisis. France responded accommodatively to the initial German challenge to her policy in Morocco, trying to buy Germany off with offers of concessions on other issues. But the Germans believed that they were the most resolved party and were not interested. They thought they could get more: humiliate France and block the French Moroccan program entirely via an international conference, and break up the Anglo-French entente by demonstrating British infidelity. Germany demanded the removal of Delcassé, the French foreign minister, believing it was Delcassé who was blocking French agreement to a conference.[55] The French cabinet acquiesced, believing that with Delcassé out the Germans would enter into bilateral negotiations. This, however, merely confirmed the German impression of French weakness. They continued to reject the French proposals, insisted on a conference, and stepped up their coercive pressure. The French attitude then stiffened, partly because they resented the German pressure, partly because they had discovered they could count on British support. With this shift in the balance of resolve, France accepted the conference, knowing she would prevail. The Germans, after some perceptual lag, began to see this, too, and indicated interest in the earlier French offers. But now these offers were no longer available. The French now held the upper hand, which they used ruthlessly to administer a resounding diplomatic defeat to Germany at the conference. Had the French taken their firm stand earlier, especially by refusing to cashier their foreign minister at German behest, their offer of an amicable bilateral settlement might have been accepted. As it turned out, their later tough strategy paid bigger dividends.

The Munich crisis could be given a similar interpretation. Chamberlain wanted a general settlement with Hitler on all outstanding issues, and Hitler himself was not averse to the idea. If in the early summer of 1938, when the issue was merely autonomy for the Sudeten Germans, the British and French had demonstrated the resolve they finally mustered in late September, a general settlement might very well have been attainable on the basis of Sudeten autonomy. It was impossible after they had projected an image of fear and irresolution that only encouraged Hitler to raise his demands.

Our point here is similar to what was said in Chapter II in the language of game models: that P-search, a phase of mutual coercion and countercoercion that clarifies relative bargaining power, must precede accommodative bargaining; otherwise accommodative attempts fail. If the mutual coercion phase reveals one party to be clearly the less resolved, any partial concessions offered then by that party are rejected. The tactics of loss-minimization discussed above simply do not work for the weaker party when bargaining power is sharply asymmetrical. This does not mean that he gets nothing; usually he does get something, as we shall see, but only because it is in the stronger side's interest to give it.

The accommodative dilemmas discussed above are most relevant when the initial coercive phase reveals a situation of roughly symmetrical bargaining power. Then a substantial reduction of initial demands by

[55] The Kaiser and perhaps some others in the German government wanted Delcassé out for another reason: they believed he stood in the way of their project for a Franco-German-Russian alliance.

both sides is necessary to avoid war and leads to a compromise. In these cases, both parties know or learn that they cannot be forced to give up everything, yet they must give up something. They are therefore highly sensitive to the loss-avoidance constraint during the convergence process; they try to manage their own bidding so as to maximize their share in the ultimate compromise settlement. Besides the tactics previously mentioned—keeping offers ambiguous and starting high—other techniques employed to minimize concessions include trying to force the opponent to make the first bid, making proposals through deniable intermediaries, and omitting from bargaining communications items that one is prepared to concede to get a settlement.

Our one case of explicit and approximately even compromise, the Agadir crisis of 1911, illustrates several of these tactics. Germany and France were agreed that Germany was to get some sort of "compensation" for France's completing its take-over of Morocco. The question was exactly what, and how much. Each faced a trade-off between expediting a settlement and maximizing its individual utilities in the settlement. Both opted for the latter by dallying tactics—waiting for the other to make the first bid—and by vagueness and "starting high" when they did start bidding. Both Cambon, the French ambassador, and Kiderlen, the German foreign minister, seemed to feel that the first bidder would be at a bargaining disadvantage because the bid would reveal information about the bidder's utilities and expectations, which the other could exploit. The first significant interviews between the two men, on June 21 and 22, seemed to illustrate that the coercive maxim "he who commits first, wins" is reversed in accommodative bargaining: "he who bids first, loses." It also illustrated the related clarity vs. ambiguity dilemma: after two days of fencing, the only thing Cambon could say definitely was what France would *not* give—compensation in Morocco itself, adding that "one may seek elsewhere." Kiderlen seemed to agree. His parting words, "bring us back something from Paris," signified his desire that France make the first bid.

It was more than two weeks before Cambon "brought anything back," and meanwhile Germany had initiated coercion (and triggered the crisis) by sending the *Panther* to Agadir. When Cambon and Kiderlen next met, on July 9, Kiderlen stated more clearly than before that Germany would not ask for anything in Morocco, that France could have a free hand there. The "ballpark" was beginning to get defined. However, Cambon's offer of limited non-territorial forms of compensation was "outside the ballpark" for Kiderlen, who rejected it. Cambon was following the principle of "starting high" in hopes of raising Kiderlen's image of the French minimum, lowering his expectations of what he could eventually get, and thereby minimizing French sacrifices.

At the next meeting, July 15, Cambon asked Kiderlen to state his demands. Kiderlen, by this time exasperated by the prolonged Alphonse–and–Gaston act, demanded the entire French Congo. He was also "starting high," and of course Cambon rejected the bid. In the subsequent negotiations, both Kiderlen and Caillaux, the French premier, made offers of concessions through unofficial intermediaries before presenting them in the official negotiations, in part to probe the adversary's probable response before getting committed to the offer.

Such "testing the water" as a loss–minimization tactic hardly ever occurs in the cases of asymmetrical bargaining power or, if attempted, the test is negative. The reason is fairly obvious: only one party is going to do virtually all the accommodating, and both sides know it, so there is no point in the weaker side testing the opponent's probable reaction to specific concessions by prior hints, ambiguous proposals, etc. Significantly, the only important instance is the one asymmetrical case that could plausibly be said to have ended in a compromise of sorts—Cuba, 1962. Khrushchev had some leverage because the U.S. leaders preferred not to use force, though they were willing to use it if necessary. But before officially proposing that the United States promise not to invade Cuba in return for his removing the Soviet missiles, Khrushchev first verified its acceptability to the United States through unofficial intermediaries. Had he not done so and the United States had rejected the bid, he would have suffered image loss that would have reduced his chances of getting any *quid pro quo*.

PUBLICITY VS. SECRECY

In crisis bargaining the parties have a choice between communicating publicly or privately. The choice involves both of the goal–constraint sets we have been discussing. In coercive bargaining, making threats public enhances their credibility, because the threatener is then more likely to be committed by maximum engagement of his prestige and bargaining reputation. Also, public opinion will expect the government to stand on a position publicly taken, and the bargainer can then cite public expectations as barring any back-down. The constraining risk, of course, is that if both parties become committed to publicized positions, their mutual inability to retreat will force them into coercive escalation as the only alternative. Also, public threats are more provocative than private ones. Risk-avoidance is best served by private communication, which is more easily "deniable," but coercive potency is reduced by the opponent's knowledge of this deniability. Similarly, in the accommodative mode, concessions made publicly tend to be committing; it is harder to make a further concession once a position has been taken. This is useful for maximizing one's own share of the bargaining object. But it runs the risk that no bargain can be reached at all. Private negotiation, by allowing more flexibility and room for maneuver makes a settlement more likely but eliminates the possibility of maximizing one's own share by getting publicly committed to a position.

The publicity-secrecy variable is also involved in the more general choice between coercive and accommodative strategies, or mixtures of them. If a party's goal is to win by becoming or appearing committed, it is likely to take public positions. However, if one or both parties are accommodative-minded, interested above all in reaching a compromise settlement, they are likely to prefer private communication for the flexibility it provides. A mixture may be preferred: perhaps a public but ambiguous statement of implied demands and hinted sanctions, combined with a more specific spelling out of one's position through private channels. The public communication then leaves room for some movement at the private level while preserving some of the pressure value of the public position. A good example of such a public-private mixture was the Kennedy–Khrushchev combination of public statements and private correspondence about Berlin and Laos in 1961.

As in other forms of the "win vs. risk-avoidance" dilemma previously discussed, the coercive potency of publicity is usually sacrificed to the constraint of avoiding risk in our cases. Even when a party is thoroughly committed to firmness or fighting, or wants to appear so, *specific* threats are most often made through private diplomatic channels. The main reason is that the threatener wants to avoid the provocative effect of a public threat. Because it breaks a tacit rule of normal diplomatic intercourse, a public threat arouses anger and engages status values of the recipient so that he probably becomes more resolved to stand firm than before.

Here we note again the importance in crisis interaction of status factors. When a threatening utterance is ambiguous—e.g., merely a menacing reminder of one's strength, an expression of displeasure, or a denunciation of the opponent's leaders—it is more likely to be stated publicly, as with Hitler's speeches in the 1938 crisis. The lack of pointedness permits the adversary to interpret what is said as "not really a threat" and thus to avoid engagement, or pretend non-engagement of, his status values. A qualification is that public threats of a quite specific kind have become more frequent in the post–1945 nuclear era than before, because nuclear weapons have raised the "provocation threshold," a point we elaborate in Chapter VI.

Parties may try to have it both ways by use of the press leak or by otherwise manipulating the press. Thus Roosevelt and Hull in 1941 vetoed proposals to announce publicly the U.S.-British staff talks and U.S. naval movements in the Far East, fearing that such deliberate announcements would provoke Japan. They compromised by letting the information leak to the press unofficially. Dulles's most threatening pronouncement during the Quemoy crisis was given out as a "background briefing" by an anonymous spokesman, and the information that nuclear-capable howitzers had been deployed on Quemoy was deliberately leaked. In June 1961, *Newsweek* published a detailed description of the administration's military contingency plans for the Berlin crisis, which was innocently and anonymously described by "officials" as "accurate enough to cause grave concern" about the leaking of military information.[56] In the Iran crisis of 1946, the U.S. government, disinclined to threaten the Soviets directly when it still nourished hopes of cooperation with them in the postwar world, instead simply released information about Soviet troop movements in Iran to the press—implicitly warning "you are being watched." A favorite Soviet gambit in Cold War crises, notably in Quemoy, 1958, was to threaten by unattributed stories in *Pravda* and *Izvestia* when they wanted to create concern but avoid official commitment.

The degree of a government's ability to manipulate the press varies widely among countries and across time periods. In the pre-1914 era, for example, the German press was virtually an arm of the government in foreign policy matters. The British press was "guided" to a degree, but much less thoroughly controlled than the German. The Germans' failure to realize that the press of England and France was more independent than their own caused them to attach more significance to newspaper comment in those countries than was justified, and led them into several serious errors of perception. For example, in 1914 the British press was generally sympathetic to Austria and critical of Serbia, an attitude not shared by most governmental leaders.[57] This contributed considerably to the disastrous German misjudgment that England would not fight if it came to war. The Chamberlain government in the 1930s was able to exercise more influence over the press than had earlier British governments. Yet the famous *Times* leader of September 7, 1938, advocating German annexation of the Sudenland was well ahead of British cabinet thinking and probably helped convince Hitler that the British would not resist. In general the use of a controlled or guided press to supplement official bargaining—e.g., to provide a precise interpretation of ambiguous government statements or to float trial balloons— was much more prominent in the pre-1914 and interwar periods than

[56] Robert M. Slusser, *The Berlin Crisis of 1961* (Baltimore and London: The Johns Hopkins University Press, 1973), pp. 31–32.

[57] Oron J. Hale, *Publicity and Diplomacy* (New York: D. Appleton Century, 1940), p. 447. This book is a valuable study of the interaction between press comment and diplomacy in German–English relations between 1890 and 1914.

after 1945. In the United States the press "leak" has occasionally been used during crises to state bargaining positions "deniably," but the government's ability to dictate editorial comment or news stories, or to prevent undesirable publication of information, has been virtually nil. A notable exception, which really proves the rule, was Kennedy's success in persuading the *New York Times* to hold up publication of a story about an impending crisis over missiles in Cuba until after he had made his speech announcing governmental policy.

THE MIX OF COERCION AND ACCOMMODATION

Besides resolving the tension between goal and constraint in the coercive or accommodative modes separately, crisis bargainers face the larger problem of choosing between or finding the appropriate mixture of these two general strategic options. Of course, at the outset of a crisis both sides are behaving primarily coercively—otherwise there would hardly be a crisis. After this initial face-off, however, they often face a choice or perhaps a series of choices about whether to coerce or accommodate the adversary, or more likely, what kind of blend of coercive and accommodative elements to adopt in particular bargaining moves or in their general bargaining stance. Finding the optimum blend is the core of the crisis bargainer's problem.

The choice between coercion and accommodation during a crisis is a micro-version of a macro-choice that states often face when dealing with each other over the long term. The long-term version is seen in the British–French disagreement in the 1920s and 1930s about how to deal with Germany—France wanting to hold down Germany with a policy of coercion; Britain wanting to conciliate Germany, to remove causes of conflict by restoring it to a self-respecting status in the family of nations. In modern times, the macro-version is seen in the debate in the United States over the policy of détente with the Soviet Union. Whether to be firm and tough toward an adversary, in order to deter him, but at the risk of provoking his anger or fear and heightened conflict, or to conciliate him in the hope of reducing sources of conflict, but at the risk of strengthening him and causing him to miscalculate one's own resolve, is a perennial and central dilemma of international relations. A rational resolution of this dilemma depends most of all on an accurate assessment of the long run interests and intentions of the opponent. If his aims are limited, conciliation of his specific grievances may be cheaper than engaging in a power struggle with him. If they are possibly unlimited, the rational choice is to deter him with countervailing power and a resolve to use it. It is not always recognized that the theory of "balance of power" has a motivational as well as a military side if "power" is conceived as *political power*, consisting not only of relative military forces but also the parties' degree of motivation to use them. A potential aggressor may be "balanced" with concessions that reduce his incentive to attack, as well as by forces or alliances sufficient to deter and defend against his attack. Or he may not be balanced by superior forces if he perceives that his opponents' interests and hence motivation to fight are inferior to his own. Thus, there was no "balance of power" against Hitler in the 1930s, despite the British and French military superiority. Again we see how broad central problems of statecraft are reflected in miniature in a crisis.

During a crisis, although a coercive or an accommodative strategy is usually dominant for each party, it is often combined with elements of the opposite strategy. The main function of the leavening from the opposite strategy is to help meet the constraint on the dominant one. This is because the goal associated with each strategy involves values similar to the values in the constraint on the other. Both "winning" and "loss-avoidance" involve maximizing one's share of whatever is in dispute. Both "settlement" and "risk-avoidance" involve shared interests in resolving the dispute short of violence. Thus a leavening of accommodative tactics in a primarily coercive strategy may minimize the risks of war, and some coercion in a dominantly accommodative strategy may reduce one's own sacrifices (or increase one's gains) in the search for a settlement. For example, a show of willingness to negotiate takes the provocative edge off a coercive strategy; it may neutralize the opponent's reaction of feeling affronted or pushed around, thus avoiding a dangerous hostility spiral or mutual lock-in of commitments. Or an actual small concession may provide him an honorable means of decommitment. Conversely, a show of firmness, possibly including a warning or threat, when making a concession, protects the conceder against looking weak and sharpens the message that he will not concede further.[58]

The choice between coercion or accommodation, or a mixture of the two, depends on a party's assessment of relative bargaining power or the "balance of resolve." Typically at the outset of a crisis, both sides adopt primarily coercive strategies of compellence and resistance. This generally means that one or both sides has miscalculated the balance of bargaining power or, for the resister, that the balance is uncertain enough to justify resisting. The initial coercive confrontation continues until the power relations are clarified. In most of our cases that did not lead

[58] We should note, in case it is not clear, that the strategy mixing we are here discussing is analytically different from the problems discussed earlier involving the striking of a balance between goal and constraint within each strategy separately. There the problem was how to modulate coercive moves or accommodative moves *themselves* to achieve the goal without serious violation of the constraint. Here we are simply saying that an admixture of the opposite strategy may also be employed to meet the constraint on each one.

to war, one side then realizes it is overpowered and begins accommodating, while the other continues coercing, but with each of these dominant strategies being leavened by elements of the other. In two cases—Morocco, 1911, and Berlin, 1958–1962 (the latter may alternatively be viewed as two crises, 1958–1960 and 1961–1962)—there was mutual recognition of rough equality of bargaining power, and both sides adopted mixed strategies from the start. Here, finding the appropriate blend between coercion and accommodation was a much more difficult problem, as the parties groped for a compromise, than it was in the one-sided cases.

Asymmetrical Bargaining Power

In the asymmetrical cases what is most interesting is the interplay of coercive and accommodative tactics at the turning point of the crisis, after one party has clearly established its preponderance of resolve. At this point the weaker party knows it must concede but needs a little help from the adversary to get itself untracked from its former coercive stance and onto the accommodative track since it has invested quite a bit of status and reputational value in a posture of firmness. Sometimes the weaker side takes the initiative by putting out an ambiguous signal that it is ready to concede. An example is Stalin's omission of the currency reform issue in a statement to an American newsman during the Berlin blockade crisis of 1948–1949. Such signals relieve the loser of the humiliation of having to say outright "I give up." The winner collaborates by arranging a procedure for accepting the other's capitulation that appears as bilateral negotiation with the element of "duress" removed—as in the Jessup–Malik talks that followed Stalin's signal.

Sometimes the stronger party takes the initiative by issuing a dramatic no-nonsense threat, *combined* with an attractive accommodative move, to jolt the adversary off the coercive and onto the accommodative track. Timing is important. Before the ultimate big stick and enticing carrot are brought out, the opponent must have had time to realize that he is without question the weaker party. Carrots offered before that point are likely to be considered evidence of weakness and to delay the perception of power inequality. But after the stronger party clearly establishes his superior resolve, the carrot can be offered without undermining his bargaining power, and it also helps the weaker side to shift strategies with minimum humiliation.[59]

---

[59] The logic of the carrot and stick combination is as follows: the carrot increases the value the adversary can obtain without risking war, thus increasing the attractiveness of accommodation as compared to firmness, which, though possibly gaining greater values, also carries the risk of disaster. The stick complements the carrot by reducing the opponent's apparent chances of getting these greater values and increasing the risk of war if he stands firm. More prosaically

Finally, after the weaker party has retreated virtually all the way, he may still need a small "face-saving" concession from the opponent to ease his final capitulation. For example, Stalin's face-saver in 1949 was a U.S. promise of a foreign ministers' meeting to discuss the German question. Face-savers are given to the loser in nearly all of our cases of one-sided capitulation. The winner provides it not so much because he has to, to gain the final victory, but to avoid unnecessary embitterment of future relations with the adversary. The winner has achieved his main objective; there is no need to humiliate his opponent further. The face-saver is usually procedural: it costs the winner little or nothing but means a good deal to the loser. It may be something that is intrinsically worth more to the loser than to the winner, such as the document Chamberlain got from Hitler at Munich promising that all future differences would be negotiated. Or it may be worth more to the loser because it provides a rationale for pretending that some sort of compromise has occurred, a rationale that can be elaborated upon and magnified post facto. The winner collaborates by accepting the pretense; he does not thereby undermine any resolve reputational gains he may have garnered in winning since no one really believes the pretense. Protagonists and bystanders all understand that what is involved is status, not power.

We do not find all three of these accommodative moves—submission signals, carrots, and face-savers—in any single crisis. If a signal of submission is given, there is usually no need for the carrot. If a carrot is given there is no need for the face-saver, since the carrot performs the face-saving as well as the turn-around function. However, it is not always easy to distinguish the three in practice. The submission signal may take the form of asking for a carrot or a face-saver. And when the turning point is close in time to the termination point of a crisis—e.g., when the turning point is followed simply by capitulation rather than by a series of concessions by the loser—it is sometimes hard to say whether the winner's accommodative move is a carrot or face-saver.

We now illustrate the preceding remarks by case materials, chiefly from the Cuba and Quemoy crises.

(and probably more realistically) the combination causes the opponent to ask himself: "Now that I am being offered at least part of what I have demanded, is the remainder really worth fighting over?" Or reasoning more from the stick: "My adversary is looking a lot tougher than I had counted upon; perhaps I had better take what I can get rather than risk having to fight him." In terms of the critical risk model presented earlier, the carrot reduces the adversary's critical risk—the risk of war he is willing to accept—while the stick increases the risk he appears to be running in continuing to hold out for his earlier demands. Alexander George and his associates have provided an excellent discussion of the carrot-and-stick tactic, emphasizing also the importance of building up a credible image of resolve before issuing either strong threats or concessions. George, Hall, and Simons, *The Limits of Coercive Diplomacy*, pp. 238–245.

For the United States in the Cuban crisis, there was no question of mixing coercion with accommodation at the beginning of the crisis. The presence of the missiles was completely intolerable, and the United States was prepared to use whatever coercive measures were necessary, including violence, to get them out. The problem was, first, to convince the Soviets of the superior U.S. resolve and, second, to find terms for their withdrawal that would minimize damage to Soviet prestige. Moreover, in the judgment of the U.S. decision-making group, the Soviets had to be convinced of their weakness gradually. Any attempt at massive coercion at the beginning—e.g. by an ultimatum—would risk provoking them into countercommitment; the Soviets needed time to reverse the apparent assumption of U.S. resolve weakness that had tempted them to install the missiles in the first place. (This, of course, was an aspect of the "risk-avoidance" consideration affecting U.S. coercive calculations.) The gradual "education" of the Soviets was accomplished by the president's television speech of October 22, the naval blockade, the build-up of American land and air forces in and around Florida, the alert of strategic nuclear forces, and demonstrative, low over-flights of Cuba. By October 26, the Soviets had realized their miscalculation and themselves suggested a U.S. accommodative gesture that would permit them to climb down—a no-invasion pledge. This was followed by another proposal: the Soviets would withdraw their missiles from Cuba if the United States would withdraw theirs from Turkey. By these messages the United States knew two things: (1) the Soviets realized they were overpowered and (2) more ambiguously, what kind of concession by the United States they would accept as the price of backing down. In other words by (1) the United States knew that the big stick—an ultimatum—could now safely be employed, and by (2) they knew the kind of carrot that would have to accompany it. Seeking to minimize the carrot, the United States accepted only the first Soviet proposal officially, but when Robert Kennedy presented the U.S. ultimatum to Ambassador Dobrynin orally on October 27, he also included an assurance that the missiles in Turkey would be gone before long.[60]

Any interpretation of the Quemoy crisis of 1958 is hazardous because of the lack of data about motivations and decision making, especially, of course, on the Chinese side. The pattern mentioned above shows up quite clearly, however.

No doubt the Chinese Communists were worried about Chiang's concentration of forces on Quemoy, worried that they would be used to spearhead an attempt to reconquer the mainland, supported by the United States. Therefore they had a strong incentive to force the troops

[60] Kennedy, *Thirteen Days*, pp. 108–109.

off at least to remove this threat, if not to capture the Quemoy and Matsu islands for themselves. Probably the Chinese had two primary motives in initiating the crisis with their artillery blockade: (1) to test the resolve of the United States to defend the islands against invasion, and (2) to actually block the flow of supplies to Quemoy, so that Chiang's troops would either have to surrender or evacuate. The Communists may also have intended to deter a potential attack from Quemoy. It is clear that they had no immediate intention of invading, since no landing craft were assembled opposite the islands, but they might have planned to attempt it had the United States shown weakness.

As in the Cuban case, the United States built up its apparent resolve gradually, waiting until its commitment was clear before making either highly coercive threats or accommodative moves. During the build-up phase from August 4 to August 23, when the Chinese shelling was light, the only U.S. reactions were some vague rumblings from the State Department, Dulles's reiteration of U.S. determination to stand by its allies, and President Eisenhower's statement that the United States "might" have to intervene.

After much heavier shelling began on August 23 (the Chinese "challenge" that opened the crisis) U.S. statements became more threatening and took the form of gradually more positive assertions that the defense of the islands was linked to the defense of Formosa and therefore was covered by Congress's Formosa Resolution of 1955. Framing the threats in this manner avoided an explicit commitment while simultaneously laying the legal groundwork for one; it also tended to undermine or at least confuse the congressional opposition. The verbal threats were strongly complemented by a build-up of U.S. air and naval strength in the Formosa area.

By September 4, Dulles was ready to trot out his verbal big guns. On that day he issued two statements, one "official," the other unofficial "for background" to the press. The official statement emphasized conciliation: the United States wished to resume the talks at Warsaw with the Chinese government, which had been in abeyance. There was an element of coercion but it was moderate: the President had not yet felt called upon to decide whether to intervene, but would do so if circumstances required. In the background statement attributed to a "briefing officer," Dulles made the coercive element more explicit. The United States *would* defend the islands, and this might include bombing the mainland. For good measure Dulles told a senator visiting his office that the government had definitely decided to prevent a Communist capture of the islands, and the senator dutifully repeated his words to reporters. On September 4 the U.S. navy also began escorting Nationalist supply ships to the islands. This combination of verbal and active coercion, combined with an accommodative gesture, brought an immediate accommodative response from the Chinese Communists. The bombardment stopped temporarily, and Chou En-lai accepted the invitation to resume the ambassadorial talks. He coupled his acceptance with some threatening language, however, thereby guarding against the danger that the acceptance might be construed as weakness.[61]

This, however, was not the real turning point of the crisis. The ambassadorial talks at Warsaw produced only statements of hopelessly incompatible positions. The Chinese were still hoping their blockade would work. Those hopes were dashed during the last two weeks of September, when the blockade was broken by a combination of airdrops and advanced amphibious techniques. But the Chinese still needed an accommodative gesture from the United States to get themselves unhooked from the blockade. Dulles provided this in a conciliatory statement on September 30: he disavowed any commitment to help Chiang return to the mainland and hinted that a formal cease-fire might bring a withdrawal of Chiang's troops from Quemoy. This combination of successful coercive action plus conciliatory declarations turned the crisis toward resolution. The Chinese would not accept a bilaterally negotiated cease-fire because they feared it would imply acceptance of the "Two-Chinas" concept, but the U.S. disavowal of offensive intent prompted them to propose a temporary "unilateral" cease-fire if the United States ceased escort operations, to which the United States readily agreed. A joint U.S.–Nationalist communiqué on October 23, which renounced the use of force, enabled the Chinese to complete their back-down. They announced that henceforth they would bombard Quemoy only on odd-numbered days. This curious device was a kind of "face-saver" that demonstrated that the Chinese had not formally agreed to a cease-fire and preserved the principle that the issues of Quemoy and Formosa were internal matters regarding which the People Republic retained the right to use force at its discretion.

We have shown, from the Cuba and Quemoy cases, how the establishment of resolve dominance must be followed by an accommodative gesture to shift the weaker party to an accommodative strategy. The stronger party is also better *able* to be conciliatory at this point than earlier in the crisis because now his concessions cannot be construed as weakness. Thus Dulles could offer a resumption of talks with the People's Republic without appearing to be capitulating to pressure. Later, he could offer a reduction of Chiang's forces on Quemoy and give a no-force pledge. In the Cuban missile crisis, President Kennedy had decisively rejected the idea of an exchange of Turkish for Cuban missiles

[61] Kenneth T. Young, *Negotiating with the Chinese Communists* (New York. McGraw-Hill, 1968), pp. 150–151.

because it would appear to be a concession under duress. But by the time Robert Kennedy issued his ultimatum to Dobrynin later in the crisis, the U.S. had established its superior resolve beyond question, so it was possible to toss in the Turkish missiles as a "sweetener" without costs in resolve reputation.

In the Cuba case, the turn-around message of the weaker side—i.e., the message indicating a shift to accommodation—was leavened with an admixture of coercion. Khrushchev's settlement proposals were accompanied by threats and denunciations and were quickly followed by two physical coercive actions: sending a single ship toward the blockade line and shooting down a U-2 plane.[62] Thus couching a concession in the context of threatening language and action tends to protect the accommodator against an interpretation of his offer as weakness, and possibly also, as with Khrushchev's threats, communicates a certain urgency of settling for that offer. The function of the coercive element for the accommodator at the turning point is to communicate that, while he is conceding, he cannot be pushed too far without excessive risk.

In some other one-sided cases the stronger side does not have to offer a carrot to shift its adversary onto the accommodative track. The demonstration of superior resolve is enough. If concessions are requested in exchange for capitulation, they are denied. Once he has turned down the accommodative road the weaker side is pushed relentlessly until he has lost all. What he does get, but only at the end when he is thoroughly beaten, is the face-saver.

For example, in the Fashoda crisis the French hung on to their demand for an outlet on the Nile until the British mobilized their fleet. This was the turning point, at which the French finally were convinced they were beaten. They then dropped their demand for an outlet on the Nile and agreed to withdraw Marchand, helped along a bit by Salisbury's agreeing to say he had not "officially" requested the withdrawal (this could be considered a small "carrot"). The French pleaded piteously for at least a British promise of negotiations in exchange, but this Salisbury refused to give. However, *after* the French capitulation, negotiations were held that delimited the boundary of the French and British spheres in Africa. This was the procedural face-saver.

In the Yom Kippur alert crisis of 1973, the Soviets did not carry out their threat to intervene in the Middle East after the United States demonstrations and warnings. Their back-down was assuaged by an agreement with the United States that each would send non-military "representatives" to observe the cease-fire—a pale facsimile of the

[62] Roger Hilsman, *To Move a Nation* (Garden City, N.Y.: Doubleday, 1967), pp. 220–221.

original Russian demand for joint U.S.–Soviet military intervention. However, it may be incorrect to interpret the Soviet non-action as a "back-down." Since their threat was to intervene if the Israelis did not stop their advance in Egypt, and the advance stopped shortly thereafter (under U.S. pressure), the Soviets' threat could be considered successful.

Symmetrical Bargaining Power

We now consider those cases in which the parties perceive each other's resolve as roughly equal. It is not clear to either party that the other can be faced down by undiluted coercion, or it is clear that such a pure strategy is too risky. A satisfactory outcome requires some mixture of coercion and accommodation from the start—a mixture carefully calibrated according to the perceived intensity of the values at stake for the adversary and for oneself, of relative military strengths, and perceptions of the opponent's perceptions of these things. The proper strategy is some combination of firmness and flexibility that will show a willingness to concede on issues not so important to oneself (but perhaps important to the adversary), plus a determination not to concede on one's vital concerns. The inherent risk is that the flexibility will be misinterpreted as a general weakness of resolve, or that the firmness will be misinterpreted as general intransigence. The optimum blend between coercion and accommodation is not easy to find. Too large a dose of coercive pressure may lead the adversary to believe that one is not willing to accommodate at all and that, therefore, the only way he can achieve his ends is through coercive means of his own. Too much firmness may also breed intransigence in the other for emotional reasons: he thinks he is being "pushed around," makes belligerent counterthreats that are reciprocated, and a hostility spiral ensues. Conversely, too obvious a willingness to accommodate may inflate the opponent's estimate of how much he can obtain, may undermine one's coercive tactics, enhance the opponent's confidence in his coercive moves, and lead to dangerous miscalculation about the extent and value of one's core interests and where one firmly intends to draw the line.

We find this pattern of mixed coercion and accommodation best exemplified in the Morocco crisis of 1911 and the long Berlin crisis (or series of crises) from 1958 to 1962. The following summaries of these two cases highlight the complexity and pitfalls of the mixed strategy. In these cases, incidentally, in contrast to most others, both sides perceived some legitimacy in the other's claim, a fact that contributed to the perception of relative equality in bargaining power.

Morocco, 1911. In the Morocco crisis, the accommodative element was somewhat dominant in the strategy mixtures. That is, France and

Germany had a common aim of negotiating a final settlement of the Moroccan problem. Germany accepted that France was to have Morocco but demanded some sort of compensation. France fully recognized the legitimacy of this demand. England was indifferent to any compensation France might grant outside Morocco itself. The stage seemed set for amicable negotiation that would provide satisfaction to all three parties. Yet the issue produced the most serious crisis between 1870 and 1914, bringing Germany and England to the very edge of war and seriously embittering Franco–German relations in the aftermath. The reason lay in the way all three parties, but chiefly Germany and England, thoroughly botched the coercive elements in their strategies.

The initial accommodative sparring between Kiderlen and Cambon has already been described. The first coercive move, Germany's anchoring of the *Panther* in Agadir harbor, was motivated by Kiderlen's belief that France would not give "acceptable" compensation unless confronted with the threat of force. The implied threat was a German occupation of Agadir and its hinterland if the French were not appropriately generous. This act sent French blood pressures soaring, especially in right-wing nationalist circles, and made it more difficult, rather than easier for the French government to offer concessions. The government itself became suspicious that Germany's ultimate aim was to get a slice of Morocco; that the German demand for the French Congo was only a sham demand that the Germans knew would be rejected; the rejection would then serve as a pretext for shifting their demands to the real object—Morocco. Thomas Schelling's principle of "connectedness" was operating here in French reasoning.[63] Normally a threat is linked in some way to the object being demanded, and gains credibility from such linkage. The principle was strengthened in this case by the fact that Agadir had been considered the place the Germans would want if they *did* demand something in Morocco. Some small German mining interests were located near there, and it was far enough south of Gibraltar not to disturb the British. The French suspicions were not allayed by Kiderlen's assurances that he would demand nothing in Morocco because lesser German officials were saying "that depends," and the French thought they knew what it depended on—capitulating to Kiderlen's unacceptable demand for the Congo.

On July 9 and 15 an accommodative process had begun with both parties agreeing to the principle of compensation and getting their initial demands out on the table. But further progress was stalled for two weeks by the overly provocative German challenge, which had precisely the opposite effect from that intended—French resolve to resist in-

[63] Schelling, *Arms and Influence*, pp. 86 ff.

creased. A struggle now took place in the German government about whether Germany should continue along the coercive path or should shift to accommodation. The Kaiser feared that his government was moving toward war and was exasperated at the delays, which he thought would give France time to secure the backing of England and Russia. He therefore urged compromise to get a quick settlement. Kiderlen argued that Germany must have the whole of the Congo, but could not get it unless she convinced France that she would fight, and this conviction could not be instilled unless Germany were *actually* determined to fight. As for the Kaiser's concern about the slow pace of negotiations, time was required, Kiderlen said, to accustom France to the idea of large concessions. Bethmann supported Kiderlen. These arguments persuaded the Kaiser for the time being.

This exchange deserves a bit of analysis. The Kaiser was concerned about the coercive constraint—avoiding war—and he focused on the accommodative goal—compromise settlement—and achieving it quickly before France could mobilize allied support, which would force Germany to accept the worst end of the bargain. Kiderlen favored flat-out coercion to gain Germany's maximum goals. He did not worry about the risk-avoidance constraint since he believed France would yield to a credible commitment.

The argument about delaying vs. speeding up negotiations reflected both a difference between coercive and accommodative logics and a difference in factual prediction between Kiderlen and the Kaiser about the effects of delay. From Kiderlen's coercive perspective, time was required for Germany to establish a credible commitment and for the French government to comprehend the commitment and adjust its aims accordingly—in short, to decide to concede. From the Kaiser's accommodative perspective, delay was dangerous because it provided time for France to build up a countercommitment with allied support, which would either lock the parties onto a collision course or work to Germany's disadvantage in negotiations. Kiderlen did not believe, however, that France's allies would intervene. Britain had interests in Morocco, but he had already told Cambon that Germany would not demand anything there, and the British did not care tuppence for the Congo. But there was a fatal flaw in this calculation, as we shall see.

Kiderlen transmitted his threat to France in an acrimonious interview with Cambon on July 20. The demand for the Congo was serious, he said, not just a sham demand or pretext as the French press was saying. If agreement could not be reached on this, Germany would demand a return to the terms of the Act of Algeciras of 1906, which restricted the French presence to coastal ports, and would enforce this demand by going to "extreme lengths." Cambon retorted that France would go as far as Germany. Kiderlen thus increased coercive pressure in support of his initial bid, and France was forced to respond in kind to maintain its position in the balance of resolve.

During these first three weeks of the crisis, the British government had been relatively quiet. The *Panther*'s spring led the government to fear that Germany would demand a share of Morocco, and that the French would acquiesce in a three-way partition between France, Germany, and Spain in disregard of British interests. The main theme struck by Foreign Minister Grey, therefore, in speaking to the French and German ambassadors, was that Britain must be let in on any discussions concerning Morocco. He stated this in fairly strong terms to the German ambassador, Metternich, on July 4, and apparently expected an early reply clarifying German intentions. However, more than two weeks went by without any German response. This silence led to further British apprehension, which was heightened by information received from the French. On July 18, when de Selves and Paul Cambon informed Bertie, the British ambassador, of Kiderlen's demand for the entire Congo, they also expressed their belief that the purpose of this move was to demand something the French would have to reject and thus to force the issue back to the partition of Morocco and German acquisition of a port there. The Frenchmen also failed to mention Kiderlen's offer of German colonies in exchange for the Congo. This conversation probably was intended to play upon British worries and get them involved.

Grey now began to fear that Germany was miscalculating that Britain had no interests in Morocco. If this miscalculation were not corrected soon, Germany might demand a partition that would precipitate a more serious crisis inevitably involving Britain. The instrument chosen to correct the supposed miscalculation was the famous Mansion House speech by Lloyd George, to which we have alluded earlier.

Unexpectedly, the speech provoked great wrath in Germany, partly because it was a *publicly* uttered threat, but mostly because it was considered a gratuitous and insulting intervention in an affair that was none of Britain's business. Kiderlen had explicitly told the French that he would not demand anything in Morocco, and of course he knew nothing of the French communications to the British, which suggested German deception on this point. The fury in Germany was answered in kind by the British press, the German ambassador gave a stiff warning to Lord Grey, and for a few days the two countries seemed on the brink of war. This subcrisis gradually subsided after an exchange of disavowals: from Kiderlen, that he had no designs on Morocco, from Asquith, that Lloyd George had not expressed "pre-eminent" government policy. But Asquith also said that England would support the French in the Congo negotiations.

To summarize the relevant aspects of the Lloyd George episode for our study: at bottom it was the result of Kiderlen's clumsiness in trying to reconcile his coercive aim and risk-avoidance constraint. He wanted to keep open, implicitly, the threat that he might either grab or demand a piece of Morocco, to maximize his leverage over France on the Congo issue. The risk to be avoided was that of activating Britain, which would surely occur if Britain suspected that the German aims lay ultimately in Morocco. Kiderlen tried to resolve this dilemma by simply not communicating with the British, and by not giving his ambassador any definite information about German aims in case the British should ask. Obtusely, he failed to see that the anxiety he wished to instill in the French would be communicated to their ally. When it was communicated, it strengthened the suspicions already generated in Britain by the ominous German silence.

The chief motive for the Lloyd George speech was to correct an apparent or possible German miscalculation of British interests in Morocco. Both war-risk-avoidance and loss-avoidance considerations were involved. If the Germans were not informed soon of British concerns, they might unwittingly commit themselves to war over Moroccan issues against an already committed France, supported by England. Alternatively, and this was the loss-avoidance motive, they might force France to grant compensation in Morocco, to the detriment of British interests there. This particular *mode* of communicating British interests was also chosen for risk-avoidance reasons—Grey reasoned that it would be less provocative than a threat sent through official channels, and would also be less committing. The unforeseen immediate effect was to set off an emotional hostility spiral between Britain and Germany, which increased rather than reduced risks of war.[64] The two governments then collaborated, both tacitly and explicitly, to control the spiral. But the strategic effect of the episode was to shift the balance of bargaining power to Germany's disadvantage.

Once the emotional consequences of the British move had died down, it ultimately facilitated a settlement. The episode made clear to Kiderlen that he could not count on British indifference if the French–German negotiations broke down, even over the Congo. He was forced to have it stated publicly that he had no designs on Morocco, which reduced his bargaining power vis-à-vis France. However, it was to take a little time to shift Kiderlen down the path of accommodation. On July 28, he told Cambon again that if France did not meet the German demand for the Congo, he would go to "extreme lengths."

[64] Charles Lockhart has emphasized the counterproductive emotional effects of threats, illustrating from the Agadir crisis, in his "The Efficacy of Threats in International Interaction Strategies," *International Studies Series,* Vol. 2 (Sage Publications, 1973).

Kiderlen may have been convinced he could still bring the French to heel in the light of signals he was getting from the German embassy in Paris. Caillaux, the premier, had initiated secret conversations with the embassy through an unofficial intermediary, going behind the back of his foreign minister, de Selves, and the tough-minded French foreign office. He had, so the German contact at the embassy reported, offered a generous slice of the Congo. Caillaux apparently expected that this bid would encourage Kiderlen to reduce his demand to meet it, but instead Kiderlen stood firm, probably expecting to get more if he waited.

However, other German leaders, notably Bethmann, were disturbed at Kiderlen's continued truculence. An important conference took place between these two men and the Kaiser immediately following the July 28th interview with Cambon. Reports of what was said at the meeting are sketchy, but it seems that it was decided to reduce the German demands to whatever extent necessary to get agreement and to drop any thought of war.

An interview between Kiderlen and Cambon on August 1 registered in official channels the new accommodative attitude on both sides, and marked the turning point of the crisis. Cambon offered a part of the Congo and some Pacific and Indian Ocean islands. The concession was not enough for Kiderlen, but he agreed to drop his demand for the whole of the Congo if the portion granted included access to the Atlantic and the Congo River. He suggested that France compose a draft treaty.

On August 4, Kiderlen turned tougher, however. He specified now just what part of the Congo he wanted; somewhat more than Cambon had offered. And he withdrew his earlier offer, on the table since July 15, to give France some German colonial territory in exchange. The *Panther* remained at Agadir, now joined by two other warships. Caillaux now felt the need to buttress *his* position with a coercive move. Through a private intermediary, he told Kiderlen that France would make no further concessions, and if there were no signs of agreement within eight days, French and British warships would move to Agadir. Kiderlen angrily branded this as a "threat" and said that if the threat were not withdrawn he would break off negotiations. Tension again rose sharply, exacerbated by talk of war in the press and by German fleet maneuvers. Caillaux was forced to climb down. It was all a misunderstanding, he said. He had merely remarked that the state of public opinion made negotiations difficult and that "hot-heads could demand sending ships." He had not intended this as a threat.

By this time, apprehensions had been heightened so much on both sides that any incident that even faintly suggested warlike action was interpreted as impending disaster. Jules Cambon in Berlin was convinced that German public opinion was so excited that unless Kiderlen were able to present some sort of gain to the Reichstag, war might well break out. The French cabinet between August 22 and 29 worked out a draft treaty. As a last resort, they were willing to concede Germany's demand for access to the Congo River, plus a strip of Atlantic coastline.

The Germans, for their part, although they were not as apprehensive about war as the French, having decided not to fight one, were constrained by the knowledge that the Caillaux cabinet was shaky and, if it fell, would probably be replaced by a more nationalistic, less conciliatory one. This prediction was probably true, but the French leaders also cultivated it assiduously in their communications with the German embassy. The Germans believed therefore, that it would be difficult for Caillaux to concede more. Thus, while the French were pushed in an accommodative direction by risk-avoidance—their fear of an "accidental," emotionally triggered war—and also by some doubts about British support, the Germans were constrained by loss-avoidance considerations—if they pushed the present French government too hard they might eventually have to settle for much less than they could get now.

An accord was reached on Moroccan issues on October 12, with Kiderlen getting "guarantees" of German economic interest, and France getting clear political control. The parties then turned to the compensation issue. Having already agreed that this issue would be settled as an *exchange* of territory (to save face for France), the question was how much was to be given on each side. Caillaux tried to keep down French concessions in the Congo by repeated allusions to the danger of his governments' falling if he gave too much. German colonial factions on the other hand, were demanding the largest possible morsel. Agreement was finally reached on October 21, when Caillaux granted the German demands in return for a somewhat larger "countercompensation" from Germany in Cameroun.

Berlin, 1958–1962. In this crisis (or pair of crises, 1958–1959 and 1961–1962), strategies on both sides were heavily mixed, but the coercive elements were somewhat dominant.[65] The functions of the accommodative elements were to minimize the risks and promote the success of the primarily coercive aims.

Khrushchev's challenge in November 1958, contained certain accommodative elements whose primary function was to take the provocative edge off the coercive aspects and to facilitate a settlement by structuring the bargaining situation as one of "normalization" rather than "redistribution."[66] Thus the demand and threat were accompanied

[65] The reader is reminded that we are using the term *coercion* for resistance and deterrence as well as for offensive "compellence."

[66] Normalization and redistribution are two of five types or objectives of negotiation suggested by Fred C. Iklé in his valuable book *How Nations Negotiate,* Ch. 3.

by an offer to negotiate. The Western powers were not presented with a non-negotiable demand; rather, they were asked to collaborate in eliminating an "abnormal" situation, a tag-end of World War II that was autonomously productive of conflict, and that it would be in the *mutual* interest of all to liquidate. Thus it was possible to interpret the note, charitably, as an invitation to engage in "integrative" bargaining, with the Soviets stating their initial position along with the invitation. Almost immediately the Soviets began hinting that they were flexible. The coercive element of the six-month deadline was quickly deemphasized and qualified: the Soviets would take no unilateral action if only the West would *begin* negotiating within six months. Khrushchev blended the coercive and accommodative features skillfully. He needed the threat and the time limit to shock the Western powers into action and to instill a sense of urgency. He also needed the accommodative features to diminish the emotional backlash, the sense of affront, that any threat arouses. Recognizing some merit in the Soviet claim that the Berlin situation was "abnormal," and knowing that large segments of world opinion would sympathize with this view, the Western powers could hardly afford to appear intransigent by flatly refusing to negotiate. De-emphasizing the time limit undercut the Western powers' protests of "duress," but the memory that it had been issued remained hanging over their heads like a kind of ethereal Sword of Damocles that the Soviets might cause to re-materialize when it suited them.

The United States–NATO response also combined coercive and accommodative aspects. The coercive part was rejection of the free city proposal. The accommodative aspect was acceptance of negotiations. However, the West proposed broad negotiations about the German problem as a whole, and advanced as their initial position the old Western proposal for German unification via free elections, which, of course, side-stepped the Berlin problem entirely. This move illustrates another principle about accommodative vs. coercive bargaining: when a party knows it cannot satisfy the opponent on the latter's preferred negotiating ground and must ultimately fall back on plain intransigence, it may shift the discussion to other grounds where the onus of saying "no" and causing breakdown rests with the opponent. Alternatively it could be interpreted simply as stalling: when one's military position is weak, as it was for the West in 1958–1959, due to its inferiority in conventional forces, broadening the scope of negotiations tends to prolong them; as long as the opponent can be kept talking, the start of the "action game" is delayed and something may turn up in the meantime that keeps it from being played.

Dulles followed up the Western notes with further accommodative gestures, saying that the West could accept East German controllers of the access routes as "agents" for the Soviet Union and that there were ways other than free elections to accomplish German unification—e.g. confederation. Thus he sought to show flexibility to persuade the Soviets that some of their aims might be obtained by negotiating from the Western terms of reference.

The result of these exchanges was misperception and mistaken optimism on both sides. In spite of repeated Soviet statements that they were interested only in talking about "ending the occupation regime" in West Berlin, not German unification, Dulles and the State Department interpreted the near-retraction of the six-month deadline and other Soviet conciliatory gestures as an indication that they were relenting on their Berlin demands and were willing to negotiate about the whole German question. And despite the Western emphasis on unification, the Soviets interpreted the acceptance of negotiations and Dulles's apparent flexibility as signs that they were making progress toward their own aims. Both sides, in short, misinterpreted the other's accommodative moves, which were intended only to "improve the atmosphere" and avoid a coercive deadlock, as a shift in the other's substantive position. This illustrates a problem inherent in any mixed strategy: that the adversary will fail to see the *mixture* and pick up only one ingredient— usually the accommodative one.

These misperceptions were corrected at the foreign ministers conference of 1959. Breakdown was avoided only by an agreement to hold a summit conference in 1960, Khrushchev apparently believing that Eisenhower, the "realist," would be more pliant about Berlin. But Khrushchev aborted the conference on its first day, ostensibly because of Eisenhower's refusal to apologize for U-2 flights over the Soviet Union.

The second stage of the crisis opened at the Vienna meeting between Kennedy and Khrushchev, June 3–4, 1961, when Khrushchev handed over an *aide-memoire* substantially identical to the 1958 "ultimatum." The Kennedy administration tried much more consciously and systematically than the previous administration had, to combine measures of countercoercion and accommodation in dealing with the renewed Soviet demand. Kennedy was determined not to yield on the essentials of the Western position in Berlin. On the other hand he was somewhat empathetic with the Soviet position, wished not to seem intransigent about negotiations, and was willing to accommodate on less essential matters. Kennedy commenced a military build-up in the spring of 1961 with increases in conventional forces to create "an alternative between atomic holocaust and surrender." He also ordered a substantial increase in nuclear missile capabilities. The military build-up, he hoped, would give Khrushchev an incentive to negotiate seriously, and to take U.S. expressions of firmness seriously when it chose to be firm. At the same time, showing a sincere desire to find a settlement would offset the element of provocativeness in his military measures, and displaying a capacity to distinguish between non-essentials and essentials would underline U.S. determination to be firm on the latter. Kennedy believed, further, that since he was arming the country so that it might realistically risk war if necessary, he had a moral duty not only to the country but to all mankind to try to find a settlement that would obviate the need to take such risks. Finally, he believed that a "diplomatic offensive" was necessary to shift onto the Russians the onus of saying "no" to apparently reasonable proposals.

This intellectual rationale was at the same time a political compromise between hard and soft line factions in the Kennedy administration, the one expounding a coercive logic, the other an accommodative one. Acheson, for example, thought that Khrushchev's primary intention was to demonstrate the presumed U.S. lack of resolve and that accepting negotiations at all would convince Khrushchev that the United States lacked nerve. It was a simple contest of wills that had nothing to do with Berlin or Germany per se. By making the United States back down on a sacred commitment, he would shatter our power and influence worldwide. Khrushchev had to be bested in this contest of wills before any meaningful negotiations could take place. That meant simply arming, refusing to negotiate, and showing readiness for a military showdown. The soft-liners, such as Adlai Stevenson and Llewellyn Thompson, thought this reasoning put the cart before the horse. The United States should first try sincerely to reach an accommodation with the Soviets; only if that effort failed should we fall back on Acheson's tough stance. "Maybe Dean is right," Stevenson said, "but his position should be the conclusion of a process of investigation, not the beginning. He starts at a point which we should not reach until we have explored and exhausted all the alternatives." [67] Superficially, the difference was simply a difference in strategic prescription—coerce first vs. accommodate first—but at its core lay a profound divergence in philosophies of international politics, comprising, among other things, divergent images of the opponent, different estimates of the proportion of common and conflicting interests in the situation, and different conceptions of the role of power in bargaining. For the Achesonians, Khrushchev was simply out to get something that rightfully belonged to the United States; even to enter into negotiations on his terms would admit to their legitimacy and would thus weaken U.S. bargaining power drastically right at the start. The situation was almost entirely one of conflict, with little or no common interest to be realized in a negotiated settlement; and in any such negotiation, the clear demonstration of power and the will to use it were neces-

[67] Schlesinger, *A Thousand Days,* p. 355.

sary conditions for success. For the Stevensonians, the Soviet demands had some degree of legitimacy: the status of West Berlin *was* abnormal, the whole German situation was awkward, ambiguous, and autonomously productive of conflict. Thus there was a good deal of shared interest between the West and the Soviets in tidying it up by negotiation. Perhaps most importantly, these soft-liners tended to see negotiation and displays of military power and resolve as contradictory—the latter would simply befoul the "atmosphere," make the opponent more intransigent, and frustrate the achievement of a mutually satisfactory settlement. Negotiation was seen essentially as a process of reasonable discussion and give-and-take; only after this failed should coercive tactics enter the picture, even for defensive or deterrent purposes.

As noted, Kennedy wished to steer a middle course, to be firm and flexible at the same time. Aside from the problem of reconciling opposed domestic factions, this approach also carried risks in the interaction with the adversary, of which Kennedy was well aware. He genuinely feared, consistent with the Acheson–DeGaulle–Adenauer view, that entering into negotiations would be interpreted by the Soviets as American lack of nerve. But this risk had to be taken; the United States could not flatly refuse to negotiate about a situation that did indeed contain the seeds of war. His fears about appearing weak may have been eased by Thompson's argument that the Soviets were more likely to be impressed by our firmness, once negotiations got under way, than by a refusal to negotiate at all. This tended to rationalize away the basic accommodative dilemma of how to be conciliatory when one is unwilling to offer any significant concessions. Kennedy also felt he needed negotiations to *communicate* his basic coercive decision: to fight a limited, non-nuclear war if necessary to hold Berlin or to prevent encroachment on the Berlin access routes. This communication was absolutely necessary to cause the Soviets to recognize the magnitude of the risks their own moves had precipitated; only then, on the basis of mutually recognized dangers would it be possible to negotiate a settlement or at least some kind of *modus vivendi* in Berlin.[68]

Kennedy's opposite fear was that in clarifying his resolve to fight, he might appear "war-mad," provoke hostility and more coercive moves by the Soviets, which might lock both sides into coercive commitments from which there could be no return.[69] Here was the coercive dilemma between firmness and disaster avoidance. Kennedy's fears were eased by hard-line advice that Communist never let themselves be "provoked" into actions that a non-emotional calculation would tell them to avoid.

Thus, his trepidations at least partially relieved, Kennedy pursued

[68] Schick, *The Berlin Crisis*, pp. 181–182.
[69] Schlesinger, *A Thousand Days*, p. 358.

his uneasy mix between defensive coercion and accommodation. He directed preparation of a negotiating position, increased conventional and nuclear forces, made speeches emphasizing both U.S. willingness to negotiate and its resolve to fight for vital interests, and issued warnings against reckless or excessively coercive Soviet behavior. The mix was reflected at various specific choice points during the crisis. Sometimes coercive and accommodative aims collided. For example, General Lucius Clay was appointed the President's personal representative in Berlin, more or less in charge of U.S. moves on the spot. This probably was intended as a coercive move, both because Clay was known as a hard-liner and because his mandate created the possibility that he might take tough or risky actions not specifically authorized by Washington. But Washington was alarmed by some of his initiatives, and his "compulsion to force issues" tended to create a climate uncongenial to negotiation.[70]

The risk run by Kennedy in pursuing a combined coercive-accommodative strategy was, as Jack Schick has pointed out, that of garbling the message he wanted Moscow to hear.[71] It was a complicated message, requiring sensitive perception and interpretation, and the Soviet receptors might not be this good.

Kennedy made an important speech on June 25, which attempted to communicate his message. It contained coercive, persuasive, and accommodative elements. In the persuasive dimension, Kennedy sought to maximize the U.S. stakes. The threat to Berlin was "not an isolated problem" but part of a "world-wide" threat. This implied that the administration considered the challenge to Berlin to be a test of U.S. resolve to meet its commitments everywhere. With the stakes so high, the test must be met with absolute firmness.

The coercive element was an announcement of the conventional military build-up. This was designed to fill a gap in the U.S. escalation ladder, so that a military response would be more credible. Behind this announcement, although Kennedy did not spell it out, were plans for a military probe along the autobahns in case the Soviets blocked them. Such a probe by a substantial task force, although not sufficient to defeat the Soviet forces, would set off a sizable and prolonged conventional battle that would give Khrushchev time to ponder the possibilities of nuclear escalation and perhaps reverse himself. But the probe itself was to be undertaken only as a later phase of a gradual escalation process that would begin with diplomacy and non-violent coercion— first an appeal to the United Nations, then economic reprisals, and so on. Thus Kennedy planned to "start low" and keep his options open.

[70] Ibid., p. 364.
[71] Schick, *The Berlin Crisis,* p. 148.

The primary accommodative element in Kennedy's speech was simply the statement that the West was willing to negotiate and that preparations for negotiation were under way. Paradoxically, Kennedy's quite specific statement of the West's vital interests in Berlin also had accommodative overtones. The interests were (1) continued presence of American forces, (2) continued access for such forces, and (3) the security and economic viability of West Berlin. From this, the Communists could infer that the Western allies had re-examined their interests (done some "*T*-search") and had decided they could make concessions on matters not covered by these "three essentials." Significantly, Kennedy said nothing about Western rights in East Berlin, and the Communists could well have perceived this as a deliberate accommodative gesture.

During the early part of the 1961 phase of the crisis, the Soviet strategy was primarily coercive—the demand for a "free city" coupled with the threat to sign a separate peace treaty by the end of the year. The accommodative leavening consisted only of a willingness to negotiate the details of the free city arrangement. Kennedy's decision for a conventional build-up was answered by cancellation of previously announced Soviet plans for a reduction in conventional forces. Khrushchev continued to claim Soviet preponderance in nuclear power and boasted of Soviet capacity to build and deliver on U.S. territory a 100-megaton bomb. Khrushchev,[72] Ulbricht, and other Soviet spokesmen also expressed disbelief in the U.S. will to fight over Berlin and risk nuclear war. Khrushchev threatened to resume nuclear testing (which had been under an informal moratorium), citing as reasons the U.S. "threats of war," his belief that the United States was about to resume testing, and pressure from his own scientists.[73]

The crisis assumed a new and more dangerous cast when the outflow of refugees from East Germany, through West Berlin, grew to over 1000 per day by mid-July. Between August 3 and August 5, the Soviets, no doubt prodded by Ulbricht, decided to stop this flow by closing off the border. They had learned from Kennedy's June 25 speech, and the utterances of other U.S. leaders such as Senator Fulbright that the United States was unlikely to respond violently to this move. To reduce this likelihood even further, Khrushchev's language shifted markedly in the accommodative direction during the first half of August, while continuing an admixture of coercion and persuasion with claims that the balance of power had shifted to Soviet advantage, warnings to the West not to risk war, and further statements about the incredibility of Western threats to use force. The accommodative elements were contained in a

---

[72] In an interview with John J. McCloy on July 27; Slusser, *The Berlin Crisis of 1961*, pp. 10, 91, 64.

[73] Ibid., p. 91.

Soviet diplomatic note that restated the Soviet general position but modified the demand and omitted mention of the sanction: the status of West Berlin could be settled *after* the signing of a peace treaty (not as part of the treaty), implying that the West could negotiate about a peace treaty without prejudicing their rights in West Berlin. The notes studiously avoided mention of the previous threat to turn over control of the access routes to East Germany after conclusion of a peace treaty. And there was no mention of any deadline. The Soviet commandant in East Berlin assured his Western counterparts that any Soviet military moves in the near future would be defensive only.

The gradual erection of the Wall, beginning on August 13, and the lack of serious Western resistance have been described earlier. The relevant point is that the Soviets accompanied the wall-building with several conciliatory statements evidently intended to reassure the West that the Wall was intended only to deal with the refugee problem and did not presage further steps against *West* Berlin or access to it from West Germany. These statements were designed for "risk-avoidance," to avert the danger that the West might interpret the Wall as only the first in a series of physical escalations, designed to force them out of West Berlin, and thus requiring a tough or even violent response. In retrospect, the building of the Wall and the western acceptance of it (after a temporary period of considerable tension) was a tacit mutual accommodation that was to emerge finally as the eventual substantive "settlement" of the Berlin crisis. But this was not recognized by either party at the time, and the crisis atmosphere continued for several more months. Once the Wall was in place and it became clear the Western powers would not take physical action against it, the Soviets resumed their diplomatic offensive against West Berlin, punctuated by a variety of harassing and resolve-testing incidents in Berlin and the access routes and the resumption of nuclear testing. These latter moves could be interpreted, not as a resumption of the crisis over West Berlin, but as a series of coercive measures designed to camouflage the fact that the Soviets had decided to give up their demand for a free city—i.e., to protect against "image loss".[74]

Problems in Optimizing Strategy Mixtures

The many pitfalls in the path of fashioning the optimum mix between coercion and accommodation are illustrated in the Agadir and Berlin cases. The cases are different in that, in Agadir, the primary aim of both parties was the accommodative one of achieving a compromise settlement, while in Berlin it was the coercive aim of obtaining a victory

[74] Ibid., p. 168.

or avoiding defeat. Problems developed when countervailing tactics from the opposite strategy were introduced to offset the inherent weaknesses of the primary one. In the Agadir case, both sides felt the need to introduce coercive moves to "dig in" and avoid the appearance of weakness after concessions, to prevent miscalculation by the adversary, and generally to maximize their respective shares of the values they were dividing up. However, every coercive threat that was issued had the backlash effect of stiffening the adversary's resistance, slowing progress toward a settlement, and increasing tension—in one or two instances, to the very edge of war. One reason was that the threatened party considered the threat to be "unnecessary," a gratuitous violation of the "rules of accommodation" (to borrow Iklé's phrase)[75] once it had been mutually decided that the aim of negotiations was to achieve a mutually satisfactory settlement. Thus France considered the "*Panther*'s spring" an unnecessary application of pressure once she had already agreed in principle that Germany was to have compensation. And Germany considered the Lloyd George speech an affront because it was an unnecessary, unjustified intervention in an affair that was none of Britain's business. The other cause of the backlash effects was that the threats were considered excessively severe by the recipients. For the French the *Panther* represented a blatant threat of force, uncalled for in an accommodative setting. For the Germans, Lloyd George's belligerent language went beyond what was necessary to accomplish Britain's purpose of simply making known her desire to participate in any talks involving a partition of Morocco. The other significant threats—Caillaux's "eight-days threat" and Kiderlen's threat to go to "extreme lengths"—shared this last characteristic of excessive bellicosity. The "rule" that seems to be operating here is that during essentially accommodative bargaining, it is legitimate for a party to indicate firmness on its various positions along the road to settlement but not to the point of overtly threatening force or challenging sensitive status values outside the ostensible object of bargaining. Kiderlen broke another rule: "do not raise demands," when he demanded an economic "condominium" with France in Morocco after having stated he had no claims in Morocco itself. (The analogy to Hitler's raising his demands at Godesberg comes to mind; it also was an "out-of-bounds" move that temporarily hardened the British position, just as Kiderlen's move did in France.) Almost all the Agadir threats, which were intended for loss-avoidance or gain-maximization in the accommodative dimension, went too far in that they violated the risk-avoidance constraint in the coercive dimension. They created risks of war greater than were justified by the bargaining ad-

---

[75] Iklé, *How Nations Negotiate*, Ch. 7.

vantage gained. Kiderlen's threats were particularly counterproductive in stiffening the moderate French government, involving the British, and causing his accommodative-minded superiors to veto any thought of war, which weakened his bargaining power in the final stages. Kiderlen also botched his attempt to resolve the dilemma of pressuring the immediate antagonist while keeping the antagonist's ally inactive. His error was twofold: choosing a locale for exercising pressure that was too close to Britain's own interest, and failing to reassure Britain that her interests were not endangered.

It is instructive to compare the accommodative-coercive mix employed by England in this case with the one she followed in 1914. In 1914, there was tension between Grey's desire to mediate and get the central protagonists to negotiate and his desire to convince Germany that if it came to war, England would fight beside her entente partners. Mediation success required restraint of France and Russia as well as avoiding the provocation of Germany.[76] Grey then stressed accommodation in his mixed strategy, watering down the coercive elements to the point that they failed to penetrate the German image of a neutral England. The consequence, of course, was German miscalculation. In 1911, German miscalculation was precisely what Grey was most worried about, and he seemed insensitive to the danger of provoking Germany, at least in the particular instance of the Lloyd George speech. Hence his mixture was overly weighted toward coercion, producing a greater war-risk than necessary, although the Germans certainly got the message about British intentions. In order to move back toward an appropriate balance, Grey later had to partially disavow the Lloyd George speech to placate Germany and to caution the French privately that it did not imply as much support as they had thought. Sadly, his attempt to shift to a better balance in 1914 came too late to stop the mobilization-countermobilization avalanche.

In the Berlin case, the difficulties were somewhat the obverse of Agadir—to find the right accommodative leavening in an essentially coercive-countercoercive situation. Khrushchev's initial accommodative gestures were quite astute in placing his coercive aims in an accommodative light and thus drawing the West into negotiations. But the Western acceptance of negotiations in 1959, and the Soviets' acceptance of their acceptance, which specified Western-preferred terms of reference, led

[76] The choice between restraining or supporting an ally is the alliance equivalent of the choice between coercing and accommodating an opponent. The two choices are linking conversely in that coercing the ally (restraint) is consistent with accommodating the opponent, while accommodating the ally (support) is consistent with coercing the opponent. The tension or dilemma between deterring or coercing the adversary while simultaneously trying to restrain the ally is discussed in Chapter VI.

to a mutual misperception that the other was willing to concede on each party's own preferred substantive claim. Later, Kennedy's attempt to appear "flexible" succeeded quite well in mitigating the possible provocativeness of his military build-up and basically firm stance—i.e., in meeting the "risk-avoidance" constraint. But it cost him in "loss-avoidance" because the Soviets and East Germans discovered from his July 25 speech that they could unilaterally seal off the border with little risk.

One finds an interesting contrast, incidentally, between the Soviets' lowering of their demands when the Wall went up and Kiderlen's raising of his demands after having made his first concession in the Agadir crisis. Kiderlen needed a coercive gesture lest his concession appear to be the beginning of a downward slide toward capitaulation. Khrushchev needed accommodative gestures lest the raising of the Wall appear to the West as the beginning of an escalation of Soviet coercion on West Berlin, which they might decide to nip in the bud by the immediate use of force.

An interesting common feature of the two cases is the occurrence of bargaining about the withdrawal or non-withdrawal of threats. There were two such bouts of subsidiary bargaining in the Agadir case: one over Caillaux's "eight days threat" (which, incidentally, was a demand for removal of a *German* threat, the *Panther*), and another over the Lloyd George speech. In both cases, Kiderlen angrily demanded retraction. Caillaux complied—at minimum cost, since he had issued his threat secretly and through unofficial channels. The British were not so compliant (partly because their threat had been issued publicly by a prominent official), and Kiderlen had to buy them off. In exchange for only a partial British disavowal, he had to renounce publicly any claim on Morocco.

During the 1958–1960 Berlin crisis, there was much skirmishing about the Soviets' six-month "ultimatum," the West refusing to negotiate under "duress," the Soviets gradually qualifying the deadline. A bargain was reached at the Camp David talks in 1959. Khrushchev agreed there would be no fixed time limit on the negotiations; Eisenhower agreed that the talks should not be "prolonged indefinitely." This incident was somewhat like the bargaining over the Lloyd George threat in that it led to an accommodative exchange (though the exchange was more explicit in the earlier instance), and unlike the Caillaux retraction, which was forced by unilateral coercion.

Two kinds of values—affective and strategic—are at stake in such skirmishes. Affectively, agreements to negotiate or concessions made under threat are humiliating because they appear to be extorted by a juridical peer who has no "right" to do so. Strategically, the sacrifice in conceding under threat is magnified by the linkage to one's bargaining reputation. To negotiate while an opponent's threat is outstanding is to acquiesce in his assertion of superior power, which by its effect on the adversary's expectations actually does enhance his bargaining power. Thus it is largely for "loss-avoidance" reasons that the target of the threat demands its removal as a condition for the continuance or initiation of substantive bargaining.

However, the memory that a serious threat has been issued, even though it is withdrawn or considerably qualified, may continue to exert some effect on subsequent bargaining. The not quite complete British disavowal of the Lloyd George threat in 1911 served mainly to dissipate the passions that the speech had aroused. What it signified about British interests and intentions continued to affect German calculations and weakened their bargaining power with the French. Khrushchev's removal of his deadline after the Camp David talks did not expunge the memory of it, which left a certain sense of urgency. When the disavowal is forced by severe coercive pressure, as with the Caillaux threat, the threatener suffers a net loss, appearing weaker than before he had threatened.

The problem of finding the appropriate mix between coercive and accommodative tactics is the central dilemma of international conflict, but finding the recipe and implementing it is beset by many uncertainties and pitfalls. Both coercion and accommodation rest on virtually self-contained but somewhat contradictory logics. Each logic has its weaknesses, which tend to be the obverse of the other's strengths. Thus, a blending of coercion and accommodation offsets the vulnerabilities of each of the pure strategies with countervailing elements of the other but without weakening too much the strengths of either. Any particular blend may be considered appropriate if the gain from offsetting the vulnerabilities is greater than the costs and risks introduced by the countervailing strategy. For example, an admixture of accommodation in a coercive strategy is desirable if it reduces the risk of "provoking" the opponent more than it increases the risk of being thought weak, or of having to concede more than one would have had to with undiluted coercion. Or, conversely, an element of coercion in an accommodative strategy is desirable if it reduces one's sacrifices in a settlement more than it increases the risk of lock-in and no settlement, or the risk of engaging passions that push the crisis beyond control. In practice, the relative bargaining power of the parties, as it becomes clarified during the crisis, is the most important variable affecting these trade-offs. The mixture may also reflect the internal balance of influence between advocates of one pure strategy or the other, more than a reasoned calculation of the pluses and minuses of each combination. A later chapter will explore the connection between internal bargaining and the coercive-accommodative choice in external bargaining.

SUMMARY

In this chapter we began with a statement of the typical kinds of values engaged in a crisis, thus providing more content to the game models of crisis "structure" presented in Chapter II. We showed how the "bargaining power" of the parties is a function of these value structures, and we made use of Ellsberg's critical risk model to give this elusive concept some precision. We then turned to an analysis of the bargaining process in terms of the basic modalities of coercion and accommodation, which correspond to the strategic alternatives in the 2×2 game models of the preceding chapter, adding a third subprocess—persuasion—consisting of attempts to change the value structure of the other party or his perception of one's own. We developed a theory of "crisis management" based on the goals and constraints in coercive and accommodative strategies, a theory that conceived of the "management" problem as achieving the optimum trade-off between goals and constraints for each strategy and an optimum mix between the basic strategies themselves. From our case materials we were able to state how these trade-offs and choices are typically made by actual bargainers. In the main the cases showed that bargainers are at least as much concerned with the constraints on coercion—avoiding mutual commitment, keeping options open, minimizing out-of-control risks—as they are with maximizing coercive gains.[77] On the accommodative side, the constraint of minimizing losses to the self was more important to bargainers than the goal of reaching a settlement per se; hence settlements were almost always reached by "hard bargaining," and in some cases no explicit settlement was reached at all—the crisis just "faded away." There were only two or possibly three genuine compromise settlements, and in these cases the problem of combining coercive and accommodative strategies was the most delicate. In most other cases, one party gradually established its superior resolve during the confrontation phase; then a turning point was reached when the weaker party shifted to accommodation, helped along sometimes by a "stick" or "carrot," or both, and then usually conceded everything—almost always, however, getting a small concession at the end as a "face-saver."

The link between the bargaining *power* discussed in the first part of the chapter and the bargaining *process* analyzed in the last part is the element of *uncertainty*. At the outset of a crisis, the parties are either uncertain or mistaken about relative bargaining power, primarily because

---

[77] This finding is similar to Oran Young's in *The Politics of Force,* Ch. 9.

they cannot know the value of each other's interests at stake and hence how firm the other will ultimately be. Coercive, persuasive, and perhaps accommodative tactics attempt to communicate one's own resolve (truthfully or deceptively), weaken the adversary's resolve by changing his values or his perceptions of one's own, and gain information about the adversary's interests and resolve. Toward the end of the confrontation stage, the parties develop fairly clear, if not correct, pictures of mutual resolve and hence relative bargaining power, and then a process of resolution occurs—either compromise or one-sided capitulation depending on the revealed power relations. Process is therefore practically inseparable from power since it is through process that the true power relations become manifest in the parties' values and perceptions. The next chapter takes up the ways information is processed during bargaining to produce adjustment of initial uncertainties and mistaken expectations.

CHAPTER IV

INFORMATION PROCESSING

> Not ignorance and uncertainty merely, but mistakenness, belief in something which in fact is false, and further, the deliberate cultivation of uncertainty and mistakenness by one party in the mind of the other, are of the essence of bargaining.
>
> —G.L.S. Shackle.[1]

In this chapter we take up information processing and develop a model of bargaining as a process of correcting initial errors of estimation and interpretation. The previous chapter looked at the bargaining process as a process of mutual influence, with outcomes being determined basically by the parties' assessments of relative power and interest. It was implicitly understood that the parties arrive at these assessments or try to change the other's assessments by sending and receiving information, but the process of interpreting information was not explored. Here we correct this omission and thus move toward a more complete theory of crisis bargaining. In this chapter, also, we begin to investigate decision-making processes. Information processing is the link between interstate bargaining and the process of decision within the state; hence this chapter serves as a natural transition between what has gone before and the analysis of decision making in the following chapter.

CODDINGTON'S BARGAINING THEORY

The one current bargaining theory that places information directly in the center of bargaining is that of Alan Coddington.[2] We will begin by summarizing the theory; then we expand the theory on the basis of our data; then we test the expanded theory against the empirical case materials of information processing to determine where it is deficient; and finally we suggest modifications that would correct the deficiencies. It turns out that Coddington's theory brings out the essential characteristics of bargaining in greatly simplified form. The changes we suggest complicate the theory to make it empirically more adequate without changing its basic structure.

The distinctive characteristic of Coddington's theory is that it integrates the acquisition of information into the bargaining process rather than treating it as a separate problem. At the beginning, the bargainers do not know each other's objectives, intentions, and strategies. They have opinions or estimates of them, but these estimates may very well

---

[1] Foreword to Alan Coddington, *Theories of the Bargaining Process* (Chicago: Aldine, 1968), p. vii.
[2] Ibid.

be mistaken. However, during the bargaining process they receive information they can use to correct mistaken estimates. As both bargainers' estimates are corrected, they develop more realistic estimates of what kind of settlement is possible, and their bids converge toward that settlement.

More specifically, at the outset each bargainer has a set of *expectations* about how the other(s) are likely to respond to his moves. He also has a preference function over possible settlements. On the basis of his expectations and preference, he works out or decides on a bargaining *strategy*. He then begins to carry out his strategy by making a bid. The other bargainers' responses, either counterbids or messages, provide information that can be used to test expectations. If the responses conform to expectations, the latter are confirmed, and the strategy continues to be carried out. But if responses disconfirm one's expectations, it is then necessary to *adjust* expectations to fit the new information. Strategy must also be reexamined; a small adjustment of expectations may require a small change of tactics, while a large adjustment or an accumulation of adjustments may require a large or even complete strategy change. The new strategy or tactic is then output as a bid or message and the bargaining process continues through another cycle.

The model illustrated in Figure 4–1 emphasizes the information aspect of bargaining and does not bring out the influence aspect, which remains implicit. It is a one-sided model, and the present chapter will be one-sided, designed to complement other theories that emphasize influence and de-emphasize information-processing.

We now expand this skeleton model and begin to apply it to international crises. (1) We distinguish between strategic and tactical decisions because new information affects these two in quite different ways. (2) Expectations are affected in our cases not only by information but

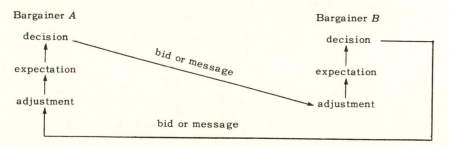

Figure 4-1. After Coddington. The Bargaining Cycle

[3] Ibid., p. 14.

also by the bargainer's belief system, including his theories of international politics and his images of self and opponent. (3) Information does not affect expectations directly; it is first interpreted, and the interpretation is affected by both belief systems and expectations and even by the previous strategy decision. In other words, there are several feedback loops in the general adjustment process. Although information is central to Coddington's model, he omits the actual interpretation of information. (4) The transmission of a message is not as uneventful as Coddington suggests. There are some feedback loops and filters in transmission, so that the message sent by A need not be the message received by B. (5) The various feedback loops allow for possibilities that are not present in Coddington's model, namely the failure to adjust mistaken expectations, or adjustment according to a nonlinear function. That is, with feedback loops expectations may remain constant throughout bargaining, or they may remain constant up to a point and then change drastically, or they may change erratically. In Coddington's model adjustment is gradual and automatic, and the system automatically converges toward a settlement; the only open question is the rate of convergence, which is controlled by an adjustment parameter.

The expanded model is shown in Figure 4–2. The figure can be interpreted by following a piece of information through it. Starting at the right, Bargainer B, let us say, makes a tactical decision to send a message

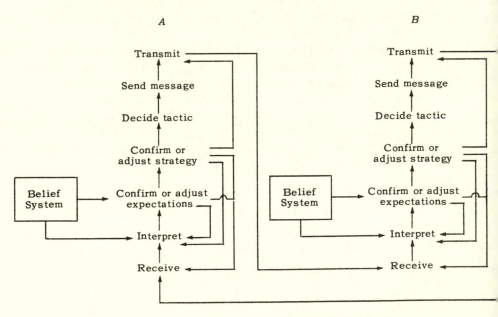

Figure 4-2. The Bargaining Cycle

to *A*. *Sending* may consist of *B*'s foreign secretary speaking through an official intermediary, or making a public statement or perhaps sending a message directly to *A*'s foreign secretary. The message that is sent may not be the same one that *B* has decided upon; the foreign secretary may fail to express himself clearly or may make changes. *Transmitting* is done by *B*'s ambassador or ad hoc emissary, who may also make inadvertent or deliberate changes based on tacit support by a faction within *B*. Thus, the ambassador or emissary, and sometimes the foreign secretary, acts as a filter that checks that the message conforms to *B*'s strategy as he understands it. The filter is not neutral; it represents control by one faction within *B* over divergent tactical interpretations of the agreed strategy. *Receiving* is done by *A*'s foreign secretary or ambassador, who may also filter out or edit messages that a faction of *A* does not want *A* to receive at that time.

So far we have referred only to messages deliberately sent by *B*; these are what Jervis calls "signals." [4] However, *A*'s information system also picks up other information relevant to predicting *B*'s behavior—the state of *B*'s public opinion, his military readiness and deployments (for instance, photos made on U-2 flights), official statements apparently intended for a domestic audience, unattributed newspaper stories and editorial comment, etc. Jervis calls these data "indices"; they are not shown on the chart, but become part of the data received by *A*.

All messages (signals) and indices that arrive at *A*'s central decision maker are then perceived or *interpreted*. We shall use the terms *interpretation* and *perception* interchangeably to denote the conscious or unconscious selection from, and attribution of meaning to received information. *Interpretation* perhaps suggests more conscious mental activity than empirically takes place, while *perception* seems to suggest too little, although it does more adequately suggest the screening-out or filtering process. Much incoming information is immediately filtered out as irrelevant; it is ignored, rejected, or sent to the foreign office for study, where it disappears into the bureaucratic labyrinth. The remainder is given meaning in two senses: (1) what is *B* trying to say? (2) Remembering that all messages may be deceptive but may also reveal more than the sender intended, what can be inferred about *B*'s actual intentions and about his probable responses to our future tactics? In the case of indices, only the second question is involved, since indices are only facts, not messages intended to communicate something. However, as Jervis has pointed out, the assumption that indices are simple facts rather than communications may be unwarranted and risky, since *B,* guessing that *A* is paying attention to them, may be able to manipulate them deceptively.[5]

[4] Jervis, *The Logic of Images,* pp. 20–26.
[5] Ibid., Ch. 3.

Interpretation is based partly on *A*'s *belief system,*[6] which includes both *theories* about the nature of international politics and a set of *images* of each bargainer including oneself. An image is a set of beliefs about the nature and characteristic behavior of some bargainer. It includes beliefs about his long-range interests and foreign policy objectives, his more specific objectives and intentions in the present crisis, the strategy he is probably following, his resources and military forces and willingness to use them, his diplomatic style, his image of one's own state, and perhaps his image of one's image of him. Images are interrelated, and in particular the self-image and the other-image are connected in ways to be discussed later. Theories are beliefs about cause-effect relationships in the international political process, regardless of the identities of the states involved. *Theory* is perhaps too grand a term for what we mean here. What we have in mind are general rules of thumb that statesmen use, indeed must use, to make sense out of the welter of international events, to predict how other states will behave under certain conditions and how they will respond to certain actions. They are "propositions" rather than "theories"; informal, unintegrated, the product of experience interacting with personal predisposition rather than of conscious cerebration.[7] Examples would be John F. Kennedy's belief that most wars result from miscalculation, Dean Acheson's belief that concessions to an aggressive opponent will always be interpreted as weakness, or Neville Chamberlain's belief that most, if not all, international conflicts can be settled by calm, reasonable discussion.

Images necessarily are important in interpretation, since the meaning of *B*'s message depends on his assumed aims, intentions, and strategy, his trustworthiness or deceptiveness, his military capabilities, and his bargaining style. For example, a verbal threat means one thing when it is sent by a habitual bluffer known to be militarily unprepared and to harbor expansionist ambition, and another thing when it is sent by a cautious, conciliatory foreign secretary who has never bluffed, representing a government that is generally defensive. That is, one interprets a message from *B* by treating it as a tactical step in *B*'s presumed strategy, and one estimates *B*'s strategy on the basis of *B*'s long-run and specific aims, capabilities, and bargaining style.

Interpretation is also influenced by *expectations*. This term we define, following Coddington, as a set of predictions of how the opponent will respond to specific tactics; collectively the set is deducible from his

[6] O. Holsti, "Cognitive Dynamics and Images of the Enemy" in David Finlay, O. Holsti, and R. Fagen, eds., *Enemies in Politics* (Chicago: Rand McNally, 1967).

[7] Klaus Knorr, "Failures in National Intelligence Estimates," *World Politics,* Vol. 16 (April 1964), p. 466.

assumed preference function and strategy. The influence of expectations on interpretations may be irrational, if the expectations came from an emotionally biased image, not from solid evidence, or are held too long in the face of disconfirming information; they nevertheless are very important in our cases. Expectations enter the interpretation process when A classifies B's message as a response to some tactic of A. Since A expects B to respond in a certain way, he unconsciously attempts to interpret the message as some version of the expected response. For instance, if A expects B to make a concession and B says "let us negotiate" the interpretation might be "B wishes to negotiate in order to make a concession." If the message is "we will never yield x" the interpretation might be that B is not yet ready to yield x but will soon, or that B is bluffing. If the message is a request for a loan, it might be filtered out as irrelevant and sent to the foreign office for study.

Since the influence of expectations on interpretation is unconscious, the interpreter does not realize at first that he has read his own ideas into the message; he thinks the ideas are objectively there in the message. Consequently he treats the fit between message and expectations as an objective confirmation of his diagnosis, which increases his confidence in the diagnosis. This makes it easier unconsciously to read his expectations into the next message, and so on.

The opposite process can also occur. Instead of interpreting a message to conform with expectations, A can interpret it as differing from expectation, and must then correct his expectations. If A expects B to concede x, and the message is "we will never yield x," A's interpretation might be "we were mistaken; B is not going to concede x." This process can also be irrational, if it involves A's giving up a well-supported expectation on the basis of one ambiguous message.

Expectations are initially deduced from belief systems and are later adjusted during bargaining to conform to new information. In this initial deduction, theories provide the major premises and images make a particular theory relevant to a particular bargainer. For example, in 1905 the German foreign office held the theories, based partly on some successful tactics by Bismarck, that opposing alliances can be broken by pressure and that other states can be attracted to an alliance with one's own state by demonstrations of power. The image of Britain was that of an untrustworthy ally who would renege on alliance obligations rather than incur sacrifices. The first theory therefore applied to Britain, and the Foreign Office "deduced" the expectation that Britain would back out of its entente obligations to France under German pressure.

Interpretations are, finally, affected by current strategy. This is a pragmatic effect. Bargainers are active entities, engaged in carrying out a strategy that is intended to make changes in other bargainers.

They turn to new information not out of a general interest in knowledge but out of a quite specific interest in finding out whether their strategy is succeeding. Bargainer A therefore asks very specific questions of a message coming from B: is B responding as expected? If not, can the desired response still be induced somehow? If not, can B's obstruction still be blocked or countered? Or if A's strategy is contingent on what type of response B is making—offer concessions if B is reasonable, dig in and prepare for war if B is stubborn—the question will be, "what type of response pattern is B showing?" Is he getting more reasonable or is he getting more stubborn? Information that is irrelevent to A's strategy, like that which is irrelevant to expectations, is likely to be filtered out or ignored. The influence of strategy on interpretation can be rational in the sense that it directs attention to important or unobvious implications of a message. But it can also involve wishful thinking if it induces an interpretation that implies incorrectly that the strategy is succeeding as desired.

When information has been interpreted and expectations adjusted accordingly, A can decide whether his bargaining strategy is still appropriate or whether it should be changed. We postpone discussion of strategic decisions to the next chapter, noting here only that strategy revision or replacement occurs only once or twice at most in a crisis. Consequently the question "Is current strategy still appropriate?" is always answered "yes," except at critical turn-around points. Tactical decisions, on the other hand, occur constantly, after nearly every message. If a message confirms expectations, the tactical decision would be to output the next tactic in the strategy. If a strategy contains tactical alternatives contingent on B's type of response, as some strategies do, the tactical decision would be to output the tactic appropriate to B's response. If B's message induces minor adjustment of expectations, the tactical decision might be to carry on with the planned tactic, or it might be to devise a tactic that could guide B's responses in the expected and desired direction. If B's responses are entirely different from expectations, the tactical decision might be to devise an information-gathering tactic to find out what B is up to. The tactic is then output, that is the message is sent and transmitted, and it is B's move.

The distinction we make between strategy and tactics is the common-sense one: a strategy is a general plan of action for winning or settling the crisis; while a tactic is a particular move within a strategy. We classify strategies according to the generalized game matrix (Fig. 2–46), which means that there are three pure types of strategies: C, make concessions; D, stand firm; E, attack. There are also mixed strategies, usually CD mixtures: make concessions if he is reasonable, dig in if he is stubborn; or, make no concessions until he has conceded our main demand, then make concessions; or, make concessions in one area but dig in firmly in another area. These are the mixtures of coercion and accommodation discussed in Chapter III. Each of these generalized strategies can be worked out in varied tactical detail to produce the variety of bargaining strategies that actually occur.

If we compare our expanded model, Figure 4–2, with Coddington's skeleton model, Figure 4–1, we see that Figure 4–1 is a special case of Figure 4–2, an ideal limit in which most of the subroutines in Figure 4–2 are empty. Coddington's model applies only to a very special, limited type of bargaining in which nearly all of the general bargaining problem has been solved beforehand, such as routine wage bargaining within a well-established labor-management relationship. In Coddington's simplification only one strategy is permitted—*C,* make concessions; therefore only tactical decisions—how much, how soon—are possible. Second, belief systems are irrelevant because Coddington assumes both bargainers are pure economic men. Consequently, each has the same correct images of self and other; his aim is to maximize utility, and his strategy is to make concessions. The only ignorance or mistakeness permitted is about the opponent's tactics, his concession rate, and this falls in the expectation category. Third, there is no need for interpretation because the only message permitted is a quantitative bid, whose meaning given a correct image is immediately clear. Fourth, the bargainers are assumed to communicate directly so there is no need for a transmission system. Fifth, the bargainers are assumed to be rational economic men free of wishful thinking or any cognitive process other than calculation, so there are no feedback loops and no possibility of the absurd confusion that characterizes some of our cases.

ANALYSIS OF THE MODEL

The problem to be investigated in analyzing our expanded model is, what factors determine whether the system converges to a settlement or diverges toward breakdown and war? That is, what subroutines and parameters in the model affect convergence and divergence? In this section we list the factors that could affect convergence, and in the following sections we examine each factor empirically. In the empirical sections we will ask, how important empirically is each factor in controlling convergence and divergence? Can some factor be omitted as negligible and do we need to add other factors? Are there important interactions among the subroutines and feedbacks that must be modeled more explicitly? The answers to such questions should enable us to construct a revised model that brings out more directly the essential characteristics of bargaining in general and also of successful bargaining.

The first factor that affects the bargaining process is the belief system, and in particular the difference between A's and B's belief systems. The amount of difference affects system performance twice: (1) since a belief system produces initial expectations and thereby initial strategies, differences in belief systems present the problem of mistaken expectations and strategies that must be overcome by later adjustments; (2) since image affects interpretation, a difference of images produces both misinterpretation of the adversary's messages and also mistaken estimates of how the adversary is interpreting one's own messages.

Some difference in images, if not theories, is probably essential to the occurrence of a crisis. If two states could agree on each other's relative capabilities, willingness to take risks, interests, and intentions, there would be little to bargain about. If each side agreed on who was weaker (though both might be mistaken), the weaker side would not challenge and, if challenged by the stronger, would yield quickly, though it might put up a brief show of resistance to save some status and self-respect. Similarly, if each side knew what the other wanted and what it was willing to pay, it could estimate immediately whether resistance or accommodation was worthwhile.

Next, at least some reduction of differences in expectations is probably necessary to a settlement. At the beginning of a crisis, each party is expecting the other to give way on some disputed point and is not expecting to give way itself, and as long as these differences persist there can be no settlement. This in turn suggests that some convergence of images is also necessary, since initial expectations are derived from images of the opponent's interests, intentions, and capabilities. One can imagine cases in which images need not converge, but these would be unusual. For instance, each side might see itself as weaker or less interested than the opponent and might expect to give way before the opponent does.

There are two possible ways to reduce the difference between initial expectations: (1) indirectly, by changing images toward convergence. This would be represented in the model by an arrow from "interpret" to a new subroutine "adjust image." (2) Directly, by somehow separating expectations from images and adjusting expectations without changing images. Since expectations control strategic and tactical decisions, this adjustment is sufficient to produce convergence on a settlement. Figure 4–2 is intended to be neutral on this issue.

The second factor that affects the bargaining process is the various filters in the message transmission system. We need to know how important quantitatively these filters are, and whether they introduce any systematic bias toward either increasing or reducing errors of interpretation.

The third factor is the three influences on the interpretation process, by image, expectation, and strategy. Generally, although there are exceptions, if the system is to converge at all, correct interpretations must ultimately outnumber or outweigh misinterpretations. We need to know the quantitative ratio of correct to mistaken interpretations, and also the variations in this ratio according to stages in a crisis, type of adversary, or whatever. We also need to know how important quantitatively each of the three influences is in producing misinterpretations, and how the three influences combine—additively, multiplicatively, or in sequence during a crisis. Since each influence can also produce correct interpretations as well as mistaken ones, we need to study each influence to see, if possible, what makes for correct rather than mistaken interpretations.

The fourth factor is the rate at which mistaken expectations are adjusted. Given that expectations are initially incorrect and that correctly interpreted messages will reveal the incorrectness of expectations, how rapidly are corrections made? In other words, how much disconfirming information is needed?

The fifth and final factor is the rate at which strategy and tactics are changed. Given that mistaken expectations are eventually corrected, it is still necessary to adjust strategy and tactics accordingly before bids can actually converge. Any lag here can increase the time needed for convergence or can eliminate convergence entirely.

We now study each of these factors empirically, beginning with initial images and the expectations that are deduced from them.

INITIAL IMAGES AND EXPECTATIONS

One can distinguish two levels or components of the image: a background or long-term component, which is how the parties view each other in general, apart from the immediate crisis, and an immediate component, which comprises how they perceive each other in the crisis itself. The opponent's ultimate aims, over-all military potential, and alignments are included in the background component, and his objectives in this crisis as well as the intensity of his interests, loyalty of his allies, and his available military power at the crisis locale are included in the immediate component. Before the crisis starts, only the background component exists, but when the initial moves of the crisis occur the immediate component, the definition of the crisis situation, is worked out. On the basis of this definition of the situation some expectations about how the opponent will react are deduced, and a strategy or at least initial moves are worked out.

We hypothesized that there should normally be some initial difference between the background image that bargainer A holds of B and the image that B holds of himself, and vice versa. However, we left open the question of whether differences of background images need to be reduced or eliminated during bargaining to produce convergence on a settlement. Table 1 summarizes our findings about background image differences and reduction of differences in the 13 cases of peaceful settlement.

Table 4–1 says that crisis settlements are usually achieved without any reduction of background image differences. This means that if adjustment of expectations is necessary for settlement, and to the extent expectations are based on the background image, expectations must somehow be dissociated from such images. What "dissociation" consists of empirically is not yet clear. The three instances of *partial* convergence of an other-image toward the other's self-image are Rouvier, 1905; Eden, 1937–1939, when he was not in the cabinet; and Truman and Byrnes, 1945–1946 Iran, a doubtful case.

The hypothesis that some initial differences of background images should normally occur is confirmed. Of the 11 substantially similar images, most were held by one party to a crisis only. That is, they are cases in which A's image of B is fairly similar to B's self-image, but B's image of A is *markedly* different from A's self-image. The cases are: Salisbury, 1898; Delcassé, 1898; Grey, 1905; Delcassé, 1905; Grey, 1908; Sazonov, 1914; Lloyd George, 1923; Poincaré, 1923; Daladier, 1938; Qavam, 1946; and Dulles, 1956 (of Britain only). In only two crises, 1898 and 1923, were *both* parties' initial images of the other substantially similar to the other's self-image.

Why do background images differ so often? The answer is located primarily in the systemic context of crises, although factors such as ideologies and the history of earlier interaction also contribute.

The aims or intentions element in the background image is largely a function of the mutual identification of the parties as adversaries, which in turn is the result of particular conflicts of interest, the structure of the international system, alignment patterns, and sometimes

Table 4–1. Background Images

Substantially similar initially		11
Initially different		31
Difference somewhat reduced during bargaining	3	
Not reduced during bargaining	28	
Doubtful, insufficient evidence		5
		47

ideologies. The causal importance of system structure and alignment patterns is often overlooked in theorizing about images, even though it is well known, for example, how the U.S. images of the Soviet Union shifted from "loyal comrade-in-arms" to "aggressive enemy, out to conquer the world for Communism" after World War II destroyed the balance of power in Europe. Similarly, alliance necessities shifted our image of the Germans and Japanese from negative to positive.

When states have identified each other as opponents, the familiar "security dilemma" operates to produce exaggerated and sometimes illusory images of the other as aggressive or at least threatening and the self as defensive. Of course, as in the case of Hitler, one side may actually be systematically aggressive and expansionist. But even when this is not so, and both sides are interested only in security, there is a tendency for each party to view the other's security measures as aggressive, and a failure to understand that one's own "defensive" policies might be seen by the other as threatening to itself and thus be the cause of the other's seemingly "aggressive" moves. The image of the peaceful defensive self reinforces the image of the aggressive opponent, for if we are "obviously" only defending ourselves, why else is he doing all these threatening things? As Robert Jervis has pointed out, even though the initial images are illusory or exaggerated, the conflicts they produce are quite real since they will often involve incompatible security interests that cannot be renounced so long as the actual intentions of the adversary cannot be known.[8]

Since crises are episodes in a long-term adversary relationship, these background images will always color the immediate crisis images. An objectively expansionist power may see itself as taking "defensive" action to remove a security threat; it will see its rival as "aggressively" creating the threat. The defensive power will fail to see how its own "defense" or the status quo itself may seem threatening to the other. To complicate matters, there are sometimes both "expansionist" and "defensive" elements in both parties' policies. Finally, there is the natural tendency to rationalize one's own actions in terms of "good" motives (often quite sincerely) and the opponent's behavior as "bad." Thus there is typically a considerable difference between the self-image and the other's image of oneself. It would be an exaggeration to say that each side sees the other as "aggressive" and itself as "defensive" apart from the imprecision of these terms. More accurately, each sees its own behavior as "legitimate"; the other's as illegitimate in some way. The difference is based on the difficulty of appreciating the other's security interests and problems, and the justice that it sees in its own cause.

[8] Robert Jervis, *Perception and Misperception in International Politics* (Princeton, N.J.: Princeton University Press, 1976).

A few examples will show some empirical variations on this pattern. In 1905–1906, Delcassé, the French foreign minister, perceived Germany as potentially expansionist, a threat to French security in the long-run. In the immediate crisis, Germany was out to humiliate France by frustrating her policy in Morocco, demanding cabinet changes, and demanding a conference to decide matters that were France's own business. Germany's background image saw the Entente Cordiale as potentially aggressive against Germany, a threat to German security; the specific French actions in Morocco were an affront since they were undertaken without consulting Germany. Both parties saw themselves in their background image as defending against a security threat; in their immediate images they were avoiding humiliation or avenging insults. In 1908, Russia and Austria perceived each other as rivals for preponderance in the Balkans after their fragile détente had broken down. Russia saw the Austrian annexation of Bosnia as illegitimate, a specific instance in the pattern of Austrian expansionism. Austria, on the other hand, regarded it as a necessary step against possible revolution fomented by Russia's client Serbia, and against a possible reassertion of sovereignty over Bosnia by the new "young Turk" regime; moreover, it was a perfectly legitimate stabilization of the thirty-year status quo of Austrian administration and de facto sovereignty. The 1914 crisis was roughly a continuation of the 1908 one for Russia and Austria, with the background hostility much intensified in the meantime. Again, Austria saw herself as defending her very existence against Serb agitation supported by an expansionist pan-Slav Russia, while Russia saw herself as defending a brother Slav nation and the balance of power in the Balkans. Both Germany and Austria failed to appreciate Russian security interests in the Balkans, while the entente powers failed to appreciate the seriousness of Austria's revolutionary problem.

The 1940–1941 case has been discussed in Chapter II. The United States did not appreciate Japan's economic problem, exacerbated as it was by a militarist definition of self-sufficiency, and perceived Japanese moves as nationalist aggression. Japan did not appreciate U.S. security worries and perceived U.S. firmness as a continuation of imperialist encirclement of Japan.

During the Cold War, background images were more potent in crises, as the structural transformation to bipolarity clearly identified the United States and the Soviet Union as enemies, and the resulting security dilemma both heightened each side's security fears and blinded each superpower to the security needs of the other. Hostility and misunderstanding were aggravated by divergent ideological images that emphasized the inherent aggressiveness of the other party and the peacefulness of the self. The 1948 Berlin crisis was precipitated by Western moves, motivated chiefly by security needs, toward consolidation of a West German state. The Soviet Union perceived these moves as violations of the Yalta and Potsdam agreements and as potentially threatening to its own security and to the economic viability of the Eastern zone. It perceived its own reaction—the blockade of the Berlin access routes—as a move to head off these threats, or at least to protect East Germany against them by incorporating West Berlin. The U.S. view was that the Soviet Union had violated U.S. access rights to Berlin and was aggressively trying to force the Western powers out of West Berlin. Both sides were right about the legal violations, but both also failed to appreciate the other's security motivation.

Again, in 1958 Khrushchev no doubt would have admitted that his demand for a German peace treaty and a free city of West Berlin involved some revision of the legal status quo—as did the U.S. demand for reunification with free elections—but he argued that his proposal was defensive, justified by the abnormality of the situation, which created constant friction and the potential for violence and war. Moreover, in his view the West was using West Berlin for illegitimate and expansionist purposes of espionage, sabotage, and subversion. Further evidence of their expansionist aim was their consistent demand for German reunification eastward. Conversely, the United States and most of its NATO allies perceived Khrushchev's demands as the second round in the persistent Soviet attempts to take over West Berlin and nullify Western rights in the city. Khrushchev saw himself as trying to realize a common interest—tranquillizing the most dangerous situation in the world—while U.S. leaders perceived the situation more as a zero-sum conflict and saw themselves as resisting a one-sided demand for Western sacrifices to the benefit of the Communists.

Other cases do not fit so well this pattern of righteous ("defensive") self and nefarious ("aggressive") opponent. In the Fashoda crisis of 1898, the French and British saw each other as long-term imperialist rivals and in this specific case were pretty much agreed about what each was doing; the French trying to get some leverage over the English position in Egypt, the British trying to block the attempt. The second Morocco crisis of 1911 featured heightened background images of enmity, as compared with the first, but the immediate crisis images were quite convergent. Both France and Germany agreed that France should have full control of Morocco and that Germany should get compensation. The issue was how much compensation. The divergence of immediate images concerned the German bargaining methods. France saw them as unjustifiably coercive, an attempt to humiliate France and to extort a German share in the control of Morocco, which had been agreed previously to be out of the question. Germany viewed them as necessary to get "fair" compensation in Central Africa from a niggardly France.

In the 1938 crisis over Czechoslovakia, Hitler viewed himself as expansionist, but legitimately so, since the German "master race" had a right to rule over the inferior breeds in the polyglot Czech state. The Chamberlain cabinet also viewed Germany as expansionist, but legitimately so, since Hitler's aims were limited to the incorporation of German minorities into the Reich. Chamberlain viewed his government as helping Hitler obtain his legitimate objective peacefully, so as to stabilize the Central European situation and remove the danger of war. Hitler's initial image of the British was ambivalent. On the one hand (congruent with the Chamberlain government's self-image) they were racial cousins, partners in anti-Communism, and natural allies since no essential conflict existed between them and Germany. But increasingly after 1936 this image of brotherhood was overcome by another component: that of an opponent, though a cowardly, pusillanimous, politically innocent one who could easily be bluffed and tricked.

When image-divergence takes the form of the "aggressive" other and "defensive" self, the effect is to increase coerciveness and hostility during the crisis and possibility to self-fulfill the image of the aggressive-other over the long-run. That is, the adversary may actually become aggressive in the future to safeguard his security against the apparently aggressive self. But the opposite error of perceiving an expansionist opponent as essentially defensive is self-correcting. Thus Hitler, in not realizing in 1938 that his adversaries did *not* share his self-image as *generally* expansionist, incorrectly perceived them as generally cowardly and developed even more grandiose ambitions.[9] His resulting behavior enabled the British to perceive and correct the error in their image of Hitler.

The typical image of the ally is, obviously, that of a friendly, generally supportive state, but often this positive component competes with a negative component of distrust. The latter is especially prominent in a multipolar system where the possibility of realignment is ever-present. In addition, supporting allies are sometimes suspected of trying to incite conflict between the state and the opponent, or the supporting ally fears the state directly involved in a crisis will give away some of the supporting ally's interests to save its own.

Suspicion that the ally is contemplating realignment was present in both Britain and France during the first Morocco crisis. In Britain it was aroused when the French cabinet fired their foreign minister, Delcassé, at German behest, and the premier, Rouvier, made overtures to Germany for a general settlement. Rouvier and some other French leaders suspected Britain of trying to incite war between France and

9 Ibid.

Germany; "perfidious Albion" would then stand aside and let the two continental powers weaken each other. A different French suspicion—that England was considering realignment—was aroused later when Britain rather timidly urged France to compromise and the French picked up rumors that Britain was ready to offer Germany a Moroccan port. In the second Morocco crisis, 1911, some British officials perceived Caillaux's negotiations with Kiderlen as part of a long-term plot for rapprochement between the two countries. Caillaux supposedly at least welcomed, if not encouraged, the *"Panther*'s spring" because it would make it easier for him to convince his domestic opponents of the need for an understanding with Germany. In the modern era, U.S. allies have a nagging fear of U.S. deals with the Soviets at their expense, or they fear that the United States might take excessive risks in a crisis without consulting them. The latter fear seemed confirmed when the United States acted unilaterally in the "alert crisis" during the Mid-East War of 1973.

HARD-LINERS VS. SOFT-LINERS

The preceding section implied that belief systems within a state are homogeneous. This necessary simplification must now be qualified. In fact, there is ordinarily some division within governments in a crisis, on general world views or "theories," images of the opponent and allies, self-image, and strategy preferences. The terms *hard-line* and *soft-line,* or *hawks* and *doves,* are familiar shorthand labels for these differences. So far as we know there has been no published attempt to describe systematically the various components of hard and soft belief systems,[10] although most sophisticated observers of politics could rightly claim that they "know one when they see one." The following is an attempt at such an explicit analysis, which we find is absolutely necessary to an understanding not only of information processing in a crisis, but also of decision making. We attempt to describe only the content of the belief systems, independent of where they come from. Our research indicates that hard and soft attitudes are more a function of personality than of governmental role, although roles of course do affect attitudes, as do a person's training and experience. We make no attempt to delve into the enormously complex question of what other personality variables correlate with these beliefs. We shall have something to say in the next chapter about the effects of roles on beliefs.

Hard-line and soft-line views, as well as "middle-line," are of course sectors on a continuous spectrum of attitudes. There are many differ-

[10] See, however, Kenneth Fuchs, "Foreign Policy Decision-Maker Lines," unpublished Ph.D. thesis, SUNY Buffalo, 1974. Our analysis draws upon Fuchs's study.

ences among individuals within each sector and some persons may be hard toward some issues and actors while soft or moderate toward others. Our necessarily brief analysis only sketches in "ideal types." Further, we simply lop off and ignore the extreme ends of the spectrum and concentrate on the more moderate types that are generally found in decision-making positions, and that, with a few exceptions, are the only types we see in our cases. Our simple typology comprises general world-views or "theories," images of the opponent, self-images, and strategy preferences. The considerable overlap among these categories cannot be avoided without distortion. The treatment of "strategic preferences" logically is more relevant to the following chapter than to this one; we include it here for the sake of completeness.

GENERAL WORLD-VIEWS

The hard-line actor typically sees world politics as highly conflict-ridden. Consequently, he is sensitive to power-strategic considerations, to the potential aggressiveness of other states, and to the need to preserve or improve the power and security positions of his own state. The best road to peace as well as security for his own state is via military strength, deterrence, and firmness in crises. If his state is expansionist, its aims are best obtained through unadulterated coercion—i.e., in a crisis, by threats unmixed with conciliation. He is typically wary of accommodative moves, fearing they will be interpreted as weakness. He is quite insensitive to the possibility that the accumulation of power and uncompromising stance of his own state, undertaken for defensive purposes, could be interpreted by the adversary as threatening. He discounts the importance of emotional factors in international politics and crises, believing that others are as cool, calculating, and "unprovokable" as he is.

The soft-liner, on the other hand, sees a considerable amount of common interest in the relations between states. Conflict there is, of course, but it should and can be dealt with by mutual accommodation; at least accommodation should be tried before coercive measures. Military strength and deterrence are necessary to a degree, but should be combined with willingness to negotiate and flexibility in negotiations. He is wary of too much reliance on military power and uncompromising firmness, fearing that it might be misinterpreted by the adversary as designed for aggression, thus causing the adversary to accumulate power and take aggressive action in the interest of *his* security. In short, the soft-liner is more sensitive than the hard-liner to the security dilemma and its potential for producing "illusory" conflict and unnecessary hostility. Conversely, he is less sensitive than the hard-liner to the risk that conciliatory moves will be exploited or taken for weakness, thus encouraging aggression by a truly expansionist adversary. His relative insensitivity to power-strategic factors in world politics is combined with a considerable emphasis on emotional factors. Wars often erupt out of "incidents" and emotionally provocative acts, more often than out of cool calculations of interest.

IMAGE OF THE OPPONENT

The typical hard-liner sees the opponent as systematically expansionist, with unlimited aims. His intention in the present crisis is to achieve some tangible subgoal in his general program of expansion, or to test the defenders' resolve, or to reveal their resolve as weak to strengthen his bargaining power for future challenges. In a state that is frankly expansionist itself, the hard-liner usually sees the adversary as upholding an illegitimate status quo, or a status quo that is threatening to his own state. The opponent's resistance in the present crisis is just another manifestation of long-standing discrimination against, or dangerous "encirclement" of, his own state. To give some obvious examples: hard-liners in the United States, such as Acheson and Dulles, viewed the Soviets as being out to dominate the world, as Churchill and Duff Cooper had earlier perceived Hitler, and as persons such as Delcassé, Poincaré, Nicolson and Crowe had viewed Wilhelminian Germany. In expansionist states, men such as Holstein in pre-1914 Germany saw "encirclement" in nearly every cordial interaction between Britain, France, and Russia, and viewed England as unjustly denying Germany her fair share in colonial territory.

For the soft-liner, the opponent's long-run aims are limited, specific and independent, not linked together in some grand design for world conquest. Moreover, the adversary's aims are, at least to some extent, legitimate. Once these particular interests and grievances are satisfied, he will be transformed into a peaceful good neighbor. His aim in the present crisis is to satisfy one of these particular grievances, not generally to expand his material power and image of resolve. Since he is essentially reasonable and will see some justice in our position as we do in his, he will be willing to compromise. The soft-liner in an expansionist state (if he does not oppose his own country's expansionist goals) likewise sees his adversary, or a faction within the adversary, as accommodating and reasonable, able to see justice in his own state's cause.

Since soft-liners are less likely than hard-liners to hold positions of power in foreign policy making, we find fewer examples in our cases. One is Briand, French foreign minister in 1922, whose objective was to turn an essentially peace-loving Germany into a good neighbor through French generosity and through agreements to resolve particular differences of interest by negotiation. Another, of course, is Chamberlain (along with most of his cabinet), who thought Hitler's aims were limited to the satisfaction of legitimate grievances against the unjust Versailles treaty and, further, that Hitler was essentially a reasonable man willing to negotiate a compromise. In the Berlin crisis of 1961 persons such as Schlesinger, Harriman, and Thompson saw some legitimacy in the Soviet demands and believed there was a chance of a satisfactory compromise. Khrushchev himself, though he advanced revisionist demands, apparently believed that Western leaders would eventually agree that tidying up the "abnormal" Berlin situation was in the common interest.

There are also characteristic differences between hard- and soft-liners in their estimates of the opponent's preference function—i.e., his valuation of possible crisis outcomes—as compared to the preferences of their own state. To a great extent, this is a result of the hard-liner's much higher valuation of his state's long-term reputation for resolve and his failure to see that the opponent may be concerned about *his* resolve image, too. This in turn is a function of the hard-liner's image of the adversary as persistently aggressive and of his own state as obviously defensive. Since the opponent is always on the lookout for signs of weakness and opportunities to expand, it is essential to maintain a *general* image of determination to resist on *all* issues. In any particular crisis the preservation of this image is more important than the specific issue at stake. The issue itself is perceived to be a test of strength in the general, long-term confrontation, for which the specific stake is merely the occasion or focus.

This viewpoint has been well stated by Arthur Schlesinger, in describing Dean Acheson's position during the Berlin crisis of 1961:

> Acheson's basic thesis . . . was that West Berlin was not a problem but a pretext. Khrushchev's *demarche* had nothing to do with Berlin, Germany or Europe. His object, as Acheson saw it, was not to rectify a local situation but to test the general American will to resist; his hope was that, by making us back down on a sacred commitment, he could shatter our world power and influence. This was a simple conflict of wills, and, until it was resolved, any effort to negotiate the Berlin issue per se would be fatal. Since there was nothing to negotiate, willingness on our part to go to the conference table would be taken in Moscow as evidence of weakness and make the crisis so much the worse.[11]

The hard-line echo in the Soviet Union, reported by the *New York Times,* was "the opposition to Premier Khrushchev tended to broaden

---

[11] Schlesinger, *A Thousand Days,* p. 355.

the East-West conflict over Berlin into a world-wide showdown, regardless of the risks of nuclear war." [12]

The same thought was expressed by Delcassé, the French foreign minister, just before his ouster by a soft-line cabinet in 1905: "If today you yield, you will be compelled always to yield, and you do not know whether you will always have, as you have today, the almost unanimous agreement of the world."

The point here is not that such views are objectively wrong in the sense of resolve reputations being unimportant. Our case research shows that nations *do* often draw inferences about an adversary's determination in a present crisis from his behavior in crises of the recent past, sometimes contributing to disastrous miscalculations, as in 1914. The present point, rather, is that (1) hard-liners tend to exaggerate the value of a resolve reputation and/or to exaggerate the degree to which inferences are made from case to case, and (2) they fail to perceive that the adversary may be concerned about his resolve image as well. We have no instances of a hard-liner thinking like Kennedy did in 1962. When Kennedy was advised by General LeMay that the Soviet Union would not respond to a U.S. bombardment of Cuba, he disagreed, saying "They, no more than we, can let these things go by without doing something." This sort of empathy for the opponent's reputation-for-resolve problem seems to be absent from hard-line thinking, although there are several individuals for whom we have no clear evidence.

There is one odd exception, namely the Japanese military, who seemed to have no concern for reputation and indeed no clear opinion of how the United States would react to their proposed moves. The Japanese thinking seemed to be oriented more to the inner-directed question of what Japan *had* to do than to the bargaining questions of influence and reputation.

In game-theoretic terms, the result may be to misperceive the game structure as Called Bluff when it is actually Prisoner's Dilemma: the opponent is seen as Chicken and a bluffer, and it is only oneself who is in Prisoner's Dilemma and cannot back down. If both sides hold this image (in reverse), the result could be disaster. In the genuine Chicken and Called Bluff cases, the error consists in underestimating the opponent's perceived cost of yielding while exaggerating one's own.

The soft-liner is much less sensitive to resolve considerations. This is in part due to his relative insensitivity to power-strategic values in general. Conflicts and crises are viewed as disputes about specific non-strategic issues, not as episodes in a continuing general rivalry for

[12] Paul Hoffmann in *New York Times,* Oct. 4, 1961, quoted by Slusser, *The Berlin Crisis of 1961,* p. 277.

power and security. The outcome has little or no consequences for the relative power of the parties. Also, since the adversary's aims are limited, there is no danger in being conciliatory and possibly "looking weak" in the present instance; there will be no future occasions when a reputation for resolve will be important. Chamberlain is a prime exhibit. He was blind not only to the material strategic value of the Sudetenland but also to the possibility that Hitler might infer a general British lack of will from their behavior in the Munich crisis. Partly this was due to trust in Hitler's word that this was his "last demand," so whatever Hitler might infer about British resolve would not matter. Of course, Hitler did make an inference of general cowardice, a disastrous miscalculation that Chamberlain might have prevented had he made clear to Hitler that British accommodativeness was bounded by the principle of national self-determination.[13]

An example of a hard-soft clash within a government on the resolve issue occurred in the Agadir crisis of 1911. British hard-liners such as Eyre Crowe saw the German challenge as a general "trial of strength" with the Entente powers; therefore the only hope of preserving peace in the long run was for Britain to present a united front with France against any and all German demands; the nature of the immediate issue was unimportant. However, the soft-liners in the cabinet wished to discriminate among issues; Britain should take a stand only if her "direct interests" became involved.[14]

The soft-line counterpart to the hard-liner's concern for resolve reputation is an interest in reputation for trustworthiness and willingness to accommodate on disputed issues. The opponent is believed to be trustworthy. If conciliatory moves are made toward him he will reciprocate, not only in the present crisis but in future disputes as well. The specific issue of the moment thus provides the occasion for taking a step toward a general settlement. This, for example, was prominent in Chamberlain's mind during the Munich crisis and earlier. He placed a high value on the document he persuaded Hitler to sign after the conference, pledging "to continue our efforts to remove possible sources of difference . . .," and which he happily waved back at London airport, saying it meant "peace in our time."

The soft-line tendency is to underestimate the amount of real conflict in a crisis, to exaggerate the value of one's own concessions to the opponent, and to exaggerate the opponent's willingness to compromise. Instances are Bulow in 1904, following soft-line advice, when he tried and failed to interest Britain in a general settlement of colonial disputes.

---

[13] Jervis, *Perception and Misperception*.
[14] Samuel Williamson, *The Politics of Grand Strategy* (Cambridge, Mass.: Harvard University Press, 1971), pp. 150–151.

He thought his proposed concessions were generous; the British thought they were an insult. In the Morocco crisis the following year, the Kaiser vastly exaggerated the chances of conciliating France on Morocco as a step toward alliance. Rouvier, earlier in the same crisis, tried for a general settlement with Germany but failed because Germany was then on a hard-line track. Chamberlain from 1937 to 1940 entertained similar illusory hopes, as did Konoye and Grew in the United States–Japan crisis of 1940–1941, and Macmillan and Khrushchev over Berlin in 1958–1959.

In game terms, the soft-liner's image of preference functions tends to overestimate the value of S for both parties—i.e., underestimate the cost of yielding—by ignoring the factor of resolve reputation. In addition, he exaggerates the value of R (compromise) for the opponent by overestimating the opponent's interest in settlement. The game is Chicken with the CC position relatively easy to reach because of the high value of R.

In sum, both soft- and hard-line figures are concerned with long-term consequences as well as the immediate issues in a crisis, and their differing conceptions of the future are closely related to their typical images of the opponent. The soft-liner sees his opponent's enmity as transient, remediable, and perhaps somewhat illusory. With reason and good will, the enmity can be transformed into friendship or at least *détente,* and his exaggeration of CC (R) payoffs and preference for C strategies represent an attempt to move toward this future. The hard-liner sees the opponent's enmity as relatively permanent, and his emphasis on deterrent and coercive strategies, on maintaining resolve reputation and curbing the aggressive opponent, are attempt to preserve his state's security in this dangerous future.[15]

There also seems to be a typical hard-soft difference in the degree of unity perceived in the adversary. The perception of a monolithic opponent seems to be more characteristic of hard-line than soft-line figures. The soft-liner is much more sensitive to divisions within the opposing government. This difference seems to follow mostly from differences in strategy preference and to some extent from differences in perceptions of the adversary's long-term aims. For the hard-liner, since the opponent is persistently aggressive, firm deterrence is the only appropriate strategy. Since this is the preferred or "dominant" strategy regardless of whether the opponent is divided between hards and softs and regardless of which faction may be in power, there is no point in paying much attention

[15] Several points in the above and following discussion are in agreement with experimental findings of Kelley and Stachelski, whose terms for "hard" and "soft" are "competitive" and "cooperative." Harold H. Kelley and A. J. Stachelski, "Errors in Perception of Intentions in a Mixed-motive Game," *Journal of Experimental Social Psychology,* 6 (1970), pp. 379–400.

to the opponent's internal divisions. If the softs come to power, they can easily be deterred or coerced. If the hards are in charge, they will either be bluffing, in which case they can be faced down by firmness, or if they are not bluffing, it is better to fight them now than later when they are stronger. The soft-liner, by contrast, tends to look for and to perceive factionalism in the adversary because the success of his preferred strategy of accommodation depends on making contact with, appealing to and strengthening the softs or moderates in the opposing government, and in not strengthening or provoking the hards and extremists. His preferred "C" strategy, in short, is not "dominant," but will work only against an opponent who also plays C.

Examples are Chamberlain and Henderson in 1937–1938, who regarded Hitler as the moderate holding back the extremist Nazis; Konoye in 1941, who desperately hoped that a personal meeting with Roosevelt would bypass the U.S. hard-liners who were ruining Japan with their embargoes; also Grew and Walker, who urged the U.S. government to support Konoye in his struggle with the aggressive militarists; and Khrushchev in 1958–1961, who kept looking for those "realists" who would join him in stabilizing peaceful co-existence. These examples also show that the soft-liner exaggerates the amount of disagreement within the opponent and the amount of agreement between the moderates and himself.

There are also characteristic differences in the image of the opponent's bargaining style. The hard-liner tends to see his opponent as calculating his moves carefully and leaving nothing to chance or impetuous subordinates. Since the adversary is engaged in a dangerous campaign of aggression and is probably bluffing at that, he has to watch his step and be ready to pull back when danger threatens. Seemingly chance incidents are probably well-planned tests of the defender's watchfulness and resolve. For instance, Eisenhower asserts in his memoirs that Communists leave nothing to chance, and argues that Nasser had probably coordinated his every move in Lebanon, Syria, etc., with Khrushchev. Similarly, Eisenhower and Dulles believed that the Soviet leaders were "behind" China's initiation of the Quemoy crisis in 1958—i.e., had collaborated in planning for it—although they would probably not support China militarily. In 1962, Acheson and others argued that Khrushchev was calmly testing U.S. courage down to the last minute, ready to move forward if the United States faltered, but also to move back if they showed resolve, even if this meant bombing the missile sites in Cuba.

The image of the cool, calculating opponent includes the further idea that the opponent cannot be "provoked" in an emotional sense. He has complete control over his own passions, so one does not need to worry that any of one's moves may anger him and throw him off his calculated track. The ultimate version of this theme is that of the "programmed opponent." The enemy will start a war when he thinks the time is ripe, and nothing one does will affect that judgment. This notion supported the German expectation in 1914 that Russia would not fight, as well as the German strategy of coercion. Russia would not be ready for war until 1916, so it would not fight now but *would* fight then; better to have the war now than later when Russia is stronger. On the opposite side, the French ambassador in St. Petersburg, Paleologue, assured the wavering Sazonov that a policy of firmness would "only lead to war if the Germanic powers have already made up their minds to resort to force to secure the hegemony of the East." General MacArthur said during the Korean War that China would enter war only if it had deliberately decided it was ready to fight the United States; nothing the United States might do, such as bombing the Yalu power plants or conquering North Korea, would affect that decision. During the Berlin crisis of 1948, General Clay voiced the same theme: "If the Soviets want war, it will not be because of the Berlin currency issue, but because they believe this is the right time." [16] This view includes the idea that the opponent cannot be provoked emotionally, but goes further in implicitly denying interdependence as such, at least in the short run—i.e., during the crisis. The opponent has *already* decided on war before the crisis begins, or he has not. If he has not, we can be as coercive as we like, even including violence, without fear of escalation; if he has, there will simply be war whatever we do. While it is usually hard-line actors who hold this mind-set, there are exceptions. For example, Sorenson reports that during the Cuban missile crisis, after a U-2 plane was shot down, all members of the U.S. decision-making unit felt that if the Soviets kept firing at U.S. planes and continued to bring their missiles to operational readiness, despite U.S. warning, it would be because they "wanted war" and if so, war would be "inevitable." [17] This ignored the possibility that the Soviets might have thought the United States was bluffing, and suggests that the idea of the "programmed opponent" might be a corollary or consequence of the phenomenon that once a party (the United States in this case) has made a firm decision and communicated it, the party tends to believe it is both clear and credible to the adversary.[18]

The soft-liner's image of the opponent's bargaining style tends to

[16] W. Philips Davidson, *The Berlin Blockade* (Princeton, N.J.: Princeton University Press, 1958), p. 106.

[17] Sorenson, *Kennedy,* p. 805.

[18] The psychologist might also call this a mechanism for relieving "cognitive dissonance"—once a close decision has been made, there is a tendency to adduce reasons why the decision was right, in fact why it could not have been otherwise. On this, see Jervis, *Perception and Misperception,* Ch. 14.

emphasize his receptiveness to conciliatory proposals (though this may apply only to his soft or moderate factions), his credibility when he takes a firm stand, the considerable role of chance and accident in his behavior, and the danger of provoking him emotionally by excessive coercion. The first characteristic requires no further comment. The second—the tendency to believe that the firm-looking opponent is not bluffing—is illustrated by Harriman, in the Berlin crisis of 1958, who believed Khrushchev when he said the Soviets would fight if the West tried to resist an East German blockade of access routes; and by Chamberlain, who was sure Hitler was not bluffing; and by Rouvier in 1905, who believed the German threats of war if they were not compensated for French advances in Morocco. In contrast to the hard-liner, the soft-line actor does not see the adversary as so very cool, calculating, and controlled; rather he is seen as improvising, subject to apparent vacillation because of the shifting influence of factions in his government, and rather unpredictable. What he does is very much a function of what oneself does; i.e., interdependence is high. Threats will only stiffen him, provoke him, and perhaps lead to an emotionally fuelled hostility spiral. The soft-liner's sensitivity to dangers of emotional provocation, contrasting with the hard-liner's tendency to ignore this factor, is in part a function of their differing images of the general dynamics of world politics. The hard-liner's image, dominated by the importance of impersonal power-strategic considerations, leaves little room for the notion of emotionally generated conflict. The soft-liner, lacking a full appreciation of power-strategic factors, falls back on an affective explanation of conflict: it is more a consequence of "feelings" than of "interests."

A few examples: Rouvier in 1905 feared that Delcassé's tough policies would provoke Germany to attack. In the 1911 Morocco crisis, British and French soft-liners vetoed a plan by the hard-line French foreign minister to send warships to Agadir as a counterdemonstration to the German *Panther,* for fear of an "incident." In 1914, Lord Grey refused Russian pleas, in the early phase, to tell Germany that England would fight alongside France and Russia. "Such a menace would but stiffen her attitude, and it was only by approaching her as a friend anxious to preserve peace that we would induce her to use her influence at Vienna to avert war." [19] Similar worries about provoking a touchy opponent were felt by Konoye, Grew, and Hull in 1940 and 1941. In the 1961 Berlin crisis, Macmillan refused a U.S. request to put British forces in West Germany on a war footing because it "would have created a thoroughly

[19] Bernadotte Schmitt, *The Coming of the War, 1914* (New York: Charles Scribner's Sons, 1930), Vol. 2, p. 90.

undesirable atmosphere of panic." [20] The appeasers' image of Hitler was a curious blend of the highly emotional and irrational, yet potentially reasonable and conciliatory, opponent:

> Most appeasers agreed that Hitler was wild, vicious and unpredictable. But they argued that his viciousness would modify, that his aims would eventually clarify, and that his wildness would end. Abrupt criticism would only anger him. Patience and kindness would bring him to reason. . . . If sensible Englishmen could meet Hitler at the right moment, and speak to him in the right tone, he would be equally sensible. Once he could be persuaded to be reasonable there was a good chance of reaching agreement with him and an Anglo–German agreement would prove as trustworthy as any agreement between two sovereign states.[21]

The soft-liner, incidentally, not only believes the opponent is highly provocable in an emotional sense, but is himself prone to react emotionally to the opponent's moves rather than in calculated power-strategic terms. For example, Lloyd George was motivated to give his famous "Mansion House" threat to Germany in 1911 largely by anger at the German "insolence" in failing to answer an official British communication for 17 days. Also in the 1911 crisis, the Kaiser, generally a soft-liner toward France, wanted to respond more toughly to a French threat than his hard-line foreign minister, Kiderlen, did. Soft-liners in the British cabinet were outraged when Hitler raised his demands at Godesberg and joined with the hard-liners in forcing Chamberlain to take a stiffer position, including a warning to Hitler. However, in all three cases (and others as well), the soft-liners' pique subsided fairly quickly and they returned to their normal stance. To complete the picture, soft-liners are also likely to respond to the opponent's conciliatory moves in affective terms; he is being "friendly," so one should be friendly to him. The hard-liner typically is skeptical, accepts or rejects the proposal according to strict cost-benefit calculations, or simply dismisses it as evidence of weakness and pushes harder.

Table 4–2 summarizes the preceding discussion. Table 4–3 shows hard and soft-line expectations about the opponent's probable response to one's own strategy, in the symbols of game theory.

Initial expectations are largely deduced from initial belief systems so Table 4–3 is easily explained. For the hard-liner, the opponent is a cool, calculating, aggressive bluffer who is playing chicken. He is likely to

---

[20] Slusser, *The Berlin Crisis of 1961,* p. 118.
[21] Martin Gilbert and R. Gott, *The Appeasers* (Boston: Houghton Mifflin, 1963), p. 47.

TABLE 4–2

TYPICAL INITIAL BELIEF SYSTEMS

	Hard Line	Soft Line
World Views ("Theories")	Emphasis on conflict; power-strategic considerations.	Emphasis on potential harmony; intrinsic (non-strategic) values; affective elements.
Image of Opponent		
Ultimate aims	Unlimited expansion or defense of illegitimate status quo	Limited legitimate expansion or defense of legitimate rights
Specific aim in present crisis	Achieve one part of expansion program; test one's resolve; defend illegitimate position	Satisfy particular interest, probably legitimate
Preference function	Chicken; overestimate S	Underestimate T and S; overestimate R
Unity of government	Monolithic	Divided
Bargaining style	Cool, calculating	Provokable, unstable, but potentially "reasonable"
Probable strategy	Opposite to one's own	Reciprocates one's own
Image of Self		
Ultimate and specific aims	Defense of legitimate status quo or legitimate expansion	Defensive
Preference function	Usually PD; low S, high P, low R	Usually Chicken: high S, low P, high R.

TABLE 4–3

INITIAL EXPECTATIONS AND STRATEGY PREFERENCE

If Our Strategy Is	Opponent's Response will be:	
	Hard-line Expectation	Soft-line Expectation
C	D	C
D	C	D
E (escalation of violence)	C	Provoked into E
Our preferred strategy	Hard-line D	Soft-line C

take advantage of any weakness (C) but cautiously to pull back if one is firm (D). He may hold out for a while, testing one as long as he dares, but if one persists he will finally give in. A D strategy is therefore bound to succeed, but even if by chance it does not, one cannot afford to yield, as that would be disastrous. In this conflict-ridden, Hobbesian world, one must preserve one's power-security position at all costs. For the soft-liner the opponent is a mixture of moderates and extremists and therefore somewhat unstable and vacillating in strategy. The greatest danger is that a rash move (E) will provoke him, or his extremists, into irreversible violence. If that can be avoided, it should be possible to convince him of the benefits of compromise and eventual cooperation. In this essentially harmonious world, cooperation is possible with mutual empathy and good will. A D strategy may produce some initial results but will gradually harden his resistance and make a cooperative solution more and more difficult. The preferred strategy is therefore a cautious C, perhaps with D as a fallback strategy.

It is also easy to capsulize hard and soft strategic preferences in terms of the goal-constraint schema for coercion and accommodation that was presented in Chapter III. On the coercive dimension, the hard-liner is out to "win" and is only minimally concerned with the constraint of risk-avoidance, although he is not blind to it. The soft-liner is much more conscious of the risks of miscalculation, or of accidental violence, or of autonomous, passion-generated escalation spirals. When the parties are engaged in accommodation, the soft-liner places a higher value than the hard-liner on settlement, per se. The hard-liner is more inclined to weigh carefully the value of settlement against the sacrifices necessary to get it, and to take tough stands on his concessions in order to minimize the sacrifice. Briefly, in the coercive process, the soft-liner is more fearful that events will get out of control; in the accommodative process, the hard-liner is more inclined to "tough bargaining."

Up to now we have pretended that there is a sharp dichotomy between hard- and soft-liners. This ignores the middle-liners, of whom our most prominent examples are Grey, Bulow, Kennedy, and Khrushchev. The middle-liner combines hard and soft features in varying degree and may seem hard in one context and soft in another. He is sensitive both to the security dilemma and to power and resolve factors, as Kennedy was; has some suspicions about the opponent's aggressive tendencies but also sees some legitimacy in his demands; is willing to move cautiously toward détente but without yielding any vital interests in the process; recognizes the existence of unavoidable conflict but is willing to define self-interest in minimal terms so that conflict can be minimized. His strategy preference is CD, a mixture of accommodation if the opponent is reasonable and firmness if he is intransigent. Examples are Kennedy's 1961 strategy and Khrushchev's 1958 strategy. Lest this account make the middle-liner seem a paragon of reasonableness, a synthesis of the best from both hard and soft, the example of Bulow reminds us that the middle-liner may be simply vacillating and inconsistent. An extreme example is Kaiser Wilhelm, who was so unstable as to be unclassifiable. There are also individuals such as Grew who are consistently hard toward one opponent (Soviet Union) and soft toward another (Japan) without combining the two sets of beliefs in any way.

Nevertheless the implication seems to be that the middle-line bargainer is most likely to interpret messages correctly during a crisis, because he is sensitive to the full range of relevant possibilities. Perhaps a still better possibility is a bargaining committee composed of *moderate* softs and hards with a middle-line central decision maker. But the closest example we have to such an ideal committee, United States 1940–1941, casts doubt on this idea, because this committee was about average in total misperceptions and in initial difference of image.

We turn now to the next two factors affecting the outcome of the bargaining cycle, namely filters in transmission and the influence of beliefs, expectations, and strategy on interpretation of messages. Both factors can best be considered together, since they both belong to the information-processing subsystem.

JERVIS ON INFORMATION PROCESSING

Robert Jervis has recently summarized the findings of cognitive psychology on information processing and applied them to diplomatic history, so his report provides a natural starting point for us.[22] The following list of some of Jervis's propositions, in paraphrase, does not reflect the richness of his analysis. We attempt to show how these hypotheses link to our own model and illustrate from our cases.

> 1. An image or theory (belief system) will have greater impact on an actor's interpretation of data, the greater the ambiguity of the data and the greater the degree of confidence in the beliefs. A corollary is that the image will be more controlling the less the amount of information that conflicts with the image.

For example, the German messages early in the Morocco crisis of 1905 were both infrequent and ambiguous, largely because the Germans did not know exactly what they wanted themselves. This allowed Rouvier and Delcassé, with their different belief systems, to interpret German messages in opposite ways. For Rouvier, the Germans were

22 Jervis, *Perception and Misperception.*

basically good neighbors who were justifiably irritated by France's failure to consult them about Morocco and who would be pacified by French concessions to German interests elsewhere. For Delcassé, who saw Germany as an implacable enemy out for much bigger stakes, to offer such *pourboires* would merely be taken as weakness; whatever Germany wanted, she had to be resisted at all costs. Later, when the Germans had adopted the aim of humiliating France at a conference, and their messages communicated this aim, Rouvier's image and strategy preference changed to resemble Delcassé's closely. On the German side, Chancellor Bulow so lacked confidence in his beliefs that he shifted ground with each major piece of new information that came in, although his vacillation was also due, in part, to conflicting pressures within his own government.

2. New information is interpreted by reference to current concerns.[23] Senders tend to believe that the receivers' immediate concerns are the same as their own; often they are not, so a message that means one thing in the context of what is on the sender's mind means something else to the receiver.

During the 1905 crisis, Lord Lansdowne suggested to the French ambassador, Cambon, that England and France should consult about "any contingencies by which they might in the course of events find themselves confronted." Lansdowne was concerned that the French, in their bargaining with Germany, might give away some British interest, such as allowing the Germans control over a Moroccan port; he simply wanted to be in a position to block this. But the French had no such thought. What was in the forefront of Cambon's and Delcassé's minds was obtaining a formal commitment from England to increase their bargaining power with Germany. So they interpreted Lansdowne's vague words as an offer of a virtual alliance. Moreover, Delcassé's political head was on the block at home because it was thought he was responsible for the crisis in not consulting Germany. If he could confront his domestic opponents with the prospect of sure victory, with British support, they would be silenced. This domestic strategy backfired, but that is another story.

Interpretation in the light of current concerns is represented in Figure 4–2 by the arrow from "strategic decision" to "interpretation." The decision maker's most important current concern is whether his strategy is working or not. The current strategy provides the categories and questions with which incoming messages are approached. Each strategy is based on several specific expectations, and the interest is in whether these specific expectations are being fulfilled. For instance (examples

[23] Ibid., Ch. 5.

are taken from our data), the 1914 German strategy was based on two key expectations:

a) Britain would stay neutral in a war between Germany–Austria and Russia–France.

b) Russia would not start such a war because of its military weakness. Consequently, the German leaders asked two main questions of incoming messages: will Russia start a war and will Britain stay neutral? Messages from France, for instance, were mainly of interest by reference to the question: Will France restrain or encourage Russia?

> 3. Incoming messages are interpreted to conform to desires and expectations.[24] Desires and expectations are usually in agreement, but when they disagree, expectations influence interpretation more than desires do. Thus interpretation in accordance with desires (wishful thinking) mostly operates indirectly through the influence of desires on expectations and the influence of expectations on interpretation.

The influence of expectations is represented in Figure 4–2 by the arrow from "expectation" to "interpretation." Given that the current strategy provides the questions that are asked of incoming messages, e.g., "Will Russia fight?" expectations suggest the answer. For example, in 1914 Germany expected that Russia would not fight; consequently Sazonov's statements that Russia would fight to preserve Serbian sovereignty were interpreted in Berlin as implying that Russia did not really want to fight and was looking for an excuse not to fight—an excuse which would be provided by the promise only to "punish" Serbia.

The influence of desires is represented by the two arrows from "strategy" to "expectation" and from "strategy" to "interpretation." A bargainer's strategy is the chosen instrument for achieving all his desired goals, and consequently all his hopes and desires are for the success of the strategy. These desires may operate directly on interpretation to produce false evidence that the strategy is succeeding (pure wishful thinking) or they may operate to increase and stabilize the expectation of success. For example, the German expectation that Britain would remain neutral was stabilized against seemingly negative information by the fact that British neutrality was essential to the success of the German strategy. Germany persistently interpreted British messages in accordance with expectations.

An apparent example of pure wishful thinking occurred in 1938, when Beneš told the French ambassador, Lacroix, that *in 1919* he had been willing to leave small portions of the Sudetenland outside the Czech

[24] Ibid., Ch. 10.

border. The ambassador interpreted this to mean that Beneš was *now* willing to give these up. Bonnet, the foreign minister, then amplified the size of the territory involved when reporting to Daladier, to make it easier for Daladier to accept the British proposal for cession of the Sudetenland. Here the ambassador was thinking wishfully, while the foreign minister was perhaps deliberately deceiving. But there was no wishful expectation intervening between the desire and the misinterpretation. Jervis argues that, of the two influences of desires, the one on expectations, represented by the arrow from "strategy" to "expectation," is the most important.

4. People use historical analogies to interpret current events, drawing especially on events experienced firsthand early in their careers that had important consequences for their own state, and also on apparently similar recent events. But these analogies tend to oversimplify the picture by neglecting differences between the present and past circumstances.[25]

Anthony Eden's misapplication of the Munich-Hitler analogy to Nasser in the Suez crisis of 1956 is well-known. The influence of a superficially similar recent event is exemplified in the expectations both Germany and England derived in 1914 from their successful collaboration in dampening the 1912–1913 Balkan crisis. For Germany, this experience, plus the fact that her recent relations with England had been good, contributed to Germany's expectation that an Austrian–Serbian war could be "localized," and that Britain would not support her entente partners to the point of war. These same recent events also supported Lord Grey's expectation that Germany would collaborate with him in mediating the 1914 crisis. Both countries overlooked the difference between the 1912–1913 crises when their respective allies, Austria and Russia, were relatively passive, and the 1914 crisis when both were deeply involved.

5. New information is interpreted to cohere with established beliefs if possible. If this is not possible, it is interpreted in such a way as to require minimum change of the established picture.[26]

A variety of tactics are used:
(a) Ignore information or dismiss it or deny that a discrepancy exists.
(b) If the message is too clear to dismiss or deny, reject the manifest content and find a hidden meaning that fits the established picture. For instance, Sazonov's blunt warning in 1914 that Russia would fight if

[25] Ibid., Ch. 6.
[26] Ibid., Ch. 7.

Serbia was invaded was rejected as a bluff. His words "We shall go to war if Austria devours Serbia" were selected out and interpreted by the German ambassador as meaning that Russia would fight only if Austria permanently annexed Serbia.

(c) Discredit the source of information. For instance, when the German ambassador to London reported in 1914 that Britain would certainly not remain neutral, his message was rejected because of his well-established pro-British bias.

(d) If the message is clear and the source trustworthy, admit puzzlement, but do not change expectations or image. For example, in 1958 Eisenhower was puzzled at Nasser's support for U.N. observers in Lebanon, since he "knew" Nasser was sending guerrillas and weapons across the Syria–Lebanon border and would be found out by the observers.

(e) If the puzzlement grows, search for additional information that will support the established image. For instance, to counter the London ambassador's repeated warnings in 1914, the Germans picked up some remarks by visiting royalty (King George to Prince Henry), ignoring the British king's figurehead status, that seemed to imply that Britain would stay neutral.

(f) If supporting information is not forthcoming, the established beliefs must be changed, that is, expectations must be adjusted, but several mechanisms may be used to minimize the adjustment. Of particular interest are "differentiation" and "transcendence." Differentiation is splitting the object into two parts, adjusting expectations only for the part that is producing the discrepant information. Transcendence is combining the established beliefs and the discrepant information at a higher level that reconciles the conflict. President Nixon used both these devices in trying to reconcile the United States–Soviet crisis during the Arab–Israeli war of 1973 with the United States–Soviet détente. He differentiated by saying the crisis had not injured the basic détente relationship, which was separate. He transcended by saying the détente had facilitated settlement of the crisis. He thus kept his basic beliefs intact by enlarging the concept of détente to include the function of crisis resolution.

Other aspects of the adjustment process, up to a complete reversal of image and expectations, will be discussed in a later section.

6. The previous points have dealt with the interpretation of received messages. An additional source of misinterpretation is located in the sender.[27] The sender too readily assumes that he has made his intentions clear. However, his message may

27 Ibid., pp. 216, 355.

have been vague or may not have been transmitted faithfully by the intervening ambassadors.

For example, in 1914 Grey felt that he had stated with unmistakeable clarity that, although Britain was not "automatically" committed to war, she could not in fact remain neutral. He therefore "knew" that Germany knew it would be up against Britain, France, and Russia in war and would be reluctant to fight such a combination. Consequently he felt that there was no immediate war danger, and he had plenty of time for the diplomatic moves he was planning to mediate the crisis. He did not know that the wishful thinking Germans had zeroed in on the "no automatic commitment," neglecting the accompanying warning, nor how they were selectively noticing his parliamentary statements, intended for home consumption, that Britain was "free," nor how they were discounting the accurate reports of their ambassador in London.

In Russia, Sazonov did not know that his bluntest warning was simply reversed in transmission by the German and Austrian ambassadors, that Bethmann was being told that he was "weak" and "conciliatory." Later, Tschirsky, the German ambassador in Vienna, deliberately failed to deliver until too late several messages from Bethmann that were intended to restrain Austria. Thus the German leaders were first misled into thinking that their strategy of coercing Russia was succeeding when it was not; later Bethmann was led to believe that his revised strategy of restraining Austria was at least being implemented, when it was not.

The above six points are by no means a complete summary of Jervis's book; several lesser points that we discuss in the next section also appear there.

INFORMATION PROCESSING IN CRISES

Jervis's report lists the general characteristics of information processing but does not give the relative importance or relative frequency of each characteristic. Nor does it answer the prize question, "What are the chances of correct information getting through the system?" To answer these questions and to test Jervis's hypotheses, we collected and coded some 350 interpretations from our crisis data.[28] Interpretations were made of both messages (signals) and indices. We examined about 272 messages (of which some 35 were uncodable because either intention or interpretation was not known) and 61 indices. In many cases two interpretations of the same signal or index were coded, thus bringing the total number of interpretations up to 351. We attempted to in-

---

[28] Data available on request (38 pp). Send self-addressed stamped envelope with request to Dept. of Political Science, State Univ. of New York, Buffalo, N.Y. 14261.

clude all the important messages and indices from our cases, that is all the information that was or could have been used to correct mistaken expectations and confirm correct ones, except for some obviously uncodable messages. However, further research would undoubtedly turn up more messages of lesser importance. We were careful to get our set of messages and indices directly from the data, that is, from our own case studies plus some good historical accounts of certain cases. We did not add examples from outside our set of cases. Adding examples ad hoc would destroy whatever neutrality might characterize the data. One can always find an example of any hypothesis if one searches long enough, but a true test of a hypothesis requires data collected on some quasi-neutral basis. So if a devotee of a particular hypothesis finds that his favorite illustration has been omitted from our sample, we can only answer that we did not try to keep anything in or out, and if his hypothesis is important, some other examples of it would have shown up in our sample.

From Table 4–4 we see that the chances of a message getting through untarnished to *someone* in the receiving government are about four in ten. The chances are higher in alliance communication. Within the "alliance" category much of the distorted communication occurs between allied adversaries such as United States–Soviet Union, 1945–1946, Iran; United States–Britain, 1956, Suez; and Japan–Germany, 1941. Between close allies such as Russia–Serbia and Britain–France, 1938, there is no distortion.

The four in ten figure, however, is very approximate. For one thing, the data are pretty bad, as bad as attitude survey data usually are, and are therefore significant only in large numbers. (1) There is probably a bias toward selecting misinterpreted messages, both for the historian and for ourselves, because these tend to be the spectacular ones. We have tried to counteract this bias by searching for additional correct interpretations in the case studies. In our initial set of data, the probability of a correct interpretation was close to three in ten, but a search for additional interpretations shifted this figure to four in ten. The total correct

TABLE 4–4

INFORMATION PROCESSING IN CRISES

	Total	Adversary	Ally	Neutral or Mixed
Correctly interpreted	139(40%)	98(39%)	40(46%)	1
Incorrectly interpreted	181(51%)	133(52%)	40(46%)	8
Distorted in transmission	31(9%)	23(9%)	7(8%)	1

interpretations could be raised higher by including more minor messages and more alliance discussions, but the total of misinterpretations could also be raised by starting our count in the pre-crisis build-up phase. The general pattern is for misinterpretations to predominate early in a crisis and to give way to correct interpretations at the end, so the farther back we begin the higher the percentage of misinterpretations. We began counting with the "precipitating incident" of a crisis when there was one, but in some crises there was no such incident and it was not quite clear where to start. (2) It was not clear how many conflicting interpretations within a government to include. We generally included one representative from both major factions within a government, such as Eden or Halifax and Chamberlain in 1937–1938, but usually omitted ambassadors and foreign office officials who largely duplicated the interpretations of their respective superiors, and omitted high-level individuals who were not in the primary decision-making group. (3) Sometimes the same message was sent several times through one or more channels: for instance, in 1940–1941, Britain several times requested that part of the U.S. fleet be stationed at Singapore, and in 1960–1961 Khrushchev several times sent a request for negotiations or discussions to Adenauer. Such series of messages were counted as single messages.

Apart from the poor quality of data, considerable judgment was involved in coding, particularly when data on interpretation were ambiguous or when the sender's intention was ambiguous due to internal conflict or when he unwittingly communicated more than he intended. For example, in 1938 the French, intending to send as firm a warning as they dared to Hitler, took up defensive stations along the Maginot Line. Hitler inferred from this that France would declare war if he attacked Czechoslovakia, but would not attack Germany. We judge that Hitler interpreted the French deterrent intention correctly but was not deterred by their timid effort. The message had the opposite of its intended effect, but the interpretation was correct. Also, in some cases, we do not have explicit evidence on how a message was interpreted and have had to infer interpretation from the response. Sometimes this is easy: if, as in 1909, Russia tells Serbia to submit to Austrian demands because Russia cannot fight a war at this time, and Serbia submits three days later, we can infer that the message was correctly interpreted. At other times the inference is not so easy, and judgment is involved in deciding whether or not to code the message at all.

The usual solution to the problem of judgment in coding is to get a panel of five judges and compare their responses for reliability. However, our judges would have had to be intimately familiar with all sixteen case studies in order to code, so this solution was not available to us.

In addition the 40-percent correct figure is too high if we consider only the interpretations of the official in charge of bargaining strategy. For instance, in 1937–1938 Eden and Halifax made several correct interpretations of messages and events that Chamberlain misinterpreted, but Chamberlain almost always persuaded the cabinet of his interpretations and thus controlled British strategy. In 1906 Moltke correctly interpreted the situation at the opening of the Algeciras conference, but Bulow was making the decisions, and he was dead wrong.

When we break down the gross figures by crises (Table 4–5), we find a great range of variation. At the one extreme there are three cases in which practically no distortion of communication interferes with bargaining. These are Fashoda, the typical Bully crisis; the Ruhr, 1923, the typical Leader crisis; and Berlin, 1948, the typical Chicken crisis. At the other extreme stand the Middle East events of 1957–1958, a morass of confusion from beginning to end. The remaining crises lie in the range of 15%–60% correct interpretations, with the median figure the 37.5% of United States–Japan 1941. The figures on Quemoy and Cuba are low because most messages in these brief crises are uncodable; we do not have adequate information of Chinese or Soviet intentions or interpretations for most messages.

We see from the subcategories in Table 4–6 that 12 instances of

TABLE 4–5

VARIATIONS IN INFORMATION PROCESSING

	Correct	Incorrect	Distorted in Transmission	Uncodable
1898 Fashoda	13	2	—	1
1905 Morocco	10	20	5	4
1908 Bosnia	22	15	1	5
1911 Morocco	8	8	2	
1914 Europe	18	19	10	1
1923 Ruhr	14	1		1
1938 Munich	13	22	5	2
1941 U.S.-Japan	9	14	1	1
1946 Iran	4	13	2	
1948 Berlin	8	1		2
1956 Suez	3	17		1
1957 Lebanon	1	18		2
1958 Quemoy	2	2		6
1958 Berlin	12	27	5	4
1962 Cuba	2	2		5

TABLE 4–6

DISTORTION IN TRANSMITTING OF MESSAGES

Sending		9
Vague or contradictory because of internal conflict within sender	4	
Diplomatic vague language	5	
Transmitting		8
Delayed or distorted by ambassador's disagreement with message	6	
Receiving		14
Misinterpret disconfirming information	6	
Filter out disconfirming information	5	
Conscious distortion to deceive one's own government	2	
	Total	31

distorted transmission are an expression of internal conflicts either within the sender or the receiver. For example, one instance of "receiving" was Bonnet's 1938 deceptive concealment of the Soviet Union's statement of willingness to provide immediate military support for a French–Czech resistance to Hitler. Bonnet used this tactic to hold down the hard-line opposition within the French and British cabinets. Most of the remainder (11) are cases of ambassadorial misperception.

In Table 4–7, category 1 interpretations serve to confirm correct expectations, while 2–7 disconfirm incorrect ones. The 2 messages are good news, whose implications we can assume are gladly accepted. Categories 3 and 4 messages are unexpected, but the cost of accepting their implications is slight since no change of strategy or tactics is required. This is an "ignore" category. Category 5 requires tactical changes only. Categories 6 and 7 are the painful ones, where the deci-

TABLE 4–7
CORRECT INTERPRETATION

1. Correct in conformity with image and expectations ....48 ⎫		
1a. Recognize a bluff .... 6 ⎭		54
2. Correct in conformity with desires but not expectations		4
3. Correct perception of duplicity		7
4. Correct in opposition to desires and expectations but not requiring change of strategy or tactics by interpreter		20
5. Correct requiring change of tactics		33
6. Correct requiring change of strategy ....14 ⎫		
6a. Requiring complete backdown .... 4 ⎭		18
7. Correct requiring changing of strategy and image		3
	Total	139

sion maker has to admit he was entirely mistaken and where in four cases he had to admit defeat. Categories 5, 6, and 7 are worth more detailed examination later.

The categories in Table 4–8 overlap considerably so the counts are suggestive rather than conclusive. The first group of categories, 8 through 13, shows the influence of incorrect images in defining the bargaining situation. We can see the effects of familiar image patterns: image of self as defensive appears in 10, image of opponent as aggressive appears in 8 and 11. The soft-line fear of accidental war by provoking the extremists shows up in 9, and the hard-line picture of the opponent as calculating and well-organized shows up in 13. Categories 8 and 10 overlap in the sense that some misinterpretations that contain one ele-

TABLE 4–8

INCORRECT INTERPRETATIONS

Misperceptions Induced by the Belief System

8. Perceiving an aggressive intent when none is intended	9
9. Exaggerating a danger or threat	3
10. Failure to perceive sender's security worries; failure to recognize own threatening behavior	13
11. Opponent is stirring up trouble in some third country	10
12. Suspicion of ally's dependability or loyalty.	6
13. Underestimate diversity of opinion within opponent . . . . .5⎤	
13a. Exaggerate diversity within opponent, reasonableness of ⎬ one faction . . . . .2⎦	7
H. Historical analogy—4 (coded in categories 8-10)	
Subtotal	48

Misperceptions Induced by Expectations and Strategy

14. Incorrect interpretation based on expectations but not desires. .	15
15. Both expectations and desires . . . . .31⎤	
15a. Exaggerated estimate of own effectiveness . . . . 7⎦	38
16. Desires, hopes, but not expectations	17
17. Ignore negative information, continue with strategy	29
Subtotal	99

Reinterpretations of Negative Information

18. Interpret as bluff	7
19. Interpret as duplicity of sender	10
20. Discredit source of message; reject message as erroneous	9
21. Admit puzzlement without changing expectations	3
22. Counter with exaggerated confirming information	5
Subtotal	34
Total	181

ment also contain the other; they could perhaps be combined, yielding a total of 22 separate instances. Categories 8, 10, 11, and 13 are hard-line categories while 9, 12, and 13a are soft-line or middle-line.

The historical analogies (H) are included in the "belief system" group because they generate or support either some "theory" about how to deal with conflict or some "image" of an opponent. In our coded instances, which included only analogies explicitly mentioned in interpretations, the history was always of some aggressive opponent who was stopped by a D strategy or who failed to be stopped by a C strategy. This sort of history, the Munich syndrome, is part of the hard-line image. The soft-line image also includes historical analogies at times, but no instances happened to show up in our sample. There may also be other analogies that do not fit either the "hard" or "soft" labels.

Historical analogies are more prevalent than indicated in our count, because they operate as background patterns used to define the situation in several other cases. In 1914 the analogy of recent wars, including the 1912–1913 Balkan wars and the 1904 Russo–Japanese war, suggested that if a European war came, it would last a few weeks or months at most. In 1938 the British cabinet reasoned from a 1914 analogy that wars arise from conflict over misplaced minorities (like the Sudeten Germans), but that actual war can be avoided by keeping calm and negotiating disputes, since no government really wants war. This was a soft-line history, part of the soft-line "theory" or world-view. At Quemoy in 1958, the 1949 invasion of Quemoy and the 1954–1955 occupation of the Tachens and Ichiang set the pattern: China intended to invade and occupy the offshore islands. In 1961 the United States was getting ready for another Berlin blockade, and in 1965 it saw the Dominican Republic as another Cuba in the making. These background historical analogies do not show up in our sample because they do not explicitly appear in the interpretation of specific messages. If we were to read them into specific interpretations, we would have to read all sorts of tacit background factors into other interpretations, and this would make coding hopelessly intuitive. At any rate, *no* examples in our sample or elsewhere in the cases of historical analogies produced a correct interpretation of a message. Jervis's hypothesis that statesmen usually draw incorrect or over-generalized inferences from historical analogies is strongly confirmed. In addition, most of the overt instances in our sample are key misinterpretations that provide the initial basis for a mistaken definition of the whole crisis.

Category 12, suspicion of ally, is more pervasive than it appears to be from the low count. It occurs as a background factor in a number of alliance interpretations but seldom is the dominating factor in a mis-interpretation. For example, during a number of months in the 1945–

1946 Iran crisis, alliance suspicion was present for both the United States and the Soviet Union. In the United States it took the form of interpreting Stalin's messages as probable attempts to deceive the United States (19). But then wishful thinking took over: perhaps, despite appearances to the contrary, Stalin was taking U.S. warnings seriously, so that the U.S. strategy might still work. In the Soviet Union wishful thinking also took over: the United States might be up to something in Iran and then again it might not; but in either case it might be better to ignore their disturbing behavior and press on with the Iran strategy in hopes of a quick success before the troop withdrawal deadline of March 2. When U.S. objections could no longer be ignored, they were reinterpreted as the consequence of meddling by the hostile Iranian government, which had stirred up U.S. suspicions (11). In both cases strategy (desire) dominated the alliance image in the final misinterpretations so the interpretations are coded under 19, 17, and 11, not 12.

Categories 14 through 17 represent the influence of expectations and desires and are quantitatively the predominating categories in information processing. Category 14 represents exaggerated fears or worries about expected dangers during a crisis, chiefly by soft-line interpreters. Category 16 represents the hope that one's strategy might still work despite strong evidence to the contrary, pure wishful thinking. Wishful thinking is also present in many of the instances coded as 17, since one reason to ignore a disturbing message is the hope or desire that the news isn't as bad as it seems; compare for example the Soviet interpretations during the 1945–1946 Iran crisis. Jervis's hypothesis that desires usually operate indirectly through their influence (or perhaps mutual influence) on expectations is confirmed. However, his hypothesis that when the two are opposed expectations will dominate is difficult to test because many instances from categories 1 and 17 are relevant to it. It does not seem to be confirmed.

Category 17 is a borderline category, because the reasons for ignoring a message vary. Some "ignores" are wishful thinking, a hope that things are really not that bad or that our luck will finally change. They hardly differ from 16. Some represent a rational reluctance to discard an organizationally well-established strategy on the basis of one or two negative messages. These may be instances of correct interpretation combined with a temporary refusal to accept the strategic implication. Some "ignores" lean toward 19 or 20, a reluctance to believe anything coming from a certain source. In many cases we just do not know the reasons why a message is ignored; if we always knew the reasons, the instances in this category might all be reclassified into other categories. Category 17 is also an important adjustment category. Many messages that behaviorally are ignored in the sense that they are rejected or not answered or produce no change of strategy or tactics are, we can infer, gradually changing expectations. Their strategic effect is therefore delayed and cumulative rather than non-existent.

Categories 18 through 22 represent clearly irrational attempts to reject or deny negative information. Most of the instances come from a few cases in which a mistaken diagnosis of the situation was tenaciously defended against persistent negative information: Austria, 1908–1909; Germany, 1914; Britain, 1938; United States, 1941; Britain, 1956; and United States, 1958, Lebanon. In the remaining cases, with a few exceptions the interpreters stop at 17; they proceed with their strategy confidently according to expectations, then rely on hope for a time, but after ignoring at most one or two unmistakably bad messages they reluctantly change what needs to be changed.

What inferences can we draw from these tables?

1. Errors in transmission cannot be disregarded in the aggregate; one message in 11 is not transmitted correctly. But the subcategories tell a different story. 40% of the errors are an expression of factional differences in the bargainer and therefore are an aspect of bureaucratic politics rather than information processing. Another 40% are instances of the ambassador's desires or expectations determining interpretation and can be included in the interpretation process. The remainder is random noise and can be disregarded; the few spectacular examples in this category are atypical. This means that transmission is a practical problem for a central decision maker who has internal opposition or whose opponent is internally divided, but need not be incorporated in an information-processing model.

2. The number of correctly interpreted messages available to disconfirm mistaken expectations is about 100 (categories 2–7 plus $\frac{1}{2}$ of 17). The number of misinterpreted messages available to confirm and preserve mistaken expectations is about 165 (8–22 minus $\frac{1}{2}$ of 17), plus 30 distorted in transmission. This means that, if it takes one correctly interpreted message to counteract one misinterpreted message, and this ratio were to hold across all cases, then many mistaken expectations will not be corrected. But since there is a great deal of correction of mistaken expectations there must be some other basis for correction. Since the basis is not quantitative, it must be qualitative, located in the specific content or pattern of messages and indices. Three possibilities suggest themselves: (a) the correctly interpreted messages, or some of them, may be more important, contain more bits of information, so that one of them can counteract a half-dozen misinterpreted messages; (b) the sequence or pattern of messages may make a difference; perhaps even the misinterpreted messages fall into some pattern that tends to destroy or correct itself; (c) perhaps a repartitioning of the data into two classes,

rational bargainers and irrational bargainers, would reveal that most of the convergence occurs in the former class and most of the divergence and oscillation in the latter class. This was the solution that Rapoport and Chammah [29] found for interpreting their data.

3. Of the three factors affecting misperception, the belief systems are *quantitatively* less important than the other two. Expectations, supported by desires, are the most important, but desires also affect interpretations independently. All three influences must be retained in the model, but no additional influences are necessary.

4. Categories 18 through 22, reinterpretations of negative information, are quantitatively negligible, particularly since most instances are contributed by a few cases. Jervis discusses a few other ways of dealing with disconfirming information which do not appear in the table since no instances occur in the sample. When we repartition the data into rational and irrational subclasses, categories 18 through 22 should appear in the irrational class while the rational class should stop at 17.

We turn now to qualitative analysis. If we search for the most important messages, that is, the ones which had the largest effect in changing expectations and strategy, we find them mainly in two groups of categories, 6–7 and 8, 9, 10, 11, and 13. There are also scattered instances of 1, 4, 5, 15, and 16. The 8–13 group occurs at the beginning of a crisis (15 instances) or near the midpoint (8 instances). The 6–7 group occurs near the midpoint (9 instances) or at the very end (6 instances). This suggests we should look at time sequences in the categories, and when we do the data immediately make sense.

A crisis frequently begins with a single message or index, the challenge: the Kaiser makes a speech at Tangier, the *Panther* anchors at Agadir, Khrushchev sends a note to the Western powers. When there is no one dramatic incident, a pattern of moves by the opponent occurs instead. This incident or series of moves is interpreted on the basis of the background image and the specific circumstances (categories 8, 9, 10, 11, 13) to produce a whole diagnosis of the crisis situation (immediate image) and a whole set of expectations: the opponent's aim is x, his strategy is y, this move y_1 is intended to accomplish z, if we do A he will probably respond y_2, and if we do B he will probably respond y_3. In some cases these expectations are reinforced by one or two additional indices or messages. These initial interpretations are very important since they produce a whole diagnosis and set of expectations. And, since initial images are substantially different three-fourths of the time, these initial misinterpretations produce the initial difference of expectations that sets the bargaining problem.

[29] Rapoport and Chammah, *Prisoner's Dilemma*.

In the three cases in which misperception was negligible (1898, 1923, 1948) the initial diagnosis was based on correct interpretations (1, 6) or was made before the start of the crisis on the basis of correct interpretations.

After the initial diagnosis is made and strategy decided, the background image recedes (with some exceptions), and immediate image and expectations dominate interpretation (14 and 15). Expectations are supported against possible disconfirmation by the initial strategy. Since the bargainer desires the strategy to succeed, his desires and hopes make him reluctant to accept evidence that his expectations are mistaken. What seems to happen is that the bargainer tries to fit new information into his pattern of expectations with varying degrees of success. Some messages fit well, some not so well; also an occasional correct interpretation (4 or 5) slips through. After a time enough piecemeal adjustments and plain negative evidence have accumulated to disorganize the original neat pattern of expectations; then wishful thinking takes over (16, 17).

Here the rational and the irrational bargainers take different paths. The rational bargainer does indulge in some wishful thinking; he puts the best possible interpretation on an ambiguous message (16) and may even ignore (17) one or two unmistakably bad messages in hopes that the situation will yet improve. However, his hopes gradually are being displaced by fears that things are going wrong, and his expectations are being adjusted to fit the new information. Finally, after a particularly clear message (6 or 7, or 1 when one bargainer gets a clear message that enables him to convince his colleagues), the new expectations replace the old and strategy is suddenly shifted.

The irrational bargainer never loses confidence in his expectations. Messages that cannot be interpreted in accordance with expectations are rejected by Categories 18–22, or in some cases 16, and expectations are never adjusted.

THE ADJUSTMENT OF EXPECTATIONS AND IMAGES

The data for this section are mainly the approximately 100 "insightful" interpretations in which new information dominated the contrary influence of image, expectation, or strategy (2–7, 17). In about half these instances the influence of information on expectations must be estimated from later behavioral changes, changes of tactics or of strategy, since the recipients did not report the effect on their expectations. Adjustment of expectations also occurs in some instances of category 16, which overlaps category 17.

The most straightforward category is 5, correct interpretations in opposition to expectations and requiring a change of tactics (33 instances). This is the type of instance Coddington had in mind in his discussion of the adjustment process. These are cases in which a message states that the bargaining situation is not quite as diagnosed and that the current tactic is not working as expected. The response is to change expectation and tactic. The fact that in practically all instances only one message is sufficient to induce adjustment indicates that tactics, in contrast with strategies, do not have any emotional (hope), ideological or bureaucratic inertia built into them.

Examples: 1905, Rouvier rejects Bulow's demands for a conference. Bulow's interpretation: threats are not working, try a hinted concession. 1923, British secure U.S. support, revive commission of inquiry plan. French interpretation: looks like trouble ahead, British seem to be moving into active opposition. Perhaps they can be stalled off for a while. 1909, Russian hint of possible realignment. British interpretation: realignment is a possibility if Russia gets no entente support, time to support Russia's client Serbia. 1938, British warning of September 2, ultimatum of September 19 to Czechoslovakia. Czech interpretation: Czechoslovakia has no choice, must submit in order to retain British support. 1957, Turkish–U.S. troop movements near Syrian border. Inferred Soviet Union interpretation: attack on Syria is possible, time to warn them off. 1959, U.S. proposes broad negotiations at foreign ministers' level. Soviet interpretation: United States has misunderstood our proposal, but let's go along anyway; at least it's negotiations.

Category 2 messages also produce immediate adjustment of expectations and the appropriate tactical shift. Example: September 13: Chamberlain proposes discussions with Hitler at Berchtesgaden. Motive: show British concern, improve communication with Hitler and support him against the Nazi extremists. Hitler (who had expected British firmness): Chamberlain is ready to make some concessions. Wonderful! Increase demands.

These are instances of the normal working of a normal, moderately successful bargaining process. Normal bargaining consists partly of a continuation of successful tactics, in which the feedback is in conformity with expectations (category 1), and partly of a change of tactics that are not working as expected (categories 2, 5).

Change of strategy is a much more convulsive process. Of the 15 instances of strategy change, 11 were preceded by a series of negative messages that were either interpreted correctly (4), or ignored (17), or misinterpreted by wishful thinking (16). Remember that wishful thinking expresses the resistance to change of a strategy that is not working. In several instances we have direct evidence of what was happening after each of these negative messages: confidence in expectations and hopes of success were incrementally declining. When the level of hope got very low there was a complete strategy shift. In several cases this shift had to be preceded by a change of government as well.

Japan 1941 is an extreme example of persistence in the face of disconfirming information. The Japanese D strategy of negotiating a settlement with the United States while preparing for war if negotiations failed was activated at least by October 1940. The United States rejected Japan's general preamble to negotiations October 5–8 and ignored Nomura's opening statement of March 8, 1941, but raised Japan's hopes with a reasonable proposal April 14. Thereafter all the news was bad: The United States obstructed negotiations with irrelevant abstract principles on April 16, rejected the Japanese conditional acceptance of their April 14 offer, added new embargoes in June, sent an insult in July (later retracted), froze Japanese assets on July 26, rejected the proposal for a Konoye-Roosevelt meeting, and rejected the proposal of October 2. Interpretations of most of these messages fell in category 4—correct but contradictory to desires and expectations. Japanese hopes for a negotiated settlement had been quite high after the (misinterpreted) "U.S." proposal [30] of April 14, but by October they were nil, and a strategy shift occurred, a shift from D to E, from coercive pressure to attack. Some other instances are: the German admission of defeat March 1906 (D to C) after a series of ever clearer messages that Germany was isolated on the Morocco issue; the 1908 Austrian shift from firmness to accommodation with Turkey (D to C) after a mistransmitted Turkish protest, a misinterpreted Turkish boycott, an ignored British warning, and German advice to negotiate that finally broke through Austrian resistance; Halifax' shift from appeasement to firmness September 1938, preceded by a series of unmistakable warnings that Hitler was planning to attack October 1 and several days of intensive foreign office discussions; Stalin's withdrawal of the Berlin blockade after mounting evidence that the airlift was succeeding; and Eden's shift in September 1956 to a unilateral strategy (C to D in Protector) after a series of discouraging and perplexing maneuvers by Dulles.

There were two instances of a sudden collapse of expectations due to one overwhelmingly clear message of failure. In January 1946, the Soviet Union suddenly cut off trade between Iran and Azerbaijan and announced they could no longer work with the Iranian Premier. Result: shift from D to C, and change of prime ministers, from Hakimi to Qavam. In November 1956, the U.S. ultimatum to Eden forced his Suez withdrawal.

Finally, Hitler's strategy shift of Sept. 28, 1938, from attack to coercive diplomacy (E to D) was produced by four nearly simultaneous

[30] The proposal actually originated with a Japanese envoy, but this was obscured in transmission from Tokyo.

messages lowering the expected value of attack and increasing that of negotiated acceptance of French–British surrender. Britain sent a warning and mobilized the fleet, France made a substantial concession giving him nearly everything he wanted, Mussolini plead for restraint, and there was unmistakable evidence of German popular unwillingness to fight.

How are expectations adjusted in these instances? In most of these instances the new information states that a key expectation on which the whole bargaining strategy is based is completely wrong. In 1940 the key Japanese expectation was that the United States would eventually appreciate the Japanese economic problem and would lend some support or at least would stop strangling the Japanese economy. In 1914 the key German expectation was that Britain would not fight; in 1948 Stalin expected that West Berlin would collapse because of the blockade; in 1956 Eden expected that Dulles, though perverse, obstructionist, and too clever by half, would not actively interfere where Britain's vital interest was at stake; and so on. In the remaining instances a set of expectations on which the strategy was based was each shown to be completely mistaken. In 1908 Aehrenthal (Austria) expected the German ally and the Russians to support him vis-à-vis Turkey, Britain to avoid involvement in Balkan affairs, and the new Young Turk regime to be reasonable, progressive domestic reformers free of ancient dynastic delusions about Bosnia.

The new information therefore requires not only an admission that one's expectations are completely mistaken at a fundamental point or points but also that one's strategy is bound to fail or has failed. These are difficult admissions to make. In contrast, the 2 and 5 type messages merely state that some expectation is slightly inaccurate and that a slight tactical shift is needed for continued success of the strategy.

The response to the new information is resistance, refusal to change expectations. Resistance takes the form of category 15 misperceptions, plus some instances of categories 18–22 in a few cases, followed by 16 and 17. Finally resistance collapses and expectation and strategy are suddenly changed. The cause of the collapse is either a gradual lowering of confidence in the key expectation (as in the Japan 1941 case), or a type 6 message that is too clear and urgent to be ignored or wished away.

Among our cases are two exceptions to the general rule of resistance plus sudden collapse of expectations. Halifax in August–September 1938 offered strong resistance to a series of negative messages indicating that Hitler was going to attack, but was persuaded to shift strategy by his friends—and then was again talked out of his strategy shift by Chamberlain. The Japanese in 1941 offered no misperception-type resistance; they interpreted the bad news from the United States correctly. But they showed extreme resistance to the implication of this news, the implication that their expectation was wrong and their strategy had failed.

Note that these data on strategy change disconfirm learning models and Markov models of bargaining. These models omit expectations and images, that is, all subjective or conscious factors, and substitute an intervening mental variable such as the propensity to play C or to play D. They then attempt to relate inputs to changes in this propensity. A learning model might have an equation that says that each input of a C bid (concession) by the opponent reduces a bargainer's propensity to play D by a certain percentage. Such models may eventually fit experimental gaming data but are wide of the mark for crisis bargaining. We find: (1) inputs affect directly a bargainer's immediate image and expectations, that is, his estimate of the bargaining situation, and only indirectly his strategy or tactics. (2) The function mapping inputs on expectations is not linear but is a step-function. That is, expectations remain constant until some critical point is reached, at which time they collapse completely and are replaced by different expectations. (3) The new strategy is based on the new expectations. (4) The propensity to play C or D, or in our terminology one's "hard" or "soft" bias, is part of one's belief system and does not change in a crisis.

We turn now to the question of adjustment of images. Image change or resistance to change is an extremely complex subject that, if treated fully, would take us far beyond our present concerns. We limit ourselves, therefore, to a few generalizations that seem fairly well-grounded in our case studies.

1. Background images usually do not change, and then only marginally during the course of a crisis. Immediate images and expectations often change without effect on the underlying image ("This is the same old opponent; it's just that he is more determined [or less determined] on this specific issue than we had expected").

2. Background image change, if it occurs at all, is a long-term process; it may be accelerated, however, by events during a crisis.

3. Background images are affected by changing system structure and changing alignments in the system.

4. In the short term—e.g., during a crisis—change in background image for a government usually results from a change of regime, or a shift in the balance of power within a regime, not from individuals changing their minds.

We look first at some of our relatively few examples of background image change during a crisis—i.e., at some counter-instances to point 1 above. Rouvier in 1905 shifted from an image of German as a good neighbor with legitimate grievances to one of Germany, the aggressive, bullying enemy. Rouvier was not a specialist in foreign policy and had no diplomatic experience; possibly his images and theories were not well established. Also in the 1905 crisis, Lord Grey, who had previously viewed Germany as little more than an irritating nuisance, came to see it more as a definite "enemy." This was the result not only of Germany's behavior during the crisis but also of the dynamics of alignment triggered by the Entente Cordiale: British support of France, forced by the need to preserve the entente, generated expressions of hostility from Germany which reinforced the image of Germany as enemy. This "vicious circle" persisted in subsequent years reinforced by the Anglo-German naval race.

In 1914 the German, in particular the Kaiser's, background image of England shifted from that of the benevolent neutral to the leader of a conspiracy of "encirclement." The Kaiser and some other German officials actually held a split image of England. On the one hand, she was a "natural ally," similar to Germany in race and customs, with interests primarily upon the sea that complemented rather than conflicted with Germany's interests on land. And in the years just before 1914, Anglo–German relations had been good. The other side of the image was that of England the unscrupulous schemer, the bourgeois "nation of shopkeepers," inciting others to wars from which she would profit, and excluding Germany from a share in colonial spoils. For the Kaiser, at least, the "good" part of the image was dominant during most of the crisis; the "bad" part jumped to the fore when it became known that England would fight with France and Russia. Note that this kind of split image is different from the one mentioned earlier, the tendency of the soft-liner to see factionalism in the opponent's government.

Though the soft-liners in Chamberlain's cabinet did not change their background image of Hitler during the Munich crisis, they swung around 180 degrees following Hitler's takeover of Czechoslovakia the following spring. For Halifax and others, that event was enough; for Chamberlain himself, the additional impetus of Danzig was required.

These four examples suggest the proposition that, when background image change does occur, it is usually from "soft" to "hard." We find no examples of hard-liners "going soft."

The Iran crisis of 1946 illustrates how background images and image changes are linked to system structure, and how a crisis at a structural transition point may accelerate image change. The United States' full image shift from Russia-the-wartime-ally to Russia-the-aggressive-opponent occurred over about a three-year span, from 1945 to 1948; similarly for the Russian image of the United States. The essential cause of this change was the defeat of Germany and weakening of Western

Europe, which left the United States and the Soviets as inevitable adversaries in a new bipolar balance of power. There was "image lag," in that it took some time for the logic of bipolarity to reflect itself in attitudes and behavior. The Iran crisis took place when both parties still had ambiguous images of each other—on the one hand, they both still hoped to collaborate harmoniously in managing the postwar world and saw the other as a plausible partner; on the other hand, numerous conflicts cast the partnership in doubt. The Iran crisis was one of these, along with earlier and later conflicts over Eastern Europe and Germany. For the United States, the apparent Soviet attempt to grab northern Iran, and for the Soviets, being haled before the United Nations like criminals, were fairly traumatic surprises that helped accelerate the mutual shift to full-blown Cold War images.

Other cases in which fairly significant image change occurred were Bosnia, 1908, and Suez, 1956. The latter produced a change in the European allies' images of the United States: they realized the United States could not be counted on for help outside the European theater, and doubts were sown even about that.

However, image change is much less prominent in our cases than resistance to change. The more important question, then, is not how images are adjusted but how they resist adjustment. Ole Holsti has investigated this question for Dulles, and has shown that Dulles's image of the Soviet Union could not be changed because any conceivable Soviet message would confirm some component of the image.[31] If the Soviets made an active move, this proved that they were aggressive; if they were conciliatory, this proved that they were in internal economic difficulty due to the inherent unworkability of Communism; if they yielded on some issue, this proved they were bluffers.

We have several instances of rigid background images that maintained themselves in the same manner that Holsti has described. Adenauer's image of the Soviet Union was change-proof because of the component belief that Communists are masters of deceit and guile. Any apparently non-aggressive Soviet move or message was immediately interpreted as a trick of some sort (category 19). Any argument by a non-Communist, a Macmillan or a Schumacher that conflicted with Adenauer's opinions was evidence that this gentleman had been taken in by Communist guile and was therefore unreliable (category 20). Another example was Eisenhower's and Dulles's belief in the monolithic unity of the Communist camp. This was maintained through 1956–1960 by several mechanisms, including puzzlement at discrepant be-

---

[31] Ole Holsti, "The Belief System and National Images: a Case Study" in J. Rosenau, ed., *International Politics and Foreign Policy* (New York: The Free Press, 1969), pp. 543–550.

havior (category 21), misinterpreting or exaggerating apparently positive information (13, 22), ignoring negative information (17), and the belief that observed disunity resulted from U.S. firmness (15a). Chamberlain, a master of wishful thinking (15, 16), managed to find a ray of hope in everything Hitler and Mussolini said and did. Category 15–16 interpretations involve a lowering of hopes, and Chamberlain's hopes did get pretty low at times, but some new message or reinterpretation of an old one would always raise them again. After Bad Godesberg, September 23, 1938, the situation looked hopeless, but then Chamberlain persuaded himself that he had finally won Hitler's confidence, that Hitler had actually made a concession for the first time, and that negotiations were finally possible. Chamberlain's persistent wishful thinking was rewarded by an illusory success, the friendship treaty with Hitler at the Munich conference. Grew, U.S. ambassador to Japan, had an unchangeable image of Japan because he saw its government as divided between the peaceful moderates and the militarists. Any bad news from Japan meant the militarists were getting stronger, and good news meant the moderates were coming back. The consequences of any conceivable U.S. move could be interpreted to fit this split image.

In short, a rigid background image resists change by providing a self-confirming interpretation for any conceivable message. However, the categories of interpretation vary from one image to another.

In summary, we find three kinds of adjustment in our cases. 1. Minor adjustment of expectations tied to tactics occurs with a single negative message (2 or 5). 2. Major adjustment of expectations tied to strategy is at first resisted by category 14, 15, and 16 interpretations if possible, or with clearer messages by 17 and 4 interpretations. After a series of such messages and/or a loud and clear one (6) expectations collapse and strategy is changed. Adjustment of immediate images accompanies adjustment of expectations. 3. Adjustment of background images occurs through changes of personnel, with a few marginal exceptions.

A REVISED BARGAINING MODEL

We have now examined all five of the factors affecting performance of the expanded bargaining model, Figure 4–2. In each case we have described the main quantitative and qualitative empirical characteristics, the range of variation, and the connections with other factors. The only topic not investigated is how strategic decisions are made, and that is the subject matter of the next chapter. We are now in a position to answer the question: What further revisions of Coddington's model are necessary to make it applicable to crisis bargaining?

Our empirical investigation has shown that much of the variation in model performance can be accounted for by dividing our bargainers into two groups, the rational and the irrational bargainers. We accordingly construct two models, a rational one and an irrational one. These models are real types, only slightly idealized; each describes rather closely the actual bargaining behavior of a group of bargainers. However, there are also bargainers whose behavior falls between the two main groups, some approximating the rational group rather closely and others falling near the midpoint of the two groups. The rational group includes the main middle-liners Salisbury, Grey, Kennedy, and Khrushchev; some hard-liners, Delcassé, Sazonov, Hitler 1937–1938, Ulbricht; and the soft-liners, Eden 1936–1937 and Qavam, plus many figures who appear more briefly in the data. The irrational group includes Holstein 1904–1906, Chamberlain, British Ambassador Henderson, Tojo, Eden in 1956, Dulles, Adenauer, and a number of lesser figures. In-betweens include Bulow, Halifax, Stalin, and Aehrenthal. These classifications do not of course refer to moral character, but to rationality in the information-processing sense, namely the ability to interpret disconfirming information correctly and to adjust mistaken expectations and strategy accordingly. Our rational bargainer is not one who "knows" at the start of a crisis what the situation is, what the relative interests, power relations, and main alternatives are, since there are few such people. He is rather one whose initial judgment may be mistaken and who knows it, but who is able to correct initial misjudgments and perceive the outlines of the developing bargaining situation in time to deal with it effectively.

The key characteristic of rational bargaining is that the background image is relatively dissociated from interpretation and adjustment. The

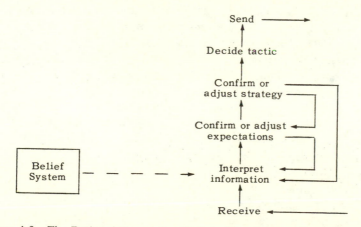

Figure 4-3. The Rational Bargaining Module (Two Modules Make a System)

first few messages or incidents in a crisis are interpreted by deduction from one's belief system and initial perceptions of crisis circumstances— there is, after all, no other basis available for interpretation—and these interpretations produce an immediate image and an initial set of expectations. But as bargaining gets under way, the belief system gradually moves into the background, that is, the arrow from "belief system" to "interpretation" gradually disappears.

This means, empirically, that the bargainer has *low confidence* in his initial diagnosis. He does not think he knows from the very start what the crisis is about, as did Eden in 1956 or Adenauer in 1958, or as Acheson for example "knew" on the first day of the Korean war that this was the next step in Stalin's drive to conquer the world. All such "knowledge" comes from the image. Rather the bargainer sets up some tentative guesses as to what the opponent's immediate aim, interests, and strategy are and how he might react, and may even admit ignorance on some points. When new information comes in, he tries to fit it into his existing pattern of expectations, and if successful feels that the expectations have been confirmed. But if it does not fit he does not reject or reinterpret it (categories 17–22). Rather he treats his tentative guesses as disconfirmed and tries to construct a new set of guesses that fit all the information that has come in so far. As bargaining progresses, more and more information comes in and hopefully some pattern is gradually stabilized as the correct diagnosis of the situation. This pattern may even make possible a correction of early misperceptions based on an initially mistaken diagnosis.

Given a basically tentative, low-confidence outlook (a "flexible image"), the rational bargainer engages in several specific practices. First, his tactics include probes or searches for information. He does not know what the opponent's specific aims and preferences are (though he "knows" what his ultimate aims are), so he must find out by testing specific points. Initial tactics therefore include probes, tentative concessions, tentative demands, specific warnings, and the like. Second, a rational bargainer builds redundancy into his messages. (Khrushchev is the primary example here.) He does not assume that the opponent "must know" what he is doing, but rather assumes that the situation is pretty confused. Consequently he tries to send a message several different ways, always through a different channel, and keeps repeating the same theme. The purpose is to break through the resistance set up by the opponent's mistaken expectations and also to give him time to test, retest, and adjust his expectations. This practice is also useful for bypassing unsuspected filters in the transmission channels.

Third, interpretation is based at first on image and expectations because there is at first nothing else on which to base it. This makes some initial misperceptions almost inevitable. If we denied this, we would not be describing human, limited rationality. But after several messages have accumulated, interpretation of new ones is based on the developing pattern of information itself, not directly on the image. It is based, not on what we "know" the opponent's fundamental characteristics and ultimate aims are, but on the specific pattern of his overt statements and actions this time. New information is, as always, interpreted by its fit with what we "know," but what we know comes from the bargaining process rather than from the image.

An example may clarify the distinction. In the 1937–1938 Anglo–Italian bargaining, Mussolini sent a number of friendly messages expressing his desire to reduce tensions in the Mediterranean, including 21 July 1937, 10–11 September 1937, and February 1938. In the last message there was a note of urgency: this may be the last chance to develop Anglo–Italian cooperation because of changes occurring in Europe. Chamberlain "understood" and agreed: there was a danger that the two dictators would get together, which might still be forestalled by British concessions to Italy. Chamberlain's expectations were confirmed and his C strategy made more urgently necessary. But Eden noticed a pattern: Mussolini had several times expressed his desire to be cooperative and accommodating, but had not yet made a single specific concession. Here was a discrepancy that showed something was wrong. And indeed something was wrong. Mussolini was actually aligning himself with Hitler and preparing for aggression in the Mediterranean.

Fourth, there is bound to be a certain amount of wishful thinking and even some ignoring of bad news. This imposes some inertia on expectations and strategy that could be costly, as an opportunity for some key move may be lost by delay. On the other hand it provides more time for additional information and may even prevent a too hasty change of strategy on the basis of some misleading message.

Fifth, during interpretation, the rational bargainer does not primarily focus on his own strategy but on the opponent's strategy. He does not ask, except occasionally, "Is my strategy working?" This question leads directly to wishful thinking, since it mobilizes and activates the hopes and fears associated with a strategy. Germany in 1914 is a prime example of this error. Had the Germans inquired into what the British strategy was, plenty of information was available for answering the question. Instead they already "knew" that Britain would not fight, so they did not inquire and were very skeptical of the negative information that forced its way through their filters.

Sixth, adjustment is a very limited affair. There is no adjustment of the background image, which may even be confirmed by instances of the opponent's brutality, deceit, and aggressiveness, or by his concessions, which confirm an image of weak resolve. What is adjusted is the estimate of the opponent's specific aims, interests, degree of resolve, and capabilities in the particular conflict. The non-adjustment of images means that both bargainers will disagree from the start and throughout the crisis and afterward in their histories and memoirs on what the issue of the crisis is, who started it, what the status quo is, who is the aggressor and who is the defender, what a just or fair solution would be, and how the solution fits into the grand scheme of history. All such ideas come from the image.

Seventh, once one has discovered the opponent's specific aims, interests, and resolve, it may still be necessary to be firm, to risk war, or even to fight. But fighting, if it occurs, will be rational in the sense that it comes after a thorough exploration of the intensity of comparative interests and power relations, and a judgment that war is preferable to acceding to the opponent's demands. And if a peaceful settlement is achieved it will be seen as a specific settlement rather than as a step to disaster or to new heights of glory: he was too strong for us on this point but we got or saved that, and in general we did about as well as could be hoped for given the existing power distribution. In this way there is no aftermath of frustration and determination to get revenge (or conversely rising aspirations) that would lay the foundation for the next crisis.

It may happen that the bargainer's image and initial expectations are correct; we have about eight examples of this. In such a case there will be no adjustment of expectation, except on tactical details. However, this does not indicate that the bargainer is unusually rational, but only that he is lucky; his images and bargaining style happened to be the right ones for the circumstances. His success in this crisis may be followed by bungling and failure in the next, which happens not to suit his particular set of images.

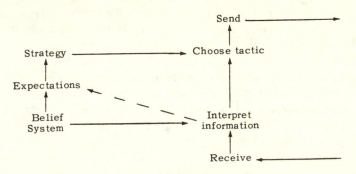

Figure 4-4. The Irrational Bargaining Module

The irrational bargainer [32] is characterized by a rigid belief system that dominates his behavior. He knows from the onset of a crisis what the opponent is up to because he has studied the opponent thoroughly and understands his ultimate aims, bargaining style, preferences, and internal political problems. He also is a keen judge of men on his side, knowing whose opinions to value and whose opinions to ignore or bypass, but he generally prefers to make his own decisions. Knowing the opponent as he does, he is not going to be duped by the opponent's tricks or deceptive statements, nor is he going to lose heart at temporary setbacks, alarms, and rumors, but continues firmly on his chosen strategy through all diversions and difficulties.

Given the bargainer's understanding of the opponent, there is only one possible strategy to use; no others have a chance of success. And if by chance this one does not succeed, then success was never possible. The purpose of interpretation is to determine which of several possible responses the opponent is making to one's actions. For each possible response there is one appropriate tactical rejoinder, and each rejoinder is included in the initial strategy as a tactical alternative. Program control thus moves directly from interpretation to tactical decision, with each message setting off its appropriate response almost automatically.

In terms of Figure 4–4, the first move or two of the crisis is interpreted by means of the belief system to produce a complete diagnosis of the situation. (categories H, 8–11). This diagnosis is held with complete confidence because it is directly in accord with the belief system. Thereafter expectations and consequently strategy are immune to change; the bargainer "knows" what is going on and is not going to be fooled by any new information. The arrow from "interpretation" to "expectations" disappears. All new information is interpreted by means of the image, and messages either agree with expectation (1, 3) or are rejected by category 17–22 reinterpretations.

A decision maker approximating this model may occasionally come through a crisis with his expectations confirmed and his objectives achieved. Chamberlain at Munich was a possible example with his illusory success, the friendship agreement with Hitler; or Dulles at Quemoy, though the Quemoy strategic situation was rather complex and some ingenuity and openness to new information was involved in devising the correct initial strategy. More often, one of two outcomes occur: (1) The decision maker is betrayed by his colleagues or allies, who take from him control over strategy. This happened to Holstein in 1906,

---

[32] This concept is roughly equivalent to Steinbruner's "Theoretical Thinking." John Steinbruner, *The Cybernetic Theory of Decision* (Princeton, N.J.: Princeton University Press, 1974), pp. 131–135.

to Adenauer in 1961, and Bethmann-Hollweg in 1914, and nearly happened to Chamberlain and Bonnet in 1938. Or (2) reality finally breaks through with an unmistakable message of defeat: Bulow 1906, Eden 1956, Tojo 1945, and Henderson September 3, 1939. In short, the rigidity of the irrational bargainer means that if he is lucky and his initial strategy happens to be correct, he will win, but if it is not correct, he will not be able to realize this in time to avoid defeat or disaster. The rational bargainer may also be lucky, but in addition he is able to correct mistakes and thereby make the most, after some fumbling and delay, of whatever opportunities the bargaining situation offers.

Note that the cybernetic bargaining model of Figures 4–3 and 4–4 is an N-person rather than a 2-person model. One need only include one module for each bargainer. Also one must then specify which bargainers, that is which modules, are permitted to receive each message: all other bargainers (public message), one other (private message), etc. One can also arrange for one bargainer to be rational and another irrational or can change one module to fit known characteristics of some empirical bargainer.

The main objection that may be made to the rational bargaining model is that the practice of taking the opponent's words and actions seriously despite his known dishonesty lays one open to being duped. The possibility of deception is indeed a problem in bargaining. One must be wary of the opponent's messages and not accept them at face value. The issue, however, is, how is one to test the truth of a message—by what one "knows" of the sender's ultimate aims, or by the pattern of his actions and messages in the present crisis? Our data suggest that the rational bargainer does the latter. He does not immediately believe any message from the opponent, nor does he ignore or reject it, but tries to fit it into a developing picture of the opponent's goals, resolve, and strategy. A message that does not fit or that is contradicted by information obtained through other channels may be deceptive and must be examined carefully. Where the pattern itself is ambiguous, seemingly contradictory, or unclear, he seeks out information to clarify it, and he may even test a clear pattern with further probes before committing himself to a strategy. Moreover he does not rely on a single channel of communication but seeks information from several different channels. This means that successful deception must involve a whole program of acts and messages over an extended period of time rather than a few direct lies, and such a program is very difficult to sustain.

Our data provide only one confirmed example of a successful program of deception continued over a long time, namely Hitler 1937–1938. But Hitler's strategy was successful because it played into the rigid images and the wishful thinking of the appeasers, not because it produced a consistent pattern of deceptive information. Plenty of contrary information could have enabled a rational man to see through the deception (which Eden did do) and which the appeasers—certainly not rational men in the present sense—had to ignore or interpret away to maintain their self-delusion. Japan was not being systematically deceptive in 1940–1941, nor was Dulles in 1956. The Soviet attempted deception in Cuba 1962 was unsuccessful.

We must distinguish here between continued, systematic deception of the 1937–1938 sort and occasional evasiveness, concealment, or ambiguity. The latter is an essential part of rational crisis bargaining and appears continually in our cases. It is necessary for a good bargainer to conceal some aspects of his strategy at some stages of a crisis, and conversely it is necessary for the opponent to try to penetrate the concealment. This is the point of the Shackle quotation at the beginning of the chapter. But in other stages or circumstances it is equally necessary to be honest and to accept the opponent's honesty. For instance if the opponent is preparing to make an offer rather above one's current minimum, it is unwise to tell him honestly he could get a settlement for less; but if he is persistently offering much less than one's minimum and a deadline is approaching, it is important to reveal one's approximate minimum. The same holds for the amount of alliance support one is getting or giving, and bargaining deadlines—these facts must be concealed at some times and revealed at others. Since the question of when to conceal and when to reveal is a question of strategy and tactics rather than information processing, it will be discussed in the next chapter.

From an information processing standpoint it is necessary to accept the high probability that the opponent, like oneself, needs to be honest at some times and evasive or even deceptive at others, and that an occasional deception or evasion does not mean that nothing the opponent says or does can ever be believed. The problem is to judge when he is being honest and when not.

A rigid image of the opponent as totally untrustworthy is as much a hindrance to solving this information processing problem as is a rigid image of him as totally trustworthy.

CHAPTER V

DECISION MAKING

In this chapter we examine how bargaining decisions are made. This completes our examination of the bargaining model of Chapter IV; but, in addition, the shift of attention to internal characteristics of decision-making units leads to revisions of the model and to a supplementary model. We will concentrate mainly on strategic decisions, of which there are about fifty documented instances in our cases. The number of tactical decisions could well run into the thousands, so it would be impossible to examine them all systematically.

Our procedure will be to use three current theories of decision making to organize and interpret the data. This will simultaneously bring out the characteristics of strategic decisions in our cases and test the adequacy of the theories. The theories are the maximizing of expected utility or "rational actor" theory, bounded rationality, and bureaucratic politics. The first two of these may be called problem-solving theories, in that they deal with the intellectual process of dealing with a problem under the assumption that the decision maker is a unitary actor. The third theory drops this assumption and looks at the political processes occurring inside the decision-making unit. All three theories will be treated as theories of the *process* of decision making.

THEORIES OF DECISION MAKING

The "rational actor" or "maximizing" theory treats decision making as a process of maximizing expected utility. It is assumed that there is a single homogeneous good, utility, that is present in all actually desired ends, and that an increased amount of any end brings with it an increased amount of utility, at a steadily diminishing rate. The latter is the assumption of diminishing marginal utility. Second, a set of well-defined and mutually exclusive alternatives is assumed, from which the decision maker is to choose one. Third, it is assumed that the decision maker is able to estimate the outcome and calculate the expected value of each alternative. Given these assumptions, the decision maker calculates the expected value of each alternative, compares all alternatives, and chooses the alternative that maximizes expected utility. In game theory versions of this theory, the decision maker selects the strategy that maximins utility or minimaxes regret, etc.

The key assumption in this theory of decision making is that there exists a single homogeneous good, utility, which is present in all other goods. Operationally, this reduces to the assumption that all concretely desired goods are comparable at the margin. That is, it is assumed that a decision maker can compare any two packages containing varying combinations of goods and know that he prefers one or is indifferent between them. To take an old example, suppose there are two desired goods, bread and tea, and $1 is to be spent on them. This means that there are 100 alternative packages, each containing a certain combination of bread and tea—1¢ worth of bread and 99¢ worth of tea, etc.— and the decision maker can compare all of these packages and know which one he prefers to all the others. Thus, the assumption that there is only a single ultimate good, utility, reduces operationally to the assumption of the *homogeneity of goals,* that is their marginal comparability. If one has two goals, bread and tea, one can compare any amount of each, or any combination of both, and decide which is preferable. The other two underlying assumptions in the strict version of the theory are *infinite calculating ability* and *omniscience.* One needs these two abilities to be able to calculate the outcome of an infinite set of alternatives and the expected value of each outcome.

The assumption of omniscience is not necessary to a maximization model, as Cross [1] among others has shown. Without this assumption, the maximizer has a set of comparable goals, some but not all possible alternatives, and some information about the expected effect of the alternatives on the goals. He then calculates the expected value of each alternative and chooses the one with the highest expected value. But in Cross's version, this simplification introduces a new complication: as each new piece of information comes in, the bargainer must recalculate all his equations, his cost and return curves, and either continue or change his current strategy accordingly. He can also calculate the cost of new information, compare it with the expected returns, and estimate how much time or effort he must expend in getting new information. Cross's version of the maximizing model thus depends even more on the assumption of remarkable calculating ability, since the calculations are done not once but continually.

One can also drop the assumption of extraordinary calculating ability, though in this case the model is no longer mathematical. The decision maker then has several crudely defined alternatives whose consequences he guesses at and evaluates; he then compares the expected consequences two at a time and by a process of elimination finally arrives at the best alternative. This loose version of the theory retains only the assumption of comparability of goals in terms of the homogeneous ultimate good, utility.

A second theory of decision making drops both the assumption of

[1] Cross, *The Economics of Bargaining.*

homogeneous goods and of perfect calculating ability in an attempt to get closer to actual practice without losing theoretical simplicity. This is the tradition of bounded rationality, which goes back to Simon, March, and their followers, and beyond them to John Dewey.[2] In this tradition one assumes first, the *heterogeneity of goods,* that is, an inability or at least a great difficulty of comparing the value of two different goods. If two goods are alternative, so that achieving one means sacrificing the other (for example, peace and national security), one cannot tell how much of one is worth sacrificing to get a given amount of the other. This makes each good almost an absolute, unique value, not expressible in terms of other values.

Second, one assumes that the whole set of available alternatives is not given at the start of decision making. New alternatives may turn up from time to time or may be constructed by modifying old ones. For example, in early July 1914, the alternatives facing the German government were either to let their ally Austria down a third time by offering limited, conditional support or to offer unconditional support. The alternative of a "halt in Belgrade," which the Kaiser and Bethmann–Hollweg found acceptable at the end of July, did not exist in early July. Third, even for the known alternatives, one is not able to calculate the probability of their achieving specific goods, except very crudely. One might be able to say that alternative 1 is likely to achieve good A and unlikely to achieve B, but would not be able to put this in percentages; nor would one be able to say what degree of modification of 1 would increase the probability by any given percent.

The second and third of these assumptions could also be included in a maximizing theory, but not the first. Given heterogeneity of goods, the term "best possible alternative" has no operational meaning, so there is no way of finding it, no way of maximizing. Instead, one searches for an acceptable alternative, one that is "good enough." Since each good represents a qualitatively unique value, one cannot compensate for the sacrifice of one good by extra achievement of a different good. Consequently, each good must be achieved; leaving even one out would be unsatisfactory. An alternative is not acceptable unless it is likely to achieve all goods. In other words, each good is a *constraint* on an acceptable alternative.

Constraints are either positive or negative. A positive constraint is a good that must be achieved by some positive action; we will call such a constraint a "goal." A negative constraint is a good already in existence that must not be damaged or, in other words, a possible evil that must

---

[2] Herbert Simon, *Models of Man* (New York: Wiley, 1957), Ch. 14; James March and H. Simon, *Organizations* (New York: Wiley, 1958), pp. 137–141; John Dewey, *Human Nature and Conduct* (New York: Random House, 1922).

be avoided. A simple decision problem is one in which there is a single goal to be achieved and two or more evils to be avoided, and in which an acceptable alternative is one that achieves the goal and avoids the evils. In another kind of problem one must prevent one evil while avoiding still others.

"Achieving a goal" is not a precise concept since some goals at least can be achieved in varying degree. If degrees of achievement are possible, one needs a criterion that says what degree of achievement is acceptable. The criterion is called the *level of aspiration*. For example, in 1908 Russian foreign minister Izvolsky had one goal, *open the Turkish Straits,* and several constraints, including *avoid alienating Serbia, France, Britain* and *avoid antagonizing Austria.* But the Straits could be opened in varying degrees: one warship could be permitted through every 24 hours, or three ships or more; they could be opened only to Russia, or to all Black Sea countries; or to all countries; and so on. If there were some level, say one ship a day, at which Izvolsky could feel he had effectively opened the Straits for the time being, that would be his level of aspiration. The level could be set in his initial strategy planning based on military advice, but more likely it would be clarified in his mind during initial discussions with other foreign ministers.

A level of aspiration can be revised either upward or downward during or after bargaining. The standard hypothesis, for which there is experimental evidence, is that level of aspiration goes up with success and down with failure. For instance, if Izvolsky had gotten an agreement to allow one Russian ship a day through, he might feel he had essentially succeeded in opening the Straits and could turn his attention to other matters; but the Russian government would probably maintain a latent interest in increasing the number allowed, and would intend to raise the issue at some opportune time. Conversely, if Izvolsky had gotten nowhere in discussions, as actually happened, he might decide he could settle for one ship a week, or even a promise by Britain and Turkey to discuss the question favorably in a year or so.

By extension, some negative constraints can also be satisfied in varying degrees. Thus the constraint *avoid war* seems at first to be absolute: a strategy either leads to war or it does not. But if a proposed strategy involves some small risk of war, the decision maker must ask himself how large a risk is acceptable, and we are back to a relative constraint. Here again the level of acceptability might be set in advance, or more likely one would decide for each proposed strategy whether it posed an acceptable risk of war. One could therefore extend the term *level of aspiration* to all constraints; but since it seems odd to speak of an "aspiration" to achieve a negative constraint, we will confine *level of aspiration* to goals and refer to *level of acceptability* for negative constraint.

If we compare the concept of aspiration level with the maxima and minima of utility theory we see that the maximum and minimum (in game terms, approximately T and P for most games)[3] are the two limits to changes in aspiration level. Initial aspiration level may be set at the maximum or initial bid, though it is usually somewhat below this in the sense that the decision maker does not expect to achieve his full initial bid and will be satisfied with somewhat less. Successive lowering of levels approaches but does not usually reach the limit or minimum. And in fact we found that our bargainers did not decide on their minimum at the beginning of bargaining and in many cases never did decide on a minimum. The minimum is thus an ideal limit concept that is seldom clearly formulated in bargainers' minds. Conversely, the maximum-minimum concepts of utility theory remind us that aspiration levels are in fact changeable, however fixed they may seem at the beginning of bargaining. They also remind us that at times a decision maker may have two simultaneous aspiration levels, a higher or "hope" level and a lower or "satisfactory" level. For instance, in 1948 Stalin hoped (T) to get a cancellation of Western plans for a consolidated West Germany, but at the worst (P) he would at least settle for inclusion of West Berlin in the East Zone. As it happened, he did not even achieve the lower level; the outcome was unsatisfactory, and Berlin remained on the Soviet agenda.

The actual decision procedure varies according to the nature of the available alternatives. If alternatives come in or are constructed one at a time, one simply accepts the first acceptable alternative. If a series of unacceptable alternatives shows up, or if one is unable to construct an acceptable alternative, one concludes that a level of aspiration was too high and lowers it. If the first alternative is acceptable, one suspects that a level of aspiration was too low and wishes it had been set higher. To avoid setting the level too low, one could start with an artificially high level and gradually settle down.

If a set of alternatives is available at the outset, one runs through the set testing each against the constraints. If several acceptable alternatives remain, one raises one or more levels of aspiration and tests the remaining alternatives, continuing this dual process until only one alternative remains. If no acceptable alternatives remain, one can either search for or construct new alternatives, continuing until an acceptable one

---

[3] The reader may wish to be reminded of what these symbols stand for in a game matrix: T=a party's valuation of his initial demand. S=a party's valuation (cost) of accepting the opponent's initial demand. P=the value (cost) for either side of no agreement. R=the value of compromise for either side.

T and S are located in the DC and CD cells of the game matrix, P in the DD cell and R in the CC cell.

appears; or one can lower one or more levels of acceptability or aspiration and test the rejected alternatives again, continuing this dual process until one alternative appears.

A third sort of procedure is necessary if alternatives are not discrete and well-defined but appear as a rather amorphous mass of possibilities. In this case one cannot test alternatives sequentially, since it is not clear where one "alternative" stops and the next one starts. Instead, as Tversky has suggested,[4] one runs the constraints sequentially against the list of possibilities, eliminating everything that does not meet each constraint. The material that is left is acceptable. If more than enough material remains to construct one alternative, one raises a level of aspiration and eliminates some more; if there is not enough material left, one either searches for more or lowers an aspiration level, etc. Tversky calls this "elimination by aspects" in contrast to the more familiar "elimination by alternatives."

In none of these procedures is any complex calculating ability required. However, it is possible to refine the procedures by making more detailed estimates and thus reintroduce some calculation.

Bounded rationality and maximizing are not as incompatible as they appear to be. They can in fact be combined in two opposite ways, by taking one theory as basic and the other as supplementary. One can, first, take maximizing as basic. One can say that decision making is, by definition, a process of finding the best alternative, and the best is the one that promises to achieve the most of various desired goods. However, it is sometimes difficult and perhaps even humanly impossible to find the absolutely best alternative, so that ordinary human decisions fall short of the ideal in various ways. It is impossible to consider *all* alternatives, but a decision maker may consider those two or three that appear most obvious, reasonable, or promising. But this involves using constraints and levels of acceptability to eliminate other alternatives—some are too risky, some too costly, and others do not achieve desired goals. Nor can one consider all possible consequences, but one can consider the more obvious or likely ones. When a particularly bad consequence appears, one can eliminate the alternative or modify it to reduce the likelihood of that consequence occurring; this again involves using acceptability levels to screen alternatives. In short, the maximization equations represent the ideal limit that a good decision approaches as it becomes more careful and exact, while the bounded rationality procedures are more nearly descriptive of actual decisions. If these procedures are used carefully they may enable one to creep up on and approximate the best under difficult conditions.

Consider the use of constraints. Maximization theory states that in

[4] Amos Tversky, "Elimination by Aspects: a Theory of Choice," *Psychological Review,* Vol. 79 (1972), pp. 281–299.

order to find the best alternative one must compare all goods at the margin; but with goods such as peace (avoid war) and security (avoid alienating the indispensable ally) this is indeed difficult. Bounded rationality accepts the difficulty and works with independent, non-comparable constraints, thereby seeming to evade and to perpetuate the problem. However, constraints must actually be compared with each other whenever no acceptable alternative can be found. If there is no alternative that satisfies all constraints, no way to achieve both peace and security, a little bit of one must be given up—one level of acceptability must be lowered—but which one? Making this decision involves comparing the two constraints at one particular level, though not yet at all levels. A similar problem occurs if several acceptable alternatives exist. One must then raise some level of aspiration until all but one alternative is eliminated, and this again involves some comparison of goods. After several such comparisons, the originally incompatible goods will have been brought into some partial preference ordering.

This does not mean that the problem of comparison is solved. Changing aspiration or acceptability levels is a difficult process and may occur only once or twice in a whole crisis, if at all, so that in practice one remains far away from the ideal limits. The maximizing theory, by focusing on the ideal limits, ignores the actual difficulties of comparing goods. The bounded rationality theory, by providing a practical way to deal with these difficulties a little, loses sight of the ideal goal of the whole process. Both theories are necessary.

There is also the question of calculation. Maximization theory states that in order to find the exact optimum settlement one must compute marginal cost and return curves and select the point at which they cross; that is, one must find the point beyond which an improved settlement costs more than it is worth. However, this is an unrealizable ideal, more a definition of "optimum settlement" than a practical procedure for finding one. And if one remembers that the calculations must be repeated each time new information on costs and returns comes in, the idealization is obvious. The bounded rationality theory, on the other hand, provides a simple procedure for approaching the optimum point: one sets an initial level of aspiration by examining similar cases and works out a strategy aiming at that level. If now the opponent is more obstinate than expected, one presently lowers the level and revises the strategy; if he is more accommodating than expected, one raises aspiration level, and so on. After many changes of level one should be close enough to the optimum point. But here again change of aspiration level may occur only once or twice in a whole crisis, so that the approximation to the ideal may be very limited indeed.

The other possible way to combine the two theories is to treat bounded rationality as basic and maximization as auxiliary.[5] One can approach this combination by considering why crises occur at all. They occur because the normal conflict of interest between great powers has become so intense as to produce an intolerable situation for at least one power, and because the attempt of that power to correct the intolerable situation makes things intolerable for one or more other powers. This specific situation is what the crisis is about, and the essential objective for the powers involved is to correct it, to make it tolerable. The objective is not the vague, abstract one of maximizing utility; it is the quite specific one of correcting the intolerable situation. If there are several ways of doing this, some may be better than others, and one certainly prefers the better to the worse. More often the problem is to find even one way; that is, finding one acceptable solution is a necessity, but finding the best possible solution is a luxury.

The bounded rationality theory focuses directly on this central point. Crisis decision making is a search for a strategy that will correct the intolerable situation, that is, a strategy that will preserve or achieve all endangered goods at an acceptable level. It is a search for an acceptable strategy, not a best strategy. When a decision maker cannot find or construct even one acceptable strategy, he does not choose the best of the unacceptable strategies, that is, he does not maximize; he stalls if possible, postponing action and searching for a way out of the intolerable situation.

If stalling is not possible, the actor will choose the best available action, but since this does not yet correct the intolerable situation he will continue searching. For example, in the 1948 Berlin crisis, Stalin's 1949 decision to end the blockade was most probably the best alternative then open to him, so that it maximized his utility. However, it did not solve the problem. One goal, to protect the East Zone against economic and political pressure from the West Zones via West Berlin, was not achieved. The Berlin problem therefore remained on the Soviet agenda, and a whole series of strategies to deal with it was devised and tried out from 1949 to 1958. A similar point could be made for Germany in the 1905 Morocco crisis and for Austria and Russia in the 1908 Bosnia crisis. In each case the search for a way to correct the intolerable situation continued although the crisis was over for the time being.

The maximization theory is relevant in cases where more than one acceptable strategy or solution is available. In such cases an acceptable solution seems assured, and the decision maker can interest himself in achieving a better rather than a worse solution. This involves comparing alternatives, estimating costs and returns, etc., that is, maximiza-

[5] The following discussion is based on Dewey, *Human Nature and Conduct,* pp. 190–194, 199, 212–216.

tion procedures. For example, by August 1911 the Agadir crisis was substantially settled; it was pretty well agreed that France was to have a free hand in Morocco and that Germany was to get substantial compensation from the French Congo, and also that peace and existing alliances were to be preserved. The issue that remained was the maximization issue of how much France would have to pay Germany in compensation.

Note that when bounded rationality is treated as basic rather than as a simplified way to maximize it focuses attention on the underlying conflict and forces one to distinguish between ending the crisis and resolving the underlying conflict.[6]

A third decision theory that has been reemphasized more recently is the "bureaucratic politics" theory.[7] This theory drops the assumption that the decision maker is a unitary actor, i.e., that a single preference function governs decision making. If the decision maker is a government, as in our cases, it is composed of a set of bureaus or departments or ministries with different responsibilities, different resources, different

[6] COMMENT BY SNYDER: I find these last five paragraphs puzzling in the way they mix up the separate notions of finding an "acceptable" resolution of a crisis and settling the underlying issue in conflict. Diesing seems to be saying that bounded rationality is basic because it focuses on finding a settlement of the underlying conflict; maximization is auxiliary because it operates only in resolving the immediate crisis. But this point seems to apply only to the first of the two scenarios; not to the second, where it is reversed. In the first example, a party that has no acceptable alternatives backs down and maximizes by accepting the best of the bad; the crisis is then over but the losing party stays within the bounded rationality paradigm by continuing to search for settlement of the underlying conflict in the future. In the second case, a party (or both parties?) have more than one acceptable alternative and thus find it easy to agree on a general crisis resolution formula by bounded rationality procedures; maximizing then takes over as the parties proceed to bargain out a detailed settlement of the underlying issue. Second, in the first case, crisis resolution is the consequence of one side having superior power; while in the second, power is by implication absent from the settlement process. That is, in the latter case, all constraints, including the "avoid war" constraint, have been met. The parties have tacitly agreed that peace is going to be preserved. But if so, what leverage do the parties have over each other in trying to maximize, to get a "better rather than worse solution"? Diesing's use of the Agadir example is inappropriate because the possibility of war was subjectively present for both Germany and France right up to the final concessions that produced the settlement. Finally, if the parties maximize when they are forced to take less than is "acceptable," and also when they can get more than is merely acceptable, it is unclear why they do not also maximize in the intermediate range, the "range of the acceptable."

Diesing may be onto something here, but it is not clearly developed. The preceding paragraphs in which maximizing is treated as basic and bounded rationality as auxiliary (although I think these labels are misleading) give a much clearer picture of the complementarity of the two theories.

[7] Graham Allison, *The Essence of Decision* (Boston: Little, Brown, 1971); Morton Halperin, *Bureaucratic Politics and Foreign Policy* (Washington, D.C.; Brookings, 1974); Richard Neustadt, *Presidential Power* (New York: Wiley, 1960).

information sources, and variable influence within the government. Each department and subdepartment develops its own preference function by working out an interpretation of its responsibilities and how they contribute to the national interest. It uses its information sources to define problems and to develop preferred strategies and operating procedures, uses its influence to get a preferred strategy adopted officially, and uses its resources—political authority, expertise, contacts—to carry out strategies.

Decision making in this theory is a process of getting one's government officially and actually committed to some bargaining strategy or tactic, and this involves getting the approval of those officials whose approval is needed, officially and actually. In game terms, decision making is a process of building a majority coalition; the strategy is the coalition agreement. (In the limiting case in which one person makes the decision, coalitions form among his advisers.) One builds up a coalition piecemeal, by persuading and bargaining with key departments and officials one by one, offering each an appropriate argument or payment for joining the coalition. The payment might consist of strategy revisions to fit B's definition of the problem and B's goals, or giving C a prominent role in carrying out the strategy, or including D's favored tactic as a preliminary move or a fallback position, or promising E support on some other issue. Some departments with similar goals and preference functions are natural allies, while others may be natural opponents. Over a period of years, semipermanent protocoalitions may develop, perhaps with one coalition generally dominating the government, or perhaps with two coalitions each sponsoring opposing strategies at the same time, trying to form a majority coalition at the expense of the other. There is a strong parallel with the politics of a multipolar international system and the politics of one alliance in a bipolar system.

What constitutes a majority or dominating coalition? *Majority* is perhaps misleading with its connotations of voting and 51 percent. Voting does take place at decision-making meetings, but votes are indicators of personal assent or dissent rather than abstract units to be added up. For instance, at the Warsaw Pact meeting of March 29, 1961 to consider the Berlin problem,[8] there was discussion and a vote on Ulbricht's proposed "wall" tactic. The crucial vote was Khrushchev's abstention, indicating that the tactic could remain under consideration, not the 5–1 vote against Ulbricht that seemed to bury the tactic. Khrushchev was an essential member of any "majority" coalition, though he could not by himself constitute a majority.

The important consideration in coalition formation is not a member's

[8] Cf. Zolling and Bahnsen, *Kalter Winter in August,* pp. 102–104.

vote but his weight, the resources he can bring to a coalition. These consist of his official position plus his personal prestige and influence in the government.[9] A coalition builder will try to get the support of members who can swing key departments—Army, Foreign Office, Treasury—behind his strategy. In particular, it is essential to get the support of a department that would have to carry out the strategy, since its active preference for a different strategy would express itself in sabotage or listless performance. For instance, Ulbricht's disapproval of the refugee-control tactic of stationing inspectors at checkpoints, adopted at the March 29, 1961 meeting, undoubtedly contributed to its failure.

In general, a majority coalition is that portion of the decision-making group that can carry out a strategy without the help of the remaining group members, and if necessary against their active opposition. If one or more members can frustrate the implementation of a strategy by their active opposition, they constitute a blocking coalition or coalitions. Blocking coalitions must be induced to at least abstain, and in some cases their "yes" vote is needed. In the previous example Ulbricht's blocking power was so great—he was in charge of carrying out any strategy decided on—that his "yes" vote was needed. Like Khrushchev, he was an essential member of any majority coalition.

One puts together a majority coalition by lining up enough "yes" votes to produce an organization capable of carrying out a strategy, and by inducing all remaining blocking coalitions to abstain. Since the gaining of assent or abstention involves changing the proposed strategy to make it more acceptable to the new member or abstainer, the strategy may change considerably in the process of building a coalition. And if the demands of potential coalition members are contradictory, as they often are, the changes needed to bring in a new member may alienate an older supporter, who may react by proposing quite different changes aimed at a different eventual coalition. Presently the protocoalition around a developing strategy can break up as the strategy itself grows fragmented. For instance, in Cuba 1962, Acheson was terribly annoyed at the way his military supporters kept modifying his "air strike" strategy so as to alienate the potential support he was trying to draw into his coalition. The military leaders in turn were merely acting defensively,

---

[9] Personal prestige and influence derives from a variety of sources, including recognized expertise concerning the issue or the nature of the opponent, and the central decisionmaker's confidence in one's judgment. For example, in the Cuban case, the influence of Llewellyn Thompson and Charles Bohlen came from their expert knowledge of the Soviets. The influence of Robert Kennedy, Sorensen, and McNamara derived from the fact that they enjoyed the president's confidence. The influence of the Joint Chiefs of Staff was weakened by the president's loss of confidence in them after the Bay of Pigs episode the previous year.

since the changes he was making in *their* "air strike" strategy would exclude them from the majority coalition. Acheson's air strike option was the "surgical" one of striking only at the missile sites; the Joint Chiefs of Staff, following Air Force plans, had a much larger set of targets in mind. And while these protocoalition partners worked at cross purposes, a still different coalition was being assembled by others.

The sponsors of a strategy must therefore estimate whether the strength a new member brings to a coalition—strength for getting the strategy adopted or for carrying it out—outweighs the weakening effect (for their goals) of his desired changes in the strategy. They have to choose between keeping the strategy they want and risk not getting it adopted, and getting a strategy adopted that no longer accomplishes what they want to accomplish. In the previous example the military supporters of Acheson chose the former option, and lost.

One way out of this dilemma is to make all the changes that new members want, thus producing a rather multicolored and even self-contradictory strategy, and then simplifying and unifying the strategy in practice. This dishonorable expedient tacitly reduces the payoff of late joiners and fringe members, particularly those whose support is no longer needed once the strategy has been officially adopted. An example is Austria, 1914, to be discussed later.

Another way out of the dilemma is to minimize the size of the coalition and maximize the abstainers. This device is equivalent to setting up a minority government in a divided Parliament. It preserves the purity of the strategy at the risk of not being able to carry it out or at the risk of interference by the abstainers. An abstention can be secured simply by not consulting someone, leaving him off the committee. Chamberlain used this tactic for most of September 1938, consulting only his inner cabinet plus Ambassador Henderson, and Grey used it in July 1914.

When a strategy is functioning as a coalition agreement, change of strategy is a matter neither of recalculating equations nor of changing aspiration level, but consists rather of renegotiating the coalition agreement. Renegotiation may involve reducing some member's payoff or even dropping a member from the coalition. Since renegotiation can be a difficult, uncertain, and time-consuming process, it will not be undertaken lightly. This fact helps to explain the rigidity of bargaining strategies in the face of negative information that we noted in the previous chapter. The reluctance to change a strategy that is apparently not working is not entirely due to individual irrationality; it is also due to the difficulty of renegotiating the majority coalition—organizational irrationality.

The bureaucratic politics theory has two components, a non-rational and a rational, which are not sharply distinguishable in current versions. The non-rational component is a theory of consciousness, i.e., attitudes and where they come from. It states that the individual's values, beliefs, and cognitive sensitivities are mainly determined by his position in government. For instance, in a typical crisis, military leaders would be sensitive to the specific incidents that might lead to war, would worry about what resources were available to them for carrying out their responsibilities in case of war, would oppose bargaining moves that might put them in a militarily weak position when war broke out. Treasury men would be sensitive to budget and economic effects of proposed moves, such as calling up reserves or guaranteeing an ally's costs during a boycott (Humphrey and Macmillan 1956, Chamberlain 1937). Foreign Office men would be sensitive to the diplomatic consequences of military or fiscal moves, would favor using military moves as components of a diplomatic strategy (Sazonov's partial mobilization in 1914), and would perceive possibilities of a negotiated solution to the crisis. The mechanisms by which an individual's consciousness is adapted to his official role include: (1) selective recruitment: recruits select and are selected by departments whose values and operating procedures are congenial to their personalities; (2) role socialization by colleagues; (3) learning by experience, which is shaped by the information, resources, and responsibilities of a particular department; (4) the rational need to cooperate closely with colleagues and therefore to develop a common cognitive and value orientation.

Government officials are divided into two quite different types of people in this theory. First there is the ordinary department member who has been socialized into the values and beliefs of a particular department and identifies the well-being of his department with the national interest. His activities in the coalition building of which decision making consists are characterized by *partisanship:* he supports the strategy favored by his department. Second there is the central decision maker, usually the prime minister or foreign secretary, plus his allies and assistants. These people have been socialized to feel responsibility for their party or their government as a whole, and identify the good of the party rather than of a department with the national interest. Their experience in office is one of being continually pulled in different directions by their various subordinates, the partisans. Each partisan with access to a central decision maker is continually pressing his case, by presenting selected information, urging selected values, offering slanted interpretations and arguments. The partisan's purpose is to capture the central decision maker for his coalition, that is to get him committed to the favored strategy. Faced with conflicting partisan pulls, the activity of the central decision maker is characterized by *uncom-*

mitted thinking,[10] by a reluctance to be captured by one department to the exclusion of other departments.

A third group, the in-and-outers,[11] occurs rarely in our cases and can be ignored.

The general picture this theory gives of the decision-making process, then, is of partisans maneuvering into alliances and oppositions, each trying to capture the commitment of the central decision maker. The latter, however, avoids committing himself, but mediates between the partisans, suggesting compromises and trying to work out a combination proposal that will satisfy most of the partisans. If he succeeds or if one of his allies or assistants succeeds, the decision has been made.

From our cases we see that this picture, despite the descriptive intent of the writers, is an idealization—more a model of rational bureaucratic decision making than a description of typical behavior. What we find instead is a continual dialectic, conflict, of centrality and partisanship, with the ideal balance rarely achieved. In many cases the central decision maker is himself a partisan, bringing his specialized bureaucratic consciousness and goals with him—finance (Chamberlain), military (Tojo), law (Dulles), agriculture (Khrushchev), or most often diplomacy. This means that a crisis receives a partisan definition from the start, with other points of view either ruled out or forced to disguise and distort themselves. The inadequate access of these points of view means that the favored strategy will be inadequately examined from these points of view; for example the diplomatically dominated strategies of Russia, Austria, and Germany 1914, all suffered from lack of attention to military considerations because the military constituted separate blocking coalitions rather than full members of the dominant coalition.

Another tendency is for the central decision-making group to be captured by a partisan viewpoint and then to exclude other viewpoints from consideration; this apparently occurred in the U.S. government during the Vietnam war. Still another tendency is for the central decision maker to fail at mediation and compromise; we have five or six examples of this type. In this case, bargaining moves are characterized by vacillation and ambiguity as one or another partisan gets into the act and shifts strategy in his desired direction.

The central-partisan dialectic is most acute in those individuals who are intermediate between a bureau and the center. These may be either career officials who have risen to so high a position that they can perceive a larger central responsibility, or they are assistants of

[10] Halperin, *Bureaucratic Politics and Foreign Policy,* pp. 24–25; Steinbruner, *The Cybernetic Theory of Decision,* pp. 128–131.
[11] Halperin, *Bureaucratic Politics,* pp. 19, 89.

the central decision maker who have been appointed to a department to control it for the center—a Robert Kennedy or Lo Jui-Ching. These intermediaries are in constant danger of being captured by the opposing position and of betraying the trust of their old associates. For example, in the late 1950s Lo was appointed head of the Chinese army to control it for the central group, but was persuaded by subordinates and captured for the army viewpoint to his own personal discomfort. Conversely, in the 1890s Delcassé was a French colonial office official who shared the colonialist viewpoint and supported the Fashoda expedition; but when he became foreign minister in 1898 he developed a loyalty to the center, became sensitized to the larger problem of keeping the shaky government from falling and preserving the shaky Russian alliance, and consequently took a stand on Fashoda that must have looked like betrayal to his former colonialist associates.

The rational component of the bureaucratic decision theory has remained implicit in recent accounts.[12] The question here is what would an ideally rational organization be like. One can approach this question by asking whether it is reasonable for officials to act as they do during a decision-making process. Their behavior is non-rational in the sense that it is conditioned by socialization and bureaucratic experience, but is it ever also rational? The answer takes us to the heart of politics, which is concerned with public action and public goods. In order to control or participate in controlling any collective action aimed at a public good, one needs power, authority, influence, however these may be defined. Any politician who wishes to participate in public action is thus faced with the imperative of maintaining or increasing his power, authority, influence. As Sam Rayburn observed, "To be a statesman you have to get elected." This is a rational imperative in the sense that it is a prerequisite for any participation in government.

For the career official, the partisan, this imperative takes two forms: (1) maintain or improve access and influence with the central decision maker; (2) maintain or improve influence with colleagues. These are prerequisites for any partisan success in forming a majority coalition or getting a central figure committed. For the central decision makers, the imperatives are more complex. (1) If the party or the government or the country is to act effectively, its power must be maintained or improved. For the party, this includes getting reelected. (2) A second way to maximize the power of a government is to minimize factional conflict, to get partisans to work together rather than against one

---

[12] For an early attempt to state the rational component, see Paul Diesing, *Reason in Society*, 1962 (reprinted Westport, Conn.: Greenwood Press, 1973), Ch. 5. Cf. also Alexander George, "The Case for Multiple Advocacy in Making Foreign Policy," *American Political Science Review*, 66 (Dec. 1972), pp. 751–795.

another; hence the attempt of central figures to mediate, to find compromises that will be acceptable to all factions, to form a grand coalition as nearly as possible. But in order to so unify the organization, the central figure must represent the whole organization, not a part that is in conflict with other parts; hence the rational necessity to remain basically uncommitted, uncaptured by any partisan group. (3) In order to remain uncommitted, the central figure must insure that no partisan group becomes strong enough to capture or dominate him, and must therefore maintain the influence, access, etc., of weaker departments.

A similar set of imperatives can be worked out with regard to information. Any government official needs influence to act at all, but he also needs information to act effectively on his colleagues and on the world. The partisan needs specialized information relevant to his concerns, and the central group needs multiple sources of information to maintain its independent central position. Information comes through organizational channels, so these information imperatives have implications for how an organization would rationally be structured. An ideally rational organization is one in which partisans have sufficient information and influence to make proposals but in which their influence is so evenly distributed that the central group can both maintain its own independence and the unity of the organization through compromise. This is the ideal that is implicit in the various accounts of bureaucratic politics, disguised as factual descriptions.

The bureaucratic politics theory plainly supplements rather than competes with the utility-maximizing and bounded-rationality theories. It focuses on the internal political imperatives of maintaining and increasing influence and power rather than on the purely intellectual problem of choosing a strategy to deal with an external opportunity or threat. Of course both of these processes are involved in actual decision making. Therefore, one can say that the same decision making behavior can be described as a process of forming and changing coalitions, or as a process of testing alternatives against constraints, lowering aspiration levels, estimating cost, etc. The problem then is to map one theory on to the other, that is to show how a process in one theory can be described as quite a different process in the other theory. A detailed amalgamation of this sort has already been worked out by Gore.[13]

A rather different way of relating the bureaucratic politics theory to the problem-solving theories is to say that the former theory applies best to some cases and the latter theories to other cases. Bureaucratic politics describes decision making as a process of forming a dominant coalition,

---

[13] William Gore, *Administrative Decision-Making* (New York, Wiley, 1964).

but coalition politics requires the participation of at least three people. Also bureaucratic politics involves a conflict between at least two different bureaus or departments, and this again requires a minimum of three participants, including a central decision maker. But some crisis decisions are made by one or two people pretty much on their own—Stalin and Molotov in the 1940s, Dulles and Eisenhower in the 1950s. It would be plausible to suppose that when one or two people make decisions, the problem solving theories apply, when 3+ people—a committee or cabinet—are involved, bureaucratic politics is more relevant. We shall test this possibility presently.

Between these two cases—decision by one or two people and decision by three or more—lies a third case. Decisions may be made by one person, usually a foreign minister, within limits vaguely set by his colleagues. If he oversteps these limits, his colleagues will get involved, perhaps to the point of taking the decision away from him entirely (Delcassé 1905, Izvolsky 1908), perhaps only to modify or even support his decision in their own fashion. As long as he stays within these limits, the foreign secretary can presumably use a rational decision procedure based on his own preference function and the advice of his subordinates, but the potential intervention or support of his colleagues is a bureaucratic background factor that necessarily enters into every step of the process.

A fourth case is also intermediate in a more ambiguous way. This is the case of a central decision maker who is advised by various officials or by a committee—Hitler on September 26–28, 1938 consulting his generals and diplomats, or Kennedy in October 1962 appointing a committee to advise him—but who does not have to take their advice. Plainly, bureaucratic politics is involved in the kind of advice that is given, and in particular the advisers are always trying to improve or preserve their influence with the central decision maker and with each other, but what about the central decision maker? Is he primarily concerned with solving the problem, settling the crisis according to his own preference function and using advice to clarify his own ideas, or is he primarily motivated by bureaucratic considerations and influences? Is his decision focused primarily on dealings and relations with the external opponent, or is it focused primarily on the internal problem of maintaining a proper distribution of influence and a proper consensus in the government? ("Proper distribution" could be defined as that which is most promising for achievement of the top man's total program, of which his aims in a current crisis are only a part.) A plausible argument could be given either way, and the evidence could also be interpreted either way.

1. One bureaucratic imperative for the central figure is "stay in

TABLE 5–1

INCIDENCE OF VARIOUS TYPES OF DECISION-MAKING STRUCTURES

Type of decision-making structure	Number of instances
1. One or two people	9
2. One person within collegial limits	11
3. Central decision-maker with advisers	4
4. Committee	10
5. Divided government	3
6. Don't know	4
Total	41

office." But in September 1938 Hitler was in some danger of being removed from office if he made the wrong decision, and Kennedy in October 1962 believed himself to be in a similar position. A central figure who ignored this imperative, acting as though his hold on office were invulnerable, would be irrational. Second, it is not enough to solve a problem in one's own head; the government, namely those same advisers, must carry out the decision, and that means they must understand and approve it to some extent.

2. The gravity of a crisis, with war an imminent possibility, takes precedence over narrower considerations of influence and office, it can be argued. The central figure must normally be sensitive to bureaucratic considerations, but in a crisis the objective of preserving or promoting vital national interests, while avoiding war, is supreme. Second, the bureaucratic imperatives can simply be included in the problem as additional constraints on an acceptable solution. Thus in the Cuban case the constraints were: get the missiles out, avoid war, maintain alliance ties, stay in office, don't alienate the military and their congressional supporters, etc.

The implication seems to be that this type of case can be described both in problem-solving and in bureaucratic terms.

The relative importance of the bureaucratic politics theory and the problem-solving theories would then seem to depend on the relative frequency of these five types in our cases. Type 1 cases, it would seem, can best be interpreted in problem-solving terms, Types 4 and 5 in bureaucratic terms, and Types 2 and 3 can be interpreted both ways or require a combined interpretations.[14]

[14] Obviously, the type will be determined in part by formal governmental structure, and the rules and roles that go with it. But it is incorrect to associate type 4 with parliamentary cabinet regimes, type 2 with presidential or separation of power structures, and types 1 and 3 with authoritarian regimes, as might be implied at first glance. For example, types 2 and 4 have been characteristic of the Soviet Union in recent years, and types 1 and 3 are often found in parliamentary or presidential structures.

The most prominent characteristic of Table 5–1 is that the categories were found to overlap considerably, forming a continuum rather than discrete types, so a slight shift of boundaries would change the numbers. For example, one instance of Type 2 was Curzon making British policy in 1923 within limits set by the cabinet. In practice these limits would be imposed by the prime minister, Baldwin, and this is not too different from Eisenhower restraining Dulles in the 1950s (Type 1). The difference is that Eisenhower and Dulles were more of a team, working together on a joint strategy, while Curzon made his own policy under the shadow of potential interference by Baldwin. Also Baldwin would not make a move unless other ministers proposed or at least supported it, while Eisenhower and Dulles could act pretty much as they pleased in crisis situations, though there still were some bureaucratic limits.

Another difficulty in the table is that the boundary between cases is pretty arbitrary. For example, the U.S. structure that made decisions in the Lebanon crisis July–August 1958 was the same one that made decisions in the Quemoy crisis August–September 1958 and the Berlin crisis beginning November 1958. Although this could be counted as one instance of a structure, we counted it as three, arbitrarily. In some cases, decision structures changed during a crisis; for instance France in 1904 was probably Type 2, by the onset of the crisis in 1905 was Type 5 (Delcassé vs. Rouvier), and then changed to 2 as Delcassé was forced to resign. Hitler's initial decision to attack Czechoslovakia was apparently made in private (Type 1) since he simply announced it in May 1938, but his September 28 decision not to attack was made after much traffic by advisers through his office (Type 3). Where such changes occurred, we counted the structure that seemed best to characterize the crisis as a whole.

However one counts, the table shows that the bureaucratic politics theory is directly relevant to most of the cases, including Types 2, 3, 4, and 5. The problem-solving theories are presumably relevant to half of the cases, including Types 1, 2, and some of 3.

Type 1, one or two people, includes Hitler, 1938; Stalin–Molotov in 1946, Iran, and 1948, Berlin; Truman–Byrnes in Iran, 1946; Dulles–Eisenhower in 1956 and the three 1958 crises; and Mollet–Pineau, 1956. Type 2 is limited to the pre-World War I cases plus England, 1923. Type 4, decision by committee, includes Britain, 1911; Germany, Austria and Russia, 1914; Britain and France, 1938; United States, 1940–1941; Britain, 1956; and Soviet Union, 1958. Type 5 is an extreme of committee decision making in which two factions are working at cross-purposes, each undoing the work of the other. It includes Germany, 1905; France, 1923; and Japan, 1940; plus brief episodes in other cases. This type is continuous with Type 4; the U.S. government in 1940 was nearly as divided as Japan in 1940, except that committee members did not send secret emissaries to the opponent or make secret pledges to the ally as the Japanese did. Types 1 and 5 are the two opposite extremes for decision structures. Type 3 is mainly United States cases: United States, 1948; United States, 1961; United States, 1962; plus perhaps France, 1914. It could easily be the largest category if one takes "adviser" in the official organizational-chart sense rather than in the political influence sense.

Though the general relevance of the bureaucratic politics theory is established by Table 5–1, there is one major divergence between the theory and our case materials. We find that the ideas and preferences of individuals are determined both by their official position, past and present, and by their personal bias, but that personal bias is much more important than the bureaucratic theorists have recognized. The evidence is the numerous instances in which the same official position is occupied by incumbents with quite different "lines," for instance Forrestal and McNamara, Briand and Poincaré, or Litvinov and Molotov, with their bargaining behavior differing accordingly. The perspectives of heads of government vary over the whole spectrum, from Chamberlain through Kennedy to Hitler. Foreign ministers are mostly hard-line, but there are a good half-dozen instances of middle-line foreign ministers such as Grey, Hull, and Byrnes, and three or four soft-liners like Briand. Foreign offices are also divided, both between hards and softs and on alliance preferences. The British foreign office was mostly anti-German in the period 1904–1914, but there were also highly placed pro-Germans. Moreover, the foreign minister may oppose the consensus of his own department, as Dulles did in Quemoy, 1958.

The military role is the clearest instance of role-derived attitudes and provides a good contrast with other decision-making roles in which personal bias is dominant.

Military representatives support accommodation as often or more often than they support a firm stand. Their preference, however, is based more on their estimates of military preparedness than on personal bias. The primary military role is to fight wars and if they do not believe the resources available to them are sufficient to fight successfully, they will oppose going to the brink. If they do advise apparently "tough" measures, these will often be measures of preparedness that they desire not for diplomatic coercion but simply to increase readiness. A general military tendency is to underestimate their own strength and overestimate the opponent's, a manifestation of the conservatism inherent in the military role.

Another manifestation of the military role is dislike of the manipulation of military force for diplomatic coercion. The use of their forces for "political" purposes is considered a corruption of their role; it diverts and disorganizes forces with respect to their primary mission of war-fighting. Thus the Russian military leaders opposed partial mobilization against Austria in 1914, which was desired by Sazonov as a political show of force, because it would delay general mobilization for war against Germany. When some actual use of force in a crisis is under consideration or after it has been decided upon, there is a military tendency to want to go further than the civilian leadership desires. In Cuba, 1962, the U.S. military leaders were not enthusiastic about the limited move of the naval blockade, and the air strike they favored was much more comprehensive than the "surgical" one the civilian leaders had in mind. The military role counsels "doing it up right" if military force is to be used at all.

However, on the whole military resistance to the "political" use of force has declined in the nuclear age, in the United States at least, because of the need to have coercive options between verbal threats and actual violence. "Doing it up right" in some situations could all too obviously escalate to catastrophe. Also, the non-violent use of force is closely related to the function of deterrence, which has become fully accepted as part of the military role.

Military participation and influence in crisis decision making tends to vary with the imminence of the use of force or the extent of its actual involvement in the crisis. When the action is entirely diplomatic, with war only a contingent possibility, the military role is limited to the relatively passive one of estimating relative strengths—in game model terms, clarifying the P-situation for those who are making bargaining decisions. However, when the use of force is actually being considered, or when force is being used in the crisis in some way, the military typically become much more assertive and influential. In 1914, for example, the German military leaders did not assert themselves strongly until the Russians began mobilizing; then they virtually took over complete control of decision making.

Military influence in crises has tended to increase in the post-1945 nuclear era, as compared, say, to the pre-1914 period, largely because of increased use of military force in non-violent ways as an instrument of coercive diplomacy.

When military representatives do get actively involved in decision making, they tend to focus on the military-strategic interests at stake rather than on intrinsic or reputational interests. For example, in Quemoy, 1958, U.S. military leaders were not so much concerned with demonstrating U.S. resolve as with preserving the morale of Chiang's army—a goal directly related to the defense of Formosa.

Perhaps "line" comes out more prominently in our cases because we are dealing mainly with top decision makers, who have more freedom to express their personal bias and are less subject to role parochialism than lower-level officials. Also, the bureaucratic politics theorists have so far concentrated their attention on the United States in the Cold War period when, as Halperin observes,[15] there was a very considerable hard-line consensus, so that differences within this consensus tended to reflect bureaucratic roles. Perhaps some attention to the multipolar period before 1941, including the United States in 1940, would rectify this omission in the bureaucratic theory. However, there were some personal line differences in the U.S. government even in Berlin, 1961, and Cuba, 1962, which the bureaucratic theorists have played down. The problem is to recognize the interplay between personal line and official position without reducing either one to the other.

INITIAL STRATEGY DECISIONS

Our crisis bargaining decisions fall into two main groups, initial strategy decisions and later decisions. Initial decisions are those that determine the first bargaining moves as the crisis begins. In cases where a crisis developed gradually, the initial strategy may have been adopted six months or a year before the dispute reached crisis proportions. In cases where a crisis began suddenly, the initial strategy decision may have been the one that started the crisis or it may have been the answering decision on how to deal with a challenge. In a few cases, perhaps two or three (Britain, 1905, 1911), there was no initial decision; the state was gradually drawn into a dispute and reacted step by step until it found itself following a strategy.

Later decisions are made after the initial strategy has failed to perform as expected; they produce either modifications of the initial strategy or a complete new strategy. The difference between initial and later decisions is that initial decisions are made before the bargaining process has begun. They therefore have no feedback available from bargaining, and must be based on the initial distribution of hard-line–soft-line biases, bureaucratic biases, theories, and images of the opponent. Later decisions are based partly on feedback and partly on initial biases and images and so are likely to be more realistic and effective than initial decisions, at least for rational decision makers.

An initial decision consists first of defining the problem; second, of setting an objective or objectives whose achievement is judged possible and would constitute a solution to the problem; and third, of selecting or constructing a strategy to achieve the objective.

1. In most of our cases, the problem is defined as a situation in

[15] Halperin, *Bureaucratic Politics*, pp. 11–12.

which the opponent is up to something dangerous or threatening and must be stopped. There are also cases in which the problem is defined as an opportunity for gain that may be frustrated by some opponent. When a state defines the crisis in the former way, we call it defensive; when it defines the situation the latter way, we call it expansionist, following the Gamson and Modigliani classification.[16] In either case one must make an estimate of the opponent's intentions and of his probable reactions to various actions. Since this is an initial decision and no feedback is available, the estimate must necessarily be based on the image of the opponent.

2. Next, the decision maker sets an objective that is regarded as achievable and would resolve the crisis problem. For a defensive power, the objective would probably be to stop the opponent or get him to withdraw his threatening move; for an expansive power the objective would be some specific gain. In some cases both a maximum and a minimum objective may be set. The objective constitutes the T-payoff or T-goal and is often stated in the initial bid. Examples: Nasser must be made to disgorge the Canal; the Cuban missiles must be removed.

3. The strategy for achieving the objective must necessarily be chosen from the set of basic strategic alternatives: $C, CD, DC, D, DE,$ and E. That is, when one is in conflict with an opponent, the conflict can be resolved either by mutual accommodation, by firm diplomatic pressure, by direct attack, or by some combination of these. Examples: C—France, 1905: Germany has some legitimate grievances against us which we must try to satisfy through limited concessions. CD—Soviet Union, 1958: We must try to negotiate a compromise settlement of the Berlin question along something like the following lines, but if the West refuses to negotiate, we will have to establish a settlement unilaterally and insist on it. DC—Britain, 1898: We must absolutely insist that the French leave Fashoda, but once they agree to this, some concessions, perhaps about boundaries, can be negotiated to maintain friendly relations with them. D—West Germany, Berlin, 1958: We must insist on the status quo and make no concessions to the Communists. DE—Austria, 1914: We will make a maximum demand on Serbia and if Serbia does not accept it immediately and completely we will attack. E—Britain–France, 1956: Attack Suez Canal.

In some cases the strategy may be only vaguely outlined, with the tactical details to be worked out as needed, as in the C example above. At the extreme, the strategic decision may consist only of the choice of

---

[16] These terms are roughly equivalent subjectively to the "external" and "internal" precipitants of a crisis which we discussed in Chapter I. Cf. William Gamson and A. Modigliani, *Untangling the Cold War* (Boston: Little, Brown, 1971).

C or *D,* as in the *D* example above. But in other cases, as in the *CD* example above, considerable tactical detail may be worked out in advance, including possible concessions and possible replies to the opponent's countermoves.

We now consider each of these topics in more detail. The first topic, defining the problem, need not be considered as it has already been discussed in the previous chapter in the section on initial images and expectations. We take up first the setting of objectives, second the devising of possible strategies, and third choosing or constructing a strategy from the set of possible strategies. In each case we shall discuss the topic in terms of the concepts of bounded rationality, seeing how far these concepts fit or are relevant to our cases. Then we shall go over the same ground again using the concepts of bureaucratic-coalition politics and seeing how relevant they are. Then we shall put the whole initial decision process together again by means of several detailed examples. The examples will also serve to bring out some of the range of variation found in the cases.

SETTING OBJECTIVES

The bounded rationality theory reminds us that a crisis bargainer always has a plurality of conflicting objectives in a crisis. In addition to the main objective of stopping the opponent or taking control of some territory, there are always other objectives: to maintain peace, to maintain the loyalty of the ally, to maintain or improve bargaining reputation, etc. Each objective is a *constraint* on an acceptable strategy, that is a strategy is acceptable only if it achieves each of the objectives. The process of setting objectives is therefore a process of listing constraints and setting levels of aspiration or acceptability for each constraint.

The constraints are normally opposed to each other, since together they constitute the bargaining dilemmas described in Chapter III.

We classify constraints as primary and secondary. The primary constraints state the main objective (stopping the opponent or making a gain) while the secondary constraints refer to other potential dangers that must be avoided in settling the crisis. A primary constraint may be either negative or positive, while secondary constraints are all negative. Primary constraints are components of T in the game matrix, while secondary constraints are mainly located in P and S.

When the primary constraint is negative, it may be expressed as *correct the intolerable situation*. The crisis has been defined as an intolerable threat or danger brought on by some opponent. The danger may have been brought on by a sudden specific move of an opponent, or it may be a gradually developing danger that is finally judged to have crossed some threshold of intolerability, or it may be a long-standing intolerable situation that the state is now finally strong enough to correct.

The first category includes the 1962 missiles in Cuba; the Soviet note of November 1958; the Berlin blockade of 1948; the Chinese artillery barrage of 1958 interpreted as a prelude to an invasion of Quemoy and Formosa; the 1956 cancellation of U.S. aid for the Aswan Dam; Nasser's subsequent nationalization of the Suez canal; Austria's Balkan moves of 1908, 1912, and 1914, which Russia interpreted as a threat to its influence and reputation; and the sudden German moves of 1905 and 1911 in Morocco, which interrupted France's takeover of Morocco.

The second category includes situations that deteriorate over a period of years until they become finally intolerable and require a drastic remedy. The 1914 Austrian government saw Serb provocations in this manner. Serbia had been sending terrorists and saboteurs into the Empire year after year, stirring unrest; the 1914 assassination was the last straw and the chance finally to end the Serb subversive threat. In 1948, U.S. moves in Germany became intolerable for Stalin: first a refusal to agree on adequate reparations, then a halt even to small deliveries, then the creation of a separate West German zone, and finally a currency reform that could ruin the exhausted East zone. In 1957–1958 Eisenhower saw another disaster building up in the Middle East: first Nasser's pact with the Soviet Union, then Syria lost to the Communists, Turkey threatened, internal aggression in Lebanon, and finally Iraq lost. It was time to save what little remained for the Free World. Similarly for the Soviet Union, the December 1957 NATO agreement to send nuclear missiles to West German territory, even though under U.S. control, may have appeared as the last straw in the military build-up of West Germany and the continuous undermining of East Germany through West Berlin. Given Adenauer's policy of negotiating from strength, his subordinates' demands for German-controlled nuclear weapons, and his goal of recovering the lost Eastern territories, the prospect of German access to nuclear weapons with which to blackmail the Soviet Union was intolerable.

The third category, a long-standing intolerable situation that finally becomes remediable, is best exemplified by German attempts in the 1930s to nullify the Versailles treaty. We have no other clear examples in our cases.

Frequently, a positive goal is mixed in with the negative constraint. The crisis is called into existence by an intolerable situation or grievance, but it soon becomes apparent that if the intolerable situation can be corrected this also opens up the prospect for positive gains. As strategy planning continues, the positive and negative aspects tend to become amalgamated into a single T-goal. For example in Iran, 1945, Stalin's main objective probably was to exclude American oil companies and American influence from the territory immediately adjacent to the Soviet Union's vital oilfields; but if in the process of keeping Americans out he could obtain an exclusive Soviet oil concession and perhaps even a friendly government in northern Iran that would be all to the good. In 1962 the essential U.S. objective was to get the missiles out of Cuba, but the process of getting them out was perceived by some as a good chance to get Castro out too. In 1948 Stalin's most urgent objective may have been to stop the consolidation of West Germany, but the prospect of picking up West Berlin along the way was also attractive. The 1958 Lebanon invasion was designed to stop the spread of Communism in the Middle East, but it was also an opportunity to put some life into the Eisenhower Doctrine and demonstrate U.S. power. Khrushchev's goals in 1958 were generally negative—get rid of the West Berlin cancer and prevent the nuclear armament of West Germany, but there was a positive aspect as well in consolidating and gaining recognition for the Ulbricht regime.

Conversely, the positive goals of the expansionist powers also usually had a negative component, which served at least as a pretext or rationalization for expansionist moves. The 1938 German move in Czechoslovakia was rationalized as correcting the intolerable oppression of Germans by Czechs; ditto for the 1912 Serb expansion into Turkey; the 1908 annexation of Bosnia could be justified as a way of ending subversive hopes for annexation by Serbia; the 1911 German interest in the French Congo could be expressed as the need to avoid the intolerable humiliation that would result from a failure to secure adequate compensation for the French seizure of Morocco.

This mixture of positive and negative components in nearly all cases complicates our original distinction between defensive and expansionist powers. Each bargainer can emphasize the negative constraint on its own strategies and the positive goal of the opponent, picturing itself as the defender or redresser against intolerable moves of the opponent. The disagreement extends to the official and unofficial historians on each side, and there may be a few borderline cases in which disagreement is not easily resolved. In these cases one can merely note that the primary constraint had both positive and negative components.

Postive constraints vary in stringency or absoluteness. The U.S. objective in Cuba, 1962, was absolute, uncompromisable: the missiles had to go whatever the risk or cost. In contrast, the German objective in 1911, "to secure adequate compensation" was highly adjustable. All the other cases lie between these two extremes, although of course there are several cases—e.g., England in Suez, 1956—of objectives that were essentially absolute but had to be given up completely through lack of power to achieve them.

SECONDARY CONSTRAINTS

These are conditions that an acceptable strategy must not infringe, as this would create another intolerable situation. The most common secondary constraint is *Avoid war,* operative in all cases except 1912–1913 Balkans. Another negative constraint is *Avoid alienating the ally,* present in all cases except 1898 and 1948. Less frequent is *Avoid activating a potential opponent,* either a partial ally of the primary opponent or his potential ally. Examples are Germany in 1908, 1911, 1914, and 1938, with reference to Britain. In 1913 Bulgaria's inability to observe this constraint led to disaster, as activated opponents attacked from four directions. A variant is *Avoid activating domestic opposition,* as in the 1958 Quemoy crisis when Dulles had to avoid activating Senate opponents. An occasional soft-line–middle-line constraint is *Don't spoil the negotiating atmosphere,* operative for Britain, 1898 and 1938; United States, 1941; Iran, 1945–1946; Soviet Union, 1960–1961; United States, 1961; and briefly for France, 1905. This implies avoiding acts that would provoke the opponent emotionally, arouse his suspicions, or complicate his domestic political situation.

In addition to these recurrent constraints, there are occasional moral and legal constraints such as Robert Kennedy's *Avoid surprise air strikes.*

The secondary constraints also vary considerably in stringency, ranging from a nearly absolute prohibition to a mild warning of possible danger. For instance, the constraint *Avoid war* presumably meant *Avoid war at all costs* for Chamberlain, 1938, while for Britain, 1898, it went more like *Postpone war until it is clear France will not yield peacefully.* This constraint in fact is an empirical version of P in the game matrices ("avoid P"), which varies greatly in value. In the nuclear age it is very strong for the nuclear powers (but see below, p. 507) while before 1914 it was rather moderate. The constraint *Avoid alienating the ally* was crucial for France in 1914 toward Russia and for Beneš in 1938 toward Britain, important for Britain in 1906 and 1911 toward France, but of minor importance for the United States in 1958 toward Chamoun in Lebanon. It is an empirical version of P in alliance matrices. Generally it is more important in multipolar crises and less important in bipolar ones.

We now shift to the concepts of bureaucratic politics. As soon as we look inside a government we see that a constraint is not simply set by "the government"; it is emphasized, pushed, by some member or faction and merely accepted by other members and factions. In a few cases a constraint may be of equal importance for all members of the decision-making group, but normally each constraint will be pushed by one part of the group and accepted by the other parts.

The various types of decision-making structures differ in characteristic ways in the distribution of constraints. In Type 2 structures there is usually one constraint that is accepted by the whole government but that is less important to the top man, the foreign minister, than to his colleagues. This constraint then sets the bureaucratic limits on his freedom: if he does not take the constraint as seriously as his colleagues would like, they will get into the action, perhaps even taking the decision away from him. This constraint then is mainly an external one for the foreign minister, and when he is in difficulty he is tempted to conceal parts of his strategy from his colleagues partly to evade the constraint. Examples: For Britain, 1905–1914, a variant of the *Avoid war* constraint was *Avoid alliance commitments that might drag Britain into a European war*. This constraint was of great importance to the left-wing Campbell–Bannerman faction but of little importance to Grey and the foreign office. It seriously limited Grey in his choice of tactics, and several times he tried to make tacit semi-commitments that would reassure the French and deter the Germans without being recognized as such by his radical colleagues. He was not always successful, and in 1911 especially his colleagues did get involved. For Russia in 1908 a variant of the *Avoid alienating the ally* constraint was *Avoid alienating Serbia*. This constraint was of secondary importance for Izvolsky, who was primarily interested in getting the Straits opened. He found that he could get Austrian support on the Straits in return for Russian support on the annexation of Bosnia, which was a bargain for him; but Serbia opposed the annexation bitterly and expected Russian support. When word of Izvolsky's bargain got back to St. Petersburg, there was a commotion; he had violated the alliance constraint, and the play was taken away from him.

In Types 3 and 4 structures all members accept the same constraints, with minor exceptions, but vary in the importance they attach to a constraint. Type 5 structures are characterized by strong disagreement on one or more constraints and goals. For example in 1940–1941 Japan, *Avoid war with the United States* was very important to a faction headed by the prime minister but of little importance to the army. The army's goal was *Pacify China,* which was of little interest to the other groups. The foreign minister's constraint *Avoid alienating the German ally* was barely shared by the others; when it took the form *Attack Singapore* and later *Invade Siberia* at Hitler's urging, the others lost interest completely. The navy's primary constraint was *Protect the Sumatran oil source,* which was important but secondary for the other factions.

The importance of a constraint to an official depends partly on his position in the government and partly on his personal bias. *Avoid war* is primarily a soft-line constraint though of course also accepted by middle- and hard-liners. The difference between soft and hard is more in the estimation of the degree of war risk than in acceptance of the constraint. *Avoid spoiling the negotiating atmosphere* is a soft-line–middle-line constraint. *Avoid alienating the ally* is a more specialized constraint usually urged on the group by the foreign minister—Grey, Matsuoka, Rusk—or some other spokesman closely involved in alliance relations. Thus in 1941 when Matsuoka was finessed out of office the alliance constraint went with him, thereby enlarging the Japanese strategy space. Hard-liners will also emphasize this constraint because it is a component of war preparedness; soft-liners are more likely to be suspicious of the ally as a source of entanglement leading to war.

The primary constraint, when it is negative, i.e., perceived as defensive, is the one most likely to be accepted equally by all factions. In 1962, United States, *Get the missiles out of Cuba;* in 1961, Soviet Union, *Protect East Germany;* in 1956, Britain, *Stop Nasser;* in 1940, United States, *Stop Japanese expansion;* in 1937, Britain, *Settle with Hitler,* were accepted equally by all. The disagreements were on the relative importance of other constraints. But a positive primary constraint, a goal, is by no means equally shared. In 1898 the French goal of expansion into the Nile valley was a Colonial Office goal, and in 1911 the German interest in the Congo was urged by the colonialist faction and rejected by the anticolonialist faction. In 1940 the Japanese expansion into China was an army goal. Thus, an expansionist faction in a government can win if it manages to get government attention focused on a negative constraint, such as stopping the opponent or avoiding humiliation, and plays down its expansionist goal. Thus in 1898 the French colonialist emphasis was on not letting "the British bully us," rather than on gaining a foothold in the Nile valley. Similarly, in 1905 and 1911 the German hard-liners stressed avoiding humiliation at French hands, rather than picking up real estate in Morocco and the Congo.

LISTING POSSIBLE STRATEGIES

Once the constraints on an acceptable strategy are set, it is necessary either to construct or to choose an acceptable strategy. In either case one needs materials to choose from or work with, a list of possible strategies or parts of strategies. There are two subheads to this topic: (1) Where do possible strategies and tactics come from? The various decision theories all postulate that a possible strategy must somehow be invented or found, and that it must then be brought to the attention of the central decision makers. It is also plausible to postulate that if the number of possibilities is large, there should be some sort of preliminary scanning and filtering mechanism to reduce the initial possibilities to a small number, say three or four. (2) How many possibilities are left for final choice? The maximization theory and the bureaucratic theory both assert that a decision cannot be rational unless at least two alternatives are considered seriously, and three to five alternatives are better than two. The bounded rationality theory asserts that it is possible to be rational after a fashion with only one alternative, though a plurality of options is preferable.

1. Source of Strategies.

The most obvious source of possibilities for a bounded rationality theory is the set of logical possibilities present in the situation. If a country is looking for allies to strengthen its position in a multipolar system, there are only a few countries available; if it is looking for a way to stop an opponent, the only possibilities are accommodation, coercion, attack (C, D, E), or some combination of these, although there may be several empirical variants of each. We have several examples of this obvious process. In 1900 when Britain, weakened by the Boer war, decided to work toward détente and, if possible, alliance with one or more of its current opponents there were four main possibilities: Germany, France, Russia, and Japan. France was a doubtful possibility because of the recent Fashoda crisis, so the other three possibilities were tried first, with the 1902 alliance with Japan as the result. Since this alliance applied only to the Far East, Britain continued the search in the European area, turning next to France.

In our crisis cases, the outstanding case in which all logical alternatives were considered was the Cuban missile crisis, when the United States considered six possibilities, although three—do nothing and diplomatic approaches to Khrushchev or Castro—were dropped rather quickly. Also in the Berlin, 1961, case several options were weighed: negotiate, refuse to negotiate, or a mixture—stand firm on some things and negotiate accommodatively on others.

These examples are atypical, however. Usually, most possibilities are either ignored or quickly eliminated as unfeasible or ineffective by preliminary scanning, and only a very few are seriously considered.

The bounded rationality theory has a second mechanism to accomplish this task of preliminary selection. It is proposed that past strategies and their outcomes are preserved in organizational memory, with strategies classified according to the type of problem to which they are suited. A strategy that has succeeded in solving some problem in the past is given a positive rating for that type of problem, while a strategy that has failed in the past is given a negative rating. Presumably when a crisis occurs, the decision maker defines the crisis as a certain type of problem; he then calls the list for that problem from organizational memory and notes which strategies have succeeded with that type of problem and which have failed. Failed strategies are excluded from consideration and successful strategies are put on the list of possibilities to be considered further.

The most familiar example of this sort of process is the Munich syndrome. A specific intolerable move, for instance Nasser's sudden nationalization of the Suez Canal, is classified as an instance of Hitler-type aggression. It is then noted that, in the 1938 instance of this sort of problem, a C strategy led to the Munich fiasco; therefore C or even mixed strategies are ruled out, and only D and E strategies are considered. The opposite is the 1914 syndrome—the belief held by Chamberlain in 1938 and Macmillan in 1958 that World War I might not have occurred if the leaders of major powers had been able to get together at a conference in time—which produces a preference for C strategies.

We have several examples where successful strategies were tried again in the next similar crisis and unsuccessful strategies were excluded from consideration. The 1914 Austro–German fait accompli strategy was a repeat of Aehrenthal's 1908 strategy on Bosnia. In 1908 a fait accompli had succeeded in bypassing Russian objections, so the same results were expected again.[17] Russia, however, had yielded then only out of military weakness. Now that it was stronger it dropped the C strategy of conciliation and conference negotiation that had failed in 1909 and 1913, and shifted to D. In Britain, Grey was preparing his favorite "restrain allies and hold a conference" strategy, which had worked in the 1909 Morocco agreement and especially in the 1912–1913 Balkan conference that he had chaired with outstanding skill. He expected that Germany would again restrain Austria as in 1912–1913 and thus contribute to his success. Germany, however, had had enough of conferences, having lost completely in 1906 and gained nothing in 1909. Moreover, the restraint of Austria in 1912–1913 had cost Germany dearly in alliance solidarity, and it was not disposed to weaken its only alliance still further for the sake of the dubious gain of another Balkan stalemate. The 1922 French threat to occupy the Ruhr was a repeat of a similar 1921 threat that had succeeded in getting Germany to agree to reparations payments; but in 1922–1923 Germany resisted, depending on a continuation of British support which had been weakened in July and withdrawn after a change of British government in October 1922. In 1960 the United States was polishing up its "airlift" response to the expected Second Berlin Blockade; but the Soviet Union had had enough of blockades after the 1949 fiasco and was determined not to make that mistake again, in spite of

17 Bernadotte Schmitt, *The Coming of the War, 1914*, Vol. 1, p. 359.

Ulbricht's pleas for a little action. In 1939 Hitler again adopted the attack strategy that had been successful against Austria and was planned against Czechoslovakia; he expected Britain and France to back down again, not realizing that they were dropping the "appeasement" strategy after it had twice failed to appease.

The miscalculations and upsets in the above cases result from the tendency to treat a successful strategy as somehow having an inherent virtue, rather than as owing its success to a particular combination of circumstances not likely to be repeated.

There are also two or three counterexamples, in which an unsuccessful strategy is repeated. As we examine the positive instances we see that while they confirm the descriptive validity of the bounded rationality theory, they disconfirm it prescriptively. In the theory it is rational to repeat a successful strategy; in our cases it is irrational. The bounded rationality theory was developed through the study of routine problems characterized by constant rules, known goals, and a predictable problem-situation: chess, geometry, pricing and ordering decisions in a department store, relocation of a factory, etc. Crises are what Reitman calls "ill-defined problems" having none of the above characteristics.[18] History is not only more complex than chess or geometry, it is qualitatively different in that it never repeats itself. The use of historical analogy to deduce mechanically a proposed strategy is always irrational insofar as it obscures the new features of the present bargaining problem. Consequently those statesmen who reason deductively from historical analogies do indeed follow the bounded rationality theory, but their reasoning is irrational, while those who try to deal with a crisis in its own terms are more likely to be rational.[19]

The bureaucratic politics theory throws more light on the source of strategic possibilities by clarifying the "organizational memory" concept. It reminds us that an organization's memory exists in the standard operating procedures and contingency plans of its partisan components plus the biased personal memory of its central members. "Calling a list of possibilities from organizational memory" consists of a meeting or meetings in which partisan leaders push the favored strategy and tactics of their department. From this standpoint it makes little difference whether a strategy has succeeded or failed before; the crucial question is whether its supporters still have influence. Sponsoring a losing strategy may result in loss of influence, but not so great a loss that the sponsoring

[18] Walter Reitman, *Cognition and Thought: An Information Processing Approach* (New York: Wiley, 1965).

[19] We do not mean to say that historical knowledge in general is irrelevant or dangerous for crisis decision making, only that decision makers in our cases do not use it well. Robert Jervis has stressed the dangers of unsophisticated application of historical analogies in *Perception and Misperception,* Ch. 6.

department is no longer consulted; and one can always argue that the loss was due to special circumstances, including the crippling amendments added by opponents of the strategy, so that it is sure to win this time. Such arguments may not be enough to get a losing strategy adopted a second and especially a third time, but they can be sufficient to get it considered again, which is our present topic.

The bureaucratic theory can account for all the examples of strategy consideration mentioned earlier, including the ones that do not fit the bounded rationality theory. First, the few instances in which a country scanned the logical possibilities for détente and alliance are explained without reference to logic. Britain considered the German, Russian, and French alternatives because there were supporters of each alternative in the government; similarly the German government contained advocates of friendship with Britain, Russia, and France. In the Cuban and Berlin crises, each alternative seriously considered had its sponsors. It may be that each option has supporters in the government because the options are logical possibilities, in which case the two theories supplement each other.

Second, the few instances when an unsuccessful strategy was adopted a second and third time can be explained by the continued presence of the strategy's supporters in the government. For example, the continuation of Britain's C strategy until spring 1939 is explained by Chamberlain and his supporters' continued influence in the government. Failure of the strategy did not convince Chamberlain to shift to D, even in 1940; instead it gradually alienated marginal supporters and encouraged opponents to oppose Chamberlain more actively.

The continued consideration and use of a successful strategy is explained in the same fashion; the success or failure of a strategy makes little difference to its continued availability as a possible strategy. An interesting instance is the disastrous German reliance on British support in 1923, after the support had been clearly withdrawn in October 1922. The reliance continued because its sponsors were still in office. Such instances suggest that the continued consideration and use of a successful strategy after the conditions for its success have changed is simply a matter of bureaucratic inertia. They are not instances of bounded rationality (or irrationality), and count against that theory rather than for it.

The few cases in which an unsuccessful strategy is eliminated from consideration or at least not adopted again are explained in part as due to change in personnel. Examples: Germany, 1906–1914 (hold a conference); Soviet Union, 1949–58 (blockade); Russia, 1909–1914 (yield to threats); Britain, 1938–1939 (appease). One cause of change in personnel, however, is that marginal supporters of a strategy react rationally to its failure and turn against it. The bureaucratic theory does, after all, allow for a small amount of individual rationality. People do learn from experience and do stop supporting a strategy that has failed. What the theory asserts is that this sort of rational thinking is a marginal phenomenon. It is always the marginal supporters of a failing strategy who turn against it first; the most committed supporters, the Chamberlains and Rostows, continue to argue that the strategy will succeed next time until they are finally removed from office.

Finally, the bureaucratic theory calls attention to a few interesting instances in which entirely inappropriate, illogical tactics are considered and perhaps even adopted. The most discussed example is from the Cuban case: the committee was "calling organizational memory" for a list of possible tactics for getting the missiles out, and the Pentagon responded with a plan to overthrow Castro, left over from 1961. Bureaucratically the explanation for the Pentagon proposal is simple: there were no contingency plans for Cuban missiles because no such things had ever existed, but there was an invasion plan because that was an issue in 1960–1961 *and because the sponsors of invasion were still in office*. Another example is Germany 1914. Germany had adopted a *D* strategy of deterring Russia, and needed a military tactic in case the Russian bluff extended to the point of mobilization. The logical tactic would be massing troops on the Russian border, but the military instead came up with the Schlieffen Plan, which was all they had available in the mobilization category (and all they wished to have). This plan involved attack rather than deterrence, and against a different country at that, but it was accepted. A reverse example from 1914 is the consideration given by British and German diplomats to a "Halt in Belgrade" tactic that did not even exist as a possibility. The Austrian military were planning to attack through Bosnia and so could not even reach Belgrade, let alone halt there. The point of these examples is that the source of possible strategies and tactics is not logic but contingency plans, standard operating procedures, and personal biases of officials.

In summary, the bureaucratic theory gives an excellent account of the immediate source of possible strategies: they come from people in office, and from the biases that stem from the roles and personalities of these people. This account is supported by all the instances in our cases. The bounded rationality theory does moderately well. It provides two principles, that possible strategies come from the logical possibilities of the situation, and that the strategies considered are those that have been successful in the past. When treated as descriptive principles, each receives some empirical support and some disconfirmation. However, the second principle is disconfirmed prescriptively—i.e., when statesmen in our cases follow this principle, they act irrationally by failing to discriminate adequately between past cases and the present crisis. The implication seems to be that the ultimate source of strategies may well be the set of logical possibilities inherent in the international situation, but this logic has to become effective through the varied sensitivities and biases of officials and departments, who respond to it only slowly and unevenly.

2. How Many Strategies are made Available for Serious Consideration?

According to the maximization theory an alternative cannot be called the best one unless it has somehow been selected from an infinite set of possibilities. This can be done by preliminary scanning that selects the two or three possibilities that dominate all the rest, and by then carefully comparing these with each other. In the simpler and more realistic version of the theory one drops the infinite set and the claim that an alternative is the absolute best; instead one postulates a small set of plausible alternatives that are compared with one another to yield a "best of the set." In either case an alternative cannot even be called better, let alone best, if it is not compared with at least one other alternative.

The bureaucratic theorists apparently agree that a decision is not rational unless at least two alternatives, and preferably more, are considered seriously.[20] Their argument is that unless a second alternative is available, that is, supported and pushed by some part of the bureaucracy, there is no way for the central decision maker to get loose from a strategy that is failing. If the whole government has been committed and involved in a strategy, the sheer inertia would prevent change in less than several years. Nor would there be any clear operational concept of an alternative strategy unless operational details had been worked out in some department.

According to the bounded rationality theory it is not necessary to consider more than one alternative to be rational. The "best" alternative is a chimera, and one should be satisfied with an acceptable alternative. But one can construct an acceptable alternative piecemeal by checking it successively against each constraint and patching it up each time it fails to satisfy some constraint. It is probably easier to do this if one starts with two or three moderately plausible alternatives, because one can take the strong parts of each alternative and glue them together to make something better than each taken separately. But the job can be done with only one strategic alternative, if one has a sizable set of tactics with which to work.[21]

[20] George, "The Case for Multiple Advocacy in Making Foreign Policy," *American Political Science Review*, pp. 751–795.

[21] Note that we are merely stating the three theories here, not asserting their empirical correctness.

TABLE 5–2

NUMBER OF STRATEGIES CONSIDERED BY DECISION UNIT

Number of strategies considered	Decision units
Two or more	15
One	13
None (Britain 1905, 1911) (cf. p. 361)	2
Don't Know (chiefly Soviet Union and China)	10
Total	40

All three theories agree that a decision is more likely to be rational if it begins with at least two alternatives.

The issue then is, are initial strategic decisions made by choosing one from a set of two or more alternative strategies (*C, CD, D, DE, E* or variants of these)? Or does the decision unit limit itself to one alternative from the start?

The answer seems to be "about half and half."

If we factor these cases by type of decision-making structure we get the following results:

TABLE 5–3

NUMBER OF STRATEGIES CONSIDERED BY VARIOUS TYPES OF DECISION UNIT

Decision unit types	Number of strategies considered		
	0	1	2+
Types 1, 2	2	12	2
Types 3, 4, 5	0	1	13

Types 1 and 2 involve decision by one or two people, while Types 3, 4, and 5 are cabinet or committee or bureaucratic decisions.

Table 5–3 asserts that when decisions are made by one or two people only one alternative is considered, while if three or more are involved at the top of the structure a plurality of alternatives is considered.[22] We are now in a position to explain Table 5–2. When one person or a two-person team is in charge, a non-decision in Bachrach and Baratz's sense occurs. That is, the "line" bias of the decision maker rules out all but one kind of strategy from the start. This bias can be rationalized by historical analogies or by theories—for instance Dulles advising a

---

[22] By "considered" we mean explicitly and seriously considered—i.e., actually articulated, tested against constraints, compared with other alternatives, etc. It might be argued that in explicitly considering and then adopting only one strategy, say, "stand firm," decision makers implicitly consider and reject its opposite, "yield" or "make concessions." However, this interpretation does not fit any of the theories we are testing, which say that for an alternative to be "considered" it must at least be articulated and discussed.

doubter to read Stalin's *Problems of Leninism* (1924) to understand Soviet behavior of the mid-fifties. It can also be rationalized bureaucratically by having committees prepare reports advocating the favored strategy, holding formal meetings with pseudo-discussion to ratify what has already been decided, etc. When a plurality of people is involved at the top, their varying biases insure that a plurality of alternatives will be considered seriously.

This conclusion is not as firm as it seems from the table. The data we have are mainly public data—cabinet minutes, records of conversations, messages, etc. A committee decision-process usually generates a record that eventually is made public, while an individual's decision is private and may never be recorded. Some private thoughts are recorded in memoirs and private letters—Chamberlain's letters to his sister for instance—but not all of our top men left memoirs, and those who did must have omitted and distorted many events. Consequently when a committee considered two or more alternatives, they went into the record and eventually into our case study, but Type 1 and 2 decision makers may also have considered alternatives without leaving any record of the fact. They may even have considered several alternatives subconsciously. Or their consideration of alternative strategies may have occurred years earlier when they were working out their beliefs and images. What we can say is that if Type 1 and 2 decision makers did consider two or more alternative strategies at the beginning of a crisis, the deliberation was brief, private, and sketchy, since these men appear in the public record with their minds already made up.

The conclusion seems to be that if there is any rational procedure at all in the Type 1 and 2 cases it is of the bounded rationality type in which a strategy is constructed according to specifications, within narrow limits. However, there may be some unrecorded choices among alternative tactics. The Types 3, 4, and 5 cases could be rational either in the form of comparison and choice or through construction of a strategy. In either case it is clear that committee structures (3, 4, and 5) are superior to individualized structures in the number of alternative strategies they make available for decision.

CHOOSING OR CONSTRUCTING A STRATEGY

Because of the scarcity of evidence on individual decision making, Types 1 and 2, we must consider mainly Types 3, 4, and 5 cases in this section. The issue now is, how is a strategic decision finally made? According to the maximization theory, the utilities of each alternative are added up and the alternative with the largest total is chosen. Or more crudely, the advantages and disadvantages of each alternative are listed, and the list with the largest balance of advantage over disadvantge is chosen. According to the bounded rationality theory each alternative is tested against the set of constraints, and an alternative that fails to satisfy all constraints is rejected. If an alternative satisfies all constraints, it is accepted. If no acceptable alternative is found, one of the unacceptable alternatives is improved at its weak points until it meets all specifications. According to the bureaucratic theory a choice is made through coalition-building. The search for an acceptable strategy is actually the construction of a majority coalition; as soon as a majority has been formed the decision has been made.

Our conclusions about initial strategy decisions are:

1. In most Type 3, 4, and 5 cases no procedurally rational decision in any of the three senses is made.

2. In those few cases where something like a rational decision occurs the bounded rationality theory most accurately describes the intellectual procedures used. This disconfirms our original hypothesis that bounded rationality would mainly apply to Type 1 and 2 structures.

3. There is no support for the utility maximizing model in its ideal-type version, though we do find a few instances of its crude approximation.

4. There is some evidence of coalition-building, but not much—though of course coalition processes could have been occurring beneath the surface so that they do not appear in data such as cabinet minutes and memos. Where coalition-building occurs, the coalition account is an alternative version of the strategy-construction account; the two theories supplement each other. The concept of coalition-building is more useful in interpreting some cases in which no decision occurred. These are cases in which continuous attempts to form majority coalitions all failed.

Table 5–4 says that a committee that is initially divided on strategy

TABLE 5–4

CHOICES FROM 2+ ALTERNATIVES

Methods of Decision	Decision units considering two or more alternatives	
No choice: vacillation, stall, self-defeating compromise	(5)	Germany 1905 France 1938 United States 1940, 1948 Japan 1940
Choice by bureaucratic political maneuvering	(4)	France 1905, 1911 Austria, 1914 United States 1973
Choice by rational discussion	(4)	Britain 1922, 1938, 1956 United States 1962
Total	13	

usually reaches decisions either by vacillation, postponement, an ambiguous, meaningless compromise that evaporates in practice, or one faction outmaneuvers the other and pushes its view through without serious discussion of alternatives. For instance in France 1905 the division between Delcassé (*D*) and Rouvier (*C*) was resolved by Rouvier's maneuvering Delcassé out of the cabinet, and in 1911 secret emissaries were used to bypass cabinet opposition. Only in a minority of cases was a procedurally rational decision reached. There is also circumstantial evidence of procedural rationality in some of the "Don't Know" cases, such as Soviet Union, Berlin, 1958. The United States 1962 Cuba case, which appears prominently in the decision-making literature, is extremely atypical in the number of alternatives considered, in the amount of deliberation, and in the complex consistency of the decision.

If we follow our committee structures (Types 3, 4, and 5) over time there is further evidence of procedural irrationality. A committee often grows more divided; when the disunity becomes intolerable, one faction expels the member or members farthest from it and reestablishes a tolerable degree of disunity. We have five instances of this, and three counterinstances of committees' maintaining a steady level of disunity over a year or more. Irving Janis's "groupthink" suggestion [23] that committees develop an artificial unanimity by non-rational psychological pressures is only half the picture: the surface unity covers and is stimulated by a structural tendency to disunity punctuated by expulsion of dissenters. Janis's example, U.S. decision making in the Vietnam war, illustrates both groupthink and its underlying opposite. In addition Janis's example is a Type 3 structure; it is doubtful whether his argument applies to Types 4 and 5.

The typical weakness of Type 3, 4, and 5 structures is the opposite of the typical weakness of Type 1 and 2 structures. The weakness of committees is disunity; a self-consistent decision cannot be made, or cannot be made to stick, or is reached through maneuvering and expulsion of dissenters. The weakness of individualized structures is narrowness; a decision is made, but on a basis of the exclusion of most possibilities at the outset. However, in a small minority of cases both these weaknesses can be overcome and a rational, effective decision achieved.

We have now narrowed our empirical base down to four cases of bounded rational decision making by committee: Britain, 1922, 1938, and 1956; the United States, 1962. Of these four, the chosen strategy was successful two times and disastrously unsuccessful two times. The reader may by now wonder whether there is any point in investigating the rationality of initial decisions further; they are, on the whole, not

[23] Irving Janis, "Groupthink," *Psychology Today* (1971), pp. 43–76.

rational. Rationality becomes prominent only in the revising or replacing of strategy, based on information feedback. However, when we analyze the procedures that occur in these four cases we can see that they also occur in some of the other cases, though less successfully. Also there is indirect evidence of rationality in some of the Don't Know cases and the Type 1 and 2 cases. The limitation, therefore, is partly in our data rather than in what actually happened.

In two of the four rational cases a sequential testing of alternatives against constraints seems to have occurred. There were two initial possibilities; one failed the test, and the other was judged acceptable, more by default than by much testing. The committee seems to have said, "*A* is unacceptable, so we are left with *B*." It then attempted to work out tactics that would make *B* acceptable. In a third case, the British discussions of March 18–22, 1938, the same procedure was followed but much more carefully and thoroughly.[24] Of the three alternatives considered by the mainly soft-line cabinet, No. 1, a grand alliance against Germany (*D*), was immediately rejected as unfeasible; No. 2, firm commitment to Czechoslovakia (*D*), was rejected on three grounds: it would not save Czechoslovakia from destruction, it would not avoid war and would in fact provoke an otherwise peaceful Germany into starting a world war that Britain was likely to lose, and it would probably break up the Commonwealth. The third alternative, appeasement (*C*), also had possible unacceptable consequences, such as weakening the alliance with France, and much discussion was devoted to estimating their likelihood and examining possible ways to prevent their occurrence. This produced some tactical revision of the strategy. There was also considerable search for additional alternative strategies and tactics. Having found no acceptable alternatives the cabinet concluded that No. 3 was the best available alternative; it was in fact the only acceptable one. In the fourth case, Cuba, 1962, six alternatives were tested, and all failed by at least one constraint. Then coalition politics took over: two protocoalitions, each united behind one alternative, tried to improve their alternative until it became acceptable to a majority. The final choice combined components of the two favored strategies, plus other changes. One could also interpret this case as a crude approximation to maximization procedures. One could argue that after all but two alternatives were eliminated by sequential testing against constraints, the remaining two—blockade and air strike—were compared in terms of estimated costs, risks, and effectiveness, and the presumed best one, the blockade, was selected.[25] The British Munich decision could also be interpreted in this fashion.

---

[24] Middlemas, *Diplomacy of Illusion,* pp. 184–197; Ian Colvin, *The Chamberlain Cabinet* (New York: Taplinger, 1971), pp. 108–114.

[25] Sorenson, *Kennedy,* p. 782.

If we use the Cuban case as a guide we find a few examples from the Don't Know category that seem to have followed a similar procedure. That is, the adopted strategy seems to have been constructed to satisfy a set of constraints and also to satisfy the committee members supporting those constraints. There are also cases in which a similar procedure was followed but failed to produce an acceptable strategy and a majority coalition. Some of these cases will be interpreted presently.

We turn now to examples, beginning with perhaps the wisest of all our initial decisions, Britain 1922. On July 15 Lloyd George asked his cabinet colleagues whether there was any way to continue the British strategy of economic aid to Germany, aimed at German recovery and reintegration. This was D in Leader, since France opposed economic aid and insisted on ruinous reparations. Given the strong French opposition manifested at the recently failed Genoa conference and the alliance constraint *Maintain the French alliance,* there was no way to help Germany officially without endangering the alliance. A private bank loan probably could not be arranged either. Since D could not be continued the cabinet chose C, letting France have its way for a while. Perhaps in the course of events the French would come to see that their strategy was not so good after all, at which time Britain might be able to do something (D).

This is one of the three cases in which a committee (Type 4) examined two or more alternatives and chose one. The procedure follows the bounded rationality scheme, and no information about bureaucratic politics is available.

Our next example, Austria, 1914, illustrates a committee arriving at a decision through parliamentary maneuvering without discussion. The hard-line group, including Foreign Minister Berchtold and War Minister Conrad, had two constraints: *Neutralize the Serbian threat* and *Avoid war with Russia.* Berchtold the diplomat was also sensitive to a third constraint, *Avoid activating France and Britain* by a too obviously aggressive move. To meet the first constraint Conrad the military man favored an E strategy, surprise attack; but Berchtold feared that such an undiplomatic action would violate constraint 3 and preferred an ultimatum followed by a properly declared war (DE). Both of these hard-liners felt that constraint 2 could be met by calling on the German ally to deter Russia. Since the game was Bully, with Germany–Austria the Bully and Russia Chicken, a German threat would be sufficient to deter Russia.

The opposition protocoalition was led by Tisza, the Hungarian premier, weakly supported by Sturgkh, the Austrian premier. Tisza felt the same three constraints as Berchtold, except that 3 read *Avoid activating Romania* with its strong claim on Transylvania. Tisza felt that any attack on Serbia would bring in both Russia and Romania, which would be disastrous for Hungary. Thus 2 and 3 were combined for Tisza, and Berchtold's preferred *DE* strategy failed by constraint 2–3. Tisza's preferred strategy was *D* with *C* components: a diplomatic demand for redress of grievances from Serbia, with willingness to compromise if necessary to keep Russia neutral. Only if Serbia proved completely intransigent would war be necessary, and such a war might well find Russia and, therefore, Romania staying out.

Both protocoalition leaders searched for support, Berchtold by contacting the German ally, successfully, and Tisza by preparing a letter to Emperor Franz Josef. At a July 7 meeting Berchtold, the chairman, arranged attendance so Tisza was in a minority of one. Tisza saw he had no hope of forming a majority coalition, though he was still in a position to block because Hungarian support was essential for war and since he officially had a veto. Then Berchtold accepted Tisza's preferred strategy: he declared there should be no surprise attack but rather strong diplomatic demands to be followed by war only if Serbia was completely intransigent. Tisza could not oppose his own strategy, so he had to abstain. Berchtold next, on July 9, got the Emperor's support by stressing the German alliance support, and Tisza, finding that the Emperor had not answered his letters and seeing his own domestic support eroding, accepted Berchtold's strategy on July 14.

However, Berchtold modified the strategy in practice. Instead of a strong diplomatic demand with room for negotiation, as Tisza had wanted, the note was an ultimatum designed to be unacceptable and to be followed automatically by war—Berchtold's original *DE* strategy. Tisza's payoff for joining the coalition was verbal only and disappeared in practice; and Hungary lost Transylvania.

The U.S. decision in the 1962 Cuban crisis does not fit the bureaucratic politics theory well because it is a Type 3 case—i.e., one man held the power to decide, with other participants acting as advisers. The difficulty with the bureaucratic politics interpretation is that the strategy decision was recommended by an advisory group whose main weights were their influence with the president and whose official positions remained in the background. Moreover, several members of the group held no official positions in the foreign policy bureaucracy. However, the case can be interpreted in terms of *coalition* politics with bureaucratic elements. Officially the president made the decision—he *was* the majority coalition—though in practice he could not afford to disagree with all his advisers or even a strong majority of them, since he needed their continued support to carry out his various policies. The military advisers in particular were a blocking coalition because they had to carry out any coercive strategy involving action, so their opposition would partly frustrate the strategy. The bounded rationality theory fits the case well. The following account combines the bounded rationality and coalition politics interpretations.

The Cuban decision is atypical in several respects: it was one of the three or so initial decisions that succeeded almost as planned, with few surprises and few modifications, and the committee that produced it had a fairly evenly mixed spectrum of hard-line–middle-line biases with a weak soft-line component and a middle-line central decision maker. Also it was the most thoroughly deliberated initial decision in all our cases.

The precipitant, the intolerable development, was the secret Soviet emplacement of "offensive" nuclear weapons in Cuba. The action was intolerable in part because of its sheer effrontery: Soviet representatives had many times assured Kennedy that they would do no such thing, Kennedy had trusted them and risked his influence in several political arenas by standing firm against hard-line charges and demands for action. Now all Soviet assurances were revealed as lies. They were burglars. They were showing contempt for Kennedy by lying to him and by disregarding his clear warnings against putting offensive missiles in Cuba. Moreover they were ignoring the Monroe Doctrine. Their purpose therefore was to test Kennedy's resolve. In order to preserve the United States' and the president's reputation for resolve, which he needed, both for international and domestic political bargaining, it was necessary to resist the challenge. A second aspect of the problem was the shift the missiles would make in the military balance, a shift that would occur as soon as the missiles became operational. Both aspects of the challenge would be met by *publicly forcing* the Soviet Union to remove the missiles before they became operational. Constraint 1 therefore read: *the missiles must be removed through public U.S. coercive measures before they become operational*. This constraint required a coercive strategy. It also added a time constraint, since the missiles would become operational in two weeks or so.

There were three negative constraints. Constraint 2 was *minimum risk of escalation and war*. Constraint 3, though less important in this case, was *consistency with alliance or U.N. obligations*. This was an alliance and community constraint; the United States must not damage its alliance relations or flagrantly disregard international law. Constraint 4, accepted by only part of the committee, was roughly *No immoral acts; do not violate the principles for which the United States stands*.

The committee considered six types of possible strategy, if we follow Sorenson's classification.[26] In the discussion, the coercive strategies were

[26] Ibid., pp. 58–61.

tested from a ML bias and the accommodative strategies from a HL bias, so all strategies failed to be acceptable. For example, strategy 5, limited air strike (E), failed by constraint 1, since the military could not guarantee removal of 100 percent of the missiles and even one operational atomic missile was too many. It also failed by constraint 2 given a SL or ML bias, since the Soviet Union might respond violently to a U.S. attack on its troops. Given a hard-line bias it met constraint 2, since the Soviet Union would retreat in the face of toughness and could not be provoked into World War III by the killing of a few troops. It also failed by the SL constraint 4, since a Pearl Harbor-type move was immoral for the United States.

The next task was to select one of the six possible strategies as the basis for construction of an acceptable strategy. This was done by coalition bargaining; the problem was to form a majority behind one strategy.

There was a strong effort by Acheson and others to form a majority coalition around strategy 5. A key move was the president's attempt to get military assurance that the strike would remove all the missiles; this would take care of constraint 1 to everybody's satisfaction. Since strategy 5 already met constraint 2 for a hard-line adviser, all HL advisers and possibly some middle-line advisers were potential members of this coalition. By giving their assurance the military representatives would be shifting from their preferred strategy 6, massive air strike and invasion (E), to 5. The military, however, refused to shift, and strategy 5 remained unacceptable to middle-liners and some hard-liners. The second and successful attempt was made by a middle-line protocoalition of Robert Kennedy, McNamara, and Sorensen. They bid strategy 4, blockade (D), thus preempting the middle ground and sweeping in moderate hard-liners and all middle-liners. Had the remaining hard-liners, Acheson and the military, immediately united around strategy 5, they might have drawn off some hard-line advisers and produced a mutual blocking situation; but they remained divided between 5 and 6, rejecting one another's arguments, and so failed to draw off anyone from 4. The soft-line adviser, Stevenson, favored strategy 2, negotiations, but could not even block and so was not needed as a coalition member.

Having tentatively adopted strategy 4, the next step was to modify it piecemeal until it met all the constraints to the satisfaction of the majority coalition. Constraint 3, legality, was met by changing the name from "blockade" to "quarantine"; also by seeking alliance approval and by flimsy legal arguments in the United Nations. Constraint 2, minimum risk of war, was met by making the blockade limited, gradual, and as non-provocative as possible for a coercive move. Constraint 1 was met by adding strategies 5 and 6 as later tactical moves if 4 had not succeeded in removing the missiles within the required time limits. In this way the unique advantages of 5 and 6, both as threats and as ultimate acts, were harnessed to 4, speaking strategically; and speaking in terms of coalition bargaining the added hard-line ingredient held the hard-line members of the majority coalition.

Thus the U.S. decision was made by a combination of coalition bargaining and bounded rationality procedures. The bargaining, however, remained within the narrow range of coalition possibilities represented by alternatives 4 and 5. In a larger sense the outcome was determined by the distribution of biases in the committee; the committee biases determined both the definition of the problem, the constraint set, and the range of possible solutions. This distribution in turn was determined partly by shifts of influence in the Kennedy administration and partly by current political pressures; for instance the 1961 Cuban invasion had reduced hard-line influence, and the hard-line pressure on Kennedy in Congress and in the executive branch closed off Kennedy's soft options. As a result the committee bias was basically distributed around a moderate hard-line mode, with a strong middle-line component. This hard-line committee produced a hard-line definition of the problem (constraint 1) and a DC strategy: moderately coercive but carried out in an accommodative manner.

It happened that this strategy was successful for the United States with minor accommodative modifications. This success, however, was not due to adequate information about the situation, particularly Soviet motives and strategy. It was due rather to the fact that the distribution of biases in the committee, and its internal bargaining process, happened to produce an appropriate strategy. In contrast, the 1914 Austrian committee produced a disastrous strategy because its pure hard-line bias produced a key misjudgment about the Russian preference function and intentions. The Cuban result, however, was not just due to bias distribution, but also to the unusual sophistication of Kennedy and certain advisers—empathy with the opponent, knowledge of Soviet governmental style and structure, understanding of international diplomatic history, and enough self-doubt to build in maximum opportunity for feedback of information and correction of strategy. In short, the committee majority was, to paraphrase Acheson, "plain lucky," but they were also good crisis managers.

The Cuban crisis illustrates a point made earlier—that constraints vary in stringency. The positive constraint (goal) for the United States was virtually an absolute imperative—the missiles had to go. Other constraints, notably "avoid war" could be relaxed. The chosen strategy, blockade plus air strike if necessary, did involve accepting some risk of war, even nuclear war. The risk was minimized by the blockade choice, but was still accepted. There is an important difference here between positive constraints and negative constraints, in that the former are *interests* that one *knows* one has, whereas the latter often are uncertainties that may or may not be violated in pursuit of the main objective. When the objective is very highly valued, as in the Cuban instance, decision makers will tend to act on the certainty of that valuation and gamble with the risks attached to negative constraints. One's actions may lead to war, but on the other hand they may not; the ally may be alienated, but then again he may not. This behavior is also illustrated by the result of an important conference of German officials in 1914, a decision (by the Kaiser) to "fight the thing through, cost what it may." Saving Austria from revolution was a highly desirable objective that could be achieved by action; the undesirable by-product—general war—might or might not occur. This phenomenon seems to be a strike against the utility maximization model, in which the risks of bad consequences are supposed to be multiplied by their disutility, and the product compared to the probability times the value of the achieving the desired objective. Had that procedure been followed in the Cuban case, using the president's estimate of the chances of nuclear war as "between one out of three and even," one supposes that the United States would have chosen an accommodative rather than a coercive strategy. However, in certain other cases (Russia, Bosnia, 1908; France, Fashoda, 1898) where war, and especially a losing war, was seen as a virtually certain consequence of firmness, this negative constraint triumphed over the positive goal at stake.

We have no information about how the initial Soviet strategy was constructed in the 1958 Berlin crisis. However, it does conform to the bias distribution in the Presidium: a dominant middle-line group including Khrushchev, with a strong hard-line component. The strategy was *CD*, mainly coercive, and the style of the first bid, the November 27 note, was coercive. The accommodative component was the proposal to negotiate a compromise settlement, complete with hints of possible concessions. The definition of the problem in the November 27 note was hard-line, since it blamed NATO for agreement violations and a long history of aggressive behavior. The main coercive component was the six-month deadline with its vague threat or ultimatum overtones, and also the separate peace treaty provision. The whole strategy including its coercive components was executed in an accommodative fashion by Khrushchev: he and Mikoyan, when they were speaking for themselves and not formally for the whole committee, immediately played down the six-month clause and played up their willingness to make concessions. "Never mind that six-month business, just make us a counteroffer" they were saying. The Soviet hard-line speeches of course were quite different; they emphasized the inevitability of the peace treaty. If the Soviet Union is seen as a unitary actor, this "vacillation" on the six-month clause may seem like shrewd manipulation of the opponent, alternating the carrot and the stick; or, to a Western hard-liner, might provide clear proof that the ultimatum and the separate peace treaty threat were nothing but bluff and bluster. But if Khrushchev–Mikoyan's behavior is seen as accommodative execution of a mixed strategy, it parallels closely Kennedy's accommodative execution of the Cuba strategy. Just as Khrushchev repeatedly softened and postponed the negotiation deadline, trying the patience of his hard-line colleagues as far as dared,[27] so Kennedy repeatedly softened the blockade—postponing it, trying to move it back, letting ships through, trying to avoid submarines—and, like Khrushchev, had to endure hard-line fuming and suspicion. "This is a hell of a way to run a blockade."

The U.S. decision on Quemoy is somewhat better documented. In this Type 1 case Dulles was hard in relation to China, and the soft antithesis was located in the Senate opposition and in the British alliance partner. SL bias therefore served as an external constraint rather than an internal critic and coalition partner. Given HL bias, the Chinese artillery-and-airfield challenge was interpreted as a test of U.S. resolve. Would the United States risk war to support its ally or would it chicken out? If it yielded to Chinese threats its ally would get discouraged, the alliance would weaken, Chiang's army would lose morale, other Asian allies would desert the United States . . . and so on to disaster. Constraint 1 was therefore an absolute constraint: *hold Quemoy.*[28] Constraint 2 was to *avoid war.* This involved restraining the Formosan ally, who was urging and asking permission for various military moves that could easily lead to escalation, involvement of the Soviet Union and war. Constraint 3 was set by the soft-line Senate opposition and the British ally. It was twofold: *do not alienate Britain* and *do not give the Senate opposition a propaganda opportunity.* Constraint 4 was *maintain alliance solidarity* with Chiang. The problem therefore was to devise a strategy that would be firm to China, accommodative for the U.S. public and Britain, restraining and yet supportive for the Formosan ally. The United States must firmly commit itself to defend Quemoy in the eyes of the Chinese (constraint 1) but must not do so in the perceptions of the U.S. Senate (constraint 3) because this would give the Senate critics an opening—Eisenhower was not authorized to defend Quemoy unconditionally. The United States must demonstrate military support for

---

[27] Hans Kroll, *Lebenserinnerungen Eines Botschafters* (Cologne: Kiepenheuer und Witsch, 1967), p. 473.

[28] Howe, *Multicrises,* p. 190.

Chiang (constraint 4) but must not do so (constraint 2) in such a way as to encourage him.

Given Dulles's hard-line bias, only a D strategy could satisfy all these constraints. We do not have data on how the strategy was constructed, but we do know that the strategy itself met all the constraints by being firmly ambiguous. It was (1) indirectly firm: there were tough statements, insults, and warnings for the Chinese, such as Dulles's August 9 speech, but no public commitment to defend Quemoy; (2) for Chiang, the Chinese threat was downgraded—the 7th fleet was elsewhere in August, the Philippines and Singapore, while Chiang was warning of imminent invasion—but for the Chinese, the 7th fleet was steadily reinforced from all over the world. Dulles and Chiang did an Alphonse–Gaston routine on Quemoy, each urging the other to resupply that already overstocked island. Finally, the United States did convoy supplies, beginning September 4—up to the 3-mile limit and beyond the range of most Chinese artillery. Since it was set in the ambiguous center of the four-constraint space, U.S. strategy could be shifted in any direction to meet specific contingencies—firm up if Chiang got worried, soften if the British got worried, and so on. Also the hope was that each target would receive the messages intended for it and ignore the rest; the Chinese were supposed to notice the firm but vague warnings, the Senate critics to notice the lack of commitment to defend Quemoy, and so on. The strategy succeeded. This is an example of how a strategy can be constructed around a single alternative (D), and confirms the bounded rationality argument that rationality of a narrow sort is possible even if only one alternative is considered.

The United States was even more constrained in Berlin 1948. There were three constraints: (1) Stay in Berlin, (2) avoid war, (3) continue unifying the western zones. These constraints left the United States with no acceptable strategy. By 2 they could not coerce, given local Soviet Union military superiority; by 3 they could not negotiate because they could not offer any concessions of interest to Stalin, whose primary interest was in blocking the unification of the western zones and consequently the division of Germany; and by 1 they could not withdraw. So they essentially had no strategy, and the contradictory nature of the constraints prevented them from constructing one. However, there was no immediate time pressure to make a decision, since the blockade was not yet effective, and they did have a small concession available in the area of West Berlin currency regulations. Consequently, instead of re-examining the constraints, comparing them and relaxing one, the United States stalled for time in hopes that something would turn up: they decided to negotiate on currency regulations, but not to discuss the concessions Stalin had asked for. Something did turn up: the airlift.

The decision to stall was not reached easily, however. A variety of tactics were suggested to satisfy constraint 1 and were vetoed on the basis of 2 or 3. For example, Clay proposed an autobahn probe, which the Washington military vetoed on grounds of 2.

German decision making in the 1905 case illustrates a Type 5 committee failing to decide between two alternatives. The decision-making group included Kaiser Wilhelm (soft toward France and Russia, hard toward Britain); Holstein (hard), chief Foreign Office adviser, and Chancellor Bulow, a vacillating middle-liner, the central decision maker. Holstein's weight lay largely in his influence over Foreign Office subordinates who had to carry out policy and who were mainly hard-line like Holstein. When the Kaiser chose to insist, he would officially get his way; but he had to govern through subordinates and must therefore allow them some discretion. Also the subordinates, including Holstein, had control over information and advice reaching the Kaiser, so if *they* chose they could withhold information or advise him to go on a cruise, as in 1914. In short, both the Kaiser and Holstein constituted a partial blocking coalition, had an intermittent veto over the carrying out of strategy, with Bulow mediating.

The problem was defined as the appearance of a potentially hostile alliance, the 1904 Anglo–French entente. Given the Franco–Russian alliance, there was even a remote possibility of a triple entente against Germany, which would be intolerable. Constraint 1 therefore read: *neutralize the entente.* Constraint 2 was *avoid war;* Constraint 3, accepted by Holstein and rejected by the Kaiser, *preserve the possibility of colonial gains in Morocco.*

There are two opposed ways to neutralize a potentially hostile entente, C and D. C is to negotiate a generous settlement with one member of the entente, thereby gaining its friendship or at least goodwill. D is to threaten one member of the entente; this will perhaps frighten off the other member and expose the weakness of the entente in time of danger. Bismarck had used a similar D strategy successfully in 1887 to prevent a Russian alliance with France.

Both C and D were considered by the German decision-making group, and both were rejected. The Kaiser proposed C, which Holstein evaluated and rejected by constraints 1 and 3; Holstein proposed D, which the Kaiser rejected by 1 insofar as he could find out what was happening. The Kaiser's strategy was to make generous concessions to France or perhaps Russia, gain their trust and goodwill, and eventually make an alliance against Britain. From a hard-line bias this C strategy fails; concessions to France will be interpreted as lack of resolve or confession of military weakness and thus will earn French contempt rather than goodwill, given French hostility over Alsace–Lorraine. Holstein's D strategy was to threaten France and if necessary go to war, thereby demonstrating to France that Germany was powerful and resolved, Britain weak and treacherous. In a crisis Britain would desert France, and the French would learn respect for Germany, would seek a détente and perhaps even an alliance. From a soft-line bias this strategy fails: threatening France would arouse hostility, stiffen resistance, perhaps strengthen the Entente, and make alliance with France impossible.

Bulow failed to reconcile these opposing views, failed to form a majority coalition, and apparently did not even try very hard. He simply accepted whatever tactics were urged on him, whether C or D. First the soft C strategy was tried but executed in a coercive fashion, and when it failed the hard D strategy was tried but intermittently modified by C tactics—perhaps the two worst possible combinations of opposites. Bulow tried the C strategy first, but toward Britain, not France. He proposed a colonial agreement similar to the Anglo–French agreement. But by the time this proposal got through the hard-line foreign office to England, it sounded more like a threat than a conciliatory move, aroused hostility, and was rejected. Next he tried the Kaiser's strategy toward Russia, sending a treaty draft that Holstein and he had composed. Russia accepted this, conditional on French approval, which Holstein was sure would never come. From Kaiser Wilhelm's standpoint a triple alliance would be excellent and the next step should be a conciliatory alliance move toward France, but Holstein had opposed this, arguing that it would show weakness and encourage French aggressiveness. And since the Kaiser's strategy had been tried unsuccessfully twice, Bulow believed that it was Holstein's turn. The German coercive tactics toward France produced an immediate deadlock, and (to simplify a good deal) at each deadlock the Kaiser, hoping for a French alliance, proposed a conciliatory move, a move that was carried out in a coercive fashion by subordinates and so aroused more French hostility. The Russian treaty also remained on the agenda and was used by Russian diplomats to induce German concessions in a deadlock. The Holstein D strategy toward France was probably doomed from the start, but the Kaiser's interventions put accommodative holes in it and added to the confusion. Conversely, the Kaiser's C strategy probably had little chance of success either, but the coercive way it was carried out by hard-line subordinates made nonsense of it. The German strategic decisions and their ineffectiveness can be explained as due to the lack of coalition bargaining, the failure to form a majority coalition, and the subsequent interference by blocking coalitions.

REVISING OR REPLACING A STRATEGY

In a few cases the implementation of an initial strategy went according to plan. The opponent responded as expected, the planned reply to his response was made, etc., and agreement was reached at or near the expected terms. In 1898 the initial British strategy eventually induced the French to evacuate the Nile Valley, and agreement was reached at the initially desired boundary . The 1923 British strategy against France worked as expected. In 1958 the U.S. strategy induced the Chinese to moderate their artillery barrage; or at any rate the Chinese did moderate their barrage, and Quemoy was held by the Nationalists, with Chiang giving up his plans for mainland raids based on Quemoy. In the 1958 Lebanon troop landing, no Communist-inspired rebellion occurred, though probably not as a consequence of the landing; the internal political bargaining prior to elections (which the United States saw as Nasser's internal aggression) had already been completed before the troops arrived, and the elections proceeded on schedule. In Cuba, 1962, the U.S. blockade worked essentially as expected. In the Yom Kippur crisis in the fall of 1973, the U.S. strategy worked as expected. But in all the other cases, and to a slight extent in Cuba as well, the opponent did not respond quite as expected and there was a deadlock. At this point it became necessary to reexamine the initial strategy and make revisions to deal with the deadlock. The revisions varied from tactical amendments in the Cuban case to extensive tactical revisions in several cases, to completely new strategies in the West Berlin and Iran cases, among others.

Half the strategy revisions are from D to C; the weaker party discovers his weakness and learns he must concede something to avoid war. The stronger party, now sure of success, simply continues coercing (D), perhaps with tactical revisions. However, there are also shifts from C to D and D to E. The count across our cases is:

D to C	9
C to D	5
D to E	2
D to DC	2
E to D	1

Strategy revisions or replacement results from adjustment of expectations, an adjustment that has been forced by new information breaking in through the barrier provided by initial expectations. As long as a strategy works as expected it is continued, but when the opponent's responses are contrary to expectations, strategy is changed. Here we must distinguish between a minor and a major adjustment. A minor adjustment produced by one or two unexpected messages is absorbed into the initial pattern of expectations and responded to with an appropriate change of tactics only. For example, in 1905, Rouvier's unexpected rejection of Bulow's demand for a conference led to a shift of tactic—

Bulow's hint that Germany needed a conference only as a face-saving device and would be conciliatory once a conference was accepted. German expectations and strategy remained basically unchanged at this point; strategy was still dominated by the initial expectation that France would back down before a show of firmness. In contrast, a series of unexpected messages produces a radical rather than piecemeal revision of expectations. The decision maker suddenly sees that his whole diagnosis of the bargaining situation was somehow mistaken and he needs to construct a new picture. For Bulow in 1906 this realization came too late to avoid defeat, but in some other cases it came soon enough to enable the decision maker to construct a new strategy based on more correct expectations. In this section we discuss the process of constructing a new strategy.

To summarize briefly the argument of this section: strategy revision is undertaken when enough new information comes in to disrupt initial expectations. The decision maker, or his successor in power, must then adjust his expectations and perhaps redefine the whole crisis problem. The adjustment and redefinition may be a quick one based on the new information already available, or it may be a careful, piecemeal process based on continuing new information and including a search for information to fill in the picture. The adjusted expectations usually require a downward revision of aspiration and acceptability levels, since the original goals and constraints cannot all be satisfied in the redefined crisis situation. In coalition cases the downward revision constitutes a renegotiation of the decision-making coalition; it is always the weakest member of the coalition that has its expected payoff reduced or eliminated, in the form of downgrading the goal or constraint belong to it. Renegotiation may happen once or twice, but not oftener. The strategy construction or revision process then proceeds as described in the previous section: a strategy is built up or revised piece by piece to satisfy the new constraints. This may be done all at once between external bargaining moves, or piecemeal during bargaining.

Strategy revisions begins when initial expectations are disrupted and destroyed and the decision maker becomes disoriented. The amount of new information needed to do this depends on the rigidity of the image and the belief system that produced those expectations. At the extreme of rigidity represented by Adenauer and Chamberlain all new information is interpreted to fit previous categories or else ignored and initial strategy is never revised. When the image is moderately flexible, as with Kennedy or Halifax, revisions and replacements of strategy occur more readily. At the other extreme, when the image of the other is already crumbling and a new image is in process of construction, as with the United States in 1945 during the Iran crisis, new information is sought from the beginning prior to adoption of any firm strategy.

In coalition cases the amount of new information needed to produce revision depends on the distribution of weights in the coalition. Since revision always involves renegotiation, there must be a weaker member who can be expelled or get a reduced payoff, and a coalition core strong enough to do the expelling. Otherwise there is no way to renegotiate and strategy cannot be revised. Examples of the latter situation are the United States, 1940–1941, and France, September–November 1923.

Because it has been initiated by new information breaking in from the outside, strategy revision is a reality-oriented process in contrast to the essentially image-oriented strategy-forming process. Initial strategy is constructed under the domination of the image and its associated expectations, while revisions are constructed on the basis of new information and a new set of expectations.

Consequently, strategy revision is usually a piecemeal process, undertaken as new information comes in. The new strategy may be sketched in outline with details filled in as needed, or only the first steps may be decided on and the remainder deferred until more information comes in. Here, however, there is some variation depending on the amount of time pressure. At the one extreme when there is no pressure for immediate action, the decision maker has time to conduct a rather thorough search for new information, with substantive moves deferred. We have three or four examples of such search strategies: United States, 1945–1946 (Iran); Qavam, 1946 (Iran); Ulbricht, 1960–1961 (West Berlin); and perhaps China, 1958 (Quemoy). These strategies were very much piecemeal strategies. At the other extreme when time pressure is acute, the decision maker must make do with whatever new information he already has. We have several examples at this extreme. In two cases, Japan, October 15, 1941, and Britain, September 7, 1956, revised expectations plus acute time pressure produced action strategies (E). In Germany, July 29, 1914, a sudden collapse of expectations plus time pressure produced a frantic attempt to find an accommodative solution.

Once the barrier of initial expectations has been broken through and the decision maker oriented to new information, he can deal with it either passively or actively. The passive way is to accept information as it comes in and to adjust expectations accordingly. The active way is to build a systematic search for information into one's strategy, to seek out information rather than merely accepting it as it comes. Most strategy revision processes in our cases combine active and passive modes; the information that happens to come in is supplemented by active search, as time permits, for pieces of information needed to complete the picture of the opponent's preferences and intentions. In our three or four examples of search strategies with no time pressure, the active search predominated. Conversely, in the 1941 and 1956 action strategies, there was no active search and in fact new information was not especially welcome. Since these were cases of rapidly deteriorating situations, with all the new information bad and getting worse daily, the lack of interest in new information is at least intelligible. It was easier for these men to decide on a desperate gamble involving almost certain ruin than to accept the new information and revise their mistaken definition of the crisis problem. In these cases new information had to break through resistance violently to announce failure of the strategy.

The new information needed to construct the new strategy is information about both ally and opponent. From the ally one needs to know the extent of his commitment—is it diplomatic, economic, defensive military, or complete? This information is needed to estimate the costs of deadlock (*DD*) and war. Sometimes a direct question is the proper way to get this information—ask him and he will tell you. Sometimes, however, a direct question will produce an evasive answer. Either the ally has not decided on his exact degree of support and does not want to decide until *he* gets enough information; or he has decided but wishes to conceal the information in order to restrain his ally from rash and dangerous moves. We have approximately 24 instances of requests for information about alliance support, and 11 of these were answered evasively.

From the opponent one needs to know his intentions and objective as well as the amount of risk he is willing to take for his objective. One also would like to know the minimum concession that would induce him to settle peacefully. In short, one would like information about his constraints and his levels of aspiration and acceptability. However, this is precisely the information the opponent wishes to keep secret, either because he is not clear about it himself and wishes to keep his options open or, if he is clear, because it can be used to manipulate him. If one knew the exact minimum concession that would induce the opponent to settle, or if one knew the exact degree of war risk he was willing to take, or if one knew the weak point in his defenses, the wavering ally or reluctant cabinet minister, one would immediately have the upper hand—and, indeed, this is precisely why one is searching for the information.

At this stage, the stage of strategy revision, bargaining becomes, indeed, a "deliberate cultivation of uncertainty and mistakenness by one party in the mind of the other," as Shackle observes (see p. 339), and conversely an attempt to penetrate the curtain of uncertainty the opponent sets up. This means that information gathering has to proceed by indirection. Direct questions about the opponent's intentions, for instance those of Truman and Byrnes in 1945 (Iran) directed to Stalin or those of Rouvier in 1905 directed to Bulow, elicit evasion and concealment, since the opponent does not want to reveal his strategy prematurely. The required information cannot, therefore, be obtained by asking him directly, but only by finding facts that enable one to penetrate his curtain of secrecy and deception. In Jervis's terminology [29] one must read indices rather than signals. Time-honored devices include the intelligence agent, the seemingly casual conversation at parties, the cracked diplomatic code; and each of these devices, as Jervis has shown, can be manipulated by the opponent to transmit false information. One can also read between the lines of his direct communications, his signals, inferring what he is trying to conceal or what he may not even be aware of. And, of course, his bargaining offers and counteroffers provide information about his goals and preferences. But the most important information-gathering device is the probe, a move designed for the purpose of getting information. Probes may be either coercive or accommodative. [30]

A coercive probe is a military or economic or diplomatic move applying pressure, force, at a specific place or issue. Coercive probes can include such moves as occupying some small location, or shelling or blockading it; or applying a boycott or inspection or tax on a specific item or at a specific locality; or requiring a pass through a specific point, or seeing or refusing to see an envoy from an insurgent group. By extension, threats to do any of the foregoing might also be used as probes, though this extension perhaps broadens the concept too much. Coercive probes are distinguished from ordinary coercive moves, including ordinary threats, (1) by their strictly and clearly limited nature, focusing on a specific issue rather than preparing the way for a larger coercive program, and (2) by the fact that their primary purpose is information gathering rather than influence.

A coercive probe asks a question of the opponent: are you willing to stand firm on this specific point? The opponent then must answer truthfully by either repulsing the probe or accepting it; he cannot evade or conceal. If the probe is repulsed it is withdrawn; the desired information has been obtained, and a new probe can be tried elsewhere. If it is

---

[29] Jervis, *The Logic of Images.*

[30] Our only clear examples of coercive probes come from the period after 1945. This suggests that coercive probes are in part a response to the need to control violence short of war; or perhaps they are a way of using the new practice of controlled violence for information-gathering purposes. The evidence is quite unclear on this. Probes should be distinguished conceptually from both "tests of resolve" and "salami tactics." The former are contrived confrontations over some minor issue intended by the initiator to enhance his "resolve image" for the crisis generally and to undermine the opponent's; their primary function is influence rather than information-gathering. Salami tactics are grabs of some small portion of whatever is at issue in the belief that the act will fall below the adversary's threshold of resistance. See Schelling, *Arms and Influence,* pp. 66–69.

accepted, the prober has made a substantive gain and also increased his information.

An accommodative probe is a hint of a possible exchange of concessions, perhaps sent through a lower-level diplomat who can be repudiated, or implied by deliberate omissions or insertions in a statement. Here there is room for evasion and counterhinting by the opponent, and the whole business can get lost in mystery and confusion, to reappear months or years later in charges of double-cross and angry denials. But hopefully the opponent either accepts or not, and the desired information about his goals is obtained.

The distinctive characteristic of probes as compared with other information-gathering activity is that they are not only searches for information but influence moves as well. An ambassadorial report on the state of public opinion (index) or a careful study of the intentions behind a diplomatic statement (signal) is pure information gathering. It does not affect the opponent because he does not know it is happening. But a coercive or accommodative probe does influence the opponent by giving him information about one's own intentions and interests at the same time that it seeks information about his. Thus it must be responded to as a regular bargaining move.

One consequence is that probes give information to both bargainers if properly interpreted. The party being probed gains information about the pattern of the opponent's concerns even as he is necessarily giving up information about his own preference function.

Another consequence is that probes force a reevaluation of aspiration and acceptability levels by both sides. When a bargainer is probed coercively, he must ask himself "Is this specific point worth a war to us?" This is not a speculative question but a practical one requiring immediate reply. When he receives an accommodative probe, he must ask "Are we willing to concede that?" These questions require an examination of constraints at specific points, at the margin, rather than in general and in the abstract. The prober must also evaluate his aspiration and acceptability levels when he is planning a probe, and also when his probes are repulsed. Probes are expensive and risky and must be limited to securing really important information; and when a probe is repulsed the question again arises "Is this specific point worth a war, or can we be satisfied with some other point instead?"

A short period of bidding, sending messages, and perhaps probing is sufficient to bring in a variety of information about the opponent's and the ally's concerns, preferences, and perhaps strategy. When this information falls into a pattern it enables the bargainer to revise his definition of the problem and his expectations.

The immediate consequence of revised definition and expectations is the realization that one's original goals and constraints can no longer all be met, and some downward revision is required. For example, when Eden finally realized about September 7, 1956 that the United States would not help him stop Nasser and that Dulles had in fact been obstructing him, his original D strategy of diplomatic and economic sanctions lay in ruins. The only remaining way to stop Nasser was military (E), and he realized the United States was opposed to this. Thus his four constraints, *Stop Nasser, Avoid War, Maintain the French Alliance,* and *Maintain the U.S. Alliance,* could not all be met. One or more acceptability levels must be reduced, and Eden chose to reduce No. 2 and to a lesser extent No. 4.

The consequence of reevaluating aspiration and acceptability levels can be called either their clarification or their change. One can argue that at the onset of a crisis deadlock, when revised strategies are being worked out, no bargainers know exactly how much or how little they will settle for or how much risk of war or alliance weakening they are willing to take. A committee may decide at the beginning of a crisis what its levels of aspiration and acceptability will be, but such decisions remain speculative until they are tested concretely and in detail. From this standpoint the result of reevaluation is a clarification of aspirations and acceptability levels. On the other hand, bargainers sometimes think they know what they will settle for and how much they will risk to get it, and in this sense the result is a change of aspiration level.

In bureaucratic terms, aspiration levels are changed by renegotiating the dominant coalition. The various constraints will be ranked differently by different coalition members, so that each member tends to become spokesman for the constraint most important to him. When not all constraints can be satisfied the constraint supported by the weakest coalition member is the one that is revised downward, thereby reducing his expected payoff or perhaps even expelling him from the coalition.

The effect of lowering aspiration levels in our cases usually was to make initially incompatible aspirations compatible. This in turn made possible a mutually acceptable settlement of the underlying issue in about one-fourth of our cases. In the other cases, excluding those that ended in war, the "settlement" consisted only of terminating the crisis, usually by the complete defeat of one side. The underlying issue in these cases remained unsettled and was reopened at a later date in another crisis or war; in one case (Berlin) it was settled later by non-crisis negotiation.

Of course, the question of which levels are lowered is crucial for a settlement. If it is the *avoid war* constraint that is relaxed or given up, as in Britain 1956 or Japan 1941, there is war rather than a settlement.

For purposes of achieving a settlement the crucial constraint is the expansionist component, the goals of new territory or some other change to one's advantage; if this can be given up, that is if the defensive faction is dominant in the decision-making group, a settlement is possible. Thus in Cuba 1962 it was essential that the United States give up its lingering interest in removing Castro—in bureaucratic terms that the "Get Castro" faction lost out; in Berlin 1961 the United States had to renounce Adenauer's interest in reunifying Germany eastward, and Ulbricht had to give up his lingering interest in West Berlin; in 1958 Quemoy Chiang had to renounce his mainland raids and perhaps invasion from Quemoy; in 1911 Germany had to do without a new German Congo; in 1898 France had to forget about a French Sudan; and so on.

In summary, strategy revision is initiated when a massive input of new information breaks through the barrier of the image and makes a decision maker realize that his diagnosis and expectations were somehow radically wrong and must be corrected. This leads him to be receptive to new information and to search for information to fill in the gaps, if time is available. If the search includes probes, these force both him and the opponent to clarify their own constraints, and at points of deadlock the clarification is downward for one or both parties. The new information provides a picture of the opponent's acceptability levels that enables the decision maker to work out a revised strategy. The strategy may be worked out piecemeal as information comes in and the pressures of bargaining force particular decisions, or it may be constructed all at once, especially if there is time pressure.

The above account of strategy revision is somewhat idealized; it represents the "rational" case in which maximally effective use is made of new information. The main deviation from rationality is the same mentioned in the previous chapter: a rigid image imposes a strong barrier to new information, so strong that, when the new information does finally break through, it is too late to do much except admit defeat. In addition there are several cases in which defeat was unavoidable even with maximal use of new information: France, 1898; Japan, 1941; Soviet Union, 1948; Britain, 1956. It takes more than information to be successful in crisis bargaining, notably power, though maximal and early use of new information enables the decision maker to achieve the degree of success the situation makes possible.

For example, the 1905 German goals were unrealistic and most probably unachievable, based as they were on wholly mistaken initial expectations about France and Britain. But if Bulow could have used Rouvier's initial accommodative communications, including his promise to remove Delcassé, to correct his expectations he could have achieved considerable gains because Rouvier was then willing to appease Germany to gain its friendship. Later, if Bulow could have correctly interpreted Rouvier's rejection of a conference and subsequent firmness, he would have reduced his demands and might have achieved token concessions in Morocco and more substantial ones elsewhere, some French good will, and a weaker entente. But his persistent misreading of messages and his persistence in a self-defeating D strategy guaranteed total defeat.

We now consider several examples to illustrate the above account of strategy revision, beginning with Soviet Union-East Germany strategy revision of 1959–1961.

The original Soviet Union strategy of 1958 was CD, primarily coercive but administered by middle-line actors who emphasized the accommodative aspects. Probably the first unexpected U.S. response occurred at the 1959 Geneva negotiations, when the opponent failed to make what the Soviet Union considered either a reasonable counter offer or a reasonable discussion of the Soviet Union's offer. However, this new information was assimilated into the original pattern of expectations: Khrushchev had never expected any results from foreign minister negotiations, since foreign offices were mired down in the well-established Cold War stances and grievances. The proper response was a tactical shift to a summit meeting with the realist, Eisenhower, who could cut through old bargaining deadlocks and work out a solution. More new information, all bad, came in 1960 with tough speeches by Dillon and Herter; then the U–2 incident; and finally Eisenhower's admission of responsibility for the U–2 and his refusal to apologize. Khrushchev's expectations were now disoriented and his strategy blocked. His image was immune to change by the new information, since in typical soft-line–middle-line fashion he saw the opponent as divided between moderates and extremists and concluded that the extremists had temporarily taken over control in Washington; but in that case his negotiating strategy could not work and he had to wait for the new president.

At this point a shift of leadership took place in the Soviet dominating coalition. Khrushchev no longer had any immediate reason to hold back the hard-line actors since he was not planning any moves until 1961. The hard-liners in any case were no longer willing to tolerate his fantasies of peaceful negotiations with the capitalist enemy, and were anxious to try their tactics. Leadership then passed to Ulbricht (hard), probably supported by hard–line members of the Presidium. Ulbricht had to stay within the general agreed–on strategy but could emphasize the D components and develop new D tactics, just as Khrushchev and Mikoyan had emphasized the C components earlier. That is, he could revise the strategy but not replace it.

Ulbricht's primary constraint was negative, *Secure the German*

Democratic Republic against West German pressures funneled through West Berlin. However, positive components had gotten mixed in, as seems to be typical of our crisis bargainers. One good defense against subversion from West Berlin was to annex the thing; so in September 1958 Ulbricht was pointing out in speeches that West Berlin was geographically part of the German Democratic Republic. Another good defense was diplomatic recognition, which would discourage the West German revisionists but also bring some bright new embassies to Unter den Linden like a string of diplomatic trophies. Additional constraints were 2) *no risk of war,* 3) *don't spoil the negotiating atmosphere by threats and tough talk.* The latter constraint was enforced by Khrushchev in preparation for 1961 summit negotiations with the new President.

Ulbricht had plenty of time, and began his piecemeal strategy revision with a series of probes.

The first probe, February 3, 1960, was East German accreditation of military missions; its objective was to see how far NATO powers would go in diplomatic recognition. The probe was repulsed when the NATO representatives insisted they were accredited only to the Soviet Union. Here Ulbricht was searching the NATO constraint, no diplomatic recognition, to see whether it was minimally compatible with his goal, security through diplomatic recognition. The next probes were in September 1960, temporary travel restrictions to West and East Berlin, and in November 1960, inspection of commercial shipments to West Berlin. Both were successful. Then there were some small probes: G.D.R. flags on the elevated line through West Berlin, which stirred up a tremendous commotion, and increased canal taxes, which went unnoticed. In late July 1961 there were more probes: East Berlin border regulations (accepted) and air traffic regulation for West Berlin (rejected). Ulbricht also got new information by studying Kennedy's July 25 speech and Fulbright's July 30 speech. During 1959–1961 there were also several NATO probes, particularly the high flights to Berlin above permitted ceiling levels, which provided Ulbricht with information about NATO concerns.

Ulbricht now had all the information he needed about U.S. preferences, and in fact the information he got after March 1961 or so merely reinforced what he already knew. He knew (1) the United States would not recognize the German Democratic Republic officially even at risk of war. (2) the United States insisted on *military* access to West Berlin. (3) The United States did not like interference with *civilian* traffic from West Germany to West Berlin and would protest strongly, but would not absolutely insist. (4) The following were of little importance to the United States: any *civilian* movement to and from East Berlin; railroad

and barge traffic between West Germany and West Berlin; political unification of West Berlin and West Germany.

Meanwhile, Ulbricht had reduced his own level of aspiration, giving
up the positive components but retaining the negative one. His essential
problem was still G.D.R. security, but if he could achieve this by
border control, diplomatic recognition was not absolutely essential. As
for West Berlin, it could wait; there were no more geographic speeches.

Given this reduced aspiration, and given the information about U.S.
constraints, Ulbricht could see that the constraints of the two sides
were compatible. He could then devise a coercive tactic, the Wall,
which solved this problem without damaging U.S. constraints or Khrushchev's constraints. It took several months of shrewd and skillful
negotiations with the Warsaw Pact colleagues from March 29 to August
5 to get the tactic accepted; and Ulbricht even had to accept accommodative amendments to satisfy the cautious Khrushchev. The amendments consisted of carrying out the tactic incrementally to get feedback
about U.S. reactions, to appease possible U.S. objections to some extent, and in other ways to make the fait accompli as non-provocative as
possible. (Cf. Kennedy's accommodative amendments to the blockade
strategy October 1962.) However, Ulbricht's inferences from the probes
were correct and the tactic succeeded as he had expected.

In November–December 1961 there was an accommodative probe
by Ambassador Kroll in Moscow. This probe was born of illusion,
developed in misinterpretations, and ended in confusion. It is a good
example of how an accommodative probe, since it is a hint, can get lost
in compounded misinterpretations. Kroll (soft-line) was still under
the illusion that Adenauer (hard-line) could be induced to negotiate
with Khrushchev, and in preparation for negotiations he put some hypothetical concessions before Khrushchev. Kroll's aim was to find the
minimum German concessions that would induce Khrushchev to settle
for German reunification with free elections and perhaps border
rectifications; like Macmillan (SL), he supposed that the Soviet Union's
main interest was in lucrative trade agreements, and thought a deal was
possible. Khrushchev, always on the lookout for a chance to negotiate,
took this ambassadorial probe as a genuine move from Bonn, and
carefully worked out his counteroffer involving deviously indirect recognition of the German Democratic Republic. Khrushchev's counteroffer was probably intended only as a working paper for further unofficial discussion with Kroll, but it was inadvertently presented to Kroll
as a regular diplomatic communication, so Kroll dutifully forwarded
it to the German Foreign Office for study. When the "counteroffer"
arrived in Bonn on December 27 there was consternation. Kroll had
interfered with Adenauer's D strategy of rejecting all Soviet moves

whatsoever; thereby he had weakened the reputation for resolve that Adenauer had been building up and possibly encouraged Khrushchev to try new bullying moves.

Ulbricht's bargaining skill becomes more apparent when one compares his probing, information processing, and strategy formation with that of some other bargainers during the crisis: DeGaulle, who thought the whole Soviet position was a bluff and should be ignored; Macmillan, who hoped a trade agreement would pave the way to a solution; Khrushchev, who thought he could get a compromise settlement if he could only manage to separate Eisenhower from Dulles; Dulles, who thought the Soviet Union was leading from weakness and imminent economic collapse; and Kroll and Adenauer.

Probably the most remarkable example of bargaining skill in our cases, exceeding even that of Ulbricht in 1961, was that of Iranian Premier Qavam as Saltaneh (soft-line) in 1946. This was an instance of a shift from D to C. Qavam's feat shows what it is possible to accomplish with no power, in bargaining with a Stalin. The problem (constraint 1) was to get Soviet troops out of Iran and to re-assert Iranian sovereignty over autonomous Azerbaijan. Constraint 2 came from Qavam's constituency, the Shah, who could dismiss him at any time: *Retain the Shah's confidence.* Constraint 3 came from the bargaining structure, which was Bully, with the Soviet Union being the Bully.[31] Since Iran had no coercive power against the Soviet Union it could only get a satisfactory payoff by an accommodative strategy (C). But Iranian unilateral accommodation would be unsatisfactory by constraints 1 and 2; if the Soviet Union continued its coercive strategy of preventing government access to the North, constraint 1 would not be met. It was necessary for the Soviet Union to be accommodative, and Qavam therefore had to persuade Stalin that he could obtain more from accommodation than from coercion. Constraint 3 then read *maintain Soviet Union hopes for negotiations,* or *don't spoil the negotiating atmosphere.* Finally, there was coercive pressure on the Soviet Union in the United Nations, where Qavam's hard-line predecessor had entered a complaint against the Soviet Union and thereby earned Soviet enmity and his own downfall. The pressure came from the United States and Britain, but Iran had to show some initiative to keep the complaint on the U.N. agenda. U.N. pressure was the one cost that could induce Stalin to abandon coercion for accommodation and was therefore absolutely essential, so constraint 4 read *keep the Iranian complaint alive in the U.N.*

---

[31] This was the bargaining structure between the Soviet Union and Iran only. In the total picture, including the United States and Britain, it was at first Leader, then shifted to Chicken.

The constraints conflicted with each other, as in the Berlin 1948 and Quemoy cases. To satisfy constraint 4 Qavam occasionally had to take some action, such as denying Gromyko's claim that the dispute had been settled; but any such action would immediately arouse Stalin's suspicion (3). To keep Stalin's hopes up (3) Qavam had to make some concessions; but any concession would arouse the Shah's suspicions (2) and those of his hard-line advisers. Qavam had one advantage: information. His predecessor's hard-line tactics had clarified the limits of U.S.–British initiative at the United Nations, given their constraints. From this information Qavam could estimate the minimum Iranian initiative needed to keep the Iranian complaint on the U.N. agenda (4). In addition Stalin's reactions to his predecessor's hard-line firmness gave information about the limits of Stalin's patience (3). Qavam could use this information both to show the Shah (2) that since firmness had failed concessions would be necessary, and to estimate the minimum rate of concession that would satisfy 3.

Qavam's C strategy was to probe the three secondary constraints to determine their limits in each specific circumstance, and to yield whenever he met opposition. This was a thoroughly piecemeal strategy. He probed the Shah's tolerance for token concessions that would keep Stalin's hopes up, but evaded Stalin's urgent demands for major concessions. At the United Nations Qavam's hard-line representative could take enough initiative to satisfy the United States, but if the Soviet ambassador complained Qavam could obligingly repudiate the representative or reverse his instructions—and reverse them once more when the United States complained. He also used his own powerlessness by playing one constraint against the other. When Stalin demanded major concessions, Qavam could say, correctly, that he was not authorized by law and by the Shah to make those concessions but would see what he could do; when the Shah's hard-line advisers felt he was selling out the country's sovereignty, he could point to the need for keeping Stalin's confidence. Soviet complaints about Iranian moves at the United Nations could be parried by explaining that these moves were required by Iranian law and U.N. regulations. Through such probing and parrying of the constraints Qavam discovered a bargaining space. In the language of a previous chapter, this was R-search. He found that Stalin's minimum demand was for an oil concession and the Shah's main interest was in sovereignty; here was room for mutual accommodation.

Having arranged a CC agreement with Stalin exchanging troop withdrawal for an oil concession, Qavam guaranteed it by tying the concessions together with technicalities. He had previously appeased Stalin by withdrawing the Iranian complaint from the U.N. agenda while keeping it on the agenda by a technicality; now he explained that the complaint could unfortunately be discharged only by a final Iranian report, and to make this report Iranian government officials must have access to Azerbaijan. So Stalin had to pressure the autonomous province to submit to central control. Qavam also explained that his oil concession must be ratified by the Iranian parliament, which could legally be elected only after Soviet troops had left the country and Iranian officials were admitted to Azerbaijan to supervise the elections. Finally when the Soviet troops were out and Parliament elected, Qavam explained correctly that he could not force it to ratify the oil agreement, which it finally refused to ratify. So after Stalin had badgered and threatened Qavam into making one concession after another, a whole series of concessions, he was finally left holding an empty bag.

Qavam received an appropriate political reward for his brilliant feat: he was fired. The Shah, worrying about Qavam's increasing prestige, had worked to undermine his power in the 1947 elections, and finally dismissed him two months after the oil concession was defeated.[32]

An instance of a shift from *C* to *D:* In 1905 Rouvier's *C* strategy was based on the diagnosis that Germany had a legitimate grievance against his opponent Delcassé's anti-German diplomacy, but once this grievance was satisfied Germany and France could again live as good neighbors, settling grievances as they came up by discussion and mutual accommodation. His initial expectation was that if he expressed willingness to accommodate, Bulow would drop his demand for a conference and state the German grievances, and France could satisfy them and restore harmony. He did not realize that Bulow was not interested in bilaterally negotiated "compensation" but in the coercive goal of frustrating France entirely and breaking up the entente. Nor could Rouvier possibly have suspected that the German government was almost as divided as his own was and that Holstein's coercive strategy was subject to arbitrary accommodative interruptions carried out in a hard-line spirit. Given the divergence between his image of Germany and the actual German situation, Rouvier's strategy could not possibly work as he expected, and the question was whether the ambiguous German feedback would enable Rouvier to correct his strategy.

Rouvier's first negative feedback came immediately, when there was no German reply to his offer to negotiate all colonial disputes and to make French concessions. His response was a tactical shift, specific new concessions in Morocco, within an unchanged basic strategy. Perhaps Bulow needed a more specific concession as evidence of good faith.

---

[32] To be sure, Qavam could not have achieved his success without U.S. and British pressure on the Soviet Union, exerted chiefly through the United Nations but also in other ways such as diplomatic protests and force demonstration.

At this point came the German argument that Delcassé's presence in the cabinet was the main barrier to good German–French relations, an argument with which Rouvier entirely agreed. Bulow meant that Delcassé was the main barrier to French yielding on Morocco, and Rouvier meant that Delcassé had in the past prevented friendly relations and was still a symbol of French enmity. So Rouvier believed he understood Bulow perfectly, and forced Delcassé's resignation as a token of good faith.

Rouvier's next negative feedback came when the Germans repeated their demand for a multilateral conference on Morocco. Rouvier then repeated his earlier offer of a general colonial settlement with Germany. When the Germans rejected this and stuck to their conference demand, Rouvier's expectations became disoriented. Delcassé had not been the barrier to good relations after all. Rouvier now realized that his image of Germany as the aggrieved but good-natured neighbor may have been mistaken and that he needed a more accurate image. Since Germany was not good-natured, it must be bad-natured; it had deceived him about Delcassé and was now trying to humiliate him. Given this new image and new expectations, a D strategy was the appropriate one. So he rejected the German conference proposal. The effectiveness of a D strategy depended, however, on the power Rouvier was able to control in the event of a DD deadlock. The main source of additional power was the British ally, so Rouvier now needed new information about the exact degree of British support, information that had been of no interest to him earlier. His inquiries in London elicited from Lord Lansdowne, the foreign secretary, the statement that Britain would follow the French lead on Morocco; if France continued to refuse the conference Britain would do so too. Lansdowne also warned Germany that British support of France was likely in case of a Franco–German war.

This information clarified the P-situation for Rouvier. In negotiations British diplomatic support was guaranteed, and in the event of war, military support was probable. This meant that a DD deadlock was more dangerous to Germany than to France, so at a conference Germany could be expected to yield. Consequently, the French constraint, *keep Germany out of Morocco,* did not rule out a conference, and the constraint, *avoid war,* did not rule out a D strategy of intransigence at the conference. His estimate of the situation thus corrected by the new information, Rouvier agreed to a conference, stood firm on all issues at the conference, and handed Germany a resounding defeat.

Japanese strategy revision in 1941 provides an example of coalition renegotiation. The Japanese bargaining strategy of July 1940 was governed by four constraints: 1. *Remove the intolerable situation* of European control of the raw materials essential to Japan's survival. 2.

Complete the "pacification" of China. 3. *Avoid war with the United States.* 4. *Maintain the alliance with Germany.* No. 1 was accepted by all, but especially the navy with its dependence on oil. No. 2, an expansionist goal, was of special importance to the army (Tojo), which was bogged down in China. No. 3 was especially important to Konoye, some advisers such as Kido, and part of the navy represented by Oikawa and Nomura. No. 4 was emphasized by Foreign Minister Matsuoka supported by civilian groups. The initial strategy was *D,* demanding guaranteed raw material deliveries from the Dutch colonies under threat of occupation if they refused. When by April and May 1941 it became apparent that this strategy was not succeeding, reexamination of the constraints was necessary to make strategy revisions possible. The first constraint to be downgraded was the alliance constraint. Matsuoka had isolated himself from his colleagues by his insistence on this constraint, and since his support was entirely from outside the government it was easy to arrange his resignation in July. The increased bargaining space derived from eliminating this constraint was used to offer a substantial concession to the United States (shift to *DC*). By early October it became clear that the revised strategy was still not inducing U.S. cooperation, and further reexamination of constraints was necessary. If constraint 2 could be downgraded, Japan could offer to withdraw from China completely (in 25 years) to get U.S. cooperation in achieving raw material guarantees. The alternative was to eliminate constraint 3 and accept war with the United States as the cost of achieving 1. Some diffuse maneuvering ensued, whose meaning gradually became clear: no one was willing to stand up to the army and suggest a downward revision of constraint 2. Konoye was not; Oikawa and other navy men were not; Kido was not. The upshot was Konoye's resignation, Tojo's elevation to premier, and the downgrading of constraint 3.

SUMMARY OF EMPIRICAL FINDINGS

We now sum up the empirical findings about the three decision theories considered in this chapter.

1. The maximization of utility theory is quite beside the point of crisis bargaining. Its basic assumptions do not hold for crises. First, the values of the bargainers are not homogeneous; they are compared only most reluctantly if at all, once or twice at most during a crisis. Second, bargainers compare two or more alternatives only in about half the cases, and when they do compare, they do not usually choose one of those considered through discussion, but resort instead to political maneuvering. Third, utility functions in many of the cases are not stabilized and worked out in detail at the start of bargaining; part of the

decision-problem is to work them out. A devotee of maximization procedures can manage to fit at most two or three cases, like the Cuban
case, into a very loose maximization interpretation.

Something like maximization does occur in the R-bargaining episode
in 1911. This was a case when all constraints had been substantially
met on both sides, the outlines of a compromise settlement (R, R) had
been achieved, and the details remained to be worked out. The aim
for both sides now was to get the best settlement at the least cost, and
this was a maximization problem. The decisions, however, were tactical
only.

The implication is that maximization is a special case of bounded
rationality. It can occur under very special conditions: all constraints
have been met and therefore the heterogeneity of goals is no longer relevant; the two utility functions are both stabilized and known; the crisis
situation therefore is determinate, and the only remaining problem is
to divide up some homogeneous good. These conditions are rare and
occur only at the end of a crisis. They correspond closely to the conditions of routine wage bargaining within a stabilized, routinized labor–
management system.

2. The fit of bounded rationality to crisis bargaining decisions is excellent, especially in the area of strategy revision. In particular, this
theory captures the central oscillation between establishing or changing
one's levels of aspiration and acceptability, and constructing or revising
a strategy. This duality incorporates directly a need for information
input, whereas in the maximization theory information has always been
an external appendage to the theory. That is, the basic decision cycle
is: establish constraints, construct an acceptable strategy, put out a
tactic, interpret feedback, test and revise levels of acceptability, test and
revise strategy, etc. This cycle improves on Coddington's cycle, since
in the latter it is only expectations about the opponent that are revised,
while in the bounded rationality cycle one's own goals are tested and
revised as well.

The concept of heterogeneous goals, constraints, is constantly applicable in our cases. These cases also support the argument that one
need not choose between two simultaneously available alternatives
but can construct a strategy to specifications.

The theory is less adequate in its account of where possible strategies
come from. The idea that possibilities come from the logical alternatives is a good one, even though logic must operate through decision
makers, i.e., very unevenly. But the concept of a typology of problems
in memory, each with a list of possible solutions to call and test one by
one, is too routinized and rigid to apply well to our "ill-defined" crisis
problems. Some of our bargainers seem to act that way in finding pos-

sible strategies, but they are the more rigid, irrational decision makers.

3. The bureaucratic theory is in part supplementary to the bounded rationality theory, relating the latter's cybernetic concepts to actual political forces. We have provided translations of several cybernetic concepts into bureaucratic terms: organizational memory, constraints, dominant coalition, renegotiating the coalition. Also the bureaucratic theory allows us to distinguish five different kinds of decision-making structures and relate these differences to the details of the decision-making process.

The theory is excellent in dealing with the immediate source of possible strategies, accounting for all the possible strategies considered in our cases. Its account of the initial decision process in type 4 and 5 cases is also sound; its emphasis on the importance of prestige, personal influence, and maneuvering debunks the supposition that consideration of alternative strategies is a rational process. It shows that bounded rationality is an idealization that is approximated in only a few initial strategy decisions though more regularly in strategy revision. It also explains the four cases in which strategy revision was also procedurally irrational—Germany 1906, France 1923, Japan 1941, United States 1941. These are all type 5 or nearly type 5 cases.

Thus the strength of the theory is in how it explains the numerous instances of organizational irrationality, as apart from individual irrationality. It brings the idealizations of bounded rationality down to political reality, showing that bounded rationality requires a type 2, 3 or 4 structure. However, this proposition needs further development. The bureaucratic theory is strong descriptively, and especially in explaining organizational irrationality, but its normative side remains vague.[33]

---

[33] See, for example Steinbruner, *The Cybernetic Theory of Decision*, pp. 341–342.

COMMENT BY SNYDER: The statement that the theory of utility maximization is "quite beside the point of crisis bargaining" is, I believe, a considerable exaggeration. We do have several cases where the "loose" version of this theory (p. 341) fits quite well. This is the only version of the theory worth testing, since one knows, without doing empirical research, that nobody behaves according to the ideal-type version. In the loose version, the only criterion for maximizing is that decision makers make *direct comparisons* of alternatives in terms of some implicit common denominator of value—one may as well call it "utility." In bounded rationality, by contrast, alternatives are tested against constraints, not directly compared with each other. We have also used a loose version of the bounded rationality theory, dropping the assumption that decision makers merely "satisfice" by accepting the first satisfactory alternative that comes along. This assumption obviously is unrealistic for crises or any situation where very important values are involved. Consequently, in both theories, the decision maker tries to find the "best" alternative; the only difference is in the intellectual procedure by which the best is identified. Diesing has obscured this important point by insisting that decision makers do not choose or attempt to find the best

BOUNDED RATIONALITY AND GAME THEORY

The decision-theoretic concepts of this chapter complement the game-theoretic bargaining concepts of Chapters II–IV. Each set of concepts deals with the same bargaining process, but from different directions Game theory, we have argued, is not suitable for describing the decision process of our bargainers, the construction, evaluation, and revision of strategies, but is suitable for describing the structure of the bargaining situation. Decision theory deals with the way bargainers come to terms with this situation, the way they learn about it and work out possible settlements. Game theory describes the bargaining structure; decision theory describes the way bargaining strategies are constructed. The two sets of concepts must, therefore, be related to each other one by one to produce a rounded picture of bargaining.

---

strategy, but only an "acceptable" one. In our cases the acceptable choice is always considered the best as well.

In the cases for which we have most data on internal decision making, we do find decision makers at certain points listing the pros and cons of all reasonable alternatives in fairly systematic fashion, then choosing the "best." This took place most clearly in the United States, Cuba, 1962; also in United States, Berlin, 1948; United States, Berlin, 1961, and England, Munich, 1938. (My hunch is there would be more such cases if our internal data were more complete.) In these instances it is very difficult if not impossible to judge whether the participants compared the alternatives to each other in terms of some implicit common denominator of costs and benefits or tested each one separately against constraints. Either theory would apply with equal validity. This is not so much because the data are ambiguous as because the intellectual procedures postulated by each theory are quite easily translatable into the other at difficult choice points. When choosing among two or more imperfect alternatives, whether decision makers choose the one with the best benefit-cost ratio or the one that least violates the constraints becomes pretty much an issue of semantics. I would argue further that the choice ultimately requires some sort of direct comparison of alternatives.

I cannot accept the statement that maximization is only a special case of bounded rationality, occurring only under the "special condition" where all constraints have been met. This might apply to non-bargaining situations, but in bargaining with an adversary, the non-satisfaction of constraints for at least one party is a necessary condition for bargaining leverage. (I have already explained, in an earlier comment, how Diesing has mis-used the Morocco, 1911, example to make his point here.) In fact, maximization occurs whenever constraints *cannot* be fully met and one or more of them must be relaxed; then some sort of comparison between alternatives must take place to find the one that requires the least modification of constraints.

I do agree that the bounded rationality theory fits our data somewhat better than the utility maximization theory. But the latter is not completely disconfirmed. In many cases a complementary synthesis of the two theories would most accurately reflect the facts.

I also agree that Diesing's *interpretation* of the "bureaucratic politics" theory is useful, but in the interpretation the "bureaucratic" element has pretty much disappeared and what is left is a theory of coalition formation. This is appropriate, since we do not find that attitudes of leading decision makers are much determined by bureaucratic role. Thus the most distinctive point of the Allison-Halperin "bureaucratic politics" theory does not survive our analysis.

	B C	B D	E
C	Compromise R, R	B wins S, T	A surrenders
D	A wins T, S	Deadlock P, P	B attacks
E	B surrenders	A attacks	War

Figure 5-1. The General Bargaining Situation

The bargaining situation consists of the preference ordering of the two main bargainers over the various possible outcomes, and the intersection of the two preference orderings determines what outcomes are possible and what the likely effect of various strategies will be. The generalized structure is given in Figure 5–1.

Variations in preference orderings produce the various possible games, each with its own dynamic pushing toward certain possible solutions, its typical misperceptions, and typical bargaining tactics. The bargainers do not at first know the opponent's preference ordering and may not be clear about their own, but they attempt to estimate the opponent's preferences in working out a strategy. Insofar as their estimates are correct and they consequently know what game they are playing, their strategy is likely to be as effective as conditions permit. Insofar as they do not know what game they are playing, their strategy may be successful by accident but may also be ineffective or even self-defeating.

The bargaining process mediates between the bargaining situation (structure) and decisions about it. A strategy decision is expressed in tactical actions, in bids, probes, threats, promises, arguments, questions, and the like; these actions affect both the actor, by getting him located in a bargaining stance, and the opponent, by changing the apparent costs and rewards of his various possible replies. The reply constitutes feedback from the bargaining situation, which can be used to evaluate the tactic and perhaps to revise tactic, strategy, or expectations. Additional situational feedback comes from the effect of the action on the actor's internal politics, which may force changes in his own preferences, resources, or goals and constraints. (A striking example is the effect of French occupation of the Ruhr on the French government, including financial weakening and the rise in influence of the Left, which forced

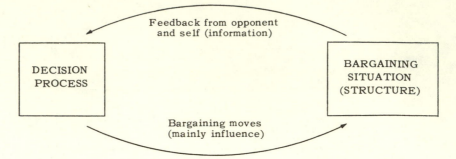

Figure 5-2. Mediation between Decisions and Bargaining Situation

Poincaré to revise his preferences sharply between September and November 1923.) The revised or reaffirmed strategy is then output again and the cycle continues (see Figure 5–2).

In theoretical terms, this means that the two related bargaining concepts of information and influence mediate between the concepts of bounded rationality and those of game theory. We argued in Chapter II that bargaining is an influence/search process, that is, every bargaining move that reaches the opponent has an influence aspect and an information aspect. This means also that all feedback, both from opponent and from self, has the same two aspects. Ordinarily the influence aspect predominates in the intentions of the actor, but in probes—actions for the sake of feedback—the information aspect predominates. Consequently, if we trace these two aspects in the movement from strategy decisions to bargaining situation and back again, we will see how far the concepts of bounded rationality can be mapped on to the concepts of game theory and vice versa.

We begin with the information aspect. The bargaining situation is the object about which information is desired. The search for information during strategy revision is the search of the successive cells of the game matrix described in Chapter 2. The search process was described originally in terms of the object searched, the cells of the game matrix; and it was argued that the dynamics of the game tended to direct the search into a certain sequence, P-T-R or P-S or S. In this chapter, search was described in terms of the searcher, the need of the decision maker for information so he could adjust his expectations. The decision maker's need is to know the aspiration and acceptability levels of the opponent's constraints, and also the amount of support he can expect from the ally.

These are two complementary versions of the same process. First, the ally's level of support determines the P-situation, the outcome of a DD deadlock, so it is a main component of P-search. The other component is the acceptability level of the opponent's *avoid war* constraint, which constitutes the opponent's preference function for the *P*-situation. Constraint 1, *remove the intolerable situation,* is the *T*-goal for both bargainers, while the positive goals of the occasional expansionist power or faction are another kind of *T*-goal. Consequently, information about the opponent's levels of aspiration and acceptability for these goals clarifies the *T*-situation. The coercive probes that yield information about the opponent's *T* also produce clarification of one's own *T,* and this is *T*-search.

R is the area of downward revision of constraint 1. The investigation of *R, R*-search or accommodative probing, is appropriate and usually occurs only late in a crisis, if at all. If it occurs earlier, for instance, Grey in 1914 with his mediation proposals or Rouvier in 1905 with his offers to settle grievances, the search will reveal nothing. The reason is that as long as constraint 1 is at its initial aspiration level, *T* or near *T,* all suggestions for compromise will be unacceptable by 1 and will be rejected. Thus, Grey's mediation proposals were unacceptable to Germany because Bethmann–Hollweg still aspired to remove Serbia from the diplomatic scene (*T*), and mediation would not accomplish this. Rouvier's proposal to settle German grievances was unacceptable to Bulow in 1905 because Bulow's *T*-goal was still the humiliation of France and destruction of the Entente, and Rouvier's proposal would not accomplish this. Aspiration level for constraint 1 must be clarified or revised downward before the *R* area has any content. Downward revision, in turn, occurs only in the strategy revision process; it is induced partly by probes and partly by information about the *P* and *T* situations, which shows that it will not be possible to satisfy both 1, *remove the intolerable situation,* and 2, *avoid war.* If 1 is revised downward this leads to *R*-search; if 2 is revised down, an increased risk of war is accepted, or, as with Japan 1941, an actual decision for war is made.

S-search is especially important in Leader and Protector games; it provides information about the needs of the ally, and what can be gotten from the situation to satisfy them. Thus in 1909 Grey argued with his colleagues that Britain must do something for Russia or Russia would become disillusioned with the Entente and would leave it. He then proceeded to search the Austrian demands on Serbia, Russia's client, to see where those demands could be beaten down a bit to help Serbia. *S*-search plainly corresponds to the alliance constraint, *do not alienate the ally.* Since the alliance constraint appears in most adversary cases, this suggests that a secondary Leader component is present in those games as well. In the Quemoy case, for example, the United States softened its stand on Quemoy, publicly at least, to satisfy British worries;

this was an *S* payoff to Britain for continuing to follow the United States.

S-search can also occur in Chicken and Bully games to discover what will mollify the defeated opponent and make his defeat more acceptable to him. The constraint that corresponds to this activity appears in Salisbury's principle (1898) that one should not drive the defeated opponent to the wall because this will preclude future friendship with him. Most of our statesmen were not that wise: they believed that once the opponent had yielded one should extract the last possible concession from him and avoid any concessions oneself. (Rouvier, 1906, toward Germany, Aehrenthal and Bulow in 1909 toward Russia, Acheson in 1962 toward the Soviet Union.)

A few constraints, including *don't spoil the negotiating atmosphere* and *retain the Shah's confidence,* relate to the game matrix more indirectly.

We turn now to the influence aspect of bargaining. In relation to the bargaining situation, influence occurs via either the clarification of one's own payoffs for the opponent or the change of his or one's own payoffs. On the decision side of bargaining, influence is the usual purpose of bargaining moves. The purpose of bargaining is to influence the opponent to move toward a desirable outcome for oneself, and one does this by arranging his payoffs, or his perception of one's own payoffs, so as to make the desired move seem advantageous to him. The detailed mapping of bargaining moves on to the situation is obvious: coercive moves (*P*-influence) mainly establish or change *DD* payoffs, and accommodative moves (*R*-influence) do the same for the *CC* cell. Persuasive moves chiefly act upon payoffs and perceptions of payoffs in the *CD* or *DC* cells. In alliance games the *DC* and *CD* cells are the main ones affected by influence moves (*S*-influence).

Influence moves can be decided only insofar as one has fairly clear expectations about the opponent (and self), that is, a fairly clear picture of the structure of the bargaining situation. One cannot choose an influence tactic unless one can predict its effect on the opponent's perceived situation. Insofar as one's expectations are vague, the usefulness of influence tactics is indeterminate, and the need for more information about the opponent becomes primary. Thus there is an oscillation on the decision side of bargaining between the need for information to clarify the situation for oneself and the need to influence the opponent by changing the situation or his perception of it. The oscillation can be diagrammed as in Figure 5–3.

As bargaining begins, the decision maker knows the least about the situation. For the challenger, initial expectations and initial strategy come more from the image and belief system than from the situation, as no feedback is yet available. The resister at least has the opponent's

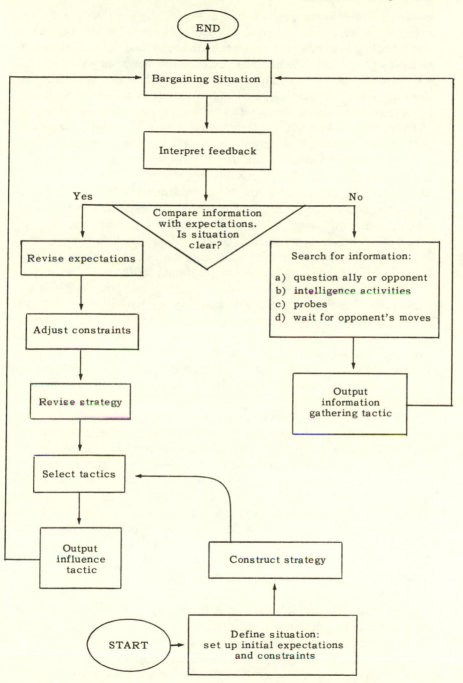

Figure 5-3. Influence and Information Search in Bargaining

challenge move as information but is still strongly influenced by his pre-crisis belief system. Having devised an acceptable strategy, each bargainer begins to influence the opponent; the mutual influencing tactics of the bargainers begin to establish the objective bargaining situation by specifying demands, committing resources, committing responses by threats and promises, etc. As long as feedback from the situation can be interpreted to conform to initial expectations, the situation remains subjectively clear and no additional information is needed. When feedback conflicts with expectations strongly enough to disorient them, the situation is no longer clear and more information is needed. New information is required until the situation is again clear. The new situation allows one to revise expectations, adjust constraints, revise strategy, and shift back to influence tactics. In some cases the oscillation between influence tactics and information tactics is rather frequent once strategy revision has begun; in some cases such as Britain, 1956, there is only one influence-information-influence oscillation and the revised strategy is carried out without any interest in additional feedback.

So far we have mapped the typology of tactics and strategy on to the game matrix via the concept of influence, and we have mapped the cells of the matrix on to the constraints and goals via the concept of information. We have also related the decision sequence of initial decision, disorientation of expectations, and strategy revision to the oscillation between influence tactics and information search in the bargaining process. We now contrast the decision perspective and the situation or game perspective.

The main difference between the game matrix and the list of constraints that control decisions is that in the matrix the outcomes are in a preference ordering while in the decision process the constraints are unique. This repeats the distinction we made early in the chapter between the homogeneous goals of utility and game theory and the heterogeneous goals of the theory of bounded rationality. The mediation between the two occurs in the strategy-revision process. When new information shows that no strategy that meets all the original constraints is possible, the decision maker must clarify or revise some aspiration level downward. But the decision as to which one to revise downward involves comparing two constraints at the margin and thereby putting them in a preference order. For instance, in 1914 when Sazonov came to realize he could probably not have both peace and an independent Serbia, he chose the latter constraint as the more important, and this made his preference ordering Prisoner's Dilemma, $S < P$. Thus at the start of a crisis the constraints are often unique, non-comparable, while later on more comparison and preference ordering has occurred.

In other words, if we take Figure 5–3 as a description of the bargaining process over time, it is a process in which the "game" or bargaining structure is gradually created and stabilized or changed. In most cases the bargainer has a preference ordering as bargaining begins but is more or less vague about the content of the cells and especially the R cell. The game does exist for him, but only in outline, and the bargaining process fills in the details and perhaps also changes his preferences. In other cases he does not have a preference ordering, either because he has no clear idea what the issues are or because his internal political process has not yet made the necessary decisions. That is, the constraints on an acceptable solution are either not clear or have not been put in a preference order. In these cases we can ascribe a structure to the crisis either by working backwards from the eventual decisions—for example the Soviet Union backed down in 1962, so the game "must have been" chicken for them—or by estimating what the decisions would have been had they been made at the start of bargaining. However, this ascribed structure is somewhat hypothetical. It refers not to an actual game, an actual preference ordering, but to various forces that would produce or that will eventually produce a game structure during bargaining.

The game structure is created and changed during bargaining in several ways. First, the initial T-payoff, and sometimes its importance relative to P and R, is established by the initial commitment to constraint 1, which is made public in the initial demand. Then the initial P-situation is set up by P-influence moves, which get resources committed and organized for action in the event of deadlock. Feedback from the opponent clarifies P further and also S, the cost of yielding to his demands. This clarification may lead to a reevaluation and change of preferences or to a stabilization of initial preferences. The opponent's responses may also engage additional values, for instance by threats, or may shift values by stimulating emotions. If there is a non-bargaining interaction this may also change constraints, payoffs, and preference ordering, by shifting the balance of internal political forces or by activating new political forces. For example in 1898 British "public opinion" (newspapers) was inflamed by certain French Colonial Office statements, thereby activating the hard-line cabinet members and increasing

TABLE 5–5

DOES THE BARGAINER HAVE A PREFERENCE ORDERING AT THE START OF A CRISIS?

Yes or probably yes	25	(70%)
No or probably not	11	(30%)
Don't know	4	
Total	40	

the political cost of minor British concessions. Finally, if there is prolonged deadlock and the initial strategy is failing, any remaining indeterminacy of preferences has to be resolved to allow for strategy revision.

Consequently the concepts of game theory should be interpreted as static reductions of a dynamic process. The bargaining game "is" not, it *becomes*. A game matrix should be treated in some cases as a time slice in a rapidly changing situation, and in other cases as describing an underlying structural possibility or tendency that gets worked into clarity and stability during bargaining. An example of the former is United States–Soviet Union bargaining relations in Poland, Germany, and Iran in 1945–1946. In Poland and Germany there was a short Leader episode from about February to April 1945—the issue in Germany being reparations vs. recovery; in Poland, what a "democratic" government should look like. The games rapidly but asymmetrically shifted to Prisoner's Dilemma, as each perceived the other's "leading" as competitive "defection." In Iran the Leader episode was somewhat more stable but shifted to Chicken during 1946. An example of the latter is Cuba, which had stabilized as Called Bluff by October 27, 1962. But the game could easily have become Prisoner's Dilemma if the United States had lowered the Soviet Union's S payoff somewhat, for instance, by issuing an ultimatum to remove the missiles, boarding and seizing Soviet ships, invading Cuba, or otherwise insisting on inflicting a humiliating defeat. The Soviet S was already pretty low, and any further lowering of it could have reduced it below P. As it was, the United States raised the Soviet S, particularly with the no-invasion pledge (S-influence), and thereby stabilized the game.

It is even possible that the game never does stabilize. If neither side makes explicit demands, because it is not sure what it wants or because its internal constraints require ambiguous expression, T and S cannot be specified, and the game remains ambiguous. Lebanon and Quemoy are the examples; both were primarily action games where explicit demands were not made and only P was clarified by the action. Quemoy, however, was plausibly becoming Called Bluff by the growing U.S. commitment to defend Quemoy.

If the "game" or bargaining structure does not clearly exist at the start of bargaining, or exists only in outline, the bargaining process has a double function. Bargaining is not only a process of resolving a crisis situation and working out a settlement, it is also a process of creating and stabilizing (or changing) the very crisis situation that is to be resolved. At the onset of a crisis its game structure is not only unknown to the bargainers, since they are without feedback about the opponent's preferences and strategy, but it has only in part come to exist, since values have not yet been fully engaged. The initial decisions and influence moves begin to set up a structure (first T, then P, then R) whose details became known via feedback; this leads to strategy revisions and further stabilization or change of the situation, and so on in a cyclical process. If there is openness to new information, the successive adjustments of expectations and revisions of acceptability levels and of strategy will follow closely the developing determination of the situation; but if initial expectations continue to dominate strategy the developing situation may diverge quite far from the initial subjective diagnoses of it.

We must, however, not exaggerate the amount of indeterminacy of crisis structures and the amount of creativity involved in bargaining. The amount varies considerably from one crisis to another, and one cannot assume in advance that any particular amount of indeterminacy will occur. The two extremes in our cases are the 1898 Fashoda crisis (high determinacy) and the 1945–1946 Iran crisis (low determinacy), and the range between them is great.

In 1898 the conventions of multipolar diplomacy and of colonial disputes in particular were pretty well established and understood. The technology of warfare and the capacities and operating routines of the two fleets were established and known—in contrast to 1948 when no one knew how the airlift would work and what the reactions of the Berliners to food and coal shortages would be. The influence pattern within the British cabinet in 1898 and the beliefs and strategy preferences of its members were established. Consequently it was settled from the start that the game was Bully, that British strategy would be D with a weak C component, and that Britain would win. The only indeterminacy on the British side was the question of how much restraint the cabinet would put on Salisbury's desire to make minor concessions to a defeated opponent, and this would depend on how strongly the leading newspapers would react to the French challenge. The main indeterminacy was on the French side, where the colonialist-anticolonialist struggle was still in doubt and the French T and constraint 1 not at all settled. The unexpected revelations of the Dreyfus affair in August seriously weakened the army and the cabinet just as bargaining was beginning. Internal feedback from these changes forced Delcassé to revise his expectations: he saw that, with the army demoralized and the cabinet about to fall, his original D strategy, to say nothing of E, would produce disaster. Consequently, he had to reduce his aspiration on constraint 1, dropping the goal of a French presence on the Nile and hoping only for some small British concession that would bolster the cabinet. This reduction made a strategy shift from D to C acceptable. Thus, on the French side, though the preference ordering was Chicken from the start, the detailed constraints, payoffs, and initial strategy were not stabilized for about a month, at which time the basic Bully structure was firmly established. Only the French S remained slightly indeterminate.

Consider now Iran in 1945–1946. In 1945 the end of the war brought a new bipolar system into existence, a system, however, whose dynamics, influence boundaries, and alignments would take several years to develop. The two main bargainers were still officially in alliance although the reason for their alliance had disappeared; the old images of each other were crumbling but new images had not yet stabilized. Both hoped to continue cooperation but no one knew how the United Nations, the instrument of cooperation, would work; it did not exist yet. Consequently neither side had clear goals or expectations. The main element of determinacy was the two divergent plans on how to cooperate (free competition plus United Nations parliamentary procedures vs. spheres of influence and foreign ministers' meetings), and these determined the basic bargaining situation as Leader with typical Leader misperceptions fated to occur. But the detailed payoffs within the Leader game were indeterminate. This was especially true of S, the follower's payoff, and P, independent action; but T was not yet stabilized and of course R was empty. For instance, the Soviet Union had no clear notion of what a sphere of influence in north Iran (T) specifically meant, as its varying policies in different localities indicated. The whole game, except for the initial Leader skeleton, had to be created by bargaining tactics and strategy decisions; and when it finally became stabilized it was Chicken.

CHAPTER VI

CRISES AND INTERNATIONAL SYSTEMS[1]

The behavior of states in a crisis is affected by the nature of the international system at the time they occur. We may call this the "external" parameter of crisis interaction. While the international system may be described in terms of many variables, two are of paramount importance for the study of crises: (1) the "structure" of the system, i.e., the number of major actors and the gross distribution of military power among them, and (2) the nature of military technology. Our historical research has encompassed two distinct international systems in terms of these variables. The system in the latter part of the nineteenth century and up to 1945 was multipolar in structure, and non-nuclear (conventional) in technology. Since 1945 it has been bipolar and nuclear. The international system at present seems to be in a transitional period leading to a new form of multipolarity and perhaps eventually to a proliferation of nuclear weapons. While one can only speculate about the possible nature of crises in this emerging system, the generalizations we draw herein about crises in historical multipolar systems provide some empirical ground for such speculation.

The following analysis seeks primarily to show the effects of these systemic variables upon crisis interaction and bargaining. One might reverse the cause-effect relationship and ask what effects crises have on the system; e.g., what is their systemic "function"? Are they stabilizing or destabilizing? How do they affect subsequent relations between the states? etc. We shall have a few things to say about such questions, but our thrust is mostly the other way: systemic environment comprises the independent variables, crisis behavior the dependent ones. To set the stage, we must first describe some general characteristics of different systemic structures.

SYSTEM STRUCTURES

The "structure" of an international system is defined by the *number* of major actors in the system and the *distribution of military power* and potential among them. In a multipolar system there are several (more than two) "Great Powers" whose military power is roughly equal, and whose rivalry and cooperation dominate politics in the system. In addition there are, of course, a number of smaller states who do not play significant roles except as they serve as objects of the Great Power

[1] This is a revised version of Snyder's essay, "Conflict and Crisis in the International System," in James N. Rosenau, Gavin Boyd, and Kenneth Thompson, eds., *World Politics* (New York: The Free Press, 1976), Ch. 29.

competition or create disturbances among themselves that engage the Great Powers. A bipolar system is one with only two Great Powers and a number of smaller states. These are definitions of ideal types, from which real international systems will deviate, more or less. The multipolar systems of 1870–1914 and 1918–1939 approximate the ideal type quite closely; the bipolar system since 1945 somewhat less so. In the latter, some of the "smaller states" were considerably more powerful than others and played roles more significant than mere objects of superpower competition. However, this "deviation" is much less important than the power inequality between the "superpowers" and all others.

Of course, the power structure among the actors is not the only important dimension of an international system. The total system comprises its structure, the pattern of relations among the state-actors, their specific interactions, and their internal attributes. In this chapter we shall concentrate on how structure affects relational patterns, chiefly alignments, and how alignment patterns in turn affect crisis interaction.

We emphasize that the "poles" in our two structural types are *states*, not alliances or "blocs" of states. Alliances and blocs are types of *relations* between states in the system that are influenced by the prevailing structure but do not constitute that structure. Thus the rough equality between the two alliances prior to 1914 did not make the system bipolar, nor did the loosening of the U.S. and Soviet blocs during the 1960s and early 1970s make that system multipolar.

The most fundamental relational phenomenon affected by structure is the identification of friends and enemies, potential or actual. For the superpowers in a bipolar system, the identity of the opponent is fully determined by structure; for the lesser powers, considerably so. The United States and the Soviet Union could not help but perceive each other as rivals after World War II, since for each one, the other was the only state in the system that posed a serious military threat to its own security or to smaller states whose independence or affiliation was deemed essential to that security. Ideological conflict had little to do with this basic identification although it did exacerbate the resulting antagonism. Specific conflicts of interest and hostile acts reflected more than they created the antagonism. Thus, while the *degree* of tension and hostility in the Cold War was undoubtedly increased by incompatible ideologies and specific hostile behavior that tended to confirm initial perceptions of threat, the initial perceptions themselves were a function of the preponderance of these two powers over all others. In short, the rivalry was structurally ordained.[2] This rivalry does not necessarily

---

[2] That the imperatives of system structure were the primary cause of the Cold War is the leading theme of Louis Halle's *The Cold War as History* (New York: Harper and Row, 1967). These imperatives are overlooked by revisionist writers,

mean unremitting hostility. While always regarding each other as the principal opponent, the Big Two have found it possible and mutually advantageous at times to cooperate, to some degree and for particular purposes, as in the current détente. But détente can never develop into entente or alliance, as it may in a multipolar system, because there is no third party powerful enough to provide a sufficient incentive for alliance.

The alignment of the lesser states in a bipolar system is determined by some combination of structural forces and specific historical, geographic, or ideological circumstances. It might be argued that their alignment is not affected by the logic of system structure at all. If left to their own devices, they will align with the superpower that appears least threatening to their own security or that is most congenial ideologically. If there is no threat, or no strong ideological affinity or repulsion, they will not align at all.

However, they will not be left to their own devices. The structural compulsions on the superpowers themselves will indirectly affect the alignment of the lesser states. Each of the giants, fearful of the other, will seek hegemony over, or alliance with, some of the states in the space between them, out of their own security concerns. When one of them starts this process, the other will perceive it as threatening, as will the rest of the small states, and these will then join in a counteralliance. This is essentially what happened in Europe after World War II. The Soviet Union asserted dominance over the Eastern European countries when it had the chance as the result of its liberation of these countries from German control. It probably did so primarily for security reasons, security against a possibly resurgent Germany backed by the immense power of the United States. The Western European countries and the United States perceived this as threatening to their security and formed NATO in response. It may be plausibly contended that something like this would have occurred in any case, whatever the detailed factual circumstances that attended the birth of the bipolar system. The superpowers, facing a power vacuum in the space intervening between them, would have each sought to fill it, or part of it, in order to preempt the intolerable security threat that would have resulted from the rival having filled all of it.

Of course the logic of structure does not fully determine which state

---

who see the Cold War as caused by the nature of the U.S. capitalist system, and also by traditional writers who find its cause in "Soviet imperialism." For analyses of the revisionists' blind spot on this point, see especially Robert W. Tucker, *The Radical Left and American Foreign Policy*, Studies in International Affairs, No. 15, The Washington Center for Foreign Policy Research, 1971, pp. 89–90; also James Richardson, "Cold-War Revisionism: A Critique," *World Politics*, Vol. 24, No. 4 (July 1972), pp. 579–613.

will be in which camp, only that alignments will form. Membership in each alignment will depend on empirical circumstances, in this case primarily geography and the limits of Soviet power. Among the states that remained outside the Soviet embrace, some (e.g., Sweden, Switzerland) did not join NATO, but they were nevertheless beneficiaries of a tacit U.S. security guarantee. The membership of some states on the periphery of the blocs may be problematical (e.g., Yugoslavia), and the superpowers may offer their protective mantle to some states for non-security reasons (e.g., the United States' tacit commitment to Israel).

Once the alignments are formed, dealignment or realignment of the lesser powers is unlikely, either because they have no incentive to realign or because, if they try, their superpower protector will prevent it. But here again, the unlikelihood of realignment results from some combination of structural necessity and specific factual circumstances. The lack of incentive to realign, for example, is largely a function of the ideology of regimes; the inability to realign, for Warsaw Pact members at least, can be traced largely to structural necessity as it determines the security interests of the superpower.

The Sino-Soviet split and the United States–China rapprochement do not violate this logic, since this realignment involved a state outside the central arena, with enough independent power to escape the embrace of its former protector. Also, China represents a potential third "pole" in a system evolving toward multipolarity. The current fluidity in world politics partly reflects this developing structural change, which is still some decades away from completion. Hence, the contemporary transitional system exhibits some of the characteristics we here ascribe to bipolarity, and some which we will attribute to multipolarity; we may speculate that the latter will grow more prominent as the system evolves.

In a multipolar system such as that of the nineteenth century, enmity and amity are not determined by structure per se. To be sure, if one state grows dangerously powerful and/or reveals generally aggressive intentions, thereby threatening a structural transformation, it will attract the antagonism of at least some others, who will typically unite against it in the familiar pattern of the balance of power. Short of this, from the structural standpoint alone, each major actor perceives all others to be equally eligible as potential allies or potential opponents. Hence the vaunted "flexibility" of a multipolar system. Some degree of determinacy is introduced, however, by *particular* conflicts of interest, ideological attractions and repulsions, geographical configuration, and traditional, ethnic or sentimental ties. Hence, the conflict of interest between Russia and Austria in the Balkans in the latter part of the nineteenth century predisposed those two states to enmity and inhibited alliance between them, as did the Alsace–Lorraine conflict between Germany and France. Various specific conflicts between Russia and England seemed to make them "natural" opponents, and alliance between France and England was likewise inhibited by imperial conflicts. Ideological similarity among the three eastern regimes exerted some attraction between them and some repulsion toward Britain and France, themselves mutually attracted by their democratic institutions. Ethnic ties predisposed Germany and Austria to friendship and exerted a weaker pull between these two and England. The upshot of these criss-crossing forces was, first, the German–Austrian alliance of 1879, which, in Bismarck's calculations, brought along England as a "sleeping partner" and produced in reaction the Franco–Russian alliance, which, notably however, was delayed 15 years, largely because of mutual ideological distaste, but also because of Bismarck's diplomatic skill in keeping Russia tied to Germany.

Such particular interests, conflicts, and affinities are more influential in determining alignment in multipolarity than they are in bipolarity. Because of them, a multipolar system is less flexible than its glorifiers have sometimes claimed. However, the "logic of particular interests' is hardly ever completely determining. It competes with, and interacts with, another logic, the "logic of flexibility," which is inherent in the structure of the system and independent of the particular interests of its members. Given that all other major states are powerful enough to be a potential threat to one's own, there is always some degree of compulsion to coalesce with some others, any others. Some states are likely to prefer the certainty of some definite allies and some definite enemies to the uncertainty of "each against each" and the disastrous possibility of "all against one." Fear of aggression or aggressive alliances by others need not be well-substantiated to trigger the first combination, and, once the first is formed, a countercoalition is likely to form in response. Particular interests and conflicts may affect the *choice* of allies, but the compulsion to align or counteralign exists apart from them, and may override them. Thus, Bismarck chose to ally with Austria, but the principal reason why he made any alliance at all was his fear that Austria might combine with France, tacitly bringing England along via her common interests with Austria in opposing Russia in the eastern Mediterranean. In a five-member system, Bismarck preferred to be in a party of three rather than two, so he simply preempted the party of three. The fact that he preempted *from France* reflected a particular conflict, but that he felt compelled to preempt at all reflected the logic of the system, as did, subsequently, the counteralliance between France and Russia that overrode the particular conflict (of ideology) between these two countries. Here we see the familiar dynamics of the Prisoner's Dilemma.

The "best" outcome (no alliance obligations) is sacrificed to "second-best" (moderate security with onerous commitments), in order to insure against the "worst" (facing a hostile combination alone).[3]

Such logic predisposes the parties toward alignment but does not specify the identity of the partners. This is determined by a process of bargaining similar to that of the *N*-person game of game theory. All actors strive to be in a "winning coalition" and to this end make competitive offers to others, offers which have as their currency, ordinarily, the firmness and scope of commitment, with side-payments in concessions on outstanding disputes. Typically, the alliances are never absolutely firm and may be quite tenuous or tacit; consequently the dangers and opportunities of realignment are ever-present. The possible combinations and variants inherent in such flexibility are many. The main point is that although there is not in multipolarity, as there is in bipolarity, much clear guidance as to what one "must" do in any specific sense, this very indeterminacy amid a plethora of dangers and opportunities exerts a powerful compulsion toward a certain kind of behavior that is governed by the rule: "Avoid isolation or being caught in a minority coalition, but get the most you can from your partners, at minimum cost and risk."

The "logic of flexibility" produces a category of *general* interests for the participants that should be carefully distinguished from the *particular* interests mentioned above. Particular interests may be "strategic" interests vis-à-vis specific other states, or they may be "intrinsic" interests—interests valued for reasons other than their strategic—i.e., power—significance. General interests are interests with respect to the general configuration of power in the system. Typical general interests are "be in a majority coalition," "resist the disturber," "preserve the balance of power," etc. States face the problem, in any situation, of predicting whether the particular or general interests of other states will be dominant, and of determining which category should guide their own behavior. Those who guess or choose wrongly may come to grief. For example, when, around the turn of this century, England made an alliance bid to Germany, the Germans asked a very high price, thinking that England's theoretical alternative of alignment with France and Russia was absolutely foreclosed because of particular imperial con-

---

[3] Admittedly, the preclusive alliance reflects only the negative or defensive incentive to defect in the Prisoner's Dilemma. In the model there is also an offensive incentive, which in alliance politics might produce an offensive alliance. However, it is the defensive incentive that puts most of the "dilemma" in the model—whether to trust the other who has an incentive to defect, or to defect oneself to avoid the worst consequences of his defection. When only the defensive incentive is operating, the Prisoner's Dilemma is equivalent to the familiar "security dilemma."

flicts. But England's general interest in ending her isolation was greater than the sacrifices necessary to resolve these conflicts. The result was the ententes of 1904 and 1907 and, it might also be argued, the defeat of Germany in World War I.

There are both particular and general interests in bipolarity as well. What is distinctive about bipolarity is the *clarity* of the general interest. The dominant general interest is the preservation of the balance of power against the other superpower—concretely, to deter and prevent the latter's expansion—or alternatively, to gain a power advantage for one's own "pole." As Kenneth Waltz has pointed out, each superpower will resist the other's attempted expansion at every point, and the other can confidently predict such resistance.[4] Waltz argues that this clarity about "who will oppose whom" is an important factor making for "stability" in a bipolar system, as compared to multipolarity where ambiguity about possible opposition may tempt an aggressor to gamble. There are several reasons for such ambiguity in multipolar systems. First, a state may think of the expanding state as a potential ally against another; hence an increase in its power should logically be encouraged rather than resisted. Second, a potential resister, while visualizing the expanding state as a threat, may face a greater threat from another quarter and be reluctant to subtract power deployed against the latter for use against the aggressor. Third, the state in question may consider both the aggressor and his target as threats to itself and prefer to stand aside and let the two weaken each other. Fourth, there is the broad consideration that the potential resister may prefer not to act until the power configuration in the system obviously represents a direct threat to itself; pending that time it will look only to its particular interests. All such uncertainties provide plenty of material for wishful thinking and possibly miscalculation in a state bent on aggrandizement.

In bipolarity there is little scope for such miscalculation because of the certainty that a power gain for one superpower means a power loss for the other. Loosely speaking, they are in a two-person zero-sum game in power terms, as compared to the more complex and more ambiguous N-person non-zero-sum game of multipolarity. Constant vigilance and resistance to the opponent's every forward move, no matter how minor, is therefore the guiding rule of behavior. Partially opposed to this clarity of interest, however, as Waltz also points out, is a relatively low *intensity* of interest. The power of the superpowers themselves is so great in relation to the power resources of the rest of the system that no particular new acquisition by one or the other, by conquest or realignment, can change the fundamental balance of power between them.

[4] Waltz, "The Stability of a Bipolar World," *Daedalus,* Vol. 93, No. 3 (Summer 1964), pp. 882–883.

Waltz considers this to be a complementary source of stability in the system: while clarity of interests inhibits attempts to change by force, low intensity of interest (in power terms) makes the changes that occur easy to absorb.[5]

In a multipolar system, while the *definition* of general power interests is often unclear, their intensity is likely to be high. That is, the expansion, defeat, or realignment of any major actor will significantly change the power distribution in the system, but the other actors may be uncertain whether the change is to their advantage or detriment. One might hypothesize that when the system is most fluid and the identity of friends and foes most ambiguous, this lack of clarity in power interests will tend to inhibit responses to change and tempt potential aggressors. Conversely, when alignments are clear and firm, the strength of the interest in preventing the defeat of an ally or an opponent's increase of power will encourage resistance and favor deterrence of aggression. The most dangerous condition is that in which alliance commitments *seem* questionable to outsiders but are in reality quite firm.

Another important difference is in the function of alliances relative to "interests." In bipolarity, alliances usually merely *register* the general interests of the members, interests already inherent in the power structure of the system. During the Cold War period, the United States had a clear interest in defending against Soviet expansion all countries outside the Soviet orbit, as the Soviet Union had likewise in its sphere, whether alliances were made or not, and the lesser states on each side had a clear interest in being protected. The formation of NATO, the Warsaw Pact, and other alliances did not create any new interests for the parties, although they did clarify and perhaps add somewhat to the strength of the existing interests, and they also served important functions in facilitating military and political collaboration and in educating public opinion.

In a multipolar system, on the other hand, alliances and alignments often actually *create* interests that did not previously exist. Alliances in multipolarity reflect the fact that no state controls enough power under its own sovereignty to meet all the threats that may arise. There is therefore an incentive to pool power, and the pooling has two major effects: first, by *identifying* friends and foes, perhaps somewhat arbitrarily, it makes clear *whose* expansion is to be regarded as threatening, and whose is to be considered advantageous. In a very real sense, the compulsion to pool power as a general systemic necessity actually creates relations of enmity and amity; it does not just reflect prior relations, although in most cases, what actually occurs is some mixture of "crea-

[5] Ibid., p. 886.

tion" and "reflection." This creation of opponents and friends obviously also creates interests in resisting the one and defending the other, interests that did not exist before, at least not so strongly. For example, when England made her entente with France in 1904, Germany, previously only a vague source of concern, became identified as an enemy and France as a partner, and these identifications were not merely clarified but also strengthened as the entente developed from a mere colonial agreement to something approaching an alliance. In fact, the gradual strengthening of the ties and sense of common interest with France, and the intensification of rivalry with Germany, reciprocally acted and reacted upon each other in a kind of vicious circle. In deciding to pool her power with France to escape isolation, England had to pay the inevitable price of "creating," for Germany, the role of opponent, a role that was previously only latent or weakly defined and might not otherwise have materialized. As for France, her conflict of particular interest with Germany over Alsace–Lorraine, which had previously inhibited but not absolutely foreclosed alliance with Germany, now became subsumed in a more general power competition with Germany as the irreconcilable foe.

The second reason why multipolar alignments "create" interests is that the pooling of power entails the obligation to defend at least some of the ally's particular interests, which may be quite different from one's own. These interests, to a degree, become one's own interests as a derivative of the interest in maintaining the alliance. Unlike bipolarity, where alliances involving the superpowers are actually unilateral guarantees by the latter to their dependent allies involving no reciprocal expectation that the clients will come to the aid of their protectors (whatever the wording of the alliance document), in multipolarity they are bilateral or multilateral exchanges of commitment. The fulfillment of, or the intention to fulfill, the commitments is a condition of obtaining the benefits and, in fact, for the continuing viability of the alliance itself. However, since the contingencies that might activate the commitments cannot be fully and exactly stated in alliance contracts, and since many alignments are no more than tacit understandings that may mean something different to each partner in concrete situations, alliances and alignments never overcome completely the basic ambiguity of interest in multipolarity. And since alignments are temporary and constantly subject to change, the interests created by them are also changeable.

Finally, as Robert E. Osgood has pointed out, the general power interests of allies tend to be *homogeneous* in bipolarity and *heterogeneous* in multipolarity.[6] In the central arena of a bipolar system, the

---

[6] Osgood and Tucker, *Force, Order and Justice*, p. 172.

dominant concern of all the partners is to deter and resist expansion by the opposing superpower or its wards, although in peripheral subsystems (e.g., the Middle East) the local threat from opponents in that subsystem may loom larger for the ward than the superpower threat, and vice versa for the superpower ally. By and large, there is little or no disagreement between allies as to *which* threat is to be resisted, since one threat dominates all others. Differences tend to center instead on *how* the threat is to be met, on the mix of resistance and accommodation to be employed in dealing with the opponent, the kind of military strategy to be adopted, the allocation of defense costs among the allies, etc. In a multipolar system, by contrast, allies are likely to have somewhat different interests, to feel threatened in different degree from different quarters. These differences are largely due to factors of geographical location and particular conflicts with different opponents. Thus in the latter part of the nineteenth century, Austria had a strong interest in resisting Russian influence in the Balkans, while for Germany, as Bismarck put it, the Balkans were not "worth the bones of a Pomeranian grenadier." Austria, conversely, cared little for Germany's interest in containing and isolating France. The mirror image of this heterogeneity occurred in the Franco–Russian alliance. The divisive effects of such differences are reduced by the common interest in preserving the alliance. Nevertheless, heterogeneity of interests is a source of conflict and strain within multipolar alliances that, in a crisis, may appear as a reluctance of the ally not directly concerned to stand firm against the opponent's demands. Typically, the supporting ally will face a hard choice between somewhat incompatible interests: preserving the alliance vs. avoiding war over the ally's special interests, which are only partly shared if at all.

The homogeneity of interest in bipolarity is qualified by its regional character. Thus, while the United States and its NATO allies share interests to a high degree in Europe, the allies have not been enthusiastic supporters of the United States in non-European crises, nor has the United States shared European interests in *their* adventures outside Europe. Obvious examples are Quemoy 1958 and Suez 1956. An extreme case was the Yom Kippur war of 1973 when the Europeans actively obstructed U.S. efforts to re-supply Israel. However, the interests involved in these cases was not primarily the *general* one of resisting the opposite superpower but rather the *particular* interests of the United States or its allies.

To summarize, in bipolarity, the identity of friends and foes and the definition of interests is largely a consequence of the structure of the system; alliances register but do not create interests; interests are clear and relatively unchanging, and are shared in high degree among allies. In multipolarity, enmity and amity are not determined by structure but by conflicts of particular interests and a systemically induced compulsion to align with others to escape the dangers of isolation; alignments create interests to some degree; interests are often ambiguous but are potentially or actually intense; interests tend to be changeable, reflecting changing alignments, and are imperfectly shared among allies.

In both systems, states play three simultaneous "games" over time: an adversary action game, an alignment game, and a preparedness game. These are the three basic dimensions of the politico-strategic "supergame," which was discussed in Chapter II. Crises and wars are typical subgames in the adversary action game; alliance formation, realignment, or negotiation about the common stance to be taken toward an adversary are typical subgames in the alignment dimension. In the two sections that follow we take up interactions between the alignment game and adversary crisis games, in multipolar vs. bipolar systems. (To simplify, we set aside the preparedness game, assuming that arms levels remain fairly constant during a crisis.)

CRISES IN MULTIPOLAR SYSTEMS

The most prominent difference between multipolar and bipolar crises is the greater salience of alignment considerations in the former. This is because the protagonists are usually highly dependent on allies or quasi-allies for coercive or resistance power in the crisis, because allied support is often uncertain, and because de-alignment or realignment is possible, either during or as a consequence of the crisis. Multipolar crises, while they are "adversary games" in the first instance, feature a high degree of interaction between the adversary game and the alliance game, between adversary bargaining and alliance bargaining. Thus they are more complex affairs than bipolar crises, in which alignments are fixed and the superpowers, at least, are much less dependent on power contributions from allies.

In both the adversary and alliance games, the parties are "interdependent," but the nature of the interdependence is different in each case. In the adversary game, interdependence consists of the parties' capacities to harm each other and their degree of conflict of interest. (Each "depends" on the other's acquiescence for the satisfaction of its interests.) Mutual assessments of interests at stake and capacities to harm produce expectations about the other's resolve to stand firm in a crisis, and bargaining generally involves attempts to manipulate these expectations by firmness or threats or to compromise the conflict by offering concessions. In the alliance game, interdependence refers to how much the allies or incipient allies need each other—i.e., how dependent each is on the other's power for meeting threats posed by adversaries. The most relevant expectations here are estimates of the degree of support the ally will provide in crisis and war, and the likelihood of his de-alignment or realignment. Alliance bargaining essentially involves trying to change the partner's expectations about oneself in these respects so as to affect the distribution of burdens, risks and benefits of the alliance to one's own advantage, or to discourage the partner from realigning. Obviously, the alliance and adversary games interact reciprocally: (1) the apparent solidarity of the alliance affects the amount of coercive or deterrent power that can be generated vis-à-vis the adversary, and (2) the perhaps differing degrees of fear of, or conflict with the adversary affects the allies' degrees of dependence and hence their capacity to influence each other.

Comparative dependence, the basic determinant of leverage in alliance bargaining, is a function of at least three factors: (1) each ally's independent military power, (2) the power of the adversary or adversary coalition, (3) each ally's alignment alternatives. Alignment alternatives are in turn a function of the state's degree of conflict with other states, including the present adversary, and the firmness ("bindingness") of the existing alliance contract, if one has been made. Allies may be interdependent in varying degree, and asymmetrically or symmetrically so.

The "stakes" in a multipolar crisis typically will be some mixture of the interests directly in dispute with the opponent and the parties' interests in the long-term alliance competition. For example, one of the motives of the challenger in precipitating a crisis may be to demonstrate the weakness of, or cause the break-up of the opposing alliance. This was one of Germany's chief motives when she challenged France over Morocco in 1905. Conversely, an important interest for one or both sides will be to preserve, strengthen, and demonstrate the cohesion of their present alliance. For supporting allies in particular this interest may outweigh their interest in the immediate issue between the direct protagonists, as England's prime interest in the Morocco crisis was to preserve the Entente Cordiale with France, rather than to exclude Germany from Morocco, which was France's primary concern. Germany's interests in the 1914 crisis were an approximately equal mix: she supported Austria partly because of her high dependence on Austria as her only reliable partner in the alliance game, but also because she shared Austria's interest in wiping out the "Serbian revolutionary nest."

Alliance considerations introduce complications into assessments of relative power by the direct protagonists in a crisis. Prior to the initiating moves, and during the course of the crisis, both parties must calculate carefully the likely degree of allied support on both sides, since such support will be critical to the outcome. Negotiating positions and threat postures will be heavily affected by expectations about the interests and intentions of allies and other third parties. Since such interests and intentions are typically unclear in a multipolar system, there is considerable scope for miscalculation, and the consequences of miscalculation may be serious. Germany in the 1905 Morocco crisis not only gravely miscalculated the degree of British support for France but also grossly overestimated the degree of support she would get from her own allies—Austria and Italy. The result was a humiliating diplomatic defeat. In the Bosnia crisis of 1908, the Russian foreign minister, Izvolsky, mistakenly expected British support for Russian control of the Straits in compensation for Austria's annexation of Bosnia–Herzegovina. In 1911, when another crisis broke out over Morocco, the Germans again mistakenly assumed a disinterested Great Britain. And in 1914, Germany at first assumed Russian passivity, then French; after correcting these mistakes, Germany continued to press ahead on the assumption of British neutrality; this miscalculation, too, was eventually corrected but too late to stop the mobilization-countermobilization juggernaut which by that time had taken control over events.

Much of the bargaining activity in a multipolar crisis will be between allies, more so than in bipolarity, where the basic alignment is not in doubt. The states directly involved will try to firm up the commitment of their allies, since the latter's power contribution is essential either for a favorable outcome of the crisis or for a successful waging of war if the crisis is not resolved. The latter will try to exploit their essentiality by insisting on bargaining positions toward the opponent that are more favorable to their interests. Usually, but not always, such pressures will be in the direction of compromise, assuming a supporting ally is less interested in the immediate stakes than its partner. But the target state may be able to counter this pressure.[7] If it has a plausible realignment option (perhaps with the crisis opponent), it can pose the following choice to its partner: "Either support me to the hilt or be prepared for my defection if I have to yield or compromise." Only if the supporter can point to its own realignment possibilities (again, perhaps, with the present opponent) or is, for other reasons, little dependent on the ally, can it credibly retort: "Retreat from your extreme position, or I will not support you if your intransigence precipitates war." Obviously the outcome of such bargaining depends less on actual degrees of dependence and realignment options as on the expectations and beliefs about these things that each partner is able to instill in the other.

The more *ambiguous* the alliance commitment, the stronger the bargaining position of the supporting ally. The crucial determinant is still

---

[7] We occasionally use the labels "target state" or "target ally" to refer to the immediate protagonists in a crisis. The term "supporting ally" denotes the ally of a protagonist.

the relative degrees of dependence, as they are perceived by the parties; but if the supporting ally has not made a formal commitment, he can more credibly issue the ultimate threat of non-support than if he has. Obviously, a formal commitment creates a moral obstacle to such a threat, or to carrying it out; it increases dependence to a degree by foreclosing or at least inhibiting realignment. If the commitment is informal or ambiguous, the supporter can more easily claim lack of obligation or lack of interest in the crisis issue, hint at realignment possibilities, and make his support contingent on the negotiating position assumed by the ally toward the adversary. Thus he can exert more control over the ally's crisis behavior.

Incidentally, we have here an interesting contrast between commitments in alliance bargaining and in adversary bargaining. Ambiguity or uncertainty of commitment enhances bargaining power over allies. But in bargaining between adversaries, the firmer and more explicit the commitment, the more coercive or deterrent power one enjoys vis-à-vis the opponent. The difference is explained by the difference in the relation of commitment to the appropriate threat in each "game." In adversary bargaining, the typical threat is to fight; commitment to an ally is consistent with this, and the clearer the commitment, the more credible the threat. However, in alliance bargaining in a crisis, the appropriate threat is that of "no support"—i.e., that one will *not* fight in a contingency—and the clearer the alliance commitment, the more difficult it is to make such a threat credible. This creates some tension between the often simultaneous goals of deterring the opponent and restraining the ally, as will be discussed below.

Threats to withhold support or to realign (or actual non-support or realignment) are inhibited, however, by the need to preserve a general *reputation for loyalty*. Reputation for loyalty is the counterpart in the alliance game of reputation for resolve in the adversary game. Just as opponents are often motivated to stand firm in a confrontation in order to create or preserve others' expectations of their firmness in future conflicts, allies too have an incentive to stick by their current partners, not only to preserve the latter's confidence in their loyalty but to create a general belief among other states that they are reliable alliance partners. As "resolve credit" with adversaries can be earned and "banked" by repeated instances of firmness, so "loyalty credit" with present or potential allies can be generated and drawn upon in the future by repeated demonstrations of support. And just as a reputation for resolve helps deter future crisis challenges by opponents, a reputation for loyalty tends to discourage thoughts of realignment in the ally. Finally, just as a concern for resolve reputation sometimes inhibits accommodative moves in an adversary encounter, so a concern for one's loyalty image may inhibit attempts to restrain the ally in alliance bargaining. Especially if the ally has been restrained once or twice in the recent past, the supporter may feel a strong need to provide support in a current crisis. Thus Germany's restraint of Austria in the 1913 Balkan crisis was an important reason for the "blank check" of 1914. This is the alliance equivalent of the "never again" phenomenon in adversary relations—after yielding several times to the same adversary, the loser vows never to yield again, in order to preserve its crumbling resolve reputation.

Incidentally, the importance of the loyalty image shows up clearly in laboratory coalition experiments, where the threat to realign is rarely made, and offers of realignment are usually rejected, once a bargain has been struck. Subjects usually explain that they want to preserve a reputation for loyalty so that they will be considered attractive alliance partners in future plays.

We see, then, that the bargaining power over allies that comes from having realignment options is somewhat weakened by reputational considerations. The same is true for the bargaining power that stems from ambiguous commitment: a state that is willing only to make a tentative or informal commitment automatically puts its loyalty in question. Although the ambiguous tie makes its threats to defect or withhold support quite credible, this leverage may be undermined by its need to keep "proving itself." The point is well illustrated by England's position and behavior vis-à-vis France and Russia in the early 1900s. In lieu of any formal assurance of its loyalty England felt the need to support France and Russia fully in the crises of 1905, 1908 and 1911, lest they become suspicious of its fealty and themselves defect. France and Russia, on the other hand, being formally bound and thus less worried about the other's realignment, could afford at least to abstain diplomatically as France did in Bosnia, 1908, and Russia in the 1911 Morocco crisis.

Formality and explicitness of commitment to an ally does not, of course, completely eliminate leverage over the ally. Asymmetry of dependence may yield bargaining power, and it is well known that states can find ways of evading clear commitments when their interests so require. The commitment or *casus foederis* may be explicitly limited to a particular contingency, or type of contingency, or a certain geographical area, etc. If the crisis issue falls outside this definition, the supporting ally can still legitimately exert influence by threatening to withhold support. Thus Bismarck was able to restrain Austria in its long crisis with Russia over Bulgaria in the mid-1880s by pointing to the fact that the Austro–German alliance was "defensive" only; Germany would fight if Austria were directly attacked, but would not join in any attempt to oust Russia from Bulgaria, either diplomatically or militarily, should Russia choose to occupy it. Still, the existence of formal alliance, whatever the wording of the contract, tends to arouse expectations of support going beyond the explicit wording of the contract; an ally who disappoints these expectations too much by hiding behind the letter of the agreement risks generating disillusion and thoughts of realignment in the partner. Bismarck reduced this risk in the 1880s by mobilizing England behind Austria in the "Mediterranean Agreements," thus filling Austria's need for more coercive bargaining power on the Bulgarian issue.

States in a multipolar system face a choice between firm, explicit alliance commitments that maximize their combined bargaining power vis-à-vis the adversary at the cost of less leverage over each other, and ambiguous understandings that keep their alignment options open and thus maximize their alliance bargaining power, at the cost of less coercive power over the opponent. In a crisis, either kind of bargaining power might be useful, so the contemplation of possible future crises probably is not the critical determinant of the degree of alliance commitment. More important is the need or lack of need for some certainty in advance as to who will be at one's side in case of actual war, and whether the prospective partner has alignment alternatives that need to be closed off.

Asymmetries in degree of dependence lead to differences in the *general* strategic interest that each ally will feel to be at stake in the crisis— notably, different valuations of continuance of the alliance itself. The bargaining between allies will also be affected by heterogeneity of their *particular* interests. Each ally may see the principal threat to its interests in a different quarter, so that a crisis arising with a certain opponent over a certain issue may directly engage the particular interests of one ally but not at all those of the other. Thus Austria had no particular interests involved in the two Morocco crises between Germany and France, while Germany was much less directly interested than Austria in the several crises with Russia in the Balkans. Even when both (all) allies have some particular interests at stake in the crisis, their interests are likely to be different in nature and magnitude. Both France and England had particular interests involved in the two Morocco crises, but those of England were quite different and smaller than those of France. Typically, the ally in the supporting role will have a lesser interest in the particular issue at stake. This may create a conflict between the allies about the degree of firmness or conciliation to be shown toward the adversary. A shrewd opponent will exploit this "gap" between the allies' interests by setting his demands just below the maximum he thinks the supporting ally is willing to concede. He may expect the latter to join in pressuring the target ally to accept these demands. This is the game that Hitler played so successfully during the Munich crisis, although he nearly overplayed his hand by increasing his demands at the Godesberg meeting with Chamberlain. This started a shift among waverers in the British cabinet toward a harder position; Hitler corrected his mistake by a conciliatory gesture at the last minute.

·The asymmetry in particular interests between the allies may be offset by an asymmetry in general interests. If the supporting ally has the greater general interest in preserving the alliance (i.e., is the more dependent), this may force it to support the target ally's bargaining position willy-nilly. Thus in the Morocco crisis of 1905–1906 England wanted France to compromise with Germany but shrank from exerting significant pressure upon France for fearing of endangering the entente; there was consequently no "gap" for Germany to exploit. Similarly, in 1908, England cared little about the Austrian annexation of Bosnia–Herzegovina but supported Russia in opposing it largely out of concern for the still fragile Anglo–Russian entente. However, in this case the German–Austrian combination prevailed because Russia was unprepared for war.

In addition to the degree of support to be expected from allies in a crisis, a further uncertainty concerns the possibility that allies may dealign or realign during the crisis or as a consequence of its outcome. This may provide a source of bargaining leverage between allies, as when Russia hinted, during the Bosnia crisis, that it might drop the French alliance and the British entente if allied support were not forthcoming. This also means that bargaining activity in a crisis may include, not only adversary bargaining between the direct protagonists and bargaining between each protagonist and its own allies, but also bargaining between a protagonist and supporting allies on the *other* side. One of the direct adversaries may offer the prospect of realignment to the opponent's ally, or at least attractive terms in outstanding disputes with it, if it will moderate or withdraw its support of the opponent. Or a supporting ally on one side may hold out the prospect of *rapprochement* to the opponent if the latter yields in the crisis. Germany made bids of the first type to England during both the first Morocco crisis and the 1914 crisis; England offered the second variant to Germany in the Morocco crisis.

In their bargaining with each other, the direct adversaries may use the stakes in one game as bargaining counters in the other, as when a party yields everything at issue in the crisis, or more than it would otherwise, to entice the adversary into realignment, or, conversely, offers the "carrot" of alliance to persuade the adversary to yield. The first possibility is illustrated embryonically by the German government's consideration of giving France all it wanted in Morocco in 1905 in order to entice France into a "continental league" against England. The attempt came to nothing because divisions within the German government caused a watering down of the offer, and because neither France nor Russia was enthusiastic about the continental league idea. The obverse is illustrated by French alliance overtures to England during the Fashoda crisis of 1898 to induce an English concession that would permit some sort of French presence in the Upper Nile valley. The English did not take the bait because they were not anxious at that time for an alliance with anyone.

Another variant is to "threaten" to settle a crisis with a state that is the opponent of another state with which one wants to strike a good alliance bargain. A conflict settlement is often a prelude to at least tacit alignment with the conflict adversary; the third state may fear this alignment, plus the prospect of the two former adversaries encroaching on its own interests when they fashion their settlement, and it may be willing to pay in the alliance game to stave off both possibilities. An example is the formation of the Anglo–Japanese alliance in 1902. Japan and Russia were involved in a mild crisis concerning Manchuria. Japan had two options: to settle her dispute with Russia by an agreement on spheres of influence or to continue the confrontation in alliance with England—an alliance which England was offering in order to get more protection for her own Far Eastern interests against Russian encroachment. By opening negotiations with Russia, Japan was able to get an alliance with England on very favorable terms.

A state may be accommodating in a crisis for fear that firmness may provoke the opponent's alignment with a third state, either during or after the crisis. Thus, Bismarck supported Russia's pretensions to control of Bulgaria in the 1880s, against the wishes of his ally, Austria, to reduce Russian incentives for alignment with France.

In a multipolar crisis, supporting allies face a number of specific dilemmas that stem from partially incompatible objectives. In the adversary game, the supporting ally is usually more interested in keeping the peace than in winning. Broadly speaking, there are two ways to keep the peace—deter the opponent or restrain the ally—but they cannot easily be pursued simultaneously. If "restrain the ally" is chosen, the most obvious and effective means is to hint or threaten withdrawal of support, but if the adversary learns of such attempts he is likely to gain confidence and become tougher. On the other hand, if the choice is to deter the opponent, the issuing of threats or underlining of alliance commitments may make the ally more confident and dangerously intransigent. If communication channels are leakproof, the dilemma can be resolved by saying one thing to the opponent and another to the ally. This may sometimes work because both the opponent and the target ally have an interest in *not* telling each other what the supporting ally has said to them.[8] If the channels are porous, however, what is said to one party will undermine the effect of what is said to the other.

[8] We are indebted to Robert Jervis for this point, and in general for his penetrating critique of the first draft of this chapter.

The parallel dilemma in the alliance game is between keeping open the option of realignment or rapprochement with the opponent and preserving the loyalty of the present ally. Here again, the policy choice is between toughness toward the opponent or restraint of the ally. Too vigorous deterrence or coercion of the adversary may provoke him, and generate or exacerbate future conflict. Too severe a restraining pressure on the ally may cause him to defect or realign. In this case, resolving the dilemma requires speaking amicably to the adversary and supportively to the ally, but it is not likely to stay resolved since each of the others will be motivated to reveal what has been said to them, or the supporting ally's intentions may be dangerously miscalculated.

Logically, knowledge of the supporting ally's dilemmas by the immediate protagonists in the crisis encourages them to compete in appearing committed to stand firm. A protagonist reasons that if he can appear absolutely committed to a particular bargaining position, his supporting ally will see that it is futile to try to persuade him to recede from it in conciliation; consequently, the supporter will see that the best hope for a peaceful outcome is to deter the adversary by taking a firm stand alongside the ally. The opponent reasons that if *he* can appear firmly committed, the opposite supporting ally will see that the only hope for peace is to induce his ally to compromise. Thus, the aphorism "He who commits first, wins," has an additional dimension in the multipolar alliance context, which reinforces the incentive to commit in order to coerce the adversary directly.

An approximate example of this phenomenon occurred in the 1914 crisis preceding the outbreak of World War I, in the communications between Germany and England and Russia and England. It is only approximate because the influencing of English intentions was not the only reason why Germany and Russia became committed, or endeavored to appear committed. Having done so, however, both tried to influence England in opposite directions, according to the logic just discussed. Russia said, in effect: "We are absolutely committed to defend Serbia against Austrian attack; therefore, the only hope for peace lies in your taking a firm stand alongside us, which will deter Germany and Austria." Germany's line toward England was just the opposite: "Since we are firmly committed to back Austria, the only way you can keep the peace is to persuade Russia to back down." The fact that England pursued neither option clearly and vigorously, but rather a confusing and vacillating mixture of both, was one of the reasons the peace was not kept.

A case where the supporting ally (again, England) did consistently select and follow one of these options was the Czech crisis of 1938. Hitler appeared absolutely committed to attack if his demands were not met. Thus it appeared to Chamberlain and the other appeasers in

England that the only hope for peace lay in persuading Czechoslovakia to accept these demands. The other option for peace—a firm deterrent stance against Hitler—was urged by the few British hard-liners and some French leaders as well, but they were outnumbered.

The deterrence-vs.-restraint dilemma exists in a bipolar crisis, too, but it is especially severe in multipolarity. Because of the typical ambiguity of interest and commitment in multipolarity, a state may be wishfully predisposed to doubt the opposite supporting ally's resolve and thus requires especially clear evidence and strong language to the contrary to dispel these doubts. The state's adversary, on the other hand, may count on its own ultimate indispensibility to its supporting ally and thus be skeptical about the latter's reservations about its support, which must then be expressed particularly forcefully and explicitly to be impressive. In other words, the contradiction between deterrence communications and restraint communications for the supporting ally is sharpened by the fact that the "logic of the system," supported by wishful thinking, can generate two quite contradictory sets of expectations, one of which is adopted by the opponent, the other by the supporter's ally.

When there are supporting allies on both sides, the opposite supporting allies face an additional dilemma between each other. If they can agree to exercise restraint and urge conciliation upon their respective partners, there is a good chance the crisis can be resolved peacefully, thus satisfying the dominant interests of the supporters, though perhaps with some discomfiture to their directly involved partners. However, it is difficult to reach such an agreement and, if reached, to keep it, because it runs athwart the interests of the target allies in winning the crisis and the interests of the supporters in preserving the loyalty of their partners. Thus, even if an agreement to restrain the protagonists is reached, there is a strong incentive to "double cross" by failing to restrain one's own ally, taking advantage of the opponent's restraint of his. This is another example of the ubiquitous Prisoner's Dilemma.

This may be illustrated again from the 1914 crisis. England sought an agreement with Germany on a plan for joint mediation between Austria and Russia and thought she had obtained such an agreement. England would try to restrain Russia while Germany exercised restraint on Austria. England kept her end of the bargain but Germany defected. Germany claimed to be trying to restrain Austria, but all this amounted to was "passing on" to the Austrians various pleas for moderation and proposals for compromise that came from the English, unaccompanied by any pressure upon the Austrians to accept them. In fact, messages from some German officials told the Austrians to ignore the British proposals; they were being "passed on" only to make the English believe the Germans were genuinely working for peace, so that the moral onus for the war, when it came, would fall on Russia.

Supporting allies, in dealing with their opposite numbers in a crisis, have a choice between three broad lines of policy. They may "hold the ring" for the target ally, threatening to fight if the opposite supporter fights, thus neutralizing the latter's coercive moves during the crisis and deterring him from intervention if war occurs. This is the coercive-deterrent option in the adversary game as between the supporting allies. Or they may agree mutually to exercise restraint and urge conciliation upon their protagonist partners as discussed above. This is their accommodative option. Or, third, they may enter into an entente or even an alliance with each other. This is a move in the alignment game that forecloses their involvement in the crisis between their other allies except in a restraining role and strengthens their capacity for restraint. In other words, it is a firmer cooperative solution to their prisoner's dilemma, more likely to "stick," than that envisaged in the second alternative. The third option is illustrated by the Anglo-French entente of 1904; a strong motivation for both countries was to eliminate the danger of becoming involved on opposite sides of the Russo-Japanese war via pressures from their allies in that war.

We have been discussing how alliance bargaining and adversary bargaining may interact *during* a multipolar crisis. From a broader perspective, the *outcome* of a crisis may have significant effects on alignments in the system, and, conversely, the outcome of an alliance negotiation may precipitate a crisis. The Russo–Turkish war of 1877–1878 and the crisis among the Great Powers that accompanied and followed it, settled finally at the Congress of Berlin, led to the Austro-German alliance. Russian resentment at Bismarck's alleged favoritism toward Austria during the congress fueled Bismarck's fears of a Russian-Austrian-French alliance, and finally forced him to choose Austria as Germany's primary ally. The Far East crisis of 1903–1904 between Russia and Japan precipitated the Anglo–French entente of 1904, which left Germany feeling affronted at being left out, leading directly to the Morocco crisis of 1905; the outcome of this crisis, a German defeat, in turn strengthened the entente, and also the German-Austrian alliance, by making Germany feel more dependent on Austria. Similarly, the Anglo–Russian entente of 1907, in which England vaguely promised to support Russian control of the Straits, led to the crisis over Bosnia the following year, precipitated by Austria's jumping the gun on an Austro–Russian deal by which Izvolsky, the Russian foreign minister, hoped to clinch the coveted prize.

Later, in 1913, a mild crisis occurred between Germany, on the one hand, and Britain and Russia on the other, over the issue of a German general assuming command of a Turkish army corps at Constantinople. England withdrew her support of Russia when the government made the embarassing discovery that a British admiral already enjoyed virtually the same powers over the Turkish navy as the German general was to have over the army. The affair was settled by compromise, but it left Russia feeling disillusioned with the Anglo–Russian entente. To restore Russian confidence, England felt it necessary to increase her own commitment by initiating Anglo–Russian naval conversations.

CRISES IN BIPOLAR SYSTEMS

The comparison with bipolar crises can be stated more briefly. Many of the differences result from the truncated nature of the alliance game in a bipolar system, due to the lack of realignment options. The superpowers and their clients compete in an adversary game and a preparedness game, but because of the clarity and permanence of friends, foes and general strategic interests, there is little point in trying to induce states in the opposing alliance to switch sides, and no need to fear such realignment by one's own allies. Thus, potential shifts of alignment are not part of the stakes in a bipolar crisis, as they are in multipolarity, and, in general, alliance relations and alliance bargaining are less prominent in the overall pattern of crisis behavior. Attention is concentrated on the adversary confrontation, and the interests involved in the crisis dispute are shared to a high degree among allies—i.e., interests tend to be homogeneous. Interallied diplomacy approaches closer to (although, of course, never reaches) the pole of "pure coordination"—developing common strategies and negotiating positions that best serve the shared interests of all—than in a multipolar crisis, where the interests of allies in both the adversary and alignment games are less fully shared. Of course, there will be differences between allies about crisis strategies, and these will have to be "bargained out," but the superpower's preferences will tend to be controlling because of the much greater dependence of the lesser states.

Calculations are simpler in a bipolar crisis because whether the challenger or resister has support from allies is either a relatively unimportant or an unambiguous matter. In crises directly between the superpowers, support from allies is insignificant in strictly power terms. When a superpower challenges a lesser state in the opposite camp, it is unquestioned that the opposite superpower will join in the resistance, though its degree of resistance may be uncertain. In crises initiated by junior partners, the senior protectors can be expected at least to "hold the ring": deter intervention by the opposite super-power beyond the level of aid in supplies and diplomatic support. In short, in bipolar crises, calculations can largely ignore the question of *who* will be in the opposition and concentrate on the probable *degree* of opposition. Attention tends to focus on the superpower's degree of interest or resolve. Although this question provides some scope for miscalculation, the chances of miscalculation are lower than in multi-polar crises.

Kenneth Waltz has advanced the theorem that multipolarity is char-acterized by flexibility of alignment and rigidity of policy; and bipolarity by rigidity of alignment and flexibility of policy.[9] In other words, the availability of alignment options in multipolarity produces a constraint to shape policy to suit the ally's interests in order to discourage the latter's defection, which would be extremely costly, given the usual high degree of mutual dependence in multipolar alliances. In bipolarity, the comparative lack of options for realignment and the insignificance of realignment by the lesser powers should it occur, make for relative freedom from alliance constraints in policy making. The superpowers, especially, can afford to ignore the preferences of their allies (although they may give some effect to them for other than strictly power-strategic reasons), but the latter, too, can afford to act independently since they can be quite sure that the structurally ordained chasm be-tween the superpowers themselves can never be entirely bridged. Thus the superpowers will always have an interest in protecting them, how-ever troublesome they become.[10] In multipolarity, strategic interde-pendence between allies is high; in bipolarity it is low.

Waltz deduces from this the further theorem that allies in multi-polarity have a lower capacity to dissociate themselves from or restrain each other in crises than the superpowers have, vis-à-vis their partners, in a bipolar system. In 1914, Germany could neither wash her hands of Austrian schemes against Serbia nor restrain Austria, because she was so dependent on Austria's power that she could not risk the latter's defeat or realignment; nor could France restrain Russia, for the same reason. But in 1956, the United States could both dissociate itself from, and bring a halt to, Britain's and France's adventure against Egypt;[11] she could also easily restrain Chiang Kai-shek from venturing to re-conquer mainland China in the Formosa Straits crises of 1955 and 1958, and avoid being drawn in, in case he attempted it.

[9] Waltz, "International Structure, National Force and the Balance of World Power," *Journal of International Affairs,* Vol. 21, No. 2 (1967), pp. 218–219.
[10] Waltz does not emphasize this reason for the lesser powers' independence as much as the military stalemate between the superpowers that makes deliberate aggression by one of them extremely unlikely.
[11] Waltz, "The Stability of a Bipolar World," p. 900.

However, certain other variables intervene to modify the force of Waltz's theorems. Although multipolarity is structurally flexible, alignment flexibility and policy rigidity at any particular time will depend on the firmness of commitments, how closely the balance of power between opposing alignments approaches equilibrium, the number of states on each side, the homogeneity of interests between allies and the degree of conflict between particular allies and particular opponents. When commitments are most tentative, the flexibility inherent in structure asserts itself most strongly, the danger of the proto-partner's shifting to the other camp is maximized, and states are most restrained by considerations of the partner's interests. Such "rigidity of policy" is reduced when commitments are firm, although, of course, the impossibility of absolute commitment still imposes some restraints. The cost of an ally's realignment and hence the compulsion to satisfy him is greatest when one's own side is the weakest, moderate when the alliances are in equilibrium, and smallest when one's own alliance is preponderant. The larger the number of states in an alignment, and consequently the lower the power contributions of each, the less each partner needs to shape its policy to suit particular others in order to head off the latter's realignment. Finally, the more nearly the interests of the partners are shared and the more deeply each is in conflict with some state on the other side, the less the degree of actual flexibility of alignment.

Conversely, both logic and the empirical record warn us not to exaggerate the degree to which the superpowers can ignore, restrain, or control their smaller allies in a bipolar crisis. In the logic of bipolarity, there is some tension between the asymmetry of power-dependence between leaders and clients, and the virtual certainty that the leader will have an interest in defending the clients. The former leads to the conclusion that the superpowers can control their allies quite easily; the latter to the conclusion that the allies can be as adventurous as they wish in the secure knowledge that they will be protected whatever happens.

Several considerations lessen, and perhaps resolve, this apparent contradiction. First, while the small ally can be sure the superpower has an interest in defending it (and this reduces the credibility of the latter's threat of no support), the client dare not assume the complete incredibility of such a threat because of the disastrous consequences for itself if it guesses wrong. The situation is analogous to the threat of a "massive first strike" with nuclear weaponry against an adversary: although, in a condition of nuclear stalemate, the threat has little credibility, it does not have to be very credible to deter, considering the enormous costs if it is fulfilled. Second, the superpowers have other means of control short of threatening not to defend the ally, notably means available from their considerable penetration of the economic life of their wards. Third, the superpower's degree of control varies among its several clients because they make varying contributions to the total power of the bloc; the superpower needs some allies more than others, and those it needs most it is less able to control. For example, while the United States could survive the loss of West Germany, or even Western Europe, these would be very serious losses, both because of their strategic contribution and because of the cultural and ideological values they represent for the United States. Therefore, the United States has less control over them in a crisis, and they have more control over U.S. policy than, say, Taiwan, or Pakistan, or even Israel.

Fourth, while it is true that allies' general strategic interests tend to be homogeneous in bipolarity—preserving the balance of power against the other superpower and its cohorts—this is not the case with their particular interests. Usually, in a crisis, the particular interests of the smaller states will be more directly and deeply involved, and the protector will feel some normative compulsion to defer to them.

In short, there are considerations on both sides of the question other than basic structural ones, but the weight of both logical and empirical factors seems to support the superpowers' capacity for control, although that capacity will vary with the identity of the allies involved and the circumstances of the crisis.

Some of the points just made may be illustrated from post-1945 crises. In the Berlin crises of 1958–1960 and 1961–1962, the United States played the leading role in confronting and negotiating with the Soviet Union and in formulating crisis strategies. Yet it could not call the tune entirely, primarily because of its considerable dependence on the power contributions of the allies should the crises have erupted into violence, and because it was their particular interests, especially those of West Germany, that were most directly at stake. Also, because of the tradition of consultation in NATO and the diplomatic value of presenting a united front, negotiating positions toward the Soviets were developed in serious and often difficult bargaining with the allies, in which the latter wielded considerable influence. In the 1961–1962 crisis, the United States also tried to reach a consensus with its allies on contingent military plans should military action be necessary, but this effort failed, despite U.S. willingness to modify its own preferences somewhat.[12] The lack of complete U.S. independence was also evident in the United States' fear during the 1961 crisis that an uprising in

[12] Schick, *The Berlin Crisis*, pp. 154–158.

East Germany might draw in the West Germans and consequently U.S. forces.

By contrast, the United States was much more thoroughly in control during the 1958 Quemoy crisis. Chiang Kai-shek had little or no influence on U.S. moves during the crisis, although, of course, his prior deployment of large numbers of his own troops on the island probably committed the United States to its defense had the Communists invaded. Otherwise, Chiang was kept strictly "leashed"; he was permitted to engage in air battles with Communist planes, but his desire to bomb mainland artillery batteries was vetoed. Had he attempted a mainland invasion, the United States could have sat on its hands. The Soviets also were able to restrain their client by making it clear that their military support would be available only to repel a major invasion of the mainland, not to aid in capturing Quemoy or Formosa.

The case of Suez, 1956, might seem to contradict the assertion made above that the small allies are less restrainable, the greater their power contribution to the alliance and the greater their particular interests at stake in a crisis. The United States not only failed to support but also condemned and helped force the back-down of two of its most important allies. What differentiates this from the Berlin case, of course, is that the allies undertook an *offensive* action against a small state, an action that the United States disapproved; moreover, they were not under serious threat from the Soviet Union. Restraint could be practiced because the general balance of power was not at stake, the allies' particular interests were not considered legitimate, and, most importantly in comparison with a multipolar system, the British and French had no realignment options.

It is also worth noting the *means* by which the United States exercised restraint and control in both the Suez and Quemoy cases. In Suez, it was a combination of moral disapproval, opposition in the United Nations and economic pressure. In the Quemoy case, it was not only the clear warning of no active support for any action against the mainland but also the U.S. ability to turn off the flow of supplies to Chiang's forces. These cases point to the fact that the superpowers have much more varied means of restraining their allies than was the case in the earlier multipolar system. Since the allies are dependent on the Big Two on a variety of dimensions other than active military defense, restraint need not depend on being able to make a credible threat of nonsupport in war. This was shown quite clearly in the Yom Kippur crisis of 1973, when the United States was able to force the Israelis first to accept a cease-fire, then to withdraw from their forward position, by the implicit or explicit threat to cut off war supplies.

Asymmetry of mutual strategic and economic dependence tends to

give the superpowers primary control in most crises, but there is a less
tangible political and moral interdependence that is more symmetrical
and tends to limit the superpowers' capacity to act independently. The
moral factor as it limited the allies in the Suez crisis has been mentioned.
The superpowers, too, have need for moral legitimization of their crisis
behavior, which their allies may grant or withhold. One need only recall
the 1954 Indo–China crisis when the U.S. consideration of intervention
foundered on the British failure to make it a "united action." Similarly
in the Quemoy case, the United States placed a good deal of value on
British support to help rally world opinion, and more importantly, U.S.
domestic opinion, behind its policy. The British obliged by sending a
battalion to Hong Kong and two more carriers to their Far East fleet—
despite their considerable skepticism, even disapproval, of U.S. policy.[13]
The Cuban missile crisis, the example *par excellence* of superpower
independence of allies in strategic terms, nevertheless provides further
evidence of the superpowers' moral and political dependence. Although
the interests of the NATO allies were not directly involved, the United
States felt obliged at least to inform them of the imminent U.S. challenge
before it was issued, and this courtesy no doubt helped to gain their
diplomatic support, especially in the United Nations. The Latin American allies were also consulted and were persuaded to give a ringing
OAS endorsement of the U.S. "quarantine." This solid support from
its allies helped to buttress the legitimacy of the United States' position
and no doubt improved its coercive leverage over the Soviet Union.

All this is only by way of saying that Waltz's theorem that "rigidity of
alignment equals flexibility of policy" (and vice versa), and the corollary
that allies are more restrainable in bipolar than in multipolar systems,
are statements of tendency that are realized only in pure types. That is,
of course, all that one expects from good deductive theory. Actual
structural deviations from the ideal types, and non-structural variables
common to both types, will modify the tendencies in a converging fashion. Still it is useful to start with the ideal types and the logical behavior deducible from them, as benchmarks for exploring the "real
world." A good deal of the deductive theory survives the empirical
test, and the complexities of the actual world are better perceived and
understood when they are viewed from the solid foundation of structural logic.

DÉTENTE AND CRISES

The condition of détente has different effects in multipolar and bipolar
systems, for both the alliance game and the adversary game. Détente may

[13] Howe, *Multicrises,* p. 226.

be defined as a reduction of conflict between adversaries via the settlement of some disputes, and/or the making of cooperative agreements that realize common interests. In a multipolar system, détente often marks the first step in the transformation of an adversary relationship into one of alignment or alliance, perhaps via the intermediate stage of entente or tacit alliance. Détente reduces alliance obstacles between former adversaries and may be stimulated by the rise of a new adversary or dissatisfaction with the fruits of an existing alliance or alignment. Thus it is a move in both the adversary and alliance games for the parties concerned, affecting also the expectations of others; it is a key transition point in the changing and often uncertain identifications of friends and foes.

In bipolarity, by contrast, détente between the superpowers can never lead to entente or alliance, simply because there is no strong third party to ally against. Nor can it ever develop into the "condominium"—an agreement to police the world jointly—so much feared by the Chinese and some Europeans; basic structural rivalry prevents that. It is simply an agreement to reduce the level of conflict behavior and hostility, and to maximize cooperation where cooperation is feasible. It does not affect the basic mutual identification of the parties as opponents. The rivalry is mitigated but it does not disappear. There is therefore an inherent tension between the big powers' desire to realize the interests they share (notably the interest in avoiding nuclear catastrophe) and their need to compete where they have important strategic interests in conflict, or where their clients are in conflict and require support. The tension is resolved, but imperfectly, by a tacit agreement to compartmentalize issues, to compete quietly and unemotionally when they have to compete, and not to let the competitive issues contaminate those on which they can cooperate. Détente is a semi-cooperative position in the Prisoner's Dilemma supergame, which the Big Two are continuously playing; only "semi" because beneath the general umbrella of a mutually cooperative attitude, defections do take place on some issues; also fragile because the defections persistently threaten to upset it.

For the theme of this book, the key questions about bipolar détente are: (1) does it reduce the likelihood of crises erupting? and (2) if crises nevertheless occur, does it facilitate their resolution? There seems little doubt that détente does reduce the likelihood of superpower crises by giving the adversary-partners an additional stake in avoiding them, and by eliminating the atmosphere of general hostility, characteristic of the Cold War, which might provide the emotional tinder for a crisis. The spirit of détente between the United States and the Soviet Union, which began developing in 1963 in the wake of the Cuban missile crisis, may have inhibited the Big Two from becoming seriously involved in several wars and crises between clients since then—notably the mid-East Six-Day war in 1967, the Syria–Jordan crisis of 1970, and the India–Pakistan war of 1972. It permitted them to compete quietly in the Vietnam War without disrupting a budding cooperation on other issues, and it probably contributed to the quasi-settlement of that war and the U.S. disengagement. The Nixon–Brezhnev agreements of 1972 and 1973 formalized and apparently strengthened the détente, specifically including the crisis-inhibiting aspect, in the agreement that the parties would do their "utmost to avoid military confrontations and to prevent the outbreak of nuclear war," and would consult if either had knowledge of a threat to peace from a third party.

However, the Yom Kippur war of 1973 and the "alert crisis" that punctuated it dramatically demonstrated the fragility of détente and especially its weak point in crisis prevention: the susceptibility of the big powers to being drawn into a confrontation by their clients. On the other hand, this crisis seemed to show, not without some ambiguity, how détente may moderate the behavior of the superpowers during a crisis so that it is more amenable to control and quick termination. Since many of the diplomatic moves of the superpowers during the Yom Kippur war are not yet publicly known, the following brief account should be considered as merely suggestive of the dynamics involved, not definitive history.

The outbreak of the war on October 6 placed the United States and the Soviet Union in a micro-version of their larger Prisoner's Dilemma supergame in which détente represents a mildly cooperative solution. They faced a choice between mutually cooperating to restrain the combatants or unilaterally defecting by aiding their respective clients. Their actual behavior was an interesting mixture of cooperation and defection at different levels of action. The Soviets apparently defected first by failing to inform the United States in advance that a war was impending. (That they knew it was coming seems evident from their evacuation of advisers and dependents from Syria and Egypt before the outbreak.) When the United States did find out a war was impending—about three or four hours in advance—it kept its part of the 1972 agreement by telephone calls to both the Egyptian and Israeli governments, urging them to hold off. Secretary Kissinger urged Ambassador Dobrynin to persuade his government to exert similar efforts. Whether such efforts were made is unknown. Premier Sadat of Egypt did report Russian pressure for a cease-fire soon after the war had begun; presumably the United States was speaking to Israel in a similar vein. But these moves were unsuccessful. After initial Arab successes, the Soviets "defected" at two different levels, first by urging new Arab states to join the conflict, then by greatly increasing their arms shipments to the

Arabs. The United States did not counterdefect immediately but reportedly suggested cooperation with a mutual arms embargo; when the Soviets failed to respond favorably, the United States stepped up its shipments to Israel. The first serious cooperative moves came only after the Israelis' dramatic thrust across the Suez Canal, which threatened to turn a modest Egyptian success into a humiliating defeat. Premier Kosygin then spent three days in Cairo urging the Egyptians to accept a cease-fire, and Communist party leader Brezhnev issued an urgent request for Secretary of State Kissinger to come to Moscow to discuss "means to end hostilities in the Middle East." [14] Out of the talks came an agreement to introduce a cease-fire resolution in the United Nations and to bring pressure on the protagonists to accept it, and to begin negotiations on larger issues. The resolution was passed by the U.N. Security Council the next day, October 22, but the Israeli forces continued to advance on the West Bank after the deadline. The Soviets considered this a U.S. "defection"—the United States had promised to control the Israelis and was not doing so. On October 24, the Russians then proposed a cooperative move at a "higher" level—joint U.S.–Soviet intervention to enforce the cease-fire, which would have meant in practice jointly forcing the Israelis to pull back. A second note the same day said that if the United States did not care to participate, the Soviets would do the job alone. [15] It is plausible that the Soviets believed joint intervention to be an implementation of détente, but much less plausible that they believed the United States would acquiesce in unilateral Soviet intervention as an "agent" for the Big Two. More likely, the go-it-alone suggestion was intended as a threat to persuade the United States to "start cooperating" by pressuring the Israelis to move back to the cease-fire line. At any rate, the United States perceived the Soviet proposals (and attendant military preparations) as Soviet "defection," not "cooperation." The United States then counterdefected by calling a global alert of its military forces and sending a sharply worded warning to Brezhnev. (Both the Soviet and American notes were described by U.S. insiders as "blunt" and "harsh." Other messages were subsequently exchanged but have not been publicized.)

It was a very short crisis, lasting less than a day. The Russions accepted a face-saving compromise: both countries would send unarmed "representatives" to observe the cease–fire, and both joined in support-

[14] *Newsweek*, October 29, 1973, p. 32. Other sources used for this summary are International Institute for Strategic Studies, *Strategic Survey, 1973*, pp. 27–35; and Marvin Kalb and Bernard Kalb, "Twenty Days in October," *New York Times Magazine*, June 23, 1974, pp. 8ff.

[15] *New York Times*, Nov. 21, 1973, p. 17. It is interesting that the Soviets made a similar proposal for joint superpower intervention in the Suez crisis of 1956.

ing a U.S. resolution that established a separate peace-keeping force.[16] However, events in the next few days suggested that the Soviet moves had not been in vain. Under intense U.S. pressure, including at least an implicit threat to cut off arms supplies, the Israelis agreed to open up a supply corridor through their lines to an isolated Egyptian army corps, and both the Egyptians and Israelis agreed to a conference to work out a permanent settlement.

What lessons can be drawn from this episode about the relationship between détente and crises? First, it demonstrates that the present détente has strict limits, especially in the domain of strategic action. Détente may inhibit the outbreak of some forms of crisis, but it is no guarantee against crises arising from temptations and pressures to support warring clients. Second, détente as a source of control during a crisis does not operate independently of the superpowers' interests in the outcome. The Soviets refused collaborative control at the level that might have been effective—a mutual arms embargo—when their side appeared to be winning. When the tables were turned and their clients appeared on the verge of defeat, they proposed a stronger form of control, which, however, was rejected by the United States because it clashed with the U.S. interest in keeping Soviet troops out of the Middle East. Third, détente does not become an effective source of control until the chances of direct superpower involvement in the conflict become dangerously high. In this case, it took a sharp confrontation between the superpowers themselves to shock them into behaving like colluding duopolists rather than competing ones.

Paradoxically, this last point may be given a favorable twist if one views the "alert crisis" as performing a positive function in operationalizing the détente in the larger conflict. The critical last-ditch requirement of détente in the dimension of strategic action is that it operate to prevent a one-sided result in a war between client states, because if this occurs superpower intervention becomes distinctly possible. The alert crisis accomplished this, curiously via the threat of Soviet involvement. Although the United States "faced down" the Soviet threat, the threat was effective, if not in itself causing the United States to bring pressure on the Israelis, at least in strengthening the credibility and hence the potency of that pressure. Along with whatever was said to the Israelis about arms supplies, their knowledge that a plausible consequence of their not conceding was a Soviet and American intervention and possibly a much larger war, left them, as Defense Minister Dayan said, with "no choice." The alert crisis also appears "functional" when viewed in terms of its overall results. From it, and the exchanges be-

[16] Ibid.

tween Mr. Nixon and Mr. Brezhnev that accompanied and followed it, there did emerge a truce, a U.N. police force, an agreement between the clients to negotiate, and an agreement between the protectors to exercise influence on their respective clients toward a permanent peace.

There may also be something to Mr. Nixon's claim that the prior existence of détente permitted a frankness of language between himself and his opposite number that otherwise might have been construed as provocative, leading to further escalaton. It made it possible for both sides to express their views and intentions bluntly and clearly, "as between friends," without engaging hostile emotions. Thus one sees dimly a two-way relatonship between crisis and détente: détente contributes to controlling a crisis, while a crisis may be a necessary catalyst for making the détente operational in resolving the unlerlying conflict.

THE IMPACT OF NUCLEAR TECHNOLOGY

We have been discussing the comparative effects on crisis behavior of differently structured international systems, defining "structure" simply in terms of the number of major actors and the distribution of gross military power among them. But another important attribute of international systems is the kind of military power possessed by the actors. What about the impact of nuclear weapons technology on the behavior of states in a crisis? Are there significant differences between nuclear-age crises and pre-nuclear ones that can be attributed specifically to technology rather than to structure? Unfortunately, the question is difficult to answer empirically since the transition to bipolarity and nuclear armament occurred almost simultaneously. But some things can be said with fair confidence.

The most general effect of nuclear weapons on crises, to which most other effects are contingent, is an enormous widening of the gap between the value of the interests in conflict and the possible cost of war, for the nuclear powers at least. Prior to the nuclear age, this gap was either comparatively narrow or did not exist at all: states were often willing to accept high risks of war or even deliberately to go to war to avoid sacrificing the object in dispute. Now it is difficult to imagine any issue that would be considered worth the costs of nuclear war or a high risk of nuclear war.

States have always faced, in a crisis, a certain tension between the goal of "winning" the crisis and the constraint of war-avoidance. The bargaining process in a crisis always involves threatening to destroy the common interest—i.e., threatening war, explicitly or implicitly—in order to get one's way in the conflict. At the same time, states must be wary of pushing such coercive and countercoercive tactics too far lest they become mutually committed to war or incur an intolerable risk of losing control of events. Obviously, this tension is greatly increased in the nuclear age, especially for crises directly involving the nuclear powers. Nuclear weapons have not changed, in general, the importance that states attach to their interests in conflict, and hence their desire to "win," but they have greatly strengthened the war-avoidance constraint, which in a nuclear crisis is equivalent to "disaster-avoidance." The increase in this tension poses a difficult dilemma: How is it possible to advance or protect one's interests by coercive threats and maneuvers, which necessarily require posing the prospect of war, without actually raising the risk of war to an intolerable level? An associated dilemma is how to exert coercive pressure at all by threats an opponent knows one cannot possibly mean if one is rational. It is the need to resolve these dilemmas that lies behind the search for principles of "crisis management." This search is still incomplete intellectually and theoretically, but some tendencies can be dimly discerned in the actual behavior of states in crises since World War II. They fall into two broad and complementary categories: (1) a greater exercise of prudence and control, to keep crisis maneuvering well within the disaster-avoidance constraint, and (2) a partial loosening of the constraint itself, by a tacit raising of the "provocation threshold," thus increasing the range of moves, especially physical moves, which the parties may use for coercion short of war.

States have been very inventive in devising methods for keeping the risks low in nuclear age crises. Adversaries are provided with face-saving loopholes for retreat, as when Kennedy in the Cuban crisis implicitly invited Khrushchev to pose as the savior of world peace. Or a party creates a loophole for itself, as when Khrushchev suggested a U.S. pledge not to invade Cuba in exchange for Soviet withdrawal of the missiles. Physical commitments are constructed gradually, to get feedback about the opponent's probable response before they are completed; a good example is the East Germans' step-by-step closure of the East Berlin–West Berlin border in 1961. Clients and small allies are strictly controlled (Suez, 1956; Quemoy, 1958). States try to make clear to their opponents the vital interests they will take high risks to protect; Kennedy's enumeration of the "three essentials" of Western interests in Berlin in 1961 is a notable example. Methods are cooperatively devised for fast communication in a crisis; e.g., the "hot line." Generally, states limit their demands to the necessary minimum: Kennedy did not demand the removal of all Soviet arms from Cuba; only the offensive missiles and long-range bombers. Coercive moves begin low on the escalation ladder and move upward only as needed, after close observation of the adversary's response at each "rung." The "big guns," such as ultimata and actual violence, are held in reserve until one's superior determination has been firmly established by interaction at a lower level. States are extremely careful not to provoke an opponent emotionally, avoiding actions that might trigger an impulsive reprisal and take events out of the realm of calculated control and into a spiral of uncontrollable interaction governed by passions; Kennedy's great fear of a Soviet "spasm response" to any U.S. violent act during the Cuban crisis is the best illustration. While fearful of provoking the adversary emotionally, statesmen try to keep their own emotions in check; rational calculation predominates, and calculations are much more careful than in pre-nuclear crises.

A related development is the much greater degree of detailed control exercised by top decision makers in a nuclear age crisis. Tight, centralized control is necessary, first, to minimize the risk of events getting out of control via irresponsible or parochially generated acts by elements of the bureaucracy, especially, of course, the military. Control is required, also, because military forces play a much more active role in modern crises as instruments of communication-by-demonstration. Whereas in pre-nuclear times, the main actors in a crisis were diplomats, with the military simply waiting in reserve or perhaps advising, nowadays verbal diplomacy and military action short of violence tend to merge in a single complex communicating machine. To run this machine effectively, or keep it from flying apart, requires a single operator in control of all its parts.

A comparison of crisis decision making in July 1914, with the Cuban missile crisis is instructive. In 1914, the crisis activity was almost entirely diplomatic activity, carried on by diplomats who viewed military forces only as instruments to be used in war. Military leaders shared this view of their role. They had plans only for war; they had no complex crisis "contingency plans" such as are commonplace today, at least in the U.S. military establishment and its NATO extension. But what is even more striking from today's perspective is that the civilian leaders in 1914 *did not know* in more than general outline, what kinds of war plans the military had made. Although the Russian and German civilian leaders shared the vague and widely held notion that somehow "mobilization meant war," they did not really *believe* this with enough certainty to integrate it into their diplomacy because they were not aware in detail of the logical and logistical compulsions that made it true. Their ignorance was one of the primary immediate causes of World War I.

By contrast, the Cuban missile crisis featured a complex mixture of military and diplomatic activity. Far more than in 1914, the United States and the Soviet Union "spoke" to each other as much by what they did as what they said. Military leaders played a role in crisis decision making, since their forces were used as instruments of crisis bargaining. Most significantly, on the U.S. side, President Kennedy and Defense Secretary McNamara inquired into the details of military plans and procedures relevant to the crisis and sought to gather into their own hands as much control of the military activity as they could— notably the implementation of the naval blockade, air surveillance of Cuba, and planning for an air strike. As Graham Allison documents in his careful study of this crisis, they were not entirely successful; [17] yet they did assert essential control over military activity and subordinate it to their political aims and tactics. Evidence on the Soviet side is sketchy but on the whole indicates a similarly high degree of control by the top leadership.

The second broad change wrought by nuclear technology is a tacit raising of the "provocation threshold," increasing the repertoire of moves open to states in a crisis to include a broad array of physical acts that in former times might have precipitated war. Prior to the nuclear age, there were not many options available between verbal diplomacy and actual war. Options were pretty much limited to an occasional naval demonstration and the mobilization of land and naval forces. Since 1945, however, the crisis "escalation ladder" has been lengthened; [18] an arena of "force short of war" has developed wherein states may use a variety of physical maneuvers to demonstrate resolve.

This development is in some logical tension with the first, the increased caution in nuclear-age crises. If states are more cautious because of the nuclear fear, one might expect them to be wary about undertaking maneuvers that bring them closer to war. However, logical paradoxes abound in international relations, and this is one of them. The paradox is that the nuclear fear faces two ways: it induces caution in oneself but also the thought that the opponent is cautious too, and therefore will tolerate a considerable amount of pressure and provocation before resorting to acts that seriously risk nuclear war. Moreover, the very desire to avoid nuclear war produces a need to have some substitute for war as a means of resolving inevitable conflicts. This need, combined with the "expectation of tolerance," has resulted in the tacit legitimization of a substitute, in the form of contests of resolve and "nerve" waged by verbal threats and physical means short of large-scale violence.

The physical means seem to fall into three rough categories: (1) the supply of military aid to client states who are directly engaged in crisis or war, (2) a considerable expansion of the ensemble of demonstrative or signaling acts, along with an increased significance attached to such acts, and (3) acts of minor violence.

The military supplying of client states who are the direct protagonists

[17] Allison, *The Essence of Decision.*
[18] Kahn, *On Escalation.* Osgood and Tucker also note this phenomenon in *Force, Order and Justice,* pp. 150ff.

in a crisis or war could be seen, not as a coercive bargaining tactic, but simply as a means by which the superpowers can help their allies while avoiding a direct confrontation between themselves. They bring their power to bear in support of their conflicting interests, but shift responsibility for its violent use to a proxy. The successive Middle East crises and wars provide clear examples. However, if the superpowers also have a common interest in dampening conflicts between their clients, their capacity to supply them can also be given a bargaining interpretation. The suppliers are in a Prisoner's Dilemma in which each tacitly communicates: "If you don't I won't" (cooperation) "but if you do I will" (defection). In the 1967 Six-Day War the United States and Soviet Union were able to cooperate in abstinence, but in the Yom Kippur War of 1973 they were not. Thus the development of military aid relationships has added an additional rung on the escalation ladder in the nuclear age. While it provides flexibility of physical maneuver for the superpowers, it also has its risks: first, the risk that clients abundantly supplied with modern weapons are more likely to use them against each other, and second, the risk that the suppliers themselves might inadvertently become directly involved.

It is in the second category—the increase of demonstrative or "show of force" options—that the expansion of the escalation ladder has been most noticeable. This is a consequence partly of technological advance, partly of pure inventiveness, and partly, again, of the need to have a means for exercising power in a crisis that is more potent than mere verbal threats, yet short of serious violence. The development of nuclear weaponry has provided several sorts of new demonstrative options— e.g., the calling of various levels of "alert" status for missiles, dispersal of bombers, putting more bombers in the air on airborne alert, deploying tactical nuclear weapons near the crisis area, putting more nuclear submarines out to sea, etc. Great inventiveness has been displayed also in devising new forms of force demonstration with conventional weapons. These include massing forces at the crisis locale (Cuba, 1962; Quemoy and Lebanon, 1958); dramatically announcing plans for increasing total forces (Berlin, 1961); alerting air-borne forces and concentrating air transports for them (Mid-East, 1973); putting military advisers in uniform (Laos, 1962); reserve call-ups, airplane flyovers, and many other variations. Some of these things were done in pre-nuclear crises, but they were less frequent, less varied, more likely to be considered "provocative" by the opponent, and often their demonstrative or bargaining character was only a byproduct of an intent to increase preparedness for war.

Some of these moves in the nuclear age derive their potency from the fact that they actually do increase a nation's capability or readiness to fight—as when the United States massed land and naval forces in and around Florida during the Cuban crisis of 1962. Others are "signals" intended solely to communicate a possible intent without significantly increasing capabilities or readiness.[19] Such signals appear to be taken more seriously in the nuclear age than before, perhaps because they fill an "information void" created by the advent of nuclear stalemate, which has made a comparison of capabilities (between nuclear superpowers) an unreliable index of comparative resolve. For example, David Hall credits President Kennedy's move, during the Laos crisis of 1961, of putting U.S. advisers in uniform and moving them into combat zones, as contributing significantly to achieving a compromise settlement and avoiding a Communist take-over.[20]

The use of minor violence is the least prominent of the three categories in practice. The tension between the requirement of prudence and the need for techniques of coercion and resistance short of war becomes high and distinctly uncomfortable in this area. So far, prudence has prevailed. The superpowers have shown great reluctance to use small-scale violence for bargaining purposes in crises because of their fear of escalation. However, this does not exclude minor violence from the ensemble of crisis bargaining moves available to the superpowers. At least one of these powers, the United States, has planned and been prepared to use limited violence in several crises if necessary, notably Berlin, 1961, and Cuba, 1962, with at least the hope and some degree of expectation that the interaction could be controlled and terminated before serious escalation took place.[21] Fortunately, and perhaps because the plans were known to the opponent, the crises ended before the plans had to be executed.

As suggested above, the expanded range of crisis tactics in the nuclear era can be linked to a new conception of crises as *surrogates* for war, rather than merely dangerous incidents that might lead to war. From this perspective, although they are still dangerous, crises are more functional than dysfunctional. Their systemic function is to resolve without violence, or with only minimal violence, those conflicts that are too severe to be settled by ordinary diplomacy and that in earlier times would have been settled by war. Perhaps former Defense Secretary McNamara had something like this in mind when he said: "There is no longer any such thing as strategy, only crisis management."[22] Churchill's famous aphorism "Peace is the sturdy child of terror" may require

[19] We follow Robert Jervis's definition of signals here. See *The Logic of Images*, pp. 20–23.

[20] George Hall, and Simons, *The Limits of Coercive Diplomacy*, Ch. 2.

[21] There is simply no data on whether the Soviet Union has had similar contingency plans in any crisis.

[22] Quoted in Coral Bell, *Conventions of Crisis: A Study in Diplomatic Management* (London: Oxford University Press, 1971), p. 2. Bell also suggests the positive function of crises as a mechanism for change short of war (pp. 115–116).

elaboration: Crisis is the big brother who mediates between the child and the parent.

In any system, there must be some mechanism for change and for resisting change. Historically the ultimate mechanism has been war, but since war is no longer a plausible option between the nuclear powers, they have turned to threats of force and the demonstrative use of force short of war as a means of getting their way. Between these powers, the only truly usable force is "psychological force." It is generated by creating some prospect, some risk, that one *might* use force. The pressure of risk substitutes for the pressure of force itself. The winner of the encounter is the one who can appear the most resolved to take risks and stand up to risks. But this competitive risk-running must be carefully "managed" lest it escalate to disaster.

A more modest proposition than the surrogate-for-war idea, though consistent with it, is that the demonstrative tactics we have discussed are more necessary in the nuclear age than before simply because the objective balance of military power is much less relevant to assessments of comparative resolve in a crisis. In pre-nuclear times, resolve perceptions depended chiefly on two kinds of indices: the comparative interests of the parties in the object of the conflict, and their comparative military strength. While the comparison of interests might be ambiguous, at least the "balance of capabilities" between the parties provided fairly clear objective data. In crises between nuclear powers, however, a comparison of their total nuclear capability is less clearly relevant when they are in a condition of nuclear stalemate: [23] when the most powerful weapons are too terrible to be used and when the use of conventional forces can easily escalate, not much can be inferred about relative resolve and bargaining power from a comparison of overall military strengths. The protagonists are thus apparently thrown back on a comparison of each other's "interests" as the only basis for estimating the "balance of resolve." [24]

However, the balance of resolve cannot always be read off directly from the "balance of interests" without the intervention of communicative and risk-taking activity that clarifies the interests of the parties. Thus one function, possibly the most important function, of the expanded ensemble of crisis maneuvers in the nuclear age is to clarify interests. He who is most willing to run risks would appear to have the most at stake. Alternatively, the manipulation of force short of war becomes

[23] Just how much less relevant is not clear and a matter for debate. Whether gross "superiority" in total nuclear strength confers some bargaining power in a crisis will be discussed below.

[24] Osgood and Tucker stress the "balance of interests" as the primary determinant of resolve and hence crisis outcomes in the nuclear age. See their *Force, Order and Justice*, pp. 148–149.

a substitute for the "balance of capabilities" that formerly supplied a partial index of relative resolve. When information about what one *can* do with one's full capability becomes less relevant, then signals and acts that communciate what one *might* start doing with *part* of it become more so.

The picture becomes more complicated, however, when one considers that a state's long-term reputation for resolve is itself one of its "interests" in a crisis, more so in the nuclear age than before. If crises rather than war are the *ultima ratio,* it becomes independently important to preserve a reputation for willingness to run risks and to stand firm in the face of risks. Just as the most important aspect of the outcome of pre-nuclear *war* was the change in distribution of material power—important for its utility in future war—the most significant aspect of a *crisis* outcome in the nuclear age may be the change in mutual expectations about resolve in future crises. Crises are likely to be perceived as tests of one's general resolve image, and resolve must be demonstrated in the present crisis as much to protect that image as to preserve or gain more tangible interests.[25]

When states consider their long-term resolve reputations to be an independent stake in a crisis, the apparent "balance of (other) interests" may be unreliable as an index of comparative resolve, and resolve-demonstrating tactics cannot be considered simply as "clarifiers" of these other interests.[26] Resolve may be demonstrated simply to preserve or enhance the adversary's image of one's resolve, for its value in future encounters. There are further complexities that cannot be gone into here; suffice it to say that the assessment of comparative resolve in crises between nuclear powers is a highly subjective matter and consequently the skill with which a state manipulates demonstrative short-of-war tactics may have a considerable effect on the outcome.

It could be argued that some of the changes attributed here specifically to nuclear technology could just as plausibly be considered consequences of a general bipolar power structure. Even without nuclear weapons,

[25] The extent to which states actually do draw inferences about their adversary's future resolve from the resolve it shows in a particular crisis is an empirical question that may be unanswerable due to lack of evidence. However, there is evidence that statesmen *think* such inferences are made, and that belief, of course, is what is relevant to their behavior. It seems, incidentally, to be a more important consideration for U.S. policymakers than for Soviet ones.

[26] The point made here should not be exaggerated; it probably applies only to situations in which the balance of interests is perceived as almost even, or only moderately asymmetrical. When one state clearly has a substantially greater interest in the tangible stakes than the other, the first state will be doubly advantaged in the resolve-communicating contest; first, by the basic asymmetry of interest and, second, by the mutual knowledge that, if it does not stand firm on this issue, its resolve reputation will be seriously depreciated on all issues where the concrete interests appear closer to an even balance.

the certainty of being opposed by a very powerful foe would make deliberate war an undesirable option and would stimulate a search for substitutes—e.g., threats of force, manipulation of risk and crises.

By the very nature of a bipolar system, the tangible stakes in a crisis tend to be small in the sense that the material outcome can only marginally affect the balance of power. Challenges are nevertheless resisted, partly because of the certainty that the opponent's gain *is* a loss for oneself, however small, but also because of the knowledge that the opponent of the moment is also the opponent of the indefinite future and the need, therefore, to preserve his image of one's resolve so as to deter future challenges and protect one's bargaining power in future crises. Although the stake in each particular instance is small, a cumulation of losses would be serious. Resolve becomes a primary stake, in other words, not so much because of nuclear weapons, but because the superpowers are involved in a permanent global confrontation. And precisely because the immediate tangible prizes are not important enough in themselves to justify an unequivocal determination to resist, such determination has to be repeatedly and actively demonstrated. Thus both a surrogate function for crises and an increased importance of resolve reputation can be adduced from the logic of bipolarity, without reference to nuclear weapons. However, these tendencies are no doubt strengthened by the overlay of nuclear technology, and it is difficult to determine which is the more important causal factor.

We return now to the point made earlier that capabilities comparisons are considerably less relevant to assessments of relative bargaining power in the nuclear age than before, at least with respect to the major nuclear states. The point was, first, that when the nuclear balance is stable— each side possessing a substantial second-strike capability—the threat of a "full first strike" is incredible; second, comparative willingness to begin gradual escalation into the nuclear range cannot logically be estimated from a comparison of total arsenals given the overriding fact that both sides could ultimately inflict damage totally incommensurate with the value of the object at stake. By extension, the balance of conventional forces is also an ambiguous index because of the risk that a conventional war would escalate.

However, "less relevance" does not necessarily mean irrelevance. Empirical cases show that conventional forces are by no means irrelevant to crisis bargaining power, especially when they can easily be deployed at the crisis locale. U.S. local superiority in conventional strength had much to do with its successes in the Cuban crisis, the Quemoy crisis, and the Syria–Jordan crisis of 1970. Western local inferiority in the various Berlin crises contributed to Western bargaining weakness, although it did not produce Soviet victories. The prime significance of conventional preponderance is that, if the crisis erupts into war, the moral onus and terrible risk of initiating nuclear warfare lies with the conventionally inferior party. His knowledge of this inhibits him from pushing his coercive diplomacy near the brink of war and undermines its credibility. The Berlin cases show, however, that conventional preponderance is no guarantee of success. That the Soviets did not achieve their aims in these crises (except for the partial success in 1961) may be attributable to their belief that, had they chosen to use their conventional superiority, the United States was prepared to escalate, or that the risk of escalation was too high to be taken. This brings us back to the importance of subjective resolve assessments. The certainty of a conventional win has to be weighed against the chances of a nuclear response; the inferior side in conventional forces may be able to increase this probability over the opponent's tolerance level by resolve-communicating tactics.

Then there is the puzzling question whether simple quantitative nuclear superiority does confer some bargaining advantage even when the nuclear balance is technically stable. Pure logic gives a clear negative to this question, for the reasons given above. But perversely, the real world does not quite follow this logic. Many policy makers do seem to believe that simple "superiority" somehow confers a crisis bargaining advantage. The belief may be explained in some cases as merely a lack of sophistication about nuclear strategic theory, an intellectual lag involving the naive application to nuclear weaponry of modes of thought traditionally applied to conventional forces. On the other hand, the belief may reflect, perhaps unconsciously, a higher sophistication, one based on psychological elements in human nature, consistent with the idea expressed above that political power in the nuclear age is a function more of "psychological force" than physical force. It may be, for example, that in the tension of a crisis there is a tendency to regress to more primitive, naive thinking and feeling, to tacitly set aside the esoteric calculations of the strategic theorists, and to adopt and act upon the simple and deeply ingrained idea that he who is superior in physical force is superior in bargaining power.

Robert Jervis has developed this "higher sophistication" more systematically in relating the "superiority" puzzle to the peculiarly subjective and self-fulfilling quality of beliefs about relative bargaining power in the nuclear age. If a nuclear state has actual superiority and believes this gives it a bargaining advantage, it is more likely to stand firm in a crisis. It is even more likely to be firm if it thinks its adversary shares the belief that superiority matters. And the inferior side is likely to retreat if it believes superiority is meaningful and even more likely to do so if it believes the opponent shares this belief. As stated, these four independent beliefs are reinforcing and give the actually superior state a considerable bargaining advantage. But, as Jervis notes, disbelief in the inherent meaningfulness of superiority or a failure to perceive the adversary's belief are also possible, and yield combinations with different effects on relative bargaining power. Thus, whether "superiority" is important depends on the parties' beliefs about it, and their perceptions of the adversary's beliefs.[27]

A belief that superiority matters may be subtly induced by the paucity or ambiguity of other evidence bearing on comparative resolve. Amidst great uncertainty on both sides regarding the other's interests, and risk tolerance, and the strongly felt need to eliminate this uncertainty, the simple fact of one side's nuclear superiority provides at least *some* "hard data" on which to build expectations. It may be given considerable weight in the absence of comparable tangible evidence about relative interests, or when the evidence available reveals no clear inequality of interest. Inequality in overall nuclear strength may provide a kind of "salience," a focus for the development of reciprocal expectations about who will or "should" concede, however irrational or non-rational this may be.

To what extent does the historical record support the notion that simple quantitative superiority in nuclear power, even in a condition of "stalemate," produces a bargaining advantage? After the Soviets launched their Sputnik and tested an ICBM in 1957 (before the United States had developed ICBMs), Soviet leaders and especially their Chinese allies often expressed the belief that they had achieved superiority, or at least parity, that the balance of power had shifted in their favor. Although they had not achieved a first-strike capability, they seemed to think they had substantially increased their coercive power, and this thought was no doubt reinforced by panicky talk about a "missile gap" in the United States during the next three years. Granted, the sophisticated theory of nuclear strategy had not yet been fully developed in the United States and the Soviets were even more innocent of it, so that these beliefs no doubt seemed more plausible then than they might today. At any rate, they apparently had something to do with the Soviet decision to open a new Berlin crisis in 1958. During the crisis, the Soviets repeatedly called attention to their newly acquired nuclear strength and the supposed shift in the balance of power. However, there is no good evidence that the Western position and resolve during the crisis was significantly influenced by these claims and the show of confidence based on them.

Certain aspects of the Cuban missile crisis may be adduced in sup-

---

[27] Jervis, "Bargaining and Bargaining Tactics," pp. 286–287.

port of the meaningfulness of simple superiority. By this time, the Kennedy administration had discovered, and informed the Soviets that it knew, that, although a "missile gap" did exist, it favored the United States rather than the Soviets; furthermore, the United States had initiated a missile-building program that would further widen the gap. It is difficult not to believe that a major Soviet motive in installing their own shorter range missiles 90 miles from U.S. shores was an attempt by "quick fix" to reduce the U.S. advantage. The fact that the Cuban missiles would have been highly vulnerable to a U.S. first strike suggests that the Soviets were thinking not in terms of strengthening their position in the strategic balance as technically defined, but in terms of the psycho-political advantage to be gained by reducing the U.S. margin of absolute superiority. Decision making on the U.S. side also suggests a consciousness of the value of simple superiority, or, more specifically, the cost of having one's margin of superiority reduced. Secretary of Defense McNamara, a strategic technician *par excellence,* at first suggested doing nothing about the missiles: they were no threat because they did not overturn the strategic balance—they did not give the Soviets a first-strike capability. No one else took this view, however, and Mc-Namara was persuaded to change his mind. The great majority of the decision-making unit, including President Kennedy, apparently believed that the missiles, if allowed to stay, would not only yield general political gains to the Soviets, especially in Latin America and Europe, by exposing the United States as irresolute, but, more specifically, would yield bargaining advantage to the Soviets in future crises, "with missiles staring down our throats from Cuba." [28] This was evident in the speculation that the Soviet aim was to strengthen themselves for a new round of the Berlin crisis. It was expressed in a more generalized way by President Kennedy's remark after the crisis that, although the Soviet deployment would not have basically changed the nuclear balance of power, "it would have politically changed the balance of power. It would have appeared to, and appearances contribute to reality." [29] No doubt he had in mind that, whatever the objective calculations of the strategic theorists, the psychological effects of the missiles' proximity, and the knowledge that they were targeted against U.S. cities, would have undermined U.S. confidence and bargaining power, and strengthened Soviet determination, in future crises wherever they might occur.

The large build-up of the Soviets' nuclear arsenal since the Cuban crisis to a level now surpassing the United States, seems to indicate that

[28] Sorenson, *Kennedy,* pp. 963–964.

[29] *Washington Post,* December 18, 1962. Quoted in Albert and Roberta Wohlstetter, *Controlling the Risks in Cuba,* Adelphi Paper No. 17, The Institute for Strategic Studies, London, April 1965, p. 12.

they believe superiority confers political advantage. Their achievement of this advantage may have contributed to their willingness to threaten intervention and risk a confrontation with the United States during the Yom Kippur war of 1973, in contrast to their relative passivity during the Mid-East crises of 1967 and 1970, when the build-up was not yet complete.

In sum: there are theoretical and some empirical grounds for believing that absolute quantitative superiority in nuclear power can be a bargaining asset in crises, although how valuable an asset is unclear.[30] Curiously, its value depends on how valuable decision makers believe it to be and their perceptions of how valuable others, especially the adversary, believe it is. Objectively, decision makers can afford to be indifferent to an adversary's superiority once the requirements of deterrence against nuclear attack are fully satisfied. Subjectively however, whether such indifference, professed or sincere, would cancel out all the political benefits that numerical superiority might confer in a crisis is problematical.[31]

CRISES AND THE "NEW MULTIPOLARITY"

By now, it is clear that President Nixon's 1971 announcement of an emerging new multipolar world was at least premature. It was primarily a piece of rhetorical casuistry, designed to rationalize a U.S. policy of military retrenchment. Whereas the global equilibrium had previously been maintained by U.S. power, in the near future (15 years was the president's outside estimate) new "superpowers" would spring up to do the job. Canning's famous pronouncement of 1820 was given a reverse

---

[30] This conclusion is reached also by Osgood and Tucker in *Force, Order and Justice*, pp. 152–153.

[31] COMMENT BY DIESING: It seems to me that the empirical evidence on whether nuclear superiority confers any bargaining advantage is so weak that no conclusions can be reached. There is almost no good evidence, to say nothing of a count of positive and negative instances. All that Snyder has presented is loose speculation plus selective interpretation of examples to fit the speculation.

A variey of different speculations and interpretations can be made to look equally plausible in this fashion. For instance, if we take Soviet statements at face value, their argument in the late 1950s was a deterrence argument, not a superiority argument. They said that the United States no longer had a monopoly of nuclear weapons, hat nuclear war was unthinkable, and that disputes now had to be settled by negotiation rather than by nuclear threats. The only superiority they claimed was human, not military, the desire of oppressed peoples to throw off oppression, which they wishfully thought favored their side. As for the United States, one can expect to hear a superiority argument from military spokesmen at budget time, just as one can expect to hear that the Soviet Union now has some kind of military superiority, or is moving toward it; in the 1950s we were hearing intelligence reports of secret Soviet decisions to attack the United States as soon as it had a military advantage. These are sincere budget arguments.

twist: the Old World was called into balance to redress the semi-withdrawal of the New.

In reality, the structure of the contemporary system is still essentially bipolar in military terms, though it contains an element of multipolarity in China's nuclear power and her considerable conventional strength in her own region. The structure may slowly evolve toward genuine multipolarity as China's nuclear strength approaches a second-strike capability vis-à-vis both the United States and the Soviet Union, and as Western Europe inches toward political unity and military self-sufficiency. But at present these changes seem problematical and some decades away.[32]

Yet it is undeniable that we are already witnessing a new pattern of flexible maneuver in the contemporary system that is reminiscent in some ways of the multipolar systems of the past. How is this to be explained? Part of the reason *is* structural—China's power has grown to the extent that her alignment is no longer a matter of small significance. Mostly, however, the explanation lies in a change in the pattern of *relations* [33] among the three greatest states, from conflictual to semi-cooperative between the United States and the two leading Communist powers, from alliance to enmity between the latter. The pattern began developing with the Sino-Soviet schism in the late 1950s and the beginning of the spirit of détente between the United States and the Soviet Union about 1963. The winding down of the Vietnam war provided both the motive and the opportunity for its consummation in three complementary U.S. foreign policy moves: consolidation of détente with the Soviet Union, rapprochement with China, and what Robert E. Osgood has called "military retrenchment without political disengagement"—i.e., a decision to limit further active military intervention, especially in Asia, but without compromising commitments to allies.[34] The complementarity is fairly obvious: the shortfall between commitments to allies, and a reduced capability and desire to fulfill them militarily, was covered by accommodations with adversaries, thus reducing the likelihood that the

[32] Nixon and others have referred to Japan and Western Europe as "economic superpowers," but what this term means precisely neither the former president nor anyone else has satisfactorily explained. It should be possible to delineate a world economic power structure in terms of relative capacities of states to benefit or harm others economically, and relative vulnerability to economic deprivation, but one suspects that such a structure would not look much different than the structure defined in terms of military strength.

[33] Kenneth N. Waltz has emphasized the important distinction between structure—the distribution of power among the major states—and relations or interactions among those states. Waltz, "Theory of International Relations," in Fred Greenstein and Nelson Polsby, eds., *The Handbook of Political Science*, Vol. 8 (Reading, Mass.: Addison-Wesley, 1975), Ch. I.

[34] Robert E. Osgood, et al., *Retreat from Empire?* (Baltimore and London: The Johns Hopkins University Press, 1973), pp. 3–10.

commitments would be challenged. In addition, the power of China was mobilized diplomatically as a partial substitute for U.S. military power to preserve the balance of power vis-à-vis the Soviet Union. However, the détentes were not seen simply as a means of retrenchment; for the United States, and probably for the Communist powers as well, détente had considerable intrinsic value in reducing the risks of war. China and the Soviet Union were agreeable to détente with the United States also because of the deepening hostility between themselves, now of greater concern to each than their traditional Cold War conflicts with the United States. China gained a counterweight to the Soviets in Asia and membership in the United Nations, while the Soviets gained a degree of security on their western front that would permit greater concentration on the threat from the East. Both gained a prospect of increased trade with the West.

The U.S. shift after the disillusionment of Vietnam is analogous in some ways to the British semi-disengagement from imperial defense in the aftermath of the Boer war. Confronted with a public weary of distant military adventures and clamoring for greater expenditures for social welfare measures at home, Britain found herself overcommitted in relation to resources politically available for military (specifically naval) use. She resolved the problem first by mobilizing Japan as an ally to help meet her Far Eastern commitments, then by negotiating imperial settlements with her two major opponents, France and Russia. The two situations are otherwise different, especially in the fact that there lurked in the British environment another potential opponent, Germany, whose existence and reaction to the French and Russian ententes gave the latter more and more the character of quasi-alliance than mere colonial settlements.

The current détentes may be viewed from two different perspectives. On the one hand, they are attempts to moderate conflict and to promote certain common interests (notably the interest in avoiding nuclear catastrophe) in what are still essentially adversary "games" between the United States and Russia and the United States and China. Especially between the first two, there is an inherent tension between their desire to realize the interests they share and their need to compete where they have important interests in conflict. The tension is resolved, but imperfectly, by a tacit agreement to compartmentalize issues, to compete quietly and unemotionally when they have to compete, and not to let the competitive issues contaminate those on which they can cooperate. From this perspective détente is a lessening of antagonism, an agreement to collaborate for common benefits and to resolve disputes by accommodation rather than coercion in a relationship that is still basically one of rivalry.

From the second perspective, the United States' accommodation with both the Communist powers, themselves bitter antagonists, implicitly sets in motion a new triangular alignment game in which accommodative moves between two parties may appear as moves toward alignment against the third. This game has some characteristics not unlike the alliance competition in past multipolar systems. Détente between rivals at least makes a closer alignment conceivable by reducing some of the conflict that previously blocked alignment. For the Soviet and Chinese leaders, this generates uncertainty and anxiety about whether the U.S. relationship with the other might deepen into something more positive, to their own detriment. They are both sensitive to this uncertainty, ultimately with respect to U.S. behavior in a crisis or war between themselves. For example, the Soviets can no longer be so sure, as they were before the Sino–U.S. rapprochment, that the United States would abstain in a Sino–Soviet war. While they probably do not worry about meeting Chinese and U.S. troops fighting side by side, U.S. logistical-supply aid to China, perhaps even including nuclear weapons, may appear quite possible. In a crisis short of war, a U.S. "tilt" toward China, either diplomatically or more actively by demonstrative alerts or force deployments, would yield bargaining advantage to the Chinese. The Chinese worry about a Soviet–U.S. "condominium" at their expense and frequently warn other intermediate powers of this danger.

Thus both of the Communist powers have a competitive stake vis-à-vis each other in their détentes with the United States, supplementing the cooperative stake they share with the United States. This inhibits each from competing too vigorously with the United States, lest its détente collapse—at the extreme, risking a crisis or war with the United States during which the internecine antagonist might take advantage of its preoccupation by attacking or threatening in the "rear." This places the United States in the enviable "swing position": a move toward further accommodation with one party creates bargaining leverage with the other. The role is not unlike that held by Russia between Germany and England during and after negotiation of the Anglo–Russian entente in 1907, before it had firmed up into a quasi-alliance. Threats to strengthen the entente were used to extract concessions from Germany, while expressions of dissatisfaction with the entente and hints of a possible rapprochement with Germany increased Russian bargaining leverage in disputes over Persia with the British, and yielded firmer British military commitments to Russia.

The United States has not exploited its swing position openly or blatantly, partly because the logic of the situation produces its own results, and partly because there are limits to its exploitability. The Chinese know, without having to be told, that they are on their good behavior in Asia; the Soviets likewise in Europe. The limits stem mostly from the United States' own stake in the détentes—both the reduction in conflict potential for its own sake and the political underpinning this provides for a domestically necessary policy of military retrenchment. Thus the United States cannot so vigorously play the Soviets off against the Chinese that one or the other finds the price of U.S. good will greater than the benefits. The ultimate restraint, of course, is the possibility of a Sino–Soviet reconciliation. This is more likely to occur as a result of changes in these two regimes than of anything the United States might do. It could be helped along, however, if the United States were to exploit the division between the others too vigorously.

Should a Sino-Soviet reconciliation become a real possibility, the swing position would disappear in a condition where each of the powers could credibly threaten realignment or deeper detente with either of the two others. Then, for example, the Chinese might use the threat of rapprochement with the Soviets to induce more cooperation from the United States or less U.S. cooperation with the Soviet Union, and similar tactics would be available to the Soviet Union.

The new détente-alignment game at the top is superimposed on and interacts with the "old" bipolar alliance game. Inevitably, accommodation between big power opponents has the effect of loosening their alliances. Especially for members of the U.S. alliances, détente sets up a tension between incentives to join the new game and the necessity to keep playing the old. Paradoxically, the members are tempted to play the new game either out of complacency—the feeling they are no longer threatened—or anxiety—the fear that the United States is not as resolved to defend them as before. On the other hand, they know their security is best assured by continued dependence on U.S. protection. In practice, they have sought the best of both worlds. While proclaiming their continued reliance on the old bipolar alliances, they seek either to reap trade benefits or to gain security insurance just in case the U.S. détentes should turn out to be a prelude to a relapse into isolationism. Japan moved toward rapprochement with both China and the Soviet Union while refraining from any steps toward an independent military role. The West European countries show interest in political accommodation and trade agreements with the Soviet Union, while urging the United States not to withdraw troops from Europe. The United States, too, is constrained in its play of the new triangular game by the imperatives of the bipolar alliance game. It dare not move too close to either China or Russia for fear its allies will declare their military independence, which the United States clearly does not want. The spectacle of India, once under implicit U.S. protection, now allied to the Soviet Union and exploding a nuclear device, dramatizes the risk.

The alignment implications and motives of the triangular détente system are not the positive ones of past multipolar systems—gaining allies for active aid in war—but negative in the sense of reducing one source of threat to be freer to concentrate on another, or, for the United States, reducing military burdens in general. For the smaller allies as well, accommodative moves toward either the superpowers or the lesser powers in the opposite camp, to the degree they are security-motivated, are aimed at reducing dangers, not gaining new allies.

The rejuvenated alignment game is only weakly subject to the logic of multipolarity that was described earlier in this chapter and illustrated from the nineteenth and early twentieth centuries. The reasons are numerous and complex; only a few can be mentioned here. First, there is the obvious asymmetry of power in the U.S.–Soviet–Chinese triangle —i.e., the fact that the structure of power is still predominantly bipolar. This means that the U.S.–Soviet détente cannot lead to anything approaching alliance. It cannot overcome the parties' basic mutual identification as adversaries, although it can, of course, moderate their rivalry. China does not represent the powerful threat to both that would be necessary to submerge this rivalry and move them toward alliance.

On the U.S.–Chinese side, the situation is somewhat different. These two have a powerful common adversary, so the structural condition for alignment is present. In fact, for both parties, their rapprochement was motivated, much more than the Soviet–American détente, by the competitive aim of containing the third party. Here the multipolar element in the present configuration was operating. However, it is difficult to imagine this relationship deepening into full alliance. It is in the U.S. interest to discourage a Soviet attack on China but the Soviets probably are sufficiently discouraged already by their uncertainty about U.S. behavior in that event, along with their appreciation of the Chinese nuclear capability. Any U.S. incentive to preempt a Sino-Soviet reconciliation by alliance with China would not be strong enough to offset the risks of becoming actively involved in a Sino–Soviet confrontation and the costs of the probable collapse of détente with the Soviet Union.

Second, the factor of nuclear weapons in the present configuration weakens the "compulsion to align" to avoid isolation that was mentioned as a feature of earlier multipolar systems. Today, as in the bipolar system of the recent past, the strategic objective of deterrence is dominant over the objective of winning or avoiding defeat in war. All three members of the new triangular balance have sufficient nuclear power to deter a deliberate large-scale attack by their most likely opponent, China perhaps somewhat problematically now but to an increasing degree as time goes on. Thus incentives to alliance are less than in earlier multipolar systems when the use of force offensively could still be considered a rational instrument of policy.

Third, a major difference between today's "multipolarity" and past multipolar systems is the increased importance of economic issues, and economic power, partly due to autonomous economic factors, partly because of the declining salience of security threats. Economic stakes are particularly important in the interplay between the United States and its allies—especially Western Europe and Japan—although they are also important to the Soviets in their détente with the United States. We are seeing the emergence of dual subsystems in the international system—the rise of a politico-economic system alongside the traditional politico-military one—each with its own power base and its own power structure, but with overlapping memberships and interacting in complex ways. For example, Western Europe and Japan are allies of the United States in the military subsystem, but they compete with the United States in the economic one. The United States can exploit its leverage in one subsystem to achieve gains in the other—e.g., as it holds over the West European states the implicit threat of troop withdrawals to influence their economic policies. Toward the Soviet Union, the carrot of trade and technological aid is held out as a reward for amenability in arms limitation negotiations. The Yom Kippur war of 1973 and its aftermath demonstrated vividly the interplay of economic and military-based coercion in a contemporary crisis.

In what other ways will this new pattern of multilateral maneuver affect the behavior of the major states in crisis situations? Can we expect to see re-appearing in future crises some of the patterns and dilemmas that we found in the pre-1914 and pre-1945 multipolar crises? A plausible guess is that we will see somewhat more interaction between the adversary game and the alignment game than was the case in the purer bipolar system of the 1950s and 1960s. But the interaction will be more shadowy, tacit, and implicit than in earlier multipolar systems, reflecting the nebulous character of the détentes upon which the new alignment game is based. For example, in a crisis between any two of the three leading powers, the third party is unlikely to play the role of "supporting ally" in the overt way it was played in the past; the role will be played tacitly and indirectly. Simple uncertainty about the third party's possible behavior would complicate the calculations of the protagonists. For example, although China could hardly act directly in a Soviet–American crisis in Europe, her diplomatic support of one side or the other, and her behavior along the Siberian frontier or opposite Formosa would not be without effect. Uncertainty about what China might do might inhibit the action or weaken the bargaining power of either protagonist, most likely the Soviet Union, so long as the conflict with China remains unhealed. Also, the stakes in a crisis are likely to include its possible effects on the existing détentes. Thus, in a Middle Eastern crisis, both the United States and the Soviet Union may be constrained by concern that too much coercion or too much support of their clients might shatter their détente and move the other closer to China. China would be inhibited by a similar concern should she consider reopening the Formosa issue by coercion or violence.

The role of "supporting ally" or "restraining ally" could be played either by some positive action or declaration in support of one party, or negatively, by threatening to break up the detente with one and move closer to the other. For example, in a Sino–Soviet crisis the United States could support China (and restrain the Soviets) by airlifting troops to Europe as a "precaution." Or it could restrain China by threatening to deepen its détente with the Soviet Union. Restraint might be exercised to gain political benefits from the opposite party or simply to control the crisis. If support were expected but denied, the détente might suffer, and the "supporter" would have to weigh this risk against the benefits of exercising restraint. As between allies in multipolar crises of the past, the credibility and effectiveness of such pressure would depend on the relative values placed on the détente by either party. It is extremely difficult to judge relative degrees of dependence on the current détente since the values gained from them are quite disparate for the parties involved.

We should distinguish between direct confrontations between two of the Big Three and their involvement in crises initiated by small clients. The first type is the least likely, since the negotiations of the détente themselves defused the two most prominent conflict issues between the United States and the Communist powers—Berlin and Formosa—although the latter was more shelved than settled. Their incentives to keep the détentes alive works against a deliberate challenge on any other issue. A Sino–Soviet crisis is the most salient possibility of this type, although a U.S.–Soviet conflict over Yugoslavia, should that state collapse into civil war after the death of Tito, cannot be ruled out. Much more likely are crises of the second type. Here the most obvious possibility is, of course, the Middle East. Tinder for a possible Soviet–China crisis is also present in the India–Pakistan antagonism, and for a China–United States confrontation if, say, a Communist Indo–China were to threaten or attack Thailand. In such situations, the two big powers in the protector relationship would face the difficult choice between supporting their clients or collaborating to pull them apart. The third member of the triangle might give diplomatic or demonstrative support to one side to increase the latter's bargaining power, or simply to reap "détente credit." Thus, nurturing the China connection apparently was the chief motive for U.S. naval demonstrations in support of Pakistan during the Indo–Pakistan war of 1972. Particular interests of China and the Soviets would probably constrain them from similar behavior in the two other situations mentioned. Chinese sympathy for the Palestinian cause would work against support of the United States in the Middle East, and Soviet ideological interests likewise in Southeast Asia. Thus, despite the general weakening of the ideological factor in contemporary world politics, it still is an obstacle to alignment flexibility in specific crisis situations.

However, one should not exaggerate the alignment implications of the present détentes. For the United States and the Soviet Union at least, if not for China, the primary motives for negotiating them were to reduce tension for its own sake, reduce the likelihood of nuclear war, pave the way for collaboration on non-security issues, and, for the United States, to support a policy of military retrenchment. Their relevance to crises, too, lies more in their contribution to crisis prevention and control than in the new pattern of multilateral maneuver they have fostered. As we have pointed out earlier, however, in discussing the Yom Kippur crisis, the crisis prevention function of détente works only when both superpowers involved want to make it work—i.e., only when they see the gains from collaborating as greater than the gains to be made (or losses avoided) from competing. The strength of détente derives entirely from the benefits generated by the relationship. One hopes that if and as the superpowers entangle themselves in more and more beneficial cooperative ventures, the tension between collaborating or competing in crisis-prone situations will more likely be resolved on the side of collaboration.

CHAPTER VII

SUMMARY AND SYNTHESIS

This book has been guided by two complementary goals: (1) to develop a theory of international crisis behavior and (2) to achieve a measure of synthesis among several important theories in international politics. For the latter objective, crises have served as an empirical focal point for theory integration, the rationale being that crises highlight in microcosm many of the essential features of international politics. Of course, we cannot claim that our synthesis amounts to a "general theory." Substantively it deals only with the politico-strategic side of international life, and the focus on crises tends to emphasize conflictual over collaborative elements. Still, the theories employed are and will remain central to the discipline and, with appropriate modification for the substance of issues, would probably be central to other dimensions now rising in importance, such as the politics of economics. They form the "core," we believe, to which other theories can best be linked in the continuing struggle to bring more theoretical order to our field.

The principle components in our theoretical ensemble are theories of bargaining, system structure and alignments, information processing, and decision making. The centerpiece is bargaining; the others we treat either as special features of bargaining or as factors external or internal to the states involved, which influence the bargaining process. We shall first try to show how these components are linked logically; second, we will summarize our empirical findings about the crisis bargaining process itself, and finally we will show empirically how that process interacts with its systemic environment and the internal decision-making process.

THE THEORETICAL SYNTHESIS

The synthesis can best be stated from the overall systemic perspective, with each component representing a different aspect of the international system and its functioning. The international system consists of its *structure*, defined as the distribution of military power among the major states; the *pattern of relations* among these states; their *interactions;* and their *internal characteristics*.[1] This definition differs from most in explicitly separating structure, relations, and interaction. Some writers have identified structure with the "pattern of relations" in the system, or, while clearly separating structure from relations or interaction, have used

---

[1] States that are not major actors are of course part of the system, but their roles are not significant enough to affect its essential nature. However, subsidiary systems (e.g., Middle East, Africa) might be analyzed in terms of these categories.

the latter terms interchangeably. But each of these terms denotes distinctly different phenomena. The distribution of military capability and potential among individual states is different from the relations, e.g., alignments, among them; and their relations or relationships are different from their behavioral interaction. Each affects the others, of course, and it is an important theoretical task to trace the causal links among them. This is what we attempted in the preceding chapter, although much remains to be done. The task becomes impossible unless the three sets of phenomena are kept separate analytically. Thus the effects of structure upon relations are simply lost from view if structure is defined as relational pattern.[2] For example, the pre-1914 system is often called structurally "bipolar" because power was distributed in rough equality between two alliance systems. But alliances are relational, not structural phenomena. The 1914 relational pattern was largely induced by a multipolar structure. The error obscures not only the structural causes of the relationship but also the enormous differences in behavioral process between the system at that time and the real bipolar system that emerged after 1945. The failure to distinguish between relational change and structural change also lies behind much of the current confusion as to whether the contemporary system is still bipolar or has become multipolar.

The failure to distinguish between "relations" and "interactions" obscures the difference between the relatively static and the dynamic aspects of the system's *functioning,* between the attitudinal and situational aspects on the one hand and the behavioral aspects on the other. Interaction is behavioral process, the actual encounters and communicative exchanges between states. But interactions so defined are not continuously occurring. We need some other term to express the continuing connectedness between the state-actors whether or not they are interacting and the best term available seems to be *relations*. It denotes "how states stand in relation to each other"—e.g., their images of others as opponents, allies or neutrals; their beliefs about each other's aims and intentions; their interdependence; their conflicts of interest and common interests; their ideological differences and affinities, and any other nonbehavioral elements which contribute to their attitudes, expectations and potential influence vis-à-vis each other.

From the politico-strategic perspective, the most important elements in relations are *alignments* and *interdependence*. We use the term *alignment* very broadly here to include both alignment "with" and align-

---

[2] Kenneth Waltz points out the confusing consequences of this error, and also of including attributes of states in definitions of structure, in "Theory of International Relations." However he apparently does not differentiate "relations" and "interactions."

ment "against" as well as non-alignment—i.e. the general stances of amity or enmity that exist between states, in varying degree, at any particular time. Alignment, at bottom, consists of states' intentions and expectations of others' intentions concerning supportive or opposing behavior in future interactions. An alliance is fundamentally a set of intentions and expectations, held with more or less certainty and confidence; so is an adversary relationship; so is détente. While *structure* means the objective distribution of military capabilities and potential capabilities among individual states, *alignment* refers to subjective beliefs about how capabilities are aggregated and focused in the system.

Interdependence means mutual dependence—the degree to which states are dependent on each other for the realization of goals and the preservation of values. We are concerned here with interdependence only in politico-strategic relations.[3] In this realm, we may distinguish between alliance interdependence and adversary interdependence. Allies are interdependent to the degree they need other's help for deterrence and defense against adversaries. The interdependence may be symmetrical and high (both parties need each other a great deal), symmetrical and low (both value the aid of the other but could go it alone at moderate risk), or asymmetrical (one party is more dependent on the alliance than the other). Adversaries are interdependent to the extent that each party can deprive the other of values it currently possesses or can give the other values it desires. Adversaries are, broadly speaking, interdependent on two dimensions: (1) military capabilities, and (2) conflicts of interest. On the capability dimension, their interdependence is simply their capacity to inflict military harm on each other—each is "dependent" on the others' refraining from exercising this capacity; or, they are "interdependent" via their common interest in avoiding war. On the conflict-of-interest dimension they are interdependent in the sense that the satisfaction of the interest of each depends on the acquiescence of the other, and the degree of interdependence is a function of the intensity with which the conflicting interests are valued. Between adversaries, as between allies, their interdependence may be high or low on

[3] The term *interdependence* has recently been applied mainly to economic relations but is equally relevant to politico-strategic relations. Among the few who have attempted to apply the concept to the latter realm are Kenneth Waltz and Richard Rosecrance. Our brief statement here attempts to build on their work. The concept seems to be the best vehicle for both clarifying the differences between, and integrating, the politico-strategic and politico-economic aspects of international politics, an urgent theoretical task that, at this writing, has hardly begun. Kenneth N. Waltz, "The Myth of National Interdependence," in Charles P. Kindleberger, ed., *The International Corporation* (Cambridge, Mass.: The M.I.T. Press, 1970), pp. 205–223; Richard N. Rosecrance and Arthur A. Stein, "Interdependence: Myth or Reality?" *World Politics*, Vol. 26 (October 1973), pp. 1–27.

either the capability or interest dimensions, and asymmetrical in varying degrees.

SYSTEM STRUCTURE AND RELATIONS

The structure of the international system has important consequences for the relations that form within it; relational patterns are quite different in multipolar and bipolar systems.

In a bipolar system, alignments are strongly influenced if not entirely determined by structure, at least in the central arena of the system (Europe since 1945). The superpowers are necessarily rivals, because for each, the other is the only other state in the system that poses a serious threat to its security. They will recruit as allies, by force or shared interests, the smaller states lying between them. Once alliances are formed, realignment is hardly conceivable, either because it is contrary to the structurally-determined interests of the lesser states or because the superpowers will prevent it by force. In subsystems outside the central arena, alignments of small states with the superpowers are less determined by structure, but structural effect is evident in the tendency of the superpowers to support opposite sides in local conflicts. The superpowers' rivalry does not preclude occasional periods of détente, but the logic of structure rules out alliance between them.

A multipolar system permits much greater variance in alignment. Structure provides incentives to align but does not affect who aligns with whom. Each major state is potentially an ally or adversary of any other one. Actual alignments are determined, not by system structure, but by the particular conflicts and common interests of states and by a process of competitive bargaining similar to the N-person game of game theory. Since the game never stops (so long as the structure persists) realignment is always possible.

Alliance interdependence is generally high, though variable, in multipolarity, and relatively symmetrical. In bipolarity it is asymmetrical. That is, in a multipolar system, alliance support is potentially crucial for all actors; in a bipolar system it is crucial only for the lesser states. The superpowers can take care of themselves, although alliance support is often useful for legitimizing purposes and the territory of allies is useful for force deployment.

The importance of allied support in multipolarity is combined with considerable uncertainty about whether it will be forthcoming. The uncertainty is a consequence of (1) the ambiguity of general strategic interests, e.g., whether the ally will perceive one's adversary as also a threat to itself, or as a potential ally, and (2) the fact that particular interests of allies are often not shared. The uncertainty of support is greatest, of course, when alignments are tentative and informal, but it exists even when they have been formalized. In a bipolar system, by contrast, it is a virtual certainty that the superpower will protect its allies against a challenge by the opposite superpower, and that in a crisis between smaller states on opposite sides the superpowers will at least "hold the ring" against each other—deter each other from direct intervention. This greater certainty of support in bipolarity follows from the greater clarity of interests in that system and the greater sharing of interests among allies. The superpowers know that a power gain for their opposite number is a power loss for themselves, in contrast to major states in a multipolar system, who may not be sure whether some other state's increase of power is a danger or a source of security.

INTERACTIONS AND RELATIONS

The power structure of the international system determines the *general* nature of relations and potential relations within it. Relations are established in detail, however, by the *interactions* of states, and conversely, interactions are affected by prevailing relations. We defined interaction earlier as "behavioral process, the actual encounters or communicative exchanges between states." We mean to include, by this definition, something more than action followed by *re*action. It includes any behavior that affects others in some way, including their expectations of the actor's future behavior, and/or which is influenced by expectations of others' responses. (Interaction does not necessarily include both of these elements. That is, states may take action affecting others without considering others' possible responses, or they may decide not to act, thus not affecting others, because of their expectations of others' responses—as in deterrence.) Action-reaction processes, such as arms competition and bargaining, in which the parties actively respond to each others' moves, form a sub-class.

Of course states interact in a great many ways, ranging all the way from ceremonial diplomatic contacts, to the exercise of political power, to warfare. In this book, we have dealt with one type, that of *bargaining,* so we confine ourselves here to a discussion of bargaining and how it affects, and is affected by, the relations of states.

Bargaining differs from most other interaction in that it is essentially a *communicative* process in which the parties attempt to influence each other's decisions in a future substantive interaction. Thus in simple bargaining over the sale of some object, the substantive interaction occurs when the object is exchanged for money; the bargaining that went before will have established the terms of the exchange. In a crisis, bargaining may set the terms for a later substantive interaction in implementing the settlement. Or bargaining may establish rules and expectations regarding a series of future interactions of substance as, for example in arms control or trade agreements. Communication in bargaining may be tacit as well as explicit—i.e., conveyed by actions as well as words—and the resulting bargain may be an implicit mutual understanding rather than an explicit agreement.

Following other writers, we said earlier that the necessary underlying condition for bargaining is the coexistence of conflicting and common interests between the parties. However, this notion needs some refinement. First, it is not enough merely that both common and conflicting interests exist; the relative strength of the two sets of interests is a critical variable. There are many conflicts in international history that the parties have a common interest in resolving, but there is no attempt to resolve them by bargaining because both parties know that the sacrifice they would have to make to get a settlement is greater than the value to be gained in settling. A good example is the Alsace-Lorraine conflict between France and Germany after 1870. A settlement would have benefited both parties by improving their general relations and removing an obstacle to their alignment, which would have increased both states' bargaining power vis-à-vis third parties. But these prospective benefits were less than what each party would lose in accepting the other's minimum conceivable demand. Thus, bargaining occurs only if the common interest in reaching agreement is strong enough and/or the conflicting interests weak enough to create a "bargaining range"— a range of conceivable settlements that both parties would prefer to no settlement.

However, it is not necessary that such a range "objectively" exist; it is sufficient that the parties *perceive* one, or some possibility of creating or discovering one. Given this perception, or hope, a motive exists for bargaining. In the United States–Japan crisis of 1940–1941, the shared interests of the parties were not strong enough to offset the severe conflict that divided them, but the parties did not know this for sure and bargained until they learned it. There seems no reason to exclude such "clarificatory bargaining" from the bargaining rubric.

It might seem, then, that simply engaging in bargaining behavior— making demands, threats, offers, etc.—is sufficient to qualify an interaction as bargaining, since the parties would not be doing these things unless the above conditions are met. This would not be correct, however, since such activity may be undertaken not in a serious effort to reach agreement but for what Iklé calls "side effects"—propaganda, impressing domestic opinion, setting up a pretext for military attack, etc.[4] The *necessary* condition for bargaining is the belief or hope on both sides that there is enough common interest in some agreement to offset

---

[4] Iklé, *How Nations Negotiate,* Ch. IV.

the sacrifice (measured either from the existing state of affairs or the desired change in it) that either party must make in order to reach agreement. The *sufficient* conditions are this belief plus a serious intention on both sides to find an agreement.[5]

We can now state certain connections between relations and bargaining. From one direction, the existing relational pattern generates the essential ingredients of interest and power that enter into bargaining encounters. Existing conflicts and commonalities of interest provide the occasions and motives for bargaining. The existing alignment pattern determines the type of bargaining that particular pairs or groups of countries are likely to engage in—alliance bargaining, adversary bargaining, innovative bargaining, etc. In any bargaining encounter, the degree and asymmetry of interdependence between the parties will roughly determine their relative bargaining power. A state's political power, in a unilateral sense, derives from other states' dependence upon it for important values. But when the state is also dependent on its bargaining partner, the latter has power as well; the power of each limits the power of the other, and their differences in mutual dependence will determine their relative power in bargaining. The parties are typically interdependent on two levels: (1) the issue in conflict, where each is dependent on the other's sacrifices (concessions) for the satisfaction of its interests, and (2) the level of common interest, where each is dependent on the other's cooperation for gaining or preserving shared values. In most bargaining situations, the parties attempt to exploit each other's dependence at the second level to achieve gains or avoid losses at the first level. Thus in an adversary crisis the parties may, by issuing threats, exploit their military interdependence—their reciprocal capacity to inflict harm and their common interest in avoiding war—to resolve the conflict in their favor. Allies exploit their dependence on each other's aid by suggesting withdrawal of support, in order to resolve conflicts about how to deal with the adversary or about the distribution of burdens, commitments, and benefits in the alliance relationship. In either relationship, however,

---

[5] It follows that any interaction that does not meet the conditions just specified is not bargaining. At one extreme there are interactions that involve no conflict, that are undertaken only to realize mutual benefits. Among these are the normal routine practices of diplomatic intercourse. Others are less routine but involve little or no conflict because the terms of the interaction have been established by previous agreement, e.g., foreign aid transactions or the use of foreign military bases. Bargaining enters into such activities only when one or both parties become dissatisfied with the existing rules of interaction; they may then be changed by negotiation. At the other extreme are interactions that have a high conflict content but little or no common interest, at least not enough common interest to provide a motive for bargaining. Included here would be most wars of the past (until the terminal phase), armaments competition (when there is no attempt to control it), and competitive manipulation of exchange rates or trade controls.

relative bargaining power derives not only from asymmetries of dependence at the second (common interest) level but also from relative intensities of interest at the first level (conflict). Thus, bargaining power overall is a net result of interdependencies at both levels.

Alignments also enter into relative bargaining power, of course, via the amount of capability allies can provide and the likelihood they will provide it. The likelihood is a function of their dependence on the alliance and the degree to which their own particular interests are at stake in the bargaining with the adversary.

Relations and interaction are also linked through the "interdependence of decision" that generally characterizes interaction episodes: the consequences of each party's decisions and actions depend on the decisions and reactions of others, and thus decisions logically must take into account what others are expected to do. Such decisional interdependence is distinct from the relational interdependence discussed above. However, the two are linked through the *images* and *expectations* that are generated by the perceptions of relational interdependence; that is, the general relational background provides the materials for estimating the other parties' decisions and responses in specific interactions. For example, whether or not a state prevails in a crisis may depend on whether an ally decides to lend its support (decisional interdependence); whether or not the state expects such support and hence decides to stand firm depends on its perception of the ally's degree of dependence on the alliance (relational interdependence). Or, as between adversaries, whether a party decides to stand firm depends on its estimate of whether the other will be firm (decisional interdependence); this estimate must take into account the other's valuation of whatever is in conflict and the parties' comparative military capabilities (relational interdependence). In addition, bargaining involves attempts to influence by communication the other party's expectations and hence his decision. Thus bargaining activates and perhaps modifies the political power that is already latent in existing relations and focuses the interplay of power on a particular issue.

The opposite linkage, *from* bargaining *to* relations, is that the outcome of bargaining often changes relationships, as when a new alliance is negotiated, or when a crisis results in a reduction (or perhaps an increase) in conflicts between adversaries, or a change in their power-dependence relations. Bargaining may establish procedures, institutions, and rules for future non-bargaining interactions between the parties, as in agreements between allies concerning exchange of information or standardization of equipment, or agreements between opponents to cooperate in preventing or dampening future crises, or, in the economic field, trade agreements or negotiated adjustments in exchange rates.

The outcome of a "bargain" is almost always a change in the parties' *intentions* and/or *expectations* regarding each other's behavior in future interactions, whether in a single transaction implementing the bargain, or a series of them, or in hypothetical future contingencies. As we said earlier, it is reciprocal intentions and expectations, along with interdependence and conflicting or shared interests, that essentially constitute the continuing "relations" between states. Bargaining and other interaction changes relations but does not constitute them. Of course, not all changes in relations occur through bargaining. Some result from the unilateral actions of states. And some may be the consequence of interaction other than bargaining, such as war. Great wars, such as World War II, may also change the basic power structure of the system, and relational changes then follow from the structural transformation. Such structurally induced changes are generally mediated through, or clarified by, a series of interactions, as the "Cold War" became manifest gradually via a series of encounters over Germany and other isues.

Actor Attributes and Decision Making

To complete the synthesis, international bargaining is also affected by *attributes* of the state-actors—their national styles and "operational codes," [6] the nature of their decision-making process, and the values, images, and relative influence of the individuals and agencies who participate in that process. The state is of course a subsystem in the international system and with modifications for the fact that the system is a government, yet with some degree of conflict within it, the same characteristics ascribed to the international system may be found within the state subsystem. There is a system structure, consisting of the relative power of the agencies and individuals involved, a set of relations between them (more formally and hierarchically defined and functionally differentiated than in the international system) and a process of interaction resulting in decisions about strategies and tactics in bargaining with other states. If the decision process takes a bargaining form, we then have an interplay between an "internal" and an "external" bargaining process— the outcome of the former becomes an input into the latter. Empirically, the interplay is a good deal more complicated and interesting than that statement suggests, as we will show later in this chapter.

Communication and information processing mediate between state-to-state bargaining and the internal decision process. Bargaining is essentially a process of communication intended to influence the other party and gain information about him. Decision makers need information in

[6] Alexander L. George, "The 'Operational Code': A Neglected Approach to the Study of Leaders and Decision-Making," *International Studies Quarterly,* Vol. 13, No. 2 (June 1969), pp. 190–222.

order to make decisions about bargaining strategies and moves. So much is obvious. But beyond that, the nature of channels of communication within the decision-making unit and the images and expectational biases of the individuals who transmit and receive information will strongly affect the interpretation of information. If the biases differ, they will enter into the internal "pulling and hauling" that produces decisions about external bargaining moves.

Thus the bargaining and other interaction between particular states is conditioned, on the one hand, by the structure of the international system and the patterns of alignment and interdependence that are generated by the structure, as these patterns impinge upon the participants and issues involved in the interaction. These relations may be conceived as external constraints on the interaction, setting outside limits on the bargaining power and the alternatives available to the participants. On the other hand, within these limits the actual bargaining power and strategies chosen in the bargaining process will depend on factors internal to the states concerned—the structure of decision-making units and the values, influence, and perceptions of their members, including their perceptions of the external constraints. The object of the bargaining, the issue in conflict, must not be overlooked, since it provides the objective context and focal point for the external-internal interplay and will exert a considerable independent influence on the interaction— especially as it engages the interests of the actors and apportions military advantages and disadvantages.

We turn now to a summary of what we have learned by the application of this framework to international crises, beginning with the bargaining process per se.

CRISIS BARGAINING: GENERAL SUMMARY

GAME MODELS AND CRISIS STRUCTURES

The best formal model for our purposes turned out to be the simple 2×2 game matrix, which we used to portray the "structure" of a crisis. Here the word *structure* obviously means something different than the structure of the entire international system in terms of the distribution of military power. It means the ordinal ranking, by the crisis participants, of their values for each of the four gross outcomes: win, lose, compromise, or breakdown. (Breakdown in most cases translates to expected cost (probability $\times$ estimated cost) of war or initiation of violence). Thus, "structure" mainly shows the interests engaged in the conflict for each party, although their relative military strength enters into the P (breakdown) values in the matrices.[7] Since interests and

[7] The reader may appreciate being reminded of the meaning attached to the

military strength are the principal components of crisis bargaining power, the game structure gives a crude approximation of the relative bargaining power of the parties.

Using the 2×2 model, we found nine different types of bargaining structures in our cases. Four were symmetrical, both parties having the same preference orderings across the four outcomes. The rest were asymmetrical, with a different ranking for each actor. Each type reflected a different combination of interests and power between the parties and each had its own dynamic of resolution and probable outcome.

Table 7–1 summarizes the crisis structures, the empirical cases of each one and their typical outcomes. (We remind the reader that Leader and Protector are alliance or détente bargaining structures that may either precede or occur simultaneously with an adversary crisis. Some of the other structures may also characterize alliance bargaining situations, not all of which are listed.)

We used ordinal rather than cardinal numbers in the game models, first because ordinal rankings were sufficient to show the general structure of the conflict situation and, second, because it was impossible, even roughly, to estimate the *amount* of value that the parties attached to various outcomes. In some cases it was possible to say, from evidence other than the outcome itself, that, for example, P (expected value of war) was considered far worse than S (losing) for one party and only somewhat worse for the other, or that war or risk of war was more negatively valued by one side than the other, or that one party's demand (T) was worth either considerably more or considerably less than the other's loss in granting it (S). For such cases, at least, it might seem that we paid a considerable cost in using ordinal numbers, by giving up the opportunity to show significant differences in bargaining power. However, the cost was small, compared to the gain in simplicity and avoiding spurious precision. For the "hybrid" games there was no cost because the asymmetry of the parties' ordinal preferences also reflected implicitly a difference in interests or strength or both, and thus clearly showed an imbalance in bargaining power. There was indeed some cost for the symmetric games, since the identity of ordinal rankings for both parties implies an equality of bargaining power, when in fact there might be considerable differences in the

---

symbols we used in the 2×2 matrix. T is the initial claim advanced by either party and the value of "winning" if it is achieved; S is the cost or value of yielding to the opponent's claim, thus "losing"; R is the value of compromise, and P is ordinarily the expected cost or value of war or some kind of violence following the breakdown of bargaining. The rankings of these outcomes in the matrices of course represented the rankings of the bargainers themselves, as best we could estimate them.

TABLE 7–1

CRISIS STRUCTURES AND OUTCOMES

Structures	Cases	Typical Outcomes
Symmetrical		
1. Prisoner's Dilemma	Agadir, 1911 Berlin, 1958–1962 Yom Kippur, 1973	Compromise
2. Chicken	Munich, 1938 (late phase) Berlin, 1948 Lebanon, 1958 Iran, 1946 (late phase)	One side capitulates
3. Leader	Bosnia, 1908 (early phase) Germany–Austria, 1914 Ruhr, 1923 Iran, 1946 (early phase)	One partner leads, the other follows; or alliance or détente breaks up
4. Deadlock	U.S.–Japan, 1940–1941	War
Asymmetrical		
5. Called Bluff (one party in Prisoner's Dilemma; other in Chicken)	Morocco, 1905 Quemoy, 1958 Cuba, 1962	Capitulation by Chicken party or unequal compromise
6. Bully (Bully-Chicken)	Fashoda, 1898 Bosnia, 1909 (later phase)	Capitulation by Chicken party
7. Bully-Prisoner's Dilemma	Germany–Austria vs. Russia–France, 1914	War
8. Big Bully (Big Bully-Chicken)	Munich, 1938 (early phase)	War (avoided in this case by shift of German structure to Chicken or Bully)
9. Protector (Bully-Leader)	Suez, 1956 (U.S.–Great Britain) Quemoy, 1958 (U.S.–Taiwan)	Dominant ally protects and restrains client

actual valuations of some outcomes that would produce some inequality of power. However, this cost was small in practice, either because bargaining power was quite equal, or, if unequal, the inequality could easily be described verbally. In a number of cases the parties did not even have their own ordinal rankings clearly in mind at the beginning. Our use of ordinal rankings therefore seemed a reasonable compromise that did not strain to capture too much of what might not be there and yet provided a theoretical tool that was good enough for our purposes.

In some cases, even the assignment of ordinal rankings involved a certain amount of guesswork. All actors were of course clear from the start about their own rankings of T, S, and R—the gross outcomes win, lose, or compromise—even though the exact empirical content of these outcomes might not be clear for a while. But for only a little more than half of them could we say with confidence that they were aware from the beginning of how they ranked P—the expected cost (value) of bargaining breakdown or war—in relation to the other three outcomes. In these cases we had to guess what their ranking would have been had they been forced to make one. For example, there is no evidence that Hitler in 1938 actually compared the costs of war with England and France against the value of his objectives in Czechoslovakia until the peak of the crisis in late September. When he did compare them, he found he was playing Chicken, but our judgment that he was playing Chicken from the beginning is only hypothetical. The example clearly suggests one reason why the P-function is not always clearly established at first: the player does not think he needs to worry about it because he is sure the opponent will *not* fight. In other cases the extent or likelihood of allied support—a vital component of expected war costs—does not become clear until later in the crisis.

In still other cases the P-value is not fully faced up to as long as diplomacy and other non-violent options are still available, and may never be evaluated if such options succeed. The critical value comparison in a crisis is between S and P—the cost of yielding vs. the expected costs of war—and people will tend not to make this comparison realistically until they absolutely have to. Take, for example, the United States in the Berlin Blockade crisis. Although President Truman made a "decision" to "stay in Berlin" at a formal National Security Council meeting early in the crisis,[8] we shall never know whether this would have extended to a forcible breaking of the blockade if the airlift had not succeeded—i.e., whether the United States was playing Chicken or Prisoner's Dilemma.

Our crisis structures in Chapter II were constructed from the actual or presumed rankings of outcomes by each party separately. But neither party could be sure of the other's rankings. This was an additional source of uncertainty about the "name of the game" for the parties, in addition to the initial uncertainty about their own rankings. Sometimes they, in effect, made an estimate of the other party's preferences fairly early on, but quite often these estimates proved to be wrong. In other words, often a party's subjective picture of the crisis structure was at variance with the actual structure. This was quite typical, in fact, for at least one party in most crises; if it were not for its mistaken guess about

---

[8] Charles E. Bohlen, *Witness to History, 1919–1969* (New York: W. W. Norton, 1973), pp. 277–78.

the opponent's value rankings, the crisis would not have occurred at all. Germany in 1905 comes to mind: France was estimated to be Chicken because England would not provide support; when the British did join the fray, France turned out to be in Prisoner's Dilemma. If they had not mispredicted British behavior, the Germans would not have challenged. Of course, it is a party's subjective estimate of the crisis structure, not the actual structure, that governs its behavior.

Critical Risk

We could not use ordinal models to describe directly the bargaining *process* since these models do not show changes in the parties' utilities and expectations during the course of play. Process was described verbally by indirect reference to these models. In principle, the *critical risk* model, which employs cardinal utilities and probabilities, could be used to portray process directly. The effects of coercive, persuasive and accommodative tactics could be shown as changes in the parties' utilities, critical (i.e., maximum acceptable) risks and estimates of actual risks. It is logically the most "satisfying" model of a crisis since it shows precisely the relative bargaining strengths of the parties, what calculations the parties logically would make in deciding whether to concede or stand firm, under what conditions a party *must* make a concession, and even the exact outcome. It is an ideal type which states precisely the reasoning that a perfectly rational bargainer would employ in making bargaining choices. As with all ideal types, its usefulness in empirical research does not depend on whether real actors behave exactly as the model specifies. The precision in the model is necessary only to show clearly its essential dynamics. If one can find only a crude non-quantitative similarity to these dynamics in the real world, the model can be said to "fit," more or less. Alternatively, the model is useful if it can serve as a benchmark from which deviations can be identified, classified and explained.

By these criteria, the model's empirical value is limited. We did find states using a variety of tactics, chiefly persuasive tactics, that were consistent with behavior implied by the model. For example, tactics intended to devalue the stakes for the adversary or to increase his expected cost of war could plausibly be interpreted as attempts to lower his critical risk—the maximum amount of risk he was able to "stand." Other tactics were clearly intended to increase the adversary's estimate of the risk that the party would stand firm—thus to increase the adversary's estimate of the risk he was facing. The model was useful, therefore, in providing a framework for classifying persuasive tactics in terms of their bargaining function.

However, the model did not fit well the parties' mental processes in making the ultimate decisions whether to yield or to stand firm. In the model, this requires a comparison between a party's critical risk and the opponent's firmness-credibility. We would have had a modest qualitative fit if we had found statesmen saying things like "The chances that our opponent will stand firm are too high to be risked," or, "There is some chance of war if we stand firm, but the chance is low enough to be worth taking." But we did not find such statements, although in some cases statesmen may have had some such comparisons in mind but did not articulate them. What we do find on the record are not quasi-probabilistic risk estimates, but judgments of a more absolute kind. "He is bluffing" or "He is committed to fight unless we yield" are the usual estimates of the opponent's threat-credibility. When strong doubt is thrown on such estimates, they change to the opposite absolute, not to some intermediate degree of "likelihood." Sometimes in the early stage of a confrontation, parties are simply uncertain about the opponent's resolve, but when the turning point is reached, the uncertainty has become a certainty.

Acceptable risks also tend to be estimated as absolutes, if they are estimated at all. At one extreme, a party says, in effect, "we *must* stand firm, whatever the risk," approximated by the United States in Cuba, 1962. This is the logical position, initially at least, for parties whose preference structure is Prisoner's Dilemma or Bully—their critical risk is 1.00. An intermediate critical risk calculation is logical only for parties playing Chicken, but even for them we do not find even qualitative estimates, although again, judgments of acceptable risk may be "felt" but unarticulated. Indeed, given the tendency mentioned above to estimate the opponent's threat-credibility at near-1.00 or near-.00, even the Chicken player need not estimate some intermediate degree of acceptable risk. The judgment that the opponent is either firmly committed or bluffing is enough.

Despite its descriptive limitations the model has prescriptive value as a guide to rational calculation. It could provide a means for decision-makers to calculate roughly their acceptable risks and the actual risks and would force them to examine closely their values and predictions. It gives some rational content to the notion of "calculated risk" which too often seems to be no more than a euphemism for "gamble."

Expanded Game

We interpreted the *expanded game* model as a model of crisis escalation or potential escalation. The model's usefulness is therefore limited to crises of the nuclear age, since before the advent of nuclear weapons there were few options lying between "standing firm" and "going to war," or at least such options were seldom considered or used. In modern times, the totally catastrophic character of all-out war has forced consideration of a variety of action options short of war, perhaps involving limited violence. One can display these options and more violent options all the way to nuclear war on an $m \times n$ matrix, with the payoffs on the NW-SE diagonal representing various degrees of escalation—as we showed in Chapter II. In our application the payoffs were ordinal and the alternatives listed for rows and columns were those which we, as hindsight observers, could see as plausible options. The "fit" of the model to cases was then determined by the extent to which those options actually were in decision makers' minds at the start or soon after the start of the crisis and whether in considering or choosing an option the opponent's possible responses and possible further escalation were considered. By those criteria the model did not provide an accurate picture of most post-1945 crises. Either the alternatives were not all clearly laid out in decision makers' minds, but appeared by accident or search during the crisis, or the consequences of choosing them were not thought through. We did get a moderately good fit for the Berlin crises of 1958–1961, and a somewhat better one for the 1962 Cuban missile crisis. In the Cuban case U.S. decision makers did take account of all reasonable alternatives and Soviet responses, and in considering the air strike option peered as many as three interactive stages "down the slippery slope." Then they saw only the nuclear void and recoiled; the recoil was important in the choice of the blockade over the air strike.

A more demanding version of the expanded model would put cardinal utilities in the payoff cells and require the estimate of probabilities for the opponent's responses and for further escalation beyond the first step. In such a version the NW-SE diagonal would consist of a series of interlocking escalatory subgames, with the *DD* cell of each subgame subsuming both the costs of mutual escalation in that game and the expected values (costs) of all further potential escalation. Such a game would fit none of our cases, since utilities and probabilities are not estimated. However, it could be a useful tool for contingency planning and crisis management because it would force decision makers to confront in detail the values, costs and risks of bargaining by escalation.

Supergame

We introduced the *supergame* model to show how crises, and specific alliance bargaining episodes as well, relate to the longer term relations between the parties. We divided the supergame into three dimensions: an adversary game, an alliance game, and a preparedness game. Crises appear as specific subgames in a continuing adversary game, although they often involve the alliance game as well, and occasionally the preparedness game. The supergame portrays how crisis outcomes, or a series of them, may change either (1) the power relations or (2) the degree of conflict between the parties. It shows how the structure of each successive crisis may be affected by the outcome of the preceding one, as it changes the distribution of bargaining power or reduces (or perhaps increases) outstanding conflicts of interests. For example, the sequence of crises in the 1930s may be shown on the power axis of the supergame model as a progressive shift of bargaining power in Hitler's favor as his adversaries repeatedly yielded and his own resolve and material strength increased. The pre-1914 sequence may be shown on the opposite (conflict) axis as mounting hostility and conflict due to the failure of these crises to remove the basic sources of conflict and the bitterness engendered on both sides by the excessive use of coercion. Transformations from an adversary to an alliance relationship may be shown as gradual movement from the *DD* to *CC* cell as the parties successfully resolve outstanding differences and mutually perceive greater conflict with, or threat from, a third party. Transformation the other way can also be shown as allies fall out, perhaps via the defeat of their common enemy.

In the supergame, states face on a larger canvas, in "macro" form, the same choice between coercing or conciliating an adversary that they face in micro-form in the context of a specific crisis. To make this choice, they must decide whether, with this particular adversary, they are operating mainly on the power-struggle axis or the conflict-harmony axis. In short, they must estimate the long-term aims of the opponent as well as their own. Toward an adversary who is bent on increasing power for aggrandizement, the proper choice usually is firmness at every confrontation. But if the adversary is simply interested in resolving specific conflicts, albeit to his advantage, the proper stance is accommodation to the degree compatible with essential interests of one's own. The stance actually chosen will depend, of course, on what we have termed one's "background image." If the image is incorrect, if, say, the opponent is seen as playing "conflict-reduction" when he is really playing "power struggle," one loses because one then underestimates one's own power interests at stake, especially the interest in fostering expectations in the opponent that one will be resolved in the future. Or if the opponent is misperceived as expansionist on a large scale but is really interested only in settling specific disputes on their merits, a policy of pure intransigence will "lose" by magnifying conflict and perhaps creating an inveterate enemy out of a merely dissatisfied rival.

From the micro-perspective of a particular crisis, the supergame model focuses attention on the future-oriented values at stake. It recognizes that the present encounter may be followed by others, and that the expectations other states form about one's likely behavior in future episodes may be as important as the immediate interests in dispute. In the adversary game, the most important of these future-oriented values is "resolve reputation"; another is the material power resources in the disputed object. Among allies or prospective allies, the chief value is "loyalty reputation," which bears on one's future attractiveness as an ally. Another is the value of improving relations with the opponent, which can be linked to either the adversary game or the alliance game— the latter because a satisfactory settlement may transform the opponent into a potential ally, and by doing so increase one's bargaining power vis-à-vis present allies.

The supergame model also makes formally explicit the differences and the linkages between "relations" and "interactions" that we discussed earlier in this chapter.

THE BARGAINING PROCESS: STRATEGIES AND TACTICS

At the start of the crisis, one or both parties have incorrect or only vague images of the crisis structure, especially the adversary's side of it. The function of the bargaining *process* in relation to structure is primarily to clarify the estimates and values of outcomes that constitute the structure, but it sometimes also changes them. Clarification occurs in two ways: (1) by deliberate information search—probes and "trial balloons"—and (2) by feedback from coercive, persuasive, or accommodative moves. What is mainly clarified for each party is the preference structure of the other, but the party's own estimates and values may be clarified as well. Thus, bargaining gradually moves the parties' subjective perception of the game structure more into line with the real structure; they gradually learn the "name of the game."

Bargaining may also *change* estimates and values of outcomes, engage new values, or subtract values previously engaged—perhaps enough to change the structure of the game. Persuasive bargaining attempts to change the opponent's values, usually to lower his estimate of the cost of yielding and to maximize his perception of the cost of concession for oneself. Threats and other coercive moves tend to increase the opponent's expected cost of war. They may also increase the cost of yielding for the threatener, by engaging additional prestige and reputational values that would be lost if the threat is not fulfilled. Coercion may also increase the adversary's cost of yielding via the emotional backlash or stiffening effect of threats. If the cost of backing down is raised enough for both parties, the game structure may change, say, from Chicken to Prisoner's Dilemma. Values may also change by reappraisal of what is at stake, or by personnel changes or shifts in the balance of influence within decision-making units. Most of such change occurs during the initial confrontation stage. At the end of this stage, the parties' perceptions of the crisis structure roughly correspond to the actual structure, perhaps changed from what it was originally, perhaps not. (The real structure changes in about half our cases—i.e., the preference structures of one or both parties become re-ranked.) The relative bargaining power then stands revealed, and the crisis is ripe for resolution. The parties then do what they can or must—yield, stand firm, compromise, or perhaps fight.

We now summarize our more specific findings about strategies and tactics in the bargaining process.

1. When a crisis is resolved expeditiously and peacefully, the alternation of coercive and accommodative strategies, and information search, follows a definite pattern. Both parties must adopt primarily coercive strategies (offensive or defensive) initially to clarify their comparative resolve and the likelihood of breakdown or war if both continue to stand firm. If accommodation is tried too soon, resolution is delayed because the recipient of the offer is not yet clear about the power relations and thinks he can get more, as the Germans did in 1905 after the French offered an early settlement. Premature accommodative attempts, like England's attempted mediation in 1914, can also be dangerous by leading the adversary to underestimate the risks of firmness. An initial period of mutual firmness is necessary to clarify the balance of bargaining power and the structure of the crisis and only then are the parties in a position to estimate whether and how much they must reduce their initial claims. After that point the process of resolution is different for Prisoner's Dilemma crises than for other types. In the former, both parties prefer war to accepting the other's demands. When this is realized, the parties each know they must reduce their goals to something the other can accept, or the outcome is likely to be war. There occurs an internal reassessment of goals, plus probing the opponent, to determine what is essential and what can be sacrificed, and what the opponent is willing to give up. The communication of reduced goals to the opponent is the turning point, after which the parties make reciprocal concessions leading to a compromise. In the Chicken cases and asymmetrical structures (Bully, Called Bluff), one or both parties prefer to yield than risk war. Therefore when one party establishes superiority of resolve it can force the other to give way completely, and usually does so.

2. During the confrontation phase, the protagonists face a choice between maximizing coercive pressure by tactics tending to commit, and preserving options that leave a way out in case the opponent becomes or is committed to a firm stance. The choice is generally a straddle: non-committing coercion. Strongly coercive tactics such as physically "irrevocable commitments" or severe committing threats are rarely used

because of fears of war by miscalculation, or fears of provoking the opponent into commitment. Threats are generally stated vaguely rather than explicitly, or framed as "warnings" to reduce their provocative effect. Threats are more explicit, however, when a threatener is highly resolved from the start and perceives the adversary as lacking either the will or the capability to fight. Except for these latter cases, there is a general pattern of threats and other verbal declarations being rather cautiously stated during the early part of the confrontation phase, then more explicitly and bluntly toward the end of that phase, especially by a party that has by then established its dominance. The reason for this pattern seems to be that bargainers wish to build up their own resolve image gradually and test the adversary's resolve thoroughly before they feel safe in committing themselves firmly. Tough talk, if uttered too early, may be considered "blustering," an attempt to cover up real weakness; the preference is "quiet firmness" until one's superior resolve is clearly established. Then the stronger party will often utter sharper threats to shock the other into yielding.

3. States seldom deliberately "manipulate risk"—i.e., increase the risk of the crisis getting out of control—as a coercive tactic. Rather, their preference is to minimize out-of-control risks. They tend to avoid actions that create a chance of accidental violence and to avoid words that might arouse uncontrollable passions in the adversary's public and press. In nuclear-age crises especially, a tight rein is kept on military forces in the crisis area to minimize the chance of "incidents." However, warnings that one's military forces are subject to uncertain control, or that popular passions and bureaucratic pressures may force one's hand, are quite often employed as coercive moves. Such warnings often are effective, since decision makers commonly hold exaggerated fears of the crisis getting out of hand. There are only one or two instances in our cases of top decision makers actually losing control of subordinates or events—Bethmann (Germany) in 1914, and Aehrenthal (Austria) almost in 1909.

4. While coercive tactics predominate in the confrontation phase of a crisis, and accommodative tactics (for one side at least) in the resolution phase, each usually is leavened with some admixture of the other. The reason is that the undiluted pursuit of one strategy or the other violates or risks violating the constraints on that strategy. Introducing elements of the opposite strategy keeps the strain on the constraints within acceptable limits. Thus conciliatory gestures accompanying coercive moves reduce the risk that the coercion will provoke more intransigence in the opponent. And words and acts indicating firmness protect the accommodating bargainer from looking generally weak when he makes particular concessions. Finding the appropriate mixture is an especially

delicate problem when bargaining power is perceived to be about evenly balanced. Then each party realizes that it cannot get its way entirely and that peaceful settlement will require a compromise, with both sides making substantial concessions. Both sides try to communicate a willingness to accommodate on some issues, but a determination to stand firm on others. The problem with such mixed strategies is that the message one wants the opponent to receive is a complex one and easily garbled, either by one's own clumsiness or the other's wishful thinking. The opposite kinds of garbling that may occur are illustrated by the Agadir crisis of 1911, when too much coerciveness in the German mixture made the crisis more severe than it needed to be and reduced the German share in the ultimate compromise; and the Berlin crisis of 1958–1960, when both sides misinterpreted as the primary component the accommodative leavening in the other's essentially coercive strategy, with consequent disappointment and resentment when no compromise developed.

Strategy mixtures take a somewhat different form in cases where the confrontation phase reveals bargaining power to be clearly unequal. During this phase the weaker party has invested a good deal of prestige and reputational value in attempting to appear resolved. He knows he must back down but needs a little help from the stronger party to get himself untracked from his coercive stance and moving toward capitulation. One of two things then usually occurs. The weaker party sends a covert signal indicating he is ready to accommodate; the stronger side then arranges a procedure for accepting the other's surrender that minimizes the latter's humiliation. Or the stronger party issues a "carrot" of some kind, perhaps combined with an especially severe threat. The latter, the "stick," allows the weaker party to feel or claim that he had "no choice" but to yield. The carrot enables him to pretend, and perhaps actually to feel, that he is really compromising, not capitulating. Carrots take many forms, including a small concession on the immediate issue, a side-payment on some other issue, a promise of future good relations, or an assurance that it is one's "last demand." In some cases, the stronger party is so overwhelmingly dominant that no carrot is is necessary to induce capitulation. Even then, however, the winner almost always grants the loser some kind of small concession at the end as a "face-saver." The face-saver is analytically different from the carrot, since it is given at or near the end of the resolution phase, not at the earlier turning point, and also because its function is not to induce capitulation but to ease the loser's status costs after he has already decided to back down. The winner's incentive to grant the face-saver is to avoid unnecessary embitterment of future relations with the defeated state.

5. *Time* is a complex variable in crisis bargaining. Some analysts

have included shortness of decision time as one of the defining characteristics of crisis. We reject this interpretation because most of the cases we studied did not involve really short decision time, yet they were certainly crises by other important criteria, such as severe conflict and a perceived high likelihood of war. These analysts, who may be grouped as the "decision-making-under-stress" school, also characteristically attribute to time pressure various pathological effects such as stereotyping of the opponent, inhibiting the search for alternatives, impairing ability to estimate consequences of actions, and limiting the estimate of consequences to the immediate future. Again, our findings tend to disconfirm such hypotheses since we find some such behavior in almost all of our cases, in only two of which—1914 and Cuba, 1962—was decision time measured in days rather than weeks or months. Moreover, the Cuban case was the one where the dysfunctional effects mentioned above were *least*. Thus one suspects that, if such distorting effects are caused by crises, the cause must lie in some other stress-producing aspect, such as having to make difficult trade-offs between important values and high risks in a situation of considerable uncertainty. The decision-under-stress writers do take account of such other aspects, but since they have not systematically compared cases of crisis and non-crisis decision making, it is not clear to what the extent the apparent "irrational" elements in crisis decision making are the consequence of stress, however produced.

Time is more relevant to the intergovernmental bargaining process than to internal decision making, but its relevance is ambiguous. On the one hand, challengers sometimes try to introduce a sense of time urgency into the situation to enhance their coercive efforts.[9] The reason urgency has this effect (or is believed to) is not quite clear, but one supposes it is a combination of the following: (1) some kind of time limit is logically necessary for compellent coercion, otherwise the other party could delay yielding indefinitely, (2) communicating urgency also implies that the coercer places a high value on the disputed object, and (3) the longer the crisis lasts, the more likely it is to get "out of control." But a deadline that is too short or too explicit may provoke the adversary by appearing to be an "ultimatum."

There is another dilemma. On the one hand, time is required for the bargaining process to clarify relative bargaining power and to correct initially mistaken expectations. Thus the party that believes itself the more resolved (and at the beginning that may be both parties) may wish to stretch out bargaining time to make sure its greater motivation is fully comprehended by the adversary. But opposed to this is the risk that the

[9] George, Hall and Simons emphasize the coercive value of creating a sense of urgency in *The Limits of Coercive Diplomacy*.

adversary, if initially less resolved, may become more resolved during the bargaining, may use the extended time to engage more values and become committed.[10] The United States faced this dilemma acutely during the Cuban missile crisis; President Kennedy elected to lengthen interaction time to give Khrushchev time to appreciate the U.S. determination and to consider his own options. This is the fairly typical choice of challengers in our cases, at least in that they do not deliberately try to shorten available time. Notable exceptions are Germany in 1909 (Bosnia), 1914, and 1938. The exceptions suggest a general rule for resolving the dilemma: if you are sure you are thoroughly dominant and sure the other side recognizes this, there is no need to avoid ultimata or to stretch out the course of events—this applies to Germany in 1909 and 1938. If you are not so sure, some delay is in order. Probably the more significant variable in 1914 was Germany's desire for a quick Austrian fait accompli to preclude involvement of other powers—the quicker the better. It should also be noted that there may be other reasons for slowing things down than the bargaining reasons mentioned; for example, the United States tried to prolong negotiations with Japan in 1941 to gain more time for preparedness and accustom public opinion to the probability of war. Or a party may stall in the hope that something will turn up that will improve its bargaining position.

INFORMATION PROCESSING

Chapter III treated bargaining as a process of mutual influencing by coercion and persuasion, and accommodating to the adversary's influence. It was implicit that these processes operate via the communication and interpretation of information, but the process of interpreting information was left unexplored. In Chapter IV we developed a theory of bargaining that placed information processing at the center of things and left implicit several elements in the influence-oriented theory. For example, such factors as the parties' interests at stake, their military capabilities, their comparative resolve and bargaining power, and their mutual assessments of these things, were simply bypassed in the information-processing theory and replaced by the concepts of image, expectations, and adjustment of expectations as the determinants of bargaining strategies and outcomes. This procedure served to highlight the reciprocal effects of behavioral expectations and the flow of information without denying that assessments of interests and power relations often lie behind expectations about the opponent's behavior and are affected by information inputs. In short, the cognitive-oriented theory of Chapter IV and the value-interest-power theory of Chapter III

[10] George, Hall, and Simons also discuss this dilemma. Ibid., pp. 241–242.

complement each other by illuminating different aspects of the same complex process.

Our most important empirical findings with respect to the information-processing theory are as follows:

1. At the beginning of a crisis, each party holds a general belief system comprising *theories* about how bargaining works and *images* of the self and the opponent. These self–other images are different about three-fourths of the time. That is, one party thinks of its own behavior as defensive or legitimate, the other's as aggressive or illegitimate; the other party holds the reverse view. Images of the other may be divided into a "background" component (views of the long-term nature and aims of the adversary) and an "immediate" component (views of the adversary's immediate goals, strength, resolve, etc. in the crisis itself). Background images do not change during the crisis, but immediate images do.

2. From the belief systems are derived a set of *initial expectations* about the other party's likely behavior during the crisis. Since these initial expectations are derived from pre-crisis images, not from interaction during the crisis, they are usually inaccurate. An initial bargaining *strategy* is chosen on the basis of these expectations.

3. *Messages* from the opponent and other information about the opponent are interpreted by reference to these existing expectations and the strategy already chosen. Expectations and strategy are resistant to change; hence incoming information is interpreted to conform to them. Interpretation by reference to strategy is "wishful thinking"—the bargainer wishes his strategy to succeed and tends to distort or block out data that indicate it is failing—but more often the interpretive screen is expectations concerning the adversary.

4. If information is too contradictory to expectations to be ignored or assimilated, expectations are *adjusted,* though as little as possible. A small adjustment of expectations leads to a change of tactics—e.g., press a little harder, make a conciliatory gesture—but not of basic strategy.

5. A *change of strategy*—say, from firm resistance to accommodation —occurs much less frequently than changes in tactics. It occurs only when new information, by a cumulative build-up or a sudden massive input, indicates clearly that a key expectation upon which the whole strategy is based is wrong.

The information-processing theory provides a set of lenses through which we see things we did not see, or saw only dimly, through the lenses of value-power oriented models and theories. If we put back on the theoretical lenses of these earlier chapters, the complementarity becomes clearer. For example, it was said earlier that the outcome of a crisis is determined by relative bargaining power, which is a function of comparative resolve as perceived by the parties. The word "perceived" provides the link. Perceptions of the opponent's resolve at the beginning and throughout the crisis are the "expectations" of the information-processing model. Changes in resolve perceptions are the equivalent of adjustment of expectations: the opponent is gradually seen to be more or less resolved; implicitly one's expectations about how he will respond to one's further moves are changed. Statements in Chapter III to the effect that usually "it takes time" for the resolve dominance of one party to become fully appreciated by the other express vaguely what the information-processing theory makes more explicit: that expectations are resistant to change. The latter theory adds a degree of explanation about why they resist change, an account of the specific psychological mechanisms that preserve expectations under the assault of contradicting information. The earlier generalization that getting the weaker party re-oriented to an accommodative strategy even after the resolve-power relations have become clear requires an especially strong coercive move, is crudely equivalent to the finding, seen through the information-processing lens, that a massive dose of information clearly inconsistent with established expectations is necessary to force a change in strategy. Here again, the information-oriented theory adds an explicit explanation of why this is so, in terms of the phenomenon of wishful thinking and other mechanisms that preserve confidence in a strategy when objectively it is clearly failing. On the other hand, the function of the "carrot" that often accompanies the coercive stick is better explained in terms of value calculations; it provides an increment of value that offsets at least some of the costs of backing down.

The information theory also helps to explain why we find so many more complete backdowns than compromises in our cases. Once one party has made a concession, the other thinks "Good, my strategy is working; keep pushing." The conceder, having lost some confidence in his original expectations, has them undermined further by the adversary's increased pressure, then loses all confidence and shifts to complete accommodation. This also partly explains why bargainers are often so concerned about "looking weak": a concession not only reinforces the adversary's initial expectation that one will back down, it also activates his "wishful thinking," his strong desire that his coercive strategy will succeed.

The information model, and our findings relevant to it, complement the value-power bargaining theories in a somewhat different way by further underlining the difficulties in carrying out the rather complex and delicate trade-offs suggested by the latter. The information model takes account of cognitive rigidity, for which there is a good deal of evidence, while the value-power model tends to assume considerable flexibility.

Efforts by the sender of communications to strike an optimum balance between coercive potency and risk-avoidance, or between coercion and accommodation, may be frustrated by cognitive rigidities in the receiver. Thus, ambiguous threats put out by a bargainer hoping to exercise a degree of coercion while preserving the option of non-fulfillment may simply be too ambiguous to penetrate the screen set up by the receiver's image and expectations; an explicit threat may be required in order to change the latter's expectations and to get any coercive effect at all.[11] Lord Grey's ambiguous statements to Germany in 1914 and Chamberlain's in 1938 come immediately to mind. In both cases the rigid expectations of the German receivers filtered out the threats as bluffs. A mixed coercive-accommodative strategy may lead to misunderstanding because the receiver's expectations and wishful thinking filter out the coercive elements. The value-power theory explains the incentives for senders to employ such mixtures; the information theory and related evidence shows the need for the sender to keep in mind the receiver's probable cognitive barriers to understanding them.

While the relation between the information-proceessing model and other bargaining theories and models is chiefly complementary, there is also an important element of contradiction. The value-power theory implies that parties develop their initial estimates of relative resolve and bargaining power by a comparison of each other's interests and military forces, and change these estimates during the bargaining process by further comparisons of the intensity of interests. The information theory says that initial expectations come from images (which may include in part estimates of the other's interests and forces) but are changed thereafter by direct observation of the other's *behavior,* without reference to his interests. Empirically, the information processing theory seems to have the edge in this matter. We do not find *on the record* more than one or two explicit estimates of the adversary's intensity of interest. We do find a number of attempts (as in the U.S. decision making in Cuba, 1962) to estimate what the adversary's motives are, but no attempt to estimate the strength of those motives, let alone any comparison of that strength with the strength of one's own motives. The lack of direct interest comparisons may be only an artifact of the record—the intensity of the opponent's interests may be "felt," perhaps subconsciously, but just not articulated. We do find, however, many instances of attempts to estimate the opponent's intentions from his behavior, verbal and non-verbal, in the present crisis as well as in the past. The empirical truth seems to combine the value-calculation of bargaining models and the behavioral observation of the information model. One's

[11] A similar point is made by Robert Jervis in *The Logic of Images,* pp. 132–133.

own "inherent resolve" is determined by reference to one's own interests, which are known with fair confidence; the *opponent's* likely resolve is determined by reference to his behavior, as a surrogate for estimates of his interests, which cannot be estimated with confidence. One's own *actual* resolve is a function of both. This is an important qualification of the theory of bargaining power presented in Chapter III: that each party's resolve, and hence comparative resolve and relative bargaining power, turn on cross-party comparisons of interests. It also helps to explain the importance many actors attach to cultivating a long-term reputation for resolve by actively demonstrating firm behavior in all encounters. They do not believe the adversary will, or is able to, estimate accurately their interests in any particular crisis.

CRISIS OUTCOMES: PEACEFUL RESOLUTION AND WAR

Fourteen of our 16 major cases ended in peaceful resolution. Two, the 1914 crisis and the United States–Japan crisis of 1940–1941, ended in war. Two of the 14 peaceful resolutions were more or less even compromise settlements—Agadir, 1911, and Berlin, 1961. Two others could be considered partial compromises, i.e., short of complete capitulation by one side. They are Iran, 1946, and Cuba, 1962. In the Iran case, the bargaining process ended with the Soviets salvaging a promise of an oil concession in northern Iran, well short of their initial goal but still not inconsequential. However, they lost this gain when the Iranian parliament later refused to approve the concession, so the "outcome" is ambiguous. The Cuban case is also ambiguous as to outcome: whether it was a partial compromise or a capitulation-with-face-saver depends on how much the U.S. no-invasion *quid pro quo* actually was worth to the Soviets. All the other cases ended in the complete defeat of one party, usually assuaged somewhat by some kind of face-saving cosmetic. The following remarks attempt to explain these outcomes.

Peaceful Resolutions

1. The two crises that ended in more or less even compromises were both Prisoner's Dilemma crises in which the parties eventually perceived that each was resolved to go to war or begin an escalation process leading toward war rather than accept the other's initial demand, but that each was willing to accept less than its own original demand. Bargaining power was perceived as about equal. These mutual perceptions led to internal reassessments of goals and a process of mutual concessions, explicit in the Agadir case, implicit in the Berlin, 1961, case.

In the cases of unequal compromise or one-sided capitulation, these outcomes resulted from a mutual recognition of inequality of resolve in crises structured as Chicken, Called Bluff, or Bully. One party's interests in the issue turned out to be much greater than the other had expected (Cuba, 1962), or a party received more support from its allies than its opponent had expected (Morocco, 1905), or a party took a firm position at first out of interest or indignation and then realized it did not have sufficient military strength to risk war (Russia in Bosnia, 1908–1909). Typically the imbalance was so great that the less resolved party had no alternative but to back down completely.

2. The outcome of a crisis reflects pretty closely the "inherent bargaining power" of the parties that derives essentially from the relative valuation of their interests and their relative disutility for war or risk of war. That is, the parties' usually mistaken estimates of their comparative values of winning, losing or fighting at the start of the crisis become adjusted during the confrontation phase so that by the end of this phase their perceptions of these things, and consequently their perceptions of relative bargaining power, correspond quite accurately to reality, and the outcome reflects this reality. To be sure, what is "inherent" may change somewhat during the crucible of struggle, as the parties reevaluate their interests and perhaps engage new values. And bargaining "skill" is by no means irrelevant. It consists, however, not so much in deception as in communicating one's interests and resolve accurately to the adversary, and gaining reliable knowledge about his, so that one gains as much in the final resolution as the basic power relations permit. There are three or four cases in our sample in which either blundering or virtuosity in bargaining led to an outcome somewhat different than the inherent power relations suggested. For example: (1) Morocco, 1905: had the German government been less divided and vacillating, less "pushy" in dealing with the French and more perceptive of the interests of third parties, especially Britain, it could have avoided total defeat. (2) Morocco, 1911: had the Germans not handled relations with Britain so clumsily, or treated France so brusquely, a better outcome could have been obtained. (3) Iran, 1946: a combination of Soviet blunders and negotiating skill by the Iranian premier produced a more complete defeat for the Soviets than the actual power relations (including relations with the U.S.) would have suggested. (4) Cuba, 1962: U.S. power would have prevailed in any case, but the cost could have been much higher but for the skillful U.S. handling of the crisis.

3. Perceptions of *legitimacy* are potent in determining bargaining power and outcomes. That is, the party that believes it is in the right and communicates this belief to an opponent who has some doubts about the legitimacy of his own position, nearly always wins. Legitimacy often derives from defense of a long-term status quo against the attempt to change it by threat of force. In our cases, the defender always wins except when both sides share the belief that some change in the status

quo is more legitimate than its perpetuation. Then the side proposing change has the advantage. Of course, the parties often differ about the justice of change or different kinds of change; what matters is the intensity of the beliefs. In all the post-1945 cases the side defending the status quo won, except in Berlin, 1961, a compromise case. Here the East Germans and Soviets got what the West conceded to be legitimate, namely border closure in Berlin, but they did not get the claim the West believed to be illegitimate—free city status for West Berlin. The Cuban missile crisis was marked by initial Soviet misjudgment of the "balance of legitimacy," then a quick revision of this judgment when they learned that the United States regarded what they had done as highly illegitimate. (It is noteworthy that Kennedy's television challenge explicitly stated that the Soviet move was "unjustified" and elaborated at length on the reasons why it was.) The Munich case was one in which both sides shared a belief in the legitimacy of change—up to a point. Hitler got the Sudetenland because the British believed he had a right to it. But he did not get it the way he wanted to take it—by immediate occupation—because the British believed this violated diplomatic "due process." Perceiving that the British and French would probably fight in defense of legitimate procedures if not substance, Hitler accepted the Munich conference, plebiscites, international supervision, etc. Before 1914 there was a general belief that an eventual French protectorate in Morocco was legitimate (legitimacy again resided in change, not preservation, of the status quo). Germany opened the first Morocco crisis because she believed the French failure to consult her was illegitimate, a belief that was also generally shared. When the Germans got their conference, this injustice was rectified. They then lost on the substance despite their superior military strength (they simply did not consider the issue worth fighting over) because the legitimacy factor favored the French on the substantive issues. In the 1911 replay the Germans were able to get some compensation because the French (and everyone else involved) believed they deserved it. Bosnia, 1908–1909, is the exception that proves the rule: there was a general belief that at least the method employed by Austria in annexing Bosnia was illegitimate (no consultation, no conference with other signatories of the Treaty of Berlin), but she was able to get away with it because the other most interested party, Russia, was simply too weak militarily to take a firm stand. These examples do not conclusively prove that legitimacy superiority always wins in the absence of gross military inequality but they do show that "being in the right" when this is recognized by others is a strong bargaining asset. It is probably the most potent element in the "balance of interest" component of the bargaining power equation. It is worth noting also, although other variables were operating, that the two cases that ended in war were cases in which opposite legitimacy beliefs were held with about equal intensity.

4. Schelling's theory of "salience" [12]—that settlements will tend to occur at certain prominent points that focus the expectations of both parties—is relevant to only a few crisis outcomes, significantly only to genuine compromises. Thus in the Agadir case, the French and German governments were agreed that Germany was to get some part of the French Congo; the issue was how much. There was no logical or obvious criterion for deciding how much, and since the parties were about equal in bargaining power, neither could enforce its preferred division. The solution had to be based on some geographical feature of the area which posed the question "if not here, where else?" Kiderlen located this feature in his demand for access to the Congo River and the Atlantic coast and the French could find no rationale for denying it. The salient feature in the 1961 Berlin crisis was of course the boundary line between East and West Berlin; it provided the rationale for the Wall as the de facto settlement. In the other cases where bargaining power was unequal, there were in some cases salient points where the weaker party tried to "dig in its heels" but unsuccessfully. Unequal bargaining power overrode salience in those cases. Salience was more relevant to the bargaining process than to outcomes. The parties often stopped short of certain points on the verbal or action escalation ladders—e.g. the invocation of "national honor" or the actual use of violence—in order to minimize escalation risks. On the other hand, some such point was occasionally breached by a highly resolved party in order to demonstrate its resolve: for example Salisbury's breach of diplomatic convention when he published a "Blue Book" containing diplomatic correspondence during the Fashoda crisis.

War

Full-scale war was the outcome of two of our cases—the European crisis of 1914 and the United States–Japan crisis of 1940–1941.

The 1914 case shows that war is likely when misperceptions about other states' intentions are not corrected soon enough to arrest the activation of military plans that must necessarily lead to war. Three of our theoretical foci are involved in this finding: information processing, bureaucratic politics, and game models (specifically, the Prisoner's Dilemma). It is quite clear that if the German civilian leaders had realized earlier that Britain would fight if France were attacked, they would have put the leash on Austria. They were willing to fight Russia and France if necessary, but they believed that British participation would result in a German defeat. Bethmann did try to hold Austria

---

[12] Schelling, *The Strategy of Conflict,* Ch. III.

back at the eleventh hour when an unmistakable message from Lord Grey corrected his miscalculation that Britain would remain neutral. But by then it was too late because the Russian announcement of partial mobilization had triggered the start of mobilization procedures by the German military that, according to their plans, had to be followed automatically by war on Russia and France. The Prisoner's Dilemma element was the general belief in military circles in all countries that "mobilization means war"; hence, when one country started mobilizing or appeared about to start, this "defection" had to be countered, resulting in a mobilization race either to get the advantage of attacking first or to avoid the costs of being attacked while still unprepared. Although it was only the special features of Germany's Schlieffen Plan that made it logically necessary that mobilization be followed by attack, it seems highly likely that the Prisoner's Dilemma dynamics of the "mobilization means war" syndrome would have resulted in war even without those special features.

Given the mobilization Prisoner's Dilemma, and given the German military plans, the causal finger points to misperception or, more precisely, the tardy correction of misperception. (The three variables are not entirely separate, since part of the misperception of civilian leaders in all countries was a lack of appreciation of the logic of mobilization, and lack of knowledge, even among *German* civilian leaders, of the war-proneness of the Schlieffen Plan. However, simple ignorance is probably a better word for this than "misperception.") Why were the Germans so mistaken about British intentions and why did they correct their mistake so late? Partly it was the recent good relations between Germany and England, especially their cooperation in containing the 1912–1913 Balkan conflicts. Partly it was German wishful thinking: indices of probable British neutrality were selectively noted; indications that Britain would fight were played down or ignored. But in large part the explanation lies in the failure of the British to make their intentions clear. And one reason for this is that they did not *have* any clear intentions because of a split in the cabinet until after the war had already begun. Thus Grey felt he could not communicate his own preferences unequivocally in the name of the government. Here is perhaps a "bureaucratic politics" causal element.

Of course, there were other causal elements. One was systemic: the multipolar system of 1914 had all active major powers aligned in two opposing alliances of apparently equal power. Each member of each alliance (with the possible exception of tIaly) was absolutely essential to the security of every other member. Thus allies under threat had to be supported lest they be defeated or defect. The Germans' failure to realize this (except for their own necessity to support Austria) lay behind their fatal illusion that an Austro–Serbian conflict could be "local-ized." The systemic cause also links up with the German miscalculation of British intentions. It was largely the diffusion of power among several (but yet few) major actors that, first, made it possible for Germany to predict mistakenly the behavior of one of them and, second, made that mistake so critical. Had the Triple Entente and Triple Alliance been solidary states—i.e., had the system been bipolar—would the war then have occurred?

The other example of the United States–Japan shows that crises become wars when correction of misperceptions reveals a conflict of interests so deep that it cannot be resolved either by unilateral retreat or by mutual compromise and therefore can only be resolved by war. The perceptual element in this case worked oppositely to 1914. As long as the two parties mistakenly believed there was some possibility of a settlement, negotiations dragged on and the outbreak of war was delayed. When finally the misperceptions were corrected and both sides realized there was no chance of either one making a concession acceptable to the other, Japan chose the only remaining option—war. In 1914 the misperception hastened progress toward war, and its correction probably would have stopped war had it come soon enough. There were deeper elements of misperception in the United States–Japan case that were part of the basic images each held of itself and the other. The Japanese leaders believed that they must have control of raw materials-producing areas in East Asia for their economic survival and security and, as a newly recognized "Great Power," thought they had a right to such control. The United States could not understand why free trading could not satisfy Japan's needs. A unique and critical element was Japan's perception of the main U.S. coercive instrument—trade restrictions on critical fuel and other materials—as actually creating those conditions of economic strangulation that they desperately wanted to avoid and whose prevention provided their strongest motivation for war.

What both of these examples have in common is wildly inaccurate estimates of the value of P—the cost of war. If either side in the 1914 crisis could have foreseen the duration and amount of blood-letting that would occur in the ensuing war, they would have been playing Chicken rather than Prisoner's Dilemma or Bully, and would have been willing to accept almost any compromise. In 1941 the Japanese leaders believed, or at least hoped, that the United States would sue for peace after initial naval defeats, even though they knew they would lose a long war. If they had more realistically estimated U.S. determination, one supposes the game might not have been Deadlock, and some compromise might have been reached. The two cases also illustrate the point made earlier about the tendency for the certainty about substantive interests to dominate the uncertainties about the consequences of acting to protect the interests. The latter are not calculated, but simply "gambled with." This tendency is stronger, the greater the substantive interests, the protection of which becomes elevated to an absolute imperative— "whatever the cost" as the Kaiser put it in 1914. In both 1914 and 1941, the nations did what they thought they *had* to do in view of their substantive interests, and the uncertainties about the outcome of war were left to fate.

If we ask the obverse question, why all our crises except those of 1914 and 1941 did *not* end in war, the simple answer is that one or both sides preferred the costs of retreat or compromise to the costs or risks of war. These crises differed from that of 1914 because the realization that the adversary was committed to war, or might be if its claims were not met, came soon enough to permit a settlement before non-bargaining elements took the crisis out of control. They differed from the 1941 crisis in that the clarification of relative interests and resolve during the bargaining process revealed that the conflict of interest was not so deep that it could not be resolved short of war.

From our limited sample and this brief analysis we cannot claim to have given anything approaching a definitive answer to that enormously complex question: what causes war? We have merely pointed to certain proximate reasons why a bargaining-type crisis may eventuate in war— chiefly faulty information processing, high interdependence among allies, preemptive compulsions, highly incompatible interests and underestimates of the cost of war. We suspect, however, that these factors would be prominent in any definitive study.

SYSTEM STRUCTURE AND CRISIS BARGAINING

Earlier we discussed how different structures of the international system—multipolar and bipolar—tend to produce different patterns of relations, including alliances and alignment possibilities, conditions of interdependence, and conflicting and common interests. Here we summarize how the relations characteristic of each structure tend to affect crisis bargaining.[13]

---

[13] This does not necessarily mean that any particular crisis in either system type will be affected by the entire pattern of relations in the system; only that part of the pattern that touches upon the "system-segment" where the protagonists are located will be relevant. For example, in a system that is bipolar overall, a crisis might occur in a regional subsystem where the superpowers are not involved and the only "relational" factor might be the alignments and potential alignments in that subsystem; the crisis might then develop as a typical multipolar crisis. In a multipolar system the relevant alignments are only those that are actual or potential for the protagonists involved, and conceivably the two parties may be alone in the field. The point should not be overstressed, however. Even when,

First, in a multipolar crisis, the relative bargaining power of the immediate protagonists will depend heavily on the intentions of their allies, especially as these are appreciated by the opponent. Second, serious miscalculations about alliance support can occur because of uncertainties concerning the ally's interests and dependence on the alliance, and misperceptions generated by the ally's attempt to deter the opponent and restrain the ally at the same time. Third, much of the bargaining activity in a multipolar crisis will be between protagonists and allies on the same or opposite sides, as the protagoinsts seek to firm up support from their own allies and weaken the opponent's support from his, or the supporting allies seek to influence the bargaining position of their directly involved partners. Fourth, the supporting ally's capacity to restrain or moderate the position of its partner is generally weaker than in bipolarity because of the supporter's typically high dependence on the alliance. However, restraint capability varies with the comparative dependence of both parties. Fifth, the stakes in the crisis for both parties, and for the opponent as well, may include stakes in the alliance game as well as the adversary game, and the stakes in one game may be used as bargaining chips in the other. Thus, an alliance may be offered, or held out as a future prospect, to persuade the adversary to make concessions in the crisis dispute.

Structural-relational effects in a bipolar crisis are different for the superpowers than for the lesser states, reflecting the greater asymmetry in alliance interdependence. Here we should distinguish between three types of bipolar crises: (1) direct confrontation between the superpowers (Cuba, 1962); (2) crises in Europe initiated by a superpower in which a smaller state on the other side is the direct target, but the opposite superpower takes the lead in bargaining (Berlin); and (3) crises outside the European "central system" in which client states on either side are the direct protagonists and the superpowers play a supporting (or perhaps restraining) role (Middle East). (Of course, there are several conceivable variations of these types.) In the first type, the role of allies is relatively unimportant. The allies have little power to restrain the superpowers or influence their bargaining positions. The stakes are strictly whatever is at issue with the adversary; the alliance game does not enter the picture. In the second and third types, where the smaller allies are directly involved as protagonists, the intentions of the supporting superpowers are even more important for them than they are for the states in a multipolar crisis. It is clear that support will be forthcoming, but how much? In the second type, that question is

_____

in retrospect, third parties did not become actively involved, their potential involvement must enter into the calculations of the participants and those who elect to abstain must consider the consequences.

answered by the superpower's taking the bargaining lead from the start, both vis-à-vis the opponent and within the alliance. The superpower's preference generally will govern the bargaining stance toward the adversary, though it will be constrained to give some effect to the preferences of the allies whose particular interests are threatened, because of alliance norms and because their goodwill and cooperation are important to the effective functioning of the alliance. The alliance game is thus somewhat involved, but not in the extreme form of possible realignment, as in multipolarity.

In the third type of bipolar crisis, the superpower plays a role more like that of the "supporting ally" in multipolar conflicts—standing at arms length as a protecting (or restraining) friend and having much less direct interest in the outcome of crises and wars than the client does. Here the client state has the decisional initiative in crises, but also needs to discover the extent of superpower support, which may range from deterring the opposite superpower, to providing arms, to covert or possibly overt participation in war. The logic of the extreme asymmetry in strategic dependence implies that the superpower is quite free to set whatever limits it likes on its support, thus can exercise much greater restraint over the ally's actions than supporting allies can in a multipolar crisis and more than in the second type of bipolar crisis, because of the greater strategic importance of allies in that type. Control may be exercised by specifying that military support will be given only for defensive purposes, not if the ally takes the offensive. (This source of restraint may not be credible in a multipolar crisis where the normally high strategic interdependence may force the supporting ally to fight regardless of who initiates the war.) Another source of control is the threat to cut off the flow of military supplies and economic aid. But these sources of restraint are undermined by several factors. First, once the local parties have built up their arsenals they may believe they can start a war and finish it before replacements are needed. Second, the Prisoner's Dilemma in which the United States and Soviet Union are trapped in the Middle East inhibits their capacity to withhold or to threaten to withhold supplies: once one of the patrons is suspected or seen to be providing supplies to its client, the other is virtually forced to do the same, and there is a strong temptation to take the initiative in such "defection" lest the client otherwise lose and the protector lose its political influence as a result. Third, the superpowers deter each other from direct intervention, but this means that the clients lack ultimate security against their local adversary. They may then be driven to attack out of security fears. This is essentially why the United States was unable to restrain Israel in 1967.

This implies that the potential for superpower crisis or even war is highest in peripheral subsystems like the Middle East where the super-powers stand at arms length from their clients and do not participate directly in decisions, and yet are somewhat trapped by the logic of events after local decisions are made. The potential for being "dragged in" is obvious. This danger is lower in the central system of Europe because here the superpowers' forces are physically present, they are constantly involved in collaborative decision making with allies and therefore have more capacity for controlling decisions that might lead to crisis, as well as decisions during a crisis.

The superpowers are highly interdependent as adversaries because of their mutual capacity to inflict enormous destruction and their de-pendence on each other to control adventurous allies or quasi-allies. When power is thus concentrated at the top, those at the top feel a con-siderable degree of joint responsibility for control of conflict in the system as a whole. The exchanges between Khrushchev and Kennedy during the Cuban missile crisis provide vivid evidence of this sense of partnership. Since then, a kind of crisis co-management role has been developing, though fitfully, as part of the maturation of détente. The Nixon-Brezhnev agreements of 1972 formalized the role by an agree-ment to collaborate in crisis prevention and control. However, the managers do not yet agree on the rules and procedures for managing, and it is not clear that they are sincerely prepared to assume the role. The role implicitly includes four dimensions: avoidance of direct con-frontation between each other, control or mediation of conflicts between other states within their own spheres of influence, control of conflicts between clients on opposite sides, and control of conflict outside the recognized sphere of either (as in Africa or Southeast Asia). They have performed well in the first two dimensions. In the third and fourth, however, the record is mixed, with some successes and some back-sliding.

The Big Two are in the position of duopolists who may either collude or compete. Collusion provides maximum joint benefits, benefits that others share to the extent they value order and peace (although others may not value these things as much as they dislike being "controlled!"). But in the familiar logic of the Prisoner's Dilemma, there are also temptations and pressures to compete for unilateral advantage. The temptations come from opportunities for gain, the pressures from their clients seeking aid. Thus the superpowers' role as joint crisis managers is in continual tension with their own underlying rivalry and their re-sponsibilities as alliance leaders and protectors.

Still, collusion comes easier between duopolists than between oligop-olists. In the multipolar world prior to 1914 it was more difficult for leading states to join with adversaries to restrain obstreperous allies because of the latter's indispensability and possible realignment options. An attempt to hold back an ally risked the ally's defection, which could be disastrous. England and Germany did assume the co-managerial role successfully but briefly during the 1912–1913 Balkan crises, restraining Russia and Austria respectively. But the legacy of resentment in the restrained powers, and anxiety in the restrainers—especially in Germany—lest failure to support the ally the next time cause its defection, made collusion virtually impossible in 1914. In general, the Prisoner's Dilemma that is inherent in co-management is more severe in a multipolar system than in a bipolar one because the potential costs of collusion loom larger relative to potential benefits.

Military Technology and Crisis Structures

One might suppose that all superpower crises in a bipolar *nuclear* world would be Chicken. Surely there are *no* political objectives that are worth a nuclear war. However, the nuclear powers have not yet faced the stark choice between yielding in a major crisis and the *certainty* of nuclear war. What they have faced is a choice between yielding or compromising and the *risk* of nuclear war, which is something different. Even if the P payoff means violence, it can be violence in a small way, at a low rung on an escalation ladder that has several more rungs to go before the nuclear one, and it may be possible to get off before that one is reached. Thus the United States seemed quite prepared to kill Russians (and Cubans) to get those missiles out of Cuba in 1962 if the Soviets had not yielded. The crisis was Called Bluff, or perhaps Bully, rather than Chicken, in part because the United States could hope that the air strike would lead at most to limited reprisals. The Berlin crisis of 1958–1961 was Prisoner's Dilemma not Chicken, in part because the first acts in a DD deadlock would have been nothing more than East Germans checking papers on the access routes, harassment, etc., a long way from nuclear war.

Technically the P-value in a nuclear crisis is the summation of the "expected values"—possible outcomes times associated probabilities—of all the escalatory sequences that may follow a DD outcome in the bargaining game. However, decision makers do not calculate utilities, probabilities, and expected values in choosing among alternatives. They choose options that meet constraints, in the manner of "bounded rationality." If no option meets all constraints, some constraints are loosened until one alternative becomes acceptable. Constraints that involve high uncertainty—such as "avoid nuclear war"—are most easily loosened. Constraints built on certainties—such as "preserve the vital interest"—are much more difficult to modify. Thus we observed in U.S. decision making in both the Cuban and 1961 Berlin crises a tendency to act upon the *interest* that one is certain about and to gamble with the uncertain consequences of action, even when a possible consequence is nuclear war. The Soviets seemed more willing to modify interest-based constraints, perhaps because their interest was in changing the status quo rather than in defending it. One suspects that in a crisis within the Soviet sphere of interests—say, if the United States had challenged in Hungary, 1956, or Czechoslovakia, 1968—Soviet decision making would have been similar to the tendency just mentioned for the United States. This tendency is another reason why nuclear-age crises are not necessarily structured as Chicken and may take more dangerous forms, especially if both sides consider their interests at stake to be "vital."

Of our eight post-World War II cases, only three—Berlin, 1948, Lebanon, 1958 and the late phase of Iran, 1946—were classified as Chicken. On the other hand there were no instances of the *most* dangerous types: Big Bully, in which one party prefers war to the opponent's capitulation, or Deadlock, in which neither party is willing to make the concessions necessary to avoid war. At least it can be said that while nuclear crisis antagonists are often determined to stand firm rather than capitulate entirely, they are also more willing than in former times to accept compromises or to grant some significant *quid pro quo* for the adversary's giving way.

One would expect prenuclear crises to be less frequently Chicken than crises between nuclear powers, and more frequently one of the other types in which at least one side prefers to fight than give in to the opponent's claim. This expectation arises, first, from the obvious fact that war between great powers was less costly than it is potentially in the nuclear era, thus more likely to be considered less costly than giving up an important interest. Second, the comparative military strength of the parties was a more reliable indicator of the probable outcome of war, and the stronger side could predict that territorial gains would offset its war costs. Third, if forces were about equal, each side might wishfully gamble on victory for itself (as both the German–Austrian and Russian–French combinations did in 1914). Fourth, a preventive war calculation could plausibly be employed to discount the costs of war (Germany in 1914 again provides the example).

Our cases support this reasoning rather strongly. Three of the eight prenuclear crises—Fashoda, Bosnia (later phase) and 1914—were Bully or Bully-Prisoner's Dilemma, in which one party preferred war to receding at all from its demand. One (Agadir, 1911) was Prisoner's Dilemma, with both parties preferring war to accepting the adversary's initial demand, though also willing to compromise. One (Morocco, 1905) was Called Bluff with one party in Prisoner's Dilemma, and one crisis (U.S.–Japan, 1941) was Deadlock in which both parties preferred to fight rather than make any significant concession.

The Munich crisis was the only pre-1945 case that we classified as Chicken. However, we recognized that this case was hard to classify and could have been interpreted differently. The Chicken classification was based on the final stage of the crisis when Hitler finally began giving some credence to possible British–French military intervention. Up to that time he had been playing Big Bully against Czechoslovakia, completely discounting the Western powers and "negotiating" only to establish a pretext for attack. It could be argued that his shift at the turning point was to Bully rather than Chicken—i.e., he shifted to preferring acceptance of his diplomatic demands over war, but was not willing to accept any significant compromise of these demands.

Finally, of the two game structures peculiar to alliances, Leader is characteristic of the pre-1945 period, Protector of the post-World War II era. The difference is more a function of system structure than of military technology. That is, Leader games are typically played in a multipolar system where the military power of allies is more or less equal and their mutual dependence is high. When the allies disagree about bargaining strategy towards the opponent, *either* may grab the lead, playing its preferred strategy; this forces the other to follow to avoid the mutually disastrous consequences of alliance break-up. Protector games are typical of alliance interaction in a bipolar system and leader games are not found. The reason, of course, is that alliance interdependence is asymmetrical; the smaller allies cannot take the lead and hold it because of their much greater dependence on the alliance than the superpower's. System structure guarantees their protection, but also their subjection to the superpower's will in critical strategy choices.

STRUCTURES, ALIGNMENTS AND IMAGES

System structures and alignments have considerable effects on states' *images* of each other, which in turn are important in determining expectations about each other's behavior in crisis bargaining. Other factors enter into images, of course, but the causal link from structure and alignment to image is often overlooked. In a bipolar system where strategic rivalry between the superpowers is inevitable, affective and cognitive images will develop consistent with this rivalry. After World War II the transformation of the U.S. image of the Soviet Union from "partner in keeping the peace" to "inveterate aggressor," as well as reverse changes in U.S. images of Germany and Japan, resulted from the transformation of system structure and the realignment that necessarily followed. The United States and Soviet Union were in the familiar "security dilemma," in which initial images of a *potentially* aggressive other are gradually confirmed and strengthened as each side's defensive moves are interpreted by the other as aggressive. Thus Stalin's probably defensive moves in securing a Communist-dominated Eastern Europe appeared to the United States and Western Europe as aggressive (since *they* were not aggressive, how could the moves be considered defensive?); the Western powers' response—the Marshall Plan and moves toward a strong and independent West German state—appeared to Stalin as aggressive, an intolerable threat to Soviet security, and so on.

A similar phenomenon also may occur in multipolarity as alignments change and become firmer; in fact, the process of alignments "becoming firmer" often works through the intervening effects on images. For example, after negotiation of the Anglo-French entente in 1904, Germany began to take on more and more malign characteristics in the eyes of the other two. German attempts to make friends with either were treated coldly or given a negative interpretation. Thus the enthusiastic German welcome to Edward VII when he visited Kiel was branded by the London *Times* as "tasteless and vain." When the Germans sent a squadron of warships to Plymouth in a cordially intended return visit, the *Times* intimated the ships had been sent to spy on the defenses of the city.[14] The British stereotype of Germany and Germans had changed completely: "Germany was no longer the land of the categorical imperative: on the contrary, she was wallowing in materialism—her ideal was profits and her cult was brute force."[15] The strategic imperative of holding the entente together also worked against the German image in French and British eyes. Every attempt by Germany to make friends with one of the other two was branded as an attempt to split the entente, and friendly initiatives toward Germany were avoided by the other two for fear the partner would take it as a sign of disloyalty. This in turn negatively affected Germany's images of the other two and strengthened her feelings of isolation and fears of "encirclement." These feelings contributed to a growing aggressiveness in German diplomacy, and an increase of conflict with the entente powers.

EXTERNAL BARGAINING AND INTERNAL BARGAINING

So far in this chapter we have considered the bargaining and other interactive behavior of *states,* viewed as unitary actors in a system. Almost half of the decision-making units in our cases *are* unitary actors, or virtually so. These are the Types 1 and 2 units, in which one or two

[14] Raymond Sontag, "German Foreign Policy, 1904–06," *American Historical Review,* (January 1928). Vol. 33, p. 285.
[15] Oran J. Hale, *Publicity and Diplomacy: With special reference to England and Germany, 1890–1914* (New York: D. Appleton Century Co., 1940), p. 270.

persons, the head of government or foreign minister or both, control decision making entirely, or within a broad range of choice.[16] For these types, the theories of bounded rationality, or perhaps crude value-maximizing rationality, are sufficient to explain decisions. The controlling values, goals, and constraints are those of the one or two persons in charge, and there is no occasion for "bargaining" with other persons who hold different views. When more than two persons or agencies are involved, decisions are a result of the differing values, perceptions, and influence of these participants. Here, the "bureaucratic politics" paradigm, or a modified version of it, is useful for explaining decision making. From this perspective, the process and outcomes of crisis bargaining are the result of an interplay between "external" interstate bargaining and internal bargaining. The main purpose of this section is to analyze this interplay. But first, we wish to mention certain limitations of the bureaucratic politics paradigm [17] when applied to crisis behavior.

First, there is a general tendency in crises to limit participation to a few top officials and to minimize involvement of bureaucracies. Usually, if more than the head of government and foreign minister are actively involved, participation is limited to some sort of inner cabinet or ad hoc committee consisting of no more than four or five persons. (The Cuban missile crisis was unique in the large number of individual participants for the United States.) Thus, while the "pulling and hauling" described in the bureaucratic politics theory does occur in these cases, the "bureau-

[16] To refresh the reader's memory, we repeat our typology of decision-making units: Type 1: One or two persons deciding alone with virtually no internal restraints. Type 2: One or two persons acting independently within broad limits established by colleagues. Type 3: One central decision maker assisted by advisers, whose advice he is not legally obliged to consider or accept, but who do have some informal influence. Type 4: Decision by committee in which all members share responsibility and power. Type 5: Divided government in which decision-making power is divided between opposing factions who block each other and prevent adoption of clear consistent strategies.
We constructed this typology with reference only to intragovernmental participation and influence, i.e., abstracting from broader influences in the domestic political setting such as public opinion, press, parliaments. In some cases our decision-making units are restrained and influenced somewhat by such factors. We simply did not have the space in this book to explore these broader domestic influences. They are not central to our theoretical objectives and not as influential in crises as often supposed.

[17] We refer, of course, to recent works on bureaucratic politics that treat the subject in a quite theoretical vein, chiefly those of Graham T. Allison and Morton Halperin. While these writers have made a valuable contribution in systematizing the subject, earlier studies should not be forgotten and are still useful. See, e.g., Roger Hilsman, *The Politics of Policy Making in Defense and Foreign Affairs* (New York: Harper and Row, 1971); Samuel Huntington, *The Common Defense* (New York: Columbia University Press, 1961); Warner Schilling, Paul Hammond, and Glenn H. Snyder, *Strategy, Politics and Defense Budgets* (New York: Columbia University Press, 1962); and Richard Neustadt, *Presidential Power* (New York: Wiley, 1960).

cratic" element is minimal. The degree of lower-level involvement does vary across cases—in general, in inverse ratio to the brevity and severity of the crisis.

Second, the bureaucratic politics theorists emphasize that attitudes of decision makers are strongly role-conditioned: "where you stand depends on where you sit." However, in our cases individuals' views seemed at least as often to be the function of personal predilection toward "hard" or "soft" strategies. These predilections were fairly consistent for given individuals on different issues, though there were a few exceptions. Dulles, for example, was rather moderate on Berlin but tough on Quemoy; Acheson the opposite. Role influences were most clearly seen in the case of military participants. All this suggests that the bureaucratic politics paradigm is useful in crisis studies mainly for its account of the internal bargaining *process* (when such bargaining does occur), not for its explanation of why peoples' attitudes differ.[18]

Third, although the bureaucratic politics paradigm has been developed by empirical reference to the U.S. decision-making structure, it seems less relevant to the United States, where the president holds the ultimate power of decision in foreign policy, than to other kinds of regimes where responsibility is shared.[19] Finally, the theory is more relevant to modern times when agencies other than the foreign office have become involved in foreign policy making, with military participation especially active, than to, say, the pre-1914 period when the foreign office and head of government had virtually all the action with the military more or less waiting in the wings until called upon.

We turn now to the interplay between external and internal bargaining.[20] The most obvious link is that internal bargaining produces deci-

[18] Here it must be said the Graham Allison's choice of the Cuban missile crisis as the empirical vehicle for his excellent exposition of the paradigm was unfortunately misleading. His Models II and III are more generally applicable to non-crisis decisions in which agency biases are freer to operate, untrammelled by constant presidential involvement and a shared sense that the "national interest" should take precedence over bureaucratic concerns. Allison, *The Essence of Decision*.

[19] See Stephen Krasner, "Are Bureaucracies Important?" *Foreign Policy*, No. 7 (Summer 1972), pp. 159–179 for a critique of the theory, emphasizing the president's primary role in U.S. foreign policy making. Also see Robert J. Art, "Bureaucratic Politics and American Foreign Policy: A Critique," *Policy Sciences* 4 (1973), pp. 467–490.

[20] We follow Allison and Halperin in using the term "bargaining" for collective internal decision making. For them it apparently means the whole process of maneuver and "pulling and hauling" by which decisions get made, a meaning more diffuse and comprehensive than the definition we gave earlier for interstate bargaining. We accept this, but point out that in crises the process of decision or coalition-formation often takes the simpler form of merely discussion and persuasion among top decision makers. See Allison and Halperin, "Bureaucratic Politics: A Paradigm and Some Policy Implications," in Raymond Tanter and

sions about strategies and tactics to be employed by the state in its bargaining with other states. Responses of other states are similarly the product of "pulling and hauling" between individuals and agencies with different interpretations of the first state's move, different interests, different influence bases, etc. From this perspective the process and outcome of international bargaining is more the adventitious result of configurations of attitude and influence *within* states than of the "balance of bargaining power" *between* states. (We shall have more to say below about how these two conceptions may be reconciled.)

There is a further, less obvious link that the bureaucratic politics theorists have missed. This is that the stances taken by individual participants tend to mirror the spectrum of external bargaining options available to the state. The salient options are coercion (offensive or defensive), accommodation, or some mixture of these two. Each of these external alternatives has a coherent logic that makes it a rational choice provided its assumptions are granted, and the proponents of each will of course argue that logic. For example, the soft-liner will argue that conciliation ought to be tried first; if it doesn't work, there will be time later to fall back on the coercive option. If coercion is tried first, this will get the opponent's back up, make him less willing to concede, set off an escalation of threats and counterthreats and block the initiation of a negotiation process through which a mutually satisfactory compromise might be found. The hard-liner will argue that accommodation at the beginning will give an appearance of weakness and make the opponent push harder for his own goals, not a compromise. The correct approach is to be firm from the start; there will be time to make concessions later if one has to. While the soft-liner underrates the danger of looking weak, the hard-liner discounts the risk of provocation and escalation. Thus, the central decision maker's problem of choosing between, or mixing, these external options is paralleled by his internal problem of building a majority coalition or compromising divergent advice so as to keep "on board" as many participants as possible. The alternatives that are "bargained out" internally come from competitive logics that are inherent in the external bargaining situation. The internal power of the proponents of each alternative will tend to vary with the potency of its logic, given the facts of the external situation, and interacting with whatever consensus does exist about the nature of the opponent and the "national interest."

The bureaucratic politics theorists miss this point because of their commitment to the notion that internal bargaining positions stem primarily from agency interests. The external situation appears only as

Richard H. Ullman, eds, *Theory and Policy in International Relations* (Princeton, N.J.: Princeton University Press, 1972), pp. 50–51.

one kind of occasion for decision, a stimulus that triggers the internal struggle, in which the policy preferences of the various participants come chiefly from internal sources [21]—notably agency role and the desire to enhance the status and influence of their agency. Power in the internal bargaining process also is said to flow mainly from internal sources. We do not deny that these internal factors are operative, but assert that the external situation—i.e., what the opposing state is doing and how it affects the interests of one's own state—is at least as important in determining bargaining positions and influence in the internal debate. Even if certain agencies or individuals can be expected regularly to take hard or soft positions, their influence will be greater or less depending on whether the external situation seems to favor an accommodative or coercive strategy, in the eyes of the central decision maker and in terms of the core of consensus in the group.

A few examples from our cases illustrate the point. In all the pre-1914 crises, beginning with Morocco, 1905, Lord Grey faced the external choice between deterring Germany and Austria while supporting France or Russia (the coercive alternative), or conciliating the former while restraining the latter (the accommodative option). This choice was mirrored in the internal division between the foreign office hard-liners and the Radical soft-liners in the cabinet. The foreign office people spoke the logic of defensive coercion: Germany was out to dominate the continent; thus she must be contained and France must be supported at all costs. The Radicals perceived little threat from Germany and felt she had a right to be consulted about and perhaps to share in the control of Morocco; the connection with France was not an alliance, thus Britain had no obligation of support; furthermore support would encourage French intransigence, which might precipitate war. In 1905–1906, when the entente was still fragile and untested, Grey leaned toward the foreign office view and managed to carry out a tough strategy against Germany by simply not informing his Radical colleagues of everything he was saying to France and Germany, or about the initiation of military staff conversations with the French. In 1911, during the early part of the Agadir crisis, Grey leaned the other way, believing the German demand for compensation to be legitimate. He took the Radicals into his confidence and adopted their preferred strategy of concilation. Later, when it appeared the Germans were after a piece of Morocco rather than just "compensation" in Central Africa, Grey's own preference shifted toward coercion, and he managed to form a new majority coali-

---

[21] Halperin, *Bureaucratic Politics*, pp. 101–112. Halperin and Allison do recognize four categories of "interest" that are held by individual decisionmakers: conceptions of the national security interest, agency interests, domestic interests, and personal interests. However, the emphasis is placed on agency interests and the influence of agency role on conceptions of the national interest.

tion around this strategy by gaining the defection of the Radical leader, Lloyd George, who had become enraged by Germany's high-handed behavior. In both these cases the internal division was linked to the international bargaining situation via the competing logical strategies for dealing with it. In 1911, as the situation changed so that British interests seemed threatened, the internal balance of power changed with it, making possible a shift of strategy.

In the 1961 phase of the Berlin crisis, President Kennedy was faced with a situation that did not seem to demand either a purely coercive or purely accommodative strategy. It was necessary that the Soviets understand that the United States would fight for its vital interests, and what those vital interests were; at the same time the United States should be willing to negotiate in search of a settlement that would leave its essential interests intact. These alternatives were reflected in the domestic debate, with the hard-liners, led by Dean Acheson, calling for a refusal to negotiate (and citing the damage to the U.S. reputation for firmness if negotiations were entered into) and simply waiting for the Soviets to carry out their threat if they dared, then putting selective, graduated military measures into play. The soft-line group favored entering into negotiations without threats and considering military steps as a last resort. In resolving his external dilemma in favor of a mixture of those two options Kennedy at the same time settled the internal struggle by giving something to everyone. The United States would negotiate, he announced, but certain things were non-negotiable, the Acheson plan for military measures was put in reserve as a threat in case negotiations failed, and military forces were increased. But it was Kennedy's personal preference for a mixed strategy that most influenced the decision; the concurrent compromise of the internal struggle was incidental.

The bureaucratic politics theorists do not deny, of course, that states can be influenced by external stimuli. However, they argue that if one's influence attempt is to succeed, there must be someone with influence in the opposite government who already wants to do what one desires of that government. Hence the prescription: if you want to influence another government, find out what group(s) in that government are already inclined to do what you want, and shape your moves so as to strengthen those groups in their own government's internal debate.[22] This point is the bureaucratic politics school's most original and interesting contribution to the theory of international politics and bargaining, as distinct from internal decision making. Let us see how it stands up empirically.

This theory implies that the first task of the international bargainers

---

[22] Allison and Halperin, "Bureaucratic Politics," pp. 57–66.

is to assess the internal configuration of attitudes and influence in the other government. Assessment or information-search is indeed, as we have emphasized, a primary component of bargaining; what the bureaucratic politics theory does is shift the focus of search from the aims, interests, and power of the other state in general to the interests and power of individuals or factions within the state—certainly a more difficult task.

Decision makers in our cases only occasionally attempted such assessments, and when they tried they did pretty miserably. A typical example was Bulow's and Holstein's estimate that the formation of a new Liberal government in Britain in 1905 was a great break for Germany since the Liberals were pro-German and would forsake the entente with France that had been negotiated by the previous Conservative government. The Germans apparently were not aware of the division within the Liberal party between rather hard-line "imperialists" and soft-line "radicals" and that the imperialists held all the foreign policy-related portfolios. On the other hand they did correctly perceive that the French foreign minister was in a weak domestic political position, which could be exploited to get rid of him. But they did not perceive the nuance that the opposition to Delcassé was based mainly on personal animus and domestic issues rather than foreign policy, so they were surprised when the French position on the Morocco issue did not change after he left. The record does not show that either the French or the British had a glimmer of the sharp split in Germany between Holstein and the Kaiser.

Consistent with the typically poor analysis of the divisions and influence patterns within the adversary was the infrequency and usual failure of deliberate attempts to affect those patterns, as prescribed by the bureaucratic politics theory. For crises the prescription boils down to "strengthen the soft-liners" or "avoid strengthening the hard-liners" in the adversary government. The few attempts that were made almost all failed, largely reflecting mistaken estimates of internal politics in the other state.

In some cases, the outline of the internal split was estimated correctly, but an inappropriate strategy was chosen for dealing with it. One of the German motives for staging a naval demonstration at Agadir in 1911 was to help the conciliatory French premier, Caillaux, overcome his hard-line opposition by creating a rationale for concessions. The move merely stiffened sentiment for resistance in the French cabinet. The error here was not so much a failure to perceive the division in the opposite government as a mistaken judgment about how to influence it, and this in turn is attributable, probably, to the peculiar German insensitivity to the emotional "stiffening" effect of tough moves on others, though they were remarkably thin-skinned themselves.

Deliberate attempts to manipulate the adversary's internal balance of power are few, but there are many instances of international bargaining moves having had such effects unintentionally. In 1905, for example, the initial German demands over Morocco were perceived by the dominantly soft-line French cabinet as appeasable by offers of compensation elsewhere. When these offers were spurned and the French leaders perceived that Germany was out to humiliate France at a conference and break the entente with Britain, the hard-line foreign ministry gained influence and the premier, Rouvier, who had taken over the foreign office portfolio, shifted his own position from soft to hard. In the Agadir crisis of 1911 the sudden public British intervention via the Lloyd George speech first produced a spasm of indignation in Germany, but its more important consequence was that the accommodatively inclined Kaiser called his hard-line foreign minister to heel, putting Germany's policy on the road to compromise. After Eisenhower refused to apologize for the U-2 incident in 1960, leading to the collapse of a summit conference, Khrushchev evidently lost standing in the Kremlin. To keep his more militant comrades at bay he was forced to adopt their line and speak in more bellicose terms on the Berlin issue when he opened it up again in 1961.[23]

When the parties are aware of each other's internal divisions, the division in one's own state may be exploited in external bargaining. Delcassé made full use of English apprehensions about the weakness of his government in the Fashoda crisis of 1898 and about the possibility of a military coup if the British pushed too hard. The turbulent political situation in Iran in 1946 enabled the Iranian premier, Qavam, to pose for the Russians the possibility of a more intransigent regime replacing his own if they refused to accept his terms. A variant is to warn, not of the downfall of one's own government, but of a shift in the balance of influence within it toward a harder bargaining position. Hence the Czar's statement to the Kaiser in 1914 that he was under "tremendous pressure" from his military to mobilize. Khrushchev says in his memoirs that at the height of the Cuban missile crisis Robert Kennedy told Ambassador Dobrynin "I don't know how much longer we can hold out against our generals" and even spoke of the president's fear of a military take-over. "We could see that we had to reorient our position swiftly," Khrushchev states, thus implying that concern about the internal power balance in the U.S. government was the most important single factor in inducing the Soviets to retreat.[24]

[23] Schick, *The Berlin Crisis*, p. 128.
[24] *Khrushchev Remembers*, trans. by Strobe Talbot, with Introduction, Commentary and Notes by Edward Crankshaw (New York: Little Brown, Sphere Books Ed., 1971), p. 459. Obviously the statements mentioned, as in any memoirs, must be treated with some skepticism. Khrushchev may have misrepresented, or mis-remembered his ambassador's report of Robert Kennedy's words,

Another kind of internal-external interaction occurs when an internal faction undertakes independently to influence another state's policy. In one variant of this, the purpose is to persuade the other state to do something that will strengthen the position of the faction in its own state. A well-known example is the attempt by German conspirators in 1938, including some high military figures, to persuade the British government to stand firm against Hitler. This, they argued, would strengthen their own position sufficiently to bring off a coup against Hitler or at least to frustrate his plans. The attempt failed basically because it did not mesh well with the image of the dominant British appeasers: the image of Hitler as a man who could be reasoned with and who had limited aims, and Chamberlain's desire to achieve a general settlement in Central Europe. More specifically Chamberlain did not wish to risk war to precipitate a revolt that might fail, and the conspirators' report that Hitler intended to attack Czechoslovakia by late September seemed only to increase the urgency of getting a negotiated settlement. A somewhat similar example, this time involving allies, occurred in 1911 during the second Moroccan crisis when Cambon, the French ambassador in London, urged the British government to bring pressure on the French government for a more conciliatory policy toward Germany; this would strengthen the French "peace faction." The attempt succeeded by producing a British statement and a French understanding that there were limits to British support. This example does support the prescription of the bureaucratic politics theory, but it is noteworthy that it required an appeal from a faction of the French government to get the British to act according to that prescription.

Sometimes minority factions in allied governments collaborate to undermine the strategy of their governments. Thus Vansittart and Churchill in 1938 privately encouraged hard-liners in the French cabinet. In turn (but whether as a result of the Britishers' urging is unclear) certain of the like-minded Frenchmen telephoned Beneš in Czechoslovakia urging him to resist the official Anglo–French "ultimatum," which insisted that he accede to Hitler's demands.[25] At the same time some members of the Agrarian party in Czechoslovakia, apparently including Hodza, the premier, were urging another faction of the French government to exert pressure on Beneš to accept the ultimatum.[26]

---

or Dobrynin could have mis-transmitted them. There has been no corroboration on the U.S. side that Robert Kennedy ever said anything like this to Dobrynin, much less that the president had any fear of a "military take-over."

[25] Keith Eubank, *Munich* (Norman: University of Oklahoma Press, 1963), p. 145.

[26] Christopher Throne, *The Approach to War, 1938–39* (New York: St. Martins Press, 1968), p. 75; Henri Nogueres, *Munich* (London: Weidenfeld & Nicholson, 1965), p. 151.

Sometimes two factions act independently toward the opponent, producing what appeares to be a calculated mixed strategy but really is not. Soviet strategy during the Berlin crisis of 1961–1962 appeared at times to be a deliberately mixed strategy, combining elements of the accommodative and coercive, but apparently was the result of two factions' following different tracks, or alternatively gaining the upper hand in the Presidium. Khrushchev, the soft-liner, constantly pushed for negotiations and entered into a private correspondence with Kennedy to that end. But Soviet hard-liners who opposed a negotiated settlement apparently were able to take decisions on their own or force them through over the chairman's opposition, e.g., to resume nuclear testing and strengthen the Soviet armed forces, which got in the way of the chairman's accommodative tactics.[27]

During the Iranian crisis of 1946 the conciliatory Iranian premier, Qavam, was often irritated by the insubordinate behavior of his U.N. ambassador, Hussein Ala, who constantly reiterated Iranian grievances against the Soviets in the Security Council. Sometimes this undermined Qavam's strategy by irritating the Soviets, but in a larger sense it contributed to the ultimate settlement by keeping the issue high on the U.N. agenda, thus keeping alive the "stick" of possible U.N. condemnation of Soviet behavior.

Examples of this kind shade over into instances where subordinates not in sympathy with official policy sabotage its implementation. In 1914, Paleologue, the French ambassador in St. Petersburg, ignored directives from his government to restrain Russia from taking precipitate action and instead urged mobilization, pledging unqualified French support. Roosevelt's licensing order of August 1, 1940, which permitted licensing of low-grade gasoline and crude oil exports to Japan, was turned into a complete embargo by hard-liners in the State Department who were in charge of implementing the program.[28]

Summarizing, we can distinguish at least five different ways in which internal bargaining may interact with the external bargaining process: (1) the internal pattern of influence and attitudes affects choices of bargaining strategy and tactics toward the other state; (2) external bargaining moves may either intendedly or unintendedly affect the configuration of influence in the opposite decision-making unit; (3) opposing factions within a state may carry out independent strategies that usually undercut each other, but may also be mutually supportive, in effect constituting a mixed strategy that is objectively more effective than either of the independent strategies alone might have been; (4) dissident individuals may sabotage official policies in implementation; and (5) po-

[27] Slusser, *The Berlin Crisis of 1961*, p. 169.
[28] Feis, *The Road to Pearl Harbor*, p. 247.

tential changes in the balance of influence at home may be used as warnings to inhibit the opponent's coercion.

What is one to make of all these examples of external-internal interaction in the light of the bureaucratic politics theory's proposition that other nations can be influenced only "when a clear signal is sent, when someone in the other nation already wants to take the desired action and the action increases that player's influence"? [29] Apparently the situation is somewhat more complicated, at least for crises. In crises the "desired action" that one presumably wants is a concession from the other side. The "someone" most likely to want to concede is the soft-liner; hence one wants to increase his influence. But how is that to be done? Logical reasoning does not provide an unambiguous answer. According to one line of reasoning the influence of the softs in the other state ought to be increased (and that of the hards decreased) by conciliatory gestures and concessions by one's own state; the softs' argument that a satisfactory negotiated settlement is possible would gain credibility. Conversely, a tough strategy by the self would strengthen the hards in the other, either by triggering emotions and status values or by giving credibility to their argument that only firmness can lead us to reason. Following another logic, the softs in the other state would gain power by a strong coercive policy that made clear the necessity to yield, and the hards would gain strength by our own accommodative moves, which show that we are weak and can be pushed farther.

The empirical evidence is highly mixed. The most meaningful thing that can be said about it is that the "logic" that prevails tends to reflect the structure of the crisis itself and the relative bargaining power between the states, and changing perceptions of structure and power relations during the crisis. The 1905 Morocco crisis was Chicken for both Germany and France in its early phase, but the dominant view in the French government was that it was Bully, with Germany as the bully and France cast in the chicken role. The initial German coercion strengthened the French soft faction and produced an accommodating response, because of the general belief that France was too weak to risk war. But then the French offers strengthened the German hard-liners by confirming their proposition that France could easily be coerced. Then the continued German toughness strengthened hard-line opinion in France by demonstrating that Germany was out for more than the redress of legitimate grievances. Meanwhile, significantly, Britain had ranged herself alongside France, which shifted France's preference structure to Prisoner's Dilemma, and further strengthened French hards. The new tough French position showed the Germans that France was

[29] Allison and Halperin, "Bureaucratic Politics," p. 60.

not to be bullied as easily as expected. The power relations were becoming clearer. The German softs then gained ascendance and tried to promote an alliance with France and Russia, which would have involved German capitulation on the Morocco issue. When this didn't work, Germany switched back to a tough policy, with hard-liners in charge. But when this strategy met rock-hard resistance from France, the external power situation was completely clear; then the German softs took over again since only their strategy seemed to make sense in a hopeless situation.

In 1914 Lord Grey's tardy declaration of British support for France produced an immediate increase in soft-line strength in Germany. The Kaiser pushed his Halt-in-Belgrade scheme (though its communication to Austria was sabotaged by subordinates) and Bethmann, previously hard-line, switched to soft-line in trying to restrain Austria. But these internal changes were merely ancillary to the fact that the German civilian leadership finally realized they had miscalculated English interests and intentions, and hence the structure of the game they were playing with England. It was Called Bluff, not Chicken.

The pattern of an accommodative move strengthening the opponent's soft-liners is found only twice in our cases and both are dubious instances. In 1941 an apparent U.S. conciliatory message may have strengthened slightly the weak "peace group" in Japan—at any rate, it brought a bid for negotiations from Japan. This is a dubious interpretation, however, since the hard-line group in control in Japan also wanted negotiations with the United States if there was any chance of success. Khrushchev, who was soft-line relative to certain others in the Kremlin, may have had this internal position strengthened by Eisenhower's agreement to a summit in 1959. The corollary—tough move strengthens opponent's hard-liners—appears somewhat more frequently. The more intransigent U.S. position in Berlin in 1960, followed by the U-2 incident and the aborted summit conference, apparently lowered Khrushchev's stock in the Kremlin and strengthened his hard-line opponents. In 1914 the Russian partial mobilization greatly strengthened the position of the military in Berlin; then when it became clear that Germany intended to attack France and Belgium as well as Russia, the evenly split British cabinet swung over to a hard-line majority. These 1914 examples again suggest a link between internal shifts and crisis structures. Germany and Russia were in Prisoner's Dilemma (simultaneous-move version) once mobilization started: one side's moves toward mobilization had to be countered, and this put the military in the center of the action in both countries. England was in Prisoner's Dilemma with respect to a German attack on France and Belgium—almost all cabinet members preferred to fight rather than see these countries overrun—and when the German intentions became clear the British soft-liners turned hard consistent with this basic preference. Bethmann's last-minute shift to soft after he discovered the British intentions reflected the fact that his preference ordering vis-à-vis a united Triple Entente was Chicken. Thus we can say tentatively that the pattern "hard move strengthens other's softs" is typical of asymmetrical crisis structures when the recipient of the move is the Chicken party. The reverse pattern of hard-strengthens-hard and soft-strengthens-soft is perhaps typical of Prisoner's Dilemma.

If these examples show anything, it is that the bureaucratic politics theorists have stated at best a half-truth in their dictum: "Ask who in another government wants to do what you want for his own reasons. If you locate him, strengthen him. If you do not, despair." [30] It is only a half-truth because the ability to influence another government in a crisis depends primarily on the balance of bargaining power, which in turn depends on the balance of interests and military forces and relative disutility for war between the two *governments*. If these things are estimated correctly, one can wield as much influence (or must submit to as much influence) as the state-to-state power relations and one's bargaining skill will permit. The power relations will indeed depend somewhat on who is in charge in each government. And the exercise of the influence may be accompanied by, or may operate through, a change in the internal balance of power in the other government. But the internal change will usually be incidental to a changed perception of general power relations between the governments. Even if no one in the opposite government *wants* to do what you want, you need not "despair," since people can be persuaded to change their minds. And if there *is* someone, "strengthening" him means persuading others to the same view, which may require the same strategy as if there were no one. And what that strategy may be depends greatly on the general context, the structure of power relations between the *states*. The element of half-truth is that it may often help to know something about the distribution of attitudes and influence in the other government in devising an optimum strategy, especially if there is a fairly wide spectrum of opinion in the other state. Then, if one faces a coercive opponent, but the opponent's majority coalition includes a few wavering members inclined to compromise, a compromise proposal that suits their views may cause their defection and the formation of a different majority coalition. Or if the opponent's strategy is accommodative, based on a tenuous soft-line coalition, one knows that care is required in implementing one's own coercive strategy to avoid the opposite kind of shift in the other state. It bears repeating, however, that governments generally do not

[30] Ibid., p. 72.

do well in analyzing each other's internal politics in crises, and indeed it is inherently difficult.[31]

An alternative and more theoretically satisfying way to link up the bureaucratic politics model with international bargaining is descriptive rather than prescriptive. If the analyst knows something about the distribution of internal attitudes and influence, he can explain and predict the outcome of bargaining episodes between states in greater detail and within narrower limits than would be possible with bargaining theory alone. In the usual bargaining model the outcome is indeterminate within a certain range; the internal factors the bureaucratic theory emphasizes provide empirical materials that reduce the range of indeterminacy.

Admittedly, there is usually a core of shared images and values on both sides, and if this core is large relative to what is not shared, an identification of individuals' values and images would not add anything useful to the analysis. In some situations, however, there is considerable divergence. Soft-line actors tend to estimate force ratios more favorably to the opponent than hard-liners, to place a greater disutility on the costs of war, and to estimate their own state's interests lower—especially since, for them, "resolve reputation" is not one of those interests whereas for the hard-liners it is extremely important. Thus, the "balance of forces and interests," i.e., the balance of bargaining power generally between the states, is affected by the relative influence of hard- and soft-line participants within the states. The analyst is able to estimate the balance of bargaining power and hence explain and predict the probable outcomes more accurately if he knows something about the hard–soft lineup in the decision-making units.

The idea can also be expressed in terms of a link between bureaucratic politics and the utility models which we presented in Chapter II. In such models each party has a "minimum position" that, in crises, is formally equivalent to the expected cost of war or bargaining breakdown. That is, the state prefers war or breakdown to accepting anything less than the minimum with respect to the object of bargaining. If the minimums overlap, there is a "bargaining range" wherein there is a possibility of compromise. The relevance of bureaucratic politics or internal coalition politics is that the internal balance of influence or compromise between hards and softs implicitly sets the minimum positions for the states and hence the limits of the bargaining range if there is one. If there is no internal compromise and the softs are in charge on both sides, the external bargaining range will be widest, and there will be the best chance of agreement; if the hards are ascendant, the range will be narrowest and may not exist at all.

[31] Halperin recognizes the difficulty; *Bureaucratic Politics,* p. 313.

In the Fashoda crisis, for example, the general balance of bargaining power in both its components—relative military strength and intensity of interest—overwhelmingly favored England. The interests were highly shared, though not completely so, in the British cabinet; less highly shared in France. Therefore it was determined from the start that England would "win" the crisis, though the exact details of the outcome were not. While the English posture was "hard" throughout the crisis, Salisbury was "soft-line" relative to his colleagues; his minimum would allow the French some kind of colonial reward in exchange for the withdrawal of Marchand. The "minimum" for a few extremists was a preventive attack on the French navy. The actual British minimum position—that Marchand must leave without counterconcessions—was a compromise in the cabinet, somewhat affected by external interaction with the French. In France, Delcassé was soft-line relative to nationalist sentiment in the Assembly and public opinion—his minimum was withdrawal of Marchand without compensation. But he was forced to take a tougher stand initially, demanding a French "presence" on the Upper Nile, for fear his government would fall if he did not. Nationalist and newspaper agitation in France in support of this French position activated and strengthened hard-liners in the British cabinet, producing the hardening of the British terms just mentioned. Eventually the obvious superiority of British naval power and resolve forced Delcassé back to his minimum where a settlement was reached. The effect of internal bargaining in this case was to eliminate the potential bargaining range that existed between Delcassé's and Salisbury's personal minimums and reduce it to a point. If these two men had been alone in the field, without any colleagues or political oppositions to deal with, Delcassé could have achieved somewhat more, but it still would have been a British victory given the distribution of inherent bargaining power between the two states.

Internal bargaining can also be linked to game models of the crisis structure. When there is internal disagreement, participants may hold different perceptions of the structure. The structure for the state is then a composite of the different preference structures of individuals and factions. As different participants rise or fall in the influence hierarchy within the state, the structure may change for the state. For instance, in the first Moroccan crisis, while Holstein was in control, the German structure was Prisoner's Dilemma—he preferred a breakdown of negotiations to accepting the French demands. When Holstein was out of action because of illness, or out of favor, the German structure was Chicken, according to the preferences of the Kaiser or Bulow. At the end Bulow, in one of his rare moments of decisiveness, overruled Holstein so the effective German structure was Chicken.

CONCLUSION

We are now able to see, in outline form, how some of the theories we have been using may be integrated via the notion of "structure." We have used the world "structure" in three senses: the distribution of military power in the international system, the distribution of influence in a national decision-making unit, and the preference structures of state-actors in a crisis. The first two usages are similar in that they both refer to the distribution of power among actors in a system. The third is different in that it is constructed out of values, not power, although it indirectly reflects relative bargaining power in a conflict. The first two stand, broadly speaking, in the position of independent variables in relation to the third as dependent variable; that is, the structure of the international system and of domestic decision-making units provide inputs from opposite directions into the estimates and valuations of outcomes that make up the crisis structures.

Crisis structures, as we have shown them in game models, reflect roughly the inherent *bargaining power* of the participants. That is, bargaining power is a function of the relative values the parties attach to the possible outcomes, especially the outcomes of losing, winning, and of bargaining breakdown and possible war. The first two reflect the parties' substantive *interests* at stake; the last is a function largely of the parties' comparative *military strength*.[32] Comparative interests and comparative military strength, as the parties perceive them, are the basic determinants of relative bargaining power and crisis outcomes.

International system structure, and the alignments that have formed within it, will strongly affect the military power potentially available to states in a crisis. This component is fairly objective, although of course there is an element of subjectivity in estimates of force ratios and the interdependence and loyalty of allies. The interest component is also a

[32] This, of course, is a considerable simplification. As we showed in Chapter III, it is more accurate to say that a state's resolve, and hence its inherent bargaining power, is a function of its "expected cost of war" and its substantive interests and not simply its "military strength" and its interests. The notion of "expected cost of war" subsumes not only a party's superiority or inferiority in military strength (which presumably determines whether it would win a war or not) but also the degree of value it places on what it would win or lose, as well as the disutility it attaches to war damage per se, and the probability of various degrees of damage. It is this package of values, modified perhaps by estimates of public morale in war, domestic political consequences of war, etc. that combine to produce the *P*-value in the crisis structure. In the modern age, the ambiguous relevance of overall *nuclear* force comparisons between the superpowers further qualifies the simple notion of "military force ratios" as a component in bargaining power. Despite all these qualifications the gross comparison of military strengths probably is the most important element in the package, and to simplify the analysis here we use the term "comparative military strength" or some synonym as shorthand for the whole package.

function, to a degree, of system structure and alignment patterns (as we showed in Chapter VI), but it is more strongly affected by the values of individuals involved in decision making, and therefore more subjective. International structure and actual and potential alignments, one might say, establish the outside limits of the potential range of comparative bargaining power between the states; internal factors determine what the relative bargaining power will actually be within these limits.

To clarify the notion of "outside limits", suppose states A and B, protagonists in a crisis, and themselves about equal in military power, are aligned with states C and D, respectively. One potential outside limit of the relative bargaining power between A and B is set by the condition: A has solid support from C while B has no support from D. Abstracting from internal factors, A then is dominant. The other potential outside limit is set by the reverse conditions of allied support, which make B dominant. The actual outside limits are of course set by the actual alignment conditions in a particular case. The notion of outside limits is an objective (though hypothetical) conception which expresses the potential range of bargaining power relations between the parties based on capabilities and alignments alone, abstracting from their perceptions of them and their valuations of the interests in dispute.

Within this range, the actual relative bargaining power of the principal adversaries is determined by subjective internal factors, chiefly decision makers' perceptions of allied support and their valuations of the interests in conflict, but including also estimates of the adversary's long-run aims, the value placed on settlement per se, and the comparative utility or disutility for the expected consequences of war, whatever the balance of military strength. Relative bargaining power will depend, of course, not just on how each decision unit values and perceives all these things but also, and probably more so, on how each perceives the other's values and perceptions.

The operative values and perceptions of the decision-making unit will depend on the balance of influence among its constituent members—i.e., its "structure" as defined in Chapter V. This structure is in part formally defined, in part a function of informal influence derived from various sources. If one or two persons are in complete control, the operational "interests" of the state will reflect their perspectives. For example, if they are hard-liners the interests directly in conflict will be valued highly, settlement for its own sake will have a low value, the adversary's aims will be considered potentially unlimited and illegitimate, the likelihood of support from the present ally will be estimated optimistically and highly valued. The state's bargaining power will then approach the high side of the outer limits. If soft-liners are in charge the state's bargaining power will approach the low side of the outer limits because of their opposite estimates and valuations. If those formally in charge are held within limits by colleagues of differing views or if these colleagues or advisers themselves participate in decision making, the state's interests, or alternatively its "crisis structure" as expressed in a game model, will reflect these internal limits or the nature of the collegial compromise.

What we have just been saying rather abstractly is illustrated by the Czech crisis of 1938. One hypothetical limit to the relative bargaining power of the parties consisted of France, Britain, and Russia, all firmly committed to support Czechoslovakia against all of Hitler's demands even at the cost of war and convinced that any German expansion would lead to further expansion and eventually a grave threat to their own security. At this limit the bargaining power of the allies would have been superior to Hitler's by virtue of superior military power as well as greater interests at stake. The opposite potential outer limit consisted of a Britain and France indifferent to the fate of Czechoslovakia, perceiving German superiority in the military balance and, beyond that, favoring German expansion into central and eastern Europe as a bulwark against the Red menace. It so happened that the distribution of values, perceptions and internal influence in the British decision-making group, and to a somewhat lesser extent the French, approached this lower limit, so Hitler's bargaining power was superior. If Churchill and like-minded persons had been in office in Britain, the power relations and the outcome of the crisis would have been different—if indeed there had been a crisis at all. A firm British and French stance also would have affected the internal balance of influence in Germany, strengthening the opposition to Hitler, thus further weakening his external bargaining power even if he had initiated a crisis.

The range of potential asymmetry in bargaining power and crisis "structures" is greater for multipolar crises than for bipolar ones in which the superpowers are involved. One reason for this is the typical cruciality of allied support in multipolarity combined with its frequent uncertainty. Objectively, the range runs from one protagonist getting full support from its allies and its adversary no support, to the opposite conditions. Subjectively, the actual bargaining power of the parties depends considerably on decision makers' *expectations* concerning the degree of allied support, both for their own state and for the opponent. Since allied support is often uncertain, there will be considerable room for disagreement among individual decision makers concerning whether it will be forthcoming. Hence the bargaining position taken by the state, and its bargaining power, will vary according to whose perceptions are dominant in decision making. The point is illustrated niccly by the sharp difference between Rouvier and Delcassé in 1905 concerning the likelihood and value of British support of France. When Rouvier forced the resignation of Delcassé, French bargaining power declined, partly because of Rouvier's skepticism about British loyalty, which the Germans also doubted. Later on, it gained strength when the reality of British support became clearer to Rouvier, and to the Germans as well.

Another feature of multipolarity that tends to increase potential variance in relative bargaining power is the ambiguity of interest which often characterizes a multipolar crisis. This ambiguity usually stems from uncertainty about "who is the real enemy" and may be reflected internally in divergent identifications of most dangerous foes and most desirable allies. Such "phobias" and "philias" with regard to other states in the system will increase the range of policy options put forward in the internal debate, beyond the usual "hard-soft" alternatives, or they will accentuate the latter. The bargaining power of the state will depend a good deal on whose alignment preferences and opponent-identifications prevail. Thus, if the decision makers in control see a third state which they consider more threatening in the long-run than the immediate crisis opponent, they will be less willing to risk war in the present crisis. Or they may wish to settle with the present opponent in order to pave the way for alliance with him, or to shift his antagonism toward the threatening third party. This will reduce the state's bargaining power in the immediate crisis.[33] In other words, interests in the "alliance game" may contradict and thus devalue interests in the "adversary game." But individuals may disagree about the extent of the contradiction or devaluation, as Holstein and the Kaiser disagreed in 1905 with respect to France.

Although uncertainty of alignment and ambiguity of interests are typical of multipolarity, these things are variables, not constants, in what we have called the "pattern of relations" in the system. The greater the uncertainty and ambiguity, the greater the potential for internal divisions; the state's bargaining position and bargaining power then more likely will depend on the accidents of internal politics, on *who* happens to hold office. In the less frequent cases when alignments are firm and interests are clear, as approximated in 1914 (except for Italy) one finds less internal division. In these conditions the state's bargaining behavior and bargaining power depend less on internal politics and more on the external pattern of relations itself. Thus, the weight of domestic causation in a multipolar system varies within limits set by the

---

[33] During the Fashoda crisis Clemenceau said: "The brutal fact is that France cannot think of throwing herself into a war for the possession of some African marshes, when the German is camped at Metz and Strasbourg." Quoted by Raymond Sontag, *European Diplomatic History, 1871–1932* (New York: Appleton-Century-Crofts, 1933), p. 64. Although the French were outmatched by England militarily, their resolve was further weakened by Delcassé's desire to nurture a possible future alliance with England.

degree of flexibility in external alignments. But since flexibility (and consequent uncertainty) is the norm, these limits are typically broad and the ratio of internal to external causation is usually high, higher than in a bipolar system.

In a bipolar crisis between the superpowers, or in which the superpowers play a leading role, the outer limits of variation in their relative bargaining power, as determined by capabilities and potential allied support, will be narrower than for states in a multipolar crisis. This follows from the rigidity of alignment in a bipolar system, and the superpowers' relative independence of allied support. The capabilities component of bargaining power is chiefly the capabilities of the superpowers themselves. However, with nuclear stalemate, the relevance of nuclear if not conventional capabilities to bargaining power is ambiguous; consequently relative bargaining power is determined primarily by the "balance of interests." Here again, of course, "interests" are subjective and will be determined for the state by attitudes and influence distribution within the decision-making unit. The range of potential variance in this component is also narrower than in multipolarity because of the clarity of interest that follows from the clear identity of the external threat. There is little tension between interests in the adversary game and interests in the alliance game and this is mirrored internally in a high degree of consensus about interests. There will of course be "hard-soft" differences among decision makers, but the soft side is limited by the absence of any motive to conciliate the adversary because a more serious threat is perceived elsewhere. Thus "hard" attitudes will tend to predominate. Soft positions will be procedural, and vague substantively (Berlin, 1961: "Let's at least negotiate and see what can be done"). Or they will center on reducing the risks of a hard strategy. (Cuba, 1962: Only one person, Stevenson, proposed a genuine compromise with the Soviet Union and he was ridiculed. Other "soft-liners" were concerned chiefly with minimizing the risks of escalation.) Thus, on the whole, the relative bargaining power of the superpowers in a bipolar crisis is less affected by internal politics, by the identity and relative influence of decision makers, than it is for states in a typical multipolar crisis.

Empirically, in none of the bipolar crises do we find anything like the range of internal variation that we find say, in 1905, between Holstein and the Kaiser, or between Rouvier and Delcassé, or between Izvolsky and the rest of the Russian government in 1908, or between Chamberlain and Churchill in 1938. In the crises of the post-1945 period for the United States there were few significant differences within the government about what the national interest was, or what it was worth (with the possible exception of Quemoy, 1958), although there were differences about tactics to be employed in the bargaining process. And there would have been little difference in the value placed on the interests involved, one supposes, whether a Republican or Democratic regime had been in office, again excepting Quemoy. Certainly this was true of the two phases of the 1958–1962 Berlin crisis when the two parties alternated in control. As the Quemoy case demonstrates, internal dissension tends to be greater in crises outside the central arena (Europe) where the opposite superpower is not the primary opponent.

For the lesser powers also in bipolarity there is little room for internal disagreement since the identity of the primary threat is as clear for them as it is for their protector, and there are no realignment possibilities to provide a focus for dissent. If there are incipient differences they are overwhelmed by the dependence on the superpower protector. Dissension within Britain during the Suez 1956 crisis was again, as in the Quemoy case, partly a function of the peripheral character of the crisis, with the Soviet Union not seriously involved. And the differences became irrelevant in the face of overwhelming U.S. (financial) power.

We may speculate that in the more pluralistic (if not "multipolar") world that has been developing since the early 1970s, there will be less internal consensus in major power crises. Straws in the wind are the divisions in the U.S. government and public over the Mayaguez incident, the Angolan civil war, and the American "tilt" toward Pakistan (China) in the Indo-Pakistan war of 1972. International pluralism produces ambiguity about a state's interests and a consequent plurality of domestic opinions as to what those interests are. Between the U.S. and Soviet Union, still the principal axis of rivalry, détente has already shifted the theme of U.S. domestic debate from how to compete with and deter a known opponent to how to compete and cooperate with him at the same time, or even whether he ought still to be regarded as an opponent at all. Sinophobe and Sinophil attitudes are less apparent but are implicit in the debate over détente. Such divisions dimly appear to be developing in China and the Soviet Union as well. In future big power crises, the bargaining power and bargaining strategies of the participants will depend more than in the past on who is in charge and on the values placed by incumbent decision makers on the going relationships with the other two members of the triangle. With changing regimes these valuations might well shift. Such internal changeability, and the inherent ambiguity of interests in a system that is at least moving toward multipolarity, augurs unpredictability. Unpredictability could, in turn, induce even greater all-around prudence than we have seen in nuclear bipolarity— or, we must add, a greater potential for dangerous miscalculation.

CASE SUMMARIES

Here we summarize briefly 12 of our case studies. To conserve space, we omit four cases that either did not contribute a great deal to our analysis or are described fully enough in the text (the Ruhr, 1923; Suez, 1956; Lebanon, 1958; Middle East, 1973). Most of the summaries are organized according to the phase model of crises presented in Chapter I. The author of each takes full responsibility for its contents. Where co-authors are named, the first is the person who wrote the first draft of the summary; the second is the writer of the much longer original case study. The short bibliographies list only the most useful of the sources consulted.

FASHODA, 1898, by Paul Diesing and Kenneth Fuchs

PRECIPITANT

The long-standing Anglo–French rivalry for control of Egypt and the Suez Canal seemed to have ended with the British in sole command in 1892. The French colonial office, however, satisfied itself that if France dominated the Upper Nile at Fashoda she could, by threatening to build dams in the area, regulate the flow of the Nile and hence hold hostage the Egyptian agricultural economy. Such a position would assure a permanent French voice in the determination of Egyptian affairs. Accordingly in 1893, 1894, and 1895 Delcassé, the colonial minister, planned expeditions into the Upper Nile valley, which was then under Arab rule from Khartoum. These schemes were disapproved by the foreign ministry, which was aware of British warnings that French claims to any part of the Nile valley would not be tolerated. In 1895 a new foreign minister approved a small non-political exploratory expedition that the colonial office quietly transformed into an expedition aimed at occupation.

CHALLENGE (SEPTEMBER 1898)

Salisbury, the British foreign minister, knew of the French expedition and instructed the British commander at Khartoum, General Kitchener, to seek it out. In early September Kitchener, with some 20,000 troops, had defeated the Arab army and taken over the Sudan. When word reached London on September 9 that the expedition had been located, Salisbury notified the French of the discovery, and for good measure added that the Sudan belonged to the British by right of conquest and was not negotiable.

CONFRONTATION

The British note arrived at an inopportune moment for the new French foreign minister, Delcassé. Revelation of the army's complicity in the Dreyfus affair had come in August, and Delcassé had been preoccupied since then with the resulting political crisis. The army was demoralized; investigations and accusations were rife; the cabinet was expected to fall at any time. When the British note reminded him of the half-forgotten Nile expedition, Delcassé hoped to extract some small gain from it to bolster the cabinet; but, seeing no immediate opportunity, he stalled, claiming that he needed more information on the whereabouts of the expedition. During September Delcassé employed various delaying techniques such as requesting British assistance in communicating with the expedition. The British position, however, was gradually becoming firmer and as it did, Kitchener's pressure on the French expeditionary group grew more intense. Delcassé also asserted that his preference for an Anglo–French alliance was being damaged by British unreasonableness, cautioned that French public opinion would not permit capitulation, and warned against a British ultimatum.

RESOLUTION

On October 5 Delcassé proposed discussing the distance the expedition should withdraw, and suggested the west bank of the Bahr el Ghazal branch of the Nile. A few days later a Paris newspaper speculated that the real French aim was a commercial outlet on some branch of the Nile. On October 21 Delcassé asserted that he could not withdraw the expedition without some assurance of negotiations about a possible commercial outlet on the Nile.

Meanwhile the British had mobilized their fleet. On October 27 the British cabinet discussed whether to declare war or grant a commercial outlet. A compromise was struck: they would demand unconditional withdrawal. Accordingly Salisbury informed the French envoy that the expedition's presence at Fashoda was "an obstacle to negotiations." Delcassé's response was a suggestion for a joint commission on boundaries, but, on November 2, under the guise of protecting the health of its members, he ordered the withdrawal of the expedition.

EXPLANATION OF THE OUTCOME

The basic determinant of the outcome was the preponderant military capability of the British. Their fleet was far superior to that of the

French, even in the Mediterranean. In addition the Russians had indicated to the French that the Russian navy would be unable to support France in a war against Britain. Consequently when bargaining got down to basics, the French had to back down in order to avert a losing war. Salisbury, however, avoided coercive diplomacy as long as he could because he had the very important goal of preserving good relations with France, and, beyond that, of keeping alive the possibility of a future alliance. Coercive measures—harsh language, threats, ultimatums, mobilization, war—would make a permanent enemy of France, and this would be disastrous for Britain in the multipolar world of 1900. Salisbury, therefore, avoided even a request for French withdrawal, countenanced territorial concessions, and did his best afterward to soften the effect of withdrawal on France. For instance, he renamed Fashoda "Kodok" to hasten the fading from memory of the French defeat. Firmness was forced on Salisbury by the cabinet hard-liners who had lost patience with him.

From the French perspective the expedition had always been controversial and was kept semisecret for that reason. The British reconquest of the Sudan in 1898 changed the expedition from a civilizing mission against the fringes of a barbarian Dervish territory into an intrusion into the British empire. With the explosion of the Dreyfus affair in late August 1898, the expedition became an annoying complication for certain politicians—e.g., Delcassé—and a rallying cause for militarist and colonialist extremists. Premature French capitulation would have given the militarists a real issue, so Delcassé, like Salisbury, avoided getting down to basics as long as he could.

SELECTED BIBLIOGRAPHY

Andrew, Christopher, *Theophile Delcassé and the Making of the Entente Cordiale: A Reappraisal of French Foreign Policy 1898–1905* (London: Macmillan, 1968).

Brown, Roger G., *Fashoda Reconsidered: The Impact of Domestic Politics on French Policy in Africa 1893–1898* (Baltimore: Johns Hopkins University Press, 1970). Best single account.

Giffen, Morrison B., *Fashoda: The Incident and its Diplomatic Setting* (Chicago: University of Chicago Press, 1930).

Grenville, J.A.S., *Lord Salisbury and Foreign Policy: The Close of the Nineteenth Century* (London: University of London, 1964).

Langer, William L., *The Diplomacy of Imperialism 1890–1902*, 2d ed. (New York: Knopf, 1968).

Sanderson, G. N. *England, Europe and the Upper Nile, 1882–1899: A Study in the Partition of Africa* (Edinburgh: University Press, 1965).

MOROCCO, 1905–1906, by Glenn H. Snyder

PRECIPITANT

French influence in Morocco increased steadily during the early 1900s, clearly aimed at establishing a protectorate or colony. After first buying off Italy and Spain, France obtained Great Britain's implicit consent in the Entente Cordiale agreements of April 1904, giving England a free hand in Egypt in exchange. The parties pledged mutual diplomatic support in executing the agreement. Germany was not consulted and regarded this as an affront; moreover, she perceived the entente as an incipient alliance against herself. However, Germany took no action against France during 1904 because of divisions in the government. Holstein, in the foreign ministry, favored a strategy of coercion. War over Morocco should be threatened unless German interests were recognized; England would provide only diplomatic support; France would have to give way because of her military weakness and that of her Russian ally; the entente would then collapse because of French disillusionment, and France thereafter would be more accommodating toward Germany. The Kaiser favored a conciliatory strategy, consistent with his favorite project of a "continental league" of Germany, Russia, and France aligned against England. First, an alliance should be made with Russia, then France induced to join; making trouble in Morocco would frustrate this plan. Bulow, the German chancellor, developed an ingenious middle course: satisfaction should be demanded in Morocco but a German–Russian alliance should also be negotiated; when the proper moment came to invite France to adhere, the Morocco demands could be dropped. The Kaiser tried his strategy first, proposing an alliance to Russia in the fall of 1904. The attempt failed but the Kaiser's hopes remained high. His opposition to the alienation of France prevented adoption of the Holstein strategy until early 1905.

The specific incident that precipitated the German challenge was the despatch of a special French mission to Fez, the Moroccan capital, in January 1905, to persuade the Sultan to accept far-reaching "reforms" that would have amounted to a French protectorate. The head of the mission told the Sultan the program was supported by all the interested European powers. This mission, and particularly this statement, infuriated the German government, since they regarded themselves as an "interested power."

CHALLENGE

The German challenge was presented by a reluctant Kaiser, whom Bulow persuaded to stop off at Tangier during one of his Mediterranean cruises and thus to dramatize the German displeasure. He made a splendid entry into the town on March 31 and gave a speech in which he supported the Sultan's independence and warned the French to respect it. His words exploded over the headlines of European newspapers, and the crisis was on.

CONFRONTATION

Although the Germans had, for the moment at least, inaugurated a coercive strategy, they had not formulated any specific demand. After three days of intense discussion, they demanded a conference of the signatories of the Treaty of Madrid of 1880, which had guaranteed the status quo in Morocco. The conference demand, they felt, was unassailable legally, in contrast to the self-interested proceedings between Britain and France the previous year. They were sure of commanding a majority at the conference. In particular, if Britain failed to support the French ambitions, the entente would collapse. The German aims then were two: to humiliate France by dragging it before the court of "Europe," which would deny the French the sole right to colonize Morocco, and to break up the Anglo–French entente. However, Germany had no intention of going to war if these aims were not achieved, although she made vague threats of war during the crisis.

Phase 1:

The French government was also divided, hence its response to the German challenge was contradictory. Delcassé, the foreign minister, rejected the conference idea and opposed concessions. He believed the Germans were bluffing. Rouvier, the premier, while not agreeing to the conference, offered Germany a general settlement similar to the Anglo–French entente, including a strip of land and a port on the Atlantic coast of Morocco. He believed that Germany would attack France unless given "satisfaction." The Germans, having adopted a coercive strategy with grander aims, turned aside Rouvier's offers and instead demanded the removal of Delcassé, whom they perceived as the chief obstacle to these aims. Rouvier decided to comply and was able to do so because of Delcassé's political weakness in the Assembly and cabinet. Delcassé tried to save himself by disclosing what he mistakenly thought was an English offer of alliance, which would enable France to face down Germany, but to no avail, since Rouvier and others saw in this "offer" an attempt by Perfidious Albion to incite war between France and Germany. Rouvier himself took over the foreign affairs portfolio when Delcassé resigned on June 5.

Phase 2:

Now the French would accept the conference, the Germans thought. Now the Germans would accept a quiet bilateral settlement, thought Rouvier. Both sides' expectations were confounded. Disappointed and angered by the continued German bluster and insistence on a conference, and fortified by an anti-German shift in French public opinion and a new English display of support (which now began to appear in a different light), Rouvier dropped his attempts at accommodation and moved close to the firm line of Delcassé. France would go to the conference only if it were first assured that matters it considered already settled by the Anglo–French accord were excluded. France was playing a "dangerous game," warned Bulow. However, when he learned of the British support of France, he signed an agreement recognizing France's "special interest" in Morocco, and promising to make no demands at the conference contrary to previous "treaties or arrangements." France then agreed to the conference.

Phase 3:

Germany had won the first round; the second round was a draw. But now the Germans changed their strategy, realizing that with England standing solidly behind France, Holstein's coercive strategy was not likely to produce results. They shifted to the Kaiser's accommodative strategy: letting France have its way in Morocco in return for joining a "continental league" with Germany and Russia. The first move was to negotiate a treaty of alliance with Russia, which provided for the later adhesion of France. The Kaiser himself, meeting alone with the Czar on a yacht in the Baltic, accomplished this remarkable feat. France, queried by Russia, refused even to discuss adhesion to the German–Russian treaty; the embarrassed Czar was then persuaded by his advisers to renounce it. With the accommodative option thus frustrated, the Germans returned to Holstein's coercive strategy.

The new Liberal government that took office in Britain in December 1905 gave somewhat stronger support to France than had the Conservatives because they were more sensitive to the German menace and hence placed a greater value on the entente. Lord Grey, the new foreign minister, informed Germany that in case of war between Germany and France it was unlikely Britain could remain neutral. Grey was less explicit in speaking to the French, citing the need for cabinet approval for any statement that could be interpreted as an alliance commitment. However, Grey's approval of staff talks between the French and British armies constituted a tacit commitment.

RESOLUTION

The conference opened at Algeciras, Spain on January 16, 1906, Delegations were sent from eight countries—France, Germany, Great Britain, Austria, Italy, Spain, Russia, and the United States. The main issue was the allocation of command over the Moroccan police in the major port towns. A secondary issue was the capitalization and control of a state bank. The initial French proposal called for a sharing of the police powers between France and Spain only, Franco–Spanish dominance in the bank, and commercial equality for all countries. Germany countered with a demand for an equal role in both the police and the bank or, alternatively, suggested that some smaller country or countries, not involved in the conflict, should assume command of the police. The Germans were astonished when all the other delegates except the Austrians supported the French plan. Yet they stood firm, hoping by maneuver and argument to split the opposition, and threatening to break up the conference if they were excluded from the police power. The turning point came when Germany allowed Austria to present a "compromise" that really amounted to German capitulation with a face-saver: France and Spain would control the police in all ports except Casablanca, where a Swiss or Dutch officer would be in charge. The latter also would have the power of inspection over all the police forces and would report to the European diplomatic corps in Tangier. But France would not even accept this, believing that Germany eventually would have to yield entirely. The British delegate forced a vote on the Austrian plan August 2; all except Germany and Austria voted against it. The full extent of the German diplomatic weakness now stood revealed, and Bulow, overruling Holstein, chose to capitulate rather than break off the conference. The conference agreed on the original French proposal, with the German face-saver reduced to near-invisibility: there would be a neutral police supervisor, but he would have no command powers and would report to the Sultan, not to the diplomatic corps.

SELECTED BIBLIOGRAPHY

Anderson, Eugene N., *The First Moroccan Crisis, 1904–1906* (Hamden, Conn.: Archon Books, 1966).

Andrew, Christopher, *Theophile Delcassé and the Making of the Entente Cordiale* (London: Macmillan & Co., Ltd., 1968).

Gooch, G. P., *Before the War: Studies in Diplomacy* (London: Longmans, Green, 1938).

Hale, Oron J., *Germany and the Diplomatic Revolution* (Philadelphia: The University of Pennsylvania Press, 1931).

Leaman, Bertha R., "The Influence of Domestic Policy on Foreign Affairs in France, 1898–1905," *Journal of Modern History,* Vol. 14 (1942), pp. 449–479.

Monger, George W., *The End of Isolation* (London: Thomas Nelson & Sons, Ltd., 1962).

Rich, Norman R., *Friedrich von Holstein,* Vol. II (Cambridge: At the University Press, 1965).

Sontag, Raymond J., "German Foreign Policy, 1904–1906," *American Historical Review* (January 1920).

Williamson, Samuel R. Jr., *The Politics of Grand Strategy* (Cambridge, Mass.: Harvard University Press, 1969).

BOSNIA, 1908–1909, by Glenn H. Snyder

PRECIPITANT

The crisis was precipitated in general by the Austrian desire to annex the Turkish province of Bosnia–Herzegovina and the Russian desire to secure free passage for Russian warships through the Straits of the Bosporus and the Dardanelles. Izvolsky, the Russian foreign minister, and Aehrenthal, the Austrian foreign minister, reached an agreement on September 16, 1908, in which they pledged mutual support for these objectives. However, the two men may have misunderstood each other concerning the procedure to be followed. According to his own later account, Izvolsky thought the plan was, first, to arrange a conference of all the signatories of the Treaty of Berlin (1878), at which other major powers would be persuaded to acquiesce in the changes; then they would be carried out. Aehrenthal claimed he told Izvolsky the annexation would take place sometime in October, after which a conference would be held to ratify that act and also to approve the change in the Straits convention, with Austria and Russia giving each other mutual support at the conference. Both men apparently thought that approval of the other powers would easily be obtained. Austria was already occupying and administering Bosnia by authority of the Treaty of Berlin, hence annexation would merely formalize an existing situation. Russia had already obtained vague assurances from Great Britain, the most interested power, that she would not oppose the Russian aim at the Straits.

After his meeting with Aehrenthal, Izvolsky set off on a leisurely tour of other European capitals to line up support for a conference. However, when he arrived in Paris on October 3, he learned from the newspapers that the annexation of Bosnia was imminent, and a letter from Aehrenthal the next day confirmed that it would take place October 7. This Austrian act was the "specific precipitant" of the crisis that followed.

If Izvolsky was surprised by the timing of the Austrian move, he received a severe jolt a few days later from his own government, a telegram stating that Russia could never consent to the Austrian move, and expressing the prime minister's disapproval of Izvolsky's own apparent complicity. Izvolsky then went to London, where he learned from Lord Grey that the British government, which was sympathetic to the new republican regime in Turkey, could not just now approve any change in the status of the Straits. Izvolsky's plans were thus thrice confounded —by Aehrenthal, by Grey, and by his own government. Thereafter he bitterly denounced the annexation and maintained he had never assented to it.

CHALLENGE

The challenge was mounted by Russia, Serbia, England, and Turkey. Serbia mobilized, protested to the powers, and demanded territorial compensation. Russia and England supported the Serbian demands and proposed a conference—not to accomplish what Izvolsky had planned but to get compensation for Serbia and Turkey. The Turks joined the demand for a conference and boycotted trade with Austria.

Aehrenthal rejected the conference idea, declaring he would only negotiate bilaterally and separately with Turkey and Serbia. He rejected the Serbs' demand for compensation and threatened to publish correspondence between Izvolsky and himself that would have revealed the former's complicity in the annexation. The Austrian army mobilized. Germany fully supported the Austrian position.

CONFRONTATION

Austria held the upper hand from the start because of Russia's military weakness, Britain's unwillingness to go beyond "diplomatic" support for Serbia and Russia, France's failure to support her ally, and the unqualified backing of Germany for the Austrian policy. The Austrian military wished to use the crisis as a pretext for war on Serbia to put a stop to Serbian intrigues among the Slavic population of the Empire. Aehrenthal at first seems to have agreed with this objective but soon decided to be satisfied with the diplomatic humiliation of Serbia. The emperor, Franz Josef, was a restraining force.

The Russians seem to have taken their stand in a fit of indignation, out of sympathy for their South Slav brethren. Knowing they could not fight, they nevertheless encouraged the Serbs in a reckless course. They did have some leverage in their capacity to withhold recognition of the annexation, as did Britain. The British motive in supporting Russia and

Serbia was to preserve the recently negotiated entente with Russia; in supporting Turkey they were motivated by ideological sympathy. Germany supported Austria because Austria was her only reliable ally; there was some fear in Germany that Austria might defect to France and Russia if not supported.

Aehrenthal moved toward Turkey first, believing that if Turkey, the party directly wronged, were to recognize the annexation, the others could hardly withhold their assent. An agreement with Turkey was soon reached, the Turks receiving financial compensation. Bulgaria, which had declared its independence from Turkey simultaneous with the Austrian move in Bosnia, also paid an indemnity to Turkey.

But the stubborn Serbs continued to demand territorial compensation and the Russians and British to refuse recognition of the annexation until Serbia received some satisfaction. Under pressure from Russia, the Serbs did drop their demand for territorial compensation and placed themselves "in the hands of the powers," hoping to get at least some kind of economic payoff. By this time, however, it was not enough for Austria that the Serbs reduce their demands. Austria began making demands on *them*: that they cancel their mobilization, reduce their army, recognize the annexation, and accept in writing a position of servile submission. Aehrenthal told Russia Serbia had until the end of March to accept these demands—then the Austrian army would invade.

At this point Germany stepped in, asking Russia whether it would accept the annexation via an exchange of notes. Russia replied evasively. Germany then, on March 22, presented Russia with a virtual ultimatum: ". . . we expect an answer—yes or no; we must regard an evasive, conditional or unclear answer as a refusal. We should then draw back and let things take their course." Izvolsky then surrendered and agreed to the exchange of notes, not without some feeling of relief, for the German démarche, as an overpowering *force majeure,* took Russia "off the hook" of its embarrassing commitment to Serbia. This was the turning point of the crisis, at which the weaker party, having realized its weakness, reversed its strategy from coercion to accommodation. Note that an especially dramatic act of coercion was required to force the turn-around.

RESOLUTION

But the crisis was not yet over. England was still committed to the diplomatic support of Serbia. When Germany asked England to recognize the annexation, Grey stuck to his guns—not until Serbia was satisfied. However, the Russian backdown made it easier for Grey to exert pressure on the Serbs, and he guessed correctly that with Russia out of the way an Austrian attack might be imminent. There followed a period of hard bargaining between Grey and Aehrenthal about the terms of a note that Serbia might send to Austria as a proposed settlement— Aehrenthal using to good effect his uncertain control over his own military. The result was a note slightly less submissive in tone than Aehrenthal had earlier demanded, but still specifying a reduction in the Serbian army and recognition of the annexation. Overall it amounted to a Serbian capitulation. Serbia accepted these terms on March 30. Acceptance came in the nick of time, for the Austrian cabinet had decided the previous day to attack. Aehrenthal could now tell his military hawks that Serbia had accepted Austria's terms, so there was no longer any reason for war. The crisis was over. It was a clear Austro–German diplomatic victory, but a Pyrrhic one in the long run, since it left in Russia a bitterness and a determination to strengthen herself and never again to back down before Austro–German threats, and conversely in Germany and Austria a feeling that the entente powers could easily be faced down—an explosive combination of attitudes that contributed much to the disaster of 1914.

SELECTED BIBLIOGRAPHY

Carroll, Malcolm E., *Germany and the Great Powers, 1866–1914* (New York: Prentice–Hall, 1938).

Grey, Edward, *Twenty-Five Years: 1892–1916* (New York: Stokes, 1925).

Langer, William L., *Explorations in Crisis* (Cambridge: The Belknap Press of the Harvard University Press, 1969), Chs. 2, 3.

Pribram, Alfred F., *Austria–Hungary and Great Britain, 1908–1914.* Translation by Ian F. D. Morrow (Westport, Conn.: The Greenwood Press, 1971).

Schmitt, Bernadotte, *The Annexation of Bosnia* (Cambridge, England: The University Press, 1937).

AGADIR, 1911, by Glenn H. Snyder and Charles Lockhart

PRECIPITANT

The Act of Algeciras of 1906, while it settled the first Moroccan crisis, did not settle the underlying conflict between France and Germany over the issue. France was determined eventually to bring Morocco fully into her empire; Germany was determined to frustrate this or at least to obtain substantial compensation. By 1911, the perennial disorder in Morocco had spread to the interior, specifically to Fez, the capital, where the French police power did not legally reach. In April, France decided to send an expedition to Fez, ostensibly to protect European lives and property. This was the specific precipitant of the crisis, for it appeared as an overt move to take control of the capital and establish a protectorate. However, a crisis did not follow immediately; the Germans merely indicated they would require compensation if France did take full control of the country.

The first serious discussions took place between Jules Cambon, the French ambassador in Berlin, and Kiderlen, the German foreign minister, on June 20 and 21. It was an Alphonse-and-Gaston conversation, each man refusing to advance a specific proposal for German compensation. Cambon warned that it could not come out of Morocco itself, it must be "elsewhere." Kiderlen did not commit himself to this but said in parting, "Bring us back something from Paris." Cambon felt justified in assuming that the principle of no compensation in Morocco had been established. Soon after this conversation the French government fell, and in the several weeks before a new one was formed, Cambon could get no decision on what to "bring back from Paris."

CHALLENGE

As at Tangier in 1905, the German challenge took the form of a coercive demonstration with no specific demands attached. The gunboat *Panther* dropped anchor in the harbor of Agadir ostensibly to "protect German citizens" although there were no German citizens there. Kiderlen's purpose was to extract more concessions from France than she was likely to give without pressure. He also believed that the conciliatory French premier, Caillaux, would be better able to overcome his right-wing opposition if he could point to the German pressure as giving him "no alternative" but to make substantial concessions.

CONFRONTATION

Phase 1: France vs. Germany:

The "*Panther's* spring" turned the situation into a crisis not only because of its inherent belligerency but also because it immediately made the French suspect the Germans were going to demand part of Morocco after all, something over which the French would rather fight than yield. (Agadir had been prominent in speculation about what Germany might want in Morocco since there were German economic interests nearby and it was far enough south not to worry the British.)

As usual, the French government was divided. The foreign minister, de Selves, wanted to take a tough line: offer no compensation and send both French and British warships to Agadir and Mogador as a counter-demonstration. Caillaux, the premier, wished to accommodate, fortified by a military judgment that France did not have more than a 70%

chance of victory in case of war with Germany. He and the British vetoed Selves's counterdemonstration idea as too provocative.

The initial British reaction was less supportive of France than in the first Moroccan crisis. This time, the Radicals in the cabinet were more involved, and they limited Grey to the demand that England must be in on the negotiations if there was to be any partition of Morocco. Grey made this statement to both the French ambassador, Paul Cambon, and Metternich, the German ambassador, on July 4.

Russia gave little or no support to France. It was resentful over the lack of French support during the Bosnia crisis and had recently established quite friendly relations with Germany. Austria, likewise, stood aloof on the ground that the Austro–German alliance did not cover Morocco.

The next Cambon–Kiderlen conversation, July 9, was acrimonious because of the intervening German coercion. Kiderlen did agree not to ask for anything in Morocco; Cambon offered some minor, non-territorial forms of compensation, which Kiderlen rejected. The Congo was mentioned vaguely, but the record does not show who mentioned it first. (In fact, Kiderlen had already decided to ask for the Congo, and nothing in Morocco, but wanted to keep open the possibility that he might revert to Morocco if France proved too intransigent about the Congo.)

Specific proposals finally were put on the table in a July 15 meeting. Cambon asked point-blank: What do you want? Kiderlen answered: All of the French Congo. To ease French sensibilities, Germany would give the Northern Cameroun and Togoland in exchange. Cambon was astounded, gave a flat rejection, and ended the conversation. The French government perceived the exorbitant German demands as deliberately intended to elicit a French rejection, which would then justify a German shift to what they really wanted—a slice of Morocco.

At his next meeting with Cambon on July 20, Kiderlen stepped up the pressure by saying that Germany was serious about wanting the whole Congo and would go to "extreme lengths" to get it. Cambon replied that France would go just as far.

Phase 2: The British intervention.

At this point of high tension Great Britain stepped in and almost provoked war, although, curiously enough, war between Germany and England rather than Germany and France. Since his last communication with the German ambassador on July 4, Grey had waited impatiently for a German reply but received none. Either Kiderlen did not interpret Grey's earlier statements as a request for clarification of German intensions (as Grey intended them), or, more likely, he wished to talk as little as possible to the British in order to keep them uninvolved. The

British, however, perceived the prolonged German silence as menacing. They feared also that Germany might perceive further British silence as indicating indifference. They had heard from the French of the German demand for the entire Congo and the French interpretation of this as a sham demand designed to force the issue back to Morocco, where British interests were involved.

Out of these considerations, Grey approved in advance a speech by Lloyd George, chancellor of the Exchequer, which invoked the inflammatory symbol "national honor" and declared that war was preferable to Britain's being treated "as if she were of no account in the Cabinet of Nations." Germany reacted angrily to the speech, though more to the British press interpretations of it as a warning to Germany than to the speech itself. The German ambassador confronted Grey: Was the press interpretation correct? If so, Germany's "dignity" required an official retraction. Grey replied that English "dignity" forbade such a thing. When Grey emerged from the interview, he immediately warned the Admirality to expect a German attack at any moment. Tempers cooled in a few days however, and dignity was preserved by a diplomatic exchange: Kiderlen allowed Asquith, the prime minister, to say in the House of Commons that Germany had promised to make no demand for a share in Morocco; in return, Asquith said Lloyd George's words did not reflect "preeminent" government policy. Asquith also said, however, that Britain would support whatever position France chose to take. The net result of the incident was distinctly to Germany's disadvantage, for Kiderlen lost leverage over the French, and the British ranged themselves more solidly alongside France.

RESOLUTION

The Lloyd George episode was the turning point of the crisis because it confounded Kiderlen's plan of keeping England uninvolved and shifted the balance of resolve against Germany. The German government, at the Kaiser's insistence, made a firm decision not to go to war, no matter how little France offered, though of course this decision was kept secret. Kiderlen became distinctly more accommodative. So did France, since the conciliatory Caillaux covertly took charge of French policy, negotiating secretly through intermediaries, and also because Grey cautioned the French not to read too much into Asquith's words of support. The new spirit of accommodation surfaced on August 1 when Kiderlen told the French ambassador he would be satisfied with part of the Congo and Cambon offered part of it, plus some islands. It was not enough, however; Kiderlen wanted access to the Atlantic Coast and the Congo River. The negotiations became deadlocked on this point, each party being constrained from yielding further by nationalist sentiment at home.

Threats were uttered by both sides and rumors of an imminent German landing at Agadir sharply increased tension once more. An agreement was finally reached in hard bargaining during October. France got her Moroccan protectorate. Germany got about a fifth of the French Congo, with access to the sea, and gave a very small piece of her own African possessions in exchange. The outcome was a compromise, somewhat shaded in France's favor, in the sense that Germany quite probably would have received more had it not been for her heavy-handed tactics and obtuse handling of England. The Morocco issue was now settled for good but French–German relations did not improve as a result. Nationalists in both countries charged their governments with a sell-out; bitterness was especially strong in France because of the bullying German tactics. The Franco–British entente emerged stronger than ever.

SELECTED BIBLIOGRAPHY

Barlow, Ima C., *The Agadir Crisis* (Chapel Hill: North Carolina University Press, 1940).

Caillaux, J., *D'Agadir a la grande penitence* (Paris: Flammarion, 1933).

Gooch, G. P., *Before the War,* Vol. 2 (London: Longmans, 1938).

Grey, Edward, *Twenty-Five Years: 1892–1916,* Vol. 1 (New York: Stokes, 1925).

Jaeckh, Ernst, ed., *Kiderlen–Waechter,* Vol. 2 (Stuttgart: Deutsche Verlag, 1924).

Lepsius, J., A. M. Bartholdy, and F. Thimme, eds., *Die Grosse Politik der Europaeischen Kabinette: 1871–1914,* Vol. 29 (Berlin: Deutsche Verlagsgesellschaft, 1925).

Lowe, C. J., and M. L. Dockrille, *The Mirage of Power,* Vol. 1 (Boston: Routledge, 1972).

Williamson, Samuel R., Jr., *The Politics of Grand Strategy* (Cambridge, Mass.: Harvard University Press, 1969).

1914, by Glenn H. Snyder and Dennis Yena

PRECIPITANT

The *general* precipitant of this crisis was revolutionary activity among the Slavs in the Austro–Hungarian empire, largely directed and organized by the "Black Hand" society in Serbia, which was led by officers of the Serbian army. As we explained in Chapter I, the term "general precipitant" does not pretend to encompass less proximate "causes" of a crisis, which in this case would have to include such things as earlier promises of Russian support to Serbia, the general tightening of bonds within the two Great Power alliances, the resolve among all the continental powers not to back down again as a legacy of crises over the previous decade, the general feeling that war was "inevitable," and many other factors. The Serbian intrigues against Austria and Austria's vulnerability to them were simply the proximate cause that fused all these broader elements into a critical mass. The specific precipitant was the assassination of the Austrian Archduke Ferdinand at Sarajevo, Bosnia, on June 28. It was not so much a "cause" as a legitimizing event that triggered an Austrian decision to do what it felt it had to do sooner or later—exterminate the Serbian "revolutionary nest."

CHALLENGE

As in many of our cases, the challenge did not immediately follow the precipitant. Although Berchtold, the Austrian foreign minister, said on June 29 that he intended to make this the occasion for "settling accounts" with Serbia, he did not actually fling the gauntlet until almost a month had passed. Time was needed for an official enquiry that would further legitimize the planned action; also Germany had to be consulted; the Austrian army would not be ready for several weeks anyway. German intentions became clear on July 5 with the famous "blank check": Austria could do what she liked with Serbia; Germany would hold Russia at bay or fight if she intervened. The Germans urged their ally to attack as soon as possible to present the Triple Entente with a fait accompli. The Kaiser did not think Russia would intervene in the face of German power and because of the nature of the precipitant: the Czar's sympathies with the aristocratic brotherhood would overcome Russian feelings for their South Slav brethren. France would restrain Russia, and England would not fight, since present German–English relations were good. The Austro–Serbian war could be "localized."

The Austrians procrastinated, chiefly because their army was not yet ready to move. Finally, they presented an ultimatum at Belgrade on July 23, to be answered in 48 hours. Its terms were very harsh, including demands for a commanding Austrian role in breaking up the subversive conspiracy within Serbia. Clearly Austria did not expect Serbia to accept the ultimatum; it was intended as a pretext for attack. The ultimatum was the challenge move; when its terms became known, all of Europe knew that a very serious crisis was at hand.

CONFRONTATION

To almost everyone's surprise, Serbia accepted almost all the Austrian demands, excepting only those that would have violated its sovereignty. Nevertheless, Austria declared the reply unsatisfactory, broke off relations, and ordered mobilization against Serbia.

In the 12 days between the issuance of the ultimatum to the outbreak of war, the behavior of the parties followed two contradictory lines: diplomatic communication that was generally aimed at settling the crisis or at least localizing an Austro–Serbian war, and military decisions that led straight to war. The story of the crisis can be told, and its outcome explained, largely in terms of misperceptions in the diplomatic exchanges and the failure to correct the misperceptions in time to stop the momentum toward war generated by mobilization decisions.

On July 24, Germany announced to all the powers her support of Austria and demanded that the conflict be "localized"—i.e., that others not intervene. England replied that this was impossible—Russia would fight. Sazonov, the Russian foreign minister, said as much the same day to the German ambassador, but the latter paid more attention to Sazonov's statement of willingness to negotiate and reported home that Russia was "weakening." Russia appealed to Britain for a declaration of support, but Grey refused. Instead he attempted a mediating role: first he proposed (to Germany) four-power mediation between Austria and Russia, then a formal conference, then that Germany and England collaborate in restraining Austria and Russia. Germany rejected the first two proposals and pretended to accept the third. However, in passing on Grey's proposals to Austria, Germany let Austria know that she opposed them. Far from restraining Austria, Germany was egging Austria on. On July 26, she advised Austria to declare war and attack as soon as possible. Although the army would not be ready to attack until Aug. 12, Berchtold, to satisfy the Germans, issued a declaration of war against Serbia July 28.

Meanwhile, military decisions were being made that would eventually control the course of events. In Russia on July 24, even before the Austrians had started mobilizing, the Czar was persuaded to authorize a "partial" mobilization—against Austria but not Germany. Sazonov intended this as a political coercive measure, a threat to deter Austria, rather than as preparation for war. From Germany he received indirect assurance from the foreign minister, Jagow, that the partial mobilization would not trigger war: Germany would mobilize only if Russia mobilized against Germany or actually attacked Austria, not if she only mobilized against Austria. After learning of the Austrian war declaration on July 28, Sazonov telegraphed all European capitals that Russia would begin mobilization against Austria the next day, and stressed that this move was not directed against Germany.

But the German war plan required not only mobilization but war against both France and Russia as soon as Russia began mobilizing at all. The dreaded two-front war was to be avoided by defeating France quickly, then shifting forces to the eastern front before the slow-mobilizing Russians had time to reach full strength. Moreover, Von Moltke, the German chief of staff, told Bethmann that the Austro–German alliance obliged Germany to mobilize as soon as Russia and Austria began mobilizing. This was contrary to what Jagow had told the French and Russians and apparently was news to Bethmann. He passed it on to Sazonov as a "friendly opinion." Sazonov, also surprised, requested advice from his military leaders. They now saw little chance of avoiding war with Germany and demanded cancellation of the partial mobilization order since it would delay general mobilization. The Czar was persuaded to authorize general mobilization, but then canceled it when he received a telegram from the kaiser urging him to cooperate in averting war. Mobilization against Austria alone was ordered at midnight, July 29. The alternative of no mobilization at all seems not to have been considered.

Meanwhile in the diplomatic channels, Grey continued his efforts to mediate and Germany pretended to collaborate. Germany suggested to Russia that she enter into negotiations with Austria on the principle of "no territorial gains," but failed to suggest this to Austria. Sazonov indicated a willingness to compromise on the harshest points of the Austrian ultimatum, but Berchtold managed to avoid the Russian ambassador in Vienna for a day and a half, until after the declaration of war against Serbia had been issued.

Grey's mediation strategy was a compromise between two factions in his government—the Liberal Radicals, who urged restraint of Russia, and the foreign office, which urged a clear British commitment to France and Russia to deter the Central Powers. Grey thought he had made clear enough to the Germans that Britain would fight in defense of France, but he did not know that the German government was heavily discounting information from Lichnowsky, their ambassador in London, because of his reputation as an Anglophile. The German leaders persisted in believing that England would ultimately stand aside.

The German complacency evaporated on July 29, when Grey finally stated unambiguously that Britain could not remain neutral. This message, combined with the near-simultaneous statement by von Moltke that Russian mobilization against Austria would force Germany to war, doubly jolted Bethmann and caused him to reverse course. During the evening and wee hours of July 29–30, he bombarded Vienna with messages urging Austria to hold back and try to compromise with Russia on the "Halt-in-Belgrade" proposal that had been suggested independently by Grey and the Kaiser. But his language was not strong enough. After what had already passed between Berlin and Vienna, the only message that could have stopped Austria would have been a flat withdrawal of support. Moreover, von Moltke was sending contradictory advice to Vienna. He wired Conrad, the Austrian chief of staff, urging immediate Austria mobilization against Russia and promising full German support.

In Vienna, Berchtold's reaction to these contradictory messages was: Who rules in Berlin? A war council decided it was the German military and therefore decided to mobilize against Russia.

In St. Petersburg, meanwhile, the Czar had been persuaded to reverse himself again and order general mobilization. War with Germany was now inevitable, his military advisers said; any delay in mobilization would be to Russia's disadvantage. When this news reached Germany on July 31, Bethmann, on the brink of nervous collapse, was persuaded to authorize German mobilization. An ultimatum was sent to Russia, demanding an end to military preparations within 12 hours. Receiving no reply, Germany declared war on August 1. Similar declarations against Belgium and France followed during the next two days. The division in the British cabinet vanished when German armies crossed the Belgian frontier on August 4. Britain declared war on Germany. When Bethmann was asked a few days later why the war had started he threw up his hands and cried "If I only knew!" We now know that the primary immediate reasons why the 1914 crisis ended in war were: (1) the compulsions inherent in war plans and mobilization schedules, (2) German misperception of English intentions until too late to block these compulsions, (3) the criminal ignorance of civilian leaderships in all countries of the logic of mobilization and military plans, and (4) the need to stand by allies lest they be defeated and the balance of power overturned, and finally the cancerous element that triggered it all, the Austrian vulnerability to revolutionary disintegration.

Selected Bibliography

Albertini, Luigi, *The Origins of the War of 1914* (London: Oxford University Press, 1966).

Fay, Sidney B., *The Origins of the World War* (New York: The Macmillan Co., 1928).

Reiners, Ludwig, *The Lamps Went Out in Europe*. Tr. by Richard and Clara Winston (New York: World Publishing Co., 1966).

Renouvin, Pierre, *The Immediate Origins of the War* (New Haven: Yale University Press, 1928).

Schmitt, Bernadotte E., *The Coming of the War, 1914* (New York: Charles Scribner's Sons, 1930).

Turner, L.C. F., *Origins of the First World War* (New York: Norton, 1973).

MUNICH, 1938, by Paul Diesing

The precipitant-challenge-confrontation scheme is inappropriate and misleading for this case. The major participants were each pursuing quite independent strategies that occasionally intersected by accident, and Czechoslovakia was so divided internally as to be unable to pursue any strategy at all. Only at the very end of the crisis, the last three or four days, were the participants operating within a fairly common frame of reference, and only then could any bargaining occur. The history of the crisis, then, is a history of how several entirely diverse frames of reference gradually merged, permitting a few days of confused bargaining, and then separated again.

German strategy was aimed at first annexing Austria and thus exposing the undefended southern Czech frontier to German attack. Then Henlein, the leading Czech Nazi, was to make impossible demands on Czech President Beneš on behalf of the Sudeten Germans. When the German army was ready, Czechoslovakia was to be attacked from three directions under the pretext of protecting the Sudeten Germans from Czech bullying, and on the pretext that Henlein's peaceful attempt to redress grievances had failed. However, this attack could not come until (1) the West Wall along the Rhine had been completed, to stop a possible French attack on behalf of its Czech ally, and (2) the army had been brought up to fighting strength. The Austrian annexation had disclosed great unpreparedness in the army. As these preparations developed during the summer of 1938, Hitler estimated that he would be able to attack Czechoslovakia on October 1, 1938. Britain was to be kept out of the action entirely by focusing attention on the pseudo-bargaining between Henlein and Beneš, with Germany acting as the peace-loving protector of its people just across the border, and by dangling the hope of good relations.

In Britain, Chamberlain's policy since 1936 had been to seek a détente with both Germany and Italy, but especially Germany. There were several reasons for this, and Chamberlain's followers emphasized them in varying degrees. First, antagonism to Germany would lead either to war or the need for heavy rearmament, both ruinous to the weak British economy (by orthodox pre-Keynesian thinking, which emphasized balanced budgets and paying off the national debt). Second, détente would buy time to complete Britain's very modest rearmament program. Third, a strong and friendly Germany would be an excellent bulwark against Socialism and Communism in Central and Eastern Europe, and a better ally than the weak, semi-socialist France. Chamberlain felt the same contempt for the 1936 Popular Front government that he felt for the Labour party.

Détente was to be achieved by unilateral concessions—support for inclusion of Austrian, Czech, and Danzig Germans within Germany, transfer of some African colonies (preferably Belgian or Portuguese) to Germany, and attempts to find what other interests Hitler had. For Chamberlain it was crucial that Germany achieve its aims peacefully, with British assistance, rather than by force: wars tend to spread, cause ruin, and lead to Communism afterward; and it was better to gain German friendship by generosity than to incur enmity by a firmness that was essentially a bluff, given British military weakness.

The French government was divided; there was Foreign Minister Bonnet's group, which thought much as Chamberlain and even hoped for a Franco–German alliance against Bolshevism and its Czech copy; anti-Germans such as Reynaud and Mandel, who wanted to rearm; and Daladier wavering in the balance. Daladier felt that France could not honor the alliance with Czechoslovakia unless guaranteed full British support, because the French forces were sufficient only for defense. French policy thus vacillated between seeking British guarantees (and commitment of a British attack force that did not exist) and urging Czech accommodation with Germany.

Czechoslovakia was divided ethnically between Germans, Czechs, Slovaks, Magyars, Poles, Ruthenes; and cross-cutting this were conservatives, Nazis, agrarians, liberals, socialists, and communists. The largest party was Henlein's Sudeten German party, and the anti-communist Slovak prime minister was sympathetic to Henlein's demands for autonomy. President Beneš spoke for the state internally because of personal prestige, but could take no foreign policy initiative because of divisions in the government. Also Beneš as an anti-communist did not want Soviet support but looked to France and Britain for help. In Beneš's view the government had tried for twenty years to appease the Sudeten Germans and gain their loyalty, but had always failed because of outside agitators. In Henlein's view the Germans had suffered twenty years of oppression. In Chamberlain's view, Czechoslovakia was an artificial creation of the unjust Versailles treaty, all but lost to Socialism, and undeserving of survival.

CONVERGENCE OF THE FRAMES OF REFERENCE: FRANCE AND BRITAIN

Daladier's aim was to secure a guarantee of British attack forces in the event of war—or perhaps to get a refusal that would give France an excuse to abandon her commitment to Czechoslovakia. Bonnet's aim was to so phrase the requests for support that Britain would have to refuse them. Chamberlain's aim was to persuade Daladier to put pressure on Beneš to concede autonomy to Henlein, thereby appeasing Hitler. In discussions in April and September 1938 the three men talked past each other: Chamberlain evaded Daladier's blunt questions (Will you support France?), and when Chamberlain portrayed British–French military weakness, Daladier replied that France would honor her commitments (with Bonnet assuring Halifax privately of the opposite). Faced with British evasiveness, the French cabinet on September 12 compromised, deciding neither to encourage nor to discourage Czech resistance to Hitler—an empty decision, because Bonnet controlled communications with Czechoslovakia, and he insisted on Czech concessions. Thereafter France mainly followed the British lead.

CONVERGENCE: BRITAIN AND GERMANY

Throughout the crisis and after it Chamberlain continued to believe that his strategy of appeasement was succeeding. He did this by interpreting evidence to fit his preconceptions and by either ignoring directly negative evidence or discrediting its source. Up to late August he carried the cabinet with him; then Halifax was convinced by a series of messages and by foreign office discussions that Hitler was planning an attack and might be deterred by a mild British warning. He was talked and maneuvered out of this opinion by Chamberlain by September 10, but the possibility had been opened up.

The next shift in cabinet thinking occurred September 17–19, when Chamberlain returned from Berchtesgaden and proposed accepting Hitler's demand of a plebiscite in areas of a German majority. This was more than some in the cabinet were willing to concede; however Chamberlain again persuaded the doubters that détente was in sight.

The next correction of the cabinet diagnosis occurred on September 23–24, when Chamberlain told Hitler at Bad Godesberg that Britain would accept the plebiscite, and Hitler responded by increasing his demands. Halifax once more shifted, and this time had a cabinet majority for warning Hitler of British involvement if he attacked Czechoslovakia.

At this point the majority diagnosis in France and Britain, excluding Chamberlain and Bonnet, was close enough to Hitler's picture of the situation to permit bargaining to occur. The diagnosis was that Hitler was not interested in good relations with Britain and intended to attack Czechoslovakia on September 28, that this would drag France and eventually Britain in against their will, and that Hitler might still be dissuaded by warnings and/or concessions. Conversely, the series of British concessions must have suggested to Hitler the possibility of achieving his aims by bargaining rather than by attack.

The resulting bargaining is described in the text. The combined British–French warnings, mobilizations, and concessions, plus appeals against war by his own generals and Mussolini, plus strong antiwar sentiment in Berlin, induced Hitler to back down. Hitler's belligerent speech of September 26 and their own boldness frightened the British and French majority into backing down; their warning had been a bluff.

SELECTED BIBLIOGRAPHY

Best Account: Middlemas, Keith, *Diplomacy of Illusion* (London: Weidenfeld and Nicolson, 1972).

German: Bullock, Alan, *Hitler, a Study in Tyranny* (New York: Harper & Row, 1964).

Speer, Albert, *Inside the Third Reich* (New York: London: Macmillan, 1970).

British: Gilbert, Martin, and Richard Gott, *The Appeasers* (London, 1963).

Various opposing interpretations: Loewenheim, Francis L., ed., *The Munich Crisis* (Boston: Houghton Mifflin, 1965).

UNITED STATES–JAPAN, 1940–1941, by Paul Diesing

BARGAINING SETTING

The 1941 crisis did not start with a specific challenge by one side, but developed gradually as each side saw itself defending freedom for all Southeast Asia against an increasingly aggressive imperialist opponent.

In the Japanese view Japan was the only remaining Asiatic country except Thailand not already ruined by Western imperialism, its raw materials looted and its population assigned an inferior status and an inferior standard of living. And the pressure on Japan was increasing: its products were excluded from Western markets by import restrictions and boycotts, its raw material sources were under Western control and could be cut off at any time, and its surplus population was confined by immigration restrictions. Japan must control its own raw material sources to survive and must develop Asiatic markets for its industrial products. Otherwise industry would stagnate, the population would starve, and the military would be rendered incapable of defense against Western imperialist takeover.

The Japanese policy, set July 1940, was, first, to expel the Western imperialists and their friends, the Chiang government, from China; second, to arrange guaranteed raw material deliveries from the United States, the Dutch Indies, and Indo-China, to be paid for with industrial exports; and third, to avoid provoking the United States.

The United States viewed Japan as one of those military dictatorships that like to invade other countries out of inherent aggressiveness. In Ambassador Grew's minority view, this was true only of a dominant militarist faction that might yet be overcome by a peace-loving faction.

The United States had a moral obligation to protect weaker countries against such aggressors, and it had a special obligation to protect the raw materials the British needed to continue the war against Hitler. Also U.S. exports to Japan would have to be reduced to make materials available to Britain and to the U.S. war preparations. Looking forward to the postwar world, the United States proposed including the British–French–Dutch possessions in an expanded Monroe Doctrine area (Feis, *Road to Pearl Harbor,* p. 63), a free trade area in which raw materials should be sold to the highest bidder rather than taken by military force.

The United States was divided about how to stop Japanese aggression. The hard-liners urged firmness, since aggressors generally bluff and are always encouraged by appeasement. The military urged caution as the United States would not be prepared for a Pacific war until early 1942. The soft-liners urged support for the Japanese peace faction in the form of conditional rewards for peaceful behavior. The middle-liners, including Hull and Roosevelt, preferred caution in order to avoid provoking more aggression, and a delay of firmness in hopes of a Japanese turn toward peacefulness. Much the same spectrum of opinion existed in the Japanese government, except that there were no soft-liners. Consequently each move by both governments was a compromise between opposite proposals.

MAJOR BARGAINING MOVES

1. We begin arbitrarily with the U.S. embargo of aviation fuel and top-grade scrap iron July 25, 1940, a compromise between a complete oil-scrap embargo and none at all.

2. August, 1940: Japanese increased demands for guaranteed oil deliveries from Sumatra to replace the embargoed oil. But a 50% compromise is accepted in November to avoid provoking the United States.

3. September: Japanese defense treaty with Germany, to deter the United States; renewed determination not to provoke United States in the future.

4. December: Unobtrusive, selective licensing of U.S. exports to Japan.

5. January, 1941: Japan reopens trade talks with the Dutch, seeking to replace licensed U.S. exports.

6. April, U.S. bargaining proposal to Japan: The United States would restore normal trade with Japan, assist Japan in obtaining raw materials from Southeast Asia and assist in blocking British aggression from Singapore, stop supporting Chiang and offer economic assistance to China and Japan. Japan would partially withdraw from China after

its pacification and would support the United States against a German attack on the United States. This proposal greatly encouraged Japanese middle-liners.

7. May, Japanese reply: Some additional concessions are requested as a test of U.S. good faith—a compromise between accepting and rejecting the proposal.

8. May, June: United States rejects whole proposal, to the middle-liners' astonishment and dismay.

9. June: More unobtrusive U.S. embargoes; Dutch suspend trade negotiations.

10. July: Japan demands air and naval bases in southern Indo–China. Since raw materials are being refused, Japan must take them by force.

11. July 26: United States freezes Japanese assets, but assures Japan that it can still apply for export licenses and that no embargo has been imposed.

At this point the desperate Japanese military pressed for a rapid decision on war or peace, as the U.S. embargo meant ruin for Japan in 18 months. They thought it extremely unlikely that Japan could win a long war, but army leaders at least hoped that the United States might agree to a negotiated peace after some initial Japanese victories. If not, honorable suicide was preferable to national ruin and degradation. The middle-liners presented five more final proposals to the United States along the line of the April "U.S." proposal, all of which were rejected. They then resigned or gave up, and a decision on war was made. U.S. rejections were a compromise between hard-liners who argued that firmness would call the Japanese bluff and soft-liners who urged continuing negotiations to prevent war. They were gentle rejections.

EXPLANATION OF OUTCOME

This case is in no way a strategic interaction between two rational bargainers. Both governments were divided throughout, and tactical decisions always reflected the relative strength of opposing factions rather than a rationally calculated strategy. Each move of the opponent strengthened the hard-liners and discouraged the soft-liners, thus increasing hard-line influence slightly and resulting in a somewhat firmer response. The result was a gradual hardening of both bargaining positions, with the middle-liners and military gradually joining the hards, until the hards took over in Japan in mid-October 1941.

SELECTED BIBLIOGRAPHY

A strongly pro-U.S. view: Langer, William and S. E. Gleason, *The Undeclared War, 1940–1941* (New York: Harper, 1953).

More sympathetic to Japan: Butow, Robert, *Tojo and the Coming of the War* (Princeton University Press, 1961).

Somewhere in between: Feis, Herbert, *The Road to Pearl Harbor* (Princeton University Press, 1950).

IRAN, 1945–1946, by Glenn H. Snyder and Charles Planck

BACKGROUND AND PRECIPITANT

Soviet, British, and American forces had occupied Iran during World War II in order to block a German move into the country, and to maintain a supply route to the Red army. By a treaty with Iran in January 1942, the Soviet Union and Great Britain promised to respect Iranian sovereignty and territorial integrity and to withdraw the troops six months after the end of hostilities. In August 1945, revolts by the Communist-led Tudeh party broke out in the Soviet-occupied northern part of the country (chiefly in Azerbaijan), with Soviet forces providing protection and aid. When a major rebellion erupted in November, the Iranian government dispatched troops to quell it, but the troops were turned back by Soviet forces. This act of force committed the Soviets to support of the rebels. It was the immediate precipitant of the crisis. By December 16 the revolt had succeeded, and the rebels had proclaimed an Autonomous Republic of Azerbaijan.

INTERESTS OF THE GREAT POWERS

The primary Soviet aim was to establish a friendly, i.e. Communist-controlled, regime in northern Iran or in the country as a whole, possibly as a security buffer zone. Although they had signed various documents during the war that on their face foreclosed "spheres of influence," the Soviets may have read a tacit assent into the Western powers' failure to demur when they insisted on "friendly governments" on their borders. A secondary Soviet objective was to obtain oil concessions in northern Iran, chiefly to preclude others' getting them and thereby acquiring political influence.

The United States was committed to the Open Door in trade and reliance on the United Nations for security and resolution of conflicts. Spheres of influence and imperialism were anathema. In Iran, therefore, the U.S. aim was to strengthen the country so that outside interference would be unnecessary, and to prevent Iran from becoming the exclusive economic preserve of other powers.

The chief British interest was to protect its strategic and oil interests in the south, though Britain also supported the U.S. opposition to the Soviets achieving a foothold in the north.

CHALLENGE

The United States and Britain had no wish for a direct confrontation with the Soviet Union, first, because they (especially the United States) still held high hopes for great power collaboration in the postwar world, and second, because they lacked the military and political means to counter the Soviets on the spot. Their response to the Soviet moves was extremely moderate, consisting of mild protests, reminders of Soviet treaty obligations, publicizing Soviet activities, and suggesting reciprocal disengagement of forces. The aims of this strategy were to convey concern and implicitly warn of further pressure, while leaving the Soviets an avenue of withdrawal by avoiding explicit charges of Soviet responsibility for the rebel regime. When this strategy clearly failed to move the Soviets, the U.S. position gradually hardened, beginning with encouragement to Iran to bring its case to the United Nations.

CONFRONTATION

Iran brought its complaint to the U.N. Security Council January 19, 1946, charging Soviet interference in the internal affairs of Iran. This was the first effective pressure on the Soviets. U.N. involvement meant worldwide publicity and Great Power opposition, which the Soviets wished to avoid because (1) it would frustrate their program of local pressure and bilateral negotiation, and (2) it would worsen their relations with the other powers on a wide range of issues. The Security Council recommended, January 30, that the two parties enter into direct negotiations but did not drop the matter from its agenda. Keeping the issue formally before the Council was useful to Iran as an implicit threat during subsequent negotiations.

The Iranian premier, Qavam, went to Moscow for a month of negotiations beginning February 19, but was unsuccessful. The Soviet demands were extreme: recognition of the autonomy of Azerbaijan, 51% Soviet share in a joint stock company to exploit oil in the northern provinces, and continued presence of Soviet troops in parts of the country. When Qavam rejected these terms, the Soviets raised their demand to full ownership of the oil company.

The peak of the crisis was reached in the weeks following March 2, 1946, when the Soviets failed to evacuate their troops and thus violated the 1942 treaty. The Soviet reasons for not withdrawing were apparently to retain bargaining leverage on the oil and Azerbaijan issues, or alternatively, to have an instrument of pressure as back-up for a possible Tudeh revolution aimed at taking over the entire country. During the first week of March, the Soviets also moved in substantial additional troops. These moves galvanized the Western powers into stronger action. The United States and Britain sent notes of protest and the U.S.

government released to the press information on the Soviet troop movements. The battleship *Missouri* was sent on a show of force to Istanbul. On March 9 Churchill made his famous "Iron Curtain" speech at Fulton, Missouri.

Iran brought its second complaint to the U.N. Security Council on March 18, this time with stronger encouragement from the United States. The Soviet Union requested postponement, on the ground that negotiations were underway, but this move failed, largely because of U.S. opposition. The Soviets were thus forced to step up pressure on Iran while also making concessions, in order to get some kind of bilateral settlement before the United Nations took up the issue on March 25. They offered troop withdrawal "in five or six weeks" and a "regional" rather than "autonomous" status for the Azerbaijan regime, in exchange for 51% control of an oil concession. Qavam expressed satisfaction with the troop withdrawal promise, but accepted Soviet terms on oil and Azerbaijan only with substantial reservations. When the Security Council convened, Gromyko, the Soviet representative, moved to remove the Iranian complaint from the agenda, claiming an agreement had already been reached and troop evacuation begun. When the motion was defeated, Gromyko walked out. The U.S. behavior at this session revealed that maintaining the wartime concert no longer held first priority in U.S. policy. Nevertheless, Secretary of State Byrnes was unwilling to antagonize the Soviet Union more than necessary. At his motion the Council voted on April 4 to postpone further discussion until May 6, when the Soviet Union and Iran were to report jointly on the status of troop withdrawal.

RESOLUTION

On this same day (April 4) Qavam and the Soviets reached agreement on all issues: Soviet troops would be removed six weeks after March 24, an oil company would be established in which the Soviet Union held 51% of the stock, and the status of Azarbaijan would be settled in negotiations between Teheran and the rebel government. Soviet troops subsequently completed evacuation by May 10.

This marked the end of the most acute phase of the crisis, but it was not the end of the story. The Soviets apparently had at least gained something for their efforts: an oil concession. However, this depended on ratification by the Majlis, which had been closed since April 11 because Tudeh agitation had prevented a quorum. Its reopening required new elections, and these required reestablishment of central government authority throughout the country. When the Soviets comprehended this situation, they exerted pressure on the stubborn Azerbaijan regime to accept Qavam's rather lenient terms. The agreement of June 14 gave Teheran official authority over the province, but made many concessions to regional autonomy, including the right to maintain temporarily an Azerbaijan army. The Soviets then overplayed their hand in attempting to increase Tudeh influence throughout the country to maximize support in the coming elections. Tudeh rioting during the summer, and Soviet pressures on Qavam and other cabinet members, led to the inclusion of three Tudeh members in the cabinet. This in turn aroused right-wing opposition. Anti-Tudeh rioting in the south and pressure from the Shah enabled Qavam to shift his political base to the right and expel the Tudeh members from the cabinet and other positions. The premier was now in a position to move physically against Azerbaijan, especially since the United States had declared publicly its support for such a move. Despite Soviet threats, the Iranian army marched on December 10. The rebel regime collapsed almost immediately. Elections were then held with only two Tudeh members gaining seats, and in October the Majlis voted down the Soviet oil concession, 102 to 2. The Soviets ended up with nothing, because of their own blundering, Qavam's diplomatic finesse, the patiently firm U.S. position, and above all, it seems, because the Soviets did not consider the issue worth damaging its relations with the Western powers when more important issues were pending in Europe.

SELECTED BIBLIOGRAPHY

Byrnes, James, *All in One Lifetime* (New York: Harper, 1958).

Hurewitz, J. C., *Middle East Dilemmas* (New York: Harper, 1953).

Lenczowski, George, *Russia and the West in Iran, 1918–1948* (Ithaca: Cornell University Press, 1949).

Skrine, Sir Clairmont, *World War In Iran* (London: Constable and Co., Ltd., 1962).

U.S. Department of State, *Foreign Relations of the United States: Diplomatic Papers,* Vols. V, VII, VIII (Washington: U.S. Government Printing Office, 1965 and 1969).

Von Wagenen, Richard W., *The Iranian Case, 1946* (New York: Carnegie Endowment for International Peace, 1952).

BERLIN, 1948–1949, by Paul Diesing and Clark Murdock

PRECIPITANT

The roots of the 1948 crisis lie in U.S.–U.S.S.R. disagreements in 1945 on policy toward Germany, with Britain supporting the United States and France supporting the Soviet Union. These disagreements parallel British–French disagreements on the same topic in 1919–1922. The Soviet emphasis was on reparations to be used in reconstructing the Soviet Union while the U.S. emphasis was on industrial recovery to facilitate recovery in Western Europe. Both policies focused on the industrial areas of the west zones. The United States first evaded reparations, beginning July 1945, by emphasizing local military control of each zone and pushing for economic recovery of the U.S. zone, then halted reparations entirely in May 1946. The Soviet Union meanwhile took what reparations it could from its zone. Continuing economic recovery required economic integration of the U.S. and British zones, and this was followed by planning in February 1948 for a separate West German state.

The Soviet Union protested these moves.

The specific precipitant was the June 7, 1948 publication of plans for a West German state, followed June 18 by a currency reform in the western zones.

CHALLENGE

The Soviet Union responded on June 21 with currency reform in the east zone and on June 24 with a blockade. The purpose of the reform and blockade were, first, to consolidate the east zone economically by stopping the flow of old currency east and of real capital and labor west through Berlin, and second to get some leverage against the proposed West German state and for a return to reparations deliveries. Stalin hoped to trade the ending of the blockade for cancellation of plans for a Western state; but if the United States refused, he at least would have West Berlin and the east zone. On July 3 the Soviet representative announced that the blockade would continue until the plans for a West German state were abandoned.

CONFRONTATION

The United States perceived the blockade as another step in the aggressive Soviet expansion program—Poland, Hungary, Czechoslovakia —to be followed by take-over of West Germany, etc. Consequently some advisers urged that the Soviet Union be stopped in Berlin before the U.S. position became still worse. Others saw West Berlin as an indefensible outpost of little value and a potential source of continuing friction, and proposed withdrawal. Truman rejected withdrawal because the United States had a legal right to be there, but he accepted military advice that breaking the blockade by force would be too risky, and he postponed decision on how to deal with the blockade. Meanwhile, the West Berlin garrisons were being supplied by air on an emergency basis.

RESOLUTION

As the fall wore on the West Berliners rejected offers of food from East Berlin and became ever more determined to resist Communist bullying, while airlift capacity steadily increased. Accordingly, the Western bargaining position steadily hardened, and by January 1949 the West had withdrawn its earlier offers to circulate Eastern currency in West Berlin. On January 31 Stalin indicated readiness to end the blockade in return for a foreign ministers' meeting. The blockade was lifted May 12, and the fruitless meeting began May 23.

EXPLANATION OF OUTCOME

The success of the airlift removed Stalin's bargaining power. The blockade consolidated West Berlin opposition to Communism, and the airlift symbolized resistance to Communist aggression. This unified the West in an anti-Communist stance and led to the formation of NATO. When Stalin realized the blockade was both ineffective and counterproductive, he called it off.

SELECTED BIBLIOGRAPHY

A traditional Cold War view: Davison, W. Phillips, *The Berlin Blockade* (Princeton: Princeton University Press, 1958).

A revisionist view: Gimbel, John, *The American Occupation of Germany: Politics and the Military, 1945–1949* (Stanford: Stanford University Press, 1968).

Gottlieb, Manuel, *The German Peace Settlement and the Berlin Crisis* (New York: Paine-Whitman, 1960).

QUEMOY, 1958, by Paul Diesing and Jane K. Holland

PRECIPITANT

In 1949 the Chinese Communist army completed conquest of mainland China, but was defeated in an attempt to capture the offshore island of Quemoy. The Nationalists continued to hold a series of offshore islands, which they used to blockade major mainland ports such as Amoy, and, with U.S. support, to stage raids on the mainland. During the early 1950s several of these islands were evacuated under mainland pressure, but Quemoy and Matsu were held and strongly reinforced. The mainland opposite Quemoy was also reinforced with artillery and airfields; on August 6 and 18, 1958, the third and fourth of these airfields were completed. By 1958 sporadic artillery duels were occurring between Quemoy and the mainland batteries.

On July 17, 1958, a Nationalist general announced that Quemoy was being converted to an offensive base preparatory to invading the mainland. This was one of a series of Nationalist pledges to invade the mainland. On the same day the Chinese radio, in a program beamed toward Formosa, announced a campaign to liberate Formosa; this was one of a series of such pledges. In August the Chinese artillery firings intensified. Most of the shells directed toward Quemoy were airburst shells that scattered propaganda leaflets, but supply convoys were also shelled.

CHALLENGE

On August 23 the Chinese Communists began heavy shelling of Quemoy and Matsu, effectively interdicting their supply lines. This heavy shelling lasted until September 6. The precise nature of this challenge was not clear, as the Chinese Communists did not declare their purpose. There had been a slow buildup of armaments on both sides. After the heavy shelling began in late August, the United States became involved in the hostile buildup, sending the Seventh Fleet to the Quemoy area, and reinforcing it greatly. Secretary of State Dulles also made statements of support for the Nationalists and hostility toward Communist China, including an intimation that the United States would defend Quemoy.

MILITARY STRENGTH

The United States Seventh Fleet controlled the Formosa Strait. On the Chinese side there were no invasion craft or other naval vessels in the area, and the bomber force on the four airfields remained quiet. The Nationalists had 100,000 troops, one third of their army, on Quemoy, well fortified in underground bunkers, and their army and air force were supplied with advanced U.S. weapons.

INITIAL EXPECTATIONS AND STRATEGIES

The Chinese strategy is not known; however, their actions suggest either a defensive strategy or a probe to test the Quemoy defenses and resupply capability. The Nationalist strategy was to stir up hostilities that would get the United States militarily involved in a mainland invasion. The U.S. strategy was to provide the Nationalists enough support to maintain their morale and to enable them to hold Quemoy, but to prevent them from attacking the mainland. U.S. intelligence in early

August estimated that there was a possibility of Chinese attack on Quemoy (approved or backed by the Soviet Union), but this possibility was discounted by the end of August when the Chinese kept their bombers grounded. Thereafter the main U.S. concern was with Nationalist morale.

RESOLUTION

On September 4 Dulles proposed reopening talks with the Chinese at Warsaw but again warned them not to attack Formosa or related positions, an oblique reference to Quemoy. On September 6 the Chinese accepted Dulles's proposal, reduced the level of their artillery barrage, and declared their desire to obtain U.S. withdrawal from Formosa through peaceful negotiations. On September 7, when it was clear that negotiations would take place, Khrushchev sent a letter to President Eisenhower. Khrushchev did not indicate that he would give material support to the Chinese Communists in their effort to settle an "internal" matter, but warned the United States not to attack the mainland. Meanwhile U.S. military advisers trained Nationalist sailors to offload supplies to small craft while beyond artillery range and to follow a zigzag path to the Quemoy landing beaches. On September 7 and September 14, supply convoys got through the artillery blockade in this fashion, and by September 21 the blockade had been circumvented. On September 24 the Nationalists won a big air battle over the Formosa Straits.

In talks at Warsaw and in speeches September 25 and 30, Dulles was conciliatory, suggesting that Quemoy be reduced to outpost status, that the United States had no obligation or interest in helping Chiang return to the mainland, and that his return was most unlikely. In statements during October 1–5 Chiang expressed shock and dismay at Dulles's speeches; he asserted that Quemoy was a purely defensive outpost, that U.S. help was needed against imminent Chinese invasion of Formosa, and that he could not understand why his friend Dulles had betrayed him. On October 6 the Chinese called off the artillery barrage, asserting that their aim was to induce the United States to leave Formosa by peaceful negotiations, and citing Dulles's September 25 and 30 speeches as evidence that the United States would eventually agree to leave.

EXPLANATION OF OUTCOME

The U.S. training in landing tactics circumvented the artillery blockade; and the blockade itself demonstrated the futility of using Quemoy as an offensive base. The additional aggressive moves that all three sides claimed to expect did not occur. The military stalemate was accompanied, on all three sides, by a shift from the hostile speeches of July and

August to more conciliatory statements emphasizing peaceful and defensive intentions.

SELECTED BIBLIOGRAPHY

Eisenhower, Dwight D., *Waging Peace: 1956–1961* (Garden City, N.Y.: Doubleday and Co., 1965).

Halperin, Morton, ed., *Sino–Soviet Relations and Arms Control* (Cambridge, Mass.: M.I.T. Press, 1967).

Howe, Jonathan T., Lt. Comdr., USN., *Multicrises* (Cambridge, Mass.: M.I.T. Press, 1971). Best single account.

Hsieh, Alice Langley, *Communist China's Strategy in the Nuclear Era* (Englewood Cliffs, N.J.: Prentice-Hall, Inc., 1962).

Tsou, Tang, *The Embroilment over Quemoy: Mao, Chiang and Dulles* (Salt Lake City, Utah: Institute of International Affairs, University of Utah Press, 1959).

Zagoria, Donald S., *The Sino–Soviet Conflict, 1956–1961* (Princeton, N.J.: Princeton University Press, 1962).

BERLIN, 1958–1962, by Paul Diesing

PRECIPITANT

When Khrushchev and his associates had overcome the anti-party group in 1957 and consolidated their position, they turned their attention to urgent domestic and foreign problems, including Germany. They found the United States preparing to introduce tactical atomic weapons into Germany as part of a general military buildup, and influential West German figures were beginning to demand German control over atomic weapons. This was perceived as a serious potential danger to the Soviet Union. If West German revanchists ever got control of atomic weapons they could use them to blackmail the Soviet Union, demanding border revisions and Soviet troop withdrawals as a price for peace. The Soviet Union took a series of actions to counter this danger: warning notes to the United States protesting the stationing of atomic weapons in Germany, a proposal for an atom-free zone in Central Europe, a proposal for mutual troop reductions December 1957, a visit by Mikoyan to Adenauer in April 1958 to discuss German rearmament and especially atomic weapons, and other notes and talks with Bonn. These actions had no effect on U.S. or West German plans.

CHALLENGE

On November 27, 1958, Khrushchev took a more dramatic step that got U.S. attention and began the Berlin crisis. He proposed that the major belligerents of World War II negotiate a German peace settlement that would stabilize existing borders and thereby end German revisionist attempts. The settlement should recognize the existing status quo: two German states, with West Berlin a free, neutral city within East German territory, and an end to the postwar occupation. If the West refused to negotiate, Khrushchev proposed to negotiate a separate peace treaty with East Germany, on the model of the separate U.S. treaty with Japan, that would end the state of war and occupation rights in Berlin. However, he undertook not to do this for at least six months, to give the United States time to negotiate a settlement.

PRELIMINARY NEGOTIATIONS

The West interpreted the Soviet note as an ultimatum intended to force the West out of Berlin as a prelude to further aggression. However, Dulles agreed to negotiate, in hopes that Khrushchev's blustering concealed some legitimate Soviet desire for security. The result was the Geneva Conference of May 11–August 5, in which the Soviet Union waited for a U.S. counteroffer on details of the peace settlement, and the U.S. again proposed German unification with unilateral Soviet withdrawal from their occupation zone, and was prepared to offer security guarantees in return. The two sides were not only far apart, they were negotiating on different subjects.

In order to keep negotiations going Eisenhower proposed that Khrushchev visit the United States. Khrushchev accepted, feeling that direct negotiations with Eisenhower would be more productive than the foreign ministers' negotiations. The outcome of this visit was an agreement to negotiate on May 14, 1960, at Paris.

CONFRONTATION, PHASE I.

In early 1960 several speeches by U.S. officials showed that the United States was not picking up the peace treaty idea and did not intend to remove its occupation troops from West Berlin nor to recognize East Germany. The U-2 incident of May 1, in which a U.S. spy plane was shot down over the Soviet Union, was either the last straw or gave Khrushchev a pretext to break up the unpromising conference. He demanded an apology, and when this was refused, broke up the conference. Khrushchev declared that Eisenhower had betrayed his confidence and proposed to wait and negotiate with the next president in 1961.

PHASE II.

While Khrushchev was waiting, Ulbricht, the East German President, went into action. From February 1960 on he made a series of probes to determine where the West would stand firm and where it would be accommodative. He tried accreditation of military missions, temporary travel restrictions to East and West Berlin, various controls over freight shipments, and the like. The West was also doing some probing, including scheduling various political meetings in West Berlin and trying new air flight patterns over East Germany. These probes clarified the position of each side to the other.

PHASE III.

In 1961 President Kennedy took a middle position between those advisers who urged firmness and those who advised negotiations. He decided to be firm on essentials but negotiate on non-essentials. After some months of study the United States decided that West Berlin was essential to its security and would not be given up, and Kennedy announced this commitment on July 25. This speech, plus Fulbright's July 30 suggestion that East Germany close the border, plus reactions to his probes, gave Ulbricht the information he needed. Ulbricht's problem was the open border, across which spies, saboteurs, and currency could move east and refugees and labor move west. He perceived West Germany, supported by the United States with its consistently expressed desire for German reunification, as using the open border to undermine the East German state. (Conversely, the open border also symbolized Ulbricht's lingering claim on West Berlin.) He now estimated that the United States would not resist a border closing, although it would resist interference with air access to West Berlin. Ulbricht convinced the East block leaders on August 3–5 to approve a border closing, and on August 13 the German Democratic Republic constructed first a fence and then a wall along the border. Khrushchev reluctantly agreed to Ulbricht's border closing proposal after tentatively opposing it earlier in 1961, and even agreed to accept U.S. troops in West Berlin if that was necessary to get the United States to accept the wall.

RESOLUTION

The border closing interrupted Kennedy's and Khrushchev's preparations for negotiations, but after a short pause both continued their strategy. During 1961 Khrushchev had sent a number of messages to Kennedy via intermediaries, hinting at concessions and restating his basic security concerns. In late August Kennedy suggested negotiations, which were quickly arranged for New York beginning September 21. In an exchange of letters with the Soviet leader beginning September 29 Kennedy wrote that the United States was not interested in reunifying Germany and that Khrushchev should be satisfied with this de facto division into two states and should not ask for formal recognition as well. Khrushchev wrote that he could get along without formal recognition if the reality of East Germany and the independence of West Berlin was tacitly understood. Satisfied by these exchanges Khrushchev dropped his December 31 deadline for a settlement on October 17. Negotiations continued in various forms until June 1962 without result. As at Geneva in 1959 the two sides were working on different topics. The United States was trying to get access guarantees to West Berlin; the Soviet Union was trying to get some indirect recognition of East Germany; and West Germany was trying to halt negotiations entirely.

In June 1964 the Soviet Union signed a separate peace treaty with East Germany, and in 1971 fresh negotiations reached agreement on access guarantees, recognition of borders, and the independence of West Berlin.

SELECTED BIBLIOGRAPHY

Best general account: Zolling, Hermann, and Uwe Bahnsen, *Kalter Winter in August* (Oldenburg: Stalling, 1967).

Soviet view: Kroll, Hans, *Lebenserinnerungen Eines Botschafters* (Cologne: Kiepenheuer & Witsch, 1967), and Embree, George, ed., *The Soviet Union and the German Question,* documents (Hague: Nijhoff, 1963).

Best U.S. account: Schick, Jack, *The Berlin Crisis, 1958–1962* (Philadelphia: University of Pennsylvania Press, 1971).

A British view: Windsor, Philip, *City on Leave* (New York: Frederick A. Praeger, 1963).

A West German view: Schultz, Klaus-Peter, *Berlin Zwischen Freiheit Und Diktatur* (Berlin: Staneck, 1962).

An East German view: Klein, Peter, ed., *Geschichte der Aussenpolitik der DDR* (Berlin: Dietz, 1968).

CUBA, 1962, by Glenn H. Snyder and Charles Lockhart

PRECIPITANT

The Soviet Union began supplying Cuba with large amounts of armaments during the summer of 1962. This produced anxiety in the U.S. government, especially in Congress, where the situation was exploited by some Republicans for domestic political purposes. President Kennedy, on September 4, announced the presence of Soviet SAM-2 anti-aircraft missiles and 3500 Soviet personnel but no offensive missiles. Were these to be installed, he said, "the gravest issues" would arise.

Tass stated on September 11 that the Soviet Union had no need to place long-range missiles outside its own borders. Khrushchev promised Kennedy not to do anything that would disturb the U.S. election campaign, and assured the president that no surface-to-surface missiles would be placed in Cuba.

The specific precipitant of the crisis was the U.S. discovery, on October 14, that Soviet IRBM and MRBM sites were under construction or already built in Cuba; in the next few days launching facilities for about 60 missiles were spotted, enough to increase the Soviet nuclear strike force against the United States by 50%. The C.I.A. estimated the missiles would be operational in about 10 days. A special Executive Committee of high-level officials was formed to decide on a U.S. course of action, and it deliberated in secret for six days. Six alternatives were considered: no action, diplomatic action (either through the United Nations or to the Soviet government directly), a secret threat to Castro, invasion, a "surgical" air strike on the missile sites, and a naval blockade. The first three options were quickly eliminated. Inaction was intolerable, since, although the missiles would not have overturned the strategic balance technically, to let them stay would sharply increase Soviet resolve and lower the Soviets' estimate of U.S. resolve in future crises, and yield a variety of other political benefits to the Soviet Union. Purely diplomatic action would be interpreted as weakness and would permit Khrushchev to stall until the missiles were in full readiness. Debate narrowed to two options—air strike or blockade—with invasion linked to the air strike as a necessary follow-up. The air strike was at first favored as a move that would dispose of the problem cleanly and finally, but considerations of morality and risks of escalation undermined its attractiveness. Moreover, the Air Force could not give assurance that it would be 100% successful. Dominant opinion eventually swung over to the blockade as a move that would dramatically demonstrate U.S. resolve, avoid violence, or at least minimize violence if it did occur, and give Khrushchev time to decide to withdraw the missiles. The air strike and invasion alternatives were to be held in reserve. Thus the committee's essential decision was to try to remove the missiles by coercive threat, but to remove them by force if necessary. Kennedy agreed to this strategy on October 20.

CHALLENGE

In a television address, October 22, the president announced the naval "quarantine" (so labeled to avoid the legal act-of-war implication of a "blockade"), demanded the withdrawal of missiles already in Cuba under threat of "further action," and said that any missile launched from Cuba on any target in the Western Hemisphere would bring "full retaliation" against the Soviet Union. U.S. military forces had already been placed on full alert and a massive buildup was underway in Florida and the Caribbean area.

CONFRONTATION

The Soviets, caught by surprise, denounced the "quarantine" as an act of piracy and at first indicated determination both to ignore it and to continue work on the missile sites in Cuba. Khrushchev threatened that if a Soviet ship were stopped, Soviet submarines would sink U.S. ships. However, the blockade was implemented with extreme care to limit provocation; for example, the first ship boarded was Soviet-chartered, not owned, and known not to be carrying missiles. The most dangerous action was Navy harassment of Soviet submarines, forcing them to surface. On the 24th, the Soviet missile-carrying ships stopped or turned back to the Soviet Union, the first indication that the Soviets shrank from risking violence.

However, the success of the blockade did not solve the main problem of removing the missiles already in Cuba. The Soviets were rushing their installation and they would be operational in a few days, at which point an attack on them would be extremely hazardous. The President ordered a step-up in pressure, including low-level demonstrative overflights and dropping of flares. The point of highest tension for the U.S. decision makers came when a U-2 was shot down over Cuba. It had been decided earlier that if this should happen, reprisals would be carried out against anti-aircraft sites. However, the president vetoed reprisals for fear they might take the crisis out of control.

RESOLUTION

Meanwhile, Kennedy and Khrushchev had been communicating almost daily. On Friday, the 26th, came the first signal that the Soviets were ready to retreat. Khrushchev said he would withdraw the missiles in return for a U.S. pledge not to invade Cuba. However, the next day a more formal letter arrived proposing withdrawal of the Soviet missiles in exchange for U.S. withdrawal of its missiles in Turkey. Since the president was determined not to remove the Turkish missiles under pressure (even though he had previously ordered them removed as obsolescent) he decided to ignore this second letter and accept Khrushchev's first proposal. About the same time this response was wired to Moscow Saturday evening, Robert Kennedy orally delivered an ultimatum to the Soviet ambassador Dobrynin: the United States would have to have by the next day a commitment to remove the missiles, otherwise the

United States would remove them itself. He told Dobrynin of the letter that had just been sent to Moscow. When the ambassador inquired, in effect, What about the missiles in Turkey? Kennedy replied that the president had ordered them removed some time ago and they would be gone shortly.

The next morning, Moscow radio broadcast a statement from Khrushchev saying he had ordered the Cuban missiles dismantled and removed. The crisis was suddenly over.

SELECTED BIBLIOGRAPHY

Abel, Elie, *The Missile Crisis* (Philadelphia and New York: J.B. Lippincott, 1966).

Allison, Graham, *Essence of Decision: Explaining the Cuban Missiles Crisis* (Boston: Little Brown, 1971).

Hilsman, Roger, *To Move a Nation* (Garden City, N.Y.: Doubleday, 1967).

Kennedy, Robert F., *Thirteen Days* (New York: W.W. Norton, 1969).

Schlesinger, Arthur M., *A Thousand Days: John F. Kennedy in the White House* (New York: Houghton Mifflin, 1965).

Sorenson, Theodore, *Kennedy* (New York: Harper & Row, 1965).

INDEX

accommodation, 195, 197, 207, 273; and critical risk model, 205; goals and constraints in, 207

Acheson, Dean, 157, 225, 271, 272, 286, 299, 300, 304, 334, 350, 383, 384, 512, 515

action game, 153

Adenauer, Konrad, 71, 73, 105, 272, 317, 331, 333, 334, 338, 364, 391, 397, 400, 401

adjustment of expectations, see expectations, adjustment of

adversary action game, 429, 440; as dimension of supergame, 165

adversary bargaining and alliance bargaining, 429–40

Aehrenthal, Alois, 134, 137, 139, 200, 237, 242, 328, 333, 370, 490

Agadir, see Morocco crisis, 1911

alert crisis, during Yom Kippur War, 1973, 447–50

alignment game, 429, 439

alignments, 472–74, 478

alliance bargaining, 73–74, 175; comparative dependence in, 430; in multipolar crises, 431–35

alliance commitments, 441; ambiguity of, 431–33

alliance formation, as dimension of supergame, 165

alliance games, 129–52; in bipolar system, 440, 466; in U.S.-Soviet-China triangle, 465

alliances and interests, multipolar vs. bipolar systems, 426–28, 441

Allison, Graham, 453, 511n, 512n

analysis of options, 64

anarchy, of international system, 164, 188

Art, Robert, 512n

Asquith, Herbert, 265

attributes, of states, 471, 479

background image, see image, background

balance of capabilities, 456–57

balance of interests, 499, 529

balance of power, 178–79, 254, 255, 422, 425, 442

balance of resolve, 255, 456

Baldwin, Stanley, 358

Balfour, Arthur James, 241

Balkans crisis, mid-1880s, 433

Balkans crisis, 1913, 433, 507

bargaining: accommodative, 22 (see accommodation); as central process in international politics, 3; coercive, 23, 195 (see coercion); innovative, 24; integrative, 24, 73; necessary conditions, 476; persuasive (see persuasion); redistributive, 23; strategic interaction (game) models, 37–65; theory, 22–23; utility models, 33–37

bargaining power, 179, 189, 190, 280, 490, 500; balance of, 513, 523; contextual effects upon, 193; determinants of, 525; effects on crisis structures, 488–89; inherent, 190, 498; internal determinants of, 526; in nuclear age crises, 193–94; outside limits of variation, 526; relative, 190, 191, 193, 492, 494, 496, 529; relevance of conventional forces, 458; relevance of nuclear forces, 458, 459

bargaining process, 195–207, 488

bargaining skill, 190, 194, 498

Bay of Pigs, 187

belief system 286, 290, 310, 494

Bell, Coral, 455n

Beneš, Eduard, 312, 366, 518

Berchtold, Leopold von, 380, 381

Berlin blockade crisis of 1948, 108, 236, 347, 483, 508; constraints, 387; game model of, 113–14; images, 294; physical commitments, 120, 227–28; stalling tactics, 387–88; summary, 559

Berlin crises of 1958–1962, 90, 96, 385, 491, 497, 499, 500, 519, 530; alliance bargaining, 443; coalition politics, internal, 398; constraints, 398–99; effects of bargaining moves on opponent's internal divisions, 517, 521; as expanded game, 156–58; feedback, 399, 400; game model of, 92–93; images, 295; internal bargaining, 515; level of aspiration, 400; mixture of coercion and accommodation, 268–75, 277; out-of-control risks, 239; P-bargaining, 103; probes, 399–400; R-bargaining, 103; strategy revision, 398–401; summary, 564; T-bargaining, 103–104; trade dispute, 1960, 121; utility model of, 69–71

Berlin crisis, 1958, 460

Library of Congress Cataloging in Publication Data

Snyder, Glenn Herald.
    Conflict among nations.

    1.   Arbitration, International.   2.   Pacific settlement of international
disputes.   3.   International relations—Research.   4.   World politics—
20th century.   I.   Diesing, Paul, joint author.

II.   Title.
JX1952.S688   341.5′2   77-72135
ISBN 0-691-05664-1
ISBN 0-691-10057-8 pbk